TAXATION FOR SOLICITORS

TAXATION FOR SOLICITORS

Editor and Co-Author

Padraic Courtney

Authors

Sean Brodie
Nuala Casey
Michelle McLoughlin and
Anne Stephenson

OXFORD
UNIVERSITY PRESS

OXFORD
UNIVERSITY PRESS

Great Clarendon Street, Oxford, OX2 6DP,
United Kingdom

Oxford University Press is a department of the University of Oxford.
It furthers the University's objective of excellence in research, scholarship,
and education by publishing worldwide. Oxford is a registered trade mark of
Oxford University Press in the UK and in certain other countries

Published in the United States of America by Oxford University Press
198 Madison Avenue, New York, NY 10016, United States of America

British Library Cataloguing in Publication Data

Data available

Library of Congress Control Number: 2024943659

ISBN 978–0–19–894052–4

PREFACE

This text has been prepared as a practice guideline for students at the Law Society of Ireland's Law School. It is not intended as a comprehensive statement of the law or practice and is designed to be read in conjunction with the Professional Practice Course in relation to *Wills, Probate and Estates, Taxation* and *Applied Land Law* Modules and material from lectures and tutorials in relation to same.

Members of the profession who consult these materials will appreciate that solicitors' practice in the conduct of cases varies and should note that it is not the intention of this material to cover all varying practices in the areas concerned. Likewise, as is the case for all legal materials, they may be superseded by legislation and/or case law.

In particular, in relation to taxation advice, the most recent Finance Act and related legislation should be consulted.

If advice on the law or on any particular set of circumstances is required, professional advice should be sought, and lawyers should do their own legal research.

While every care has been taken in the production of these materials, no responsibility is accepted by the Law School or the Law Society or by any author of these materials for any errors or omissions.

This book could not have been written without the valued contribution of many practitioners who have lectured, tutored, and written on this subject for the Law Society's Law School down the years.

Padraic Courtney,
Editor
February 2024

AUTHORS

Sean Brodie has lectured on the Law Society's VAT and Landlord and Tenant Law modules on the Professional Practice Course and electives and on the Law Society's diploma in Commercial Conveyancing. He has also lectured on VAT for the Irish Tax Institute. He is currently a partner with PriceWaterhouseCoopers where he advises on all aspects of VAT. Prior to joining PriceWaterhouseCoopers he worked in the office of the Revenue Commissioners

Nuala Casey (BCL) was admitted as a solicitor in 1977 and is a consultant solicitor with Shiel Solicitors LLP. She has extensive experience in the area of Probate Practice. She is a consultant, tutor, and internal examiner for the Professional Practice Courses in the Law School, and lectures in Probate and Applied Land Law for the Law Society's Continuing Professional Development (CPD) programme. She is a registered Trust and Estate practitioner and a former member of the Committee of the Society of Trust and Estate Practitioners (STEP) Ireland, and has lectured and tutored on the Law Society/STEP Diploma in Trust and Estate Practice. She is editor and co-author of the Oxford University Press *Conveyancing* manual, an author on the Law Society's *Wills, Probate & Estates* Manual, and co-editor and co-author of the Law Society's *Complex Conveyancing* Manual.

Padraic Courtney qualified as a solicitor in 1994 and has worked for the Law Society's Law School as a course manager, specialising in Probate and Taxation, for more than twenty years. He holds the Law Society Diploma in Property Tax. A registered Trust and Estate Practitioner and former Committee member of STEP Ireland and secretary to the Law Society of Ireland Probate, Administration and Trusts Committee, he has lectured and tutored on *Wills, Probate & Estates* and *Taxation* on the Law Society Professional Practice Course and electives and has delivered seminars for CPD, Skillnets, the DSBA, STEP Ireland, and regional Bar Associations. He runs the *Wills, Probate and Estates* Masterclasses offered by Law Society Professional Training.

Michelle McLoughlin is a solicitor practising in M. Mc Loughlin & Co., in Sligo. Michelle advises on employment, company, and commercial law queries and transactions. She also has extensive experience in providing taxation advice, in particular in stamp duty and Capital Acquisitions Tax, and in structuring commercial transactions. She is an associate of the Irish Taxation Institute and achieved first place in their final examinations and went on to receive the Findlater Scholarship for achieving first place overall in the Law Society examinations. She lectures and tutors for the Law Society at PPC I, PPC II, and CPD in the areas of Stamp Duty, Capital Acquisitions Tax, and VAT.

Anne Stephenson is the Principal of Stephenson Solicitors, a specialist practice providing advisory services for solicitors and financial institutions in the area of Wills, Trusts, Administrations, and Tax Planning. She is a member of STEP, the DSBA Probate and Taxation Committee and Mental Health and Capacity Committee, the Probate Liaison Committee of the Law Society, the Probate, Administration and Trust Committee of the Law Society, and the Committee of SFE Ireland. She lectures, examines, and tutors on the Law Society's

Professional Courses on the *Wills, & Estate, Taxation* and *Conveyancing* Modules and on the STEP Diploma in Wills, Trust & Estate Planning. She also lectures on the Law Society's CPD Courses, and to the DSBA and numerous other professional bodies including the Stephenson series of Probate Practice Seminars. She regularly contributes articles to various other publications, including the Law Society Gazette, The Parchment, and the Tax Review. She is also co-author of the OUP manual on *Wills Probate and Estates*, 8th Edition 2024, and the OUP manual on *Conveyancing*, 9th Edition 2023.

ACKNOWLEDGEMENTS

Copyright in all forms and materials produced by the Revenue Commissioners remains the property of the Revenue Commissioners and such publications are reproduced here under the terms of the Re-use of Public Sector Information Regulations 2005 (SI 279/2005). For all revenue publications, it is recommended that practitioners obtain the most recent version of same from the Revenue Commissioners website <www.revenue.ie>.

Copyright in all forms and materials produced by the Law Society Copyright vests in the Law Society save and except the chart set out in Chapter 3, para **3.13**, copyright of which vests in Brian Bohan and Fergus McCarthy, authors of *Capital Acquisition Tax* 3rd Edition, Tottel Publishing 2008 on page 291 thereof and the same is reproduced here by kind permission of the authors. Copyright in this chart vests with the original authors and publisher of same and their kind permission to the Law School and Oxford University Press to use same for illustration purposes in this chapter is acknowledged and appreciated.

OUTLINE CONTENTS

DETAILED CONTENTS

TABLE OF CASES

TABLE OF PRIMARY LEGISLATION

TABLE OF SECONDARY LEGISLATION

TABLE OF INTERNATIONAL INSTRUMENTS

TABLE OF EU LEGISLATION

Directives

Regulations

INTRODUCTION AND OVERVIEW

This introduction briefly outlines the topics to be covered in the succeeding chapters, their relevance in relation to specific areas of practice covered in other Law Society of Ireland Manuals, particularly *Wills, Probate & Estates* (Courtney: OUP, 2024), and *Conveyancing* (Casey and Brennan: OUP, 2023).

Chapter 1: Capital Acquisitions Tax—Introduction and Basic Concepts

Chapter 1 introduces CAT, giving a brief legislative history and equitable background. It outlines some basic issues including territoriality, the distinctions between a 'gift' and an 'inheritance', the elements of each showing how 'taxable value' and the 'valuation date' are arrived at, and the distinction on occasion between 'date of death' and 'valuation date' in the case of an inheritance.

The chapter goes on to deal with how different limited interests in land, including right to reside, life interest, interest for a period certain, and ownership subject to such limited interest are valued for CAT purposes, whether for interests in land or otherwise.

Chapter 2: Calculation of CAT Payable: Computation and Aggregation, and the Role of the Solicitor

Chapter 2 details how, once the taxable value of the benefit is calculated, the CAT payable and interest (if any) is calculated whether payment is by instalments or otherwise, concentrating on the role of the solicitor when the benefit arises in the course of administration of an estate or as a voluntary transfer of an interest in land. It also deals with the different types of appeal against assessment that can be made.

Chapter 3: CAT, Valuation of Benefits and Anti-Avoidance, Introduction to Reliefs

Chapter 3 outlines the principles involved in valuing certain types of benefit, primarily private company shares, revocable or contingent gifts, and bequests free from tax, and details some anti-avoidance measures in place, including dispositions enlarging the value of a property and dispositions by or to a limited company. The chapter goes on to deal with the major reliefs and exemptions from CAT that are available, describing the conditions which must be met and any clawback provisions.

Chapter 4: Agricultural Relief

Chapter 4 discusses agricultural relief—when it arises, the conditions which must be met, and how it is calculated, including combining agricultural relief with dwelling-house exemption and the clawback which will apply.

Chapter 5: Business Relief

Chapter 5 concentrates on business relief, outlining distinctions between business relief and agricultural relief, the conditions which must be met, and how it is calculated, including combining business relief with dwelling-house exemption and the clawback which will apply.

Chapter 6: 'Favourite Nephew/Niece Relief' and Combinations of Reliefs

The discussion of CAT reliefs concludes in Chapter 6, which deals primarily with favourite nephew relief—when it arises, the conditions which must be met, how it is calculated, and the clawback applying. The chapter also deals with combinations of reliefs, including situations when agricultural and/or business relief, favourite nephew relief, and dwelling-house exemption all apply to the same disposition.

Chapter 7: Stamp Duty

Chapter 7 introduces the principles of Stamp Duty, giving a brief legislative history and focusing on transfers or conveyances, voluntary or otherwise, of real property. The chapter deals with residential property, commercial, agricultural and mixed property, certification and stamping, and any penalties or interest provided for. The chapter goes on to deal with Stamp Duty on leases of property, focusing on the nature and term of the lease, any particular terms of the lease including covenants to improve and terms of payment to include premium, penal terms, voluntary leases, exemptions and reliefs to the duty, calculation of tax where payment is uncertain, sub-sales, partitions, and exchanges. It goes on to deal with administrative matters including time for stamping, penalties and interest, and revenue powers and appeals.

Chapter 8: Capital Gains Tax and Other Tax Charges

Chapter 8 introduces the principles of Capital Gains Tax, giving a brief legislative history and focusing on transfers or conveyances, voluntary or otherwise, of real property, including the principal private residence and development land and any extra-territorial issues arising. The chapter then goes on to focus on CGT arising with leases and other wasting assets. It also deals with particular reliefs and exemptions available and property passing between spouses and on death. The chapter then goes on to review other property taxes, including Local Property Tax, the Non-Principal Private Residence Tax, the Household Charge, the Vacant Homes Tax, and the Residential Zoned Land Tax.

Chapter 9 Value Added Tax

Chapter 9

Chapter 10: Income Tax

Chapter 10

Chapter 11: Corporation Tax

Chapter 11

Chapter 12: Taxation and the Conveyancer's Responsibilities

Chapter 12 deals with the tax issues arising in the course of buying and selling immoveable property on behalf of clients and the obligations on the solicitor acting to ensure tax compliance. This chapter should be read in conjunction with *Conveyancing* (Casey and Brennan: OUP, 2007).

Chapter 13: Wills, Estate Planning, and Taxation

Chapter 13 discusses the options available when advising clients on how they may pass on assets in as tax efficient a manner as possible, primarily by means of drafting a will but also looking at the other means available, attempting to minimise all taxes payable while protecting the client's wider interests. It should be read in conjunction with Chapters 1 to 5 of *Wills, Probate & Estates* (Courtney: OUP, 2024).

Chapter 14: Taxation Issues in the Administration of Estates

Chapter 14 covers the tax issues arising in the course of administering the estate of a deceased person, highlighting the duty of care owed by the solicitor to the personal representative and the procedures involved in ensuring compliant yet tax-efficient administration of the estate. In addition to the taxes dealt with in this manual, Estate Duty, Residential Property Tax, Probate Tax, and Income Tax may all arise to be dealt with. This chapter should be read in conjunction with Chapter 8 and Chapters 14 to 19 of Wills, Probate and Estates (Courtney: OUP, 2024).

FURTHER READING

This book is designed to be read in conjunction with the following OUP Manuals: *Wills, Probate and Estates* (Courtney, OUP, 2024), *Conveyancing* (Casey and Brennan, OUP, 2023), and *Landlord and Tenant Law* (Brennan et al, OUP, 2007).

General

WEBSITES

Institute of Taxation in Ireland <http://www.taxireland.ie>

The Law Society of Ireland <http://www.lawsociety.ie>

The Revenue Commissioners <http://www.revenue.ie>

JOURNALS

Institute of Taxation in Ireland, *Irish Tax Review*

The Revenue Commissioners Tax Briefing

The Law Society of Ireland Gazette

Capital Acquisitions Tax

LEGISLATION

Capital Acquisitions Tax Consolidation Act, 2003, as amended by Finance Acts, 2003 to 2010, and Finance Acts (No.1 to No.3), 2011.

SUGGESTED READING

Aileen Keogan, Law of Capital Acquisitions Tax (Finance (No.3) Act 2011 Edn, due to be published in autumn 2011, Institute of Taxation of Ireland)

Brian Bohan and Fergus McCarthy, *Capital Acquisitions Tax* (3rd Edn, Butterworths, 2008)

John Condon, *Capital Acquisitions Tax* (Finance Act 2007 Edn, Institute of Taxation of Ireland)

Anne Corrigan with Anne Williams, *Trust and Succession Law* (Finance Act 2007 Edn, Institute of Taxation of Ireland)

Denis Cremins, *Valuation of Shares in Unlisted Companies* (Finance Act 2005 Edn, Institute of Taxation of Ireland)

Hilary Delany, *Equity and the Law of Trusts in Ireland* (4th Edn, Thomson Round Hall, 2007)

Aidan McLoughlin (editor) and others, *Pensions: Revenue Law and Practice: Finance Act 2010* (Institute of Taxation of Ireland)

John Wylie, Aileen Keogan, and John Mee, *The Law and Taxation of Trusts* (Tottel, 2007) 2nd Edn due in 2011

Revenue Commissioners leaflets are available from the Revenue website, <www.revenue.ie>

Stamp Duty

LEGISLATION

Stamp Duties Consolidation Act, 1999 as amended by the Finance Acts, 2001 to 2010, and the Finance Acts, 2011.

SUGGESTED READING

Aoife Goodman, *Stamp Acts* (Finance Act 2011 Edn, Institute of Taxation of Ireland)

David Donegan, Raymond Friel, and Amanda-Jayne Comyn, *Irish Stamp Duty Law* (5th Edn, Tottel, 2009)

Monroe & Nock on the Law of Stamp Duties (Sweet & Maxwell, looseleaf)

Tom Power and Emmet Scully, *Law and Practice of Irish Stamp Duty* (Finance Act 2010 Edn, Institute of Taxation of Ireland)

Sergeant and Sims on Stamp Duties (Butterworths, looseleaf)

Revenue Commissioners leaflets are available from the Revenue website, <www.revenue.ie>

Capital Gains Tax

LEGISLATION

Taxes Consolidation Act, 1997 as amended by Finance Acts, 1997 to 2010, and the Finance Acts, 2011.

SUGGESTED READING

Tony Appleby and Finola O'Hanlon, *The Taxation of Financial Gains* (Finance Act 2008 Edn, Institute of Taxation of Ireland)

CHAPTER 1

CAPITAL ACQUISITIONS TAX—INTRODUCTION AND BASIC CONCEPTS

1.1 Introduction to CAT

Capital acquisitions tax (CAT) is a tax on gifts and inheritances (benefits) received by individuals (beneficiaries) from other individuals (donors). The calculation of the tax payable is primarily based on:

- value of benefit;
- the relationship between the beneficiary and the donor;
- any prior benefits received by the beneficiary from either that donor or from any other donor in relation to whom the beneficiary bears a similar relationship.

1.1.1 LEGISLATIVE HISTORY

In 1975 the old death duties (i.e. estate duty, succession duty, and legacy duty) were replaced by CAT. This tax, introduced by the Capital Acquisitions Tax Act, 1976 (CAT Act, 1976), taxes both gifts and inheritances.

The CAT Act, 1976 was constantly amended by succeeding Finance Acts and in 2003 was repealed and replaced by the Capital Acquisitions Tax Consolidation Act, 2003 (CAT Consolidation Act, 2003), which in its turn has been amended by the Finance Acts, 2003 to 2024 inclusive.

All references to legislation in this chapter are to CAT Consolidation Act, 2003 as amended, unless otherwise stated.

1.1.2 EQUITABLE BACKGROUND

The succession and legacy duties already referred to were in fact acquisition duties and the draftsman of the CAT Act, 1976 and, subsequently, CAT Consolidation Act, 2003 has drawn to a large extent on the fundamental concepts of those obsolete acquisition duties. For example, the valuation date in CAT is based on the date of retainer in the old legacy duty legislation.

The CAT legislation follows closely the rules of property law and equity and study of the interpretation section (CAT Consolidation Act 2003, s. 2) is of great importance in order to understand the underlying principles of this tax.

CAT is a tax on benefits, howsoever arising. In CAT Consolidation Act 2003, s. 2, benefits are defined as including 'any estate, income or right'.

In CAT the emphasis is on what the **beneficiary** (i.e. the person receiving the benefit) acquires. Tax is calculated and charged on the beneficiary's acquisition from the **disponer** (i.e. the person 'giving' the benefit taken by the beneficiary). The benefit is referred to in CAT Consolidation Act, 2003 as a 'disposition'. In CAT Consolidation Act, 2003, s. 2, disposition is defined very widely.

1.1.3 TAXABLE GIFT OR INHERITANCE

CAT consists of two taxes: a gift tax and an inheritance tax. These taxes are distinguished by the fact that an inheritance is taken **'on a death'** (as defined in s. 3) while a gift is not so taken. The importance of the distinction between the two types of tax is now largely irrelevant but it is of some importance in specific circumstances.

This phrase is utilised in s. 6 (gift) and s. 11 (inheritance) of CAT Consolidation Act, 2003, to indicate the territoriality rules referable to gift and inheritance tax.

1.1.4 TERRITORIALITY OF THE TAX

Gifts or inheritances of all property situated in the State are taxable regardless of the domicile/residence/ordinary residence of the disponer or beneficiary.

1.1.5 RESIDENT/ORDINARILY RESIDENT RULES

Gifts or inheritances of non-Irish situated property, taken on or after 1 December 1999, are liable to tax where either the disponer or the beneficiary is resident or ordinarily resident in the State. 'Resident' and 'ordinarily resident' are defined in Part 34 of the Taxes Consolidation Act, 1997.

1.1.5.1 Residence and ordinary residence

An individual is regarded as **resident** in Ireland for a year of assessment if he or she:

- is present in the State for a period of 183 days or more; or
- if in the year of assessment and the year before that he or she is in the State for a period of 280 or more days. If the individual does not stay in the State for more than 30 days in a year of assessment, that stay is not taken into account in calculating the 280 days.

An individual is regarded as **ordinarily resident** in Ireland for a year of assessment if he has been resident in the State for the preceding three years. He or she does not cease to be ordinarily resident in Ireland until he or she has been resident outside the State for the preceding three years.

Domicile is dealt with in **Chapter 13** but essentially is residence plus intention to live in a State. Sections 6 (4)—gifts and 11(4)—inheritances further provide that a person domiciled outside the State is treated as not resident or ordinarily resident on the date of a gift or inheritance unless they have been in the State for the five consecutive years of assessment prior to the date of the gift or inheritance and they are either resident or ordinarily resident on the date of the gift or inheritance. See also Bohan and McCarthy, *Capital Acquisitions Tax* paras 3.23 to 3.46 for a more detailed review of the law of domicile as it applies to CAT.

1.1.5.2 Pre-1 December 1999 rules for trusts

Special provisions apply for non-Irish ordinarily resident persons and for gifts or inheritances taken under a **trust or settlement** existing on 1 December 1999 where the settlor was not resident or ordinarily resident.

1.1.5.3 Example

A, who is resident or ordinarily resident in the State at the date of the disposition, transfers a portfolio of Irish shares and a portfolio of English shares to his cousin B, who is resident or ordinarily resident in England and Wales.

As A is resident or ordinarily resident in the State at the date of the disposition, B is liable to gift tax on both the Irish and the English portfolios.

If A was not resident or ordinarily resident in the State at the date of the disposition, B would pay tax on the portfolio of Irish shares only.

Section 11 of CAT Consolidation Act 2003 states that the whole of an inheritance is taxable in a case where:

- the disponer is resident or ordinarily resident in the State at the date of the disposition under which the successor (defined as the person who takes an inheritance) takes the inheritance; or
- the successor is resident or ordinarily resident in the State at the date of the disposition.

In effect there is global liability to inheritance tax in a case where the disponer or beneficiary is resident or ordinarily resident in the State at the date of the disposition (providing that the non-domiciled person has been resident in the State for the five consecutive years of assessment immediately preceding the year of assessment in which the date of death falls). The residence/ordinary residence rules came into full force on 1 December 2004. When completing the Statement of Affairs (Probate) online form SA 2 (see Chapter 6 of *Wills, Probate and Estates*) of any deceased person resident or ordinarily resident in Ireland after that date, details of all assets affected by the will, the intestacy rules, or Part IX or s. 56 of the Succession Act, 1965 wheresoever situate, must be included.

Difficulties may arise in the administration of estates where the deceased was resident in Ireland for a considerable period but retained substantial assets outside the jurisdiction which have not been made known to an Irish personal representative (possibly because they pass under a separate non-Irish will). The situation may also arise where a non-national has left the country in the past year but is still 'ordinarily resident' and dies outside the country. A liability to CAT may arise, but this will be very difficult to enforce.

Where neither the disponer nor the successor are resident or ordinarily resident in Ireland but any property passing is situate in Ireland then the benefit arising from that property is taxable. This includes shares in any Irish company. It also includes shares in any foreign company that owns property or assets in Ireland. The market value of those shares will be multiplied by the value of the Irish assets and divided by the total assets. For the purposes of this course we will not be dealing to any great extent with the extra-territorial effect of taxation.

The practice implications for solicitors where either the beneficiary or the personal representative is non-resident at the date of death are dealt with in Chapter 14 para 14.7.2 of the Wills, Probate & Estates OUP Manual and on the Advanced Probate & Taxation Elective.

1.2 Gift or Inheritance

Initially when the tax came into force different rates applied whether the benefit taken was a gift or an inheritance. With the exception of the small gift exemption (see below and **3.10.3**), 'connected gifts' (see **3.9.1**), and the dwelling-house exemption (**3.13**), the distinction between a gift and an inheritance is largely moot. See **2.6.2**.

1.2.1 'ON A DEATH'

Section 3 of the CAT Consolidation Act, 2003 defines '**on a death**' in relation to a person becoming beneficially entitled in possession. It is not limited to property passing under the will or intestacy of the deceased person and includes all assets passing on a death. For example, property passing by survivorship or by nomination or a remainder interest vesting on the death of a life tenant are assets passing outside the will or intestacy but are all chargeable to tax.

The definition is not confined to the death of the disponer, which would be the normal situation. It includes a situation where the disponer could still be alive.

For example, Andrew by *inter vivos* disposition settles property on Brian for life with remainder to Conor absolutely. Brian dies and Conor is deemed to take an inheritance on the death of Brian, from Andrew the original disponer, who may still be alive at that date. This is considered an inheritance 'on a death'. It is possible therefore to take an inheritance from a living disponer.

Similarly, for example, Andrew by *inter vivos* disposition settles property on Brian for a fixed period (say ten years) with remainder to Conor absolutely. Andrew dies five years later. After the ten-year period Brian's interest lapses and Conor receives a gift of the property from Andrew (even though Andrew is now dead). It is also possible therefore (for tax purposes) to receive a gift from a dead disponer.

Thankfully we do not come across situations like these very often!

The definition also makes provision at s. 3(1) (c) for the situation where the disponer dies within two years of the date of the gift. For CAT purposes the gift is converted to an inheritance. This used to have relevance when gift tax was chargeable at 75 per cent of inheritance tax. This is no longer relevant for gifts received since 1 December 1999, but may be significant for gifts received prior to that date. It is also relevant in relation to certain *inter vivos* trusts where the disponer died within two years of setting up a discretionary trust; for example, any payments out by the trustees after the death of the disponer would be taxable as an inheritance and not a gift.

It should be noted that the small gift exemption of €3000 (which will be referred to at **3.10.3**) still remains although the gift has become an inheritance. Apart from how the valuation date is ascertained, this is the only effective difference between a gift and an inheritance since 1 December 1999.

1.2.2 GIFT TAX

Section 4 of CAT Consolidation Act, 2003 creates a charge of gift tax on the **taxable value** of every **taxable gift** taken by a **donee** (beneficiary who receives a gift).

A gift is further defined in s. 5(1) as arising where a person becomes beneficially entitled in possession otherwise than on a death to any benefit and otherwise than for full consideration. For example, if I transfer property valued at €150,000 to someone for consideration or payment of €50,000, in effect I have given that person a 'gift' of €100,000.

1.2.3 INHERITANCE TAX

Sections 9 and 10 of CAT Consolidation Act, 2003 similarly charge inheritance tax on the **taxable value** of every **taxable inheritance** taken by a **successor** (beneficiary who inherits) where the date of the inheritance is on or after 1 April 1975.

Before considering the phrases and words highlighted in **bold** above it is necessary to examine what constitutes a gift or an inheritance.

Section 5(1) of CAT Consolidation Act, 2003 sets out the elements which must be present in order that a gift is deemed to be taken; and s. 10(1) of CAT Consolidation Act, 2003 sets out those elements in connection with an inheritance.

1.2.4 ELEMENTS OF A GIFT OR INHERITANCE

A person is deemed to take a gift/inheritance:

(a) where under any **disposition**

(b) that person becomes **beneficially entitled** in possession

(c) otherwise than on a death (in the case of a **gift**), or on a death (in the case of an **inheritance**)

(d) to any **benefit**

(e) otherwise than for full **consideration** in money or monies worth paid by that person.

Each of these elements will be considered in more detail below.

1.2.4.1 Regarding element (a) 'disposition'

The word '**disposition**' is widely defined in CAT Consolidation Act, 2003, s. 2. It includes any act or omission by a person as a result of which the value of that person's estate immediately after such act or omission is less than it would be but for such act or omission.

It includes trusts, covenants, and any agreement or arrangement whether made by a single operation or associated operations. Apart from positive acts of transfer (e.g. A transfers his lands to B in consideration of natural love and affection), the definition covers acts of omission, for example a failure to exercise a right.

This latter aspect of the word 'disposition' has been given added importance by the enactment of the Finance Act, 1994, s. 146, now contained in CAT Consolidation Act 2003, s. 62. That section was enacted to ensure that a possessory title to lands is not used as a method of evading payment of tax and is of particular significance to conveyancers.

Apart from the *inter vivos* aspects of the word 'disposition' it also covers a will, an intestacy, payment of a share as a legal right under Part IX of the Succession Act, 1965, and a *donatio mortis causa*.

In any other case, the 'date of the disposition' is the date on which the act (or, where there is more than one act involved, the last act) of the disponer was done by which that disponer provided or bound himself/herself to provide the property comprised in the disposition.

If there is a disposition there must of necessity be a '**disponer**' and this is also defined in s. 2:

> *'disponer', in relation to a disposition, means the person who, for the purpose of the disposition, directly or indirectly provided the property comprised in the disposition, and in any case where more than one person provided the property each is deemed to be the disponer to the extent that that disponer so provided the property . . .*

The section goes on to confirm the type of disponer for different types of disposition. For example, where a person inherits on intestacy, the person who died intestate is the disponer. The disponer is in fact the true source of the benefit and it is important to pinpoint him or her because the disponer's consanguinity (relationship)—or the lack of it—to the beneficiary will decide the tax threshold applicable in any particular case. In very blunt terms, the more distant the relationship the lower the threshold and thus the more tax paid.

1.2.4.2 Regarding element (b) 'beneficially entitled in possession'

An underlying principle of CAT Consolidation Act, 2003 is that a gift or an inheritance is not taxed until it comes into possession.

'**Date of the gift**' is defined as meaning the date of the happening of the event upon which the beneficiary becomes beneficially entitled in possession to the benefit. Likewise, the definition of date of the inheritance is defined as meaning the date on which the beneficiary becomes beneficially entitled in possession. It follows that if possession is postponed, tax is also postponed.

'**Entitled in possession**' is defined in s. 2 as meaning '*having a present right to the enjoyment of property as opposed to having a future such right*'.

The definition also states that a person shall be **deemed** to be entitled in possession to an interest in a partnership, a joint tenancy, or the estate of the deceased person whether testate or intestate.

This is because it could be argued on legal grounds that a person was not entitled in possession to a share in a partnership or an interest as a joint tenant or to the estate of the deceased person. For example, in the case of a share in the estate of a deceased person, it could be argued that the right to such share was a chose in action against the estate and did not give the beneficiary any right to any specific part of that estate. However, because the definition states that for the purpose of CAT Consolidation Act, 2003 a person is deemed to be entitled in possession, this argument does not arise.

Finally, the definition states categorically that a person who has an interest in expectancy is not deemed to be entitled in possession to that interest until it ceases to be an interest in expectancy. There is one minor exception to this general principle, which will be dealt with in **Chapter 4**: agricultural relief when applying the 'farmer test'.

'**Interest in expectancy**' or future interests will be dealt with in more detail later in this chapter.

1.2.4.3 Joint tenants

Section 7 specifically deals with joint tenants and tenancies and simply states:

> *The liability to gift tax in respect of a gift taken by persons as joint tenants is the same in all respects as if they took the gift as tenants in common in equal shares.*

A similar provision is found in s. 13 for persons who inherit as joint tenants. The provision at s. 13 also deals with surviving joint tenants who are deemed for CAT valuation purposes only to inherit at tenants in common in equal shares. See also **2.9.3**.

1.2.4.4 Regarding element (c) 'gift' or 'inheritance'

Element (c) indicates the distinction between a gift and an inheritance. An inheritance is taken on a death and a gift is not taken on a death. In CAT Consolidation Act, 2003 this is referred to as 'otherwise than on a death'.

1.2.4.5 Regarding element (d) 'benefit'

The word '**benefit**' is defined as including any estate, interest, income, or right. As we shall see later, it is the benefit which is taxed. This benefit may be a life interest, an annuity, or a right of residence. An interest in expectancy is also a benefit, but as already stated, it will not be taxed until it comes into possession.

1.2.4.6 Regarding element (e) 'consideration'

This indicates that there is no question of a gift or an inheritance if '**full consideration**' is paid '**in money or monies worth**'. Tax will arise if the consideration is partial or inadequate. However, allowance will be made for such partial consideration in arriving at the taxable value of the gift or inheritance.

The consideration however must be paid by the beneficiary, but not necessarily to the disponer.

Example: Adam transfers his house to Brian absolutely on condition that Brian gives €20,000 to Chris.

In such a case there are two gifts (or two taxable events occur):

(1) Brian takes a gift of a house less €20,000, which he must pay to Chris.

(2) Chris takes a gift of €20,000 from **Adam**. Note that the gift is deemed to be from Adam, even though Brian is actually paying the money. This is because Chris is deemed to receive the money because of a disposition made by Adam. The importance of this will be explained in **Chapter 2**.

1.2.5 TYPES OF INTEREST (ABSOLUTE AND LIMITED)

As already stated, the word '**benefit**' includes any estate, interest, income, or right.

The word '**property**' is defined as including rights and interests of any description. The CAT legislation taxes two types of interest:

(1) an absolute interest; and

(2) a limited interest. (Limited interests will be dealt with in more detail later in this chapter.)

1.2.5.1 Powers of appointment (general and special)

'**Absolute interest**' in relation to property includes the interest of a person who has a **general** power of appointment over the property. This is as opposed to a **special** power of appointment, which is a power to appoint out to members of a particular class.

Example: Adam transfers property to Brian for life with remainder to whomsoever Brian would by deed or will appoint. As Brian can appoint the remainder interest to himself, he is regarded as taking an absolute interest in the property.

If, however, Adam transfers property to Brian for life with remainder to those of Brian's children that Brian would by deed or will appoint, then Brian merely receives a life interest. Powers of appointment are dealt with in more detail in **Chapter 13**.

1.3 Discretionary Trusts

Sections 14 to 25 of CAT Consolidation Act, 2003 deal with discretionary trusts, defining them and dealing with the imposition of an initial levy (CAT Consolidation Act, 2003, Chapter 2) and an annual levy (CAT Consolidation Act, 2003, Chapter 3). Taxation of discretionary trusts is taught as part of the Advanced Probate and Taxation Elective.

1.4 Value of Property for Tax

Part 4 of CAT Consolidation Act, 2003 deals with ascertaining the value of property for tax purposes. This entails moving from the **market value** of a property to the **taxable value** of the property.

1.4.1 MARKET VALUE

Section 26 defines the market value of property as being

> *the price which, in the opinion of the Commissioners, such property would fetch if sold in the open market on the date on which the property is to be valued in such manner and subject to such conditions as might reasonably be calculated to obtain for the vendor the best price for the property.*

The legislation therefore postulates a fictitious sale in arriving at the market value of the property comprised in the benefit.

Furthermore, that market value is ascertained by the Revenue in such manner and by such means as it thinks fit (s. 26(4)). It is usual for the beneficiary lodging the tax return to include an auctioneer's valuation of the property. The Revenue may accept this, or in the case of the valuation of immovable property refer the question of value to the Commissioner of Valuation for his opinion.

1.4.2 SURCHARGE FOR UNDERVALUATION

It should be noted that s. 53 of CAT Consolidation Act, 2003 provides for a surcharge where an estimate of the market value of the gift/inheritance, which is an undervaluation, is included in the self-assessment return. The percentage of the surcharge depends on the percentage of the undervaluation as against the ascertained value and is as follows:

Estimate of the market value supplied in the return, expressed as a percentage of the ascertained value of that asset	Surcharge
67–100%	Nil
50–66%	10%
40–49%	20%
0–39%	30%

For example, if the property was valued by the taxpayer at €100,000 but Revenue valued the property at €160,000 then the taxpayer would face a surcharge of 10 per cent of the re-calculated CAT liability:

$$€100{,}000/€160{,}000 \times 100\% = 62.5\%$$

$$\frac{€100{,}000}{€160{,}000} \times 100\% = 62.5\%$$

Interest is payable on any surcharge raised.

The 'ascertained value' means the market value of the property as valued by the Revenue.

1.4.2.1 Appeals against surcharge

An accountable person aggrieved by the imposition on him or her of a surcharge can appeal the imposition of the surcharge to the Appeals Commissioners in accordance with section 949 I of the Taxes Consolidation Act 1997 within 30 days of notification. The appeal can be made on the grounds that, having regard to all the circumstances, there were sufficient grounds on which he or she might reasonably have based his estimate of the market value of the asset.

Appeals will not be dealt with in detail here.

1.4.2.2 Best practice

However, as the taxpayer's legal representative, solicitors should not:

(1) value property themselves; and/or

(2) accept a client's valuation of property.

Best practice is to always engage a reputable auctioneer or valuer.

1.4.3 ARRIVING AT THE TAXABLE VALUE

Having ascertained the market value of the property, the next step is to arrive at the taxable value of the property. The phrase '**taxable value**' was referred to in the charging sections for gifts and inheritances. This taxable value is arrived at under the provisions of CAT Consolidation Act, 2003, s. 28.

Whether dealing with an **absolute** or **limited** interest, one always begins with the market value.

Example:

(1) Adam transfers an asset valued at €260,000 to Brian **absolutely**; or

(2) Adam transfers an asset valued at €260,000 to Brian **for life** with remainder to Chris absolutely; or

(3) Adam transfers an asset valued at €260,000 to Brian **for ten years** with remainder to Chris absolutely.

We will deal with arriving at the taxable value for examples (2) and (3) (i.e. limited interests) later in this chapter.

In example (1) Brian has taken an absolute interest in possession. In arriving at the taxable value of Brian's benefit, you should begin with the **market value** of the asset, that is, €260,000.

1.4.3.1 Liabilities, costs, and expenses

The next step in the sequence in arriving at the taxable value is set out in CAT Consolidation Act, 2003, s. 28(1). Allowance can be made for liabilities, costs, and expenses that are properly payable out of the taxable benefit. After deduction of those liabilities, costs, and expenses from the market value of the property in which the benefit is taken, we arrive at the '**incumbrance-free value**'.

These liabilities, costs, and expenses could include, in the case of a gift:

- the **legal costs and expenses** in connection with the legal transfer of the property,
- **Stamp Duty** if paid by the beneficiary and
- the **expenses of preparing the return** including any auctioneer's costs.

In the case of an inheritance, the liabilities, costs, and expenses might be the payment of funeral and testamentary expenses properly payable out of the benefit.

If the property taken by the beneficiary is subject to a mortgage, that mortgage would also be a good deduction under this sub-section as a mortgage is a liability on a property.

Practitioners should be aware of the provisions of s. 47 of the Succession Act, 1965. Remember that not all beneficiaries under a will have to pay the funeral and testamentary expenses. They are normally paid according to the First Schedule to the Succession Act, 1965. See Chapter 2 of *Wills, Probate and Estates*.

1.4.3.2 Incumbrance-free value

The market value of the property less the value of any mortgage charged on the property and/or any costs or expenses payable is the **incumbrance-free value**.

1.4.3.3 Consideration

Section 28(2) states that the **taxable value** of the benefit where the benefit is an **absolute interest** is ascertained by deducting from the incumbrance-free value the value of any *bona fide* consideration (in money or monies worth) paid by the beneficiary for the benefit. These are defined as including:

(1) any liability of the disponer which the donee or successor undertakes to discharge as their own personal liability, and

(2) any other liability to which the gift or inheritance is subject under the terms of the disposition under which it is taken.

As already stated, it is not necessary that such consideration should be received by the disponer, and quite often it is payable to a third party under the terms of the disposition, particularly if passing by will.

1.4.3.4 Taxable value

The incumbrance-free value of the property less the value of any consideration paid for the property is the taxable value. Obviously, any deductions already made as a cost, liability, or expense cannot be deducted again as consideration.

Section 28(4) sets out the position in arriving at the taxable value of a benefit where that benefit is a **limited interest** and will be dealt with in later in this chapter.

Section 29 of CAT Consolidation Act, 2003 deals with benefits taken subject to a contingency. For example: 'I leave my farm to my wife Mary for her life or until she re-marries with remainder to my son Francis absolutely'. The contingency is ignored until Mary re-marries. Contingent benefits will be dealt with in more detail in **Chapter 3**.

To sum up therefore, the sequence from market value to taxable value may be shown as follows:

- **Market value**
- Less **liabilities, costs, and expenses**
- Equals **incumbrance-free value**
- Less **consideration**
- Equals **taxable value**

1.4.4 EXAMPLE OF TAXABLE VALUE

Taking example (1) in **1.4.3** a few steps further, Adam transfers his house, valued at €260,000 and subject to a mortgage of €50,000, to his brother Brian absolutely on condition that Brian pays their sister Cynthia €20,000. The costs, including stamp duty and solicitor's fees, etc., are €10,000 and are paid by Brian.

The costs of €10,000 and the mortgage of €50,000 are deductible from the market value and the payment of €20,000 is deductible from the incumbrance-free value of Brian's benefit.

Applying this example to the sequence above, we get the following:

Market value		€260,000
Less **liabilities, costs, and expenses**		
Liability (mortgage)	€50,000	
Costs and expenses (stamp duty, etc.)	€10,000	(€60,000)
Equals **incumbrance-free value**		€200,000
Less **consideration** (payment to Cynthia)		(€20,000)
Equals **taxable value**		€180,000

It should be noted that Cynthia also has a taxable benefit with a market value and taxable value of €20,000. We are not aware of any liabilities, costs, expenses, or consideration payable by Cynthia.

1.5 Valuation Date(s)

The valuation date is a very important date in CAT as it determines when the tax is due. The pay and file deadline will depend on when the valuation date falls. Where the valuation date falls on or before 31 August in any tax year the pay and file deadline will be 31 October of that year.

Where the valuation date falls after 31 August in any tax year the pay and file deadline will be 31 October of the following year. As can be appreciated, identifying and planning for the valuation date is of significant importance.

There is a short extension granted each year where the taxpayer both files and pays using ROS, the Revenue Online System. This will be dealt with in **Chapter 2**.

The valuation date differs when dealing with a gift or an inheritance.

1.5.1 TAXABLE GIFT

Section 30(1) provides that for a taxable gift, the valuation date is the date of the gift and there is no need to differentiate between the date of the disposition (gift) and the valuation date.

Section 30(7) states one exception to this rule, which is unlikely to arise. It states that if a taxable inheritance in respect of which the valuation date has not arrived (for example, a future interest) is gifted by the beneficiary to a donee, the valuation date of that gift will be taken as the valuation date of the original inheritance.

1.5.2 TAXABLE INHERITANCE

Section 30 goes on to provide for a taxable inheritance where the position is slightly more complex. In general the valuation date will be some date later than the date of the date of the disposition.

It is important to remember that the tax regime applicable is fixed at the 'date of the disposition' and the tax becomes due at the 'valuation date'. By this it is meant that the tax chargeable will be based on the rules applying at the date of death even if the tax is not due until months or even years later. This can be important where a person dies in, for example, December of any year.

1.5.3 DATE OF THE DISPOSITION

'**Date of the disposition**' is defined as meaning:

- In the case of a will, the date of the testator's death.
- In the case of an intestacy or a partial intestacy, the date of death of the intestate.
- In the case of a benefit taken under Part IX of the Succession Act, 1965 (spouses and children's rights) the date of death of the deceased.

1.5.4 VALUATION DATE AND RETAINER

As already stated, the valuation date concept in CAT particularly in relation to inheritance tax is derived from the date of **retainer** concept in the obsolete legacy duty legislation.

The meaning of 'retainer' was analysed in *Lord Advocate v Wotherspoon's Trustees* (1930) SLT 82. It was stated in that case that the retainer which gives rise to a right of the Crown to demand payment of the duty must be a retainer in the right and for the benefit of the legatee. The judgment also referred to a retainer as denoting delivery, payment, or other satisfaction or discharge of a legacy, something of analogous character to actual delivery or payment.

The point of 'retainer' may be reached prior to the point of actual handover or transfer. It arises when the beneficiary is entitled to have the benefit transferred, not at the time of actual transfer. The obsolete legacy duty was not payable until the date of retainer had arrived. So it is with CAT legislation, where the tax is only due and payable at the valuation date.

Accordingly, if the valuation date has not arrived, the tax is not due and payable.

1.5.5 EXCEPTIONAL CASES

Section 30(2) states that in the following exceptional cases, the valuation date is the date of death of the person on whose death the inheritance is taken:

- *Donatio mortis causa*, that is, a gift made in contemplation of death which becomes effective only if that death occurs.
- An inheritance taken by a person when a disponer, who had power to revoke the disposition, dies without revoking it. A disposition subject to a power of revocation by the disponer will be dealt with in **3.5**.
- An interest which is taken in possession following the cessation of a prior life interest will always give rise to an inheritance (CAT Consolidation Act, 2003, s. 3(1)(d) and 3(2)).

1.5.6 VALUATION DATE NOT NECESSARILY DATE OF DEATH (INHERITANCE)

Section 30(4) deals with valuation date of a taxable inheritance other than already referred to above. Here the basic concept is that of the 'date of retainer' already referred to. That is the date on which it might reasonably be said that the successor takes identifiable property into his or her possession and that the transfer or assent by the personal representatives may take place.

This valuation date may be the date of the inheritance but is much more likely to be at a later date, during the course of administration. The valuation date is a question of fact in the circumstances of each estate. It is in order to meet this variety of circumstances that fairly flexible rules are laid down in sub-section (4). According to that sub-section the valuation date of a taxable inheritance will the *earliest* of the potential valuation dates discussed in **1.5.7**.

1.5.7 POTENTIAL VALUATION DATES

The potential valuation dates are:

(1) the earliest date on which a personal representative or trustee or the successor or any other person is entitled to retain the subject matter of the inheritance for the benefit of the successor or any person in right of the successor or on his behalf; or

(2) the date on which the subject matter of the inheritance is so retained; or

(3) the date of delivery, payment, or other satisfaction or discharge of the subject matter of the inheritance to the successor for his or her own benefit or to or for the benefit of any person in right of the successor or on his or her behalf.

According to the legislation, therefore, the valuation date is the earliest of three possible dates. The legislation envisages a situation where a personal representative could retain a benefit for a successor before the successor was entitled to so retain.

In this context it should be noted that the definition of personal representative in CAT Consolidation Act, 2003, s. 2 means the executor or administrator for the time being of a deceased person and includes any person who takes possession of or intermeddles with the property of a deceased person. This definition is wider than the definition of personal representative in the Succession Act, 1965, s. 3.

As already stated, the rules regarding a valuation date are very flexible, and deliberately so as they must take account of every eventuality in the administration of an estate.

It can be stated however that a valuation date would not arrive in the case of intestacy until the date when the administrator extracts letters of administration intestate. However, even in this case it appears that a person intermeddling with an estate could trigger a valuation date prior to letters of administration being obtained.

1.5.7.1 Valuation date prior to grant of representation

It appears therefore that a valuation date could arrive prior to the date of the grant of probate in the case of an inheritance under a will; for example, where a residence is passed to an individual already residing in it, or a business (such as a farm) passes to a beneficiary who has an active role in running it for the deceased and begins to run it for his or her own benefit from the date of death.

The line between a beneficiary who is active in a business entering onto a property as a caretaker to ensure that the value of the property or business is maintained while the estate is being administered, and a beneficiary who is to inherit a business entering onto a property and taking it over on the death may be a thin line, which is not easily identified. However, if the profits of the business or any income from the property are passed on to the executor's account for the estate, rather than going directly to the beneficiary, that would indicate that the beneficiary is not yet entitled to the asset.

1.5.7.2 Litigation

On the other hand, it could be argued that the valuation date should not arrive prior to the date of the grant of probate as the will could be contested and might never come to probate. There may be a challenge to the validity of the will arising from alleged undue influence, or the incorrect execution of the will or the lack of capacity of the donor, and any such claim would affect the devolution of the entire estate and would push back the valuation date for any benefit passing through the estate.

Other common actions against an estate would include claims by a surviving spouse or civil partner for a legal right share under s. 111 of the Succession Act, 1965, and such a claim could affect the assets passing to all of the other beneficiaries. It should be noted that these claims only affect assets passing through the estate, and an asset passing by operation of law outside the estate (such as an interest in a joint property passing by survivorship) will not be affected.

The valuation date for the joint property will be the date of death, but the valuation date for other benefits taken from the estate should not arise until the spouse's claim is settled.

Another common type of claim against an estate is a claim by a child that although he or she does not have a right to a set portion of the estate the court should make provision for him or her under s. 117 or in some cases s. 67A of the Succession Act, 1965, on the basis that the parent failed in his or her moral duty to make proper provision. Any such action will defer the valuation date for any benefits affected. Section 117 is dealt with in detail in Chapter 4 of the *Wills, Probate & Estates* OUP Manual.

However, the mere fact that there is litigation in the estate will not defer the valuation date for any beneficiary whose interest is not directly affected. For example, if there is a dispute among children who inherit the residue under s. 63 of the Succession Act, 1965, this would not affect specific beneficiaries.

Alternatively, there may be a dispute about the level of benefit received giving rise to a claim for legitimate expectation or a claim for *quantum meruit*, that is, a claim that there was an implied promise that work done would be paid for and therefore the estate owes the value of the work to the claimant. Any such claim is likely to affect the residue but may not impact on other benefits if the residue is clearly larger than the level of the claim.

1.5.8 SEVERAL VALUATION DATES

It is possible that one inheritance could have several valuation dates.

For example, in the case of a residuary legatee the personal representative might make advance payments out of the inheritance. In the case of each advance payment the valuation date for that advance payment would be the date of that advance payment and there could be several of these valuation dates before the personal representative was finally in a position to retain the balance of residue for the beneficiary.

A tax return should be lodged on 31 October each year in respect of each advance made on or prior to 31 August in that year, regardless of whether the advance (or advances) exceeds 80 per cent of the relevant group threshold in the particular case. This is so because an estimate must be made of the balance of the residue, and this must be aggregated in arriving at the tax referable to the advance. This point is often missed and results in a payment of interest on the advance, as the valuation date of that advance is the date of the advance.

In the case of settled property where the life tenant dies, the valuation date in respect of the inheritance now taken by the remainderman who becomes entitled in possession on the death of the life tenant is the date of death of the life tenant.

1.5.9 MAIN VALUATION DATES—SUMMARY

Type of Benefit	Valuation Date
Gift	Date of gift
Gift made in contemplation of death	Date of death
Revocable gift	Date of death of disponer
Gift made within two years of disponer's death	Date of gift *but* gift treated as inheritance for tax purposes save that it benefits from small gift exemption
Inheritance	Earliest of (1), (2) or (3) at **1.5.7**

1.5.10 TREATMENT OF IRISH ASSETS WITH FOREIGN DISPONER

Where the disponer is not resident or ordinarily resident in the State the draftsman had a problem in arriving at the quantum of the taxable inheritance. This was so because the valuation date is different from the date of the inheritance (normally the date of death of the deceased disponer).

In some cases, during the course of administration of the estate, the locality of the estate or parts thereof may change between the date of the inheritance and the valuation date. For example, Irish shares may be sold in the course of administration and the proceeds of sale remitted to the UK prior to the distribution of the estate.

The draftsman therefore decided that the *situs* or locality of each asset of the estate would for inheritance tax purposes be regarded as frozen at the date of the inheritance (i.e. the date of death).

Accordingly, the entire or a proportion of any benefit which was payable out of Irish assets would remain unchanged, although at the valuation date the locality or *situs* of the assets might be foreign. In the case of a specific bequest of Irish property under the will of a foreign resident disponer the whole of that specific bequest is taxable because the whole property, which was to be appropriated to the inheritance, was Irish at the date of death of the deceased.

In the case of a share of residue or a pecuniary legacy payable out of residue, where the entire residue was Irish at the date of the inheritance the whole inheritance is taxable. Locality of the residue might change in the course of administration but for inheritance tax purposes it remains Irish.

Provision is also made for a situation where a part or a proportion of the benefit was payable out of Irish assets as at the date of the inheritance. For example, where a foreign testator leaves all his shares to a beneficiary and the shares are partly Irish and partly foreign. The part referable to the Irish shares is taxable although the portfolio of shares may change between the date of death and the valuation date.

Another example would be where a pecuniary legacy under the will of a foreign resident or ordinarily resident disponer is payable out of a residue which at the date of death was half Irish and half UK. In such a case one half of the pecuniary legacy would be liable to inheritance tax although at the valuation date the proportion of Irish and foreign assets in the residue may have changed considerably.

It will be appreciated that this problem of freezing the locality of the assets of an estate did not arise in connection with gift tax, as the valuation date in connection with the gift was the date of the gift.

1.5.11 IMPORTANCE OF VALUATION DATE

(1) Tax is due and payable on the valuation date (CAT Consolidation Act, 2003, s. 51(1)).

(2) The market value of the property subject to tax is ascertained as at the valuation date.

(3) If the tax is being paid by statutory instalments under CAT Consolidation Act, 2003, s. 54, the first instalment is due on the 31 October immediately following the valuation date. See **2.9.8** for instalments.

(4) Where the valuation date arises before 31 August in any year, the tax should be paid and a return filed by 31 October that year. If the valuation date arises after 31 August in any year, the tax should be paid and a return filed by 31 October the following year.

A return should be filed where:

(i) CAT is due and payable.

(ii) Where no CAT is payable, if the total of the value of the current benefit together with any aggregable prior benefits is more than 80 per cent of the relevant group threshold (see para 2.5.2).

(iii) Where no CAT is payable, whether the total value of the current benefit and any aggregable prior benefits is more than 80 per cent of the relevant group threshold or not where either is claimed in order to claim the relief. Agricultural and Business Relief are dealt with in Chapters 4 and 5.

For the tax year 2011 only, the file and pay date was 30 September for benefits taken on or before 31 August that year. The pay and file date reverted to 31 October the following year and has remained unchanged.

Failure to do so will lead to a surcharge and interest at the appropriate rate of interest (see CAT Consolidation Act, 2003, s. 51) being applied as and from the valuation date up to the date of payment of the tax. See **2.9.7**. There is a further provision in s. 58 of the CAT

Consolidation Act, 2003 for a penalty of €3,000 where a person fails to comply with the provisions of s. 46. This would usually arise in the course of a Revenue prosecution.

The current regime which applies from April 2010 replaced the earlier regime whereby if tax was paid within four months of the valuation date no interest accrued. Otherwise, interest was charged from the valuation date to date of payment.

In connection with agricultural relief (to be dealt with in **Chapter 4**) the property of the beneficiary must be valued as at the valuation date for the 'farmer test'.

In view of the fact that tax is not due and payable until the valuation date arrives, s. 30(6) gives power to the Revenue to determine the valuation date in respect of the whole or part of any inheritance. The taxpayer has the right to appeal against this determination under the provisions of s. 30(9), which appeal will be held under the auspices of s. 67.

In cases of doubt under s. 30(8) the Revenue may come to an agreement with the taxpayer on the particular valuation date to be applied in the estate. This might arise in a situation where many advances had been made say out of the residue and in order to avoid a multiplicity of valuation dates.

1.5.12 DISTINCTION BETWEEN DATE OF INHERITANCE AND VALUATION DATE

It is crucial that students distinguish between date of the disposition (gift/inheritance) and valuation date. The date of the disposition (gift/inheritance) is the date at which the disposition (gift/inheritance) is made. The tax regime applicable is fixed at this date. That means that the indexation factor/current group threshold (see **2.5**) to be applied, the rate of CAT payable on any taxable excess (see also **2.5**), the amount of any reduction applicable to agricultural or business property (see **Chapters 4** and **5** respectively), and the rules to determine whether dwelling exemption (see s. 86, discussed in **Chapter 3**) applies are fixed at the date of the disposition.

The valuation date is the date at which the tax due is payable under the regime in existence at the date of the disposition (gift/inheritance).

For example, if a person dies in November 2024 leaving property to a sibling and the valuation date is January 2025 (the date the grant of probate issued) the amount of tax payable is calculated under the rules in force in November 2024—not January 2025.

This may be of significance if there is an increase or decrease in thresholds in the Budget (usually held in mid-October of each year).

For example, on 8 October 2019 the group threshold for group A increased from €320,000 to €335,000, to take effect on 9 October 2019.

A death immediately prior to that date with a valuation date afterwards would have to use the group A threshold as at the date of death and not the date of valuation.

Where there is an intervening life or other limited interest the relationship is determined at the date of the original gift or inheritance but it will be the threshold amount arising at the date of the residuary beneficiary becoming beneficially entitled in possession that will be applied. This will be dealt with in Chapter 2.

1.6 Introduction to Life, Limited, and Lesser Interests

So far, we have looked at how to ascertain the taxable value of a present absolute interest in possession in property. In this section we will deal with ascertaining the taxable value of lesser interests in property and also how to deal with future interests or interests in expectancy. The chapter will then go on to deal with ongoing interests in property and valuing the property subject to the ongoing interest.

Before continuing it is opportune to list and differentiate between the different interests that can be held in property including but not limited to:

(a) absolute interest (sole);

(b) joint interest (joint tenants);

(c) interest in common (tenants in common);

(d) limited interests which fall into two categories:

 (i) an interest limited for a period certain.

 (ii) a life interest.

(e) a remainder interest;

(f) an ongoing interest.

1.6.1 TYPES OF INTEREST IN PROPERTY

An '**absolute interest**' as sole holder of the property is the highest interest one can hold in property. An absolute interest in property is 'alienable'; that is, it can be sold or transferred. It is also 'heritable', which means it is capable of being passed on a death. As discussed earlier, for CAT purposes, this includes a life interest in property together with a general power of appointment.

A '**joint tenancy**' in property means that more than one person owns a property with the right of survivorship; on the death of one of the joint owners, the property vests in the survivor(s). Property held under a joint tenancy is not heritable until there is only one owner surviving. All the joint tenants own all the property simultaneously. The joint tenancy can be 'severed' by a Deed of Severance resulting in a tenancy in common.

A '**tenancy in common**' means that there is undivided possession of property by more than one person but there is no right of survivorship; the interest of a tenant in common is heritable. It passes on death as part of his or her estate. Tenants in common can hold unequal shares in a property.

A '**limited interest**' is an interest in the property which is less than an absolute interest and, as noted, can fall into two broad categories:

An '**interest for a period certain**' is an interest in a property for a fixed term: for example, until a beneficiary reaches the age of 35 or until, say, 22 November 2030.

A '**life interest**' is a limited interest in property for life, ending on the termination of that life. It is usually the life of the tenant but can (rarely) be for the life of another ('pour autre vie').

Limited interests can be subject to conditions, but as noted in Chapter 2 of the Wills, Probate & Estates OUP Manual, these are frowned upon by the Courts.

A '**remainder interest**' is a present right to a future interest in property, usually on the cessation of a limited interest. The most common type is 'to A for life, remainder to B'. On the death of A, B becomes entitled to the property absolutely. Until then, all B has is the right in the future to become entitled to the property. This is sometimes referred to as an interest in expectancy or a future interest, and the person holding the interest in expectancy is usually referred to as the remainderman.

This future interest in the property could be:

- absolute ('to A for life, then to B absolutely');
- joint tenancy/tenancy in common ('to A for life, then to B and C as joint tenants/ tenants in common');
- life ('to A for life, then to B for life then to C absolutely'—B has a future life interest arising on the death of A; C, the remainderman, has a future absolute or full interest arising on the death of A and B);

- a limited interest to arise at some date in the future; either a fixed date (to A for ten years or until his 35th birthday or until 21 February 2030 and thereafter to B absolutely) or on the occurrence of a contingency or event, such as the re-marriage of a life tenant ('To A for life or until her re-marriage and thereafter to B'). This does not include a reversion expectant on the determination of a lease.

Remainder interests are not taxed until the remainderman becomes beneficially entitled in possession to the interest in property concerned. An **'ongoing interest'** is where someone has an ongoing right to an interest in a property, for example a right to reside in a property or an annuity. They do not 'own' the property as such but have a right which can, in some cases, be charged on a property. Ongoing interests are dealt with in **1.10**.

1.7 Limited Interests and CAT

'Limited interest' is defined in s. 2 as meaning:

(a) an interest (other than a leasehold interest) for the duration of a life or lives or for a period certain or

(b) any other interest which is not an absolute interest.

The First Schedule to CAT Consolidation Act, 2003 deals with the valuation of various limited interests. The First Schedule and the tables contained therein are reproduced below.

1.7.1 PART 1

Part 1 contains the rules relating to the valuation of the different types of limited interest.

Part 1

Rules relating to the valuation of limited interests utilising Tables A and B in Parts 2 and 3 of this Schedule

1. *The value of an interest for a single life in a capital sum shall be that sum multiplied by the factor, contained in column 3 or 4 respectively of Table A, which, is appropriate to the age and sex of the person in respect of the duration of whose life the interest is to be valued.*
2. *The value of an interest in a capital sum for the joint continuance of two lives shall be the value of an interest in that sum for the older life, ascertained in accordance with rule 1, multiplied by the joint factor in column 2 of Table A which is appropriate to the younger life.*
3. *The value of an interest in a capital sum for the joint continuance of three or more lives shall be the value of an interest in that sum for the joint continuance of the two oldest of those lives, ascertained in accordance with rule 2, multiplied by the joint factor of the youngest of those lives.*
4. *The value of an interest in a capital sum for the longer of two lives shall be ascertained by deducting from the total of the values of an interest in that sum for each of those lives, ascertained in accordance with rule 1, the value of an interest in the capital sum for the joint continuance of the same two lives, ascertained in accordance with rule 2.*
5. *Where an interest is given for the longest of more than two lives, it shall be valued, in accordance with rule 4, as if it were for the longer of the two youngest of those lives.*
6. *The value of an interest in a capital sum for a period certain shall be the aggregate of—*

   (a) *the value of the capital sum, multiplied by the factor in Table B which is appropriate to the number of whole years in that period (or zero if that period is less than a whole year); and*

(b) where the period is not an integral number of years, a fraction (of which the numerator is the number of days in excess of the number of whole years, if any, in that period and the denominator is 365) of the difference between—

(i) the value of an interest in the capital sum for one year longer than the number of whole years, if any, in the period; and

(ii) the value ascertained under the provisions of paragraph (a) (or zero, where so provided in the said paragraph).

7. In the case of a limited interest where the interest is for a life or lives, but is guaranteed for a period certain, the value shall be the higher of—

(a) the value of an interest for such life or lives, ascertained in accordance with the appropriate rule in this part of this Schedule; and

(b) the value of an interest for the period certain, ascertained in accordance with rule 6.

8. The value of a limited interest for which the other rules in this Part of this Schedule provide no method of valuing shall be ascertained as if the interest taken were a series of absolute interests in the property applied in satisfaction of the interest from time to time, taken as separate gifts or inheritances, as the case may be.

1.7.2 VALUING LIFE INTERESTS

Part 2 of Sch. 1 contains Table A, which values an interest for a single life in a capital sum. This table is based on the age and sex of the beneficiary (i.e. the person in respect of the duration of whose life the interest is to be valued). The legislation makes no provision for the state of health of that person.

The First Schedule, Part 1 further indicates how an interest for the joint continuance of two lives, the joint continuance of three or more lives, or the longer of two lives is calculated for tax purposes. These will not be discussed further here.

For example: if property valued at €1,000,000 was left to a woman aged 38 for her life, the value of that inheritance would be calculated as follows:

Years of age	Joint factor	Value of an interest in a capital of €1 for a male life aged as in column 1	Value of an interest in a capital of €1 for a female life aged as in column 1
38	.95	.8549	.8821

$$€1{,}000{,}000 \times .8821 = €882{,}100.$$

1.7.2.1 Age in whole years only

It does not matter whether the woman is aged 38 years, 11 months and 29 days or 38 years and 1 day. It is the age in whole years at the date of the disposition (as defined in **1.5.3**) that matters.

Consideration in its entirety (if any) is always deducted from the incumbrance-free value (absolute or discounted for limited interest). See **1.8** below.

As noted in earlier, it is possible for both a limited interest and a full interest to pass at the same time: for example, a life interest in a house and €20,000 absolutely.

1.7.2.2 Part 2, Table A

Part 2, Table A of CAT Consolidation Act, 2003, Sch. 1 is set out in full at **Table 1.1**.

1.7.3 VALUATION OF INTERESTS FOR A PERIOD CERTAIN

Part 3 of the First Schedule to CAT Consolidation Act, 2003 contains Table B, which shows how the value of an interest for a period certain is arrived at; that is, here, if the house valued at €1,000,000 was left to a person (gender is not relevant) for ten years.

Number of years	Value
10	.4913

$$€1,000,000 \times .4913 = €491,300$$

This is the taxable value of a ten-year interest in a property valued at €1,000,000. Gender is irrelevant in this case.

Again, consideration in its entirety (if any) is always deducted from the incumbrance-free value (absolute or discounted for limited interest). See **1.8** below.

1.7.3.1 Part 3, Table A

Part 3, Table B of CAT Consolidation Act, 2003, Sch. 1 is set out in full at **Table 1.2**.

1.7.4 VALUATION FOR PART OF A YEAR

Part 3, Table B deals with whole years but provision is made in para. 6 of Part 1 of the First Schedule for valuing an interest where the period is not an integral (i.e. whole) number of years, for example 3 years 36 days. This may arise where a beneficiary is given an interest in a property until he or she reaches the age of 35 years, for example.

This is unlike the treatment of life interests in Table A, which as we have seen in **1.7.2.1** is calculated in whole years. In that case the calculation is as follows:

- the value of the capital sum for three years, and
- a fraction, in this case 36/365 of the difference between the value of the capital sum for four years and three years.

Again, let us say that the capital sum is a house valued at €1,000,000.

The value of the capital sum for four years is €1.000,000 × .2370 = €237,000.

The value of the capital sum for three years is €1,000,000 × .1836 = €183,600.

The difference between the value of the capital sum for four years and three years is

$$(€237,000 - €183,600) = €53,400$$

Thus, the value of the capital sum for the entirety of the fourth year is €53,400.

The value of the capital sum for the thirty-six days of the fourth year is:

$$€53,400 \times 36/365 = €5,266.80$$

Total value of the capital sum for three years and thirty-six days is:

the value of the capital sum for three years	€183,600.00
together with the value of the capital sum for the 36 days of the fourth year	€5,266.80
	€188,866.80

The value of the capital sum for the part of year is always divided by 365, whether the year is a leap year or not (CAT Consolidation Act, 2003, Sch. 1, Part 1, para. 6(b)).

TABLE 1.1 CAT Consolidation Act, 2003, Sch.1, Part 2, Table A

PART 2
TABLE A

1	2	3	4
Years of age	**Joint factor**	**Value of an interest in a capital of €1 for a male life aged as in column 1**	**Value of an interest in a capital of €1 for a female life aged as in column 1**
0	.99	.9519	.9624
1	.99	.9767	.9817
2	.99	.9767	.9819
3	.99	.9762	.9817
4	.99	.9753	.9811
5	.99	.9742	.9805
6	.99	.9730	.9797
7	.99	.9717	.9787
8	.99	.9703	.9777
9	.99	.9688	.9765
10	.99	.9671	.9753
11	.98	.9653	.9740
12	.98	.9634	.9726
13	.98	.9614	.9710
14	.98	.9592	.9693
15	.98	.9569	.9676
16	.98	.9546	.9657
17	.98	.9522	.9638
18	.98	.9497	.9617
19	.98	.9471	.9596
20	.97	.9444	.9572
21	.97	.9416	.9547
22	.97	.9387	.9521
23	.97	.9356	.9493
24	.97	.9323	.9464
25	.97	.9288	.9432
26	.97	.9250	.9399
27	.97	.9209	.9364
28	.97	.9165	.9328
29	.97	.9119	.9289
30	.96	.9068	.9248
31	.96	.9015	.9205
32	.96	.8958	.9159
33	.96	.8899	.9111
34	.96	.8836	.9059
35	.96	.8770	.9005
36	.96	.8699	.8947
37	.96	.8626	.8886
38	.95	.8549	.8821
39	.95	.8469	.8753
40	.95	.8384	.8683
41	.95	.8296	.8610
42	.95	.8204	.8534
43	.95	.8107	.8454
44	.94	.8005	.8370
45	.94	.7897	.8283
46	.94	.7783	.8192
47	.94	.7663	.8096
48	.93	.7541	.7997

Continued

TABLE 1.1 Continued

1	2	3	4
Years of age	**Joint factor**	**Value of an interest in a capital of €1 for a male life aged as in column 1**	**Value of an interest in a capital of €1 for a female life aged as in column 1**
49	.93	.7415	.7896
50	.92	.7287	.7791
51	.91	.7156	.7683
52	.90	.7024	.7572
53	.89	.6887	.7456
54	.89	.6754	.7335
55	.88	.6598	.7206
56	.88	.6445	.7069
57	.88	.6288	.6926
58	.87	.6129	.6778
59	.86	.5969	.6628
60	.86	.5809	.6475
61	.86	.5650	.6320
62	.86	.5492	.6162
63	.85	.5332	.6000
64	.85	.5171	.5830
65	.85	.5007	.5650
66	.85	.4841	.5462
67	.84	.4673	.5266
68	.84	.4506	.5070
69	.84	.4339	.4873
70	.83	.4173	.4679
71	.83	.4009	.4488
72	.82	.3846	.4301
73	.82	.3683	.4114
74	.81	.3519	.3928
75	.80	.3352	.3743
76	.79	.3181	.3559
77	.78	.3009	.3377
78	.76	.2838	.3198
79	.74	.2671	.3023
80	.72	.2509	.2855
81	.71	.2353	.2693
82	.70	.2203	.2538
83	.69	.2057	.2387
84	.68	.1916	.2242
85	.67	.1783	.2104
86	.66	.1657	.1973
87	.65	.1537	.1849
88	.64	.1423	.1730
89	.62	.1315	.1616
90	.60	.1212	.1509
91	.58	.1116	.1407
92	.56	.1025	.1310
93	.54	.0939	.1218
94	.52	.0858	.1132
95	.50	.0781	.1050
96	.49	.0710	.0972
97	.48	.0642	.0898
98	.47	.0578	.0828
99	.45	.0517	.0762
100 or over	.43	.0458	.0698

TABLE 1.2 CAT Consolidation Act, 2003, Sch.1, Part 3, Table B

PART 3
TABLE B
(Column (2) shows the value of an interest in a capital of €1 for the number of years shown in column (1)).

1	2	1	2
Number of years	**Value**	**Number of years**	**Value**
1	.0654	26	.8263
2	.1265	27	.8375
3	.1836	28	.8480
4	.2370	29	.8578
5	.2869	30	.8669
6	.3335	31	.8754
7	.3770	32	.8834
8	.4177	33	.8908
9	.4557	34	.8978
10	.4913	35	.9043
11	.5245	36	.9100
12	.5555	37	.9165
13	.5845	38	.9230
14	.6116	39	.9295
15	.6369	40	.9360
16	.6605	41	.9425
17	.6826	42	.9490
18	.7032	43	.9555
19	.7225	44	.9620
20	.7405	45	.9685
21	.7574	46	.9750
22	.7731	47	.9815
23	.7878	48	.9880
24	.8015	49	.9945
25	.8144	50 and over	1.0000

1.8 Taxable Value of Limited Interests

In **1.4.3.1** and **1.4.3.2**, liabilities, costs, and expenses are deducted from the market value of an asset to arrive at the incumbrance-free value of an absolute interest applying the provisions of s. 28(1)–(3).

For limited interests, s. 28(4) provides that it is this incumbrance-free value (the value of the asset after the deduction of costs, liabilities, and expenses but prior to the deduction of any consideration paid) that is reduced by use of Tables A and B as described in **1.7.1** and **1.7.2**. Consideration (in its entirety) is then deducted from this 'limited interest' value.

The incumbrance-free value will therefore be reduced to take account of the fact that the interest taken is a limited interest (examples (2) and (3) from **1.4.3**).

(2) *Adam transfers his dwelling house valued at €260,000 to Brian for life (Table A) with remainder to Cynthia absolutely, or*

(3) *Adam transfers his dwelling house valued at €260,000 to Brian for 10 years (Table B) with remainder to Cynthia absolutely.*

The incumbrance-free value already ascertained is reduced, not the taxable value according to the rules and tables in the First Schedule to CAT Consolidation Act, 2003. So, applying the formula applied earlier: in this case the incumbrance-free value is reduced for limited interests according to the appropriate table, and the formula looks like this:

Market value	
Less	liabilities, costs, and expenses
Equals	incumbrance-free value
Reduced for limited interests according to the appropriate Table (either A or B)	
Gives incumbrance-free value of limited interest	
Less	consideration
Equals	taxable value

1.8.1 TAXABLE VALUE OF LIFE INTEREST

Taking example (b) a few steps further: Adam transfers his house, valued at €260,000 and subject to a mortgage of €50,000, to his 65-year-old brother Brian for his life with remainder to their sister Cynthia on condition that Brian pays their other sister Deirdre €20,000. The costs, including stamp duty and solicitor's fees, etc., are €10,000 and are paid by Brian.

The costs of €10,000 and the mortgage of €50,000 are deductible from the **market value** and the payment of €20,000 is deductible from the reduced **incumbrance-free value o**f Brian's benefit.

Applying this example to the sequence above, we get the following:

Market value	€260,000
Less liabilities, costs, and expenses	
Liability (mortgage)	€50,000
Costs and expenses (stamp duty, etc.)	€10,000
	(€60,000)
Equals incumbrance-free value	€200,000
Applying age and gender factors to limited interest (male aged 65) .5007	
€200,000 × .5007 =	€100,140
Less consideration (Payment to Deirdre)	€20,000
Equals taxable value	€80,140

The **incumbrance-free value** of Brian's benefit is (market value of €260,000 less mortgage of €50,000 and costs and expenses of €10,000) = €200,000.

Brian is a male aged 65 years. The value of his **limited interest** according to Table A of the First Schedule to would be €200,000 multiplied by .5007, that is, €100,140.

This sum represents the value of the interest taken by Brian and would be the taxable value if not for the conditional payment to Deirdre.

Less ***consideration*** *(Payment to Deirdre) €20,000*

That €20,000 would be a good deduction as part consideration. It would be deducted *in its entirety* from the discounted incumbrance-free value. Even though the interest passing is a life interest, the payment is an absolute payment and so is deducted in its entirety.

*Equals **taxable value** €80,140*

This leaves the taxable value of Brian's benefit at €80,140.

1.8.2 TAXABLE VALUE OF INTEREST FOR A PERIOD CERTAIN

Taking example (c), the interest for a period certain from above, and applying the same costs and consideration.

Adam transfers his house, valued at €260,000 and subject to a mortgage of €50,000, to his brother Brian for ten years with remainder to Cynthia on condition that Brian pays their sister Deirdre €20,000. The costs, including stamp duty and solicitor's fees, etc., are €10,000 and are paid by Brian.

The costs of €10,000 and the mortgage of €50,000 are deductible from the market value and the payment of €20,000 is deductible from the reduced incumbrance-free value of Brian's benefit. In this case the incumbrance-free value is reduced in accordance with Table B (value of interest for a period certain).

Market value	€260,000
Less liabilities, costs, and expenses	
Liability (mortgage)	€50,000
Costs and expenses (stamp duty, etc.)	€10,000
	(€60,000)
Equals incumbrance-free value	€200,000

In this case the incumbrance-free value of Brian's benefit is the same (market value of €260,000 less mortgage of €50,000 and costs and expenses of €10,000) = €200,000.

1.8.2.1 Applying factors to limited interest (ten years' interest in house)

Brian has an interest in the property for ten years. The value of his limited interest according to Table B of the First Schedule already referred to would be €200,000 multiplied by .4913, that is, €98,260.

€200,000 × .4913 =	€98,260
Less consideration (Payment to Deirdre)	(€20,000)
Equals **taxable value**	€78,260

1.8.3 FULL INTEREST AND LIMITED INTEREST PASSING AT SAME TIME

As discussed earlier, it is possible to receive a limited interest in one property and a full interest in other property at the same time, for example: 'I leave my house [valued at €500,000] to A [a male aged 47] for his life with remainder to C and I leave €100,000 to A for his own use and benefit absolutely'. In this case, no costs or consideration are payable by A and there is no mortgage on the house.

- As a male aged 47, the age and gender factor applicable is .7663.
- In this case, A received a life interest in a house valued at €500,000 together with €100,000 absolutely.
- The taxable value of the house is €500,000 × .7663 = €383,150.
- This, added to his absolute interest in €100,000, gives a total benefit of €483,150.

1.9 Remainder Interest/Interest in Expectancy

As noted earlier, a remainder interest or interest in expectancy is a present right to a future interest and is not taxed until the remainderman is beneficially entitled in possession.

Example: Adam, the disponer (by *inter vivos* disposition or by testamentary disposition), settles property on his son Brian for life with remainder to his (Adam's) daughter Cynthia absolutely.

Brian's interest is taken in possession and he is taxed accordingly for a life interest.

Cynthia's interest, although vested in interest, is not vested in possession, and her interest will only become a present right on the death of Brian the life tenant or alternatively if Brian releases his life interest to Cynthia. Cynthia will always be deemed to take the property from Adam and for the calculation of tax, her Tax group (which is based on her blood relationship to the disponer: see **Chapter 2**) will be fixed as at the date of the original disposition. The value of the group threshold will be the indexed value at the date Cynthia becomes beneficially entitled in possession. This is also outlined in **Chapter 2**.

Example: if Adam settled the property on his son Brian for life in 2008 with remainder interest to his (Adam's) daughter Cynthia then Brian's tax threshold would have been the group A threshold in 2008 of €521,208.

Cynthia pays no tax until Brian dies or unless Brian assigns his life interest to her. Alternatively, Cynthia could assign her remainder interest to Brian or to a third party. They could further decide to split the property between them either as tenants in common in equal or unequal shares or as joint tenants. Any of these transactions are referred to as the breakup of a settlement and have complex CAT implications.

CAT considerations in the breakup of settlements are dealt with in Part V of the CAT Consolidation Act but are not dealt with on the PPC.

If Brian died in 2025, then Cynthia's group A threshold in 2025 would be €400,000.

The crucial point to remember about interests in expectancy is that they are not taxed until they become interests in possession. When that happens, they are taxed at the current market value at that date and at the indexed group threshold applying at that date as outlined above. Until then, they are ignored (with the exception of applying the 'farmer test' for agricultural property which will be dealt with in **Chapter 4**).

It is important to distinguish between an interest in expectancy and a contingent interest in expectancy. For example: 'to my wife for life with remainder to my son Paul' is an interest in expectancy; 'to my wife for life with remainder to my son Paul on his reaching the age of 21' is a contingent interest in expectancy. The benefit is contingent on Paul (in this example) reaching the age of 21. The case of *Jacob (Bridget Kathleen) v Revenue Commissioners* 3 ITR 105 is relevant in attempting to distinguish between the two.

1.10 Ongoing Benefits 'Slice' Principle

1.10.1 INTRODUCTION

This principle is utilised by the draftsman in taxing a benefit which is not a one-off benefit but an ongoing benefit.

Ongoing benefits were referred to in the list of types of benefit receivable in para **1.6** and would include a benefit taken by way of an **annuity** or a **right to reside** in property or, as is more common in the rural community, a right of **residence, support, and maintenance** on the lands in question.

To fully understand the operation of this principle it is vital to be aware of the different interests in property that can be received by people, and in particular that practitioners understand the difference between a right to reside; a right to residence, support, and maintenance; an exclusive right to reside; and a life interest.

1.10.2 DIFFERENT TYPES OF ONGOING INTERESTS IN PROPERTY

A **right to reside** is a right to live in the property only. It may be even further limited to a right to reside in a particular bedroom and a right to use the kitchen, bathroom, and living room in common with others. This right is not an exclusive right and gives the holder no ownership in the property. The right to reside vests in the individual for their lifetime only: that is, it is not heritable (cannot be passed on by will or intestacy) and cannot be alienated (sold) to a third party. It can however be surrendered to the present owner in possession of the property for consideration.

Someone else is the present owner in possession of the property subject to or 'blighted with' this right to reside. This right can be a charge on the property, and may be found on Land Registry Folios from time to time. Where a farm is charged with a right to reside, that right to reside affects the farmhouse only, not the farmland. This distinction is important when calculating the value of the right to reside.

A **right to residence, support, and maintenance** is a right to reside along with a right to be supported and maintained on or out of the lands. This is a right charged on the land and is enforceable against the entire property and any income derived from it. For that reason it is charged against the farmhouse and the farmland in its entirety and is of greater value than a mere right to reside.

An **exclusive right to reside**, however, is considered by the Revenue Commissioners to have a right equivalent to a life interest, following the UK case of *IRC v Lloyds Private Banking Ltd*. In particular, since the passing of the Land and Conveyancing Reform Act, 2009, which removed the power of sale of the life tenant, the position of the holder of an exclusive right to reside and that of a life tenant are increasingly indistinguishable.

The person who has an exclusive right to reside in a property can allow others to reside in the property by permission but in the event of a dispute can order the others to leave. Someone else owns the property subject to (and 'blighted with') that person's exclusive right to reside, but for taxation purposes is treated as if they were a remainderman for the lifetime of the person with the exclusive right to reside. As noted, the remainderman only becomes beneficially entitled in possession for CAT purposes on the death of the life tenant.

1.10.3 WHERE THE BENEFIT OR 'SLICE' IS A CHARGE ON PROPERTY

Section 5(2) of CAT Consolidation Act, 2003 states that a gift shall be deemed to consist of the *appropriate part* of the property in which the donee takes a benefit or on which the benefit is charged or secured or on which the donee is entitled to have it charged or secured, while s. 10(2) provides that the same principles apply to an inheritance.

The effect of this is that the person granted the right to reside is, for tax purposes, considered to receive a 'slice' of the property for their lifetime, and the person who receives the property itself receives that property 'burdened' with that 'slice'. This burden is only lifted when the 'slice' is terminated, usually on the death of the person who has the right to reside.

1.10.4 CALCULATING THE MARKET VALUE OF THE SLICE

This 'slice' and the effect of the 'slice' on the owner of the property both need to be valued for CAT purposes. Section 5(5) of the Act does this by defining **'appropriate part'**. It means that part of the entire property in which the benefit subsists which bears the same proportion to the entire property as the gross annual value of the benefit bears to the gross annual value of the entire property.

In other words, if a person is, for example, left or given a right to reside in a house, the annual value of that right to reside is deemed to be a percentage of the annual rental value of the entire house. The taxable value of that right to reside is then that percentage of the market value of the house. Figures for the annual values and market value can be obtained from an auctioneer/valuer.

The difference in values is comparable to the difference between renting a room in a house as a lodger (annual value of right to reside) and renting the entire house as a tenant (annual value of the property).

The 'appropriate part' or the 'slice' is arrived at by using the following formula:

$$\frac{\text{Gross annual value of right to reside}}{\text{Gross annual value of the property charged with the right to reside}} \times \text{by market value} = \text{capital value of right of the property}$$

To apply the formula to the example given above: Brian is left a house subject to Adam's right to reside in a house for his lifetime. Adam is a male aged 57 and does not have to pay any costs, liabilities, expenses, or consideration.

An auctioneer's valuation has valued as follows:

Annual value of right to reside	€12,000 (€1,000 per month)
Annual value of the property	€486,000 (€4,000 per month)
Market value of the property	€600,000

$$\frac{\text{Gross annual value of right to reside}}{\text{Gross annual value of the property charged with the right to reside}} \times \text{by market value} = \text{capital value of right of the property}$$

$$\frac{€12{,}000}{€48{,}000} \times \text{by } €600{,}000 = €150{,}000$$

The market value of Adam's 'slice' of the property is €150,000. As Adam pays no costs, liabilities, or expenses, this is also the incumbrance-free value. This is then discounted for age and gender as part of the sequence already dealt with in arriving at the taxable value of his benefit.

$$€150{,}000 \times .6288 = €94{,}320$$

As Adam pays no consideration, the taxable value of his benefit is €94,320.

1.10.5 DEALING WITH THE REST OF THE PROPERTY

We now have to calculate Brian's taxable benefit.

Brian has been left an absolute interest in property subject to Adam's right to reside. The absolute market value of Adam's right to reside has been valued at €150,000.

Brian receives the rest of the property (€600,000 less the absolute market value of Adams's slice of €150,000), that is, €450,000.

Note: The deduction to be made is to the capitalised *market* value of the slice and *not* the value of the slice discounted for age and gender. Deducting the discounted value of Adam's rights in the inheritance tax return of Brian is a very common error. The correct position is clearly set out in s. 28(8) and (9) of CAT Consolidation Act, 2003:

(8) Where a taxable gift or a taxable inheritance is subject to a liability within the meaning of subsection (9), the deduction to be made in respect of that liability under this section shall be

an amount equal to ***the market value*** *of the whole or the appropriate part, as the case may be, of the property, within the meaning of section 5(5).*

(9) *For the purpose of subsection (8), 'liability', in relation to a taxable gift or a taxable inheritance, means a liability which* ***deprives*** *the donee or successor, whether permanently or temporarily, of the use, enjoyment or income in whole or in part of the property, or of any part of the property, of which the taxable gift or taxable inheritance consists.*

What this means is that where a benefit is subject to a liability which means that the beneficiary does not have full use of the property, the market value of that liability is deducted from the value of the benefit.

This means that where a person is given a property subject to somebody else's right to reside, there are two taxable benefits accruing to two different people:

(1) the right to reside, which is taxed according to the life interest in the market value of the right; and

(2) the property subject to the right to reside, which is taxed at market value less the market value of the right to reside without taking the life interest factor into account.

Both of these are current benefits and are taxable at the appropriate valuation date.

1.10.6 DEALING WITH THE CESSATION OF THE LIMITED INTEREST IN THE PROPERTY

However, the interest is a life interest and will come to an end at some stage. When Adam dies, Brian will take a further benefit from the original testator. That benefit arises by reason of the cessation or cesser of Adam's right to reside and this is provided for in s. 37 of CAT Consolidation Act, 2003.

This provides that the 'slice' of the property is 'set free' on Adam's death and is now taken by Brian absolutely. This is dealt with as a current benefit from the original disponer of an absolute interest in the 'slice' of the property at current values.

Again, an auctioneer must provide current valuations for the market value of the property, the annual right to reside, and the annual value of the property. Let us say, in this case, that property values have increased.

Annual right to reside	€15,000 (€1250 per month)
Annual value of the property	€60,000 (€5000 per month)
Market value of the property	€750,000

One of the dangers when providing a right to reside is that the person residing in the property is not motivated to spend money on necessary maintenance of the property, and the value of the property may be adversely affected by such neglect over a number of years.

Applying the formula again:

$$\frac{\text{Gross annual value of right to reside}}{\text{Gross annual value of the property charged with the right to reside}} \times \text{by market value} = \begin{array}{c}\text{capital value of right}\\ \text{of the property}\end{array}$$

$$\frac{€15{,}000}{€60{,}000} \times \text{by } €750{,}000 = €187{,}500$$

Brian is deemed to receive a current benefit of €187,500 from the original testator on Adam's death. The valuation date will be the date of Adam's death. This will be aggregated with the prior benefit of (€600,000 – €150,000 = €450,000) to calculate the current tax payable. Aggregation will be dealt with in detail in **Chapter 2**.

As this is a benefit received on a death, it will always be an inheritance, and the small gift exemption (SGE) cannot be availed of. The SGE will be covered briefly in **Chapter 2** and dealt with in more detail in **Chapter 3**.

A 'rule of thumb' applied by the Revenue Commissioners is that they will accept a valuation of up to 10 per cent of the property for a right of residence *simpliciter* and a valuation of up to 20 per cent of a right of residence, support, and maintenance per person. For example, if a couple transferred their farm to a child subject to their joint residence, support, and maintenance, the Revenue Commissioners would accept a 40 per cent reduction in the valuation of the property to take this into account.

Real property (i.e. an interest in land) is not the only type of property that can be subject to a burden of this nature. Personal property can also be 'sliced' in this manner. This is not dealt with in this book.

CHAPTER 2

CALCULATION OF CAT PAYABLE: COMPUTATION AND AGGREGATION, AND THE ROLE OF THE SOLICITOR

2.1 Introduction

Once we have established the taxable value of a benefit, whether absolute, limited, lesser, or ongoing, we then have to establish the CAT payable on that taxable value, pay that tax, and file a return.

The date the tax is due depends on the valuation date and a return should be filed with the tax due on the appropriate 31 October following the valuation date. Depending on the nature of the benefit and whether there are any reliefs claimed, the return can either be a paper return (IT38S) or done online, or in some cases has to be done online. Where a relief (other than the small gift exemption (SGE)) is claimed or where the benefit is anything other than a full interest in property, the return has to be done online. It is proposed to move CAT to an entirely online tax in the future.

The CAT payable depends on the consanguinity (relationship) between the disponer (i.e. donor/testator/intestate) and the beneficiary (i.e. donee/successor). It also depends on prior benefits taken from any disponers in relation to whom the beneficiary bears the same relationship he or she does to the current disponer.

For example, a prior benefit from someone's mother will be taken into account when calculating tax payable on a current benefit from that person's father. However, a prior benefit from a brother will not. These classes of relationship are known as 'Groups'.

As was noted earlier in **1.9**, where there is a limited and future interest passing (i.e. in that example, from Adam to Brian for life and remainder to Cynthia absolutely), on the death of Brian Cynthia is deemed to inherit from Adam, and her 'group' (i.e. her relationship to Adam) is ascertained at the time of the initial gift/inheritance.

The taxable value of the full interest passing, and her Group Threshold, would be ascertained at the time that she becomes beneficially entitled in possession, that is, at the cessation of Brian's life interest.

2.2 Relationship Groups for CAT Purposes

These relationship groups are defined in the Second Schedule to CAT Consolidation Act, 2003 as amended, particularly by the Finance (No. 3) Act 2011, which dealt with the taxation provisions of the Civil Partnership and Certain Rights and Obligations of Cohabitants Act 2010.

2.2.1 GROUP A

Where the beneficiary is a child, minor child of a deceased child of the disponer or of the civil partner of a disponer, minor child of a civil partner of a deceased child of the disponer, or minor child of a civil partner of a deceased child of a civil partner of the disponer, or where a parent inherits an absolute interest from a child on the death of that child.

The definition of '**child**' for the purpose of establishing group A threshold is extremely wide for CAT purposes. 'Child' includes: natural child (marital or non-marital); adopted child (adopted under an adoption order within the meaning of s. 3 (1) of the Adoption Act 2010 or the subject of an inter-country adoption effected outside the State and recognised under that Act); child of a 'social parent' as defined in the Birth Information and Tracing Act, 2022; step-child; natural child validly adopted by other adoptive parents (CAT Consolidation Act, 2003, Sch. 2, paras 9 and 10); and in some cases foster children.

The definition of 'parent' has not been redefined to include 'civil partner of parent of child'. The tax position of children of civil partners is analogous to that of step-children.

2.2.1.1 Certain foster children

As noted above, a foster child who satisfies certain criteria may be considered a 'child' for CAT group classification. The criteria for foster children are to be found in CAT Consolidation Act, 2003, Second Schedule, para. 9.

While the foster child is considered a child of the disponer, no other relationship can be inferred from this. For example, the foster child is not a grandchild of the disponer's parent.

Certain difficulties can be foreseen in the application of these criteria:

(1) The lack of an official regulatory system for fostering prior to 1995. An earlier register established in 1983 apparently did not cover fostering by relatives.

(2) The level of proof required in the case of inheritances. It might be helpful if the foster parent acknowledged the status of the foster child while alive (possibly in the will itself).

(3) Other proofs that may be accepted by the Revenue Commissioners include information from school rolls or census forms.

(4) Foster children have not been excluded from qualifying as group A beneficiaries in respect of gifts/inheritances from their natural parents. They would appear to have the same 'advantage' in this regard as adopted children.

(5) It could be possible for a child to have been fostered twice.

(6) CAT Consolidation Act, 2003 provides that the relief will not be available based solely on the uncorroborated testimony of one witness.

2.2.1.2 Minor child of a deceased child

A minor child of a deceased child is also a group A beneficiary.

'Minor child of a deceased child' arises where the deceased parent of that minor child is a child of the disponer (where a grandparent makes a bequest to a minor child whose deceased parent is a child of that grandparent). See also notes on s. 42 of CAT Consolidation Act, 2003 at **2.9.5.3**, which deals with the tax treatment of such bequests. See also notes on s. 98 and the '*Per Stirpes*' Rule in *Wills, Probate and Estates* (Courtney: OUP, 2021).

According to the Age of Majority Act, 1985, a minor child is one who is under the age of 18 years.

In general, a group B threshold applies where a grandchild takes a benefit from his or her grandparent regardless of whether the child is a minor child or not. However if the parent of the minor child who is also a child of the grandparent is dead, the benefit taken by that minor child from the parent of his or her parent is taxed under group A.

Example: Adam, a grandfather, makes a gift to his minor grandson Brian after Chris, the father of Brian and the son of Adam, has died. Brian's benefit is taxed under group A.

A few years later, Adam makes a further gift to his grandson Brian, who has now attained 18 years. Brian's benefit is now taxed under group B.

A minor child of the child of a civil partner would benefit from this but the adult child of a deceased child of a civil partner is group C.

This is a case where a beneficiary can take benefits from the same disponer under different class thresholds.

The situation where a parent inherits an absolute interest from a child will be dealt with in **3.14.1**.

2.2.2 GROUP B

Group B applies where the beneficiary is a lineal ancestor (i.e. parent, grandparent, great grandparent, etc.), a lineal descendant other than a child or a minor child of a deceased child (i.e. grandchildren, great grandchildren, etc., except of course minor children of a deceased child), brother or sister, or child of a brother or sister.

> *where the donee or successor is on that day, a lineal ancestor, a lineal descendant (other than a child, or a minor child of a deceased child), a brother, a sister, or a child of a brother or of a sister of the disponer;*

A step-brother or sister is not a brother or sister for this purpose.

2.2.2.1 Nephew/niece or child of a brother or sister

Note the distinction between 'nephew/niece' and 'child of a brother or sister'. The words nephew and niece are equivocal and should not be used in designating the relationship between the disponer and the beneficiary. For example, I am the 'nephew' of my mother's brother; I am not the nephew of my mother's brother's wife. When completing the relevant forms, 'child of disponer's brother or sister' should be used instead of simply 'nephew' or 'niece'. The child of a sibling's civil partner is included under group B even though there is no blood relationship.

2.2.3 GROUP C

Group C applies where the beneficiary is anybody else. This will include uncles, aunts, step-brothers and sisters, grand-nephews and nieces, natural parents of adopted children, cousins, and of course strangers in blood. As noted above, a step-brother or sister is group C.

> *where the donee or successor (who is not a spouse of the disponer) does not, on that day, stand to the disponer in a relationship referred to in subparagraph (a) or (b);*

2.2.3.1 Uncle/aunt to nephew/niece and nephew/niece to uncle/aunt

Note that while a benefit received by a nephew/niece (child of brother or sister) from an uncle/aunt (brother/sister of a parent) is group B, a benefit received by an uncle/aunt from a nephew/niece (child of brother or sister) is group C.

2.2.3.2 Step-children and other relationships

As we have seen, 'child' includes a step-child. A step-child of a sibling will be a 'child of a brother or sister' and group B. However, a step-sibling is not a brother or sister and thus the child of a step-brother or sister is group C.

2.3 Prior Tax Regimes

There have been four different regimes in place since the CAT Act was introduced. The current regime came into force on 1 December 1999. This is the regime that this book will be concentrating on, and which is taught on the Professional Practice Course Part I.

We will be dealing with tax planning and the calculation of tax arising from current benefits under the current regime. This may involve ascertaining the taxable value of benefits received in the past and may (particularly in the case of agricultural relief) involve dealing with the calculation of agricultural relief under the previous regime(s).

Where practitioners have to deal with a situation where it is necessary to calculate the tax payable on a current benefit arising before the present regime came into force (i.e. before 1 December 1999), see the reading list provided at pp. xxxix–xl.

2.3.1 STAGE ONE

Initially, there were four different tables of rates of tax payable depending on the relationship between disponer and beneficiary. Each of the tables of rates had a fixed threshold or nil band, again based on the consanguinity factor, and tax was payable on an ascending scale, that is, the first £X,000 at 20 per cent, the next £X,000 at 30 per cent, and so on.

Only where a beneficiary received successive benefits from the same disponer were benefits aggregated. Aggregation in this sense means that the prior benefit was added to the current benefit for the purpose of calculating tax paid on the total benefit. The tax payable on the prior benefit was then subtracted from this figure to get the tax payable on the current benefit.

2.3.2 STAGE TWO

Under the provisions of the Finance Act, 1982 the scope of aggregation was widened and benefits taken from all disponers in the same class were aggregable. This is similar to the present regime; however, there was still a table of rates.

2.3.3 STAGE THREE

Under the provisions of the Finance Act, 1984, a system of full aggregation of all benefits taken by any beneficiary from any disponer, regardless of relationship, was introduced.

2.4 Present Regime of Aggregation

As noted, the current regime has broadly been in force since 1 December 1999 and essentially provides for aggregation within groups only.

People fall into groups depending on their relationship to the disponer, as detailed at **2.2**. To aggregate means to include prior gifts along with the current gift when calculating the value of the total gifts received from any persons in relation to whom the beneficiary is in the same group threshold. This information is required for the Individual Beneficiary Screen when completing the Statement of Affairs (Probate) online Form SA 2, as dealt with later in this chapter and in *Wills, Probate and Estates*, Chapter 8.

The table at **2.4.1** explains which prior benefits have to be aggregated with the current benefit and how far back one has to aggregate from.

Under the current regime for benefits taken since 5 December 2001, aggregation applies to benefits taken since 5 December 1991 from persons within the same group threshold as defined. Thus, if I received a gift in January 2024 from a parent (group A) and had received a gift in 1998 from an uncle (brother of parent) (group B) I would *ignore* the 1998 benefit for aggregation purposes. Any benefit received prior to 5 December 1991 is ignored completely, no matter from whom it was received.

2.4.1 TABLE OF AGGREGATION DATES

Date of current benefit	Relevant prior disponers to be aggregated with the current benefit	Date from which aggregation accrues
From 5 December 2001 (present regime)	Disponers within the same group as the current disponer only	5 December 1991 (Gifts/inheritances prior to this date can be ignored)
From 1 December 1999 to 4 December 2001	Disponers within the same group as the current disponer only	2 December 1988
From 2 December 1998 to 30 November 1999	All disponers	2 December 1988
Prior to 2 December 1998	All disponers	2 June 1982

2.5 Threshold Amounts and Indexation

The threshold amount for each group is the amount below which no tax is payable. The amount (if any) in excess of the group threshold is known as the '**taxable excess**'.

Up until 7 December 2011 the threshold amount for each group was indexed each calendar year on 1 January according to the Consumer Price Index for the year immediately preceding the year in which the benefit was taken (CAT Consolidation Act 2003, Schedule 2, para. 1).

Indexation was abolished on this date.

On 7 April 2009, as part of the supplementary budget announced on that date and in addition to increasing the rate of CAT from 22 per cent to 25 per cent (see **2.6.1**), the threshold amounts were decreased by 20 per cent. These measures took effect at midnight on 7 April 2009 and remained in force until 31 December 2009. Indexation took place as usual on 1 January 2010 and on 7 December 2010, as part of that year's budget, the threshold amounts were decreased again to take effect from midnight on that date. These threshold figures were maintained for most of the calendar year 2011.

On 6 December 2011 the group A threshold was reduced from €332,084 to €250,000 to take effect from midnight on 6 December 2011. The group B and C threshold figures were subsequently rounded up to €33,500 from €33,208 and up to €16,750 from €16,604 respectively and these thresholds were backdated to 7 December 2011. As noted above, annual indexation was abolished from this date.

On 6 December 2012 the thresholds were reduced by a further 10 per cent to take effect from that date: that is, for Group A, from €250,000 to €225,000; for Group B, from €33,500 to €30,150; and for Group C, from €16,750 to €15,075.

On 13 October 2015 the group A threshold was increased from €225,000 to €280,000 but the other group thresholds were not changed.

On 12 October 2016 the group A threshold was increased from €280,000 to €310,000, the group B threshold was increased from €30,150 to €32,500, and the group C threshold was increased from €15,075 to €16,250.

On 10 October 2018 the group A threshold was further increased from €310,000 to €320,000 and on 9 October 2019 the group A threshold was again increased from €320,000 to €335,000. The other thresholds were not changed on this date.

On **2 October 2024** all three thresholds were changed as follows: group A was increased from €335,000 to **€400,000**; group B was increased from €32,500 to **€40,000** and group C was increased from €16,250 to €20,000. These are the current thresholds.

Where the aggregate current and prior benefits exceed 80 per cent of the group threshold the taxpayer is obliged to submit a return even if no tax is payable. See **2.5.2**.

Tax is paid on the amount of current and aggregable prior benefits in excess of the threshold amount for the relevant period.

2.5.1 GROUP THRESHOLDS FROM 2000 TO CURRENT THRESHOLD

Relevant period	Group A	Group B	Group C
2 October 2024	**€400,000**	**€40,000**	**€20,000**
9 October 2019 Change to Group A threshold only	€335,000		
10 October 2018 Change to Group A threshold only	€320,000		
12 October 2016	€310,000	€32,500	€16,250
14 October 2015 Change to Group A threshold only	€280,000		
6 December 2012	€225,000	€30,150	€15,075
7 December 2011	€250,000	€ 33,500	€ 16,750
8 December 2010	€332,084	€33,208	€16,604
1 January 2010	€414,799	€41,481	€20,740
8 April 2009	€434,000	€43,400	€21,700
1 January 2009	€542,544	€54,254	€27,127
2008	€521,208	€52,121	€26060
2007	€496,824	€49,682	€24,841
2006	€478,155	€47,815	€23,908
2005	€466,725	€46,673	€23,336
2004	€456,438	€45,644	€22,822
2003	€441,198	€44,120	€22,060
2002	€422,148	€42,215	€21,108
2001	€492,253 (IR£316,800)	€40,225 (IR£31,680)	€20,113 (IR£15,840)
2000 (Effective from 1 December 1999)	€381,000 (IR£300,000)	€38,100 (IR£30,000)	€19,050 (IR£15,000)

2.5.2 REQUIREMENT TO SUBMIT A RETURN ('80% RULE')

Section 46 (4) provides that where the aggregate current and prior benefits exceed 80 per cent of the Group threshold the taxpayer is obliged to submit a return even if no tax is payable.

For the current Group thresholds the obligation to file a return would apply when the current benefit together with aggregable prior benefits exceeds:

Group A €400,000@80% = €320,000
Group B €40,000@80% = €32,000
Group C €20,000@80% = €16,000

There is one exception to this rule: where a benefit comprises agricultural or business property and agricultural or business relief applies, a return must be filed in all cases. This is regardless of whether there is tax payable or not, of the taxable value of the agricultural or business property, and of its proportion of the particular group threshold. Agricultural Relief will be dealt with in **Chapter 4** and Business Relief in **Chapter 5**.

2.6 Rate of Tax

From 1 December 1999 to 19 November 2008 the rate of CAT for the taxable excess was a flat rate of 20 per cent of the taxable excess (i.e. the amount by which the current and prior benefits exceed the threshold) whether the benefit is a gift or an inheritance.

On 20 November 2008 the rate of tax was increased from 20 per cent to 22 per cent for gifts or inheritances occurring on or after 20 November 2008.

On 7 April 2009 the rate of tax increased from 22 per cent to 25 per cent for gifts or inheritances occurring on or after 8 April 2009.

On 6 December 2011 the rate of tax increased from 25 per cent to 30 per cent for gifts or inheritances occurring on or after 7 December 2011.

Finally, on 6 December 2012 the rate of tax increased from 30 per cent to **33 per cent** for gifts or inheritances occurring on or after 6 December 2012.

This is the current rate of CAT.

2.6.1 APPLICABLE RATES OF TAX AND DATES

Date of current benefit	Rate of CAT payable
From 6 December 2012	**33%** – Current rate
From 7 December 2011 to 5 December 2012	30%
From 8 April 2009	25%
From 20 November 2008 to 7 April 2009	22%
From 1 December 1999 to 19 November 2008	20%

2.6.2 DISTINCTION BETWEEN GIFT AND INHERITANCE TAX (BEFORE DECEMBER 1999)

Under the old regime (pre-1 December 1999) there was a distinction between Gift Tax and Inheritance Tax. Gift Tax was paid at a special rate of 75 per cent of inheritance tax. This was to encourage disponers to pass on assets during their lifetime. There was a clawback provision, however. If the disponer died within two years of the gift, the 25 per cent discount was clawed back as the gift was now treated as an inheritance. This was to discourage people making 'gifts' on their deathbed.

This old gift tax rate (i.e. 75 per cent of the equivalent inheritance tax) no longer applies. The only effective difference between Gift Tax and Inheritance Tax is the SGE of €3,000 allowed for all gifts received. This is not clawed back if the disponer dies within two years of making the gift (see **3.10.3**).

This also applies to payments out of *inter vivos* trusts, where the settlor dies either within two years or outside two years of the creation of the *inter vivos* trust. Taxation of trusts is not dealt with on the PPC I.

2.7 Completion of Form IT38S (Paper Return)

2.7.1 INTRODUCTION

On 14 June 2010, s. 147 of the Finance Act, 2010 came into force. The section brought in far-sweeping changes to the administration and payment of the tax as opposed to the calculation of same.

Among the changes were the introduction of fixed file and pay deadlines (see **2.7.3**) with surcharges attached for late filing and interest due for late payment (see **2.9.7**).

The section also introduced two versions of the CAT Self-Assessment Form IT38—the 'Short Form' or paper IT38S and the online version. Both forms came into effect on 14 June 2010, when s. 147 of the Finance Act, 2010 came into force.

2.7.2 FORM IT38S

The Short Form IT38S is a short paper-based return that can be used for payment of tax only where the following conditions are met:

(1) No relief/exemption/credit is claimed, apart from small gift exemption (see **3.10.3**).

(2) The benefit taken is an absolute interest without conditions or restrictions.

(3) The property included in the return was taken from only one disponer and is not part of a larger benefit or series of benefits taken by a beneficiary on the same day.

In all other cases the online version of the return must be used. See **2.7.4**.

Revenue will have the Statement of Affairs (Probate) and, based on the information contained in part 8—see para 6.9.8 of the OUP Wills, Probate & Estates Manual—will automatically issue an IT38 to any individual who it understands may have a requirement to pay and file a CAT return in a tax year.

If for some reason the valuation date does not arise in the anticipated year—see Chapter 1 Section 8—the beneficiary simply notifies Revenue (either in writing or by completion of a tick box on the IT38 form) and Revenue note their records accordingly.

The Form is updated each year and provides for a file and pay deadline of 31 October where the valuation date arises prior to 31 August in that year; see **2.7.3**.

The paper return requires the filer to compute the liability. If Revenue are satisfied based on the data in the return that the tax is correctly computed, an acknowledgement will issue. However, if Revenue determine a higher liability (say due to the application of a late filing surcharge), an amended assessment will be made.

While the Short Form IT38S is available online it cannot be completed and saved online and cannot be returned online. If the client did not receive an IT38 from Revenue, the paper version must be collected or ordered from the Revenue Commissioners at <custform@ revenue.ie> or 24-hour telephone number 1890 30 67 06 or 00353 170 23 050 for callers outside the Republic of Ireland.

2.7.2.1 Completion of the form

The form itself is relatively straightforward. Taking each part in turn:

1. **Beneficiary details**

   These are self-explanatory and this form would be completed where the valuation date arises on or before 31 August in any year. Where the benefit arises after 31 August in any year the return would be filed prior to 31 October the following year.

FIGURE 2.1

1. Beneficiary details

Beneficiary's PPSN

Return of gift and / or inheritance tax for the year ending 31st August 2 0

Forename

Surname

Address

Eircode

PPS numbers are dealt with in *Wills, Probate and Estates* at 6.6.3.1.

2. **Filer details**

   These are for the tax adviser concerned (solicitor; tax consultant; accountant). TAIN is 'Tax Advisor Identification Number', which can be obtained by registering with the TAIN section in Revenue's North Dublin City office 9–15 Upper O'Connell Street Dublin 1 (tel: 01-865 5000; email dublinagents@revenue.ie). The application process will not allow a representative to make an application on behalf of a client without a TAIN number.

FIGURE 2.2

2. Filer details (if different from 1 above)

Forename

Surname

Address

Eircode

Telephone No.

TAIN -

e-mail

DX Number (if applicable)

Client Ref.

3. **Disponer Details**

   These are also self-explanatory, and it should be known whether the benefit is a gift or an inheritance and whether it consists of real or personal property (or both). As noted, the date of the gift/inheritance may differ from the valuation date and the date of death of the disponer (if dead) should be included. If there is any form of limited interest or condition attached, then the online version of the form must be used.

FIGURE 2.3

Disponer details

Disponer's PPSN

Forename

Surname

Address

Eircode

Place ☒ in the appropriate box to indicate the nature of the benefit — Gift ☐ Inheritance ☐

Place ☒ in the appropriate box to indicate whether the property is — Real property ☐ and/or Other property ☐

	D D	M M	Y Y Y Y
Date of gift/inheritance	/	/	
State the valuation date	/	/	
In the case of an inheritance, state the date of the disponer's death	/	/	

Place ☒ in the appropriate box to indicate applicable Group Threshold — A ☐ B ☐ C ☐

4. Assessment of Capital Acquisitions Tax

Tax is calculated as per the table below. This table and amended versions of same are provided for students as part of the PPC I course to calculate the tax 'on paper'.

FIGURE 2.4

Assessment of Capital Acquisitions Tax

	Millions	Thousands	Hundreds
A. Taxable Value of this gift/inheritance	,	,	
B. Small Gift Exemption (where relevant)	,	,	
C. Net Taxable Value of the benefit (A - B)	,	,	
D. Relevant Threshold	,	,	
E. Less Taxable Value of Prior Aggregable Benefits within this Group Threshold	,	,	
F. Available Threshold for this Benefit (D - E)	,	,	
G. Taxable Excess (C - F)	,	,	
Tax on Current Benefit (Rate____%)	,	,	

5. Declaration

The declaration should be signed by the beneficiary in his or her capacity as beneficiary, as only the beneficiary can state accurately in relation to prior benefits.

FIGURE 2.5

DECLARATION

I/We declare that the information given is true and complete and that the return is in accordance with the provisions of the Capital Acquisitions Tax Consolidation Act, 2003.

Signed

Capacity ____________________ Date D D / M M / Y Y Y Y

(Agent/beneficiary/trustee, etc.)

6. Payslip

Details to be completed in the payslip are self-explanatory and methods of payment are outlined on the following page.

FIGURE 2.6

€ Payslip Return of gift and/or inheritance tax for the year ending 31st August 2 0 _ _

PPSN:		Inheritance Tax	___,___,___ .00
Name:		Gift Tax	___,___,___ .00
Signature:			
Date:	/ /	TOTAL NET AMOUNT	___,___,___ .00

CAT

The payslip should be posted to Collector-General PO Box 354 Limerick.

2.7.3 PAY AND FILE DEADLINE

As noted earlier, the due date for CAT is entirely based on the valuation date. Where the valuation date falls on or before 31 August in any year, any tax due should be paid and a return filed by 31 October in that year. This is known as the 'pay and file deadline'. Where the valuation date arises after 31 August in any year, the pay and file deadline will be 31 October of the following year.

For example, A makes a taxable **gift** to B on 22 August 2024. The valuation date will be 22 August 2024, and the pay and file deadline will be 31 October 2024.

This should be compared to the scenario if A died on 22 August 2024 and left a taxable **inheritance** to B in his will. If the grant of probate issued on 22 October 2024 (for example) and this was accepted as the valuation date, then the file and pay deadline would be 31 October 2025.

Where the return is not filed and tax paid by the deadline, penalties, referred to as 'surcharges', are applied and interest on any outstanding tax is payable. These are two separate charges and will be dealt with in **2.9.7**.

Part 3 of the Capital Acquisitions Tax Tax and Duty Manual ('CAT TDM') gives instructions on completion of same and should be referred to as necessary.

2.7.3.1 Extension of deadline when paying and filing online using ROS (Revenue Online System)

Where the taxpayer or his/her agent is both paying and filing online, there is an extension of the deadline from 31 October (30 September 2011) to mid-November each year.

For 2024 this date is Thursday 14 November 2024. See Revenue eBrief No. 116 of 2024.

For 2023 this date was Wednesday 15 November 2023. See Revenue eBrief No. 88 of 2023. For 2022 this date was Wednesday 16 November 2022. See Revenue eBrief No. 88 of 2022.

For 2021 this date was Friday 19 November 2021, extended from Wednesday 17 November 2021. See Revenue eBriefs No. 211/21 and No. 088/21 respectively.

For 2020, because of COVID, the extension was moved from 12 November 2020 to Thursday 10 December 2020—see Revenue eBrief 174 of 2020.

CAT ROS extensions of Pay and File Deadlines for the previous years are as follows:

12 November 2019

14 November 2018

14 November 2017

10 November 2016

12 November 2015

13 November 2014

14 November 2013

15 November 2012

30 September 2011 to 16 November 2011.

As noted, 2010 was a 'transition' year.

Revenue usually announce each year an extension to this pay and file deadline to mid-November where the taxpayer both files and pays online using the Revenue Online System (ROS). This extension has been granted on a discretionary basis by the Revenue Commissioners and is usually published in April each year, but practitioners should ensure that it has been granted for the current year before relying on same.

2.7.4 ONLINE COMPLETION OF THE FORM IT38 USING ROS

As noted above, since 14 June 2010, when paying CAT, a Revenue online version of the Form IT38—*Gift/inheritance tax Self-Assessment Return* has to be completed where the conditions allowing for use of the short form are not met. See **2.7.2**.

Instructions on completing the form IT38 can be found online and were last updated in February 2021.

It is not intended on this course to deal with the online application in any great detail. It is intended instead to focus on understanding the basis of the tax and calculating tax payable without using ROS.

Practitioners may find the Revenue Guidelines on CAT and ROS which deals with technical issues of use where they are applying online.

https://www.revenue.ie/en/online-services/support/ros-help/popular-ros-services/pay-and-file/capital-acquisitions-tax.aspx

Before this can be completed, the practitioner has to register for ROS (Revenue Online Service) in order to 'e-file' the Form IT38. Presently, the Revenue Commissioners do not supply a printable version of the current IT38. It only exists in its online format. Instructions on completing the form online can be found at: <www.revenue.ie/en/tax/cat/leaflets/it39.html#register>.

It is not intended on this course to deal with the online application in any great detail. It is intended instead to focus on understanding the basis of the tax and calculating tax payable without using ROS.

2.7.4.1 Expression of doubt

It is possible to 'express a doubt' if you are unsure of the tax treatment of any item in the online version by simply ticking the 'express a doubt' box and attaching a covering letter setting out clearly the point at issue.

'Expression of Doubt' was added to CAT Consolidation Act, 2003 by the insertion of a s. 46A by s. 146 of the Finance Act, 2003. Put simply, this allows an accountable person completing IT38, where a genuine doubt exists as to the 'correct application of law to, or the treatment for tax purposes of, any matter', to complete the form but to draw attention to the doubt in an accompanying letter for the Revenue to deal with. Where the Revenue accepts that a genuine doubt exists and this was not merely a device to delay, avoid, or evade tax, even if more tax is due, penalties and interest will not arise.

2.7.5 APPLYING TO REGISTER FOR ROS

This three-stage registration process can take a number of weeks, as documents need to be received by post, and should be done well in advance of any filing date. It involves applying online for a Revenue Access Number (RAN). This involves supplying the firm's taxation number (TAIN) among other details. The RAN will arrive in the post and, using that, the practitioner then has to apply for a ROS Digital Certificate. On receipt of the application for a ROS Digital Certificate, the Revenue will post out a password. Having received the password, you can then download the ROS Digital Certificate to your computer and pay CAT online. Detailed instructions on how to register for ROS can be found online at: <www.ros.ie/PublisherServlet/info/setupnewcust>.

2.8 Calculation of Taxable Value

Calculating CAT payable on a benefit depends on three key pieces of information:

(1) Taxable Value of Current Benefit

(2) Group Threshold

(3) Taxable Value of Prior Benefits.

Prior gifts or inheritances received by the same beneficiary under the same group threshold since 5 December 1991 are to be aggregated with any benefits taken on or after 5 December 2001 for the purpose of arriving at the tax payable on that benefit.

2.8.1 TAXABLE VALUE OF CURRENT BENEFIT

The current standard tax calculation template is in two parts: Calculation of taxable value and Tax Payable on taxable value. When dealing with agricultural property (**Chapter 4**) and Business Property (**Chapter 5**), this basic template will be expanded upon.

In this section we will focus on calculation of taxable value and in Section **9** we will deal with calculating tax payable on taxable value.

Taxable Value is established as follows:

- Establish Market Value of Benefit
- Deduct Market Value of Exempt Property (if any). Exempt Property will be dealt with in **Chapter 3**
- This gives you Market Value of Taxable Property
- Deduct Liabilities, Costs & Expenses [LCE]
- This gives you the Incumbrance-Free Value [IFV]
- Take into account the value of any Limited Interest (if any)*
- Deduct Consideration from this figure to arrive at
- Taxable Value.

* For tax calculations involving absolute interests, this line can be ignored, and for the basic template used in tutorial exercises involving absolute interests, this line will not be included.

Taking each of these headings in turn:

2.8.1.1 Market value of benefit

Market value will include everything passing, giving the market values even where a limited interest is passing. In the case of a gift, full details should be provided. In the case of an inheritance, the details of all assets passing will have already been sent in as part of the Statement of Affairs (Probate). The Statement of Affairs (Probate) will be dealt with at **2.9.2** and is also dealt with in *Wills, Probate and Estates* at 6.9. The most common type of exempt property is Dwelling-House Relief, which will be dealt with in **Chapter 3** at **3.13**.

2.8.1.2 Liabilities, costs, expenses, and consideration

These are discussed in **Chapter 1**. As noted, the full value of liabilities, costs, and expenses and consideration are entered even where a limited interest is passing.

Practitioners should list all liabilities, costs, and expenses payable. This would include any charge on the property (mortgage etc.), any costs (including solicitors' fees, stamp duty, Property Registry Authority fees, etc.) payable by the beneficiary, and any expenses arising. Rights reserved (for example, a right to reside) are a liability charged on the land and as such are a liability. Where an exempt property is received, the costs relating to the exempt property will not be allowable as an expense against the taxable benefits passing. This will be dealt with in more detail in **Chapter 3**.

Remember, the beneficiary client may not be responsible for all the costs of the estate, depending on the nature of the inheritance and the drafting of the will. For example, someone receiving a specific or a pecuniary benefit is not necessarily responsible for the debts of the estate. Please refer to *Wills, Probate and Estates* and s. 47 of the Succession Act.

2.8.1.3 Incumbrance-free value and limited interest

The factors for limited interests (life or period certain) are always based on the incumbrance-free value. These have been dealt with at **1.8**.

2.8.1.4 Consideration

Consideration in its entirety (if any) is then deducted from the incumbrance-free value (absolute or discounted for limited interest). List any consideration paid for the benefit—for example if a property was being transferred at less than market value or subject to the payment of monies to a third party. For example, 'I leave my farm to my daughter Felicity, subject to her paying the sum of €100,000 to my son John'.

Also included as consideration is a situation where the beneficiary assumes a debt of the disponer, which is not legally enforceable against the beneficiary. For example, X gives his car valued at €20,000 to Y in consideration of Y paying €5,000 to pay off a creditor of X.

Again, as noted for liabilities, costs and expenses, consideration in relation to exempt property cannot be set off against taxable property.

2.8.1.5 Taxable value of benefit

As we will see in later chapters, where particular reliefs and exemptions apply, these will be taken into account when arriving at the taxable value of the current benefit.

Once we have arrived at taxable value, we then calculate the tax payable on this taxable value where the beneficiary of a current benefit has an aggregable prior benefit.

2.8.2 CALCULATION OF TAX PAYABLE ON TAXABLE VALUE IN 2024

This is the second part of the standard tax calculation referred to above and this calculation is at the heart of every CAT calculation, no matter how involved or complex it seems at first.

FIGURE 2.7

Assessment of Capital Acquisitions Tax

		Millions	Thousands	Hundreds
A. Taxable Value of this gift/inheritance				
B. Small Gift Exemption (where relevant)				
C. Net Taxable Value of the benefit (A - B)				
D. Relevant Threshold	Millions Thousands Hundreds			
E. Less Taxable Value of Prior Aggregable Benefits within this Group Threshold				
	F. Available Threshold for this Benefit (D - E)			
	G. Taxable Excess (C - F)			
	Tax on Current Benefit (Rate____%)			

Essentially, once the taxable value of the current benefit has been established, the **group threshold** and the **taxable value of any aggregable prior benefits** establish the tax payable.

In all cases the procedure is as follows (as taken from the paper Form IT38S):

Calculation of Tax Payable on Taxable Value

A.	Taxable value of this gift/inheritance	€
B.	Less small gift exemption where relevant	€3,000 or NIL
C.	Net taxable value of benefit (A – B)	€
D.	Relevant threshold Group A, B or C in 2022	€
E.	*Less* Taxable value of prior aggregable benefits	€
F.	Available threshold for this benefit	€
G.	Taxable excess [C–F]	€
H.	Tax on taxable excess @ 33%	€

**	A	€ 400,000	B	€ 40,000	C	€20,000

Prior to 2 October 2024

A	€335,000	B	€ 32,500	C	€16,250

[insert name] should file and pay [delete "and pay" if a return is necessary but no tax is payable] by 31 October 2024 / 2025 14 November 2024 if paying and filing using ROS / No extension of deadline if paying and filing using ROS has been announced for 2025.

2.8.2.1 Taxable value of this gift/inheritance

Taxable value has been dealt with above. There are a number of reliefs and exemptions which may be applicable. For the most part the minor reliefs and exemptions are dealt with in **Chapter 3**. Agricultural Property and Business Property will be dealt with in **Chapters 4** and **5** respectively, while Favourite Nephew/Niece Relief will be dealt with in **Chapter 6**.

Where the current benefit is a gift the small gift exemption may apply. Where the current benefit is an inheritance, it will not apply.

2.8.2.2 Small gift exemption

The SGE is dealt with in detail at **3.10.3** but for current gifts, a SGE of €3,000 may be deducted from a disponer once every calendar year. As noted above at **2.6.2**, this is one of the few surviving distinctions between gifts and inheritances. It is important to note, when calculating the taxable value of prior gifts, that the SGE applicable at the date of the prior gift should be deducted from the market value of the gift.

2.8.2.3 Net taxable value of benefit

This is the taxable value of the benefit after the small gift exemption has been taken into account and either applied or ignored.

2.8.2.4 Relevant threshold

This is the group threshold relating to the current benefit. As discussed, this will depend on the blood or family relationship between the disponer and the beneficiary and the date of the current benefit (not necessarily the valuation date). The group threshold should be identified.

2.8.2.5 Taxable value of prior aggregable benefits

The next figure is the taxable value of prior aggregable benefits. The important word here is '**aggregable**'. For current benefits received on or after 5 December 2001 only prior benefits received on or after 5 December 1991 from a disponer in relation to whom the beneficiary is in the same tax group as the current disponer are listed—that is, if the current disponer is a parent (Group A disponer) then gifts or inheritances from siblings (Group B disponers) can be ignored.

When calculating the 'taxable value' of the aggregable prior benefits, this information should be to hand by checking any prior IT38(s) delivered to the Revenue Commissioners at the time. If tax was due at the time and was not paid on the prior benefit at the time, then the client is facing penalties and interest. Calculation of tax due and owing prior to 1 December 1999 is not covered in these materials.

Assuming any tax due was paid at the time, the figure for the taxable value should be entered at line E.

Double-check to ensure that the taxable value of any prior gift takes into account the SGE applicable at the time of the gift. See **3.10.3** for more detail on the SGE.

For the relevant periods the applicable SGE (rounded up to the nearest euro) was as follows:

Relevant period	Small gift exemption
From 1 January 1978 to 31 December 1998	£500 (€635)
From 1 January 1999 to 31 December 2002	£1000 (€1270)
From 1 January 2003 to date	€3000

2.8.2.6 Available threshold for this benefit

If the current group threshold is greater than the taxable value of the prior benefit, the 'unused' portion of the threshold can be carried forward to be used against the current benefit and will be entered in line F.

If the aggregable prior benefits are greater than the current group threshold, then the figure '0' is entered at line F and the effect of this is that tax will be payable on the entire amount of the current benefit. The figure in line F is never less than '0'.

2.8.2.7 Taxable excess [C – F]

The taxable excess is obtained by subtracting available threshold for this benefit (F) from net taxable value (C). This figure is entered in line G.

2.8.2.8 Tax on taxable excess @ 33 per cent

Taxable excess (line G) is then multiplied by 33 per cent (the current rate of CAT). This may seem obvious, but 33 per cent is not the same as one third: one cannot simply divide by three.

It is important to remember that the rate of tax is fixed at the date of the gift or inheritance while the tax may not be due until after the valuation date. If so, the earlier rates may apply. The distinction between date of the gift or inheritance and valuation date has been dealt with in **Chapter 1**. If dealing with a benefit where the valuation date arose prior to these dates, penalties and interest may apply. See **2.9.7**.

2.8.3 SAMPLE CAT CALCULATION USING THE PRO-FORMA TAX TEMPLATE

Joe Bloggs inherited €100,000 from his father in 2009. In November 2024 his mother gave him €400,000 and this is the taxable value of the current benefit.

Calculate the CAT payable by Joe Bloggs in 2024

Standard Tax Calculation Template 2024: Absolute Interest

Calculation of Taxable Value:

Market value [MV]	€ 400,000
Less exempt property	**€______ 0**
Equals market value of taxable property	€ 400,000
Less allowable liabilities, costs & expenses [lce]	**€______ 0**
Equals incumbrance-free value [ifv]	€ 400,000
Less allowable consideration [in money or monies worth]	**€______ 0**
Equals taxable value [TV]	€ 400,000

Tax Payable on Taxable Value in 2024

A.	Taxable value of this gift/~~inheritance~~	€400,0000	
B.	Small gift exemption where relevant	€3,000	~~NIL~~
C.	Net taxable value of benefit (A – B)	€397,000	
D.	Relevant threshold Group A ~~B C~~ in 2024*	€400,000	
E.	*Less* Taxable value of prior aggregable benefits (SGE?)	€100,000	
F.	Available threshold for this benefit	€300,000	
G.	Taxable excess [C–F]	€97,000	
H.	Tax @ 33%	€32,010	

**	A	**€ 400,000**	B	€ 40,000	C	€20,000

Prior to 2 October 2024

*	A	€335,000	B	€ 32,500	C	€16,250

As the valuation date for the current benefit will be the date of the gift, that is, November 2024, Joe Bloggs should file and pay by 31 October 2025 or the pay and file date for mid November 2025 if both filing and paying online.

Clawback should not arise as no relief or exemption was claimed.

2.8.4 CONVERTING PRIOR BENEFITS FROM PUNT TO EURO

Prior benefits received in 2002 and beyond will have been received in euro and taxable in euro at the then current rate. Prior benefits received prior to 2002 have presumably been received in and taxed in punts at the then current rate. Difficulties arise when calculating prior benefits received in punts when an aggregable benefit is subsequently received in euro.

2.8.4.1 Example: prior benefits received in punts

Joe Bloggs inherited £100,000.00 from his mother in June 1996. He subsequently inherits €500,000 on the death of his father in May 2024. This is the taxable value of the current benefit.

In calculating the euro value of the prior benefit, €1 = IR£0.787564. Thus, to find the value in euro of a benefit received in punts, divide the benefit by 0.787564.

To compute the inheritance tax liability you must convert the IR£ benefit amount to €, that is, £100,000.00 = €126,973.8078. It is permissible in practice to round up or down to the nearest euro, which would give €126,974.

Applying the formula explained earlier:

Tax Payable on Taxable Value in 2024

A.	Taxable value of this ~~gift~~/inheritance	€500,000	
B.	Small gift exemption where relevant	€ ~~3,000~~	NIL
C.	Net taxable value of benefit (A–B)	€500,000	
D.	Relevant threshold Group **A** ~~B C~~ *	€335,000	
E.	*Less* Taxable value of prior aggregable benefits (SGE?)	€126,974	
F.	Available threshold for this benefit	€208,026	
G.	Taxable excess [C – F]	€288,974	
H.	Tax @ 33%	€95,361.42 rounded down to €95,361.	

**	A	€ 400,000	B	€ 40,000	C	€20,000
Prior to 2 October 2024						
*	A	**€335,000**	B	€ 32,500	C	€16,250

Assuming the grant issues after 31 August 2024, Joe Bloggs should file and pay by 31 October 2025 or mid November 2025 if both filing and paying online.

Clawback should not arise as no relief or exemption was claimed.

2.8.5 TWO BENEFITS ARISING ON THE SAME DAY

It may arise that a beneficiary may receive two benefits from the same disponer on the same day, for example a limited interest in a property and a full interest in a specific bequest. If a man aged 47 inherited €100,000 absolutely and a life interest in a house valued at €500,000 at the same time (the funeral and testamentary expenses to be paid out of the residue) from a parent, the taxable value of the benefits passing would be calculated as follows:

Basic Calculation:

		Full Interest	**Limited Interest**
	Market value [MV]	€100,000	€500,000
Less	Market value of exempt property (if any)	€ N/A	€ N/A
	Market value of taxable property	€100,000	€500,000
Less	Liabilities, costs & expenses relating to taxable property [LCE]	€ NIL	€ NIL
=	Incumbrance-free value [IFV]	€100,000	€500,000
X	Value of limited interest 0._7663		€383,150
Less	Consideration [in money or monies worth] relating to taxable property	€ NIL	€ NIL
=	Taxable value [TV]	€100,000	€383,150

Total Taxable Value of Current Benefit will be €483,150.

Tax would be paid on these current benefits in the normal fashion, assuming no prior benefits and that the grant issues prior to 31 August 2025.

Tax Payable on Taxable Value

A.	Taxable value of this ~~gift~~/inheritance	€483,150	
B.	Small gift exemption where relevant	€ ~~3,000~~	NIL
C.	Net taxable value of benefit (A–B)	€483,150	
D.	Relevant threshold Group **A** ~~B C~~ *	€400,000	
E.	*Less* Taxable value of prior aggregable benefits (SGE?)	€ 0	
F.	Available threshold for this benefit	€400,000	
G.	Taxable excess [C –F]	€83,150	
H.	Tax @ 33%	€27,439.50 rounded up to €27,439.	

**	A	**€ 400,000**	B	€40,000	C	€20,000
Prior to 02 October 2024						
*	A	€335,000	B	€ 32,500	C	€16,250

The beneficiary should file and pay [delete 'and pay' if a return is necessary but no tax is payable] by 31 October 2025 or mid November 2025 if both filing and paying online using ROS.

Clawback should not arise in this case.

2.8.6 MORE THAN ONE DISPONER—SAME GROUP THRESHOLD

It may arise that a beneficiary could receive two benefits from different disponers during the same tax year—even, albeit rarely, on the same day.

If two people who own a property jointly transfer that property to a beneficiary, that is a benefit arising from two disponers on the same day—for example, where parents who own a family home jointly transfer their interests to a child.

Another example of where benefits from different disponers arise on the same day would be where initially a husband leaves the family home to his wife for life (ignoring legal right share, etc.) and to his daughter in remainder. On the death of the wife, the daughter could receive an inheritance from her mother's estate and the remainder interest from her father on the same day. Both of these are absolute interests arising on the same day.

In both of these examples, the beneficiary was the same group threshold in relation to the disponers, group A parent(s) to child.

Even if the valuation dates differ, they may both arise in the same tax year and are covered by the same return. Should this arise, the online version of the return must be completed.

It could also arise, for example, if the wife (and mother) died in November 2024 and the grant issued in March 2025, that the valuation date for the remainder interest in the house would be November 2024—pay and file deadline 31 October 2025, and the valuation date for the inheritance from her mother's estate would be February 2025—pay and file deadline also 31 October 2025.

In this case, however, the date of the inheritance is fixed at November 2024.

Each case must be examined on the facts and the valuation date(s) and pay and file deadline(s) identified.

Take the example of (widow and) mother dying and daughter inheriting remainder interest in property from father and residue of estate from mother and assuming that the current taxable value of the remainder interest from the father is €300,000 and the current taxable value of the inheritance from the mother is €200,000:

Assuming (as above) that the valuation date in both cases arises during the same taxable period, total tax payable on all current benefits is calculated as follows:

Calculation of Taxable Value:

Market value [MV] €200,000 (Mother) + €300,000 (Father)	€500,000
Less exempt property	€______0
Equals market value of taxable property	€500,000
Less allowable liabilities, costs & expenses [LCE]	€______0
Equals incumbrance-free value [IFV]	€500,000
Less allowable consideration [in money or monies worth]	€______0
Equals taxable value [TV]	€500,000

Tax Payable on Taxable Value in 2024

A.	Taxable value of this ~~gift~~/inheritance	€500,000	
B.	Small gift exemption where relevant	€ ~~3,000~~	NIL
C.	Net taxable value of benefit (A–B)	€500,000	
D.	Relevant threshold Group **A** ~~B C~~ in 2024*	€400,000	
E.	*Less* Taxable value of prior aggregable benefits	€ NIL	
F.	Available threshold for this benefit	€400,000	

continued

continued

G.	Taxable excess [C–F]			€100,000		
H.	Tax @ 33%			€33,000		
**	A	€ 400,000	B	€ 40,000	C	€20,000
Prior to 2 October 2024						
*	A	€335,000	B	€ 32,500	C	€16,250

The daughter should file and pay by 31 October 2025 or mid November 2025 if both filing and paying online.

Clawback would not arise unless Dwelling-House Exemption (see para 3.13) has been claimed.

The total CAT payable on the current benefits is apportioned between the two benefits. This is done as follows:

The taxable value of the benefit from the father is placed 'above the line'.

The taxable value of all the *current* benefits is placed 'below the line'. The taxable value of the referable benefit is divided by the taxable value of all the current benefits and the result is multiplied by the total tax payable. This gives us the fraction of the total tax payable that applies to the referable benefit.

Taking the example above and dealing with the inheritance from the mother first:

$$\text{Tax on all current benefits}\left(€300{,}000 + €200{,}000\right) = €33{,}0000$$

$$\text{Taxable value of the benefit from mother} = €200{,}000$$

$$\text{Taxable value of all current benefits} = €500{,}000\left(€200{,}000 + €300{,}000\right)$$

$$\textit{Share of CAT payable on inheritiance from father}\ \frac{€300{,}000}{€500{,}000} \times €33{,}000 = €19{,}800$$

The process is repeated in the second IT38, with the one difference being that in this case it is the taxable value of the father's benefit that goes 'above the line'.

$$\text{Taxable value of the benefit from father} = €300{,}000$$

$$\text{Taxable value of all current benefits} = €500{,}000$$

$$\textit{Share of CAT payable on inheritiance from mother}\ \frac{€200{,}000}{€500{,}000} \times €33{,}000 = €13{,}200$$

In any event, the same amount of CAT will be paid, but in two separate payments relating to two separate benefits received on the same day.

If the valuation dates fall in different taxable periods the amount of tax paid would be exactly the same. For example, if the person died in June 2024 but the grant did not issue until September 2024, a return would be filed for the inheritance from the father in October/November 2024 and a further return for the inheritance from the mother in October/November 2025.

2.8.7 MORE THAN ONE DISPONER—DIFFERENT GROUP THRESHOLD

It can also arise that a beneficiary could receive more than one benefit in a tax year, and even on the same day, from disponers from different Group thresholds.

For example, if my father and uncle own a property jointly and they transfer it to me, that would be a benefit from a group A Disponer and a group B disponer on the same day.

Similarly, if my uncle left a property to my father for his life with a remainder interest to me, on the death of my father, I could inherit from my father (group A) and my uncle (group B) on the same day.

It can also, and quite often does, arise that a beneficiary can receive two different benefits from two (or more) different disponers on different dates in the same year, for example if my mother gave me €50,000 in January 2025 and my brother gave me €30,000 in March 2025.

In each case, an online return would have to be filed using the Revenue ROS system, but in order to advise on tax payable, two separate calculations would be made 'on paper' in advance of this.

2.9 CAT and Solicitors

2.9.1 INTRODUCTION

The remainder of this chapter deals with CAT as it relates to probate practice and goes on to deal with payment of the tax and solicitors' obligations in various circumstances. As dealt with in Chapter 8 of *Wills, Probate and Estates*, the first time CAT is an issue when administering any estate is the completion of the Statement of Affairs (Probate) the online Form SA 2 formerly the Inland Revenue Affidavit.

2.9.2 STATEMENT OF AFFAIRS (PROBATE) ONLINE FORM SA 2

Section 48A of CAT Consolidation Act, 2003, as inserted by s. 63 (1) (b) of the Finance Act, 2019, deals with the Statement of Affairs (Probate), a document which must be completed and filed online with Revenue prior to any application for a grant of representation. The Statement of Affairs (Probate) replaced the Inland Revenue Affidavit, which was a sworn document dating back to 1894 (predating the introduction of CAT by some eighty years) and was initially used to calculate death duties.

The current version of the Statement of Affairs (Probate) was introduced in September 2020 and must be completed online, usually by the solicitor on behalf of the personal representative. Practitioners are also referred to the Capital Acquisitions Tax (Electronic Probate) Regulations 2020, No 341/2020 and to the Revenue Commissioners Guide to Completing a Statement of Affairs Probate Form SA 2: <https://www.revenue.ie/en/gains-gifts-and-inheritance/documents/guide-to-completing-statement-of-affairs-probate-form-sa.2.pdf>.

The Inland Revenue Affidavit was sworn by the personal representative(s) and while the online document is no longer a sworn affidavit, it must be accurate in all respects, and a declaration to this effect is given by the personal representative(s). In addition, an undertaking is given by the personal representative confirming that they will amend the SA 2 if any significant omissions or errors come to light. The SA 2 incorporates the Corrective Affidavit Form CA 26 and the Form A3 (C) which was completed for a De Bonis Non Grant, but only where the original Form CA 24 was lodged with Revenue on or after 5 December 2001.

Essentially the SA 2 provides details of the deceased, the applicant(s), and the beneficiaries. It provides an account of the assets and liabilities of the deceased as at the date of death. Apart from listing assets and liabilities as at the date of death, quite an amount of further information is required.

Where the current benefit taken by a beneficiary other than a spouse/civil partner or charity is greater than €12,000 then full details of that beneficiary, the value of the benefit received, their relationship to the deceased, and group threshold and all aggregable prior benefits since 5 December 1991 will be furnished to Revenue as part of the statement. Revenue will be in direct contact with these beneficiaries in due course.

Where a beneficiary or indeed the personal representative is non-resident, the Revenue Commissioners will be alerted to this by the detail provided in the SA 2. The SA 2 is the first indication to the Revenue Commissioners as to possible beneficiaries and to the extent of potential Inheritance tax due.

Of particular interest from a taxation point of view is the Mandatory Questionnaire. This deals with details of property held jointly by the deceased with others and details of any dispositions made by the deceased during his/her life, including dispositions subject to a power of revocation, surrenders, free use of property, discretionary trusts, and nominations. It also asks if the deceased had an interest in expectancy, which would now go to someone else, if the deceased failed to exercise a power of appointment, and if so what the consequences were. It goes on to enquire about payments outside the estate under superannuation schemes or insurance policies or elsewhere.

It should be noted that the values in the Statement of Affairs (Probate) are as of the date of death of the deceased. In general these are not the values on which inheritance tax will be paid. The values on which tax will be paid are the values as at the valuation date already dealt with in **Chapter 1**.

After the Statement of Affairs (Probate) is filed with Revenue, a Notice of Acknowledgment (Probate) is generated by Revenue and made available to download. This Notice of Acknowledgment is lodged with the rest of the probate papers to the Probate Office/ District Probate Registry.

Since June 2010, payment of CAT is almost entirely a matter for the beneficiaries and the estate has no responsibility to ensure the tax is paid. There are exceptions to this where any beneficiary or the personal representative resides outside the jurisdiction. Prior to then, CAT was a charge on any immovable property comprised in the estate and the estate was secondarily liable for the payment of CAT. A certificate of discharge from CAT (called a CA 11) was made available on payment of the CAT. Best practice was to either pay the tax on behalf of the beneficiary from the funds due to that beneficiary held by the estate and a certificate obtained prior to releasing funds or ensure that tax had been paid and a certificate obtained or assenting to the transfer of immovable property to a beneficiary.

Since June 2010 this is no longer necessary unless the beneficiaries and/or the personal representatives are out of the jurisdiction. See **2.9.6.1**.

Under s. 48(3) an account has also to be delivered by the trustees of a settlement under which the deceased person had a limited interest, and this account should give full details of inheritances arising under that settlement on the death of the deceased, including the names and addresses of the successors.

2.9.3 JOINT PROPERTY

As outlined in **1.2.4.3**, s. 7 of CAT Consolidation Act, 2003 states:

> *The liability to gift tax in respect of a gift taken by persons as joint tenants is the same in all respects as if they took the gift as tenants in common in equal shares.*

When persons take property as joint tenants they have the right to sever the joint tenancy and divide the property, each taking their own share absolutely. The draftsman decided therefore to treat a benefit taken by beneficiaries as joint tenants as if they took as tenants in common. This is for the purpose of calculating the taxable value of that benefit and tax liability arising only and has no other application.

Section 2 of CAT Consolidation Act, 2003 defines entitled in possession as follows:

> *'entitled in possession' means having a present right to the enjoyment of property as opposed to having a future such right, and without prejudice to the generality of the foregoing a person is also, for the purposes of this Act, deemed to be entitled in possession to an interest or share in a partnership,* ***joint tenancy*** *or estate of a deceased person, in which that person is a partner, joint tenant or beneficiary, as the case may be, . . .*

However, it was difficult to quantify the interest of each joint tenant. In theory each joint tenant owns all the property, and yet he owns none of it and he has a contingent right to take the entire property by survivorship. Treating the beneficiaries who take as joint tenants as if they took as tenants in common for tax purposes simplified the problem posed in calculating the actual interest of each joint tenant in the joint property.

Section 13(2) of CAT Consolidation Act, 2003 followed s. 7 by stating that the liability to inheritance tax in respect of an inheritance taken by persons as joint tenants is the same in all respects as if they took the inheritance as tenants in common in equal shares.

Section 13(1) deals with the position where persons are joint tenants and one of them dies. That sub-section states that the survivor or survivors are deemed to take the deceased's share as an inheritance derived from him. The rationale behind this is that the deceased could have made himself absolute owner of his or her share of the joint tenancy at any time up to the date of death.

It should be noted that the sub-section refers to persons who are *beneficially and absolutely* entitled in possession as joint tenants.

It is necessary to distinguish between the following examples;

(1) Annette by will devised lands to her daughter **Brenda** and son in law (Brenda's husband) **Charles** as joint tenants absolutely. For inheritance tax purposes Brenda and Charles are treated as if they take half of the lands each as tenants in common from Annette the disponer.

Brenda subsequently dies and Charles is treated as taking an inheritance from Brenda of one half of the current value of the lands on the grounds that Brenda up to the time of her death could have severed the joint tenancy and made herself absolute owner of her share. Charles, as a surviving spouse, will not pay any CAT: see **3.11**.

(2) Annette by will devised lands to Brenda and Charles as joint tenants for life with remainder to the survivor for life with remainder to her grandson (their only child) David absolutely.

Brenda and Charles each take a limited interest in one half of the lands for their respective lives from the disponer Annette.

Brenda subsequently dies and Charles is treated as taking a limited interest for his life in Brenda's half of the lands from the disponer Annette. Section 13(1) does not apply in this case as Brenda and Charles are not absolute joint tenants. (Note that valuation of an interest for the continuation of two lives is not dealt with in this book.)

The question frequently arises in CAT as to whether joint tenants are beneficial joint tenants or whether on the facts of any particular case the presumptions of a resulting trust or of advancement might apply. Joint property is covered in detail in Chapter 12 of *Wills, Probate and Estates*.

For many of the assets listed in the Statement of Affairs (Probate) the question will be asked if the asset was held solely by the deceased, as a joint tenant or as a tenant in common. Where the asset was held as a joint tenant, a number of other questions have to be answered.

It is vital, when administering an estate, to determine whether on the death of a joint tenant the property is acquired by the survivor or whether in fact there is a resulting trust in favour of the deceased joint tenant's estate.

FIGURE 2.10

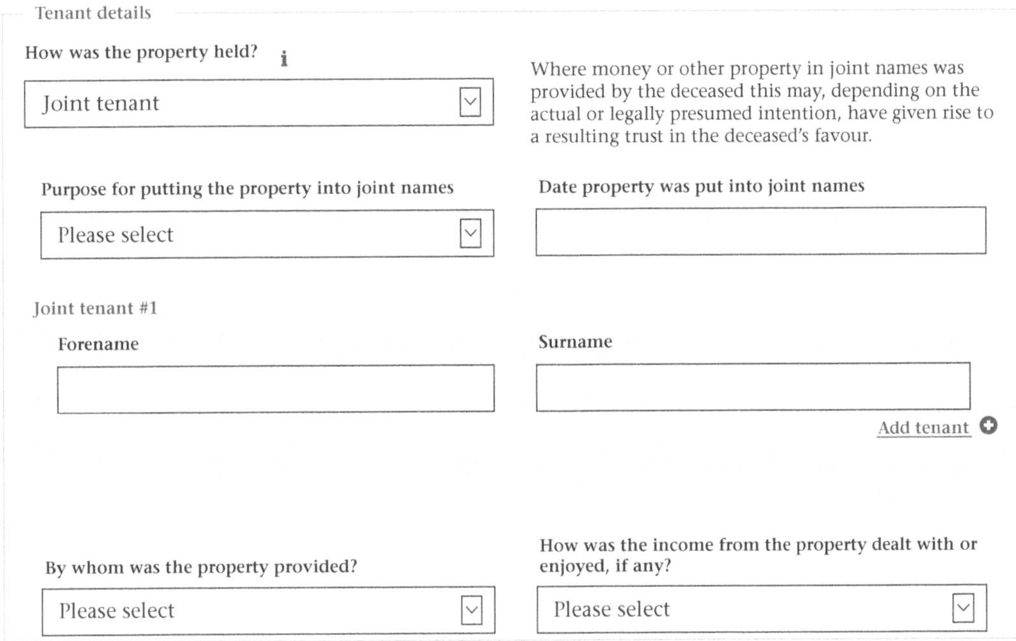

Tenant details

How was the property held?

Joint tenant

Where money or other property in joint names was provided by the deceased this may, depending on the actual or legally presumed intention, have given rise to a resulting trust in the deceased's favour.

Purpose for putting the property into joint names

Please select

Date property was put into joint names

Joint tenant #1

Forename

Surname

Add tenant

By whom was the property provided?

Please select

How was the income from the property dealt with or enjoyed, if any?

Please select

It will be appreciated that the tax liability will follow the legal position in any particular case.

Part 6

2.9.3.1 Distinction between real property and personal property held jointly

The rules relating to joint property distinguish between personal property and real property and there is much case law dealing with the various equitable presumptions.

Note the case of *Lynch v Burke and Allied Irish Banks Plc* [1996] ILRM 114 SC, which overruled a long-standing decision in *Owens v Greene and Freeley* [1932] Irish Reports. The High Court judgment in this case, which was appealed to the Supreme Court, is also reported at [1991] IR 1.

On the facts of the case, the Supreme Court held that in the case of bank monies in the joint names of the deceased and another the concept of resulting trust, which was devised primarily to defeat the misappropriation of property as a consequence of potentially fraudulent or improvident transactions, was not to be used to defeat the clear intention of the depositor to benefit the surviving account holder on death. In the particular case, the bank deposit book stated that monies were to be paid to 'Frances McFadden only or survivor'. The Court held that this created a contractual obligation on the bank to pay to the survivor, thus bypassing the presumption of resulting trust.

The question of whether the survivor takes the property as against the estate of the deceased person depends on the evidence to be submitted in each particular case and the survivor does not have to argue against the presumption of a resulting trust to the estate of the deceased. In the above case, both the High Court and Supreme Court judges agreed that no other possible interpretation of the testator's intention was possible. Students are referred to the *Law Society Practice Note on Joint Bank Accounts* (December 2008) and para 6.6.7 of *Wills, Probate and Estates.*

2.9.3.2 Monies standing in joint names

Section 109 of CAT Consolidation Act, 2003 (as amended) deals with joint accounts (other than current accounts). It deals with the situation where a sum of money exceeding €50,000 (€31,750/IR£25,000 from 26 January 2001 to 14 June 2010 and £5,000 prior to that date) is lodged or deposited otherwise than on a current account in the State with a banker in the joint names of two or more persons and one of such persons dies. Where these conditions are met, the surviving joint account holder(s) can either use the Form SA 2 or complete a Revenue Form CA4 (which can be completed on screen and printed off from the Revenue website, <www.revenue.ie>) and returned to the Revenue signed but not sworn by the beneficiary. A letter of clearance (IT8) will issue from the Revenue and on production of this letter of clearance a banker can pay out the money to the survivor or survivors without a grant of representation.

Revenue may also issue a letter of consent to such payment or part thereof pending the ascertainment and payment of the tax, for example where a joint account forms part of a greater inheritance by the beneficiary from the disponer.

The word 'banker' is widely defined and includes a building society, Post Office Savings Bank, Industrial Credit Company Limited, and other corporations.

It should be noted that producing a Grant of Probate or Letters of Administration to the bank does not entitle the bank to pay over the monies to the survivor. This section makes provision for penalties on a bank which contravenes the provisions of the section. It should also be noted for the purposes of this section that the tax is deemed to be due and payable on the date of death of the deceased.

Sub-section (7) as amended by the Finance (No. 3) Act, 2011 provides that this does not apply where the joint monies are deposited in the joint names of two persons, one of whom dies on or after the coming into force of CAT Consolidation Act, 2003 and is at the time of his death the spouse or civil partner of that other person. This follows on from the provision that an inheritance taken by one spouse or civil partner on the death of the other spouse or civil partner is exempt (see **3.11**).

Whenever dealing with property—whether immoveable (land and buildings) or moveable (personal property such as bank accounts)—held jointly, the questions that are 'opened up' by clicking on joint ownership in the SA 2 must be answered to ensure that the property passing actually goes to the correct person, apart at all from the taxation considerations arising.

2.9.4 INTEREST IN ASSURANCE POLICIES

Section 41 deals with the question of when tax is payable where the gift or inheritance consists of an interest in a life assurance policy. Where life assurance is provided by an employer as part of the insured's pension arrangements this is dealt with under s.80, which deals with retirement and employment benefits. See **3.14.6**.

Life assurance policies can be taken out on the basis that sums shall be paid out after a fixed term or on the death of the life insured. If a disponer gifts an interest in a policy of assurance on his or her own life to a beneficiary, then obviously this will not be an interest in possession until either the policy matures or the disponer dies.

Section 41(1) recognises this and states that an interest in a policy of life assurance will not become an interest in possession and therefore not be taxable until either:

(1) the policy matures (by virtue of reaching the maturation date, or by the death of the disponer) or

(2) the policy is surrendered by the beneficiary to the insurer for a consideration in money or monies worth or

(3) the insurer makes a payment to the beneficiary in full or partial discharge of the policy.

In short, the charge to CAT is postponed until some value emerges from the policy.

2.9.4.1 Example

A disponer is the owner of a policy on his own life, valued at €40,000, and in respect of which he has paid all the premiums. He assigns the policy to his sister and dies two years later. The charge to CAT against the sister will arise not when the policy was assigned to her, but on the death of the disponer when the proceeds of the policy are paid out to her.

It is possible that if all of the premiums on the policy had not been paid by the disponer before assigning it to his sister, and thereafter she paid the premiums, then she would be treated as having paid partial consideration for her inheritance of the proceeds of the policy, and this would be calculated rateably.

2.9.4.2 Non 's 72/73' policies only

Section 41 relates to policies which are not 's. 72' policies. A s. 72 policy left specifically to one person for the purposes of paying that person's CAT will not in itself be taxable insofar as it is used to pay his CAT. These policies were formerly known, and often still are referred to, as 's. 60' policies. Section 72 and 73 policies will be dealt with in **3.7**.

2.9.4.3 Section 41(2) deferred annuity

Subsection (2) states that where the gift or inheritance consists of a contract for a deferred annuity, the gift or inheritance will be deemed to have been received when the first instalment of the annuity falls due and will therefore be taxable then, and on the *entire* value of the annuity. Capitalising the value of annuities is not dealt with on this course.

2.9.5 PROVISIONS TO APPLY WHERE EXCEPTIONS TO THE DOCRTRINE OF LAPSE APPLY (SECTION 42)

Under the general rules of succession, if a beneficiary under a will predeceases the testator, then a devise or bequest in favour of that beneficiary will lapse and fall into the residue. If a residuary beneficiary predeceases the testator, then the residue may also lapse, and a portion of the estate may pass on intestacy. See para 2.9 of *Wills, Probate and Estates* and s. 91 of the Succession Act, 1965.

2.9.5.1 Testate—Succession Act, 1965, section 98

There are some exceptions to this rule where a bequest is in discharge of a legal or moral obligation or to an individual on trust or where the will provides for a 'gift over'. The main legislative exception is contained in s. 98 of the Succession Act, 1965. See paras 4.6.8.3 and 8.8 of Wills, Probate and Estates.

This section provides that where a person who is a child or other issue of a testator, and to whom property is left under a testator's will, predeceases the testator and leaves issue of his own who are living at the date of the testator's death, then the devise or bequest in favour of that deceased child will not lapse, but the child will be deemed to have died immediately after the testator. The effect of this is that the property left by the testator will therefore devolve under the will or intestacy of his *deceased child* or other issue. See Chapter 4 of *Wills, Probate and Estates.*

2.9.5.2 Intestacy—per stirpes rule

A similar provision arises on intestacy under s. 67(2) 67B (2), which provides for issue of predeceased issue of the deceased, and in s. 69 (1) in certain cases, children of a predeceased sibling. See para. 9.5 of *Wills, Probate and Estates.*

The effects of lapse on testate and intestate estates are very different and the legal effect should be clarified before any tax consequences are examined.

2.9.5.3 Taxation consequences (section 42)

Potentially, therefore, for the purposes of CAT where someone other than the child inherits in these circumstances (see *Wills, Probate and Estates,* Chapter 4, para. 4.5.8.3; Chapter 8, para. 98.5; and Chapter 9, para. 9.8 for examples) this situation could give rise to two charges to tax, the first by allowing the legacy or bequest to be taken by the estate of the deceased issue, and the second when the property is passed on in accordance with the will or intestacy of the deceased issue.

Section 42 of CAT Consolidation Act, 2003 specifies that in circumstances such as this the first of these inheritances, that is, the deemed inheritance by the deceased issue, shall not be deemed to be an inheritance and therefore not give rise to a charge to tax.

Subsection (2) goes on to state that when the property is administered through the estate of the deceased issue, the person becoming beneficially entitled to it will be regarded as having derived the benefit from the *original testator* and not the testator's predeceased issue.

2.9.5.4 Example of Section 42

A testator Albert dies, a widower having by his will bequeathed all of his estate to his only child, his daughter Diane. Diane had predeceased her father, leaving her husband Edward and their two children Fiona and Gerard surviving.

FIGURE 2.11

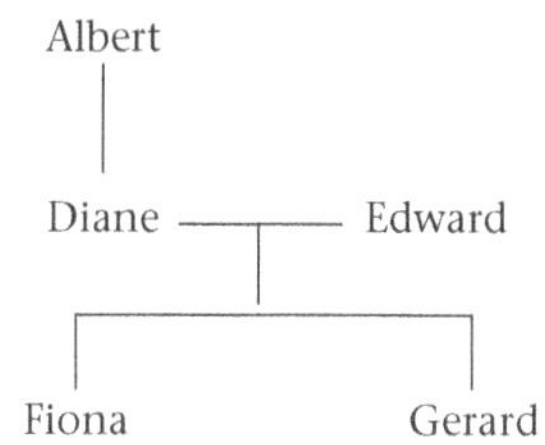

Diane had by her will left all of her estate to her two children Fiona and Gerard.

By virtue of s. 98 of the Succession Act the devise in favour of the testator's daughter does not lapse, but instead goes to her estate, and her children inherit all of the testator's estate on his death.

The inheritance tax consequences are:

(1) The estate of Diane, the daughter, is not taxed in respect of the bequest to her (notwithstanding that s. 98 of the Succession Act deems her to have died immediately after the testator); and

(2) the two children, Fiona and Gerard, are taxed on the basis of an inheritance from their grandfather as disponer.

2.9.5.5 Minor child of a deceased child

If the children in the example above are minor children of a deceased child at the date of the testator's death, they would receive the benefit of the group A €400,000 tax threshold (see **2.2.1.2**). Otherwise, they would be taxed as 'ordinary' lineal descendants/grandchildren (group B) and their threshold would be €40,000.

2.9.5.6 Surviving spouse of a deceased child

Taking the example above, suppose the daughter, Diane, had left her entire estate to her husband. By virtue of s. 98 of the Succession Act the devise in favour of the testator's daughter would not lapse, but instead goes to her estate and thus to her husband (widower). The children of a predeceased child who kept the bequest alive do not benefit in this case.

The surviving spouse would be deemed to inherit directly from his late father-in-law.

'Surviving spouse relief' (see **3.12**) provides that the surviving spouse would be deemed to acquire his late wife's group threshold in relation to her father; that is, he would go from Group C stranger in blood to Group A child: a significant increase.

2.9.5.7 Illustrating Section 42 (children)

The figure below illustrates the operation of s. 42 where a child predeceases.

FIGURE 2.13

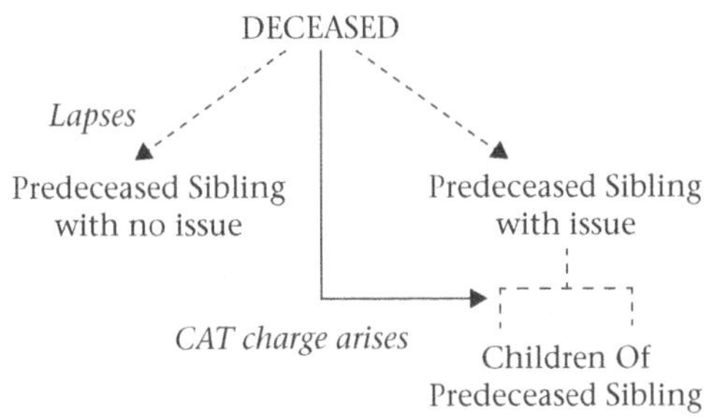

2.9.5.8 Illustrating Section 42 (children of siblings)

Please also note that where a person dies intestate without spouse or children or parent, the surviving brothers and sisters inherit equally. Children of a predeceased sibling take their late parent's share in equal shares.

The figure below illustrates the operation of s. 42 on intestacy where a child of a predeceased sibling inherits.

FIGURE 2.14

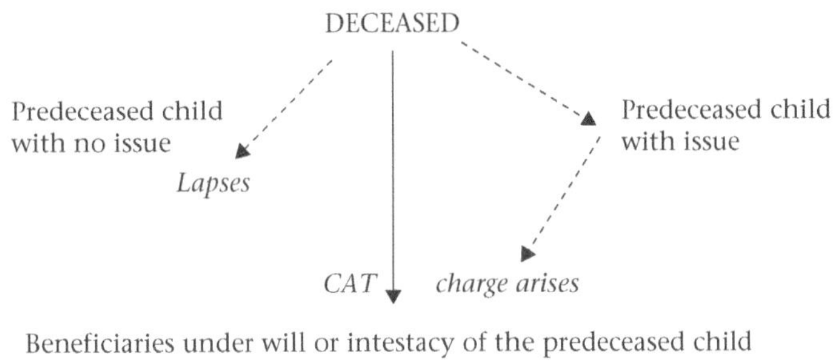

The relationship applicable for the charge to CAT is that between the testator and the ultimate beneficiaries, in this case group B from sibling of parent.

It is important to realise that s. 98 only applies in testate situations.

Should a person die intestate, leaving predeceased children, who have themselves children alive, the doctrine of *'per stirpes'* will apply and the grandchildren will take the share that would have gone to their parent in equal shares directly from their grandparent.

Practitioners should refer to Chapter 8 of *Wills, Probate and Estates* and para 28 on page 23 of *The Succession Act 1965 and Related Legislation: A Commentary* (Spierin: Bloomsbury, 2017).

2.9.6 ACCOUNTABLE PERSONS AND THE CHARGE TO TAX

Having calculated the tax payable and observed the relationship between CAT and probate practice, we will deal with payment of the tax, covering accountable persons, enforcement, and interest payable on outstanding tax.

Section 45 of CAT Consolidation Act, 2003 was substituted in its entirety by s. 147(b) of the Finance Act, 2010 to take effect from 3 April 2010. Prior to that date, the estate (inheritance tax) or the donor (gift tax) were secondarily liable for the payment of the tax. Since 3 April 2010 the successor (inheritance tax) or the donee (gift tax) are entirely responsible for the payment of the tax and the estate or the donor have no responsibility.

There is an exception to this where there are non-resident beneficiaries and/or a non-resident personal representative.

2.9.6.1 Non-resident beneficiary

Currently it is not possible to enforce a charge to taxation outside the jurisdiction, so in order to protect its tax base where it appears that a beneficiary is non-resident, s. 45AA of the CAT Consolidation Act, 2003 as inserted by s. 147(1)(d) of the Finance Act, 2010 provides for a form of liability for the personal representative. Practitioners are referred to the Revenue Commissioners CAT TDM Part 02 Statement of Affairs (Probate) and Part 04 The Certificate of Discharge (Form CA 11) published on the Revenue website: <https://www.revenue.ie/en/tax-professionals/tdm/capital-acquisitions-tax/index.aspx>.

Section 45AA (1) provides that the personal representative will be assessable and chargeable for the tax to the same extent as the non-resident beneficiary.

There are certain protections provided for the personal representative; for example, where the non-resident beneficiary fails to disclose prior benefits having been asked to do so by the personal representative, the personal representative will not be liable for the resulting charge to tax. The liability is limited to tax due on property that they have 'control' over or should have had control over but for their 'own neglect or default'. 'Neglect' or 'default' are not defined in the legislation.

The personal representative has the authority to sell or mortgage property due to the non-resident beneficiary to pay the tax, if necessary, but this may be of little practical benefit as such 'forced sales' do not achieve a full market value for the property being sold.

Where the personal representative is satisfied that all due tax has been paid and all relevant returns filed, the Revenue Commissioners have agreed a procedure by which the personal representative can write to the Revenue Commissioners at Dublin City Centre District, Revenue Commissioners, 9–15 Upper O'Connell Street, Dublin 2 indicating that they intend distributing the remaining assets to the non-resident beneficiary in one month's time.

If the Revenue Commissioners do not respond in that one-month period, advising that the file may be audited, the personal representative is at liberty to distribute the assets. Should a subsequent liability arise, provided that the personal representative acted honestly and in good faith and did not deliberately fail to comply with his or her obligations, then the Revenue will only seek to enforce liability on the resident personal representative to the extent of any assets remaining under his or her control. Any excess liability will be sought by the Revenue directly from the non-resident beneficiary and liability for the excess liability will not be enforced against the resident personal representative.

2.9.6.2 Non-resident beneficiary and personal representative

Section 48(10) of the CAT Consolidation Act, 2003 as inserted by s. 147(1)(l) of the Finance Act, 2010 goes on to deal with the situation where there is a non-resident beneficiary *and* there is no personal representative resident in the State. Again, the same issue of enforceability of the charge to tax outside the jurisdiction arises. In those circumstances a grant of representation will not issue unless a 'solicitor who is lawfully practicing in the State' is appointed by the intended applicant(s) to act in the administration of the estate. This solicitor will be broadly subject to the same liability for the tax as the personal representative under s. 45AA.

Section 115 of the Finance Act, 2012 further clarifies this and confirms that the solicitor referred to in s. 48(10) shall be assessable and chargeable for the tax to the same extent as the beneficiary.

Solicitors should be very careful before taking on such a role and should consider the Practice Note issued by the Probate, Administration & Trusts Committee on 13 December 2018 (Issue 103 of the Legal eZine: <http://ezine.lawsociety.ie/xk2p3qaciyk?a=2&p=54316318&t=28930673>) before proceeding.

2.9.6.3 Tax no longer a charge on property

Up until 14 June 2010 the Revenue, in addition to their right (*in personam*) to follow the person accountable for tax, also had a right *in rem* against the property comprised in the benefit.

Section 147(1)(r) removed this charge retrospectively save and except for applications to be registered as owner of property based on adverse possession. See **Chapter 4** in this manual and para 4.3 of the Revenue Manual.

2.9.6.4 Registration of Title Based on Possession—Section 62 CAT Consolidation Act, 2003 (Form CA 12)

If a person wishes to be registered as owner of property based on possession under the Land Registry Rules 2012, they are required to present a certificate issued by the Revenue Commissioners to the effect that the property in question did not become charged to CAT during the relevant period or that any such charge shall be discharged to the satisfaction of the Commissioners.

A copy of the sworn Land Registry Form 5 and application Form C.A.12 should be submitted. If these forms are in order, then the Form C.A.12 can be certified.

There is also a Self-Certification Form I.T.76 that can be used by solicitors in situations where the property involved is under a certain value, as set out in s. 62.

2.9.7 SURCHARGES AND INTEREST

As noted earlier, the payment and filing deadlines have been dramatically altered by s. 147 of the Finance Act, 2010. The current pay and file due date is 31 October where the valuation date arises prior to 31 August in any tax year. If the return is filed late, there is a surcharge for late filing, and interest is also due.

It should be noted that there are two separate penalties:

1. A surcharge for late filing of the CAT return (either paper or online) and
2. A charge to interest on late payment of the tax due.

Both penalties are based on the amount of tax due and delay in payment of the amount of tax due.

2.9.7.1 Surcharge for late filing

The amount of the surcharge is based on the amount of tax due and whether or not the payment was made inside two months of the due date.

(1) Where the tax is paid and a return filed within two months of the due date, a surcharge of 5 per cent of the tax due will apply. This 5 per cent surcharge is 'capped' at €12,695.

(2) Where the tax is paid and the return is filed later than two months of the due date, the surcharge increases to 10 per cent of the tax due, subject to a maximum surcharge of €63,485.

Interestingly, where a return is required but no tax is due (i.e. the current and prior aggregable benefits are over 80 per cent of the group threshold), the surcharge is nil. In those circumstances, Revenue have the power to impose a penalty of €3,000 together with a charge of €30 per day until the return is filed.

Where no tax is due, however, it would be extremely rare for such a penalty to be imposed, and the penalty usually arises in cases of criminal prosecution for failure to pay and file.

2.9.7.2 Interest on late payment of CAT

Where the tax is paid after the pay and file deadline of 31 October, s. 51 of CAT Consolidation Act, 2003 (as amended) provides for simple interest payable at the rate of 0.0219 per cent of the tax due per day (including part of a day) from the pay and file deadline.

This is in addition to and separate from any surcharge for late filing.

Originally the rate was 1.5 per cent per month or part of month (18 per cent per annum). This was reduced to 1.25 per cent per month (15 per cent per annum) from 5 July 1978 and further reduced to 1 per cent (12 per cent per annum) per month from 27 March 1998.

From 1 September 2002, the rate was converted to the then current daily rate of 0.0322 per cent per day and this was further reduced to 0.0273 per cent per day or 9.9645 per cent per annum from 1 April 2005 to 30 June 2009. The rate was most recently lowered from 1 July 2009 to the current rate of 0.0219 per cent per day (approx. 8 per cent per annum).

From 1 July 2009 onwards, when calculating interest on outstanding tax, the following daily rates are to be used:

(Period) **(1)**	**(Daily Percentage)** **(2)**
From 31 March 1976 to 31 July 1978	0.0492%
From 1 August 1978 to 31 March 1998	0.0410%
From 1 April 1998 to 31 March 2005	0.0322%
From 1 April 2005 to 30 June 2009	0.0273%
From 1 July 2009 to date of payment	**0.0219%** (Current Rate)

The formula for calculating interest is tax due multiplied by Number of Days Delay multiplied by Daily Percentage Rate.

Interest is recoverable in the same way as if it was part of the tax.

Clawback of Reliefs

Subsection (3) provides that in the case of various reliefs (agricultural relief, heritage properties, business relief, dwelling relief), interest due to the tax payable on the withdrawal of the relief will only run from the date the relief or exemption ceases to apply. The interest does not run from the original valuation date.

Payments on Account—Interest Taken First

Subsections (5) and (6) provide for a payment on account of tax, which can be made at any time but is always applied first in discharging any interest which has accrued due on outstanding tax, with the balance if any set against the tax.

However, even in that case any overdue instalments will still be charged to interest at 0.0219 per cent per day.

2.9.7.3 Rates of interest for agricultural or relevant business property

Where tax is being paid by instalments (see **2.9.8.2**), s. 55 of CAT Consolidation Act, 2003 (as amended) provides that the rate of interest on outstanding instalments will be 0.0164 per cent per day or a part of a day where the benefit consists of agricultural property or relevant business property. This rate was formerly:

- 0.0204 per cent from 1 April 2005 to 30 June 2009;
- 0.0241 per cent from 1 April 1998 to 31 March 2005; and
- 0.0307 per cent from 8 February 1995 to 31 March 1998.

(Period) (1)	(Daily Percentage for Agricultural or Relevant Business Property) (2)
From 8 February 1995 to 31 March 1998	0.0307%
From 1 April 1998 to 31 March 2005	0.0241%
From 1 April 2005 to 30 June 2009	0.0204%
From 1 July 2009 to date of payment	0.0164% Current Rate

2.9.8 PAYMENT OF TAX BY INSTALMENTS (SECTION 54)

Section 54 of CAT Consolidation Act, 2003 (as amended) makes provision for payment of tax by instalments where the benefit passing is not personal property. The taxpayer has the option to pay tax (usually) by monthly instalments over a period not exceeding five years by arrangement with the Revenue Commissioners.

Interest at the rates outlined above will be payable on such instalments. The first instalment would be due on 31 October immediately following the valuation date. Instalment payments can be paid before they are due.

Prior to June 2010, instalments were paid on an annual basis of five equal payments and the first payment was due on the anniversary of the valuation date.

Where and to the extent that the property comprised in the benefit is sold or compulsorily acquired, all unpaid instalments shall be paid on completion of the sale unless the interest of the beneficiary is a limited interest.

2.9.8.1 Provisions for 'personal' agricultural or business property

Section 55 of CAT Consolidation Act, 2003 provides that the instalment provisions apply to the payment of tax on agricultural property and/or relevant business property, which consists of personal property taken absolutely.

As noted above, where the property comprised in the benefit is sold or compulsorily acquired, all unpaid instalments shall be paid on completion of the sale.

An exception is again provided in respect of agricultural property and/or relevant business property. Payment by instalments in respect of an absolute interest in such properties will no longer come to an end in the event of a sale within the instalment period provided that the proceeds of sale are re-invested in other agricultural property and/or relevant business property within one year of the sale or six years of the CPO.

As noted earlier, the interest rate for agricultural or business property is 0.0164 per cent per day or a part of a day.

2.9.8.2 Life tenant dies before all instalments paid

Section 54(5) applies to life tenants only, that is, individuals whose interest in the property ceases on their death. It provides that where a life tenant inherits property and whether they chose to pay by instalments or not, where that life tenant dies before the final instalment would have been due, either

(a) where the life tenant was paying by instalments, they do not have to pay any further instalments; or

(b) where the life tenant paid the CAT due by the initial pay and file deadline, a calculation is made of the sum of any such instalments which would have been due had the life tenant chosen to pay by instalments and this sum is refunded.

For this purpose, Revenue assume that the life tenant chose to pay by instalments on a monthly basis (sixty monthly payments over a five-year period commencing on the relevant 31 October after the valuation date).

For example, where a life tenant has a CAT liability of €30,000:

(a) where that life tenant chooses to pay by sixty equal instalments of €500 per month (ignoring interest), paying the first instalment on 30 October 2022, and dies on the 12th of April 2025, the 30* instalments which have not yet been paid are exempt and do not have to be paid.

(b) where that life tenant pays the CAT due by 31 October 2022 and dies on 12 April 2025, a refund is due of the thirty instalments that would have been due.

A sum equivalent to any instalments due but unpaid before his or her death, had he or she paid by instalments, will be refunded to the estate of the life tenant. In this case, this would be 30 instalments of €500 each: a total of €15,000.

* €30,000 is due in sixty equal instalments and the first instalment is paid on 31 October 2022. 12 Instalments of €500 each would be paid by 30 September 2023 (ignoring interest); a further 12 (total 24) instalments would be paid by 30 September 2024 and a further six (total 30) instalments would be paid by 31 March 2025.

It follows that if the life tenant dies before the first instalment is due, all the tax will be refundable or, if it has not been paid, will cease to be payable. It should be noted that the taxable value of the limited interest taken by the life tenant still stands for the purposes of aggregating with benefits taken by that life tenant before death.

The relief applies only to an interest limited to cease on the death of the life tenant and does not therefore apply to a limited interest, which would be for a period certain.

A common error in dealing with the tax liability of a life tenant who dies within the instalment period is to re-assess the liability for a period certain. This is totally incorrect and will only arise where the limited interest is subject to a contingency (to be dealt with in **3.3**).

2.9.9 OVERPAYMENT OF TAX

Section 57 of CAT Consolidation Act, 2003 (as amended) deals with overpayment of tax and provides in subsection (2) that 'the Commissioners shall . . . give relief by means of repayment of the excess or otherwise as is reasonable and just'.

Subsection (3) (as amended) provides that the claim for repayment must be applied for within four years of 31 October in the year in which that tax was due to be paid.

Where the valuation date is (for example) 1 January 2023 any claim for refund of any overpayment of tax must be made within four years of 31 October 2023.

Subsection (6) provides for interest at the rate of 0.011 per cent per day or part of day (approx. 4 per cent) from either:

1. three months (93 days) after the date the taxpayer notified the Commissioners of the overpayment;

   or

2. where the Commissioners were mistaken in their operation of the tax from the date of the overpayment.

However, Subsection (8) provides that where interest is less than €10 it shall not be paid.

CHAPTER 3

VALUATION OF BENEFITS AND ANTI-AVOIDANCE, INTRODUCTION TO RELIEFS

3.1 Valuation of Private Company Shares (Section 27)

Section 27 of CATCA 2003 deals with the market value of shares in private trading companies and is mainly aimed at reducing the tax advantage of incorporating a family business.

Although protected to some extent by the Companies Act, 2014, in particular s. 212 of same, a minority shareholder can be outvoted on essential questions such as dividend policy and director's remuneration. When valuing a shareholding in a private (i.e. unquoted) company significant discounts apply depending on the amount of the shareholding held.

For example, a shareholder with less than 10 per cent of the shares is in a fundamentally weak position and has very limited rights, particularly if another shareholder holds all the remaining shares. Many of the protections under the Companies Act, 2014 are not afforded such a minority shareholder, whose only recourse would be through the courts. A shareholder with between 10 per cent and 25 per cent has some protection under the Companies Act, 2014 but is still in a very weak position *vis à vis* a single shareholder holding all the other shares.

This is taken into account when valuing a minority shareholding and the value of such a shareholding is normally discounted to take this into account. Section 27 provides that this 'discounting' does not apply when calculating the value of minority shareholdings in a 'Private Family Controlled Company'.

A Private Family Controlled Company is a company 'controlled' by five people or fewer. As we will see below, 'control' in this context is different to our usual understanding of control and where relatives have a shareholding in a company they are treated as being one person for the purpose of establishing the number of people who control the company and whether they number five or fewer.

3.1.1 EXAMPLE OF PRIVATE FAMILY CONTROLLED COMPANY

Andrew, Bernadette, Christopher, Daisy, and Eamon E are siblings who own a business with a net assets value of €5,000,000.

Each 'sibling' has an asset worth €1,000,000. If they incorporate the business each sibling will own 20 per cent of the shares in the limited company which owns that business.

Each 20 per cent shareholder has a minority shareholding, and as such the shareholding would be much less in value than 20 per cent of the value of the entire shares of the company. In essence, with shares, the sum is greater than the whole of the parts.

Such restrictions however would not be genuine in this case, where family members taken together are in a position to run the affairs of the company as they wish.

3.1.2 EFFECT OF SECTION 27

Accordingly, s. 27 of CAT Consolidation Act, 2003 deals in a specific way with the market value for CAT purposes of shares in a private company provided that on the date of the benefit and after taking that benefit the company is a company 'controlled' by the beneficiary.

The value of each share is ascertained as if it formed part of a group of shares sufficient to give the owner of the group control of the company. In relation to a private company, a 'group of shares' is the aggregate of the shares in the company that belong to:

- the beneficiary;
- relatives of the beneficiary (as defined below at **3.1.3**);
- nominees of the beneficiary; and
- the trustees of a settlement whose objects include the beneficiary or relatives of the beneficiary.

3.1.3 DEFINITION OF 'PRIVATE COMPANY' AND 'RELATIVE'

A 'private company' is defined in s. 27(1) as a body corporate wherever incorporated which:

(1) is under the control of not more than five persons; and

(2) is not a company which would fall within s. 431 of the Taxes Consolidation Act, 1997, which deals with 'Certain Companies with Quoted Shares Not to Be Close Companies'.

Section 431 is quite complex and necessitates a public beneficial holding of at least 35 per cent of the voting shares, quotation on a recognised stock exchange within the past 12 months and the five largest shareholders not holding more than 85 per cent of the voting shares.

The word 'relative' referred to above in connection with control is defined in CAT Consolidation Act, 2003, s. 2(4) as amended by s. 103 (2) of the Finance Act, 2013 to include:

(1) a spouse/civil partner of the beneficiary;

(2) the father, mother, grandparent, or any child, uncle, or aunt of the beneficiary;

(3) any child (other than the beneficiary himself) and any child of a child of any person who is a relative by reason of (1) or (2) above (which would include siblings and nephews and nieces and children of a civil partner); and

(4) the spouse/civil partner of a person who is by (2) or (3) above a relative of the beneficiary.

The spouse/civil partner of a relative is regarded as a relative while that relative is alive. However, if the relative has died, the widow/widower or surviving civil partner of such a relative is not regarded as a relative.

For a graphic illustration of who the 'relatives' of a beneficiary are, see *Capital Acquisitions Tax* (Bohan and McCarthy: Tottel, 2008, para 10.7), also reproduced at Figure 3.1.

Please note that this illustration has not been updated to include civil partners and relations of civil partners as outlined above. The beneficiary and his relatives and nominees are all considered a single person for the purpose of the five-person rule. For example, in the example of private family business above at **3.1.1**, all five persons would be considered a single person for this purpose. In other circumstances you could have a limited company with many more than five shareholders, which would be considered to be five or fewer when all the related shareholders are taken into account and grouped together.

FIGURE 3.1

'Relatives' as defined by CATCA 2003 s.2(4)

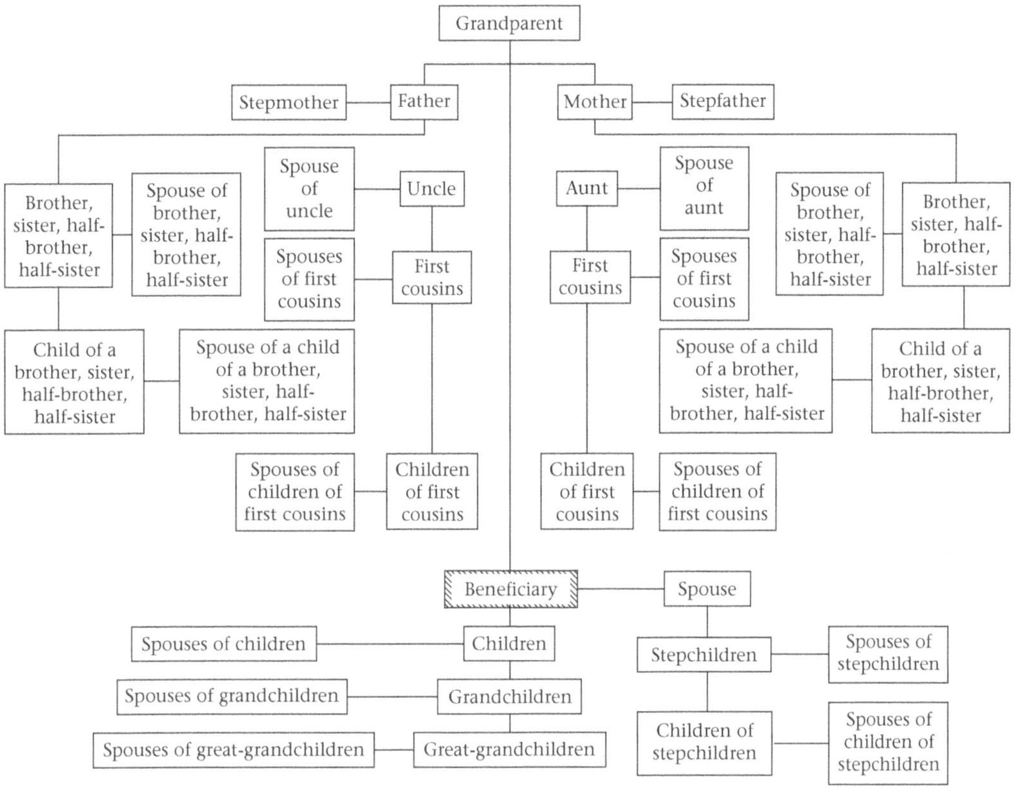

3.1.4 DEFINITION OF 'CONTROL'

Under CAT Consolidation Act, 2003, s. 27(3) and (4), a person is deemed to have control of a company if that person:

(1) can control more than 50 per cent of the votes of the company on all questions affecting the company or could obtain that control by exercising a power reserved to him or her or at his or her direction or with his or her consent, for example by way of nominee holdings;

(2) has the control or the capacity to control or can direct the control in general of the Board of Directors, including the powers of the governing director and any powers of a like nature;

(3) is in receipt of or has the right to receive more than half of the dividends and interest on debentures of the company whether declared or not; and

(4) has an interest absolute or limited in the shares of the company of an aggregate nominal value representing half or more of the aggregate nominal value of the shares of the company.

While it is necessary to have control over 50 per cent of the votes of the company or to have the right to receive more than half of the dividends of the company, it should be noted that 50 per cent ('one half or more') of the aggregate nominal value of the shares of the company will be sufficient to give control.

3.1.4.1 Example of 'control'

Andrew and Brian each own 50 per cent of the shares of company X Ltd. and they are unrelated. Both Andrew and Brian are regarded as having control of that company. Each has 'one half or more' of the aggregate nominal value of the shares of the company.

3.1.4.2 Further example of 'control'

A disponer who has 100 per cent shareholding of a private company makes a gift of 20 per cent of those shares to his son. That 20 per cent shareholding is valued as if it was a part of a 100 per cent shareholding, which means in effect that the value of the 20 per cent shareholding represents one fifth of the net value of the company with no discounting for a minority holding.

If the disponer was a stranger to the beneficiary the 20 per cent shareholding would be valued as a minority shareholding, which would give a much lower market value for CAT purposes.

While ostensibly an anti-avoidance measure, s. 27 is used to define 'control' for the purposes of business relief, as outlined in **Chapter 5**.

3.2 Dispositions by or to a Company (Section 43)

Following on from the CAT treatment of the gift/inheritance of company shares, s. 43 of CAT Consolidation Act, 2003 deals with how gifts or inheritances are treated for CAT purposes if given to or taken from company. The section is an anti-avoidance section concerned with preventing individuals wishing to pass property on to other individuals from endeavouring to 'conceal' it by first transferring the property to a company and then granting to the individual a gift or inheritance of the shares in that company.

The section applies only to a company as defined in CAT Consolidation Act, 2003, s. 27(2) as discussed above.

3.2.1 'LOOK THROUGH' PROVISIONS

Section 43 provides that for the purposes of assessing a CAT liability the company which has either given or received the gift or inheritance will be 'looked through' to ascertain who are the ultimate shareholders in the company. Those ultimate shareholders as individuals will be treated as having made or having received the gift or inheritance. The proportions in which they will be regarded as having made or received the gift or inheritance will be the same proportions as they each would receive if the company were wound up voluntarily on the date of the dispositions and its assets realised.

The same 'look through' provisions will apply to locating the owners of any liabilities incurred by the company, but only where those liabilities are incurred otherwise than wholly and exclusively in connection with any business of the company.

3.2.2 EXAMPLE: DISPOSITION TO A COMPANY

Mr White makes an interest-free loan (gift) of €100,000 to a company Colours Limited. The shareholdings in Colours Limited are as follows:

- Mr White 50%.
- Ms Black (his niece) 25%.
- Mrs Red (his sister) 25%.

On a voluntary winding-up of the company the assets of the company would be distributed in these same proportions.

Section 43 will impute the following gifts:

- Mr White to himself €50,000 (no charge, s. 83 as discussed at **3.14.11**).
- Mr White to his niece Ms Black €25,000.
- Mr White to his sister Mrs Red €25,000.

3.2.3 CHAIN OF 'LOOKING THROUGH' (SECTION 43(4))

Section 43(4) provides for a possible chain of 'looking through' by stating that where a shareholder in a company which has given or received a gift or inheritance is itself a company then that company shall also be looked through to find its shareholders in the same manner as provided for in subsection (1).

3.2.3.1 Example: looking through

Take the same circumstances as in the example in **3.2.2** above, where Mr White makes an interest-free loan of €100,000 to Colours Limited.

The shareholdings in Colours Limited are as follows:

- Mr White 25%.
- Ms Black (his niece) 25%.
- Yellow Limited 50%.

The shareholdings in Yellow Limited are in turn as follows:

- Mr White 50%.
- Mrs Red (his sister) 50%.

The following benefits would be imputed for CAT purposes:

- Mr White to Mr White €50,000 (his 25 per cent shareholding in Colours Limited and his 50 per cent shareholding in Yellow Limited)—again no charge to tax (CAT Consolidation Act, 2003, s. 83).
- Mr White to Ms Black €25,000 (25 per cent shareholding in Colours Limited).
- Mr White to Mrs Red €25,000 (half of the amount given to Yellow Limited).

3.2.4 DISCRETIONARY TRUST (SECTION 43(5))

Where the shareholders are the trustees of a discretionary trust, sub-section (5) makes look through provisions again applicable, and the dispositions will be regarded as having been made by the disponer who set up the trust.

3.3 A Benefit Taken Subject to a Contingency (Section 29)

Section 29 of CAT Consolidation Act, 2003 deals with a benefit, which under the terms of the disposition creating it may cease on the happening of a contingency.

In such a case the contingency is ignored in computing tax on the initial benefit.

If the contingency happens, the tax will be adjusted as if the person took a limited interest for the actual period during which that person enjoyed the property. Tax will however be payable in respect of any property substituted for the benefit which was given up by reason of the happening of the contingency.

3.3.1 EXAMPLE: A BENEFIT SUBJECT TO A CONTINGENCY

Andrew, by will, leaves property to his widowed daughter-in-law Belinda (widow of his predeceased son, Christopher) for her life or re-marriage with remainder to the children of Belinda and Christopher equally absolutely.

In the event of Belinda's re-marriage she was to receive a legacy of €30,000 absolutely.

Initially, B is taxed on the basis of a life interest depending on her age according to the tables in CAT Consolidation Act, 2003.

Four years later, B re-marries. The tax payable by her on the basis of her life interest is adjusted and re-assessed on the basis that B took a limited interest for a period of four years. This would normally give rise to a refund situation.

B is also now taxed on a benefit of €30,000. This sum would be reduced from the value of the benefit received by her children as it is consideration for the benefit.

It is extremely important to distinguish this example from a situation where a life tenant dies within five years of receiving the life interest (see **2.9.8.2**).

3.4 A Liability Subject to a Contingency

Section 28(5) of CAT Consolidation Act, 2003 states that a deduction shall not be made in respect of any liability the payment of which is contingent on the happening of some future event. If and when the event happens a re-assessment of the tax is made on the same lines as in s. 29.

3.4.1 EXAMPLE: A LIABILITY SUBJECT TO A CONTINGENCY

David by will leaves his dwelling-house (market value at the valuation date €100,000) to his sister Eimear absolutely, subject to her paying €10,000 to her son Fionn if and when Fionn (who is currently aged 16 years) attains 21 years.

Eimear B is taxed on the basis of a taxable value of €100,000 without allowance for the €10,000. The fact of the matter is that Eimear enjoys the entire dwelling-house until her son Fionn attains the age of 21. If Fionn does not reach 21, the €10,000 is not payable by Eimear.

If and when Fionn attains 21, Eimear will be allowed relief for the €10,000 as follows: the tax assessed on the €100,000 will be re-assessed on €100,000 less €10,000 (i.e. €90,000).

However in addition Eimear will be treated as having enjoyed the €10,000 for five years up to the date of payment. Under Table B of CAT Consolidation Act, 2003, Sch. 1 the value of an interest in €10,000 for five years would be .2869 of €10,000 (i.e. €2,869).

The new adjusted taxable value of Eimear's inheritance will be €90,000 plus €2,869 equals €92,869. As tax has already been paid on a figure of €100,000 the tax overpaid will be refunded with interest from the date of payment to Fionn (if more than 93 days).

3.4.2 LIABILITIES NOT ALLOWABLE AS DEDUCTIONS

It should be noted that there are other liabilities, which are not allowable as deductions in arriving at the taxable value. They are listed in CAT Consolidation Act, 2003, s. 28(5).

3.4.2.1 Example: where a liability can be reimbursed

Deduction cannot be made for a debt in respect of which a right of reimbursement exists.

Aoife gifts her dwelling-house to Brian. The dwelling-house is already security for a loan given by a bank to Ciara. If the bank calls on Brian to pay, a deduction will not be made in respect of Brian's gift since he can insist on Ciara reimbursing him. However if and to the extent that Brian cannot recover from Ciara the debt is allowable.

3.4.2.2 Example: exempt property

Section 28(5)(e) provides that no deduction is allowed for a liability incurred in acquiring exempt property.

If as part of a benefit, a beneficiary receives a dwelling for which he or she obtains dwelling-house exemption, any mortgage on that property is not taken into account when ascertaining the taxable value of the entire benefit. Also, as mentioned earlier in this chapter, any costs, liabilities or expenses applicable to the entire property are apportioned and the relevant portion set against the taxable element of the benefit.

This will be dealt with in further details when dealing with dwelling exemption.

3.5 A Gift Subject to a Power of Revocation (Section 39)

One contingency which is specifically excluded from the provisions of s. 29 (as dealt with above at **3.3**) is a contingency which consists of a power of revocation by the disponer.

Section 39 of CAT Consolidation Act, 2003 provides that a person who takes property under a disposition, which can be revoked by the disponer, will not be taxed on the market value of that gift unless and until the power to revoke is released or is no longer exercisable; for example when the disponer dies without revoking the disposition.

While a power of revocation is no longer common, a disponer who wishes to reserve to himself the power to revoke a gift should be advised as to the taxation consequences of that power.

3.5.1 EXAMPLE: TAX CONSEQUENCES OF POWER OF REVOCATION

Andrew makes a gift of lands to Barry absolutely but reserves to himself the power to revoke the gift.

Section 39 states that although the beneficiary becomes beneficially entitled in possession to the lands he is deemed for tax purposes not to be so beneficially entitled in possession to the lands unless and until the power of revocation is released by the disponer or otherwise ceases to be exercisable; for example on the death of the disponer without releasing the power.

In the meantime however the provisions of s. 40 (free use of property) apply and Barry is deemed to take a gift at the end of each year during which he is allowed to have the use, occupation or enjoyment of the property.

3.5.2 FREE USE OF PROPERTY (SECTION 40)

The gift taken by Barry each year is deemed to consist of a sum equal to the difference between the amount of any consideration in money or monies worth given by Barry for such use, occupation, or enjoyment and the best price obtainable in the open market for such use, occupation or enjoyment.

On the assumption therefore that such use, occupation, or enjoyment would be worth €18,000 per annum (€1,500 per month) on the open market, Barry is regarded at the end of each year as taking a gift of €18,000 from Andrew the disponer. The small gift exemption would apply to this annual benefit.

Section 40 also applies when a person has the use of a property for no consideration or for less than a commercial rent or interest rate. For example: Alice loans €200,000 to her brother Brendan repayable on demand but free of interest.

In this case 'the best price obtainable' would be the income obtainable from the investment of the cash. This would be the best payable on demand deposit rate available from the main Irish banks for such a sum

It is important to note that it is the interest 'lost by the donor' and not the potential interest chargeable to the beneficiary by a bank or other financial institution that is the taxable rate.

On the assumption that the going rate of interest on such a deposit would be €20 (i.e. 0.01 per cent) annum, Brendan is treated as receiving a gift of €20 in a full year each year until the loan is repaid. Brendan will have the benefit of the small gift exemption each year and in this example, given current historically low deposit interest rates, no tax would accrue.

Should deposit rates rise, this annual benefit could potentially use up a lot of a group threshold over a period of time, particularly if between siblings.

3.6 Disclaimers

The law certainly is not so absurd as to force a man to take an estate against his Will. Prima facie, every estate, whether given by Will or otherwise, is supposed to be beneficial to the party to whom it is so given. Of that, however, he is the best judge, and if it turn out that the party to whom the gift is made does not consider it beneficial, the law will certainly, by some mode or other, allow him to renounce or refuse the gift.

Abbot CJ, in Townson v Tickell And Another [1819] Eng R 658, (1819) 3 B and A 31, (1819) 106 ER 575

Section 12 of CAT Consolidation Act, 2003 deals *inter alia* with disclaimers. Students should read Chapter 8 para 08.10 and Chapter 15 para 15.4 of *Wills, Probate and Estates* (Courtney: OUP, 2025) to fully understand the legal background to disclaimers, the distinction between disclaimers of a testate estate and disclaimers on intestacy and their application. Students are also referred to the Revenue CAT Tax and Duty Manual Part 06 Disclaimers of Benefits, which can be found on the Revenue website at <https://www.revenue.ie/en/tax-professionals/tdm/capital-acquisitions-tax/index.aspx>, and the Revenue website, which has general notes on disclaimers at <www.revenue.ie/en/tax/cat/guide/disclaimer.html>.

The crucial thing to remember about a disclaimer is that a disclaimer for CAT purposes is *not* a disposition. It is the extinguishment of a right before it comes into possession. Accordingly, one of the main elements of a benefit is missing and the act of disclaimer of itself does not give rise to a CAT liability.

The disclaimer must be a 'pure or simple' disclaimer, that is, a disclaimer where the person disclaiming does not nominate the person who is to benefit by reason of the disclaimer but rather where the rules of law establish who is to benefit as a result of the disclaimer. Practitioners should take great care when advising clients on disclaiming, particularly disclaimers on intestacy.

3.6.1 EXAMPLE: 'PURE OR SIMPLE' DISCLAIMER

Alfred by will devises his land to his son Brian absolutely and the residue of his estate to his nephew Cillian absolutely.

Brian disclaims his inheritance of the land and the devise falls into the residue of the estate and thus to Cillian. This disclaimer benefits the residuary legatee Cillian, who however takes that benefit from the testator, Alfred, and not from Brian, the person disclaiming.

When a person disclaims a benefit, that person ceases to have any liability in respect of the gift/inheritance disclaimed (s. 12(1)).

3.6.2 'DISCLAIMERS FOR CONSIDERATION'

If however the person disclaiming receives any consideration for the disclaimer, such consideration will be considered as a substituted gift/inheritance taken from the person who provided the original benefit which is disclaimed, rather than from the person who actually pays the consideration.

3.6.2.1 Example: disclaimer for consideration

Taking the example above, but this time Brian disclaims his inheritance of the lands in consideration of receiving a sum of €250,000 from Cillian.

Brian will pay Inheritance Tax on €250,000 (s. 12(3)) as an inheritance from Alfred. Cillian will take the lands as part of the residue and will be allowed to deduct a sum of €250,000 consideration in arriving at the taxable value of his inheritance from Alfred.

3.6.3 DISCLAIMER IN FAVOUR OF A NAMED PERSON

In the case above, it should be noted that Brian did not disclaim in favour of Cillian. It was still a 'pure and simple' disclaimer where by operation of law the devise went to Cillian.

It is very important to be aware that a disclaimer in favour of a named person is not pure or simple. It will be considered as an acquisition by the person purporting to disclaim, and a subsequent disposal of his benefit to the named party. Similarly, a deed describing itself as a 'Directed Disclaimer' will have the same effect of acquisition and subsequent disposal.

Taking the example above, instead of merely disclaiming, Brian disclaims in favour of Dermot, his brother. Then Brian has inherited the full value of the bequest from Alfred and Dermot receives a gift of the full value of the bequest from Brian.

This in effect gives rise to a double charge to CAT: a charge to Inheritance Tax on the original beneficiary Brian from the original disponer, Alfred, and a charge to gift tax from the eventual beneficiary, Dermot, from the original beneficiary, Brian. The deed of disclaimer in this case will be stampable under the conveyance head of charge. It is not the description of the deed but the effect of the deed that matters. The recent High Court case of *Kieran Egan and Michael Egan Junior v Helen Egan and Alan Egan* 2023 IEHC 259 is instructive in this regard.

3.6.4 SUMMARY OF EFFECTS OF DIFFERENT TYPES OF DISCLAIMERS

A disclaimer can be useful for tax planning purposes and the operation of a disclaimer in various situations can be summarised as follows:

(1) Where a person disclaims a benefit they no longer have a liability to CAT in respect of that disclaimed benefit and a disclaimer is not itself a disposition for CAT purposes.

(2) While a person can disclaim for consideration, any such consideration being treated as a benefit moving from the original disponer to the person disclaiming (i.e. a substituted gift or inheritance), a disclaimer in favour of a named person is considered as an acquisition and a subsequent disposal and therefore there is a double charge to CAT.

(3) A legacy if it is disclaimed falls into the residue of the estate subject to the testator expressing a contrary intention in the will.

(4) Should a sole residuary legatee disclaim, that portion of the estate will be distributed as on intestacy.

(5) A residuary inheritance cannot be partially disclaimed. If any portion of the residue is claimed then the entire is claimed.

(6) A disclaimer by a residuary beneficiary in common of the share of the residue means that that share of the residue is distributed as on intestacy. This of course will only apply when the residue is divided, that is, words of severance are used and one of the residuary legatees and/or devisees in common is disclaiming his or her share.

(7) Separate legacies in a will can be disclaimed subject to them not being interdependent on each other. A part of a legacy cannot be disclaimed.

(8) A disclaimer of a limited interest has the effect in general of accelerating forward the remainder interest. For example: to A for life and remainder to B. If A disclaims, B inherits an absolute interest in the property from the original testator.

(9) It is not possible to disclaim a share of a joint tenancy. One joint tenant may subsequently release his or her interest but may not disclaim the interest *ab initio* unless the other joint tenants become parties to the disclaimer (*Re Schar* [1951] Ch 280).

This is particularly important where (for example) a testator leaves property (for example) to his son and daughter-in-law as joint tenants. The daughter-in-law may wish to disclaim so that the son gets the entire property subject to the Group A threshold as opposed to her paying CAT on half the property subject to the Group C threshold.

Students are also referred to s. 3 of the Land And Conveyancing Law Reform Act, 2009, which includes 'disclaimer' in its definition of conveyance and in s. 30 requires the consent of the other joint tenants before a conveyance (which includes a disclaimer) can be made. This, however, only applies to land.

(10) A disclaimer of an entitlement under an intestacy is covered under s. 6 of the Family Law (Miscellaneous Provisions) Act, 1997. That section inserts a new s. 72A into the Succession Act, 1965 to clarify the law in relation to the distribution of a disclaimed estate or part of an estate on intestacy.

The section states that the person disclaiming the benefit taken under an intestacy is treated as if he or she had died immediately before the death of the intestate and as if he or she had died without leaving issue unless the person disclaiming is the spouse/civil partner or a direct lineal ancestor of the intestate. See *Wills, Probate and Estates*, Chapter 8, para. 08.12.

Note that the date of the gift/inheritance taken by the person who benefits by reason of the disclaimer is the date of that gift/inheritance and *not* the date of the deed of disclaimer.

3.7 Section 72 and 73 Policies

Section 60 of the Finance Act, 1985 introduced a new concept into CAT. The purpose of the section was to provide a concession in relation to the use of an insurance policy for paying Inheritance Tax by exempting from such tax monies payable under what is called a 'qualifying insurance policy' provided those monies are utilised in paying the Inheritance Tax. Section 60 and all the subsequent amendments and additions to it are now consolidated into ss. 72 (inheritance) and 73 (gift) of CAT Consolidation Act, 2003. The proceeds of any qualifying insurance policy taken out by an insured person and their spouse/civil partner will be exempt from Inheritance Tax insofar as any proceeds are used to pay that tax arising on the death of the survivor of the two, or within a year of the latter's death under dispositions made by them whether by will or by *inter vivos* disposition. Any part of the proceeds not so used will be liable to Inheritance Tax.

'Qualifying insurance policy' is a policy of insurance:

(1) in a form approved by the Revenue Commissioners;

(2) in respect of which annual premiums are paid by the insured during his life (in this context a single premium policy would not qualify);

(3) which is expressly effected under the section for the purpose of paying relevant tax.

'Relevant tax' means Inheritance Tax due and payable in respect of an inheritance taken under a disposition made by the insured where the date of the inheritance is the date of death of the insured or within one year after that death.

In assessing Inheritance Tax the interest in a qualifying insurance policy is ignored.

'Relevant tax' includes not only Inheritance Tax payable on the insured's death under his or her will or intestacy but also Inheritance Tax payable on death on property passing absolutely by survivorship, nomination, and so on.

3.7.1 EXAMPLE: INSTRUCTION TO PAY 'ALL RELEVANT TAX'

Michael Murphy effects a policy under s. 72 for €60,000, the proceeds to be payable to his personal representatives to pay all relevant tax. Michael Murphy died on 1 November 2024 and by his will he bequeathed his estate to his brother John and his sister-in-law Mary (John's wife) in equal shares.

The net estate of Michael Murphy, excluding the s. 72 policy and after payment of all debts and funeral and testamentary expenses, is valued at €120,000.

Michael Murphy's only other asset was a house valued at €240,000, which he held as joint tenant with his surviving sister Ann, who owns another house jointly with her husband. None of his beneficiaries had any aggregable prior benefits.

The following taxable inheritances (excluding proceeds of policy) are taken on Michael Murphy's death.

The following taxable inheritances (excluding proceeds of policy) are taken on Michael Murphy's death.

	Name	**Taxable value of inheritance**	**Group threshold**	**Taxable excess**	**Tax @ 33%**
1	John	€60,000	B €40,000	€20,000	€6,600
2	Mary	€60,000	C €20,000	€40,000	€13,200
3	Ann	€120,000	B €40,000	€80,000	€26,400
					€46,200

The total tax due from the three successors (i.e. €46,200) is payable out of the policy as there is an instruction to pay 'all relevant tax'. This leaves €13,800 which was not used to pay tax.

This sum, the balance of the proceeds (i.e. €13,800), goes back into the estate and under the terms of the will is taken equally by John and Mary. Therefore John and Mary take a further inheritance of €6,900 each.

Additional tax of €2,277 is payable by each of them on this further inheritance @ 33% of €6,900

This is accounted for as follows:

	Tax payable on benefit	**Tax on s. 72 surplus**	**Total tax payable**
Total tax liability of John	€6,600 +	€2,277	€8,877
Total tax liability of Mary	€13,200 +	€2,277	€15,477
Total tax liability of Ann	€26,400 +	NIL	€26,400
			€50,754

3.7.2 EXAMPLE 2: NO INSTRUCTION IN WILL

Taking the same facts as before but this time there is no provision that the proceeds of the policy were to be used to pay all 'relevant tax' arising on his death.

The same initial taxable inheritances (excluding proceeds of policy) are taken on Michael Murphy's death.

	Name	Taxable value of inheritance	Group threshold	Taxable excess	Tax @ 33%
1	John	€60,000	B €40,000	€20,000	€6,600
2	Mary	€60,000	C €20,000	€40,000	€13,200
3	Ann	€120,000	B €40,000	€80,000	€26,400

As Michael Murphy made no specific provision in his will relating to the proceeds of the policy (€60,000), John and Mary take €30,000 each, and in their cases their CAT is paid out of the proceeds of the policy, with the surplus in each case being a further taxable bequest.

Payment is available out of the proceeds of the policy as follows:

	John's liability	Mary's liability	Ann's liability
s. 72	€30,000	€30,000	NIL
Tax due	€ 6,600	€13,200	€26,400
'Surplus' from policy	€23,400	€16,800	NIL

The 'surplus' is taxable at 33 per cent in each case as the threshold has already been used. The effect of this is:

1. Ann: pays €26,400 out of her own resources
2. John: takes further inheritance of €23,400—pays further tax at 33% of €7,722
3. Mary: takes further inheritance of €16,800—pays further tax at 33% of €5,544

	Tax payable on benefit	Tax on s. 72 surplus	Total tax payable
Total tax liability of John	€6,600 +	€7,722	€14,322
Total tax liability of Mary	€13,200 +	€5,544	€18,744
Total tax liability of Ann	€26,400		€26,400
Total tax liability			€59,466

3.7.3 SUMMARY OF EFFECT OF POLICIES

3.7.3.1 No policy

	John	Mary	Anne
Tax	€6,600	€13,200	€26,400
Payable	Own resources	Own resources	Own resources

3.7.3.2 Policy—provision in will to pay 'relevant tax'

	John	Mary	Anne
Tax	€8,877*	€15,477 *	€26,400
Benefit from policy	€ 6,600	€13,200	€26,400
+ share of unused policy	+ €6,900	+ €6,900	NIL
Total	€13,500	€20,100	€26,400

*Original tax plus tax of €2,277 on surplus of €6,900

3.7.3.3 Policy—no provision re payment of 'relevant tax'

	John	Mary	Anne
Tax	€14,322	€18,744	€26,400
Benefit from policy	€30,000	€30,000	NIL

3.7.4 MULTIPLE LIVES

Originally s. 60 applied to a single life policy only. However, by Finance Act, 1989, s. 84 the concession is now extended to a policy effected by two spouses/civil partners, the proceeds of which are payable on the death of the survivor of the spouses/civil partners or on the simultaneous deaths of both.

Section 118 of the Finance Act, 1991 extended the provisions of s. 60 further in order to allow a life tenant to effect a single life s. 60 policy to provide for the Inheritance Tax arising on his or her death under a disposition made by his or her spouse/civil partner.

Both these provisions are now incorporated into CAT Consolidation Act, 2003, s. 73 as amended.

3.7.4.1 Example

Husband Andrew by his will bequeathed his real estate to his wife Belinda for her life with remainder to his cousin Cynthia absolutely. The personal estate went to Belinda absolutely

The wife can effect a s. 72 policy on her life and the Inheritance Tax payable on her death, on the benefit taken at that time by her husband's cousin under the husband's will, is the 'relevant tax' for the purposes of s. 72.

Section 72 also incorporated an amendment introduced by allowing a life tenant to take out a s. 72 policy to cover events arising out of a disposition made by any person after 28 March 1996.

3.7.5 GIFTS (SECTION 73)

Section 119 of the Finance Act, 1991 introduced a concession in relation to certain policies of insurance in a case where the proceeds of the policies are used to pay Gift Tax or Inheritance Tax arising in connection with gifts made by the insured. The amended section is now to be found at CAT Consolidation Act, 2003, s. 73.

The section exempts from gift tax the proceeds of an approved policy insofar as such proceeds are used to pay Gift Tax or Inheritance Tax on a gift made by the insured within *one year* of the proceeds of the policy becoming payable. There must be a minimum funding period of eight years in respect of the policy.

In addition, the proceeds can be used at any time during this eight-year period if the insured dies or becomes critically ill.

There is a certain amount of interchangeability between the relief under s. 72 and the relief under s. 73. Practitioners should review CAT Tax & Duty Manual Part 15 (Insurance), which can be found on the Revenue website at https://www.revenue.ie/en/tax-professionals/tdm/capital-acquisitions-tax/index.aspx and which sets out examples of when they can be used.

Depending on the facts of each particular case, these policies can be very useful in providing a tax-free fund for the payment of Gift/Inheritance Tax.

3.7.5.1 Example

Dermot by will settles property on Elaine for life with remainder to Fern absolutely. Elaine, the life tenant, effected a qualifying insurance policy in favour of Fern under the provisions of s. 60 now covered by s. 72. Elaine by her will left all her property to Fern absolutely. In her will she directed that all relevant tax as defined in s. 60 as amended would be paid out of the proceeds of the policy.

On the death of Elaine the proceeds of the s. 72 policy will cover not only the benefit taken by Fern under Elaine's will but also the benefit taken by her as remainderman under Dermot's will.

Should the proceeds of the policy be greater than all relevant tax the balance will be treated as an inheritance taken by Fern one day after the date of death of Elaine.

Section 72/60 policies were extremely popular in the past as a tax avoidance mechanism. However, since the introduction of the present regime for CAT and in particular business relief and dwelling exemption, the policies are not as popular. In addition, depending on the age of the disponer, policies can be quite expensive. When advising clients about ss. 72 or 73 policies, always remember that you are advising your clients to spend their money so that a beneficiary can save tax. This may not always be an attractive proposition to the client!

3.8 Benefit of Freedom from Tax s. 87

Section 113 of CATCA 2003 states that Inheritance Tax is a death duty for the purposes of the definition of pecuniary legacy in s. 3(1) of the Succession Act, 1965.

That definition states *inter alia* that a pecuniary legacy includes any general direction by a testator for the payment of money including all death duties free from which any devise, bequest, or payment is made to take effect. Accordingly, a direction by a testator that a devise or a bequest be made free of Inheritance Tax will itself be a pecuniary legacy of the amount of that tax.

Section 87 of the CAT Consolidation Act, 2003 provides that where a benefit is stated to be 'free from tax' the benefit taken shall be deemed to include the amount of tax chargeable on such benefit but not the amount of tax chargeable on such tax.

3.8.1 EXAMPLE OF FREEDOM FROM TAX

Gerard, who died in 2025, leaves a legacy of €40,000 free of Inheritance Tax to his cousin Harry, who has not received any prior benefit, and the residue of his estate to Ian absolutely.

The tax on Harry's legacy is calculated as follows:

- Tax on the threshold amount of €20,000 is NIL.
- Tax on balance of €20,000 @ 33% is €6,600.
- Tax is also chargeable at 33% on the further benefit of €6,600 and amounts to a further taxable benefit of €2,277.

Accordingly, Harry takes a benefit of €40,000 clear of tax and tax of €8,877 (i.e. €6,600 on the original benefit plus €2,277 on the tax payable on the original benefit) is paid out of the residuary estate and is a valid deduction in arriving at the taxable value of Ian's benefit.

3.8.2 REMAINDER OF ESTATE

There is little point leaving a residuary interest to a beneficiary 'free of tax' to an individual, if the debts of the estate (including tax, in this particular circumstance) are to be paid out of the residue of the estate.

A testator could however leave the residue of his estate to a beneficiary 'tax free' with a specific instruction in the will that the CAT due by that residuary beneficiary be paid by a specific beneficiary.

3.9 Anti-Avoidance

Various measures have been introduced to defeat tax avoidance schemes over the years and in this paragraph we will be looking at two of the main schemes arising: connected gifts and gift splitting.

3.9.1 CONNECTED GIFTS (CAT CONSOLIDATION ACT, 2003 SECTION 8)

Section 8 provides that where gifts are made by different disponers of the same property or connected property within three years, the second gift is deemed to come from the original disponer to the eventual beneficiary and not from the actual disponer of the second gift.

The object of s. 8 was to prevent avoidance of tax by using a series of connected gifts from a first party, via a second party, to an eventual third party where the intention all along was that the third party benefit from the largesse of the first party but by availing of larger thresholds and/or exemption by using the second party.

This is best shown by way of example.

3.9.1.1 Example: 'connected gifts'

John makes a gift valued at €200,000 to his son Kieran in January 2025. Within three years Kieran makes a subsequent gift of the item to his daughter Lisa. Without s. 8, no tax liability would arise, as the two gifts are under the group A threshold if treated in isolation.

However, under s. 8 the gift from John to his son Kieran stands, but the gift from Kieran to his daughter Lisa is treated for tax purposes as if it was a gift directly from John to his granddaughter Lisa (group B threshold). The gifts are 'connected', that is, Revenue make a connection between the two gifts.

Similarly, without s. 8 tax avoidance would be possible in the following circumstances:

Michael makes a gift of property to his son Noel. Within three years of that gift Noel transfers the property into the joint names of himself and his wife Olivia. Section 8 applies and Olivia is deemed to have taken the half share of the property from her father-in-law Michael and is taxed accordingly under group C. Again, there is a connection made between the gifts by Revenue; they are 'connected'.

The anti-avoidance legislation refers to two gifts only and not to a gift and a subsequent inheritance or to an inheritance and a subsequent gift. It could be argued in that case if Peter makes a gift to Quincy and dies within two years, then the gift is treated as an inheritance.

It is not necessary that the same property be involved and whether s. 8 applies or not will depend on the facts in each particular case. For example, if in the earlier example Kieran sold the gift valued at €200,000 and used the proceeds of sale to buy a house which he then transferred to Lisa, then the Revenue would treat the voluntary transfer of the house as a connected gift.

The section will not apply if the Revenue is satisfied that the first gift was not made with a view to facilitating or enabling the second gift to take place.

In a case where the same property is involved in each gift it will be very difficult to satisfy the Revenue that s. 8 does not apply. On the other hand, if different property is involved in each gift it can be argued that the gifts are not connected, unless of course it appears that one gift was made with a view to enabling or facilitating the making of the other gift.

One very common circumstance that arises is where, taking the example above and altering the facts slightly:

Michael makes a gift of a site to his son Noel (this is exempt in certain circumstances from Capital Gains Tax (CGT) up to a value of €500,000. See Revenue Tax and Duty Manual

Part 19 -07-2A) found at <https://www.revenue.ie/en/tax-professionals/tdm/income-tax-capital-gains-tax-corporation-tax/index.aspx>.

Noel and his wife Olivia wish to take out a mortgage and build a house on the site. The financial institution will, invariably, insist that both the site and any mortgage on the property built on the site be in the joint names of Noel and his wife Olivia.

Provided that the Revenue is satisfied that the reason the property is placed in joint names is primarily to satisfy the requirements of the financial institution, the Revenue will accept that such a gift is not a connected gift for the purposes of s. 8.

See Revenue CAT Tax and Duty Manual Part 19 General Issues on the Revenue website at <https://www.revenue.ie/en/tax-professionals/tdm/capital-acquisitions-tax/index.aspx>.

As noted above, the section applies to gifts only and not to inheritances.

3.9.2 DISPOSITIONS ENLARGING THE VALUE OF PROPERTY (CAT CONSOLIDATION ACT, 2003, SECTION 38)

Section 38 of CAT Consolidation Act, 2003 is an anti-avoidance section designed to prevent 'gift splitting'.

The section applies where:

- a disponer gives a donee property (property 1) and later the same disponer gives the same donee further property (property 2);
- joined together property 1 and property 2 are of a greater value than the two properties valued and owned separately (i.e. the whole is greater than the sum of its parts).

In this situation the second gift or inheritance of property 2 will be regarded as two separate benefits. The first of these benefits will be the actual value of property 2, and the second benefit will be regarded as the increase in value of property 1 by virtue of the fact that the beneficiary now owns property 2 along with it.

This is best shown by way of example.

3.9.2.1 Example: gift enlarging the value of existing property (land)

Property 1 consists of a house and large rear garden. The very large rear garden does not have access to the public road at present.

Property 2 consists of the neighbouring corner property, which enables the beneficiary to provide access to the very large rear garden of property 1. This greatly increases the value of property 1, as the back garden could now be sold as land with development value as it has access to the public road. The consequent increase in value of property 1 would be the second benefit deemed to be taken under s. 38(3).

A further example of where a subsequent gift can enlarge the value of an earlier gift relates to private company shares. We have already noted at **3.1** that valuation of private company shares will be discounted for minority interests (ignoring s. 27 and 'control'). Where a subsequent gift or inheritance of shares has, in addition to the value of the subsequent gift, a secondary effect of increasing the value of the original gift of shares as they are no longer a minority shareholding, this increase in value is also taxable.

3.9.2.2 Example: gift enlarging the value of existing property (shares)

X Ltd is a private limited company with an issued share capital amounting to 100,000 €1 ordinary shares. The disponer (D) is the owner of 40 per cent of the shares. The other 60 per cent of the shares are owned by 12 strangers in blood in varying amounts making D the dominant shareholder but not a majority shareholder in X Ltd, which is not a Section 27-type company.

In April 2023 D gives 10,000 of these shares to his niece. As this constitutes a minority shareholding the shares are at that time valued at €2 each, thus valuing the gift at €20,000.

In June 2025 D dies, having by his will bequeathed to the same niece his remaining 30,000 shares in the same company. His niece is now in possession of a dominant shareholding of 40 per cent of the company, and the value at that date of a majority share in the company was the sum of €4 each for all the 40,000 shares.

In addition to the original benefit in April 2023 of 10,000 shares at €2 each totalling €20,000, the CAT Consolidation Act, 2003, s. 38 deems the following benefits to be taken by the niece from the disponer in 2025:

1. The second or actual benefit of an inheritance in June 2025 of 30,000 shares at €4 each	= € 120,000
2. A further inheritance in June 2025 of the increase in value of the original 10,000 shares of €2 per share	= € 20,000

Total value of the inheritance in June 2025 (€120,000 + €20,000) = €140,000

The section does not arise where a donee or successor became entitled to 'the original property' before 28 February 1969.

3.9.3 ANTI-AVOIDANCE (SECTION 38(4))

Sub-section (4) of s. 38 provides for further anti-avoidance by stating that the section will apply to property even where the donee or successor had disposed of the 'original property' within five years prior to the disposition granting them the 'additional property' where the disposal was for otherwise than full consideration *or* where the disposal was to a company of which the donee or successor was at any time within that period of five years deemed to have control within the meaning of CAT Consolidation Act, 2003, s. 27, whether or not such a disposal to the company was for full consideration or not.

3.10 Introduction to Reliefs

Having calculated the taxable value of a benefit, ascertained the relationship between the disponer and disponee, and aggregated prior benefits within the same threshold, we calculate the tax payable.

The next step is to ascertain whether any of the reliefs and exemptions available under CAT Consolidation Act, 2003 apply to the particular bequest. These exemptions and reliefs are largely to be found at Part 9 of CAT Consolidation Act, 2003:

- general reliefs (listed below);
- agricultural relief (see **Chapter 4**);
- business relief (see **Chapter 5**);
- favourite nephew relief (see **Chapter 6**).

This is an extremely important tax planning device and where practical, a client should be advised of the most effective way of transferring assets to intended beneficiaries while avoiding CAT to the greatest possible extent. The most important reliefs and exemptions are listed below along with other reliefs and exemptions which may arise from time to time. We will deal with the more straightforward reliefs first, moving on to the more complex. We will also deal with circumstances where more than one relief or exemption is being applied for in respect of the same benefit.

3.10.1 MAIN GENERAL RELIEFS AND EXEMPTIONS

- Small gift exemption.
- Spouses/civil partners.
- Surviving spouse/civil partner relief.
- Dwelling-house exemption (formerly close relative/brother–sister relief).

3.10.2 OTHER GENERAL RELIEFS AND EXEMPTIONS

- Child to parent relief and exemption.
- Exemption of certain objects.
- Retirement payments.
- Government securities.
- Exemption for certain receipts.
- Qualifying expenses of incapacitated persons.
- Favourite grandchild relief.

3.10.3 SMALL GIFT EXEMPTION (SGE)

One exemption, which should be considered at all times when a donee receives a taxable gift, is the SGE (CAT Consolidation Act, 2003, s. 69). This exemption is referable to a gift only and not to an inheritance. It is an annual exemption per calendar year from each disponer. The present SGE is €3,000.

For the relevant periods the applicable SGE is as follows.

Relevant period	Small gift exemption
From 1 January 1978 to 31 December 1998	£500 (€634.87)
From 1 January 1999 to 31 December 2002	£1,000 (€1,270)
From 1 January 2003 to date	€3,000

In effect, for current benefits, the first €3,000 of any gift is exempt.

Even if the disponer dies within two years of making the gift which thereby becomes an inheritance the €3,000 SGE remains. It is never clawed back.

It applies to one donee in respect of all benefits taken from any one disponer during a particular calendar year. However, if a beneficiary were to receive two separate gifts from the same disponer in the same calendar year, only one SGE of €3,000 could be claimed.

In effect, a donee can take gifts from the same disponer in different calendar years and the first €3,000 of these gifts will be exempt. A donee can take a gift from numerous different disponers during the same calendar year and the first €3,000 of each gift will be exempt.

For example, if your parents made a gift to you of €10,000 from a joint account held by them, the first €6,000 (two by €3,000) of that gift would be exempt and the taxable value of the gift would be €4,000.

When calculating the taxable value of prior gifts, the SGE applicable at the time of the gift should be taken into account. For example, if the prior gift was in 1996, only the first €635 is exempt.

3.10.4 RELIEFS, EXEMPTIONS, AND FILING ONLINE

Apart from the SGE outlined above, in order to claim any of these reliefs, as noted at **2.7**, the beneficiary or their agent would have to complete the online version of the IT38 even when no tax is due. This is so that the Revenue Commissioners have an electronic record of each relief claimed and the sums involved. This will make tracking the 'revenue cost' of each relief a much more straightforward task.

Failure to file the return could lead to a Revenue demand for the tax due on the market value of the benefit regardless of relief. The beneficiary would then have to apply within four years for repayment of that tax.

There is a provision for a penalty of €3,000 for failure to comply with the requirement to furnish a return, but this is usually in the context of a Revenue prosecution.

3.11 Spouses/Civil Partners

Sections 70 and 71, respectively, of CAT Consolidation Act, 2003 2003 provide that gifts (s. 70) and inheritances (s. 71) passing between spouses are not subject to CAT.

Under the original CAT Act, 1976, exemption was not provided for spouses or surviving spouses. Interspousal benefits were charged to tax under group A.

However, under s. 59 of the Finance Act, 1985 an inheritance taken by a successor who is at the date of the inheritance the spouse of the disponer is exempt from tax and is not taken into account in computing tax. This exemption took effect in respect of an inheritance taken on or after 30 January 1985 and is now reflected in s. 71 of CAT Consolidation Act, 2003.

Interspousal gifts were however still liable to gift tax, but were also exempted by s. 127 of the Finance Act, 1990, which stated that a gift taken by a donee who is at the date of the gift the spouse of the disponer is exempt from tax and will not be taken into account in computing tax. This exemption took effect in relation to a gift taken on or after 31 January 1990.

The Finance (No. 3) Act, 2011 extended the relief to civil partners for both gifts and inheritances backdated to 1 January 2011. Since the coming into force of the Marriage Act, 2015 spouses can be of the same sex and the same exemption applies to all married couples.

To sum up the rules regarding spouses/civil partners:

- any bequest from a spouse/civil partner is not taken into account at all for CAT purposes;
- it is as if the gift/inheritance never occurred.

3.11.1 FORMER SPOUSES AND CIVIL PARTNERS

Section 88 of CAT Consolidation Act, 2003 as amended by Finance (No. 3) Act, 2011 provides that certain transfers between spouses and civil partners following the dissolution of a marriage or civil partnership are exempt from CAT. The Acts under which such orders can be made are listed in the section as amended and include the main Family Law Acts and the Civil Partnership Legislation as well as include analogous orders made by a court in a separate jurisdiction. To avail of this extended exemption, the dissolution must be entitled to be recognised as valid in the State.

The effect of this is that 'gifts' and 'inheritances' between former spouses ordered by the court on the dissolution of a marriage or civil partnership or afterwards on application by either spouse or civil partner are exempt from tax. This could also cover a court order dealing with Succession Act rights such as the legal right share.

This also means that any 'voluntary' gift or bequest between former spouses, either inter vivos or testamentary in nature, is taxable under group C—strangers in blood.

3.11.2 COHABITANTS

Section 88A as inserted by s. 3 of the Finance (No. 3) Act, 2011 and Schedule 3 Item 21 of same provides that similar gifts or transfers between qualified cohabitants ordered by the Court under Part 15 of the Civil Partnership legislation will similarly be exempt from tax.

No other gift or inheritance between qualified cohabitants whether currently cohabiting or not will be exempt from CAT and will be taxed at the group C rate. See also Dwelling Relief at **7.5**.

3.12 Surviving Spouse and Civil Partner Relief

The Second Schedule to CAT Consolidation Act, 2003 details the calculation of tax payable. Paragraph 6 of the Second Schedule (as amended) provides:

6. *Where any donee or successor is, at the date of the gift or at the date of the inheritance,*
    (a) *the surviving spouse of a deceased person or*
    (b) *the surviving civil partner of a deceased person, and, at the time of the death of the deceased person that deceased person, was of nearer relationship than such donee or successor to the disponer, then such donee or successor is, in the computation of the tax payable on such taxable gift or taxable inheritance, deemed to bear to the disponer the relationship of that deceased person.*

The effect of this is that if a person makes a gift or leaves an inheritance to the surviving spouse or civil partner of a deceased relation, the surviving spouse or civil partner 'steps into the shoes' of the deceased spouse or civil partner and takes on the Group Threshold that the deceased spouse or civil partner would have in relation to the disponer.

Example:

Alexander makes a gift to his widowed daughter-in-law Bernice, the surviving spouse of his late son Conor. Bernice 'steps into the shoes of' her late husband for CAT purposes and is taxed under the group A threshold as a 'child' of Alexander.

The spouse does not assume the tax history of her late husband, just the group threshold.

The widow or widower or surviving civil partner of a nephew or niece will obtain group B threshold on a benefit taken from the aunt or uncle of the deceased spouse or civil partner. It would also appear that the surviving spouse or civil partner of a deceased nephew or niece *may* qualify for favourite nephew/niece relief provided all other conditions are satisfied.

Favourite nephew/niece relief is dealt with in Chapter Six.

It is possible therefore for a beneficiary to change thresholds as regards the same disponer.

Example: John makes a gift to his daughter-in-law Susan, whose husband, Robert, the son of John, is still living. This gift is taxed under group C. Robert subsequently dies.

John makes a further gift to his daughter-in-law Susan who is now widowed. She stands in the shoes of her deceased husband and takes the benefit from John under group A. In effect, she has been able to avail of two different group thresholds when receiving benefits from the same person.

3.12.1 SURVIVING COHABITANTS

No such relief exists for surviving cohabitants, qualified or otherwise.

3.12.2 SURVIVING SPOUSE AND SECTION 42

It was noted earlier at **2.9.5** that where a bequest is left to a predeceased child who leaves children surviving the testator the gift does not lapse but goes under the will or intestacy of the predeceased child. It was further noted that the eventual beneficiary is deemed to inherit from the original disponer. The situation where a widow inherits directly from a parent of her predeceased husband in this manner was dealt with in **2.9.5.6**. In those circumstances, surviving spouse relief would apply and for CAT purposes the surviving spouse would inherit as a 'child' of that parent of the predeceased husband.

3.12.3 COMPULSORY NATURE OF THE RELIEF

There is no discretion about whether or not a donee in this situation should change 'class' or 'group'.

Ironically, this 'relief' could lead to a charge to tax which otherwise would not have arisen—for example, if a widow had received a substantial benefit from her own parents, prior to inheriting from her late husband's father.

3.13 Dwelling Exemption

Dwelling Exemption is a very important exemption as most clients own their own property and should always be considered when advising a client making a will.

Section 86 of CATCA 2003 (as amended) deals with an exemption provided for dwellings, which are occupied by a beneficiary as his or her only or main residence. Essentially, where the conditions are met, the beneficiary can be given or can inherit the dwelling he or she lives in (but does not own) free from CAT.

A dwelling is defined in s. 86 (1) as 'any building or part of a building, . . . used or suitable for use as a dwelling', and includes grounds of up to .4047 hectares (one acre) occupied and enjoyed with the dwelling and includes houses and apartments. If the grounds are greater than .4047 hectares then that part most suitable for occupation with the dwelling will qualify and the rest will be taxable. As we will see below, a dwelling must also be a 'relevant dwelling' in order for the exemption to be applicable.

Revenue Guidelines in this regard are found in Part 24 of the Revenue CAT Manual: <https://www.revenue.ie/en/tax-professionals/tdm/capital-acquisitions-tax/cat-part24.pdf>.

3.13.1 BRIEF HISTORY

This exemption had its genesis in 'Brother–Sister Relief', a relief introduced by Finance Act 1990 which came into force on 30 January 1991. The relief initially applied to siblings (as the name suggests) over 55 who resided in the same property for at least five years immediately prior to the inheritance and didn't own any other home.

If those conditions were met, the taxable value of the dwelling inherited by surviving sibling was reduced by £50,000 or to 50 per cent, whichever was the lesser. These rates and ceilings were increased throughout the 1990s and in December 1997 the relief was extended to all group B successors, that is, surviving parent or grandparent, grandchild, child of a sibling, as well as siblings. It also increased the relief to 80 per cent of the value of the dwelling or £150,000, whichever was the lesser.

This was known as 'Close Relative Relief'. In order to qualify, siblings over 55 had to continually reside in the property for five years but all other successors (including siblings under 55) had to be there for ten years immediately prior to the inheritance. The extended relief was also backdated to 3 December 1992.

Section 151 Finance Act, 2000 provided that gifts and inheritances of a dwelling taken on or after 1 December 1999 regardless of relationship and value would be exempt from CAT, and this is Dwelling Relief as we know it. Since December 1999 the relief has been amended substantially on numerous occasions and for the purposes of this book we will only be dealing with the current iteration of Dwelling Relief. While there have been significant changes to the relief since then, the lack of both a relationship requirement and a cap on value have been constant.

Section 86 of the CAT Consolidation Act, 2003 (as replaced in its entirety by s. 52 of the Finance Act, 2016 and subsequently amended by s. 71 Finance Act, 2017; s. 52 Finance Act, 2018 and s. 64 Finance Act, 2019) deals with the exemption provided for inheritances (and some very limited transfers) of relevant dwellings. The exemption is commonly referred to as 'Dwelling-House Exemption' but applies to all dwellings.

The exemption applies when a relevant dwelling is inherited by a successor which has been occupied both by that successor and by the disponer as his or her only or main residence at the time of the inheritance. Also, the successor cannot own nor have an interest in any other dwelling at the time of the inheritance.

Essentially, where these conditions are met, the successor can inherit (or if a dependent relative, receive) the dwelling or an interest in the dwelling he or she lives in (but does not own outright) free from CAT.

The relief is limited to inheritances of property except where the beneficiary is a 'dependent relative'. For the purposes of this section we will focus on inheritances. See below at **3.13.3**.

3.13.2 CONDITIONS

The following pre-conditions must be met.

1. In order to be considered a 'relevant dwelling' as defined in s. 86 (2) the dwelling must have been occupied by the disponer as his or her only or main residence at the date of his or her death, with two exceptions:

    (a) The disponer will be deemed to be in occupation of the dwelling even if he or she is residing elsewhere due to his or her illness or infirmity.

    (b) Where dependent relative relief applies, the disponer does not have to reside in the property at the date of the gift. See **3.13.3**.

2. The successor must have occupied the dwelling continuously as his or her only main residence throughout the period of three years up to the date of the inheritance.

    There are some exceptions where the property is sold and replaced during this pre-inheritance period but the successor must have resided in a dwelling owned by the disponer for at least three of the four years immediately preceding the date of the inheritance.

    There is a similar exception provided for in s. 86 (3) to cover situations where the successor will be deemed to be in occupation of the dwelling even if he or she is residing elsewhere due to his or her illness or infirmity.

3. The successor cannot be beneficially entitled to an interest in any other dwelling at the date of the gift or inheritance. They may be a part owner of the dwelling they currently reside in, the subject of the inheritance. For example, a joint owner of a dwelling can inherit from the other joint owner. It is important to note that the successor can own other property, just not another dwelling.

    For example, the successor may own or simultaneously inherit farmland or office or commercial property, but not another dwelling.

    As will be seen later in **3.13.4**, this deals with situations where a successor acquires an interest in two houses under the terms of a will or intestacy.

Section 86 (2A) is a further anti-avoidance measure. It provides that if the successor owned or had an interest in another property that they placed in a discretionary trust of which they are an object, then they are deemed to be beneficially entitled to that property and do not qualify for the relief.

The following **ongoing** conditions must be met **after** claiming the relief:

1. The successor must retain ownership of the property for **six years** after the date of the inheritance.
2. The successor must continue to occupy the dwelling as his or her only or main residence for six years from the date of gift or inheritance, but can own other property including other dwellings after the gift or inheritance.

There are exceptions to these conditions which will be dealt with in **13.3.6**.

3.13.3 DEPENDENT RELATIVE

The only time a gift of a qualifying property will be exempt is where the beneficiary is a 'dependent relative' as defined in sub-section 9 (a) of s. 86. Firstly, 'relative' is limited to: lineal ancestor (parent, grandparent, etc.), lineal descendant (child, grandchild, etc.), brother, sister, uncle, aunt, niece, or nephew of the disponer or his or her spouse or civil partner.

Following on from this, a 'dependent relative' means one of the above who is over 65 or who is permanently and totally incapacitated by reason of mental or physical infirmity from maintaining himself or herself.

Where these conditions are met, the gift is treated as an inheritance at the date of the gift and the disponer does not have to reside in the house at the date of the 'inheritance'. All the other conditions still apply.

3.13.4 INTEREST IN ANY OTHER DWELLINGS

This has historically been the most contentious element of the pre-conditions applying to the relief and has been the subject of numerous applications to the Tax Appeals, the Commission, their predecessors the former Office of the Appeal Commissioners and the High Court, leading to similarly numerous amendments to the legislation culminating in Section 86 (4A) as inserted by Section 64 of the Finance Act, 2019.

Section 86 (4A) of the Act provides that the dwelling will not be regarded as a 'relevant dwelling-house' and thus is not liable for the relief where the successor is beneficially entitled to any other dwelling-house or to have any beneficial interest in any other dwelling-house at:

(a) the date of the inheritance or

(b) the valuation date of the 'exempt' dwelling if the further dwelling comes from the disponer.

If so, then the relief will not apply.

While there is nothing to prevent the successor from having owned a dwelling prior to inheriting the exempt dwelling, if they own or are beneficially entitled to an interest in any other dwelling-house at the date of the inheritance, the relief will not apply.

As noted, the exemption is never available where the successor owns or has an interest in another dwelling at the date of the inheritance. The amendments brought in by the Finance Act, 2019 are to cover situations where the beneficiary acquires an interest in another dwelling from the disponer, after the date of inheritance (i.e. the date of death), and up to the date of distribution of the estate or the residue; for example, where a disponer leaves his entire estate (which comprises a number of dwellings, including a dwelling the successor resides in) to his children in equal shares—or dies intestate leaving children and a number of dwellings, including a dwelling the successor resides in.

As also noted, owning an interest in a commercial property or agricultural land at the date of the benefit will not affect the availability of the relief so long as there is not a dwelling contained on the commercial property or on the farmland.

The sub-section refers to the successor acquiring an entitlement by virtue of that inheritance. This is relevant in the following circumstance: as noted, a beneficiary could own a property subject to a limited interest (e.g. a right to reside). On the cessation of that limited interest, where the beneficiary receives a further interest (or 'slice') in the same property the relief will apply, as they did not have an interest in any other dwelling.

Similarly, as already noted, there is nothing to stop a joint tenant from receiving a greater interest in the property they already jointly own. For example, where a cohabiting couple own a property as joint tenants, on the death of one of the joint tenants the surviving joint tenant could claim dwelling-house exemption on the share of the dwelling now inherited, provided the other conditions are met.

Where a difficulty can arise for a beneficiary is where he or she inherits an absolute interest in a dwelling and a shared interest in another dwelling on the same day; for example, where a parent leaves the family home where that child resides to one child and the residue of the estate between all the children and the residue includes a holiday home.

In that circumstance, it could be argued that the beneficiary acquires an interest in two dwellings at the date of the inheritance.

This has long been a source of contention between taxpayers and the Revenue Commissioners. There have been a number of Circuit Court cases, culminating in a case stated to the High Court on this point: <https://www.courts.ie/acc/alfresco/4af67fc7-6d26-4de0-97d3-eed19b3a460c/2018_IEHC_519_1.pdf/pdf#view=fitH>.

In this case, the disponer died in October 2010, leaving his entire estate equally between his two children by way of residuary clause, there being no specific legacies in the will.

The estate included five houses, one of which was in Spain and one in which the appellant had lived her entire life, together with a business and business premises.

The net estate was ascertained in March 2011 and the Grant of Probate issued in May 2011, and the assets were distributed to the two beneficiaries in August 2011.

Prior to ascertainment of net estate and applying for the grant, the appellant entered into a deed of family arrangement with her brother wherein she got the 'family home' (i.e. the dwelling in relation to which she claimed dwelling-house exemption) and he got the business assets prior to the grant of representation issuing and final distribution. The remaining dwellings were to be divided 50/50.

She applied for dwelling-house exemption and was refused,, appealed to the Tax Appeals Commission and won in a determination issued in 2017.

The appeals commissioners found that neither child was beneficially entitled in possession to any individual asset of the estate at the date of death ('the date of the inheritance'). They also found that by the time the net estate was ascertained prior to the grant of representation issuing, the deed of family arrangement ensured that the appellant was the sole owner of only the family home and did not have any interest in any other dwelling, and that the relief would apply.

This decision was appealed to the High Court on a case stated and the judgment of Ms Justice Costello was delivered on 25 September 2018 (see above). In the lengthy judgment, Costello J found for the appellant on the basis that on the 'date of the inheritance' as defined in s. 2 (1) of the CAT Consolidation Act, 2003 and as referred to in the 'old' S. 86 (3) (b) of the Act, the appellant (along with her brother) did not have an interest in any specific property in the estate, but merely an interest in the due administration of her share of the estate.

Since the date of the judgment, as noted above, s 64 of the Finance Act, 2019 has amended s. 86 significantly to ensure that in such circumstances the successor who inherits an interest or a right to two or more houses will not qualify for the relief. Revenue have confirmed that this provision is to give effect to the policy intent that a beneficiary can only be entitled to the exemption where they inherit a right or interest to a single 'relevant' dwelling from the deceased.

3.13.4.1 Best practice

More than ever, it is important to recall the difference between 'date of the inheritance' and 'valuation date' in this context.

Even taking this recent decision into account, when taking instructions for a will where the testator has more than one dwelling and one successor may be able to avail of the relief, it is still best practice to advise the testator to not prevent the relief from applying by having that successor also inherit a share or an interest in another property.

3.13.4.2 Two homes in estate

For example, where there is a family home that one child is residing in with the testator and a holiday home, and the testator's intention is to leave the family home to the child residing there and share the residue of his estate including the holiday home between all his children, an option may be to have bequests of:

- the family home to the child residing there;
- the holiday home to the other children as joint tenants or as tenants in common with a suitably drafted gift over clause; and
- the residue of the estate between all the children.

In all cases, full instructions should be taken from the client and appropriate advice provided.

3.13.5 CONTINUOUS OCCUPATION BY BENEFICIARY PRIOR TO INHERITANCE

The successor has to reside in the dwelling for at least the three years prior to the inheritance. If the dwelling has been replaced during this three-year period, then the successor must have occupied the original dwelling and the replacement property for at least three out of the four years up to the date of death of the disponer.

Since 25 December 2016 the disponer must reside in the dwelling at the date of death as his or her only or main residence. However, the disponer does not have to have resided in the dwelling for the three or four-year period prior to the inheritance and does not have to own the dwelling throughout this period.

There is also a provision in the substituted section that either or both of a disponer or successor is deemed to occupy a dwelling even if they are not physically present in the dwelling due to infirmity. Therefore, if (for example) a parent was living in the family home and subsequently went into a nursing home and a child lived in the family home for three years prior to the death of the parent, they may be in a position to obtain the relief.

This offers some very limited opportunity to plan for tax.

3.13.6 OCCUPY AND RETAIN OWNERSHIP FOR SIX YEARS

Section 86 (6) provides that the beneficiary must 'continue to occupy that dwelling-house as that donee or successor's only or main residence throughout the relevant period'.

The beneficiary is not precluded from buying any other dwelling or dwellings during this period.

Section 86 (7) provides that if the dwelling is sold within the six-year period the exemption will be clawed back unless:

1. the successor replaces the property during the six-year retention period. The original and replacement properties must be occupied as the successor's only or main residence for at least six out of seven years, starting at the date of the inheritance. The entire sale value of the original property must be spent on the replacement property or there is a clawback of the excess—see below at **3.13.7**; **or**
2. the successor is over the age of 65 at the date of the inheritance; **or**
3. the successor must leave the dwelling during the six years because he or she needs long-term medical care in a hospital or nursing home because of infirmity (this infirmity must be certified by a registered medical practitioner). Where this infirmity is certified the dwelling can be sold without incurring a clawback; **or**
4. the successor is required by his or her employer to work (and thus reside) elsewhere.

When advising a client in relation to this relief, it is imperative that the client is fully advised in relation to clawback.

3.13.7 CLAWBACK

Section 86 (8) deals with calculating clawback where the sale price of the exempted (for clarity referred to as the 'sold') dwelling is greater than the purchase price for the replacement dwelling.

The legislation provides that the value of the sold dwelling-house which is chargeable to tax shall be reduced in the same proportion as the consideration for the acquired dwelling-house bears to the consideration for the sold dwelling-house.

This is best demonstrated by way of example.

Example:

Michael inherits a house ('the original dwelling') valued at €450,000 in 2023 and claims dwelling-house exemption. Two years later, he sells the house for €600,000 and 'replaces' it with an apartment purchased for €300,000 ('the acquired dwelling').

The value of the acquired dwelling is 1/2 (€300,000/€600,000) the value of the original dwelling at the date of sale and acquisition.

The clawback will be based on 1/2 of the date of inheritance value of the sold dwelling, that is, €225,000.

The exemption on the other half (€225,000) will continue but Michael will now have to re-calculate his tax calculation for 2023 with an additional taxable value of €225,000. The valuation date will be the date of purchase of the acquired property.

Tax may be payable, depending on group threshold, prior benefits, and so on. Even if the property was sold at a 'loss', a tax liability may arise.

For example, if Michael sells the house for €400,000 and 'replaces' it with an apartment purchased for €300,000, the value of the acquired dwelling is 3/4 the value of the sold dwelling (€300,000/€400,000).

There will be a clawback of the remaining 1/4 of the date of inheritance value of the sold dwelling. In this case 1/4 of the date of inheritance value of €450,000 would be €112,500 and this would be treated as a taxable benefit.

The clawback also arises where a dwelling has already been replaced. For example, I inherit a house in 2023 valued at €400,000 and I sell it in 2025 for €500,000 and buy a house for €600,000—clawback is not triggered. If, however, I sell the replacement house within six years of 2023, the clawback provisions still apply, and if I sell the replacement house and the proceeds of sale are greater than the acquisition price, clawback will arise. The clawback will be based on the replacement house and not the original house inherited.

3.13.8 DWELLING EXEMPTION AND TAX PLANNING

Since the repeal and replacement of s. 86 in its entirety, the utility of dwelling exemption as a tax planning tool has been severely limited. As a rule, people do not plan to die as a tax planning mechanism. While there is no 'cap' or upper limit on the value of a dwelling in all cases or relationship requirement for inheritances, it is now far less flexible and is limited to cases where the disponer resides in the property with the successor at the date of his or her death.

It is important, when drafting a will for a testator where a potential successor may qualify for the relief, that the successor is advised not to do anything to jeopardise that. However, this may have adverse consequences should the testator change his or her mind and leave the dwelling to somebody else in a later will.

Similarly, if a client inherits both the dwelling they resided in with the disponer and a share in a holiday home as part of their share of the residue, as outlined in **3.13.4**, it may be possible for the client to disclaim their share of the residue in order to maintain the right to claim dwelling exemption.

In this case, as a partial disclaimer is not possible, the client should calculate the tax payable if they take their share of the residue and lose the exemption and compare this with the value of their share of the residue. A disclaimer for consideration could be considered in these circumstances but all necessary calculations must be made before executing any document.

As previously stressed, when advising a client in relation to this relief, it is imperative that the client is fully advised in writing in relation to clawback.

Where a beneficiary inherits a dwelling that they resided in and a number of other properties in common with another or other beneficiaries, it may be possible, following the High Court judgment referred to earlier, to execute a deed of family arrangement prior to the valuation date; however, full tax and legal advice should be obtained by all parties to the deed.

3.13.9 DWELLING EXEMPTION AND EXPENSES

As the inheritance is exempt, any costs, liabilities, and expenses relating to the benefit cannot be deducted from the taxable value of any taxable benefit passing with the dwelling. If the dwelling is the only asset passing; for example:

> *I leave my House to my daughter Linda . . .*

this is not an issue, as the entire benefit passing is free from CAT.

However, if the dwelling is passing with other assets, for example:

> *I give devise and bequeath all of my estate of whatsoever nature and wheresoever situate to my daughter Linda and appoint her my Universal Legatee and Devisee . . .*

and the estate includes a relevant dwelling, then the costs, liabilities, and expenses have to be apportioned between the exempt asset and the non-exempt assets. See the CAT Consolidation Act, 2003, s. 28(5).

Any mortgage or charge on the exempt property would also be ignored for the purposes of calculating the taxable value of the non-exempt property.

Example: Consider the example of Linda, the universal legatee and devisee.

Assume that in November 2024 she inherits a house valued at €400,000 and other assets valued at €600,000. The general debts, funeral, and testamentary expenses amount to €100,000 and she has no aggregable prior benefits.

Her tax calculation will be as follows:

- The general debts, funeral, and testamentary expenses relate to the entire estate including the house, which is exempt.
- That portion of the general debts, funeral, and testamentary expenses ('GD, F&TE') relating to the house which is exempt cannot be deducted from the taxable value of the remainder of the estate.

To calculate the 'taxable' or 'allowable' value of the general debts, funeral and testamentary expenses ('the general debts etc.') we use the following formula:

$$\frac{\text{Value of Taxable Assets}}{\text{Value of Entire Estate}} \times \text{the general debts etc.} = \text{Allowable portion of general debts}$$

In Linda's case this will be:

$$\frac{€600,000}{€1,000,000} \times €100,000 = €60.000$$

This €60,000 is the portion of the general debts, funeral, and testamentary expenses relating to the taxable assets and is the 'Allowable' portion of the general debts, funeral, and testamentary expenses that can be deducted from the market value of the taxable portion of her benefit.

The template is completed as follows:

Calculation of Taxable Value

	Market value	**€1,000,000**
Less	Exempt property	€400,000
Equals	Market value of taxable property	€600,000
Less	Allowable liabilities, costs & expenses	€60,000
Equals	Incumbrance free value	€540,000
Less	Allowable consideration [in money or monies worth]	€ 0
Equals	**Taxable value**	€540,000

Tax Payable on Taxable Value

	Taxable value of this ~~gift~~/inheritance		**€540,000**
Less	SGE where relevant		0
Equals	Net taxable value of benefit		€540,000
	Relevant threshold group A ~~B C~~	€400,000	
Less	Taxable value of prior aggregable benefits (SGE?)	€ 0	
Equals	Available threshold for this benefit		€400,000
Taxable excess [taxable value less available threshold]			€140,000
Tax @ 33% of taxable excess			€46,200

** A **€ 400,000** B € 40,000 C €20,000

Prior to 2 October 2024

A €335,000 B € 32,500 C €16,250

Assuming a valuation date prior to 31 August 2025, Linda should file and pay by 31 October 2026, or by mid November 2026 if both filing and paying online.

For the first time, we need to warn our client about clawback. We need to warn Linda, in writing, of the potential liability to CAT should she sell the dwelling within six years without using the entire proceeds of sale to purchase a replacement property.

This is the first time when using the template that the Market Value of Exempt Property is deducted from the Market Value of Benefit to arrive at Market Value of Taxable Property

3.13.9.1 Dwelling exemption, expenses, and a charge on the dwelling

A further complicating factor arises where there is a mortgage on the exempt property. In that case, when apportioning the costs between the exempt and the non-exempt assets, it is the net or equitable value of the exempt property that is used.

Take the example of Linda again, but this time in addition to the general costs, liabilities, and expenses, the house is subject to a mortgage of €200,000. The value of the mortgage itself cannot be deducted from the value of the estate as it relates in its entirety to the exempt property. It will however affect the apportionment of general debts, funeral, and testamentary expenses.

In this case the calculation will be as follows:

Equitable value of 'exempt' house

$$\frac{\text{Equitable Value of Taxable Assets}}{\text{Equitable Value of Entire Estate}} \times \text{the general debts etc.}$$

$$= \text{Allowable portion of general debts}$$

In Linda's case this will be:

Equitable value of taxable assets remains unchanged: €600,000

Equitable value of entire estate equals value of entire estate (€1,000,000) less mortgage (€200,000) = €800,000.

$$\frac{€600{,}000}{€800{,}000} \times €100{,}000 = €75.000$$

This €75,000 is the 'allowable portion' of the general debts, funeral, and testamentary expenses relating to the taxable portion of the equitable value which can be deducted from the value of the non-exempt assets.

Taxable Value is then calculated as follows:

Calculation of Taxable Value

	Market value	€1,000,000
Less	Exempt property	€400,000
Equals	Market value of taxable property	€600,000
Less	Allowable liabilities, costs & expenses	€75,000
Equals	Incumbrance free value	€525,000
Less	Allowable consideration [in money or monies worth]	€ 0
Equals	**Taxable value**	**€525,000**

We then calculate tax payable in the usual manner:

Tax Payable on Taxable Value

	Taxable value of this gift/inheritance		**€525,000**
Less	SGE where relevant		**0**
Equals	Net taxable value of benefit		€525,000
	Relevant threshold group A ~~B C~~	€400,000	
Less	Taxable value of prior aggregable benefits (SGE?)	€ 0	
Equals	Available threshold for this benefit		€400,000
Taxable excess [taxable value less available threshold]			€125,000
Tax @ 33% of taxable excess			€ 41,250

** A € 400,000 B € 40,000 C €20,000

Prior to 2 October 2024

A €335,000 B € 32,500 C €16,250

Again, assuming a valuation date prior to 31 August 2025, Linda should file and pay by 31 October 2025, or by mid November 2025 if both filing and paying online.

3.14 Other Less Common Reliefs

These reliefs arise less frequently but should be considered depending on the assets owned and/or family circumstances.

3.14.1 GROUP A RELIEF IN THE CASE OF ABSOLUTE INHERITANCES TAKEN BY PARENTS FROM THEIR CHILDREN

It was noted in **Chapter 2** that group A also includes the parents of a predeceased child where that parent inherits an absolute interest from a child. Obviously, this has to be an inheritance and not a gift. Gifts from children to parents are taxable under group B, the parent being a lineal ancestor. A 'child' does not have to be a minor.

The relief applies where:

(1) the interest taken by the successor parent is not a limited interest; and

(2) the inheritance is taken on the death of the disponing child.

It applies only to an absolute inheritance taken by a parent or parents whether under the will or intestacy of the child. It would not apply to a limited interest taken by the parent under the will of the child. It would appear that an absolute interest inherited in the death of the child of a civil partner would not qualify for this relief.

3.14.2 ABSOLUTE RELIEF ON PARENT INHERITING FROM A CHILD (SECTION 79)

As outlined above at **3.14.1**, group A includes a parent inheriting an absolute interest form a child. Section 79 of CAT Consolidation Act, 2003 extends this and exempts from CAT an inheritance taken by a parent from a child on the death of the child where the child had taken a non-exempt gift or inheritance from either or both its parents within the period of five years immediately prior to the date of death of the child. This goes further than the group A relief referred to above and is an absolute relief on all inheritances passing, not just a group A relief. An absolute interest inherited in the death of the child of a civil partner would not qualify for this relief.

This is to cover tragic situations such as, for example, where parents give their farm to their unmarried son with no children, who dies intestate shortly afterwards, leaving everything to them. It was felt that in those circumstances it would be invidious to tax the 'benefit' received by those parents on the death of their child. However, the section goes further than this example and includes any taxable benefit received by a child from either parent in the previous five years. A 'taxable benefit' is anything over €3,000 in any one year.

It should be remembered that where dwelling-house exemption is successfully applied for by the child beneficiary on the death of a parent or as a dependent relative, such a benefit is not a taxable benefit. Practitioners should also advise clients who are making taxable benefits to children to keep a record of such benefits.

3.14.3 CREDIT OF CAPITAL GAINS TAX AGAINST CAT (SECTION 104)

In the case of a gift, particularly, it is quite common that such a disposal will give rise to both Gift Tax and to CGT. Capital Gains Tax is payable on any disposal of property, even a voluntary disposal.

Section 104 of CAT Consolidation Act, 2003, states that where both taxes arise on the same event, in this case the gift, the CGT is allowed as a credit against the gift tax. See also **9.16.5**.

3.14.3.1 Example: set off

Niall makes a gift to Oliver and the CAT amounts to €10,000, for which Oliver is primarily accountable. The disposal of the property also gives rise to a CGT liability, which amounts to €4,000. The disponer Niall is primarily accountable for this tax. The legislation states that the €4,000 CGT can be credited against the gift tax of €10,000; accordingly the net gift tax chargeable is €6,000 and the charge for CGT remains at €4,000.

Niall still pays €4,000 CGT but Oliver is allowed a credit for the CGT that Niall has paid.

It is difficult to see the logic of such a credit system in view of the fact that different persons are accountable. However, it does address the problem of double taxation, in that the sum of both taxes will not exceed the larger of the tax liabilities.

3.14.3.2 Both taxes payable on same transaction

It is important to realise that to gain the relief, both taxes must arise out of the same transaction. For example:

- Patrick gives to his grandnephew Quentin some shares.
- The CAT liability payable by Quentin is €6,000 while the CGT payable by Patrick is €2,000.
- Patrick must pay the CGT liability.
- Quentin has a credit of €2,000 to set against the CAT liability of €6,000 (net CAT of €4,000).

If, taking this example, Patrick sold the shares and gave the proceeds of sale to Quentin, then the CGT charge payable by Patrick cannot be set against the CAT charge payable by Quentin, as there are two separate taxable transactions:

1. the disposal by Patrick of his shares (CGT liability) and
2. the gift from Patrick to Quentin of cash (CAT liability).

The fact that the cash paid by Patrick to Quentin is the proceeds of sale is not relevant and the relief cannot be claimed.

3.14.3.3 Clawback since 21 February 2006

For gifts of this nature provided (either by gift or inheritance) since 21 February 2006, a clawback of the relief occurs if the property the subject of the gift is disposed of within two years. This is an anti-avoidance measure to cover situations such as the following:

Robert receives an offer on a property that he intended to transfer to his daughter Sinead. Robert transfers the property to Sinead as a voluntary transfer, valued at the amount of the offer. Any CGT payable by Robert would be set off against the CAT payable by Sinead.

Now, however, if Sinead then sells the property for the offered amount within two years, any set off of CGT against CAT would be clawed back.

The section was further amended in 2011 to correct a drafting error that enabled a beneficiary to dispose of the asset on the same day as the gift and avoid the clawback. The word 'after' was replaced with 'commencing on' and applies to gifts and inheritances taken on or after 21 January 2011.

3.14.4 CHARITIES (SECTION 76)

A benefit taken for public or charitable purposes is deemed to be taken beneficially by a person who would be treated as a stranger and taxed under group C for the purposes of computing the tax on the benefit taken.

However, sub-section (2) gives exemption to a benefit which is taken for public or charitable purposes if the Commissioners are satisfied that it has been or will be applied to public or charitable purposes in Ireland, or, if applied outside Ireland, that it has been or will be applied to purposes which in accordance with the law of the State are public or charitable.

Regardless of the situation of the charity, an exemption would be given provided the charity would be recognised as such by the general law of the State.

See s. 3 of the Charities Act, 2009 for details of charitable purposes recognised.

For more information on registering a charity for tax see Revenue Guidelines on charitable tax exemptions: <https://www.revenue.ie/en/companies-and-charities/charities-and-sports-bodies/index.aspx>.

The purposes must be public or charitable and, being an exemption, the onus is on the tax payer to prove this.

Until the establishment of the Charities Regulatory Authority ('CRA') on 16 October 2014 under the terms of the Charities Act 2009, there was no official register of charities in Ireland. Until then the only available list was of charities who had been issued a 'CHY' number by the Revenue Commissioners. All of these charities were automatically included in the database of charitable bodies initially published by the CRA in 2015.

For further details please see the CRA website: <https://www.charitiesregulator.ie/en>.

See also Chapter 13, Para 13.2.7 of *Wills, Probate and Estates* for further information on procedures to be applied when administering an estate where there are charitable bequests.

Subsection (3) goes on to provide that any money provided by the State for public or charitable purposes is not taxable. For example, grants provided by the IDA are not taxable as a benefit.

3.14.5 EXEMPTION OF CERTAIN HERITAGE OBJECTS (SECTIONS 77 AND 78)

This exemption applies to pictures, prints, books, manuscripts, works of art, jewellery, scientific collections, and other things *not held for the purposes of trading* (such assets, if passing as part of the assets of a business, may qualify for business relief as dealt with in **Chapter 5**) and

(1) which on a claim being made to the Revenue appear to the Revenue to be of national, scientific, historic, or artistic interest;

(2) which are kept permanently in the State except for such temporary absences outside the State as are approved by the Revenue; and

(3) in respect of which reasonable facilities for viewing are allowed to members of the public or to recognised bodies or to associations of persons.

Provided the object in question complies with these conditions and is comprised in a benefit both at the date of the benefit and at the valuation date the exemption will be granted and the object in question will not be taken into account in computing tax unless and until the exemption ceases to apply.

It would be normal that the beneficiary should apply for the exemption, although the legislation does not state specifically who should make the claim for exemption. The application to the Revenue would normally include an inventory of the item or items for which exemption is claimed, a valuation of such item, and the grounds of exemption, setting out the place where the objects can be seen by the public and attaching such items of publicity which would tend to support the claim for exemption.

As the facilities for viewing must be given to members of the public, recognised bodies of persons, or associations of persons, it appears to be possible to obtain the exemption without actually putting the objects on view to the general public. However, the underlying reason for providing such exemption is the benefit conferred on the general public who would have access to such objects.

For anti-avoidance reasons, the objects must be comprised in the benefit at the date of the benefit and at the valuation date. Otherwise, it would be possible in the administration of an estate for the executors to purchase an object which would be exempt under s. 77 and which would be part of the inheritance at the valuation date.

3.14.5.1 Clawback of exemption

Loss of the exemption can arise on two grounds:

(1) A sale of the object within six years after the *valuation date* and before the date of death of the beneficiary, unless the sale is by private treaty to: the Chester Beatty Library, the Crawford Art Gallery Cork, the Irish Museum of Modern Art, the National Archives, the National Concert Hall, the National Gallery of Ireland, the National Library of Ireland, the National Museum of Ireland, the Commissioners of Public Works in Ireland, the Irish Heritage Trust, any university in the State or any constituent college of that university, a local authority, or the Friends of the National Collections of Ireland, when the exemption shall continue to apply.

(2) Loss of exemption will also apply if there is breach of any of the conditions regarding keeping the objects permanently in the State and allowing reasonable facilities for viewing.

Under sub-section (4) a breach of any of the two conditions referred to above may cause a loss of the exemption if at any time after the valuation date such breach occurs

(1) before the sale of the object;

(2) before the death of the beneficiary and

(3) before such object again forms part of the property comprised in a benefit in respect of which benefit an absolute interest is taken by a person other than a spouse of that beneficiary.

Subsection (5) provides that any work of art normally kept outside the State, but which is in the State at the date of death of the disponer, will be exempt from tax where the

Revenue Commissioners are satisfied that it was brought into the State solely for public exhibition, cleaning, or restoration.

Subsection (6) extends the exemption to a house or garden that is situate in the State and not held for the purposes of trading, provided:

(1) on a claim being made to the Revenue it appears to the Revenue to be of national, scientific, historic, or artistic interest;

(2) in respect of which reasonable facilities for viewing were allowed to members of the public during the three years immediately before the date of the benefit; and

(3) in respect of which reasonable facilities for viewing are allowed to members of the public.

It should be noted that reasonable facilities for viewing are for members of the public alone and the facilities do not apply to recognised bodies or to associations of persons.

The exemption will cease if the property is sold within six years, except to the bodies specified in sub-section (3).

Sub-section (7) details what the Revenue Commissioners deem to be 'reasonable facilities for viewing'. However, the facilities for viewing by members of the public will not be regarded as reasonable unless Bord Failte has been provided with particulars of the name, if any, and the address of house and garden, the days and times during the year when access to the house is afforded to the public, and the price, if any, payable for such access. The price payable for such access must be 'reasonable in amount' and must not 'operate to preclude members of the public from seeking access to the house or garden'.

3.14.5.2 Heritage property owned by a company (Section 78)

Section 78 extends this relief to relevant heritage property owned by a company.

The company must be a private company within the meaning of s. 27 of CAT Consolidation Act, 2003 (i.e. a 'family company') and the benefit must consist of shares in that private company both at the date of the benefit and at the valuation date. After the taking of the benefit, the company is a company controlled by the beneficiary within the meaning of the aforesaid section. If the relevant heritage property forms part only of the assets of the company, then a proportion of the shares referable to the relevant heritage property will be exempt provided the conditions set out in s. 77 of CAT Consolidation Act, 2003 as amended are complied with.

If the particular shares obtain business relief, then that proportion of the shares which is attributable to the relevant heritage property is left out of account in determining what proportion of the shares is attributable to the relevant business property. This exemption for heritage property held by a company is subject to the condition that the relevant heritage property was held by the company or a subsidiary of that company on or after 12 April 1995. Any heritage property acquired by a company after 12 April 1995 will not qualify for the exemption, so this is of limited utility. Similar clawback provisions apply.

3.14.6 PAYMENTS RELATING TO RETIREMENT (SECTION 80)

Section 80 states that any payment to an employee out of funds provided by the employer or any other person *bona fide* by way of retirement benefit, redundancy payment, or pension (as defined) is not to be regarded as a gift or an inheritance.

Sub-section (3) of s. 80 includes anti-avoidance legislation, so that exemption may not be applicable if the employee is a relative of the employer or the employer is a private company within the meaning of s. 27.

Sub-section (5) states that any benefit taken by a person, other than the person in respect of whose service the benefit arises (e.g. a wife taking a benefit in respect of her deceased husband's service), under the provisions of any superannuation fund or under any superannuation scheme established solely or mainly for persons employed in a profession, trade, undertaking, or employment and their dependants shall be deemed to be a gift or an inheritance, as the case may be derived under a disposition made by the person in respect of whose service the benefit arises and not by any other person.

In effect the employee is regarded as the disponer in respect of payments made to his dependants by his employer under a superannuation scheme as defined in the section.

It should be noted that an *ex gratia* payment made by the employer to such dependants is also taxable as a benefit coming from the employee as the disponer.

3.14.6.1 Exemption in relation to retirement benefits (Section 85)

Section 85 deals with employers' contributions to an 'approved retirement fund' (Taxes Consolidation Act, 1997, s. 784A). These are essentially lump sums held by a pensioner on retirement to be used to provide for themselves in old age and are an alternative to pension annuities as we know them. These should not be confused with a payment by an employer as covered above and provided for in s. 80. There are provisions for tax-free drawdowns of a lump sum at retirement and mandatory drawdown at the marginal rate of tax each year.

Benefits payable from an ARF can be passed to a spouse or civil partner without payment of CAT or income tax. (A tax rate of 20% applies subsequently on the death of the spouse or civil partner).

Benefits payable to a child under 21 are subject to CAT but not to income tax.

Benefits payable to a child over 21 are subject to 30 per cent tax if inherited by a child over age 21.

Benefits inherited by anyone else are subject to marginal rate Income Tax and CAT.

3.14.7 EXEMPTION OF CERTAIN SECURITIES (SECTION 81)

Government securities, most commonly issued by the National Treasury Management Agency ('NTMA'), are exempt from CAT when they are given by a disponer and taken by a beneficiary who is neither domiciled nor ordinarily resident in the State at the date of the benefit.

The exemption also applies to units held in certain unit trust schemes provided the assets in these schemes are confined to securities within the exemption.

The exemption applies to mainstream CAT only and does not apply to discretionary trust tax.

Where the disponer is either domiciled or resident in Ireland and the beneficiary is neither, the exemption can still apply but conditions must be met.

3.14.7.1 Conditions

Certain conditions have to be fulfilled in order to obtain the exemption:

- the securities or units must be comprised in the disposition (e.g. where they were held by a trust) continuously for a period of 15 years immediately before the date of the benefit where the stocks or securities are acquired after 26 February 2003.
- Prior to this they could be held for a shorter period of time prior to transfer but they had to be held by the beneficiary for at least one year. As noted, where the disponer is not domiciled or ordinarily resident in Ireland, the period of ownership is disregarded.
- The security or units must be comprised in the benefit both at the date of the benefit and at the valuation date. The donee or successor that is the beneficiary must be neither domiciled nor ordinarily resident in the State at the date of the benefit.

The requirement that the securities or units be comprised in the disposition for the six or 15-year period will not apply where the *disponer* was neither domiciled nor ordinarily resident in the State at the date of the disposition (or, in the case of securities or units purchased before 26 March 1997, where the disponer was neither domiciled nor ordinarily resident in the State at the date of the gift or inheritance).

For the purpose of calculating the 15- (or six-) year period prior to the date of the benefit, the period of ownership during which the security or units were at any time in the beneficial ownership of the disponer would be counted as part or maybe the entire of the 15- (or six- or three-) year period during which it was comprised in the disposition.

3.14.7.2 Non-Irish domiciled or resident beneficiary of government securities

A benefit taken by a beneficiary who is neither domiciled nor ordinarily resident in the State from a disponer who was neither domiciled nor ordinarily resident in the State at the date of the disposition will obtain the exemption regardless of whether the 15-year condition applies or not (subsection (3)).

This exemption of certain securities is an important exemption to be kept in mind in the administration of an estate where one or more of the beneficiaries are foreign.

It should be remembered that a personal representative can utilise his power of appropriation under s. 55 of the Succession Act, 1965 in directing such securities towards foreign beneficiaries.

It is important that the will of a testator should include a power to the personal representative to appropriate under s. 55 without the agreement of the beneficiaries. See Chapter 3 of *Wills, Probate and Estates*.

3.14.7.3 Payment of tax using government securities at par value

One further relief applicable to government securities is found in s. 56 of CAT Consolidation Act, 2003. This allows for the payment of CAT due by transfer of government securities at par. Without going into detail on the valuation of securities, in general the lower the ECB interest rate, the higher the price of the stock and vice versa, and at the time of writing the majority of government securities are trading above par so this relief is of little assistance. The current position in relation to government securities should be ascertained prior to the sale of any government securities.

3.14.8 CERTAIN ASSURANCE POLICIES (SECTION 74)

Section 74 of CAT Consolidation Act, 2003 exempts from Inheritance and gift tax certain policies of life assurance issued after 1 December 1992 and comprised in the benefit at the date of the benefit where both the disponer and beneficiary are non-ordinarily resident and domiciled.

If the disponer had purchased the policy prior to 15 February 2001, the exemption will apply where the proper law of the disposition was foreign, and the donee or successor is neither domiciled nor ordinarily resident in the State at the date of the gift or inheritance.

3.14.9 CERTAIN SPECIFIED COLLECTIVE INVESTMENT UNDERTAKINGS (SECTION 75)

Units of an investment undertaking or a common contractual fund, which are comprised in a gift or an inheritance, will be exempt from tax where neither the disponer nor the beneficiary is domiciled or ordinarily resident in the State at the date of the disposition.

However, as respects units of an investment undertaking purchased prior to 15 February 2001 which are taken by a foreign beneficiary as a gift or inheritance from an Irish disponer, the exemption will apply, provided the proper law of the disposition was foreign.

3.14.10 EXEMPTION OF CERTAIN RECEIPTS (SECTION 82)

Certain receipts are exempt from CAT:

- The receipt by a person of any sum *bona fide* by way of compensation or damages for any wrong or injury suffered by him or her in person, property reputation, or means of livelihood.
- The receipt by a person of any sum *bona fide* by way of compensation or damages for any wrong or injury resulting in the death of any other person.
- The receipt by a person of any sum *bona fide* by way of winnings from betting, lotteries, and so on.
- Any benefit arising out of a payment made to the official assignee in bankruptcy of money which has been provided by friends of a bankrupt. This exemption also covers the remission or abatement of debts by creditors of a bankrupt.
- Payments from the competition 'Your Country, Your Call' launched by the President on 17 February 2010.
- The receipt by any women who were admitted to and worded in Magdalene Laundries of ex gratia payments pursuant to the Magdalene Commission. The exemption applies to payments made by the Minister for Justice, Equality and Defence under the scheme on or after 1 September 2013.

3.14.10.1 Support, maintenance and education of children

Section 82 also provides an exemption for certain benefits passing to children in 82(2) and 82(4).

The support is limited to actual support and maintenance when the need for such support and maintenance could be shown and provided they were part of the normal expenditure of a person in the circumstances of the disponer.

The exemption applies to:

- a minor child of the disponer or of the civil partner of the disponer; or
- a child of the disponer, or of the civil partner of the disponer, who is more than 18 years of age but not more than 25 years of age who is receiving full-time education or instruction at any university, college, school or other educational establishment; or
- a child of the disponer or of the civil partner of the disponer who, regardless of age, is permanently incapacitated by reason of physical or mental infirmity from maintaining himself or herself.

For the purposes of s. 82 'receiving full time education or instruction' includes undergoing training for any trade or profession in such circumstances that the child is required to devote the whole of his or her time to such training for a period of not less than two years.

Revenue have published a Guide to the CAT Treatment of Receipts by Children from their Parents for their Support, Maintenance or Education: https://www.revenue.ie/en/gains-gifts-and-inheritance/documents/cat-treatment-receipts-by-children.pdf

in which they state that 'normal' in this context refers to the nature of the expenditure rather than the amount and that it means expenditure that might typically be incurred by a person in the circumstances of the disponer:

> *For example, payment of fees and accommodation costs for a dependent child attending college would be normal and would be exempt from gift tax—albeit that not all parents would incur such costs.*
>
> *Revenue's long held interpretation of the exemption provided by Section 82(2) is that it does not cover all payments by a parent to a child notwithstanding that such payments may meet the tests of 'normal' and 'reasonable' outlined in the foregoing paragraphs.*

The exemption only applies to the provision of support, maintenance or education. This implies at least some level of financial dependence on the part of the child.

Revenue does not accept that gifts to a child who is financially independent can come within the terms of the exemption. Neither does it accept that gifts of a capital nature to a child are exempt from gift tax under this section.

Revenue give some examples in the Guide of benefits that would be taxable, such as:

- A gift of a house
- A gift of a deposit for a house that exceeds the annual small gifts exemption €3000
- Gifts of money in excess of the annual small gifts exemption of €3,000
- Free use of a house by a child who is not attending college

Revenue also specify some benefits that they accept are exempt, such as:

- The free use of a house by a child attending university.
- The non-exclusive occupation of the family home by a child of any age or the spouse/ civil partner of that child. This is in line with their 'long standing approach' that living at home with one's parents is not a taxable benefit.
- Payments to a child attending college.
- The cost of family functions (such as a wedding) paid for by a parent.

3.14.10.2 Payments to children on the death of the disponer

Prior to December 2014, the receipt by a minor child of the disponer or the civil partner of a disponer of money or money's worth for support, maintenance, and education, at a time when the disponer and the child's other parent were both dead, was not deemed to be a gift or inheritance.

Since 23 December 2014, the relief is now extended to a child of the disponer or the civil partner of a disponer who is older than 18 but not older than 25 and who is in full time education, subject to the provisos contained above.

Also, since that date, benefits which would not be taxable if received directly from a parent as outlined above will not be taxable if received by a child of the disponer or the civil partner of a disponer when the disponer and the child's other parent were both dead.

3.14.11 EXEMPTION WHERE THE DISPOSITION WAS MADE BY THE BENEFICIARY (SECTION 83)

Tax is not chargeable where the benefit taken by the beneficiary is under a disposition made by himself.

Example: Sandra settles property on Terence for life with remainder to Sandra absolutely. On the death of Terence, Sandra takes a benefit, but it is exempt because she takes the benefit from herself.

Similarly, where an individual gives another right to reside in a property he or she owns, on the death of the person with the right to reside, there is no tax payable.

Also, an employee is deemed to take a pension from himself.

This exemption also arises where the gift is made through the vehicle of 'associated' companies, that is, if one company owns at least 90 per cent of the other or a third company owns at least 90 per cent of the two companies involved.

3.14.12 EXEMPTION RELATING TO QUALIFYING EXPENSES OF INCAPACITATED PERSONS (SECTION 84)

Section 84 exempts a benefit which is taken exclusively for the purpose of discharging qualifying expenses of an individual who is permanently incapacitated by reason of physical or mental infirmity. The Revenue must be satisfied that the benefit has been or will be applied for such purpose.

Qualifying expenses are defined as meaning expenses relating to medical care including the cost of maintenance in connection with such medical care. This exemption is preferable to benefits taken on or after 28 March 1996.

The Revenue position is reflected in Part 22 of the Revenue CAT Manual, most recently updated in July 2024: <https://www.revenue.ie/en/tax-professionals/tdm/capital-acquisitions-tax/cat-part22.pdf>

In short, Part 22 states that the Revenue Commissioners interpret the phrase 'taken exclusively for the purpose of discharging qualifying expenses' as referring to the intention in the mind of the disponer and that evidence must be provided 'either by will or otherwise' to prove that the disponer intended to provide the benefit exclusively for this purpose. In short, 'taken' in the context of s. 84 was a technical phrase, and a reference to the mechanism by which a gift or inheritance was received by a beneficiary.

This interpretation was controversial and was the subject of a recent determination of the Tax Appeals Commissioners published in September 2019.

<https://www.taxappeals.ie/_fileupload/Determinations/2019/32TACD2019(1).pdf>

The facts leading to the appeal were that the applicant inherited a significant sum from an uncle and used or intended to use the entire sum on providing suitable living conditions and medical care and assistance for his children who both suffer from a neurological condition. The children were not the beneficiaries under the will; the applicant was. Revenue refused the relief on the grounds that the will did not specify that the benefit was to be used for this purpose and that the applicant was the beneficiary under the will, not his children.

The hearing concerned itself with the use of the word 'taken' in the section.

The Appeal Commissioners found, applying the decision of the Supreme Court in Inspector of Taxes v Kiernan [1981] 1IR 117, more recently applied in Coleman v Revenue Commissioners [2014] IEHC 662, that:

> *(w)here statutory provisions are addressed to the public generally, a word should be given the meaning which an ordinary member of the public would intend it to have when using it ordinarily.*
>
> *when the word which requires to be given its natural and ordinary meaning is a simple word which has a widespread and unambiguous currency, the judge construing it should draw primarily on his own experience of its use. Dictionaries or other literary sources should be looked at only when alternative meanings, regional usages or other obliquities are shown to cast doubt on the singularity of its ordinary meaning, or when there are grounds for suggesting that the meaning of the word has changed since the statute in question was passed.*

In this case, the word 'taken' was considered to be 'simple and unambiguous' meaning 'acquiring the ownership or possession of' and the commissioners determined that it is the intention of the recipient of a gift or inheritance and not the disponer that is relevant when applying s. 84 relief.

Revenue did not appeal this determination to the High Court as a case stated and the time for lodging such an appeal has passed. Revenue have not amended their guidance in relation to s. 84 since the publication of the determination and are not bound by the determination. It is understood that Revenue are waiting for a similar appeal to the Tax Appeals Commissioners, which they will then appeal to the High Court as a case stated if such determination is expressed in similar terms to this one.

3.14.12.1 Best practice

In all cases when drafting a will for a client it remains best practice when taking instructions for a will to inquire as to whether any beneficiary is incapacitated as provided for in s. 84 and leaving the bequest to that beneficiary or their trustees for the sole purpose of discharging qualifying expenses of that beneficiary.

3.14.13 QUALIFYING TRUST FOR INCAPACITATED PERSONS

Section 82(3) further provides that a 'qualifying trust' set up using 'trust funds' raised by public subscription for the benefit of an incapacitated person that meets the standards set down in s. 189A of the Taxes Consolidation Act, 1997 (as inserted by s. 12 of the Finance Act, 1999) will not be considered to be a gift.

Originally, s. 189A provided that on the death of the incapacitated person (or the last of them, if more than one) any remaining funds had to be applied for charitable purposes or appointed in favour of the trustees of charitable bodies.

This was amended by s. 10 of the Finance Act, 2014 to provide that the undistributed part of the trust funds on the death of an incapacitated individual, or of the last surviving incapacitated individual, as the case may be, should form part of the estate of the individual provided they have a surviving spouse, civil partner, or child.

3.14.14 FAVOURITE GRANDCHILD RELIEF/MARRIAGE SETTLEMENT

Paragraph 8 of Part I of the Second Schedule to CAT Consolidation Act, 2003 provides a relief in relation to marriage settlements which had been made many years prior to the introduction of the CAT legislation.

It applies only to a disposition which is referred to as a 'specified disposition'. A 'specified disposition' means a disposition:

(1) the date of which is a date prior to 1 April 1975;

(2) in relation to which the disponer is a grandparent of the beneficiary; and

(3) in which the marriage of the parents of the beneficiary was at the date of the disposition expressed to be the consideration.

Furthermore, the parent or parents of the beneficiary must have been entitled to a limited interest in the settled funds. Normally the settlement would allow for a life interest for each parent with the remainder on the death of the surviving parent to go to the child or children (grandchild or grandchildren of the original disponer).

For example, the trust would be set up on trust for settlors:

- to the son for life;
- remainder to the wife of the son for life;
- remainder to a grandchild absolutely.

If these conditions are satisfied, then for the purpose of computing tax payable on that benefit the beneficiary is deemed to bear to the original disponer, the grandparent, the relationship of a child.

CHAPTER 4

AGRICULTURAL RELIEF

4.1 Introduction

Agricultural relief is an extremely important relief, affecting most farms in the country. If applicable it can provide relief of up to 90 per cent on gifts or inheritances of qualifying agricultural land and property. It can, in some circumstances, be quite complex in its application.

Students should review Part 11 of the CAT Tax and Duty Manual dealing with Agricultural Relief, which can be found at: <https://www.revenue.ie/en/tax-professionals/tdm/capital-acquisitions-tax/cat-part11.pdf>.

The statutory basis for the relief is to be found in s. 89 of the CAT Consolidation Act, 2003 as amended.

[Section 100 of Finance Act 2024 introduced an entirely new Section 89A intended to replace Section 89 in its totality but this section and Section 101are subject to a Commencement Order and at time of going to press, this Commencement Order has not been enacted.]

Essentially s. 89 provides that insofar as any gift or inheritance consists of **agricultural property**:

(1) at the date of the gift or the date of the inheritance; and

(2) at the valuation date; and

(3) is taken by a donee or successor who is, on the valuation date, and after taking the gift or inheritance, **a farmer** as defined,

the market value (100%) of the **agricultural property** is replaced by the **agricultural value (10%)** in arriving at the taxable value of the benefit.

4.2 Agricultural Property

The purpose of defining an asset as 'agricultural property' is two-fold. Firstly, agricultural relief only applies to agricultural property as defined, and secondly, a beneficiary must qualify both as a farmer as provided for in 4.3 in terms of assets and as an 'active farmer' as set out at 4.3.8.

Section 89(1) states:

> *'agricultural property' means agricultural land, pasture and woodland situated in the EU* [since 20 November 2008—prior to that date only agricultural property in the State qualified]

and crops, trees and underwood growing on such land and also includes such farm buildings, farm houses and mansion houses (together with the lands occupied with such farm buildings, farm houses and mansion houses) as are of a character appropriate to the property, and farm machinery, livestock and bloodstock on such property.

The Finance (No. 2) Act 2008, s. 89(1) extended the definition of 'agricultural property' to include agricultural property situate in an EU Member State in respect of benefits taken on/after 20 November 2008. Previously the definition was limited to agricultural property situate in the State.

The effect of this is that a person who takes a gift/inheritance of agricultural land situate elsewhere in the EU which falls within the charge to CAT (either because the disponer or beneficiary is resident/ordinarily resident in Ireland on the date of the disposition/benefit) can claim agricultural relief on any CAT payable.

Also, if a beneficiary inherits a farm that 'straddles' the border, they will be able to claim agricultural relief on the entire farm, not just that portion of the farm in the State, and the entire value of the farm will be taken into account for the farmer asset test at 8.3.

Section 66 of the Withdrawal of the United Kingdom from the European Union (Consequential Provisions) Act 2019 as amended by Section 74 of the Withdrawal of the United Kingdom from the European Union (Consequential Provisions) Act 2020 provides that, when the United Kingdom withdrew from the EU, agricultural land in the UK and formerly in the EU would still qualify as agricultural land for this purpose and for the purpose of the farmer asset test, by adding the words 'or in the United Kingdom' after 'Member State'. Section 74 commenced on 31 December 2020 at 11:00 pm.

See also 4.2.7 Solar Farms.

4.2.1 SHARES

Shares in a company deriving their value from agricultural property do not qualify as agricultural property and therefore do not qualify for agricultural relief, but may qualify for business relief.

Business Relief is covered in Chapter 5.

We will also be dealing with the situation where a beneficiary who is not farming the land as an 'active farmer' can lease the land to a limited company where the main shareholder of that company is a working director, and that working director/main shareholder must farm the agricultural property on behalf of the company.

4.2.2 FARMHOUSE

The farmhouse/mansion house has to be of a character appropriate to the property. This has been interpreted as meaning 'suitable' and also as physically close to. 'Suitable' is dealt with on a case-by-case basis. The farmhouse does not have to be part of the same folio as the farmland and can even be a short distance away from the land. Again, this is dealt with on a case-by-case basis. The farmhouse could be in the United Kingdom and be close enough to the farm in question (when passing with the farm—see below).

The UK case of *Starke (executors of Brown deceased) v IRC* [1996] 1 All ER 622, and the circumstances in which 2.5 acres of land with a farmhouse and certain buildings was held not to be agricultural land, is also of interest in this regard. Therefore, in the context of the *Starke* decision it is the agricultural land that determines whether the relief applies—hence the danger of separating the farmhouse and other buildings from the land by separate transfers.

The farmhouse etc., without the land, is not agricultural property. Therefore, if a farmhouse on its own is transferred to a farmer, it will not qualify for agricultural relief (e.g. a gift of a farmhouse to a child) and will be taxed at its full value. However, if the farmland is then subsequently gifted or devised to the same beneficiary thereby 're-joining' the house and land, the house will count as agricultural property for the purpose of the 80 per cent farmer asset test in respect of the later benefit of the farmland taken by that beneficiary.

On the other hand, if the land is gifted to the donee farmer and the donor separately retains the house, the house will not be 'agricultural property' on its own assuming it is later gifted or devised to the same beneficiary, and although it may rejoin the agricultural property and become, again, agricultural, it was not agricultural property at the date of the gift or the inheritance. This underlines the importance of planning prior to implementing any transfers of agricultural property. It may be more beneficial to transfer the farmhouse with the land subject to a right to reside.

4.2.3 SMALL PLOTS OF LAND

Claims for Agricultural Relief in relation to small acreages of land are determined by reference to the circumstances of each case. However, in general, the Revenue Commissioners consider that small parcels of land do not constitute agricultural property and do not therefore qualify for agricultural relief. In this regard the Appeal Commissioners, in February 2012, determined that a small parcel of land of 0.14 acres was not agricultural property. Revenue appear to take the view that a viable farming unit is required. They interpret this to mean that at least two acres must pass before the land will be considered agricultural and that anything smaller than this may be too small to constitute agricultural property. They refer to the UK case of *Rosser v IRC* (2003) SpC 368, in which two acres with a barn on it was regarded as agricultural whereas a house on the same holding was not. In that case the definition of farmhouse employed was 'a dwelling for the farmer from which the farm was managed'.

4.2.4 FARM MACHINERY, LIVESTOCK, AND BLOODSTOCK

In order to qualify for the relief, any farm machinery, livestock, or bloodstock must be physically situated on agricultural land. It should be noted, however, that the agricultural relief is allowed on farm machinery, livestock, or bloodstock once they are situated on agricultural lands and irrespective of whether or not the lands are actually owned by the disponer. For example, they could be on land leased by the disponer.

A gift or inheritance of livestock, bloodstock, or machinery on their own would not qualify. The farm machinery, livestock, or bloodstock must pass with agricultural land, even if not situate on that land at the time of the gift or inheritance.

For example, such assets owned by a dealer in livestock or bloodstock or by a vendor of farm machinery and not situate on any agricultural land would not qualify for agricultural relief but may qualify instead for business relief.

4.2.5 CROPS, TREES, AND UNDERWOOD

While crops, trees, and underwood growing on agricultural land qualify for agricultural relief, cut crops or lumber would not qualify, as they are not 'growing on such land'.

It is not necessary to be a 'farmer' in terms of the 'asset test' in respect of a gift/inheritance consisting of trees or underwood. A gift/inheritance of trees and underwood growing on agricultural land qualifies for agricultural relief. However, this applies only to growing trees and underwood and not to cut trees or lumber.

4.2.6 EU DIRECT FARM PAYMENT ENTITLEMENT

The EU Single Farm Payment Entitlement replaced livestock premia (headage payments) and arable aid schemes. The scheme came into force on 1 January 2005 and the entitlements became the property of the farmer who farmed during the relevant period 2000–2002, and he or she could sell, transfer, or bequeath those entitlements with or without land.

Since the passing of the Finance Act, 2006, the Single Farm Payment Entitlement has qualified as agricultural property, when passing with agricultural land. This change applied retrospectively from 1 January 2005.

Since 2015 the Single Farm Payment Entitlement scheme has been being phased out and replaced by the Direct Farm Payment Scheme. The Direct Farm Payment Scheme includes payments designed to replace the Milk Quota scheme.

Initially the Direct Farm Payment Scheme focused on a Basic Payment Scheme similar to the Single Payment Scheme, but which has since expanded to include a 'Payment for Agricultural Practices beneficial for the Climate and the Environment' (Greening Payment); a Young Farmers Scheme which provides an additional payment to anyone who qualifies as a 'Young Farmer'; and a scheme to provide Aid for Protein Crops.

A very significant element of the national ceiling (44%) is allocated to the Greening Payment each year and all farmers who participate in the Basic Payment Scheme must also implement the Greening provisions.

The Basic Payment Scheme is based on entitlements based on land held and a farmer will apply based on which hectares are eligible for payment and must declare one eligible hectare for each entitlement he holds. All entitlements are subject to a 'two-year usage' rule which provides that any entitlement that remains unused for two consecutive years will revert to the National Reserve.

Initially these single payments and direct payments were not directly connected to land in the way that the payment schemes they replaced (livestock premia and arable aid schemes abolished in 2005 and Milk Quotas abolished in 2015) were. Entitlements were not attached to land but were allocated to a person and became the property of that person, and from 2016 onwards entitlements could be transferred with or without land.

Since 21 November 2017, where there are entitlements under the EU Basic Payment Scheme, these will now pass with the land where the will is silent unless there is a legal impediment preventing the transfer. Full details can be found in SI 639 of 2017. It is not intended that practitioners be aware of the ever-changing minutiae of these schemes but it is important to recognise that these direct payments are a specific asset of the estate and, depending on our client's instructions, can pass with the land or (more unusually) separate from the land.

When drafting a will for a farmer, specific advice should be taken as to the schemes (if any) availed of by that farmer and his or her intentions in relation to any payments due out of these schemes. It should be noted that any beneficiary receiving these would need to have land in order to claim the entitlement and although treated as 'agricultural property' for CAT purposes, if they are not passing with the land, they may not qualify as 'agricultural property'. This scheme is now referred to as the Basic Income Support for Sustainability (BISS) Scheme.

The beneficiary must also be an 'active farmer' as outlined in 4.3.9.

The most recent (September 2024) Department of Agriculture, Food and the Marine publications in relation to the terms and conditions relating to the BISS Scheme is available from the Department website: <https://www.gov.ie/en/service/4ae67-basic-income-support-for-sustainability-biss-scheme/>.

The Inheritance Enquiry Unit (see page 78 of the booklet for contact details) are extremely helpful in assisting family members and the legal personal representatives of deceased farmers to:

- Identify those schemes in which the deceased person participated and establish whether there are any outstanding payments due to the estate of the deceased.
- Assist the legal personal representatives in contacting various sections of the Department.
- Advise on what legal documents are required.
- Make arrangements for the issue of any outstanding payments due to estate of the deceased and for the transfer of payment entitlements (if any).

The Unit will act as a single repository for legal documentation submitted by representatives of the deceased, thus removing the necessity for forwarding duplicate copies to several sections within the Department.

4.2.7 SOLAR FARMS

Section 72 of the Finance Act, 2017 deals with 'solar farms' (agricultural land placed under solar infrastructure) and provides that for the purpose of CAT agricultural relief and CGT retirement relief, agricultural land placed under solar infrastructure will continue to be classified as agricultural land (formerly it would no longer have been deemed agricultural land), but with a condition restricting the amount of the farmland that can be used for solar infrastructure to 50 per cent of the total farm acreage.

See pages 7 and 8 of the Revenue CAT Manual Part 11 dealing with Agricultural Relief.

4.3 Farmer

The beneficiary must comply with the definition of 'farmer' as outlined in the CAT Consolidation Act, 2003, s. 89(1) as amended by the Finance Act, 2006, s. 118, the Finance Act, 2007, s. 117, and the Finance (No. 2) Act, 2008, s. 89; the Finance Act, 2012, s. 114; and most recently by the Finance Act, 2014, s. 82, which introduced the concept of the 'active farmer'. As noted earlier, Brexit did not affect the definition of 'farmer'.

Therefore, for the purpose of meeting the conditions of 'agricultural relief', a 'farmer' must pass two tests: the 'asset test', which has been a condition of agricultural relief since its introduction, and the 'active farmer test', which was introduced for gifts or inheritances taking place on or after 1 January 2015.

Taking the '**asset test**' first:

*'farmer', in relation to a donee or successor, means an **individual** in respect of whom not less than **80 per cent** of the market value of the property to which the individual is **beneficially entitled in possession** is represented by the **market value** of property in a member State which consists of agricultural property, . . . and for the purpose of this definition—*

(a) no deduction is made from the market value of property for any debts or encumbrances (except debts or encumbrances in respect of a dwelling-house which is the only or main residence of the donee or successor and which is not agricultural property for benefits taken after 1 February 2007).

(b) the individual is deemed to be beneficially entitled in possession to:

(i) an interest in expectancy notwithstanding the definition of 'entitled in possession' in s 2 [of the CAT Consolidation Act, 2003], and

(ii) to property which is subject to a discretionary trust under or in consequence of a disposition made by the individual where the individual is an object of the trust.

(iii) For the purpose of paragraph (a) of the definition of 'farmer' in subsection (1), a loan secured on the dwelling-house referred to in that paragraph which is not used to purchase, repair or improve that dwelling-house will not be treated as a debt or an encumbrance.

4.3.1 DOMICILE AND RESIDENCE NO LONGER APPLICABLE

It is no longer necessary for the beneficiary to be either domiciled or resident in Ireland.

Up until 31 March 2006, to qualify as a farmer, the individual had to be domiciled in the State. This condition was removed by s. 118 of the Finance Act, 2006 to take effect after the passing of the Finance Act, 2006 on that date.

Up until 8 February 2012, the beneficiary had to remain resident in the State for the three years of assessment immediately following the year of assessment in which the valuation date fell to retain the relief.

This condition was removed by s. 114(1)(b) of the Finance Act, 2012 and it no longer applies in respect of gifts and inheritances taken on or after 8 February 2012. However, the new 'active farmer' conditions will apply in respect of gifts and inheritances taken on or after 1 January 2015.

The beneficiary never had to be resident in the State on the date of the gift or inheritance.

4.3.2 MARKET VALUE OF LAND IGNORING DEBTS OR ENCUMBRANCES

When calculating the 'farmer asset test', that is, whether 80 per cent of a beneficiary's assets are agricultural in nature, it is the market value that is used, even if the beneficiary takes a limited interest in the property.

Debts and encumbrances on the property are not taken into account. This is an anti-avoidance measure to cover a situation where, for example, a person who owns non-agricultural assets could otherwise take out a mortgage prior to the valuation date, use the money to purchase agricultural assets with an option to return within a short period, qualify as a 'farmer', return the assets, and repay the mortgager. This provision in the CAT Consolidation Act, 2003 prevents this.

4.3.2.1 Off farm principal private dwelling

Since 1 February 2007 there is one exception to this rule. Where the beneficiary has an 'off farm principal private dwelling', that is, a dwelling that would not qualify for agricultural relief as it is not sufficiently close to the farmland (e.g. where the beneficiary resides in a house in the nearest village), any debts or encumbrances in respect of that dwelling would be deducted from the market value of the dwelling when calculating the value of non-agricultural assets. See s. 117 of the Finance Act, 2007.

Example:

Joe Bloggs, a farmer, wishes to leave farmland, livestock, bloodstock, and farm machinery (l, b&fm) valued at €1,000,000 to his daughter, Mary. Mary lives in the next town and owns a house there. The house is valued at approximately €300,000 and there is a mortgage of €200,000 on the house. She does not have any other assets.

For the purpose of the 'farmer test' her house will be valued at (€300,000 – €200,000) = €100,000. Prior to this coming into force, she would not have been allowed to take the mortgage into account and the house would have been valued at €300,000.

Secured Borrowings used to purchase, improve or repair

Section 114 (1) (a) Finance Act, 2012 inserted s. 89(1A), which has narrowed the applicability of this exception since 8 February 2012. Borrowings secured on an individual's off farm principal private dwelling are only deductible if those borrowings were used for the purchase, improvement, or repair of that dwelling.

4.3.3 ANTI-AVOIDANCE (INTERESTS IN EXPECTANCY AND DISCRETIONARY TRUSTS)

These conditions are further anti-avoidance measures.

Taking the first condition, dealing with **an interest in expectancy**: for example, consider a disponer who leaves his farm valued at €2,000,000 to his son and the rest, residue, and remainder of his property (i.e. his non-agricultural assets) valued at €1,000,000 to his wife for life, with remainder to his son absolutely.

For the purposes of ascertaining whether the son is a 'farmer' the present value of the interest in expectation of rest, residue, and remainder of the estate will be included as an asset of the son. This is calculated by subtracting the value of the life or lesser interest from the market value of the property. This is for the purpose of the 'farmer test' *only* and is not used in any other fashion.

The residuary property is not included when calculating the taxable value of the benefit received. When calculating the taxable value of the benefit received, only the benefit comprising an interest to which the beneficiary is beneficially entitled in possession is included, and not any future interest.

Taking the second condition: for example, a person who owns non-agricultural property worth €1,000,000, on inheriting a farm worth €2,000,000, could place all his property in a discretionary trust, naming himself as a trustee and an object (potential beneficiary) of the trust; the trust property would not be considered his and he would qualify as a farmer. A week later, he could appoint all the property to himself out of the trust. As this would be a benefit to himself it would not be taxable under s. 83. This provision in the CAT Consolidation Act, 2003 prevents this.

4.3.3.1 Pension

The Revenue Commissioners accept that any interest which a beneficiary may have in a pension or pension fund can be ignored when calculating whether a beneficiary meets the 80 per cent agricultural assets 'farmer' test.

4.3.4 FARMER TEST AT VALUATION DATE

The individual must qualify, that is, be 'a farmer' on the valuation date. In circumstances where the valuation date is after the date of the gift or inheritance, there may be scope for some planning to ensure that the individual qualifies, for example, by disposing of some of his own non-agricultural assets. When dealing with inheritances, while the market value of the property at the date of death is the value for the Statement of Affairs (Probate), it is the market value of the various assets at the valuation date which is relevant for the farmer test.

For this reason, it is extremely important to advise a beneficiary of agricultural property about the implications of selling livestock immediately after the death of the disponer. Also, crops growing are agricultural property but cut crops are not. However, it may be that the beneficiary has no choice but to cut crops and/or sell livestock for sound agricultural reasons.

4.3.5 FINANCIAL NATURE OF THE 80 PER CENT ASSET TEST

This is a financial test. There is no requirement that the individual has actually worked as a farmer prior to the gift or inheritance. This is now dealt with in the 'active farmer test'. The 'Asset Test' is applied as follows:

Agricultural Property—Asset Test

Market value* of all assets of beneficiary [including benefit]

	Non-agricultural assets	Agricultural assets	Total assets
Property owned prior to the benefit	€	€	€

(Continued)

(Continued)

Property the subject of the benefit	+	€	+	€	+	€
Total	=	€	=	€	=	€

$$\frac{\text{Agri Assets}}{\text{All Assets}\left[\text{Agri} + \text{Other}\right]} \times 100 = \_\_\_\%$$

*taking into account any mortgage, debt, or encumbrance on a sole or main dwelling-house which does not qualify as agricultural property in itself (see **4.3.2.1** above).

The first line details the market value of the beneficiary's assets, agricultural and non-agricultural, listed separately but not including the current gift or inheritance; that is, all the beneficiary owns prior to the gift or inheritance.

The second line details the market value of the gift or inheritance, again divided into agricultural and non-agricultural, listed separately.

The total agricultural assets and other assets are brought down and used in the 'Formula', which is simply total agricultural assets above the line over total agricultural and total other assets (i.e. total agricultural over total assets). If the result (multiplied by 100 to give a percentage) is greater than 80 then the individual qualifies as a farmer.

$$\frac{\text{Agri Assets}}{\text{All Assets}\left[\text{Agri} + \text{Other}\right]} \times 100 = \_\_\_\%$$

Example: Taking the earlier example of Mary at **4.3.2.1**. She inherits a farm and agricultural assets valued at €1,000,000 from her late father Joe Bloggs. Her house in the local village has a net value of €100,000 (market value €300,000 less mortgage €200,000). She did not inherit any non-agricultural assets nor own any agricultural assets prior to the inheritance.

All assets of beneficiary [including benefit]

		Non-agricultural assets		**Agricultural assets**		**Total assets**
Property owned prior to the benefit		**€100,000**		**€ 0**		**€100,000**
Property the subject of the benefit	+	**€ 0**	+	**€900,000**	+	**€900,000**
Total	=	**€100,000**	=	**€900,000**	=	**€1,000,000**

$$\frac{\text{Agri Assets €1,000,000}}{\text{All Assets}\left[\text{Agri} + \text{Other}\right]\text{€1,100,000}} \times 100 = 90.90\%$$

Mary is a 'farmer'.

4.3.6 COMMON ERRORS

There are several errors which are often made in relation to agricultural relief. The first is to use the *gross market values* of assets for the purposes of the farmer asset test and to continue to use those gross values when applying the relief where for example there is a debt or encumbrance on agricultural property passing or the benefit is a limited interest.

The second common error is to include the farmhouse as an agricultural asset and not claim dwelling-house relief when calculating the tax due.

A third potential error is, having included *all assets* including the assets already owned by the beneficiary when applying the farmer test, then to continue to include all those assets when calculating the tax due.

Another common error is to include *remainder property*, which was properly included for the purposes of the farmer test. CAT is not paid on a remainder interest until it becomes an interest to which the beneficiary is beneficially entitled in possession.

4.3.7 'ACTIVE FARMER TEST'

Having established that for asset purposes, the individual is a farmer, it is now necessary to establish whether the individual is an 'active farmer'.

Section 82 Finance Act, 2014 introduced an activity requirement for agricultural relief to encourage beneficiaries to ensure that the land is actively farmed. This will be referred to as the 'active farmer test' and applies where the date of the gift or the date of the inheritance takes place on or after 1 January 2015.

The test is to be found in s. 89(1) of the CAT Consolidation Act, 2003 as amended, which now goes on to define 'farmer' as someone:

who—

i. *is the holder of any of the qualifications set out in Schedule 2, 2A or 2B to the Stamp Duties Consolidation Act 1999* [as listed in Appendix 2 on page 24 of the Revenue Stamp Duty Manual Part 07, https://www.revenue.ie/en/tax-professionals/tdm/stamp-duty/stamp-duty-manual/part-07-exemptions-and-reliefs-from-stamp-duty/section-81aa-transfers-of-land-to-young-trained-farmers.pdf], *or who achieves such a qualification within a period of 4 years commencing on the date of the gift or inheritance, and who for a period of not less than 6 years commencing on the valuation date of the gift or inheritance farms agricultural property (including the agricultural property comprised in the gift or inheritance) on a commercial basis and with a view to the realisation of profits from that agricultural property,*

ii. *for a period of not less than 6 years commencing on the valuation date of the gift or inheritance spends not less than 50 per cent of that individual's normal working time farming agricultural property (including the agricultural property comprised in the gift or inheritance) on a commercial basis and with a view to the realisation of profits from that agricultural property, or*

iii. *leases the whole or substantially the whole of the agricultural property, comprised in the gift or inheritance for a period of not less than 6 years commencing on the valuation date of the gift or inheritance, to an individual who satisfies the conditions in paragraph (i) or (ii).*

Since 1 January 2015, in order to qualify as a 'farmer' for CAT relief purposes, the beneficiary needs to hold one of the 'trained farmer' qualifications required for stamp duty relief on farmland or be in a position to show that he or she is an active or a trained farmer. Broadly speaking there are three ways to meet this new active farmer test, as follows:

- be a 'trained farmer' and farm the land commercially;

  or

- spend more than half the working week farming the land as an active farmer;

  or

- lease the land to an active farmer who will actively farm the land on a commercial basis or a trained farmer who will farm the land commercially.

For this purpose, as noted earlier, the beneficiary can lease the land to a limited company where the main shareholder is a working director who farms the land on behalf of the company. Where land is leased to a company that is owned equally by a person and his or her spouse or civil partner, then at least one of them must satisfy the working director and farming requirements to qualify for the relief.

To be an 'active farmer' when not a 'trained farmer', the individual must spend no less than 50 per cent of his or her normal working time farming agricultural property, for a period of not less than six years, starting on the valuation date. The farming activity must be on a commercial basis, and carried on with a view to the realisation of profits.

Revenue have indicated that they will accept that 'normal working time' (including on farm and off farm working time) approximates to 40 hours per week. They confirmed that farmers with off farm employment would qualify for the relief if they spend a minimum of 20 hours working on the farm each week, averaged over a year, regardless of how many hours they spend at their off farm employment.

If a farmer can show that his or her 'normal working time' is less than 40 hours a week, then the 50 per cent requirement may be applied to the actual hours worked provided that the farm is being farmed on a commercial basis with a view to the realisation of profit. If it can be shown that (in exceptional situations) 50 per cent of normal working time is not needed to farm the land on a commercial basis and realise profits, Revenue will take this into consideration in deciding whether the relief is due. Revenue recognise in the CAT Manual that this may apply to forestry, as forestry is far less labour-intensive than other types of farming and is typically carried out by 'contractors' who may well have been contracted by the disponer on a multi-year basis.

The relief is subject to the 'active farmer' condition for six years after the valuation date. This differs from the six-year clawback period from the date of the gift or inheritance, which applies to a sale of the agricultural property if it is not reinvested in other agricultural property. See Clawback in general at section 4.7.

The new legislation was intended to encourage land owners to make property available for agricultural use rather than to restrict agricultural relief. There are scenarios in which the strict wording of the legislation could preclude relief or result in a clawback, but Revenue, following intensive lobbying, have provided greater clarification of the original briefing note published by them and these further clarifications are now available in the Revenue CAT Manual at Part 11 Agricultural Relief para 11.6.3: <https://www.revenue.ie/en/tax-professionals/tdm/capital-acquisitions-tax/cat-part11.pdf>

Example: The legislation refers to an individual who 'spends not less than 50% of . . . normal working time farming agricultural property'. John is a farmer working part time in PAYE employment (22.5 hours a week) and farming part time (an average of 20 hours a week).

John's normal working week is 42.5 hours so 50 per cent would be 21.25 hours, and he is only farming for 20 hours. However, the Revenue Manual states that 'farmers with off-farm employment may qualify for agricultural relief where, averaged over a year, they work on the farm for at least 20 hours per week'. Under the legislation John would not qualify as a farmer, but Revenue confirm in the Revenue Manual that he can be considered an 'active farmer' for agricultural relief purposes.

Where, as it often happens, farmland is inherited by a person whose spouse is an active farmer, then either the beneficiary actively farms the land or leases the land to their spouse.

Where two or more persons inherit land, all must actively farm the land or a lease must be entered into to an active farmer who may be one of the owners. In the event of a dispute or deadlock, the relief will not apply if the land is not actively farmed either by the beneficiaries or a lessee.

Where the beneficiary inherits farmland, animal stock, farm machinery, and a farmhouse and is leasing the farmland to an active farmer but is (e.g.) selling the animal stock and farm machinery and holding onto the farmhouse, either as a main residence or as a holiday home, there will not be a clawback on the farmland or farmhouse where the leased property is at least 75 per cent of the property by value; however, there will be a clawback on the sale of the animal stock and farm machinery.

If land is used for bloodstock purposes, it (together with appropriate buildings) will qualify for the relief; market gardens however do not qualify for the relief, but may qualify for business relief.

Where the beneficiary is the main shareholder and working director of a limited company which carries on a farming trade and inherits land, the beneficiary can lease the land to that company. Any beneficiary can lease land to an unrelated company which is carrying on a farming business where (as outlined earlier) the main shareholder and working director of the company meets the 'active farmer' test.

4.4 Applying the Relief

Agricultural relief does not apply automatically; it must be claimed, and the applicant must demonstrate to the Revenue Commissioners that he or she passes the farmer test as outlined.

In order to claim the relief, a return must be filed online within the appropriate deadlines even if no tax is payable.

Where the relief applies, it operates by substituting the 'agricultural value' for market value.

As stated earlier, it is the date on which the benefit 'is taken', that is, the date of the gift/inheritance (not the 'valuation date'), which determines which relief applies to a particular benefit. Since 23 January 1997 the agricultural value is the market value reduced by 90 per cent and since 1 January 2015 the active farmer test requirements must be met on the date of the gift or inheritance.

Section 89(2) sets out provisions in relation to the treatment of liabilities, costs, expenses, and any consideration paid in respect of agricultural property attracting relief. Such expenditure, insofar as it relates to agricultural property, must first be reduced in proportion to the relief. If the market value of the agricultural property is reduced by 90 per cent, then so too are the liabilities and consideration (if any).

4.4.1 AGRICULTURAL RELIEF CALCULATION TEMPLATE

For the purposes of calculating the taxable value and tax payable on agricultural property, the following template is used: It consists of:

1. The 'Farmer Asset Test' (along with a reminder to check the active farming requirements)
2. Taxable value of 'ordinary' or non-agricultural assets
3. Taxable value of agricultural assets
4. Tax payable on taxable value of all assets (agricultural and non-agricultural).

The first consideration should be if the active farmer requirements are met or can be met. If these requirements can be met then the following template can be used to carry out the financial test and calculate the tax payable.

Agricultural Property—Farmer Asset Test:

Market Value* of all Assets of Beneficiary [Including Benefit]

		Non-agricultural assets		**Agricultural assets**		**Total Assets**
Property owned prior to the benefit		€		€		€
Property the subject of the benefit	+	€	+	€	+	€
Total	=	€	=	€	=	€

$$\frac{\text{Agricultural Assets}}{\text{Total}\left(\text{Agricultural} + \text{Non} - \text{Agricultural Assets}\right)} \times 100 = \_\_\_\%$$

. .. . is / is not a farmer—Check Active Farmer Test

Taxable Value of Non-Agricultural or 'Other' Property

	Market value		**€**
Less	Market value of exempt property (if any)		€
Equals	Market value of taxable property		€
Less	Relevant portion of liabilities, costs & expenses		€
Equals	Incumbrance free value		€
X	Value of limited interest	0.________	€
Less	Relevant portion of consideration [in money or monies worth]		€
Equals	Taxable value		€

This is the 'standard' template for arriving at the value of property with one difference. It is only the 'relevant' portion of liabilities, costs & expenses and of consideration that can be deducted; that is, those liabilities, costs & expenses and of consideration that relate to the non-agricultural or 'other' assets passing.

In examples, unless the interest is stated to be a life or limited interest, the value of limited interest will not be included.

Taxable Value of Agricultural Property

	Market Value		**€**
Less	Market value of exempt property (if any)		€
Equals	Market value of agricultural property		€
Less	Agricultural relief [90%]		€
Equals	Agricultural value [10%]		€
Less	Relevant portion of liabilities, costs & expenses **[reduced to 10%]**		€
Equals	Incumbrance free value		€
X	Value of limited interest	0.________	€
Less	Relevant portion of consideration [in money or monies worth] **[reduced to 10%]**		€
Equals	**Taxable value**		**€**

As can be seen here, the additional lines dealing with agricultural relief and agricultural value deal with the reduction in the value from market value to agricultural value before liabilities, costs & expenses and/or consideration are taken into account.

In both cases, liabilities, costs & expenses and/or consideration are reduced by 90 per cent to 10 per cent and only the relevant liabilities, costs & expenses and/or consideration are deducted from the agricultural value.

Tax Payable on Taxable Value

	Taxable value of this gift/inheritance	
	TV of agricultural € +	
	TV of non-agricultural €	€
Less	Small gift exemption where relevant	€3,000/NIL
Equals	Net taxable value of benefit	€
	Relevant threshold group A B C	
Less	Taxable value of prior aggregable benefits (SGE?)	€
Equals	Available threshold for this benefit	€
Taxable Excess [Taxable value less available threshold]		€
Tax @ 33% of Taxable excess		€

**	A	€400,000	B	€40,000	C	€20,000
Prior to 2 October 2024						
	A	€335,000	B	€32,500	C	€16,250

. . ..[insert name] should file and pay [delete "and pay" if a return is necessary but no tax is payable] by 31 October 2024 / 2025 14 November 2024 if paying and filing using ROS / No extension of deadline if paying and filing using ROS has been announced for 2025.

As referred to in 2.5.2, regardless of the taxable value of the benefit passing and its proportion of the applicable group threshold, the applicant must always file a return where agricultural relief is being claimed. See s. 46(4) of the CAT Consolidation Act, 2003 as amended by s. 55 of the Finance Act, 2020.

Clawback is dealt with in section 4.7.

This is the standard tax calculation template but the taxable values of the agricultural and non-agricultural assets are added together to get the taxable value of all assets passing.

It should be noted that the small gift exemption of €3,000 is never reduced by 90 per cent.

4.4.2 EXAMPLE WHERE ALL ASSETS PASSING ARE AGRICULTURAL IN NATURE

Daniel transfers land with livestock to his son Edward on 13 November 2024. The market value of the benefit is €2,000,000. There are liabilities, costs, and expenses of €85,000 (bank charge, stamp duty, and costs) paid by Edward, who also pays part consideration of €100,000. The entire benefit passing is agricultural. Edward has no other assets and has always worked on the land with his father.

Edward qualifies as a 'farmer' and has no aggregable prior benefits.

When calculating Edward's taxable value, the agricultural value of the property will be €200,000 (i.e. €2,000,000 less agricultural relief of 90 per cent €1,800,000).

Because the value of the property has been reduced by 90 per cent, the value of any deductions will also be reduced by 90 per cent and so he will only be allowed €8,500 and €10,000 respectively in respect of the liabilities and consideration.

We will not be using the 'Non-Agricultural' or 'Other' calculation part of the template.

The agricultural template for calculating the taxable value of an asset is calculated as follows:

Taxable Value of Agricultural Property

	Market value	**€2,000,000**
Less	Market value of exempt property (if any)	€ 0
Equals	Market value of agricultural property	€2,000,000
Less	Agricultural relief [90%]	€1,800,000
Equals	Agricultural value [10%]	€200,000
Less	Relevant portion of liabilities, costs & expenses **[reduced to 10%]**	€8,500
Equals	Incumbrance free value	€191,500
X	Value of limited interest 0.________	
Less	Relevant portion of consideration [in money or monies worth] €100,000 **[reduced to 10%]**	€10,000
Equals	**Taxable value**	**€181,500**

Tax is calculated on this taxable value in the normal manner, but using the agricultural template. When tax is calculated on this taxable value, then the SGE of €3,000 is deducted if appropriate. As noted above, the SGE is not reduced by 90 per cent.

Tax Payable on Taxable Value

	Taxable value of this gift/inheritance	
	TV of agricultural €181,500 +	
	TV of non-agricultural €0	**€181,500**
Less	Small gift exemption where relevant	€3,000/
Equals	Net taxable value of benefit	€178,500
	Relevant threshold group A ~~B C~~	€400,000
Less	Taxable value of prior aggregable benefits (SGE?)	€ 0
Equals	Available threshold for this benefit	€335,000
Taxable Excess [Taxable value less available threshold]		€ 0
Tax @ 33% of taxable excess		€ 0

** A € 400,000 B € 40,000 C €20,000

Prior to 2 October 2024

A €335,000 B € 32,500 C €16,250

Even though no tax is payable and the amount received is less than 80 per cent of the Group A Threshold, Edward should file an online return prior to 31 October/Mid November 2025 to comply with s. 46(4) as introduced by Section 55 Finance Act, 2020.

In all cases where agricultural relief is claimed on behalf of a client, the clawback provisions should be explained in writing. Clawback is dealt with in section 4.7.

This was a straightforward example where the entire property passing was agricultural and the liabilities and consideration could be deducted from the agricultural property after reducing them by 90 per cent.

4.4.3 APPORTIONMENT BETWEEN AGRICULTURAL AND NON-AGRICULTURAL PROPERTY

Where a gift or inheritance consists partly of agricultural property and partly of non-agricultural property, it may be necessary to apportion liabilities and consideration. It is only those liabilities referable to agricultural property which are reduced by 90 per cent (as above).

In general, liabilities which would be unsecured are payable rateably over the entire property comprised in the benefit. Accordingly, these liabilities must be apportioned between agricultural property and non-agricultural property comprised in the benefit. An example of these kinds of liabilities would be funeral and testamentary expenses when a farm and other assets are inherited as the residue of an estate.

Similarly, consideration must be apportioned between agricultural property and non-agricultural property comprised in the benefit.

4.4.3.1 Example of apportionment between agricultural and non-agricultural property

Francis inherited his late uncle's (sibling of a parent) entire estate, comprising a farm and various non-agricultural assets, on 12 November 2024. Probate issued on 22 February 2025 and this has been accepted as the valuation date. He has to pay all the various costs, liabilities, and expenses, none of which are secured on the land. He has no other assets. He did not live with his late uncle so Dwelling Relief does not apply. He did not work on the farm during his late uncle's lifetime and is not a 'favourite nephew' as defined in the second schedule to the CAT Consolidation Act, 2003 and covered in detail in **Chapter 6** of this manual.

He will lease the land, livestock, and machinery to a full time farmer for a period of ten years after taking the inheritance so he meets the active farmer requirements.

The values of the various assets and liabilities are as follows:

- Agricultural property (market value €900,000)
- Non-agricultural property (market value €100,000)
- Unsecured costs, liabilities, and expenses €10,000

Applying the farmer asset test:

Agricultural Property—Farmer Asset Test:

Market Value* of All Assets of Beneficiary [including Benefit]

		Non-agricultural assets		Agricultural assets		Total Assets
Property owned prior to the benefit		**€ 0**		**€ 0**		**€ 0**
Property the subject of the benefit	+	**€100,000**	+	**€900,000**	+	**€1,000,000**
Total	=	**€100,000**	=	**€900,000**	=	**€1,000,000**

$$\frac{\text{Agricultural Assets}}{\text{Total}\left(\text{Agricultural} + \text{Non} - \text{Agricultural Assets}\right)} \times 100 = 90\%$$

Francis **is** a farmer.

The next thing we have to do is apportion the costs between the agricultural and non-agricultural elements of the inheritance.

Proportion of debts referable to the **agricultural** element of the inheritance is:

$$\frac{\text{Agricultural}}{\text{Agricultural} + \text{Non Agricultural}} \times \text{Costs} = \text{share of costs relating to agricultural assets}$$

$$\frac{€900{,}000}{(€900{,}000 + €100{,}000)€1{,}000{,}000} x\, €10{,}000 = €9{,}000$$

Thus, of the €10,000 general costs, €9,000 refers to the agricultural assets passing.

This amount must be reduced by 90 per cent to 10 per cent to take agricultural relief into account giving allowable debts to set off against the agricultural assets of €900.

The proportion of debts referable to the **non-agricultural** element of the inheritance is:

$$\frac{\text{Non} - \text{Agricultural}}{\text{Agricultural} + \text{Non Agricultural}} \times \text{Costs} = \text{share of costs relating to non} - \text{agricultural assets}$$

$$\frac{€100{,}000}{(€900{,}000 + €100{,}000)€1{,}000{,}000} x\, €10{,}000 = €1{,}000$$

Thus, of the €10,000 general costs, €1,000 refers to the non-agricultural assets passing and this amount is not reduced.

The taxable value of the current benefit is calculated as follows:

Taxable Value—Non-Agricultural Property Calculation of Taxable Value:

	Market value	**€100,000**
Less	Exempt property	€ 0
Equals	Market value of taxable property	€100,000
Less	Relevant portion of liabilities, costs & expenses	€1,000
Equals	Incumbrance free value	€99,000
Less	Allowable consideration [in money or monies worth]	€ 0
Equals	Taxable value	€99,000

Taxable Value of Agricultural Property

	Market value	**€900,000**
Less	Market value of exempt property (if any)	€ 0
Equals	Market value of agricultural property	€900,000
Less	Agricultural relief [90%]	€810,000
Equals	Agricultural value [10%]	€90,000
Less	Relevant portion of liabilities, costs & expenses €9,000 [reduced to 10%]	€900
Equals	Incumbrance free value	€89,100
Less	Relevant portion of consideration [in money or monies worth] [reduced to 10%]	€ 0
Equals	Taxable value	€89,100

Tax Payable on Taxable Value

	Taxable value of this gift/inheritance	
	TV of agricultural €89,100 + TV of Non Agricultural €99,000	188,100
Less	Small gift exemption where relevant	~~€3,000~~/NIL
Equals	Net taxable value of benefit	€188,100
	Relevant threshold group ~~A~~ B ~~€~~	€40,000
Less	Taxable value of prior aggregable benefits (SGE?)	€ 0
Equals	Available threshold for this benefit	€
Taxable Excess [Taxable value less available threshold]		€148,100
Tax @ 33% of taxable excess		€ 48,873

**	A	€400,000	**B**	**€40,000**	C	€20,000
Prior to 2 October 2024						
	A	€335,000	B	€32,500	C	€16,250

Francis should pay and file prior to 31 October 2025 or mid November 2025 if both paying and filing using ROS.

In all cases where agricultural relief is claimed on behalf of a client, the clawback provisions should be explained in writing. Clawback is dealt with in section 4.7.

4.4.4 APPORTIONMENT BETWEEN EXEMPT, AGRICULTURAL AND NON-AGRICULTURAL

To further complicate matters, where the beneficiary is in a position to claim dwelling-house relief on the farmhouse along with agricultural relief on the farmland it may be necessary to apportion the costs three ways:

(1) **Non-deductible** for that portion of costs relating to the exempt farmhouse

(2) **Deductible at 10 per cent only** for that portion of costs relating to the agricultural property

(3) **Fully deductible** for that portion of costs relating to the non-agricultural property

4.4.4.1 Example of apportionment between agricultural, non-agricultural, and exempt

On 10 September 2024 Francis Rourke died and left his entire estate to his only child, Michelle Rourke. The Grant of Probate issued on 25 March 2025 and this has been accepted as the valuation date. All values are as at that date.

The inheritance consisted of a farm with a market value of €2,400,000 (consisting of a farmhouse valued at €200,000 and farmland valued at €2,200,000) together with livestock valued at €80,000 and a Bank of Ireland Deposit Account standing at €20,000 at the date of the inheritance.

Michelle had lived in the farmhouse with her late parents all her life and did not have any interest in any other dwelling. She inherited €60,000 on the death of her late mother in 2014 and of this she has €40,000 of non-agricultural assets remaining.

The general debts, costs, and expenses in connection with the administration of the estate amounted to €40,000.

Firstly, we consider if Michelle meets the active farmer requirements, and if she can meet these requirements we carry out the 'farmer asset test' to ascertain if Michelle Rourke is a farmer.

Assuming that Michelle intends to continue farming on a full time basis, the formula for the asset test is as follows:

All Assets of Beneficiary [Including Benefit]

Agricultural Property—Farmer Asset Test:

Market Value* of All Assets of Beneficiary [including Benefit]

		Non-agricultural assets		Agricultural assets		Total Assets
Property owned prior to the benefit		**€40,000**		**€ 0**		**€40,000**
Property the subject of the benefit	+	**€20,000**	+	**€2,480,000** *	+	**€2,500,000**
Total	=	**€60,000**	=	**€2,480,000**	=	**€2,540,000**

* For the purposes of the farmer asset test, we include the farmhouse as an 'agricultural asset' even though we will be claiming dwelling-house relief later on.

Total assets: €2,540,000 of which €2,480,000 consists of agricultural property and €60,000 of non-agricultural property. It is important to note that **all** current assets of the beneficiary are included, not just prior gifts. Current values for all assets are used.

Applying the test:

$$\frac{\text{Agricultural Assets}}{\text{Total}\left(\text{Agricultural} + \text{Non} - \text{Agricultural Assets}\right)} \times 100 = \_\_\_\%$$

$$\frac{€2{,}480{,}000}{€2{,}540{,}000} \times 100 = 97.64\%$$

Accordingly, Michelle is a farmer for inheritance tax purposes.

Calculating Taxable Value Payable—apportionment of costs

Our next step is to calculate the taxable value of the current benefit, the exempt, and the agricultural and non-agricultural parts of it. Prior benefits, while used for the farmer test, are not taken into account when calculating the taxable value of the current benefit.

Costs of €40,000 will have to be apportioned between: the Exempt Property of €200,000; the Agricultural Property of €2,280,000; and the Non-Agricultural Property of €20,000.

Exempt property

As Michelle has been living in the farmhouse that she has inherited and does not have an interest in any other dwelling, she should obtain Dwelling-House Exemption on the farmhouse. This means that the farmhouse will not be included in the agricultural property.

It also means that the portion of the costs relevant to the farmhouse will have to be calculated and deducted from overall costs, as these are non-deductible.

The formula used to calculate this is as follows:

Proportion of debts referable to the **exempt** element of the inheritance is:

$$\frac{\text{Exempt Assets Inherited}}{\text{Total Assets Inherited}} \times \text{Costs} = \text{share of costs relating to exempt assets}$$

$$\frac{€200,000}{€2,500,00} x\, €40,000 = €3,200$$

Of the costs of €40,000 incurred, €3,200 relates to the exempt farmhouse and cannot be deducted from the value of either the agricultural or non-agricultural assets.

See Dwelling-House Relief and Expenses at 3.13.3.

Agricultural Property

We now establish how much of the costs relate to the agricultural property, and the formula used to calculate this is as follows:

Proportion of debts referable to the **agricultural** element of the inheritance is:

$$\frac{\text{Agricultural Assets Inherited}}{\text{Total Assets Inherited}} \times \text{Costs} = \text{share of costs relating to agricultural assets}$$

$$(\text{Agricultural Assets Inherited}) / (\text{Total Assets Inherited}) \times \text{Costs}$$
$$= \text{share of costs relating to agricultural assets}$$

$$\frac{€2,280,000*}{€2,500,000} x\, €40,000 = €36,480**$$

$$(€2,280,000*) / €2,500,000 \times €36,480**$$

* The figure for agricultural assets will not be the same as the figure used in the farmer test, which included the exempt farmhouse. Only the farmland (€2,200,000) and the livestock (€80,000) are included.

** This figure of €36,480 will be reduced by 90 per cent to €3,648 when calculating the taxable value of the agricultural property as the market value of the agricultural property will be reduced by 90 per cent.

Non-agricultural (other) property

Finally, we establish how much of the costs relate to the non-agricultural and non-exempt or 'other' property, and the formula used to calculate this is as follows:

$$\frac{\text{Other Assets Inherited}}{\text{Total Assets Inherited}} \times \text{Costs} = \text{Share of costs relating to other assets}$$

$$(\text{Other Assets Inherited}) / (\text{Total Assets Inherited}) \times \text{Costs}$$
$$= \text{Share of costs relating to other assets}$$

$$\frac{€20,000}{€2,500,000} x\, €40,000 = €320$$

$$€20,000/€2,500,000 \times €40,000 = €320$$

This figure is not reduced.

To double-check our figures we add up:

Exempt €3200

Agricultural €36,480

Other €320

Total costs €40,000

Taxable values

Now that we have established the treatment of costs, we can establish the taxable value of the current benefit as follows:

Taxable Value—Non-Agricultural Property

Calculation of Taxable Value:

	Market value	**€20,000**
Less	Exempt property	€ 0
Equals	Market value of taxable property	€20,000
Less	Relevant portion of liabilities, costs & expenses	€320
Equals	Incumbrance free value	€19,680
Less	Allowable consideration [in money or monies worth]	€ 0
Equals	Taxable value	€19,680

Taxable Value of Agricultural Property

	Market value	**€2,480,000**
Less	Market value of exempt property (if any)	€200.000
Equals	Market value of agricultural property	€2,280,000
Less	Agricultural relief [90%]	€2,052,000
Equals	Agricultural value [10%]	€228,000
Less	Relevant portion of liabilities, costs & expenses	€3,648
Equals	Incumbrance free value	€89,100
Less	Relevant portion of consideration [in money or monies worth] [reduced to 10%]	€224,352
Equals	Taxable value	€224,352

The Exempt Property (the farmhouse) is always deducted from Agricultural Property because it was treated as agricultural property for the value part of the farmer test and if it did not qualify as exempt property, we would be claiming agricultural relief on it.

Tax Payable on Taxable Value

	Taxable value of this gift/inheritance		
	TV of agricultural €224,352 +		
	TV of non-agricultural €19,680		**€244,032**
Less	Small gift exemption where relevant		**~~€3,000~~/NIL**
Equals	Net taxable value of benefit		**€244,032**
	Relevant threshold group A ~~B C~~	€335,000	
Less	Taxable value of prior aggregable benefits (SGE?)	€60,000	
Equals	Available threshold for this benefit		**€275,000**
Taxable Excess [Taxable Value less Available Threshold]			**€NIL**
Tax @ 33% of Taxable Excess			**€NIL**

** A €400,000 B €40,000 C €20,000

Prior to 2 October 2024

A **€335,000** B €32,500 C €16,250

Michelle should file a return by 31 October 2025/mid November 2025 to comply with s. 46(4) as introduced by s. 55 Finance Act, 2020.

Clawback will be dealt with at **4.7**.

4.4.5 SECURED OR SPECIFIC LIABILITIES OR EXPENSE

Section 28(11) of the CAT Consolidation Act, 2003 provides generally that any deduction in respect of a liability that is an incumbrance on property is made against that property. As noted at Dwelling Exemption Expenses and a Charge on the Property in **3.13.4**, this means that where an item of property is specifically charged with a liability it must be deducted from that property in the first instance, for apportionment purposes. For example, a mortgage charged on lands is a secured liability. It is the *net or equitable* value (less the mortgage) that is used when calculating the apportionment of liabilities and consideration.

Similarly, if there is an expense which is applicable solely to the agricultural property, for example Stamp Duty and Land Registry Fees on farmland, it is not apportioned between agricultural and non-agricultural property and is deducted from the agricultural property only (at 10 per cent). This is not deducted from the market value of the agricultural assets in order to ascertain the net value for apportionment of unsecured liabilities, but is deducted directly from the agricultural property. In this manner its treatment is slightly different to a secured liability on agricultural property.

If in a particular case there were secured and also unsecured liabilities, the unsecured liabilities are chargeable rateably on agricultural property and non-agricultural property comprised in the benefit. Before apportioning those unsecured liabilities, the mortgage must first of all be deducted from the value of the agricultural property.

The apportionment of the unsecured liabilities is made over the *net* agricultural property (i.e. after deducting the mortgage) and the other non-agricultural property.

We deal first with an apportionment between agricultural and non-agricultural property where there is a charge on property, and then go on to deal with apportionment between agricultural, non-agricultural, and exempt property where there is a charge on property.

4.4.5.1 Example of apportionment between agricultural and non-agricultural with charged property

Reverting to the example of Francis at **4.4.3.1**: the beneficiary inherited agricultural property valued at €900,000 and non-agricultural property valued at €100,000 except that in addition to the costs of €10,000 the lands are **mortgaged** for €200,000.

For purposes of apportioning the unsecured debts, the secured debt of €200,000 must be deducted from the market value of the lands on which it is charged before apportioning debts.

While it is the **gross** value of land that is used for the farmer asset test, it is the **net** value (or the net equity in the land after deducting the mortgage) that is used in the apportionment of liabilities/consideration.

The Net Value of the Agricultural Property is calculated as follows:

Agricultural Value   Less Mortgage   Equals Net Agricultural Value

In this case

Agricultural value	**less mortgage**	**equals net agricultural value**
€900,000	less €200,000	equals €700,000

Net total costs are calculated as follows:

Net agricultural value	plus non-agricultural assets	equals net total assets
€700,000	plus €100,000	Equals €800,000

The proportion of debts referable to the agricultural element of the inheritance is:

$$\frac{\text{Net Agricultural Assets Inherited}}{\text{Net Total Assets Inherited}} \times \text{Costs} = \text{agricultural costs @ 10\%}$$

The proportion of debets referable to the agricultural element of the inheritance is:

$$\frac{700{,}000}{700{,}000 + 100{,}000} \times €10{,}000 = €8{,}750 @ 10\% = €875$$

The proportion of debets referable to the non-agricultural element of the inheritance is:

$$\frac{100{,}000}{700{,}000 + 100{,}000} \times €10{,}000 = €1{,}250$$

The full value of this can be deducted.

When calculating the taxable value of the agricultural property, the mortgage (at its 'agricultural value' of 10 per cent) is deducted as a cost liability and expense along with the allowable proportion of the 'shared' costs, liabilities, and expenses, as can be seen below:

The mortgage is €200,000, so the agricultural value of the mortgage will be €20,000 (i.e. 10 per cent).

We have already established that Francis is a farmer passing both the activity and the asset tests.

Taxable Value—Non-Agricultural Property

Calculation of Taxable Value:

	Market value	**€100,000**
Less	Exempt property	€ 0
Equals	Market value of taxable property	€100,000
Less	Relevant portion of liabilities, costs & expenses	€1,250
Equals	Incumbrance free value	€98,750
Less	Allowable consideration [in money or monies worth]	€ 0
Equals	Taxable value	€98,750

Taxable Value of Agricultural Property

	Market value	**€900,000**
Less	Market value of exempt property (if any)	€ 0
Equals	Market value of agricultural property	€900,000
Less	Agricultural relief [90%]	€810,000
Equals	Agricultural value [10%]	€90,000

(Continued)

(Continued)

Less	Relevant portion of liabilities, costs & expenses €8,750 [reduced to 10%] €875		
	Mortgage €200,000 [reduced to 10%] €20,000		€20,875
Equals	Incumbrance free value		€69,125
Less	Relevant portion of consideration [in money or monies worth] [reduced to 10%]		€ 0
Equals	**Taxable value**		€69,125

Tax Payable on Taxable Value

	Taxable value of this gift/inheritance		
	TV of agricultural €69,125 +		
	TV of non-agricultural €98,750		€167,875
Less	Small gift exemption where relevant		~~€3,000~~/NIL
Equals	Net taxable value of benefit		€167,875
	Relevant threshold group ~~A~~ B ~~C~~	€40,000	
Less	Taxable value of prior aggregable€ benefits (SGE?)	0	
Equals	Available threshold for this benefit		€40000
Taxable excess [taxable value less available threshold]			€127,875
Tax @ 33% of taxable excess			€42,198.75 Rounded up to €42,199

**	A	€400,000	B	**€40,000**	C	€20,000
Prior to 2 October 2024						
	A	€335,000	B	€32,500	C	€16,250

Francis should file and pay by 31 October 2025 or by mid November 2025 if both filing and paying online.

Clawback will be dealt with in section 4.7.

4.5 Full Example of Exempt, Agricultural, and Non-Agricultural Property with a Charge on Property

To give a further example of dealing with agricultural relief from start to finish:

On 20 October 2024 John Peterson died. He was a widower and left his entire estate to his adult daughter Jenny (date of birth 10 May 1995), who had always resided with him and his late wife in the family farmhouse. His assets were as follows:

Farmhouse	€ 200,000
Farmland	€1,800,000

(Continued)

(Continued)

(Note that the farmhouse and farmland are part of the same folio, which is subject to a bank charge of €120,000)	
Livestock, bloodstock, and farm machinery ('lb&fm')	€60,000
Bank account	€60,000
Total	**€4,180,000**

Funeral and testamentary expenses of €24,000 were incurred by Jenny. John Peterson's general debts (apart from the bank charge) amounted to €16,000. The Grant of Probate issued on 10 March 2025 and this has been agreed as the valuation date.

Jenny inherited €40,000 on the death of her mother in 2018. She drives a car valued at €12,000 and has €8,000 in a Credit Union account. These are her only assets.

The farmhouse, farmland and livestock, bloodstock, & farm machinery all meet the definition of 'agricultural property' and agricultural relief should be available in respect of these assets if Jenny qualifies as a 'farmer' on the valuation date. Jenny intends to continue to farm the land as an active farmer to meet the active farmer requirements.

4.5.1 FARMER ASSET TEST

Agricultural Property—Farmer Asset Test:

Market Value* of All Assets of Beneficiary [including Benefit]

		Non-agricultural assets		Agricultural assets		Total assets
Property owned prior to the benefit		€20,000		€ 0		€20,000
Property the subject of the benefit	+	€60,000	+	€2,060,000*	+	€2,060,000
Total	=	€80,000	=	€2,060,000	=	€2,140,000

$$\frac{\text{Agricultural Assets}}{\text{Total Assets}} \quad \frac{[€2{,}060{,}000]}{[€2{,}140{,}000]} \times 100 = 96.26\%$$

Jenny **is** a farmer.

* For the purposes of the farmer asset test, we include the farmhouse as an 'agricultural asset' even though we will be claiming dwelling-house relief later on.

Jenny is a 'farmer' as defined in s. 89 of the CAT Consolidation Act, 2003 (as amended) and can claim agricultural relief.

The next step is to calculate the taxable value of Jenny's inheritance.

4.5.2 DEALING WITH THE MORTGAGE

The mortgage is a charge on the entire farm including the farmhouse, which is exempt. That portion of the mortgage relating to the farmhouse cannot be deducted from the taxable value of the remainder of the farmland. See s. 28(5) and **3.13.3.**

To calculate the 'exempt' value of the mortgage, the following formula is used:

$$\frac{\text{Value of 'exempt' farmhouse}}{\text{Value of entire farm and farmhouse}} \times \text{value of mortage} = \text{exempt portion of mortgage}$$

$$\frac{€200,000}{€2,000,000} \times €120,000 = €12,000$$

€12,000 of the mortgage relates to the exempt dwelling-house and cannot be deducted from the non-exempt portion of the farm.

The 'net' or 'equitable' value of the farmhouse is €188,000. It will be this net or equitable value which will be used when apportioning the general debts between exempt, agricultural, and ordinary.

The remainder of the mortgage (€120,000 – €12,000 = €108,000) will be deducted from the value of the farmland before apportioning the general debts and funeral and testamentary expenses between the agricultural and non-agricultural assets passing as outlined in **4.4.3.1.**

Market value of farmland	€1,800,000
Less mortgage relating to farmland	€108,000
Net (or equitable) value of farmland	€1,692,000

The general debts, and funeral and testamentary expenses of €40,000, will be apportioned between the net equitable value of the exempt farmhouse, the net equitable value of the agricultural assets including the farmland, and the non-agricultural assets in the proportions set out in the following section.

4.5.3 APPORTIONMENT OF COSTS

Exempt	(Net value of farmhouse)	€188,000
Agricultural	(Net value of farmland) €1,692,000 + livestock, bloodstock & farm machinery of €60,000	€1,752,000
Non-agricultural	(bank account)	€60,000
Total net value		€2,000,000

The **Exempt** portion of the €40,000 is calculated as:

$$\frac{\text{Net Value of Exempt farmhouse}}{\text{Net Total Assets Inherited}} \times \text{General Costs} = \text{Exempt portion of costs}$$

This gives us:

$$\frac{€188,000}{€2,000,000} \times €40,000 = €3,760$$

This portion of the costs will be exempt and cannot be deducted against any non-exempt asset passing.

The agricultural portion of the €40,000 is calculated as:

$$\frac{\text{Net Value of Agricultural assets}}{\text{Net Total Assets Inherited}} \times \text{General Costs} = \text{Agricultural portion of costs @ 10\%}$$

This gives us:

$$\frac{€1,752,000}{€2,000,000} \times €40,000 = €35,040@10\% = €3,504$$

This will be reduced by 90 per cent to 10 per cent to allow €3,504 to be deducted against the agricultural value of the agricultural assets after agricultural relief has been allowed.

Of the remaining mortgage of €108,000, only €10,800 would be deducted from the agricultural value of the agricultural assets after agricultural relief has been allowed.

The €10,800 relates to the allowable agricultural value of the mortgage.

The non-agricultural or '**Other**' portion of the €40,000 is calculated as:

$$\frac{\text{Net Value of } \textbf{Other} \text{ assets}}{\text{Net Total Assets Inherited}} \times \text{General Costs} = \textbf{Other} \text{ portion of costs}$$

This gives us:

$$\frac{€60,000}{€2,000,000} \times €40,000 = €1,200$$

These three figures (€3,760 + €35,040 + €1,200) add up to €40,000.

Having established how the general costs are apportioned, we now go on to establish the taxable value of firstly the agricultural assets and then the other (non-agricultural) assets.

4.5.4 TAXABLE VALUE OF ASSETS

Taxable Value of Non-Agricultural Property:

Calculation of Taxable Value:

	Market value	**€60,000**
Less	Exempt property	€ 0
Equals	Market value of taxable property	€60,000
Less	Relevant portion of liabilities, costs & expenses	€1,250
Equals	Incumbrance free value	€58,800
Less	Allowable consideration [in money or monies worth]	€ 0
Equals	**Taxable value**	€58,800

Taxable Value of Agricultural Property:

Calculation of Taxable Value:

	Market value	**€2,060,000**
Less	Market value of exempt property (if any)	€200,000
Equals	Market value of agricultural property	€1,860,000
Less	Agricultural relief [90%]	€1,764,000
Equals	Agricultural value [10%]	€186,000
Less	Relevant portion of liabilities, costs & expenses €35,040 [reduced to 10%] €3,504 +	

(Continued)

(Continued)

	Mortgage €108,000 [reduced to 10%] €10,800	€14,304
Equals	Incumbrance free value	€171,696
Less	Relevant portion of consideration [in money or monies worth] [reduced to 10%]	€ 0
Equals	**Taxable value**	€171,696

4.5.5 TAX PAYABLE ON TAXABLE VALUE

	Taxable Value of this gift/inheritance		
	TV of Agricultural €171,696 +		
	TV of Non-Agricultural €58,800		€230,496
Less	Small gift exemption where relevant		~~€3,000~~/NIL
Equals	Net taxable value of benefit		€230,496
	Relevant threshold group A ~~B C~~	€400,000	
Less	Taxable value of prior aggregable benefits (SGE?)	€40,000	€40,0000
Equals	Available threshold for this benefit		€360,000
Taxable excess [taxable value less available threshold]			€ NIL
Tax @ 33% of taxable excess			€ NIL

** A	**€400,000**	B	€40,000	C	€20,000
Prior to 2 October 2024					
A	€335,000	B	€32,500	C	€16,250

Jenny should file an online return by mid November 2025 to comply with s. 46(4) as introduced by s. 55 Finance Act, 2020, even though no tax is payable.

Clawback is dealt with in **4.7**.

4.6 Conditional Gift

Section 89(3) provides that where a gift or inheritance (e.g. cash) taken by a donee or successor on condition that it be invested in agricultural property is so invested within two years of the date of the gift/inheritance, then such gift/inheritance will be deemed to have consisted of agricultural property at the date of the gift/inheritance and at the valuation date. This ensures that, all other conditions being satisfied, such gift/inheritance will qualify for relief, despite the fact that the benefit did not consist of agricultural property at the date of the gift/inheritance *and* at the valuation date, as required in s. 89(2).

For the purposes of the farmer asset test, the conditional bequest is treated as agricultural property.

This can be a very useful tax planning device where, for example, an estate is 'cash rich' at certain times of year (post-harvest, for example), or where the disponer intends giving a sum of money to a 'farmer' to ensure that the money can be received as tax-efficiently as possible. However, when drafting a will clause to this effect it is important to ensure that the gift does not lapse if the beneficiary fails to invest in agricultural land within the two-year period, by providing for a substitutionary benefit.

A clause giving effect to the testator's wishes could be drafted as follows:

> *I give and bequeath the sum of €X, 000 (X thousand Euro) to my [state relationship if any] [state full name and address] [if necessary, further identify the beneficiary, for example: my nephew Patrick Murphy, son of my sister Mary Murphy of address . . .] on condition that the whole or part of the aforementioned sum of money be invested in agricultural property within two years of the granting of representation to this my will.*

However, when drafting a will clause to this effect it is important to ensure that the gift does not lapse if the beneficiary fails to invest in agricultural land within the two-year period, by providing for a substitutionary benefit.

As this is a conditional bequest, care should be taken to confirm with the client what is to happen if the condition is not met, that is, if the beneficiary fails to invest in agricultural land within the two-year period. If the will is silent on the matter, the bequest will lapse and fall into the residue of the estate.

> *In the event that the whole or any part of the aforementioned sum has not been so invested by my aforementioned [identify beneficiary] within two years of the granting of representation to this my will, then and in that event, I give and bequeath the remainder of the aforementioned sum to my aforementioned [identify beneficiary] for his/her [delete as appropriate] own use and benefit absolutely without any condition attached.*

Please note that this clause does not refer to special powers of the executors/trustees to ensure that their secondary liability to tax is not incurred by the beneficiary not investing the money.

4.7 Clawback of Relief

Throughout this chapter, in every calculation of tax payable, it has been noted that clawback will be dealt with at **4.7**. Students have dealt with clawback in relation to dwelling-house exemption and we will now deal with clawback of agricultural relief as it arises.

4.7.1 INTRODUCTION

Section 89(4), as amended, deals with potential clawback of the relief. Since the coming into force of the amended clawback, clawback is now two-fold: disposal of agricultural property and ceasing to be an active farmer.

4.7.2 DISPOSAL OF PROPERTY

This provides that where agricultural property or any property *directly or indirectly replacing it* (except crops, trees, or underwood—see below) are sold or compulsorily acquired within six years of the date of the gift/inheritance and are not replaced:

(1) within one year if sold; and

(2) within six years if compulsorily acquired (note that prior to 25 March 2002 the period was four years)

then the agricultural relief relating to that amount of the proceeds of sale or compulsory acquisition not re-invested in agricultural property is 'clawed back' and that portion of the benefit is charged to tax as if agricultural relief never applied.

It should be noted that the clawback provisions do not normally apply to agricultural property, which consists of farm machinery, livestock, and blood stock which are sold and replaced in the normal course of farming, as these are constantly sold and replaced by farmers on an ongoing basis. However, if for example a beneficiary were to inherit a farm with livestock and farm machinery and if that beneficiary were to lease the farm and sell the livestock and farm machinery with no intention of replacing those assets, then in that case such sale would be considered a disposal subject to clawback.

As noted at **4.3.1**, it is no longer a specific requirement that the beneficiary be resident in the State for the three years succeeding the year of the benefit. However, if farming as an 'active farmer' then residence would be required.

The Revenue Commissioners accept that the proceeds from a disposal of agricultural property that needs to be expended in acquiring other agricultural property in order to avoid a clawback of the relief are the net sale proceeds after Capital Gains Tax is paid, where the Capital Gains Tax is paid out of the disposal proceeds.

It is not necessary that reinvestment is made in the same type of agricultural property. For example, the proceeds from the sale of land could be reinvested in livestock or machinery without losing the relief.

The expenditure of sale proceeds on the construction of new agricultural buildings on other land owned by the farmer or the expenditure of sale proceeds on the demolition of old agricultural buildings on such other land and their replacement by the construction of new agricultural buildings will not result in a clawback of the relief. This is the situation where the construction of the new or replacement agricultural buildings improves the value of the agricultural lands on which they are built.

4.7.3 CLAWBACK AND THE 'ACTIVE FARMER'

As noted earlier, s. 82 of the Finance Act, 2014, when introducing the concept of the 'active farmer', also brought in for the first time clawback where the beneficiary or the lessee ceases to actively farm the land within six years of the valuation date other than on the death of the beneficiary or the lessee during this period.

As noted above when dealing with the 'active farmer', it is not envisaged that the Revenue Commissioners will spend vast amounts of time seeking out 'inactive farmers'; however, appropriate records should be maintained and stored. Clawback will be calculated as outlined below and where the lease to the active farmer is terminated or surrendered within the six year period, the beneficiary has one year in which to re-lease the farm for at least the remaining portion of the six-year period.

Since 1 January 2015, there are three separate clawback provisions, as follows:

1. The six-year disposal clawback—agricultural relief is clawed back where agricultural property is disposed of or compulsorily acquired within six years of the gift or inheritance and the proceeds are not reinvested in other agricultural property within one year of the sale or within six years of the compulsory purchase.
2. The six-year activity clawback—agricultural relief is clawed back if the agricultural land is not actively farmed, or leased to an 'active' farmer throughout the six-year period beginning on the valuation date.
3. The development land clawback—if development land is sold during the period running from the sixth to the tenth anniversary of the date of the gift or inheritance, relief is claimed back. During this time there is no reinvestment option to avoid a clawback of relief. See **4.7.7** below.

Strictly read, the revised legislation requires the 80 per cent financial test to be met throughout the six-year 'clawback' window. Revenue have confirmed that in practice the 80 per cent farmer asset test only needs to be met on the valuation date.

4.7.4 CLAWBACK OF MARKET VALUE

The legislation was amended in 2005 (s. 135(1) (a) Finance Act, 2005) with regard to quantifying the clawback amount and it was confirmed that the criteria is market value, not acreage of land involved, and if there is partial reinvestment the clawback is confined to the amount not reinvested.

In order to ascertain the amount to be clawed back, the formula applying is based on the following figures:

1. Original Market Value of Agricultural Property at Time of Acquisition
2. Proceeds of Disposal
3. Proceeds of Disposal not Re-invested in Agricultural Property

And is applied as follows:

$$\text{O M V of Agricultural Property} \times \frac{\text{Proceeds of Disposal not Re-invested}}{\text{Proceeds of Disposal}} = \text{Clawback}$$

It should be noted that this applies to a 'Disposal', not just a 'Sale'. The act now defines proceeds from a disposal as an amount equal to the market value of the consideration (not just cash) received for the disposal. This means that where the farm is sold to a family member (e.g.) for less than its market value or for assets that are valued at less than the market value of the farm, there is a clawback of any sum received.

Where the 'disposal' is a gift of the agricultural property with no proceeds received, it is treated as a disposal, and agricultural relief is clawed back. This has been confirmed by Revenue in the most recent version of the CAT Manual Part 11 Agricultural Relief, part 11.10.1: <http://www.revenue.ie/en/tax-professionals/tdm/capital-acquisitions-tax/cat-part11.pdf>

The change in the calculation of clawback was to avoid the situation where a beneficiary inherited, say for example, 10 acres of land with a development value of €5,000,000 per acre, sold it, and 'replaced' it with 10 acres of poor land in a remote area with a value of €5,000 per acre. If such a case were to occur now, the beneficiary would have to invest the entire proceeds of sale in agricultural property to avoid clawback.

An example of this would be a situation where agricultural property valued at €600,000 was inherited in 2017. In 2020 the entire property is sold for €800,000 and replaced with other agricultural property valued at €500,000. In this case, €300,000 is not re-invested in agricultural property:

1. Original Market Value of Agricultural Property at Time of Acquisition €600,000
2. Proceeds of Disposal €800,000
3. Proceeds of Disposal not Re-invested in Agricultural Property €300,000

And is applied as follows:

$$\text{O M V of Agricultural Property} \times \frac{\text{Proceeds of Disposal not Re-invested}}{\text{Proceeds of Disposal}} = \text{Clawback}$$

$$€600{,}000 \times \frac{€300{,}000}{€800{,}000} = €225{,}000$$

In this case the agricultural relief on €225,000 will be clawed back and taxed at the full rate.

4.7.5 ANTI-AVOIDANCE

The reason why the sub-section refers to property directly or indirectly replacing it is an anti-avoidance measure. Otherwise a person could inherit farmland, sell it and replace it with other farmland of the same value, and then sell that farmland without clawback.

The legislation was further amended in 2010 to cover the following scenario:

A married individual owns farmland which is not subject to clawback.

He inherits further farmland which he wishes to sell so he transfers his original farmland into the sole name of his spouse. He sells the inherited farmland within six years and 'buys back' the farmland he had transferred to his spouse with the proceeds of sale.

This 'loophole' was 'plugged' by s. 146 of the Finance Act, 2010 for transfers executed on or after 4 February 2010.

The section was further amended by s. 3 and Schedule 3 of the Finance (No. 3) Act, 2011, which deleted the word 'spouse' and replaced it with 'spouse and civil partner' in respect of gifts and inheritances after 1 January 2011.

The section was further amended in 2011 to correct a drafting error that enabled a beneficiary to dispose of the farmland on the same day as the gift and avoid the clawback. The word 'after' was replaced with 'commencing on' and applies to gifts and inheritances taken on or after 21 January 2011.

Since the coming into force of the 'active farmer' requirements on 1 January 2015, any sale of the property, replacement, and subsequent sale of the replacement property would fall foul of the 'active farmer' requirements.

4.7.6 DEATH OF BENEFICIARY DURING CLAWBACK PERIOD

A proviso states that this provision shall not have effect where the beneficiary dies before the property is disposed of or compulsorily acquired. For example, if a person receives agricultural property and dies after three years but within six years, passing the property on to a second beneficiary, then in that case there is no clawback.

Death is not seen as a tax-avoidance scheme. However, a sale or compulsory acquisition by the second beneficiary within six years of the date of the first disposition to the original beneficiary would be subject to a clawback.

4.7.7 FURTHER CLAWBACK IF SOLD AFTER SIX YEARS AND BEFORE TEN YEARS

Section 118(2) of the Finance Act, 2006 introduced a new Chapter 2A: Clawback of Agricultural Relief or Business Relief: Development Land to the CAT Consolidation Act, 2003, contained in a new s. 102A. This new 'extended partial' clawback applies to benefits taken after 2 February 2006.

This clawback will apply if a benefit is granted agricultural relief and the benefit includes 'development land' as defined in the section. 'Development land' for this purpose is land whose market value exceeds its current use value and 'current use value' is defined in the section as the market value of the land if it were and would remain unlawful to carry out development on the land.

If this development land is disposed of in whole or in part in the period between end of year 6 and end of year 10 after the date of the gift or inheritance, a clawback will arise, based on the development use value (market value less current use value at the valuation date) of the development land.

The development value of the land (market value less current use value) will be taxed as if no relief applied.

Section 68 of the Finance Act, 2011 also applies to this section for gifts and inheritances taken on or after 21 January 2011, substituting the word 'commencing' to ensure that the clawback applies where a disposal takes place on the sixth anniversary of the actual date of the gift/inheritance itself.

A further clarification in 2007 confirmed that interest in such a clawback would run from the date of disposal of the development property for clawback events triggered after 1 February 2007.

This also applies to business relief, and the consequences of such a clawback are outlined in more detail at 5.15.5.

4.7.8 ADVISING A CLIENT IN RELATION TO CLAWBACK

Whenever a client claims agricultural relief, the potential clawback, including a failure to remain an 'active farmer', must be pointed out to that client, in writing, for future reference.

When acting on behalf of a client who is considering selling farmland, one of the factors that must be ascertained is whether that client has obtained agricultural relief in the past and any potential clawback that may accrue.

The solicitor should be in a position to make a rough calculation of the potential clawback arising in order to ensure that the client makes an informed decision whether to sell or not.

However, as in all commercial decisions, taxation—while an important factor and one that the client has to take into account—may not be the primary factor in taking such a decision.

4.8 Appropriation

A personal representative under s. 55 of the Succession Act, 1965 may appropriate a holding of land in satisfaction of a legacy. Provided the land was part of the disponer's estate at the date of his death, the appropriation will be read back to that date to enable the legatee to qualify for agricultural relief. Section 89(5) treats the lands as being comprised in the inheritance both at the date of the inheritance and at the valuation date.

Section 55 of the Succession Act gives power to the personal representative to appropriate assets towards a particular legacy with the consent of the legatee and if the other legatees have no valid objection. A will of the deceased testator can give power to the personal representative to appropriate without the consent of the various legatees.

The power of appropriation can therefore be used to direct agricultural property towards a beneficiary who would qualify as a 'farmer' and away from a beneficiary who might not qualify as a 'farmer'.

The Revenue would normally accept any *bona fide* appropriation, keeping in mind that under s. 55 of the Succession Act the personal representatives must deal equitably with the rights of the various beneficiaries.

For further detail on s. 55 and appropriation, see Chapters 3 and 12 of *Wills, Probate and Estates*.

4.9 Timber

Section 89(6) of the CAT Consolidation Act, 2003 states that agricultural relief applies to trees or underwood which are part of the definition of agricultural property even though the beneficiary may not be a 'farmer' as defined. Furthermore, a sale or compulsory acquisition of such timber at any time does not cause a clawback of the agricultural relief.

It appears from the wording of s. 89(6) already referred to, that timber standing on woodland can be regarded as agricultural property independently of that woodland. It follows that a subsequent sale of standing timber will not trigger a clawback of agricultural relief already given in respect of that timber whether or not the woodland on which it stands is sold at the same time.

4.10 Business Relief on Agricultural Property

Where a gift or inheritance of 'agricultural property' is taken on or after 10 February 2000 it is possible to consider a claim for business relief where an individual does not qualify for agricultural relief.

Section 102 of the CAT Consolidation Act, 2003 provides that:

> *Where the whole or part of the taxable value of any taxable gift or taxable inheritance is attributable to agricultural property to which s 89 (2) applies, such whole or part of the taxable value is not reduced under this Chapter* [i.e. Chapter 2, the Business Relief Chapter].

The Revenue Commissioners interpret this section as meaning that a beneficiary can only apply for business relief on agricultural property where the beneficiary does not qualify as a farmer under the CAT Consolidation Act, 2003, s. 89(2).

The margin note beside s. 102 says 'Avoidance of Double Relief' and initially solicitors interpreted the section as meaning that it was not possible to claim agricultural relief successfully and then claim business relief on the taxable value *after* applying agricultural relief (reducing the market value by 90 per cent to leave a value of 10 per cent and then to reduce by a further 90 per cent of that 10 per cent, leaving a taxable value of 1 per cent of the market value), but Revenue go a step further, stating that a beneficiary cannot claim business relief on agricultural property unless that beneficiary fails the farmer test.

The procedure adopted by the Revenue Commissioners is that a beneficiary applies for agricultural relief first, and if the beneficiary fails to qualify as a farmer, he or she then applies for business relief.

There are distinctions between the two reliefs, which, although similar in intention (to provide a 90 per cent relief) are quite different in their application. These will be dealt with in the next chapter and this particular topic shall be revisited in **5.14**.

CHAPTER 5

BUSINESS RELIEF

5.1 Introduction and Brief History

Agricultural relief was provided from the coming into force of the CAT Act, 1976 but there was no similar relief for anyone intending to pass on a business. A form of business relief was available in the UK, and it was felt that a similar relief should be introduced in Ireland. Sections 124 to 135 inclusive of the Finance Act, 1994 introduced a relief in respect of **relevant business property** comprised in a benefit taken by a beneficiary on or after 11 April 1994.

These sections, which were much amended by subsequent Finance Acts, are now replaced in their entirety by Part 10, Chapter 2 of the CAT Consolidation Act, 2003 (ss. 90–102A) as amended by subsequent Finance Acts.

Practitioners are referred to the Revenue CAT Work Manual, in particular Part 12, which can be downloaded from the Revenue website at <www.revenue.ie> and to the CAT Consolidation Act, 2003 (as amended by subsequent Act) Notes for Guidance up to Finance Act, 2023 also available from the Revenue website.

The purpose of the relief has been stated as being to prevent the sale or break-up of businesses, especially family businesses, to pay CAT liability and to encourage and reward enterprise. For this reason, the relief is aimed at donors transferring a business, which they have owned and run, to beneficiaries who will continue to own and run the business. For these reasons the relief is limited to a 'trading' business or assets of a trading business which are going to people who will own, run, and/or control that business.

At present the relief is 90 per cent and has been since 23 January 1997. This is provided for in s. 92 of the CAT Consolidation Act, 2003.

The relief applies to gifts or inheritances taken of **relevant business property** comprised in the disposition (or owned by the disponer or his/her spouse) for the **relevant period** immediately prior to the gift/inheritance.

It should be noted that it is the **taxable value** of the relevant business property, which obtains business relief. This differs from agricultural relief where the **market value**, the first step in arriving at the taxable value, obtains the relief.

5.1.1 'MAINSTREAM CAT ONLY'

It should also be noted that while the relief applies to limited and remainder interests (s. 90(4)), it applies to mainstream CAT only and does not apply to Discretionary Trust Tax (s. 91); that is, business relief is not available on Discretionary Trust Tax. Business assets held in a discretionary trust can avail of the relief (if applicable) on being appointed out of the trust.

5.1.2 CLAIMING THE RELIEF

In a similar fashion to agricultural relief, a return must be filed online within the appropriate deadlines in order to successfully claim the relief even if no tax is payable. As noted earlier at **3.5.2**, in order to successfully claim business relief, the taxpayer has to file a return regardless of the taxable value of the business property passing and its proportion or percentage of the applicable group threshold.

5.2 Business Relief Calculation Template

For business relief the standard template is amended once again to reflect the particular requirements applicable to business relief. The business property template consists of:

- Relevant Business Property Test including Relevant Ownership Period
- Taxable Value of Non-Business Property (if any)
- Taxable Value of relevant business property
- Tax Payable on Taxable Value of All Assets.

5.2.1 RELEVANT BUSINESS PROPERTY TEST

Relevant Ownership Period Insert 'Yes' or 'No' as appropriate

Did the disponer own the business property for the relevant period?

Two years if an inheritance directly from the disponer

Five years in every other case

Relevant Business Property Test Insert 'Yes' or 'No' as appropriate

In order to be eligible to qualify for business relief either question 1 (a) or (b) must be answered 'Yes'.

1. Is the 'Relevant Business' Property

   a) A qualifying business or an interest in a qualifying business—e.g. a sole trader or a partnership?

   And/Or

   b) Unquoted shares in a limited company carrying on a qualifying business (See Question 3)

If business assets are passing outside a business (either a limited company or a partnership) then question 2 must be answered 'yes' if the business assets are to qualify for business relief.

2. Are there business assets owned by the disponer and used by either a qualifying business s/he was a partner in or a limited company s/he 'controlled' 50%+ passing with the qualifying business or an interest in the qualifying business?

This will be dealt with in **5.3.1**.

If unquoted shares in a limited company are passing then at least one of questions 3 (a), (b) or (c) must be answered 'Yes' in order to qualify for business relief.

For question 3 the relevant amount of shares means the current gift/inheritance together with any shares already owned by the beneficiary.

3. If the Relevant Business Property consists of unquoted shares in a limited company carrying on a qualifying business does the Beneficiary:

   (a) have 10% or more of the voting shares if a full-time officer or employee of the company

   And/Or

   (b) more than 25% of the voting shares

   And/Or

   (c) control the company within the meaning of s. 27 (Five or fewer family members control 50%+ of the voting shares).

'Section 27 control' will be dealt with in **5.4**.

5.2.2 TAXABLE VALUE OF NON-BUSINESS PROPERTY

	Market Value of Property	€
Less	Market value of exempt property (if any)	€
Equals	Market value of taxable property	€
Less	Applicable liabilities, costs & expenses (if any)	€
Equals	Incumbrance free value	€
X	Value of limited interest 0.________	
Less	Consideration [in money or monies worth]	€
Equals	**Taxable value of non-business property**	€

This is similar to the 'standard' taxable value of property or the taxable value of non-agricultural property dealt with in **Chapter 4**. Again, it should be noted that for the rest of this chapter we will not be dealing with limited interests. It should also be noted that treatment of costs, liabilities, and expenses, and consideration are different to the treatment of same under agricultural relief. Costs and liabilities will be dealt with in **5.12**.

5.2.3 TAXABLE VALUE OF BUSINESS PROPERTY

	Market value of relevant business property	€
Less	Liabilities and consideration	€
Equals	Taxable value	€
Less	Value attributable to excepted assets	€
Equals	Value of relevant non-excepted business property	€
Less	Any property subject to replacement / successive benefit rules	€
Equals	Incumbrance free value of relevant business property on which relief is granted	€
Less	90% business relief	€
Equals	Taxable value of all qualifying relevant business property	€
Plus	Excepted assets and assets not eligible for relief	
Equals	**Taxable value of all business property**	

This will be dealt with in detail in **5.4.2** but it is important to note that liabilities, costs, expenses, and consideration are deducted from the Market Value to arrive at the Net Market Value for Taxation.

See for example where someone inherits the family business with a market value of €4,100,000. Costs, liabilities, and expenses amounted to €100,000 and there was no consideration leaving a Net Market Value for Taxation of €4,000,000.

Assuming business relief applies to all these assets, the taxable value will be reduced by 90 per cent to 10 per cent, that is, €400,000.

5.2.4 TAX PAYABLE ON TAXABLE VALUE OF ALL ASSETS

	Taxable value of this gift/inheritance **TV of Business € + +** **TV of Non-Business €**	**€**
Less	Small gift exemption where relevant	€3,000 / NIL
Equals	Net taxable value of benefit	€
	Relevant threshold group A B C	€
Less	Taxable value of prior aggregable benefits (SGE?)	€
Equals	Available threshold for this benefit	€
Taxable excess [taxable value less available threshold]		€
Tax @ 33% of taxable excess		**€**

** A € 400,000 B € 40,000 C €20,000

Prior to 2 October 2024

A €335,000 B € 32,500 C €16,250

. . . . should file and pay [delete 'and pay' if no tax is payable] by 31 October 2025 ormid November 2025 if both filing and paying online using ROS.

As referred to in **2.5.2**, regardless of the taxable value of the benefit passing and its proportion of the applicable group threshold, the applicant must always file a return where business relief is being claimed. See Section 46 (4) of the CAT Consolidation Act, 2003 as amended by Section 55 of the Finance Act, 2020.

This is similar to the calculation of taxable value as dealt with in para 4.7 for agricultural and non-agricultural assets but in this case business and non-business assets are added together to get the taxable value of all assets passing.

It should be noted that, as with agricultural relief, the Small Gift Exemption of €3,000 is never reduced by 90 per cent.

5.2.4.1 Clawback?

Clawback is dealt with in s. 5.15.

5.3 Relevant Business Assets

A 'relevant business asset', as the name suggests, is an asset of a business where both the business and the asset qualify for business relief.

5.3.1 WHAT IS A BUSINESS?

The word 'business' is not defined but is stated in s. 90, the interpretation section, to include:

> *A business carried on in the exercise of a profession or a vocation but does not include a business carried on otherwise than for gain.*

A business includes all the various types of business carried on for profit (including the professions, law, medicine, accountancy, etc.) whether incorporated or not. A conacre letting, for example, has recently been held to be a business, as the owner of the land in that case had certain supervisory and management duties (*AE v Revenue Commissioners* [1994] 2 ITR 668).

It has been stated that the word business means almost anything which is an occupation as distinguished from a pleasure. There are a number of English cases which are quoted by the Revenue Commissioners with approval—these include 'anything which occupies the time and attention and labour of a man for the purpose of profit' (Jessel MR in *Smith v Anderson* [1880] 15 ChD 247, at 258).

5.3.2 EXCLUDED TYPES OF BUSINESSES

Certain types of businesses are specifically excluded from being relevant business property and are thus specifically excluded from the relief.

5.3.2.1 Investment business

Section 93(3) excludes a business or interest in a business dealing in currencies or securities or stocks or shares or lands or buildings or making or holding investments *on its own behalf*. This excluded list would include businesses of stockbrokers and discount houses investing their own money. It is presumed that a business dealing in land or buildings would not include a business consisting mainly of building construction or land development, that is, that such a business would be able to avail of the relief. Other problematic issues that arise when acting for a business dealing in land or buildings include caravan parks, chalets, and other cases involving the admission of people onto land.

The Revenue CAT TDM Part 12 at pages 11 and 12: <http://www.revenue.ie/en/tax-professionals/tdm/capital-acquisitions-tax/cat-part12.pdf>

gives guidelines as to whether a business is wholly or mainly an investment business.

In deciding whether a business is wholly or mainly an investment business the Revenue Booklet states that regard will be had to the following:

- the ratios of asset value and profit attributable to trading and investment respectively;
- the ratio of turnover to investment income;
- whether the employees are engaged more on the trading side than on the investment side and vice versa;
- whether there are any particular reasons for low trading profits;
- the use to which the investments or the income from investments is put.

If the business consists *wholly or mainly* of any one of the above excluded businesses the entire business is denied business relief. It is worth remembering that businesses that engage in investment on behalf of others, such as estate agents, merchant bankers, investment brokers, and stockbrokers, are not excluded businesses. This should be distinguished from a business whose primary function is to invest on its own behalf.

5.3.2.2 'Wholly or mainly'

In general, 'mainly' means more than 50 per cent, looking at the business over a reasonable period prior to the gift or inheritance, to allow for temporary fluctuations in activity or performance. If, however, there has been a clear and definite change in direction, only the position after that change will be taken into account.

If, on the other hand, the business does not consist wholly or mainly of a business excluded by sub-section (3), the entire business is treated as relevant business property, but the part referable to the excluded portion of the business is ignored for the purpose of calculating the relief (s. 100(3)).

5.3.2.3 Gift of a 'wholly or mainly' investment business

Taking the example at **9.2.3** where a person inherited a family business with Net Market Value for Taxation of €4,000,000 after deduction of all costs, liabilities, and expenses:

If 60 per cent of that business was an investment business and 40 per cent a trading business that person would not obtain business relief. If the percentages were reversed (i.e. 40 per cent investment business and 60 per cent trading business) the business would be relevant business property but 60 per cent only of the taxable value would obtain relief ((€2,400,000 would be reduced by 90% to €240,000) while the other 40 per cent, that is, €1,600,000, would be taxed at the full value.

This would give a total taxable value of (€240,000 plus €1,600,000) €1,840,000 as follows, completing Panel 2 of Appendix B—business relief calculation.

5.3.2.4 Holding companies Section 93 (4)

On the assumption that all the other conditions for granting the relief are satisfied, s. 93 (4) provides that shares of a holding company will qualify as relevant business property if the business of the holding company consists wholly or mainly in being a holding company for subsidiaries that carry on non-excluded businesses.

The value of those shares, for the purpose of the relief, will, however, be determined on the basis that any subsidiaries or associated companies carrying on excluded business are ignored.

'Holding company' and 'subsidiary' are defined in the Companies Act, 2014 s. 8 (1) and s. 7 respectively.

5.4 Relevant Business Property (Section 93)

The intention of the legislation is that a business engaged in non-excluded activities is controlled and run by a disponer and then passed on to a beneficiary who will then control and run that business. For this reason, the type of property that can avail of the interest is limited in a number of ways.

The relief applies to the business of a sole trader or a partnership and where the business is run by a limited company the shares of that company.

Section 93 defines 'relevant business property', that is, business property eligible for business relief, in terms of level of ownership of the business (**5.4.1**), business assets passing with the business (**5.4.2**), and business property received by the same beneficiary but not necessarily from the same disponer (**5.4.3**).

5.4.1 LEVEL OF OWNERSHIP OF BUSINESS

(1) The property consisting of a business or an interest in a business (as defined). This covers a sole trader or a partnership, for example, a corner shop, public house, solicitor's practice, or any other unincorporated business. Individual assets of the business will not qualify for relief if transferred to a beneficiary separately from the business (see **5.4.2**).

(2) The unquoted shares of a company (engaged in a business as defined) whether incorporated in the State or otherwise. These shares on the valuation date (either by themselves or together with other shares in that company) in the absolute beneficial ownership of the beneficiary have to give the beneficiary on that date:

(a) **more than 25 per cent** of the voting rights affecting the company as a whole; or

(b) if the company is on that date a company controlled by the beneficiary within the meaning of s. 27 of the CAT Consolidation Act, 2003: s. 27 deals with the valuation of private company shares and deals with situations where family members own shares of a company. Essentially, where family members between them own a controlling interest in a company, which has not more than five shareholders, each family member shareholder is deemed to have 'control' of the company regardless of numbers of shares actually held. In this case, the transfer of one share would qualify for the relief. See **3.1** for further detail on s. 27 including the definition of 'relation', which is extremely wide; or

(c) shares having an aggregate nominal value which represents **10 per cent or more** of the aggregate nominal value of the entire share capital of the company provided the beneficiary has been a full-time working officer or employee of the company or, if that company is a member of a group, of one or more companies which are members of the group throughout the period of five years ending on the date of the benefit.

It is important to note the distinction between 'more than 25 per cent' where the beneficiary was not an officer or employee of the company and '10 per cent or more' where the beneficiary was an officer or employee.

5.4.1.1 Certain quoted shares

Normally quoted shares are considered an investment and would not qualify for business relief. There is one exception. Certain quoted shares are also allowed to qualify for the relief provided that such shares would have qualified for the relief if they were unquoted and were in the beneficial ownership of the disponer immediately prior to the disposition and were unquoted at the date of the commencement of that beneficial ownership or on 23 May 1994, whichever is the later date.

This is to cover a situation where a company was initially a limited company but which was subsequently floated on the stock exchange, NASDAQ, and the like. In those circumstances only, shares held by the original shareholders can qualify for business relief provided they meet the other conditions.

5.4.1.2 Types of share

Where a company has shares of a class which limits the voting powers to either or both of the following:

(1) the question of winding up the company, and

(2) any question primarily affecting shares of that class

such shares are not taken into account in determining whether 'control' exists.

5.4.2 BUSINESS ASSETS PASSING AT THE SAME TIME AS THE BUSINESS

This is an exception to the rule that relevant business property must be a business or an interest in a business (shares). The relief will also apply to any land or buildings, machinery, or plant owned by the disponer and which immediately before the benefit was used wholly or mainly for the purposes of a business carried on by:

- the disponer;
- a partnership of which the disponer was then a partner;
- a company of which the disponer then had *control* by reason of voting power passing with the business. This is not a 's. 27' type control; the disponer (by himself and not as part of a family group of shares) must have more than 50 per cent of the votes over a limited company.

There is one exception to this. Many limited companies are owned '50%–50%' by spouses or civil partners, and as such neither would be deemed to have 'control' of the company as defined, and so neither could pass on any asset owned by them but used by the company and claim business relief on the asset.

Section 83 Finance Act 2014 addressed this, in relation to gifts or inheritances taken on or after 23 October 2014, by providing that the control requirement is satisfied in the case of spouses and civil partners where, taking their shareholdings together, they control the company.

Revenue also accept that if a disponer has 50 per cent of the votes in the relevant company and has a casting vote he/she would satisfy the control requirement of s. 93(1)(e).) Having a casting vote but less than 50 per cent of the shares is insufficient.

5.4.2.1 Limited company, premises, and 'control'

Example: John owns of the shares in 60 per cent of John Ltd, a trading company. John transfers his entire 60 per cent shareholding in John Ltd to his son, Keith, along with the premises, owned by John, that John Ltd operates from. Keith will obtain business relief on the shares and the premises because John had 'control' of the limited company.

On the other hand, if John owned 40 per cent of the shares of John Ltd. and transferred his shareholding in John Ltd. to his son, Keith, along with the premises, then Keith will obtain business relief on the shares but not on the premises because John did not have 'control' of the limited company.

This point should be raised with a disponer who owns a limited company and assets used by but not owned by that limited company, and who intends on giving some shares in that limited company to beneficiaries but holding onto some shares and the assets used by but not owned by that limited company. If that person gives away 'control' of the limited company as defined, then a future disposition of the remaining shares and the assets may not qualify for business relief on the assets when those assets not owned by that limited company are passing with the remaining shares in that limited company.

Example: Liam owns 60 per cent of the shares in Liam Ltd and the premises from which Liam Ltd operates. If he transfers 30 per cent of the shares to his son Michael, then Michael will receive business relief on those shares. If he makes a further transfer of the remaining 30 per cent of the shares along with the premises to Michael, then Michael would receive business relief on those shares but not on the premises because Liam did not have 'control' of Liam Ltd at the time of the transfer of the premises.

5.4.2.2 Asset and business together

Business relief cannot be obtained where an individual asset of a business is comprised in the benefit without transferring the business (or relevant shares in the business) itself. There has to be a simultaneous gift/inheritance of both the business/interest in the business and the asset used by but not owned by the business.

Example: Noel, who is a sole trader, gives the premises, which is part of his business assets, to his daughter Ondine. Ondine will *not* obtain business relief on that asset. Neither would an individual asset or assets of a business obtain relief on the grounds that the asset or assets represent an interest in the business. Again, the intention of the legislation is to award relief on the passing on of a business and not merely assets which can be used for a business purpose.

The following individuals would be regarded as having an interest in the business:

- a partner has a share in the partnership carrying on a business;
- a life tenant would have an interest in the business if he or she is entitled to the income from a business comprised in the trust property.

As already stated, land, building, machinery, or plant of the disponer will be regarded as relevant business property provided such property is used wholly or mainly for the purposes of a business:

- carried on by the disponer as a sole trader;
- carried on by a partnership of which the disponer was then a partner; or
- carried on or by a limited company of which the disponer then had 'control' (as defined).

5.4.3 BUSINESS BENEFITS MUST BE RECEIVED BY THE SAME BENEFICIARY, BUT NOT NECESSARILY FROM THE SAME DISPONER (SECTION 93(6))

This is very important when dealing with settled property, as can be seen from the following example.

5.4.3.1 Life tenant and sole proprietor of business

Peter, by will, devises a building to Raymond for his life with remainder to Simone. Raymond starts a business in the building and is the sole proprietor of that business. Raymond leaves his business to Simone in his will.

On the death of Raymond, Simone inherits the business from Raymond but the building in which the business is carried on is inherited from Peter, the original disponer of the building.

Under s. 93(6) of the CAT Consolidation Act, 2003, once Raymond had a beneficial interest in possession immediately before the inheritance the building will qualify as relevant business property even though the business comes from a different disponer. The building was 'comprised in the disposition' for the requisite period.

5.5 Minimum Period of Ownership (Section 94)

The next of the criteria which must be clarified before business relief can be obtained is: was the relevant business property comprised in the disposition (or owned by the disponer or his/her spouse) for the **relevant period** immediately prior to the gift/inheritance?

The purpose of this is to ensure that a person planning to pass on wealth to a beneficiary does not acquire a relevant business, whether incorporated or otherwise, merely or solely for the purpose of obtaining business relief.

For this reason s. 94 of the CAT Consolidation Act, 2003, provides that the relevant business property must have been owned by the disponer and/or the disponer's spouse for a minimum period of ownership. For this purpose 'relevant business property' is the business itself, not each individual asset of the business.

5.5.1 RELEVANT PERIOD

The relevant period will be:

(1) in the case of an inheritance, which was taken on the date of death of the disponer, a period of two years immediately prior to the date of the inheritance, or

(2) in any other case, for example a gift, or on the death of a life tenant, a period of five years immediately prior to the date of the gift or the inheritance.

In the example above at **54.3.1**, Peter and Raymond must have owned the building for a period of at least five years (combined total of period held by Peter prior to benefit and period held during life tenancy of Raymond together) for the building to be considered relevant business property for Simone as it is passing on the death of a life tenant. The business itself must have been owned by Raymond for a minimum period of two years for it to be considered relevant business property for Simone.

Any period immediately before the date of the disposition during which the property was continuously in the beneficial ownership of the disponer or of the spouse of the disponer (for example, gifts or inheritances out of settlements) will be deemed to be a relevant period immediately before the date of the gift or inheritance. For example, if the disponer incorporated during this period, arguably the property changed hands, but the real effect is that the business stayed in the possession of the disponer.

5.5.2 'DATE OF THE DISPOSITION'

The 'date of the disposition' is important for the purposes of s. 94 in that the relevant period cannot be calculated until the date of that disposition has occurred. See Elements of a Gift or Inheritance at **1.2.4.1** for further details, including a definition of the phrase 'comprised in the disposition'.

According to s. 2 of THE CAT Consolidation Act, 2003 'date of the disposition' includes inter alia:

(1) the date of death of a testator in the case of a will;

(2) the date of death of the intestate in the case of an intestacy;

(3) in the case of a disposition occurring as a result of a failure to exercise a right or power, the latest date when the disponer could have exercised the power.

(4) in any other case, the date on which the act (or where more than one act is involved, the last act) of the disponer was done by which that disponer provided or bound that disponer to provide the property comprised in the disposition (for example when the disponer placed the asset in trust).

The following are some examples of the working of s. 94.

5.5.3 BUSINESS PASSES BY WILL ABSOLUTELY

Alice by will gives business property to Brian absolutely. The date of the disposition is the date of death of Alice.

Brian's inheritance is taken on the date of death of Alice and accordingly the two-year condition must be satisfied.

Assuming that Alice was the beneficial owner of the property for more than two years immediately prior to his death, the two-year condition is satisfied because the period of ownership prior to his death is greater than two years. Brian will qualify for business relief.

5.5.4 BUSINESS PASSES BY WILL WITH INTERVENING LIFE INTEREST

Alice by will gives 'relevant business property' to Brian for his life with remainder to Cynthia absolutely.

Assuming that Alice has been the beneficial owner of that property for more than two years immediately prior to her death, the benefit taken by Brian which is a limited interest will obtain business relief on the grounds similar to that as set out in **5.5.3** above.

Subsequently Brian dies and Cynthia takes an inheritance from Alice. As this inheritance is not taken on the death of the disponer, Alice, the five-year period must be looked at.

For the purposes of calculating that five-year period two periods are added together:

(1) the period prior to Alice's death when she was the beneficial owner of the property; and

(2) the period during the life tenancy of Brian.

If the total of these two periods exceeds five years the benefit taken by Cynthia will obtain business relief.

5.5.5 *INTER VIVOS* TRANSACTION ABSOLUTELY

Alice, by *inter vivos* disposition, transfers business property to Brian absolutely. Accordingly, the five-year period must be satisfied. In the circumstances Alice, or her spouse, must have been the beneficial owner of the property for five years immediately prior to the date of the disposition.

If this is the case Brian will avail of business relief. Even if Alice dies within two years of the date of the disposition thereby making the gift an inheritance (see s. 3(1)(c) of The CAT Consolidation Act, 2003 and **1.2.1**), the five-year period will still apply as the gift (now an inheritance) would not have been taken on the death of the disponer.

5.5.6 *INTER VIVOS* TRANSACTION PRECEDED BY TRANSACTION BETWEEN SPOUSES ON DEATH

Alice acquired relevant business property in 2018. She died in 2020 and by her will gave the relevant business property to her husband, Harold, absolutely. Harold made a gift of the same relevant business property to their son Brian absolutely in 2025. The five-year period applies to that gift and B will obtain business relief in respect of the benefit from his mother. The five-year period is satisfied because the business property has been in the beneficial ownership of the disponer Mrs A and her spouse since 2018, that is, a total of seven years.

5.6 Replacement Property (Section 95)

Because of the nature of business, it often arises that a businessman will buy and sell various businesses during his lifetime. Relevant business property can be replaced with other relevant business property and the replacement business property does not necessarily have to be of the same type of business. The minimum ownership period is relaxed slightly for replacement property.

In dealing with replacement property the periods of two years and five years referred to in s. 94 are relaxed somewhat in order to take account of the fact that the replacing property may not be acquired for some time after the sale of the original property.

Accordingly, in the case of a benefit of the replacing property arising on the death of a disponer:

- if the original property and the replacing property have been owned by the disponer for at least two years out of the three years immediately preceding the date of that benefit;
- the replacing property will be treated as complying with the provisions of s. 94 (apart from the continuity element, that is).

In the case of all other benefits the original and replacing properties have to have been owned by the disponer (comprised in the disposition) for five years out of the six years immediately preceding the date of the benefit.

5.6.1 REPLACEMENT PROPERTY PASSING ON DEATH

Edward owned a software business since 2012. He sold it in October 2022 for €2,000,000 and acquired a data analysis business in May 2023 for €2,000,000. He died in 2025 and left his data analysis business to Fiona absolutely.

Fiona will obtain business relief because both businesses will be deemed to have been owned by Edward for at least two years falling within the three-year period immediately prior to the death of A (his date of death being the date of the disposition). It is assumed that the software business was such that (apart from the provisions of s. 94) it would have obtained business relief if it had been the subject of a benefit taken prior to the replacement.

5.6.2 LIMITS ON REPLACEMENT PROPERTY (SECTION 95(2))

However, the relief is limited by s. 95(2). The maximum amount of business relief available will be the relief applicable to the original property if no replacement had been made. The way this operates is shown by taking the example above and assuming that:

(1) Edward paid €2,500,000 for the data analysis business in 2023 (instead of €2,000,000)

(2) The value of the data analysis business in 2025 is €3,000,000.

The maximum relief available is how much of that €3,000,000 relates to the original business. This is calculated using the following formula.

$$\text{Current value of replacement business} \times \frac{\text{Sale value of original business}}{\text{Purchase value of replacement business}} = \text{Allowable value replacement business}$$

Applying this formula to the example above:

$$€3{,}000{,}000 \times \frac{€2{,}000{,}000}{€2{,}500{,}000} = €2{,}400{,}000$$

Only €2,400,000 of the value of the replacement business of €3,000,000 is allowed the relief. There are exceptions to this provision to be found in s. 95(3); for example, if replacement is made in the context of a dissolution of a partnership or where a company controlled by the owner of a business takes over the business.

It is not necessary that one type of business be replaced by a similar type of business so long as both the original and the replacement businesses are relevant businesses.

5.7 Succession (Section 96)

Section 96 states that for the purposes of ss. 94 and 95 already dealt with, where a disponer becomes beneficially entitled to any property *on the death of another person*, the disponer is deemed to have been beneficially entitled to it from the date of the death of that person, not just from when the property is vested in them. This means that the disponer is in fact credited with ownership during the administration of the first disponer's estate.

Example: Liam, who died in May 2023, bequeathed relevant business property to Michelle absolutely. The valuation date of Michelle's inheritance was January 2024.

Michelle died in July 2025 and bequeathed the same relevant business property to Nicholas absolutely.

For the purposes of ss. 94 and 95, Michelle is regarded as having been the beneficial owner of the business property since May 2023. Two years elapsed before her death in July 2025.

Nicholas is entitled to business relief. This is because Michelle's two-year beneficial ownership is deemed to start from the date of death of Liam in May 2023. This section in effect repeats standard CAT legislation which would regard Michelle as beneficial owner since the date of death of Liam.

5.8 Successive Benefits (Section 97)

Section 97 introduced a type of quick succession relief which was a feature of the old Death Duties and Probate Tax regime. It waives the two-year minimum ownership rule where the beneficiary (or the spouse/civil partner of the beneficiary) of a gift/inheritance dies within two years of the gift/inheritance, provided of course that the original gift/inheritance was eligible for relief. This is illustrated in **5.8.1** below.

5.8.1 QUICK SUCCESSION

Last year Oscar gave 100 shares (the entire issued share capital) in Oscar Ltd, valued at €1,000,000, to Felix absolutely. All the conditions for business relief were satisfied and Felix obtained business relief.

Felix dies this year and leaves the same 100 shares to Penny absolutely. As Felix's acquisition was the previous year, the two-year period required in s. 94 is not satisfied; that is, Felix did not own the business assets for a two-year period prior to the inheritance by Penny. Normally business relief on Penny's benefit would be refused on that ground.

However, under s. 97 Penny's benefit obtains business relief despite the fact that that benefit did not satisfy the provisions of s. 94.

Penny's benefit must be an inheritance. The relief would not apply if Penny's benefit were taken by way of a gift.

5.8.2 RESTRICTIONS ON QUICK SUCCESSION RELIEF

This is restricted to the 'gift/inheritance' portion of the benefit, which is not necessarily the market value.

Example: If Oscar, in the example at **5.8.1** above, 'sold' 100 shares in A Ltd valued at €1,000,000 to Felix for consideration of €150,000 in 2023 and Felix dies in 2024 at which time the 100 shares in Oscar Ltd are valued at €1,200,000:

The relief is calculated as follows:

Market value of earlier benefit	€1,000,000
Taxable value of earlier benefit (market value of benefit less consideration)	(€1,000,000 – €150,000) = €850,000

In the preceding example, the benefit consisted of €850,000 (i.e. 85 per cent of the value of the assets passing), so business relief would have applied to the €850,000 in 2023.

On the 'quick successive' death of Felix in 2024 only 85 per cent of the value of the relevant business property passing will be available for the relief as B only received relief on 85 per cent of the value of the relevant business property passing to him.

In the example the shares were valued at €1,200,000.

85 per cent of this is €1,020,000.

The remaining 15 per cent of the shares would be taxed at their full value of €180,000.

Of the €1,200,000 in shares passing, €1,020,000 would get business relief @90%, giving a taxable value of €102,000, giving a total taxable value of (€180,000 + €102,000) €282,000.

5.9 Non-Qualifying Business Assets (Section 100)

Certain individual assets of a business are left out of account in calculating the taxable value of relevant business property although they are assets of the business at the date of the benefit. Under s. 100:

- this includes certain assets of a business called **excepted assets** (subsection (2)) and
- that part of the value of shares in a holding company which is attributable to an entirely new business (i.e. not a replacement of an existing business) acquired during the minimum ownership period is **excluded** from the relief (subsection (8)).

5.9.1 EXCEPTED ASSETS

When dealing with s. 100 and 'excepted assets' we are not dealing with whether the company itself is a 'relevant business asset'; we are looking at individual assets of the company.

An asset of the company is an excepted asset if it was not used wholly or mainly for the purpose of the business concerned throughout the whole or the last two years of the relevant period. That relevant period is the period referred to in s. 94 and is two years for an inheritance and five years for any other disposition.

An excepted asset will not qualify for business relief. Section 100(6) provides that where an asset was purchased by the company and used by the company inside, that is, for less than the relevant period, it does not necessarily mean that it will be excepted. For example, if a company buys a new van and the sole shareholder dies six months later, the van was used 'wholly or mainly for the purposes of the business concerned throughout the whole . . . of the relevant period'; that is, for the entire period of the ownership of the van, it was used by the business.

Section 100(7) specifically provides that where an asset is used wholly or mainly for the personal benefit of the disponer or of a relative of the disponer, it will be deemed not to have been used for the purposes of the business and will be excepted. An example would be a car used by the disponer or a relative of the disponer as well as being used in the business.

In general the question of whether an asset has been used wholly or mainly for the purpose of a business will be a question of fact to be decided in the circumstances of each particular case. Assets which fluctuate or change from time to time may cause difficulties, for example stock-in-trade. A flexible approach is taken by the Revenue provided that the change or fluctuation is reasonable in the circumstances. For example, as discussed, a current account proportional to the level of trade should qualify as a business asset, but a large deposit account probably will not qualify.

An issue that arises on occasion is seasonal variations in the amount of cash/current accounts. For example, a toy store will usually have a lot of cash on hand in the immediate aftermath of Christmas, and a sweetshop will have cash on hand after Christmas and after Easter.

In these circumstances, such seasonal fluctuations can be demonstrated to the Revenue Commissioners by showing bank accounts over a number of years showing the same fluctuations each year.

In addition, Revenue have accepted that cash held by a company was not an excepted asset in a situation where the company specifically built up the cash to fund the construction of a new premises. The cash was accepted as being held wholly and exclusively for the purposes of the company's business/trade. The cash was generated by the profits of the company and had been set aside for the construction of the new premises.

Similarly, cash representing the proceeds of the sale of land by a company which was sold in order to fund the construction of new showrooms and related facilities and credited to the current account of the company was allowed business relief provided the cash was used for the purpose of the business either in expanding the showroom premises or the purchase of new stock and the like.

A recent determination of the Tax Appeals Commissioners 132TACD21 <https://www.taxappeals.ie/en/determinations/132tacd2021-cat> issued on 18 August 2021 is instructive in this regard.

In that case, the Appellant received a gift from her father of 12.5 per cent of the shares in her father's company which carried on a supermarket business. The company had significant accumulated cash reserves, investment assets, and residential properties. While both parties agreed that the shares were relevant business property, as the business was a trading business, the question arose whether these assets were 'excepted assets' within the meaning of s. 100 (2) of the CAT Consolidation Act, 2003 or not.

The appellant gave evidence that the residential properties had been purchased with a view to expanding the existing business premises and that the cash and investments had been accumulated to pay for the construction project and to provide for liquidity in day to day trading and administration of the business.

Finding on the facts of the case, the Appeals Commissioner determined that the cash, investments, and residential properties were held for this purpose and not for the shareholders' personal gain.

5.9.2 EXAMPLE: EXCEPTED ASSET OF A BUSINESS

Daniel, an importer, owns a large warehousing facility which has been used wholly or mainly for the purposes of his importing business Daniel Ltd. In 2021, due to a recession in the importing business, Daniel let the warehousing facility to an outside business for a four and a half-year lease.

Daniel died in 2025 and by his will left Daniel Ltd and his warehousing facility to Estelle absolutely. Daniel Ltd qualified for business relief but the value of the warehousing premises was left out of account because for the whole of the relevant period (on the facts of the case the last two years) it was not used wholly or mainly by Daniel Ltd.

When calculating taxable value of business assets, the value of the warehouse would be deducted from the taxable value of the relevant business property as an 'excepted asset' but added back in to the penultimate panel (excepted assets and assets not eligible for relief). This figure would then be added to the taxable value of all qualifying relevant business property to give taxable value of all business property.

If on the facts above Daniel did not die in 2025 but made a gift of his business property to Estelle at that time, the warehousing facility would again be left out of account because for the last two years of the relevant period (in that case a five-year period) the warehousing facility was not used wholly or mainly for X's business.

This only applies where the asset has been owned by the company but not used by it in the course of its business.

5.9.2.1 Group of companies

Where the business concerned is carried on by a company which is a member of a group of companies and the asset was immediately before the date of the gift or inheritance being used by another member of the group, it will qualify for relief.

5.9.3 PART OF THE PROPERTY IS USED FOR NON-BUSINESS PURPOSES

Section 100(5) makes provision for a situation where a part but not the entire of lands or buildings is used exclusively for the purpose of a business; for example, where the ground floor of a licensed premises is used for the licensed business and the upper floor is used for residential purposes by the owner or his family.

Staff accommodation would be considered a business use of the portion of the premises.

In this situation an apportionment of value is made, so that the value of the downstairs premises is given the appropriate business relief and the residential portion upstairs is not taken into account. In any event the residential portion may qualify for dwelling exemption.

However, a difficulty may arise if there is a mortgage on the premises. The mortgage will cover the entire premises (business and residential). It is extremely unlikely that a financial institution would grant a mortgage that does not cover the entire property for a variety of reasons, conveyancing and otherwise.

In that circumstance the mortgage would be apportioned in the same way as the building is between the business and the non-business, each portion carrying its share of the mortgage.

Appendix 3 to Form IT39 (October 2003 Edition) states:

> *Note: In the event that the building [licensed premises with private dwelling] is mortgaged, the mortgage will have to be apportioned between the licensed premises and residence. The portion of the mortgage applicable to the licensed premises should be deducted from the business assets i.e. licensed premises and the portion applicable to the residence deducted from the non-business assets i.e. residence.*

It is arguable that this is a misapplication of the Revenue practice of deducting 'general debts' from the non-business assets first. However, it is equally arguable that the mortgage is a business mortgage, which should be taken off the business only.

Applying the Revenue practice: if the non-business element qualifies for dwelling-house exemption, that element of the mortgage relating to the business element of the property will be deducted from the business element and the remainder of the mortgage will not be taken into account at all.

5.10 To Sum Up 'Relevant Business Property'

A disposition will qualify as 'relevant business property' if:

- it consists of a business or an interest in a business (i.e. shares);
- where that business 'wholly or mainly' carries on a 'non-excluded business' as defined (i.e. no investments on its own behalf);
- and the beneficiary receives sufficient interest in the business, that is, a sole trader's business, a share in a partnership, or shares: either more than 25 per cent of the voting shares; 10 per cent if a full time officer or employee; or nominal shares where the beneficiary, along with other family members (not totalling more than five) will exercise 's. 27 type' control;

- where a business asset is not owned by the business (limited company or partnership) the disponer (not the beneficiary) must either have been a partner or had overall voting (not just s. 27 type) control by means of voting power over the limited company prior to the disposition;
- that asset must pass to the beneficiary at the same time as the business, whether by the same disponer or two or more separate disponers;
- the disponer must:
  - (a) have owned the business (the business must have been comprised in the disposition) for at least two years prior to an inheritance of the business (two out of the last three if a 'replacement' business); or
  - (b) must have owned the business for at least five years (the business must have been comprised in the disposition) if passing in any other fashion (five out of the last six if a 'replacement' business);
- replacement property is subject to certain limitations where the value of the replacement property is greater than the value of the 'replaced' or original property;
- where a disponer originally inherits the property, the period of ownership runs from the date of death of the original disponer;
- where a person receives a disposition of relevant business property and dies within two years of the original disposition the two-year rule is waived for the subsequent beneficiary.

Now that we have established whether a gift or inheritance qualifies for business relief, the next step is to calculate the effect of that relief. The first step is to calculate the taxable value of the business assets.

5.10.1 RELEVANT BUSINESS PROPERTY

In order to calculate the taxable value of business assets, firstly, we have to establish whether the property is 'relevant business property' as discussed above at **5.2.1**.

Relevant Ownership Period Insert 'Yes' or 'No' as appropriate

Did the disponer own the business property for the relevant period?

Two years if an inheritance directly from the disponer

Five years in every other case

Relevant Business Property Test Insert 'Yes' or 'No' as appropriate

1. Is the 'Relevant Business' Property

   a) A qualifying business or an interest in a qualifying business—e.g. a sole trader or a partnership?

   And/Or

   b) Unquoted shares in a limited company carrying on a qualifying business (See Question 3)

If business assets are passing outside a business (either a limited company or a partnership) then question 2 must be answered 'yes' if the business assets are to qualify for business relief.

2. Are there business assets owned by the disponer and used by either a qualifying business s/he was a partner in or a limited company s/he 'controlled' 50%+ passing with the qualifying business or an interest in the qualifying business?

If unquoted shares in a limited company are passing then at least one of questions 3 (a), (b) or (c) must be answered 'Yes' in order to qualify for business relief.

For question 3 the relevant amount of shares means the current gift/inheritance together with any shares already owned by the beneficiary.

3. If the Relevant Business Property consist of unquoted shares in a limited company carrying on a qualifying business does the Beneficiary:

   (a) have 10% or more of the voting shares if a full-time officer or employee of the company

   And/Or

   (b) more than 25% of the voting shares

   And/Or

   (c) 'control' the company within the meaning of s. 27 (Five or fewer family members control 50%+ of the voting shares)

These questions have to be answered in the affirmative if we are to confirm that the property is 'relevant business property'.

5.11 Calculation of Taxable Value of Business Assets

Once this is established we can then calculate the taxable value of business assets, taking all the exceptions detailed above into account as provided for in the template in para 5.3.3.

	Market Value of Relevant Business Property	€
Less	Liabilities and consideration	€
Equals	Taxable value	€
Less	Value attributable to excepted assets	€
Equals	Value of relevant non-excepted business property	€
Less	Any property subject to replacement / successive benefit rules	€
Equals	Incumbrance free value of relevant business property on which relief is granted	€
Less	90% business relief	€
Equals	Taxable value of all qualifying relevant business property	€
Plus	Excepted assets and assets not eligible for relief	
Equals	**Taxable value of all business property**	

Again, it should be noted that this template is for full interests passing only and does not take into account valuations for limited interests.

5.12 Liabilities and Consideration (Lines 1 to 3)

Section 98 of the CAT Consolidation Act, 2003 states that the value of a business or of an interest in a business is to be its net value; that is, the market value of the assets used in the business less the liabilities incurred for the purpose of the business.

It is not easy to reconcile this with s. 92, which states that it is the taxable value of the relevant business property which is given business relief. Appendix 3 of IT39 (October 2003 Edition) provides that in the case of a business carried on by a sole trader every asset owned by the sole trader and used by him or her wholly or mainly for the purposes of the business will be taken into account in arriving at the net value as will all liabilities incurred for the purposes of the business.

As regards liabilities and consideration, Page 24 of the Revenue Commissioners Tax and Duty Manual Part 12 in relation to CAT and business relief should be consulted:

> *In calculating the taxable value attributable to the value of the business (or interest) the following general rules should be applied to the treatment of liabilities/consideration where the acquisition consists of both relevant business property and other property e.g. an inheritance of residue consisting of a business, land, etc. and other non-business property:*

deduct from the value of the business:–	*all liabilities payable out of residue which were incurred for the purposes of the business (section 98); and—all liabilities payable out of residue which were an encumbrance on the business (section 28(11), CAT Consolidation Act, 2003) whether or not incurred for the purposes of the business;*
deduct from the value of the other property:–	*any other liabilities (or consideration) provided that where the value of the other liabilities exceeds the value of the other property then the excess should be deducted from the value of the business*

'Where a

The first three lines of the computation deal with arriving at this figure.

Inserted in line 1 is the market value of the relevant business property.

Inserted in line 2 is the liabilities and consideration. Taking liabilities and consideration from the market value gives us the taxable value, inserted at line 3.

5.12.1 TREATMENT OF GENERAL COSTS, LIABILITIES, EXPENSES, AND CONSIDERATION

This is a concession granted by the Revenue to people applying for business relief. It is important to note that this is utterly different to the treatment of liabilities and consideration for agricultural relief. There is no apportionment of costs, liabilities, expenses, and consideration between business and non-business assets as there is between agricultural and non-agricultural assets. However, this Revenue practice favours the taxpayer as it gives more business relief.

As noted in the example below at **5.12.2**, the crucial point to remember is *general debts* are *not apportioned* between business and non-business assets for the purpose of calculating the net taxable value of the business assets and the non-business assets. General debts in this case would include, for example, where a beneficiary inherits the entire estate, including business and non-business assets, and the funeral and testamentary expenses. Debts specifically relating to the business are deducted from the business assets and assets specifically relating to the non-business assets (for example, a mortgage on the house) are deducted from the non-business assets.

General debts are taken off the non-business assets in their entirety. If the general debts are greater than the non-business assets, the remaining general debts are taken off the business assets. This type of calculation arises where both business and non-business assets are received by a beneficiary as part of the same benefit. If only business assets are received it does not arise.

In the case of a partnership, partnership assets and partnership liabilities only will be taken into account. Property owned by a partner but used by the partnership would not be an asset of the partnership. Neither would a personal liability incurred by any partner be regarded as a liability of the partnership.

In some cases there will be assets owned by the business (sole trader, partnership, limited company) but which do not qualify for business relief. These are known as **non-qualifying business assets** and have been dealt with at **5.9**.

5.12.2 EXAMPLE: DEDUCTING LIABILITIES/CONSIDERATION WHERE THERE ARE BUSINESS AND NON-BUSINESS ASSETS

Joe, a sole trader, owns a grocery business, which has not been incorporated. He died on 20 October 2024 and left his entire estate, which consisted of business and non-business assets, to his son Barry, subject to Barry paying €200,000 to his sister (Joe's daughter) Josephine. Barry did not have any prior benefits.

Probate issued on 22 February 2025 and this has been accepted as the valuation date.

At the valuation date, the estate consisted of the following assets and liabilities:

Assets:	
Shop premises	€3,000,000
Stock-in-trade	€150,000
Business current account	€10,000
Deposit account	€30,000
Dwelling-house (Barry does not qualify for dwelling exemption)	€450,000
Liabilities	
Mortgage on shop premises	€1,000,000
Trade debts	€12,000
Administration costs	€ 5,000
Funeral expenses	€ 3,000

The taxable value of the benefit taken by Barry is ascertained as follows:

Taxable Value of Non-Business (Other) Property

	Market Value of Property **Dwelling-house €450,000 + Deposit account €30,000***	**€480,000**
Less	Market value of exempt property (if any)	**€ 0**
Equals	Market value of taxable property	**€480,000**
Less	Applicable liabilities, costs & expenses (if any) Admin costs €5,000 Funeral expenses €3,000	**€ 8,000**
Equals	Incumbrance free value	**€472,000**
Less	Consideration [in money or monies worth] Payment to sister Josephine	**€ 200,000**
Equals	**Taxable value of non-business property**	**€ 272,000**

Taxable Value of Relevant Business Property

	Market Value of Relevant Business Property Shop €3,000,000 + Stock €150,000 + Business current account* €10,000	**€3,160,000**
Less	Liabilities and consideration Mortgage on shop premises €1,000,000 Trade Debts € 12,000	**€1,012,000**
Equals	Taxable value	**€2,148,000**

Less	Value attributable to excepted assets	€ 0
Equals	Value of relevant non-excepted business property	**€2,148,000**
Less	Any property subject to replacement / successive benefit rules	€ 0
Equals	Incumbrance free value of relevant business property on which relief is granted	**€2,148,000**
Less	90% business relief	**€1,933,200**
Equals	Taxable value of all qualifying relevant business property	**€ 214,800**
Plus	Excepted assets and assets not eligible for relief	€ 0
Equals	**Taxable value of all business property**	**€ 214,800**

*As discussed, the treatment of bank accounts is a grey area. Where the account is a current account of a reasonable amount for the use of the business, paying suppliers, and so on, it will be treated as a business asset. Where the account is a savings or deposit account used for the accumulation of profit (for example) it will most likely be treated as an investment and not as an asset of the business. In some cases where it can be shown that the sum of money was being saved to purchase an asset of the business, then the relief has been applied.

See **5.9.1**.

In this case, the general debts, funeral and testamentary expenses, and consideration are deducted from the non-business assets and only the specific business debts deducted from the business assets.

$$\text{Taxable value of Barry's benefit}\left(€272{,}000\,\text{plus}\,€214{,}800\right) = €486{,}800$$

Tax is calculated in the standard way as follows:

Tax Payable on Taxable Value of All Assets

	Taxable Value of this gift/inheritance **TV of Business €214,800 + +** **TV of Non-Business €272,000**	**€486,800**
Less	Small gift exemption where relevant	**€3,000 / NIL**
Equals	Net taxable value of benefit	**€486,800**
	Relevant threshold group **A** ~~B C~~ € 400,000	
Less	Taxable value of prior aggregable € 0 benefits (SGE?)	
Equals	Available threshold for this benefit	**€400,000**
Taxable excess [taxable value less available threshold]		**€86,800**
Tax @ 33% of taxable excess		**€ 28,644**

** A **€ 400,000** B € 40,000 C €20,000

Prior to 2 October 2024

[insert name] should file and pay [delete "and pay" if a return is necessary but no tax is payable] by 31 October 2024 / 2025 14 November 2024 if paying and filing using ROS / No extension of deadline if paying and filing using ROS has been announced for 2025.

A €335,000 B € 32,500 C €16,250

Barry should file and pay by 31 October 2025, or by mid November 2025 if paying and filing online using ROS to claim business relief and avoid surcharges and interest.

Clawback of Business Relief will be dealt with in **5.15**.

5.13 Dwelling-House Relief and Business Relief

It is possible to obtain dwelling-house relief and business relief at the same time. In the example in **5.11.2** above, if Barry had been living at home in Joe's house for the past three years and did not have any interest in any other dwelling, he would be entitled not only to business relief on the business as outlined, but also to dwelling-house relief on the house.

The effect of this is that as a proportion of the general debts now relate to the exempt property, following s. 28(5) we have to apportion between the exempt assets and the ordinary assets. Unlike agricultural relief, however, the general debts are apportioned between the exempt and ordinary assets only and not the business assets. The taxable value of the business assets remains unaffected.

In Joe and Barry's case, the specific business debts are still deducted from the business assets in the usual fashion but the general administration and funeral expenses of €8,000 are split or apportioned between the exempt element of the non-business assets of €450,000 and the ordinary element of the non-business assets of €30,000 as follows:

$$\frac{€30{,}000}{(€30{,}000 + €450{,}000)} \times €8{,}000 = €500$$

A similar calculation for the consideration would look like this:

$$\frac{\text{Ordinary Non} - \text{Business Assets}}{\text{All Non} - \text{Business Assets}} \times \text{Consideration} = \text{Allowable Portion of Consideration}$$

$$\frac{€30{,}000}{(€30{,}000 + €450{,}000)} \times €200{,}000 = €12{,}500$$

Applying these figures to the market value of the property, the taxable value of the non-business assets taken by Barry is ascertained as follows:

Taxable Value of Non-Business Property

	Market Value of Property **Dwelling-house €450,000 + Deposit account €30,000***	**€480,000**
Less	Market value of exempt property (if any)	**€450,000**
Equals	Market value of taxable property	**€ 30,000**
Less	Applicable liabilities, costs & expenses (if any) Admin costs €5,000 + Funeral expenses €3,000 = €8,000 x (€30,000/€480,000) =	**€ 500**
Equals	Incumbrance free value	**€ 29,500**
Less	Consideration [in money or monies worth] Payment to sister Josephine €200,000 x (€30,000/€480,000)	**€ 12,500**
Equals	**Taxable value of non-business property**	**€ 17,000**

Taxable value of business property is unchanged at €214,800.

Tax Payable on Taxable Value of all assets

	Taxable Value of this gift/inheritance **TV of Business €214,800 + +** **TV of Non- Business € 17,000**	**€231,800**
Less	Small gift exemption where relevant	**€3,000 / NIL**
Equals	Net taxable value of benefit	€231,800
	Relevant threshold group **A** ~~B C~~ €400,000	
Less	Taxable value of prior aggregable € 0 benefits (SGE?)	
Equals	Available threshold for this benefit	**€400,000**
Taxable excess [taxable value less available threshold]		**€ NIL**
Tax @ 33% of taxable excess		**€ NIL**

** A **€ 400,000** B € 40,000 C €20,000

Prior to 2 October 2024

A €335,000 B € 32,500 C €16,250

Even though no CAT is payable, Barry should file by mid November 2025 in order to comply with s. 46 (4) as introduced by s. 55 Finance Act, 2020 to claim Business Relief and Dwelling Exemption.

Clawback of business relief will be dealt with in **5.15**.

5.14 Business Relief on Agricultural Property

Agricultural property which is eligible for 'agricultural relief' was originally excluded because it has its own built-in system of relief, but since the Finance Act, 2000 agricultural property which fails to qualify for 'agricultural relief' can qualify for business relief, providing it meets the 'tests'.

The approach taken by the Revenue is that a beneficiary receiving agricultural property should apply for agricultural relief first and only if he or she fails to qualify for agricultural relief is business relief applied for. This is according to their interpretation of s. 102, as outlined in **4.10**.

As stated in the conclusion to **Chapter 4** on agricultural relief, there are differences in the treatment of business property and agricultural property. Briefly, these are:

(1) There is no minimum ownership period for agricultural relief, while there is a two-year (inheritance) or five-year (every other case) minimum ownership period for business relief.

(2) It is possible to use non-agricultural bequests to buy agricultural property prior to the valuation date and obtain the relief under s. 89(3) of the CAT Consolidation Act, 2003; no such possibility exists for business relief.

(3) The farmhouse will usually qualify for agricultural relief but not for business relief.

(4) If the farmland is let, a doubt arises as to whether it will qualify for business relief, whereas if it is let to an 'active farmer' it should still qualify for agricultural relief.

(5) General debts are distributed between agricultural and non-agricultural assets proportionately. For business relief they are deducted from non-business assets first and if there are any remaining general debts, then they are deducted from the business assets.

(6) There is no 80 per cent test for business relief.

(7) Business Relief is subject to clawback if the business 'ceases to trade' by becoming (for example) a majority investment business or if there is a 'change of use' by letting assets formerly used by the business. Clawback is dealt with in **5.15**. This type of clawback does not apply to agricultural relief per se but the new 'active farmer' conditions should be met.

In general it is more beneficial to have agricultural relief apply to the property. One exception may arise if:

- the farmhouse qualifies for dwelling-house exemption;
- the assets qualify for business relief; and
- there are a large amount of general debts and/or expenses and/or consideration which can be set off solely against the non-business assets.

It is unlikely that applying for business relief will provide a more favourable outcome than applying for agricultural relief, but the solicitor should make both calculations on behalf of the client.

5.15 Clawback of Business Relief (Section 101)

The withdrawal of relief provisions are contained in s. 101. Essentially, clawback occurs in two ways, described in **5.15.1** and **5.15.2** below.

5.15.1 CHANGE OF USE

Clawback will occur if the benefit ceases to be '**relevant business property**', that is, if the business or any business which replaced it ceases to ceases to qualify as such, at any time within the relevant period of six years commencing on the date of the gift or inheritance, for whatever reason (ceasing to trade for example), or if the non-trading activity (such as property holding or investments) became more than 50 per cent of the value of the business, thus failing the 'wholly or mainly' test.

The test applied is that at the date the property ceases to be 'relevant business property', s. 101(2)(a) provides for a **notional gift** of the property by the disponer to the beneficiary of that property. If however the benefit becomes relevant business property within a year of this event, the clawback is ignored on the basis of a further notional gift of the property.

The cessation of a business of a sole trader or a partnership by reason of bankruptcy, or the cessation of a business operated by a company on a *bona fide* winding up on grounds of insolvency, do not cause a clawback.

5.15.1.1 Example: asset ceases to be 'relevant business property'

Michael died in 2021 and by his will gave his share in a partnership business to his son Nigel absolutely. Nigel obtained business relief. In 2022 the partnership business let its main premises to another business on a short-term letting at its convenience and wound down the activity that it was carrying on at that premises so that now the business of the partnership was wholly or mainly dealing in property as defined in s. 93(3).

Assuming a notional gift of Nigel's share in the partnership business at that time: that share would not be relevant business property. This situation would cause a clawback of the relief originally given in 2021.

However, within a year, in 2023, the partnership business terminated the letting and recommenced trading from its main premises and accordingly its business was not now wholly or mainly dealing in property.

A notional gift of Nigel's share of the partnership at that latter date would have qualified for business relief. In the circumstances the business relief obtained by B is not clawed back and the period of ownership envisaged in s. 94 is ignored.

5.15.2 DISPOSAL OF PROPERTY

If any relevant business property is **sold, redeemed, or compulsorily acquired** within the six-year period and not replaced within a year of the sale, redemption, or compulsory acquisition, by other 'relevant business property' (quoted shares are specifically excluded as replacement property), then a similar notional benefit is applied.

Section 101(3)—as inserted by s. 136 of the Finance Act, 2005 in relation to relevant business property which has been replaced by other property on or after 3 February 2005—clarifies that the relief granted will be reduced where the property in respect of which relief was granted is replaced by other property whose value is less than that of the original property. The relief will be reduced in the same proportion as the market value of the replacement property bears to the market value of the original property.

5.15.2.1 Sale of property

If in the example above Nigel sold his share of the partnership (or it was compulsorily acquired) at some stage within the relevant period and Nigel did not replace it within one year of the sale (or compulsory acquisition) by another business property, the clawback will occur.

The replacing property must be relevant business property (apart from s. 94) in relation to a notional gift taken by Nigel from Michael on the date of the replacement.

5.15.3 TREATMENT OF NOTIONAL GIFTS

Neither of these 'notional gifts' apply the minimum period of ownership rules in s. 94.

In both cases, tax is chargeable as if the property were not relevant business property and a fresh return has to be completed. Interest is chargeable if the tax is not paid within four months of the clawback. The clawback does not apply if the event took place after the death of the beneficiary.

5.15.4 A BRIEF HISTORY OF CLAWBACK: 23 JANUARY 1996 TO FINANCE ACT, 2000 (10 FEBRUARY 2000)

Section 101(1) of the CAT Consolidation Act, 2003 specifies a clawback period of six years. Prior to this, different clawback periods applied at different times and were subject to variations in the amount clawed back.

When business relief was first introduced in 1994, the clawback period was six years from the date of the gift or inheritance.

In 1995, this was amended to six years from the valuation date (which as discussed elsewhere can be different from the date of the inheritance).

In 1996, the clawback period was increased to ten years from the valuation date in relation to a benefit taken on or after 23 January 1996 (s. 127 of the Finance Act, 1996). That latter section added that where the event which causes the clawback occurs after the expiration of the period of six years commencing on the valuation date and before ten years have elapsed from that date, one-third only of the business relief would be clawed back.

In 1997, in respect of benefits taken on or after 26 March 1997 that one-third clawback was increased to four-ninths (s. 141 of the Finance Act, 1997).

Finally, in 2000 (from 10 February 2000) the clawback period was reduced to six years from the date of the gift or the inheritance and all reference to partial clawback was removed.

5.15.5 EXTENSION OF CLAWBACK TO 10 YEARS FOR DEVELOPMENT LAND (FINANCE ACT, 2006)

Section 118(2) of the Finance Act, 2006 introduced a new Chapter 2A: Clawback of Agricultural Relief or Business Relief: Development Land to the CAT Consolidation Act, 2003, contained in a new s. 102A. This new 'extended partial' clawback applies to benefits taken after 2 February 2006 only.

This clawback will apply if a benefit is granted either agricultural or business relief and the benefit includes 'development land' as defined in s. 648 of the Taxes Consolidation Act, 1997. If this development land is disposed of in whole or in part in the period between end of year 6 and end of year 10 after the date of the gift or inheritance, a clawback will arise, based on the development use value (market value less current use value at the valuation date) of the development land.

As noted at **4.7.2**, this section was further amended in 2011 to correct a drafting error that enabled a beneficiary to dispose of the farmland on the sixth anniversary of the date of acquisition of the gift or inheritance and avoid the clawback. This applies to gifts and inheritances taken on or after 21 January 2011.

The development value element of the land will be taxed as if no relief applied. A further clarification in 2007 confirmed that interest in such a clawback would run from the date of disposal of the development property for clawback events triggered after 1 February 2007.

5.15.5.1 Example: tax treatment of 'extended' clawback for development value

Patrick inherits a business on 7 November 2024 valued at €2,500,000 from his father. He has had no prior benefits and the entire business qualifies as relevant business property for the relevant periods of ownership.

There is a current use value of €750,000 but the market value of the business because of development potential of the business premises is €2,500,000.

The business relief provided in 2024 would be 90 per cent of €2,500,000, that is, €2,250,000.

The taxable value of that business would be €250,000 and as such no CAT would arise. A return would be filed prior to 31 October / 14 November 2025 as follows:

Tax Payable on Taxable Value of all assets

	Taxable Value of this gift/inheritance **TV of Business €250,000 + +** **TV of Non- Business € 0**	**€250,000**
Less	Small gift exemption where relevant	**€3,000 / NIL**
Equals	Net Taxable value of benefit	**€250,000**
	Relevant threshold group **A** ~~B €~~ €400,000	
Less	Taxable value of prior aggregable € 0 benefits (SGE?)	
Equals	Available threshold for this benefit	**€400,000**
Taxable excess [taxable value less available threshold]		**€ NIL**
Tax @ 33% of taxable excess		**€ NIL**

Patrick sells the business (primarily the site the business operates from) on 7 November 2032 (eight years later) for €25 million because of the development potential of the site.

In addition to any CGT due, there will be a clawback of the business relief on the development or 'hope' value of the business (i.e. the difference between current use value of €750,000 and market value of €2,500,000).

In 2032, Patrick will have to re-calculate the taxable value of the benefit originally taken in November 2024 as follows:

Market value in 2024	€2,500,000
Current use value in 2024	(€ 750,000)
Development value in 2024	€1,750,000

Business relief is provided on 90 per cent of the current use value of €750,000 = €675,000 only. The taxable value of the current use value is 10 per cent of €750,000 = €75,000.

Development value	€1,750,000
and 10% of current use value	€75,000
Taxable value	€1,825,000

Tax is charged on:

The tax will be calculated as if the benefit was taken in 2024. The valuation date will be 7 November 2032 and the return should be filed and tax paid by 31 October/mid-November 2033 to avoid interest and surcharges (assuming no further changes to pay and file deadlines in the meantime).

Amended tax payable on taxable value in 2024

Tax Payable on Taxable Value of all assets

	Taxable Value of this gift/inheritance **TV of Business €1,825,000 + +** **TV of Non- Business € 0**	**€1,825,000**
Less	Small gift exemption where relevant	**€3,000 / NIL**
	Net taxable value of benefit	€1,825,000
	Relevant threshold group **A** ~~B~~ ~~C~~ €400,000	
Less	Taxable value of prior aggregable € 0 benefits (SGE?) benefits (SGE?)	€ 0
Equals	Available threshold for this benefit	€400,000
Taxable excess [taxable value less available threshold]		**€ 1,425,000**
Tax @ 33% of taxable excess		**€ 470,250**

** **A** € 400,000 **B € 40,000 C €20,000**

Prior to 2 October 2024

A €335,000 B € 32,500 C €16,250

In addition to any CGT payable, a further €470,250 will have to be paid in 'clawed back' CAT on the original inheritance in 2024. As noted above, return would have to be filed and the tax paid by 31 October/mid-November 2033.

5.15.6 ADVISING A CLIENT IN RELATION TO CLAWBACK

Whenever a client is the beneficiary of a qualifying business asset, the potential clawback must be pointed out to that client, in writing, for future reference.

In acting on behalf of a client who is considering selling a business, one of the factors that must be ascertained is whether that client has obtained business relief in the past and any potential clawback that may accrue.

As with agricultural relief, a rough calculation of the likely clawback should be provided to the client. However, as in all commercial decisions, taxation—while an important factor and one that the client has to take into account—may not be the primary factor in taking such a decision.

CHAPTER 6

'FAVOURITE NEPHEW/NIECE RELIEF' AND COMBINATIONS OF RELIEFS

6.1 Introduction and Outline

This chapter deals primarily with 'favourite nephew relief' as provided for in the Second Schedule of the CAT Consolidation Act, 2003 (as amended) and goes on to deal with how the relief can potentially be applied for simultaneously with other reliefs, primarily business and/or agricultural relief, but also dwelling-house exemption.

Paragraph 7 sub paragraphs (1) to (4) of Part 1 of the Second Schedule to the CAT Consolidation Act, 2003 deal with favourite nephew/niece relief. That paragraph deems such a beneficiary to be a child of the disponer for CAT purposes when certain conditions are satisfied:

(1) where the beneficiary is a **child of a brother or sister** of the disponer or the child of the civil partner of the disponer's brother or sister;

(2) who has worked **substantially on a full-time basis** for the period of **five years** ending on the date of the benefit;

(3) in carrying on or assisting in carrying on the **trade, business. or profession** of the disponer or in carrying on work of, or work connected with, the office or employment of the disponer; and

(4) the benefit consists of **property**, which was used **in connection with such** trade, **business**, profession, or employment or office of the disponer or consists of **shares in a company** owing such property.

The effect of this relief is profound. A qualifying nephew/niece moves from Group B (currently €40,000) to Group A (currently €400,000), a substantial increase. For this reason, the relief gave rise to much argument at Appeal Commissioner level and beyond and each of the conditions listed above have been tested.

6.2 Child of a Brother or Sister

'Child' is defined in s. 2 of the CAT Consolidation Act, 2003 and at **2.2.1** as including a step-child or an adopted child; non-marital children have already been included under the terms of the Status of Children Act, 1987. Section 2(5) goes on to confirm that where a child is adopted any other relationship can be construed from as if the adopting parents were the actual parent; that is, the sister of my adoptive mother will be my aunt for CAT purposes.

A foster child, however, is defined as a 'child' for CAT purposes only in relations to dispositions from the foster parent in para. 9 of the Second Schedule. The foster child will not be able to claim favourite nephew/niece relief in relation to any benefit from a sibling of the foster parents. A step-child will be able to claim favourite nephew/niece relief in relation to any benefit from a sibling of the step-parent. However, a child of a step-sibling would not be able to claim the relief. To clarify, my brother's step-son could be my favourite nephew; my step-brother's son could not.

The words 'nephew' and 'niece' or 'aunt' and 'uncle' are not used in CAT legislation, as they are not precise enough. There must be a blood relationship. The beneficiary must be a child of a brother or a sister of the disponer. For example, a person's mother's brother's wife is not their aunt for CAT purposes; they are their aunt-in-law, a stranger in blood. That person will not be a child of a brother or sister and thus not a 'favourite nephew/ niece' for CAT purposes.

6.2.1 CHILD OF THE CIVIL PARTNER OF A BROTHER OR SISTER

For the purpose of the relief, child has been extended to include the child of a civil partner of the disponer's brother or sister for benefits taken since 1 January 2011. Strictly speaking, such a child would be a stranger in blood to the disponer and would be the 'favourite child of the civil partner of a brother or sister' instead of a favourite nephew or niece.

For the purpose of this chapter any reference to 'favourite nephew or niece' includes any such 'favourite child of a civil partner of a brother or sister'.

6.3 Substantially on a Full-Time Basis

Originally, the legislation referred to 'substantially on a full-time basis' for a period of five years but did not define the term. In *AE v Revenue Commissioners* 1994 ITR 119 the deceased disponer had let his lands for many years to others for the grazing of livestock, which agreement involved the lessor walking the lands twice a day herding the livestock and keeping a lookout for disease, proper fencing, and the elimination of overgrowth.

His niece called in daily to attend to this work on his behalf, and the Circuit Court found that such a daily visit would be considered 'substantial' and 'full time' as she attended on a daily basis for varying lengths of time each day. Since then, the phrase 'substantially on a full-time basis' has been defined in the legislation to mean, in addition to the earlier accepted definition:

A beneficiary shall not be deemed to be working substantially on a full-time basis for a disponer or a company unless he or she works:

(1) more than 24 hours a week for the disponer at a place where the business is carried on; *or*

(2) more than 15 hours a week for the disponer at a place where the business is carried on and such business is carried on exclusively by the disponer, any spouse or civil partner of the disponer and the beneficiary.

This means that the Revenue Commissioners will firstly look at the number of hours per week that the nephew/niece worked in the business, and only if they work more than fifteen or twenty-four hours a week will Revenue look at whether this would be considered 'substantially on a full-time basis', taking into account the earlier case law. See commentary in *Capital Acquisitions Tax* (Bohan & McCarthy: Bloomsbury 2013), para. [8.07].

6.4 For a Period of Five Years

The relief originally applied only to cases where the business property was acquired directly by the beneficiary and therefore did not cover a situation where the beneficiary obtained the property only after an intervening life interest.

Section (1) now defines the 'relevant period' as:

(a) the period of five years ending on the date of the disposition; or

(b) where at the date of the disposition, the disponer **retains an interest in possession**, limited to the disponer under the disposition; for example to self for life remainder to the nephew, the period of five years ending on the coming to an end of that disponer's life interest.

There are two types of intervening life interests:

(1) where the disponer provides for a life interest in favour of a third party and remainder to the nephew/niece;

(2) where the disponer provides for a life interest in favour of himself and remainder to the nephew/niece.

In both cases, the period allows for 'the exclusion of reasonable periods of annual or sick leave from that period of five years'.

The distinction between the two and the different treatments arising are best displayed by way of contrasting examples.

6.4.1 INTERVENING LIFE INTEREST IN FAVOUR OF THIRD PARTY

Where the disponer provides for a life interest in favour of a third party and remainder to the nephew/niece, the date of the disposition is the date of the third party becoming beneficially entitled in possession.

Example: Where a disponer by his will leaves his business to his wife for her life with remainder to his nephew (child of his brother) absolutely. That nephew has to satisfy the pre-conditions applicable at the time of death of the disponer. This means he has to have worked substantially on a full-time basis, and so on, for the requisite five-year period prior to the date of death of the disponer.

If he has not fulfilled the conditions at the date of death of the disponer, he will not qualify for favourite nephew relief when he becomes beneficially entitled in possession to the business on the death of the life tenant. Whether he works in the business after the death of the disponer and during the period of ownership of the life tenant is irrelevant.

If he had worked less than five years prior to the death of his uncle but continues working for the life tenant (his aunt), that latter period would not count in making up the five-year period. He could in fact have worked for more than five years for his uncle and then left the business during the life tenancy of his aunt. On her death he would be entitled to favourite nephew relief.

6.4.2 INTERVENING LIFE INTEREST IN FAVOUR OF SELF

Where at the date of the disposition an interest in possession is taken by the disponer for his life, the relevant period is the period of five years ending on the coming to an end of the disponer's life interest.

Example: By deed dated 1 July 2019 **Steven** transferred his business on trust for himself (Steven) for his life with remainder to **Trevor**, his nephew, absolutely. Trevor started working full time for Steven on 1 July 2019.

Steven dies in August 2025. Trevor is entitled to favourite nephew relief in 2025 because he has worked full time for his uncle for a period of five years ending on his uncle's death.

6.4.3 DISCRETIONARY TRUSTS

It is stated specifically at para. 7(4) that the relief will not apply in the case of a benefit taken by a beneficiary under a discretionary trust.

6.4.4 RIGHT TO RESIDE

The definition of 'relevant period' specifically excludes any period during which the property was subject to a right to reside or a right to residence, support or maintenance, or an annuity, that is, a 'slice' as defined in **1.10**.

Example: By deed dated 1 July 2019 Steven transferred his business to his nephew Trevor absolutely subject to and charged with rights of residence, support, and maintenance for Steven for his life. Trever started working full time for Steven on 1 July 2019.

Steven dies in August 2025. Trevor does not receive favourite nephew relief for the first gift taken on 1 July 2019 as at that time he had not been working full time for five years ending on the date of the disposition. On 1 July 2019 he had never worked prior to that date. The period spent working in the business since that date is irrelevant.

Furthermore, Trevor does not receive favourite nephew relief on the 'slice' inherited on the death of the uncle in 2025 as the uncle did not 'own' the business during this period.

6.5 Trade, Business, or Profession

In the case of *AE v Revenue Commissioners* referred to above, the Revenue Commissioners claimed that the letting agreement entered into by the uncle was not a 'business'. The Court was satisfied that while the farm was not being run efficiently, letting the land in this manner was a business, albeit not a very successful one.

Following on from this, the definition of a business is far wider for 'favourite nephew/niece' purposes than it is for business relief purposes and refers to a trade, business, profession, office, or employment. Favourite nephew/niece relief existed before business relief and the use of the term 'business assets' is far wider than would be accepted for business relief, which is more strictly defined.

For example, a 'business' for favourite nephew/niece purposes could consist of an apartment block owned by the donor that the donor rented out and the nephew/niece managed. Provided there is sufficient activity by the nephew/niece, this could qualify as a business asset for favourite nephew/niece purposes. This would not qualify as an asset for business relief purposes.

6.5.1 PROPERTY USED IN CONNECTION WITH THE BUSINESS

The relief applies only to property used in connection with the business. This has given rise to much argument as to whether assets shown in a balance sheet of a business are in fact used in the business or represent profits arising from but not used in the business. There is a very clear distinction made between 'working capital' and 'investment assets'. Revenue is of the opinion that investment assets included in a balance sheet are not necessarily business assets. This is a similar treatment to business relief.

Furthermore, in the case of, say, a residuary estate taken by the nephew or niece as the case may be, the residue would include business and non-business assets and apportionment is necessary in order to tax the business assets under Group A and the non-business assets under Group B.

6.5.2 FARMHOUSE

As noted, Para 7(2) (a) Schedule 1 the CAT Consolidation Act, 03 deals with calculating favourite nephew relief on a gift or inheritance which consists of property used 'in connection with that trade business or profession'. A farmhouse has been defined as the building a farm is run from.

6.5.3 SHARES IN A COMPANY

In addition to a business, the relief applies to shares in a company running a business owning such property.

6.5.4 PRIVATE CONTROLLED TRADING COMPANY

The definition of company for this purpose is limited to a '**private company**' '**controlled by the disponer**' and of which the disponer is a director, and which is **not** a '**private non-trading company**'.

'**Private Company**' has been defined in s. 27 of the CAT Consolidation Act, 2003 and is dealt with in **Chapter 3**, but essentially is a company controlled by five persons or less (who do not have to be related to each other).

'**Controlled by the disponer**' is defined as a company controlled by the disponer, nominees of the disponer, or trustees of a settlement made by the disponer. Control, in this case, has the meaning given to it in s. 27(4)(b) of the CAT Consolidation Act, 2003, which is narrower than the 'normal' definition of 'control' for CAT purposes in s. 27(3) of the CAT Consolidation Act, 2003, which extends control to include family members of the disponer.

A **'private non-trading company'** is one whose income consists 'wholly and mainly' of investment income or and whose assets consist 'wholly and mainly' of property from which investment income is derived. 'Investment income' is defined as being analogous to income which is not 'earned income' as defined in s. 3 of the Taxes Consolidation Act, 1997. This would include income from letting of property in the State.

The central point here is that a business renting property may get the relief, but shares in a limited company running a business renting property will not.

6.6 Calculating the Tax Payable

When claiming favourite nephew/niece relief, in the overwhelming majority of cases, either business or agricultural relief will also be claimed. It is possible in some cases that the entire 'favourite nephew/niece business' passing is one where business relief would not apply, such as an investment or property ownership and rental business, but in most cases one of those two reliefs will also be claimed. In those cases, apportionment is done under the terms of the agricultural or business relief claimed first and then (if applicable) between Group A and Group B, respectively.

This is illustrated by the example in **6.6.1** (Agricultural) and **6.6.2** (Business).

6.6.1 EXAMPLE OF APPORTIONMENT (AGRICULTURAL)

John is the sole beneficiary of his uncle Paddy's (his father's brother) estate on Paddy's death on 18 March 2025. The estate consists of the following:

(1)	Farm (including farmhouse and livestock, bloodstock and farm machinery)	€2,500,000
(2)	Savings bonds	€75,000
(3)	Bank balance	€10,000

There are general debts of €10,000 and legal costs and funeral and testamentary expenses amount to a further €10,000. John qualifies both as a farmer and as a favourite nephew and has had no prior benefits from anyone. He did not reside in the farmhouse at any time prior to his uncle's passing. The Grant of Probate is issued on 23 June 2025 and this has been agreed as the valuation date. Debts, legal costs, and funeral and testamentary expenses are 'split' between the Group A and Group B assets as follows:

Group A

$$\frac{\text{Agricultural assets}}{\text{All Assets}} \times \text{Costs@}10\% = \text{Agricultural costs@}10\%$$

This gives us:

$$\frac{€2{,}500{,}000}{€2{,}585{,}000} \times €20{,}000 = €19{,}342\text{@}10\% = €1{,}934$$

Group B

$$\frac{\text{Non Agricultural assets}}{\text{All Assets}} \times \text{General Costs} = \text{Non-Agricultural costs}$$

This gives us:

$$\frac{€85{,}000}{€2{,}585{,}000} \times €20{,}000 = €658$$

AGRICULTURAL PROPERTY CALCULATION

	Market Value	**€2,500,000**
Less	Market Value of Exempt Property (if any)	€ NIL
Equals	Market Value of Agricultural Property	€2,500,000
Less	Agricultural Relief [90%]	€2,250,000
Equals	Agricultural Value	€250,000
Less	RELEVANT PORTION of Liabilities, Costs & Expenses [LCE] €19,342 [reduced to 10%]	€1,934
Equals	Incumbrance Free Value [IFV]	€248,066
Less	RELEVANT PORTION of Consideration [in money or monies worth] [reduced to 10%]	€ 0
Equals	**Taxable Value [TV]**	€248,066

TAXABLE VALUE—NON-AGRICULTURAL PROPERTY

	Market Value [MV]	**€85,000**
Less	Market Value of Exempt Property	€ NIL
Equals	Market Value of Taxable Property	€85,000
Less	RELEVANT PORTION of Liabilities, Costs & Expenses	€658
Equals	Incumbrance Free Value [IFV]	€84,342
Less	Applicable Consideration [in money or monies worth]	€ NIL
Equals	**Taxable Value [TV]**	€84,342

Normally at this stage in an agricultural relief calculation, the two taxable values would be added together to provide the taxable value of the current benefit, but in this case the agricultural property is inherited as a favourite nephew and as such has a **Group A** threshold while the other (non-agricultural property) is inherited as an 'ordinary' nephew and as such has a **Group B** threshold. There is no aggregation between Groups.

Tax on the two benefits is calculated as follows:

Group A

	Taxable Value of this ~~gift~~/inheritance		**€248,066**
	TV of Agricultural €248,066 +	+	
	TV of Non- Agricultural € NIL		
Less	Small Gift Exemption where relevant		~~€3,000~~ / € 0
Equals	Net Taxable Value of benefit		€248,066
	Relevant Threshold Group **A** ~~B C~~		€400,000
Less	Taxable Value of Prior Aggregable Benefits (SGE?)		€ 0
Equals	Available Threshold for this benefit		€400,000
Taxable Excess [Taxable Value less Available Threshold]			€ 0
Tax @ 33% of Taxable Excess			€ 0

** A	**€400,000**	B	€40,000	C	€20,000
Prior to 2 October 2024					
A	€335,000	B	€32,500	C	€16,250

Tax Payable on Taxable Value of 'Ordinary' assets

Group B

	Taxable Value of this ~~gift~~/inheritance		**€84,342**
	TV of Agricultural € NIL +	+	
	TV of Non-Agricultural €84,342		
Less	Small Gift Exemption where relevant		~~€3,000~~ / 0
Equals	Net Taxable Value of benefit		€84,342
	Relevant Threshold Group ~~A~~ B ~~C~~		€40,000

(Continued)

(Continued)

Less	Taxable Value of Prior Aggregable Benefits (SGE?)	€ 0
Equals	Available Threshold for this benefit	€40,000
Taxable Excess [Taxable Value less Available Threshold]		€44,342
Tax @ 33% of Taxable Excess		€14,632.86 rounded up to €14,633

**	A	€400,000	**B**	**€40,000**	C	€20,000
Prior to 2 October 2024						
	A	€335,000	B	€32,500	C	€16,250

John pays €14,633 tax on a net estate valued at €2,565,000 received from his uncle.

John has to file online via ROS in order to comply with Section 46 (4) as introduced by s. 55 Finance Act, 2020. If he files online but pays separately, he should file and pay by 31 October 2025. If he both files and pays online, he has until mid-November 2025 to claim the agricultural and favourite nephew reliefs and avoid interest and surcharges.

The usual warnings about clawback of agricultural relief should apply.

As we will see in para 6.8, there is no clawback of favourite nephew/niece relief.

6.6.2 EXAMPLE OF APPORTIONMENT (BUSINESS)

James Sheehan inherits the following assets from the estate of his uncle John, who was a sole trader, on 1 February 2025. The grant of probate issued on 16 May 2025 and the valuation date has been agreed at that date. The inheritance consists of:

(1) business assets, i.e. shop premises with a market value of €4,000,000 and stock in trade valued at €200,000; and

(2) non-business assets valued at €150,000.

The unsecured debts and funeral and testamentary expenses amount to €50,000 and debts specific to the business are €120,000.

James qualifies for both business relief and favourite nephew relief in respect of the business assets, that is, the shop premises and stock in trade, and has had no prior benefits from anyone.

Under the rules prevailing for business relief, James can set the entire €50,000 unsecured debts and funeral and testamentary expenses against the non-business assets.

Taxable Value—Non-Business Property

	Market Value of Property	**€150,000**
Less	Market Value of Exempt Property (if any)	€ NIL
Equals	Market Value of Taxable Property	€150,000
Less	Applicable Liabilities, Costs & Expenses (if any)	€50,000
Equals	Incumbrance Free Value	€100,000
Less	Consideration [in money or monies worth]	€ NIL
Equals	**Taxable Value of Non-Business Property**	€100,000

Taxable Value of Relevant Business Property

	Market Value of Relevant Business Property	**€4,200,000**
Less	Liabilities and Consideration	€120,000
Equals	Taxable Value	€4,080,000
Less	Value Attributable to Excepted Assets	€ 0
Equals	Value of Relevant non-Excepted Business Property	€4,080,000
Less	Any property subject to Replacement/Successive Benefit rules	€ 0
Equals	Incumbrance Free Value of Relevant Business Property on which Relief is Granted	€4,080,000
Less	90% Business Relief	€3,672,000
Equals	Taxable Value of All Qualifying Relevant Business Property	€408,000
Plus	Excepted Assets and Assets not Eligible for Relief	€ 0
Equals	**Taxable Value of All Business Property**	**€408,000**

Again, normally at this stage in a business relief calculation, the two taxable values would be added together to provide the taxable value of the current benefit, but in this case the business property is inherited as a favourite nephew and as such has a **Group A** threshold while the other (non-business property) is inherited as an 'ordinary' nephew and as such has a **Group B** threshold. There is no aggregation between Groups.

Tax Payable on Taxable Value of Business Assets

Group A

	Taxable Value of this ~~gift~~/inheritance	**€408,000**
	TV of Business €408,000 + +	
	TV of Non- Business € NIL	
Less	Small Gift Exemption where relevant	€ 0
Equals	Net Taxable Value of benefit	€408,000
	Relevant Threshold Group A B C	€400,000
Less	Taxable Value of Prior Aggregable Benefits (SGE?)	€ 0
Equals	Available Threshold for this benefit	€400,000
Taxable Excess [Taxable Value less Available Threshold]		**€8,000**
Tax @ 33% of Taxable Excess		**€2,640**

**	A	€400,000	B	€40,000	C	€20,000
Prior to 2 October 2024						
	A	**€335,000**	B	€32,500	C	€16,250

Tax Payable on Taxable Value of Non-Business Assets

Group B

	Taxable Value of this ~~gift~~/inheritance	**€100,000**
	TV of Business € NIL + +	
	TV of Non- Business €100,000	
Less	Small Gift Exemption where relevant	~~€3,000~~ / €0 0NIL
Equals	Net Taxable Value of benefit	€100,000
	Relevant Threshold Group ~~A~~ **B** ~~C~~	€40,000
Less	Taxable Value of Prior Aggregable Benefits (SGE?)	€ 0
Equals	Available Threshold for this benefit	€40,000
Taxable Excess [Taxable Value less Available Threshold]		€60,000
Tax @ 33% of Taxable Excess		€19,800

** A	€400,000	**B**	**€40,000**	C	€20,000
Prior to 2 October 2024					
A	€335,000	B	€32,500	C	€16,250

James pays (€2,640 + €19,800) a total of €22,440 on assets with a net value of €4,180,000.

Again, the extremely important point is that although the benefits all come from the same beneficiary (his late uncle), the business portion of the benefit is taxable under Group A and the non-business portion of the benefit is taxable under Group B.

However, because there is only aggregation between gifts in the same Group threshold, the nephew has the benefit of two separate Group thresholds. This, in effect, gives a favourite nephew an advantage over a child.

A further point to note is that business assets may qualify for favourite nephew relief but may not qualify for business relief. The example was given earlier of a business letting property which would qualify for favourite nephew/niece relief but not for business relief.

6.7 Combining Benefits: Favourite Nephew, Agricultural/Business, and Dwelling-House Relief Arising on the Same Benefit

A final point to note is a situation where a nephew/niece qualifies for favourite nephew/niece relief, agricultural/business relief, and dwelling-house relief. Treatment of liabilities—particularly a mortgage covering the entire property—should be examined with great care.

Because the dwelling is exempt, the portion of the mortgage relating to the dwelling is not taken into account at all. (See **3.4.2**—liabilities not allowable as deductions.) The mortgage covering the entire property is apportioned between the exempt and the non-exempt part and only that proportion of the mortgage relating to the business is allowable against the business.

Similarly, general liabilities will have to be apportioned between the exempt, the business (favourite nephew), and the non-business (ordinary nephew). The treatment of general liabilities differs between agricultural and business relief, and this will have a similar effect when dealing with a favourite nephew claiming either relief along with favourite nephew relief and dwelling-house relief.

6.7.1 FAVOURITE NEPHEW, AGRICULTURAL RELIEF, AND DWELLING-HOUSE EXEMPTION

Taking the example from earlier at **6.6.1** and adding a few details:

John is the sole beneficiary of his uncle (father's brother) Paddy's estate. Paddy died on 18 March 2025 and the Grant of Probate is issued on 23 June 2025. This has been agreed as the valuation date, at which time the estate consisted of the following:

(1)	Farm including a farmhouse valued at €250,000 and livestock, bloodstock, and farm machinery	€2,500,000
(2)	Savings bonds	€75,000
(3)	Bank balance	€10,000

There is a mortgage of €200,000 on the farm, general debts of €10,000, and legal costs and funeral and testamentary expenses amount to €10,000. John qualifies as a farmer, as a favourite nephew, and for dwelling-house relief. He has had no prior benefits from anyone.

Calculate his Inheritance Tax, if any:

John will qualify as a farmer and, as noted before, the farmhouse, although exempt, will be an agricultural asset for the farmer test.

Costs are now apportioned between the exempt, the agricultural, and the ordinary assets as follows.

First, the mortgage is divided between the agricultural land and the exempt farmhouse in proportion as follows:

$$\frac{\text{Exempt Assets}}{\text{Agricultural Assets}} \times \text{Mortgage on land} = \text{Exempt Element of Mortgage}$$

$$\frac{€250{,}000}{€2{,}500{,}000} \times €200{,}000 = €20{,}000$$

The €20,000 of the mortgage relating to the exempt farmhouse will not be deducted from the taxable value of the benefit (s. 28(5)).

$$\frac{\text{Farmland}}{\text{Agricultural Assets}} \times \text{Mortgage on land} = \text{Portion of Mortgage deducted from farm}$$

$$\frac{€2{,}250{,}000}{€2{,}500{,}000} \times €200{,}000 = €180{,}000$$

The €180,000 of the mortgage relating to the agricultural property will be reduced by 90 per cent to 10 per cent of its value (i.e. €18,000) as the agricultural property is also deducted in this fashion.

The net value of the exempt farmhouse is (€250,000 – €20,000) = €230,000.

The net value of the farmland is (€2,250,000 – €180,000) = €2,070,000. It is these net figures that are used when apportioning the general costs and funeral and testamentary expenses between exempt, agricultural, and non-agricultural along with the value of the non-agricultural assets of €85,000.

This apportionment takes effect as follows:

$$\frac{\text{Equitable Value of } \textbf{Exempt} \text{ Assets}}{\text{Equitable Value of All Assets}} \times \text{General Costs} = \text{Exempt costs}$$

Equitable value of all assets (€230,000 + €2,070,000 + €85,000) = €2,385,000

Exempt Costs

$$\frac{€230{,}000}{€2{,}385{,}000} \times €20{,}000 = €1{,}929$$

€1,929 of the general debts relate to the exempt property and cannot be deducted from the value of the benefit.

Agricultural Costs

$$\frac{\text{Net Agricultural Assets}}{\text{Equitable Value of All Assets}} \times \text{General Costs @ 10\%} = \text{Agricultural Costs}$$

$$\frac{€2{,}070{,}000}{€2{,}385{,}000} \times €20{,}000 = €17{,}358 \text{ @ } 10\% = €1{,}736$$

€1,736 will be deducted from the agricultural value of the farm.

'Ordinary' or Non-Agricultural Costs

In this case, the exempt property, the farmhouse, was included with the agricultural costs, so all the non-agricultural assets are included in the 'Ordinary' costs, which will not be reduced.

$$\frac{\text{Non Agricultural assets}}{\text{Equitable Value of All Assets}} \times \text{General Costs} = \text{Non-Agricultural costs}$$

This gives us

$$\frac{€85{,}000}{€2{,}385{,}000} \times €20{,}000 = €713$$

€713 will be deducted from 'value after reliefs and exemptions'.

Of these costs:

- €1,929 relate to the exempt property and as such are not allowable under s. 28(5);
- a further €17,358 relate to the agricultural property and as such are reduced by 90 per cent to 10 per cent 'agricultural value', that is, €1,736;
- and the final €713 relating to the non-agricultural assets can be deducted against the non-agricultural assets, in its entirety as noted above.

In addition, the non-exempt portion of the mortgage (€180,000) will be deducted from the agricultural property after being reduced to 10 per cent.

Taxable values will be calculated as follows:

Taxable Value—Non-Agricultural Property

Group B

	Market Value	**€85,000**
Less	Exempt Property	€ 0
Equals	Market Value of Taxable Property	€85,000
Less	Relevant Portion of Liabilities, Costs & Expenses	€713
Equals	Incumbrance Free Value	€84,287
Less	Allowable Consideration [in money or monies worth]	€0
Equals	**Taxable Value**	**€84,287**

Taxable Value of Agricultural Property

Group A

	Market Value	**€2,500,000**
Less	Market Value of Exempt Property (if any)	€250,000
Equals	Market Value of Agricultural Property	€2,250,000
Less	Agricultural Relief [90%]	€2,025,000
Equals	Agricultural Value [10%]	€225,000
Less	Relevant Portion of Liabilities, Costs & Expenses General Costs €17,358 **[reduced to 10%]** €1,736 Mortgage (on farm only) €180,000 **[reduced to 10%]** €18,000	€19,736
Equals	Incumbrance Free Value	€205,264
Less	Relevant Portion of Consideration [in money or monies worth] **[reduced to 10%]**	**€ 0**
Equals	**Taxable Value**	**€205,264**

Tax on the two benefits is calculated as follows:

Tax Payable on Taxable Value of 'Ordinary' assets

Group B

	Taxable Value of this ~~gift~~/inheritance	**€84,287**
	TV of Agricultural € NIL + +	
	TV of Non-Agricultural €84,287	
Less	Small Gift Exemption where relevant	€ 0
Equals	Net Taxable Value of benefit	€84,287
	Relevant Threshold Group ~~A~~ **B** ~~C~~	€40,000
Less	Taxable Value of Prior Aggregable Benefits (SGE?)	€ 0
Equals	Available Threshold for this benefit	€40,000

(Continued)

(Continued)

Taxable Excess [Taxable Value less Available Threshold]		€44,287
Tax @ 33% of Taxable Excess		**€14,614.71 rounded up to €14,615**

** A	€400,000	B	€40,000	C	€20,000
Prior to 2 October 2024					
A	€335,000	B	€32,500	C	€16,250

Tax Payable on Taxable Value of Agricultural Assets

Group A

	Taxable Value of this ~~gift~~/inheritance		**€205,264**
	TV of Agricultural €205,264 +	+	
	TV of Non-Agricultural €0		
Less	Small Gift Exemption where relevant		**€0 €3,000 /**
Equals	Net Taxable Value of benefit		**€205,264**
	Relevant Threshold Group **A** ~~B C~~	€400,000	**€335,000**
Less	Taxable Value of Prior Aggregable Benefits (SGE?)		**€ 0**
Equals	Available Threshold for this benefit		**€400,000**
Taxable Excess [Taxable Value less Available Threshold]			**€ 0**
Tax @ 33% of Taxable Excess			**€ 0**

** A **€400,000** B €40,000 C €20,000

Prior to 2 October 2024

A €335,000 B €32,500 C €16,250

John pays €14,615 tax on a net estate valued at €2,365,000 received from his uncle.

John should file and pay by 31 October 2025 or by mid November 2025 if both filing and paying online using ROS in order to comply with Section 46 (4) as introduced by Section 55 Finance Act, 2020 to claim the agricultural, dwelling-house, and favourite nephew reliefs and avoid interest and surcharges.

The usual warnings about clawback of agricultural and dwelling-house relief should be issued in writing.

6.7.2 FAVOURITE NEPHEW, BUSINESS RELIEF, AND DWELLING-HOUSE RELIEF

The treatment of charged assets and general debts now has to be demonstrated for business relief combined with favourite nephew relief and dwelling-house relief.

Taking the earlier example of James Sheehan at **6.6.2** and adding in the following details:

James Sheehan inherits the estate of his uncle John on 1 March 2025. The grant of probate issued on 1 June 2025 and the valuation date has been agreed at that date. The inheritance consists of:

(1) Shop premises with a market value of €4,000,000, of which €400,000 is composed of an apartment above the shop premises. There is a mortgage of €100,000 charged over the entire premises.

(2) Stock in trade valued at €200,000.

(3) Non-business assets valued at €150,000.

(4) The unsecured debts and funeral and testamentary expenses amount to €50,000 and debts specific to the business are €120,000.

James lived with his uncle while assisting him in his business and thus qualifies for dwelling-house, business, and favourite nephew relief. He has received no prior benefits from anyone in the past.

Calculate the tax payable by James.

First, the mortgage of €100,000 is apportioned between the exempt portion and the business portion as follows:

$$\frac{\text{Exempt portion of premises}}{\text{Entire premises}} \times \text{Mortgage} = \text{Exempt portion of mortgage}$$

$$\frac{€400{,}000}{€4{,}000{,}000} \times €100{,}000 = €10{,}000$$

This €10,000 cannot be deducted from the value of the non-business assets.

Normally, under the rules prevailing for business relief, James can set the entire €50,000 unsecured debts and funeral and testamentary expenses against the non-business assets but because a portion of the unsecured debts and funeral and testamentary expenses relates to exempt assets, the amount relating to the exempt assets must be ascertained and the deductible expenses reduced by that amount.

Unlike agricultural relief, however, only the exempt and the non-exempt assets are apportioned, and all the non-exempt portion of the debt can be taken off the non-business assets using the formula

$$\frac{\text{Equitable value of taxable non-business assets}}{\text{Equitable value of all non-business assets}} \times \text{Unsecured debt} = \text{Allowable debts}$$

$$\frac{€150{,}000}{€540{,}000} \times €50{,}000 = €13{,}889$$

It is the market value of the property and the market value of the exempt property, not the equitable value, that is used in the first two lines of the calculation to determine the taxable value. This has no effect on the market value of the taxable property.

Taxable Value—Non-Business Property

	Market Value of Property	**€550,000**
Less	Market Value of Exempt Property (if any)	€400,000
Equals	Market Value of Taxable Property	€150,000
Less	Applicable Liabilities, Costs & Expenses (if any)	€13,889
Equals	Incumbrance Free Value	€136,111
Less	Consideration [in money or monies worth]	€ NIL
Equals	**Taxable Value of Non-Business Property**	**€136,111**

Taking the business assets next:

First, the mortgage of €100,000 is apportioned between the business portion and the exempt portion as follows:

$$\frac{\text{Business portion of premises}}{\text{Entire premises}} \times \text{Mortgage} = \text{Allowable portion of mortgage}$$

$$\frac{€3,600,000}{€4,000,000} \times €100,000 = €90,000$$

This €90,000 is deducted from the market value of the relevant business property.

The business assets are the business portion of the premises of €3,600,000 and the other business assets of €200,000 totalling €3,800,000. The allowable debts against the business assets are the allowable mortgage of €90,000 and the exclusively business debts of €120,000 totalling €210,000.

The taxable value of the business assets is ascertained as follows:

	Market Value of Relevant Business Property	**€3,800,000**
	Shop (business portion of premises) €3,600,000	
	Stock in trade €200,000	
Less	Liabilities and Consideration Business debts €120,000 Allowable portion of mortgage €90,000	€210,000
Equals	Taxable Value	€3,590,000
Less	Value Attributable to Excepted Assets	€ 0
Equals	Value of Relevant non-Excepted Business Property	€3,590,000
Less	Any property subject to Replacement/Successive Benefit rules	€ 0
Equals	Incumbrance Free Value of Relevant Business Property on which Relief is Granted	€3,590,000
Less	90% Business Relief	€3,231,000
Equals	Taxable Value of All Qualifying Relevant Business Property	€359,000
Plus	Excepted Assets and Assets not Eligible for Relief	€ 0
Equals	Taxable Value of All Business Property	€359,000

Tax Payable on Taxable Value of Business Assets

Group A

	Taxable Value of this ~~gift~~/inheritance	**€359,000**
	TV of Business €359,000 + +	
	TV of Non- Business € NIL	
Less	Small Gift Exemption where relevant	~~€0,000~~NIL
Equals	Net Taxable Value of benefit	€359,000
	Relevant Threshold Group **A** ~~B C~~	€400,000
Less	Taxable Value of Prior Aggregable Benefits (SGE?)	€ 0

(Continued)

(Continued)

Equals	Available Threshold for this benefit	€400,000
Taxable Excess [Taxable Value less Available Threshold]		**€ 0**
Tax @ 33% of Taxable Excess		**€ 0**

**	A	**€400,000**	B	€40,000	C	€20,000
Prior to 2 October 2024						
	A	€335,000	B	€32,500	C	€16,250

Tax Payable on Taxable Value of Non-Business Assets

Group B

	Taxable Value of this ~~gift~~/inheritance	**€136,111**
	TV of Business € NIL + +	
	TV of Non- Business €136,111	
Less	Small Gift Exemption where relevant	**€ 0**
Equals	Net Taxable Value of benefit	€136,111
	Relevant Threshold Group ~~A~~ **B** ~~C~~	€40,000
Less	Taxable Value of Prior Aggregable Benefits (SGE?)	€ 0
Equals	Available Threshold for this benefit	€40,000 0
Taxable Excess [Taxable Value less Available Threshold]		**€96,111,**
Tax @ 33% of Taxable Excess		**€31,716.63 rounded up to €31,717 34,192**

**	A	€400,000	B	**€40,000**	C	€20,000
Prior to 2 October 2024						
	A	€335,000	**B**	**€32,500**	C	€16,250

James pays €31,717 and should file and pay by 31 October 2025 or by mid November 2025 if both paying and filing online using ROS in order to comply with s. 46 (4) as introduced by s. 55 Finance Act, 2020 to claim the reliefs and avoid surcharges and penalties.

As always, the relevant warnings should be provided in writing in relation to clawback of business relief and dwelling-house relief.

6.8 Clawback and Favourite Nephew Relief

Unlike many of the reliefs dealt with, there is no provision in the legislation for a clawback of favourite nephew relief.

However, where the relief is claimed along with any other reliefs or exemptions such as agricultural, business, or dwelling-house the normal clawback provisions apply, and the solicitor should inform the client in writing in clear unambiguous terms of the nature and extent of such clawback.

CHAPTER 7

STAMP DUTY

7.1 Introduction

This chapter deals with stamp duty.

The current law relating to stamp duty is principally contained in the Stamp Duties Consolidation Act, 1999 ('the SDCA 1999'), which became law on 15 December 1999, and subsequent amending Finance Acts. Prior to this the law of stamp duty was found inter alia in the Stamp Act, 1891, and substantive amendments were made in subsequent Finance Acts.

Stamp duty is a tax on 'instruments'; that is to say, on various types of written documents, and not on transactions. If there is no instrument or document to stamp then no stamp duty can arise unless the legislation provides otherwise. When dealing with the question of whether a stamp duty exposure arises, the first question that needs to be asked is, 'is there a document?' These documents are referred to as 'instruments' in the stamp duty code. Not every instrument is liable to stamp duty. To be liable an instrument must be listed under one of the headings in Schedule 1 to the SDCA, 1999, which contains a list of those instruments liable to stamp duty.

With the exception of the CREST share transfer system, where no document exists, the general rule is that there is no exposure to stamp duty. If assets can be transferred without the use of a document, stamp duty can be avoided on the transaction.

The documents listed in this Schedule are usually referred to as 'heads of charge'. The three main heads of charge are conveyance on sale, lease, and mortgage. Schedule 1 also specifies the appropriate rates of duty, which may be ad valorem or fixed, applicable to each instrument. The rates of stamp duty outlined at **7.4.2** in respect of residential property apply to instruments (written documents) executed (signed, sealed, and delivered) on or after 8 December 2010.

7.1.1 'AD VALOREM'

When a document is charged to stamp duty at the ad valorem rate, the value of the property is subject to stamp duty based on the appropriate table of rates and will depend on the type of the property, whether residential or non-residential. Currently the rate of stamp duty applicable to residential property is 1 per cent where the consideration does not exceed €1,000,000, 2 per cent on any excess over €1,000,000 up to €1,500,000 and 6% on any excess over €1,500,000.

Stamp duty at the rate of 15% per cent is payable on the cumulative purchase of ten or more residential houses in a twelve-month period. This applies since 2 October 2024.

A flat rate of 7.5 per cent applies to instruments executed on or after 9 October 2019 in relation to all non-residential/commercial/agricultural property (other than policies of insurance). There is a refund scheme available to reduce the 7.5 per cent rate of stamp duty to 2 per cent on certain residential development property transfers. This scheme has been extended to 31 December 2025.

There is no stamp duty payable on contents as these pass by delivery.

7.1.2 FIXED

When a document is charged to stamp duty at the fixed rate, stamp duty of €12.50 is payable. An example might be a duplicate or counterpart lease.

7.2 The Mandatory Nature of Stamp Duty, The Finance Acts, 1991 and 2012, and Penalties

With effect from 1 November 1991 the payment of stamp duty became mandatory. Prior to this date the payment of both ad valorem and fixed duties was voluntary. This was so because although a liability arose to stamp instruments the Revenue did not have any method of enforcing the payment of duty. Section 2(3) of the SDCA, 1999 provides that an instrument which is subject to stamp duty must be stamped within thirty days after it is first executed. The Finance Act, 1991 is of importance to solicitors because it created a number of obligations and imposed a duty of disclosure on professional advisers and their clients in relation to the payment of stamp duty. Penalties were imposed for late stamping of instruments chargeable to duty, and surcharges were imposed where property had been undervalued in returns to the Revenue Commissioners. The Finance Act, 2012 ('the 2012 Act') introduced a range of changes in the administration of stamp duty that came into effect on 7 July 2012 in respect of instruments executed on or after that date. The provisions of the 2012 Act are now contained in ss 8, 14, 16, and 127 to 134A of the SDCA, 1999. In addition to the fact that the payment of stamp duty is compulsory (s. 2) and that late payment of stamp duty will give rise to interest (s. 14), ss 127 to 134A of the SDCA contain a number of provisions/penalties to help to ensure that returns are filed on time through the Revenue Online System ('ROS') for instruments which are chargeable to stamp duty. Late filing surcharges were introduced. Section 8 of the SDCA, 1999 provides for a penalty of €3000 for failing to file a return, setting out all of the relevant information. Section 8A of the SDCA, 1999 provides that all facts and circumstances affecting the liability to stamp duty or affecting the amount of duty are to be fully disclosed to the Revenue Commissioners in the returns. This section puts the onus on a person to bring to the attention of the Revenue Commissioners all the facts and circumstances affecting the liability of an instrument to stamp duty and these must be stated in the instrument itself. In some cases it will not be practicable for the instrument to contain all relevant facts and circumstances. In such cases it is permissible to set out any facts or circumstances not set out in the instrument in an accompanying statement. This statement is not required to be delivered to the Revenue where the instrument is stamped under the e-stamping system.

Evidence in relation to the chargeability of an instrument to duty must be retained by an accountable person for audit purposes for six years from the date of stamping of the instrument under the e-stamping system should the Revenue wish to examine it. In addition, s. 128A provides that an accountable person is obliged to retain records relating to a stamp duty liability or to a relief or exemption claimed for a period of six years from the date a stamp duty return is filed or the date the duty is paid, whichever date is the later. The 2012 Act introduced new fixed penalties on each accountable person for failure to file a stamp duty return. The obligation would appear to apply to solicitors involved in the preparation and filing of stamp duty returns on behalf of clients.

These penalties apply to instruments executed on or after 7 July 2012. Section 8A provides for a penalty of €3000 where an incorrect electronic or paper return relating to an instrument is filed with the Revenue in circumstances where the person is aware that the facts filed are incorrect.

Section 8B provides for a penalty of €3000 where an accountable person fails to cause an electronic or paper return relating to an instrument to be filed before the time specified in s. 2(3) of the SDCA, that is, before the expiration of thirty days after the first execution of the instrument.

Section 8(3) provides that in the case of fraudulent or negligent execution of an instrument where facts affecting liability are not fully set forth in the instrument, a penalty of €1265 applies together with the amount of difference of duty. This penalty applies to a person 'employed or concerned in or about preparation of the instrument'. This applies to solicitors and any other professional adviser to any parties executing instruments that may be liable to stamp duty.

The penalties outlined in ss 8 and 134A SDCA must be considered carefully by all practitioners. There is no de minimis threshold on the application of these penalties which could theoretically apply even where there is no stamp duty payable on the unfiled return.

Section 15 of the SDCA, 1999 reiterated the provisions of the Finance Act, 1991 in relation to surcharges imposed where the value of the property is understated to the Revenue Commissioners. This section has however been abolished in respect of instruments executed on or after 7 July 2012. For such instruments where an undervaluation of property is included in the stamp duty return filed under the e-stamping system, penalties relating to the filing of an incorrect return will be incurred (s. 134A).

7.2.1 PENALTIES FOR LATE FILING OF RETURNS: THE FINANCE ACT, 2012

7.2.1.1 Section 14 of the SDCA, 1999

An instrument that is chargeable to stamp duty must be duly stamped within 30 days after its first execution, otherwise penalties for late filing will be imposed (s. 2 and s. 14 of the SDCA, 1999 refer). Where the correct amount of stamp duty is not paid within the time limit set down in s. 2 of the SDCA, that is, if the deed is stamped after thirty days from the date of first execution of the instrument under s. 14 SDCA, 1999 interest is payable at the rate of 0.0219 per cent per day or part of a day. The 2012 Act did not change the specified return date for the filing of stamp duty returns, which is thirty days after first execution, nor was the rate of late filing interest (0.0219 per cent) changed. The Revenue has confirmed that they will continue to accept returns filed up to forty-four days after first execution, in line with previous practice.

7.2.1.2 Section 14A of the SDCA, 1999: late filing of returns

The penalty regime for stamp duty has undergone a very substantial change since the Finance Act, 2012 became law on 7 July 2012. A self-assessment regime was introduced and, for instruments executed on or after that date, a new late filing surcharge was introduced. Solicitors must continue to file e-stamping returns as previously. The e-stamping system will ensure that returns for instruments executed on or after 7 July 2012 will be treated automatically on a self-assessed basis. Adjudication was abolished and the Revenue will no longer examine instruments prior to stamping and the stamp certificate will issue immediately after the return is lodged, provided all charges are paid. The new system of penalties include tax geared surcharges for late filing of returns, tax geared penalties for failing to file a return, and a number of other penalties that will not be dealt with in this text.

The new surcharge is based on a percentage increase of the stamp duty payable and is subject to a grading of the surcharge by reference to the length of the delay in filing the stamp duty return as well as being subject to an overall cap on the level of the surcharge.

7.2.1.3 The surcharge

For instruments executed on or after 7 July 2012 a new late filing surcharge applies equal to 5 per cent of the unpaid duty where the stamp duty return is filed after the specified return date (44 days) subject to a maximum of €12,695. Where the stamp duty return is filed later than ninety-two days of the date of execution of the instrument a late filing surcharge of 10 per cent of the unpaid duty applies, subject to a maximum of €63,485. The surcharge is not a penalty and therefore forms part of a stamp duty charge. Late filing interest is charged on the amount of the original stamp duty liability plus the surcharge amount.

On 1 June 2011 it became mandatory to file stamp duty returns online using the ROS, subject to very limited exceptions. Payment of stamp duty must also be made online from that date by ROS, or in limited cases payment can be made by electronic fund transfer ('EFT').

7.2.1.4 Section 134A SDCA, 1999 penalties: solicitors' liability and obligations

In cases of fraud or negligence penalties will also apply. A voluntary conveyance must be brought to the attention of the Revenue by ticking the relevant box in the return. Failure to do so will result in a presumption of negligence or of acting deliberately under s. 134A SDCA, 1999. Tax geared penalties apply in addition to a fixed penalty of €1265 in instances of fraud and negligence. The penalty is determined by the number of defaults by the person, whether the category of default is deliberate or careless (failure to take reasonable care) but not deliberate, the level of cooperation, and whether a prompted or unprompted qualifying disclosure is made. The penalty can be 100 per cent of the underpayment.

If an error is neither deliberate nor careless, action must be taken without undue delay on spotting the error to rectify same to prevent it being treated as a deliberate action.

Other obligations to be aware of include s. 129 SDCA, 1999, which provides that any person who enrols, enters, or registers an instrument that is not properly stamped will incur a penalty of €630.

Mitigation of penalties under s. 1065 of the Taxes Consolidation Act ('TCA'), 1997 applies to stamp duty penalties.

Pursuant to s. 128 SDCA, 1999 there is an obligation to produce documents, provide information, and permit access to Revenue officials. Failure to comply is an offence under s. 1078 TCA. Section 129A SDCA, 1999 provides an obligation to retain records of a true return for six years from the date the tax was paid or return made. This is subject to a penalty of €3000 for failure to comply. Failure to produce records where a relevant person (including a solicitor) is retaining records on an accountable person's behalf can lead to a penalty of €19,045 plus €2535 per day until compliance. Employees of a relevant person can also be held liable (s. 128B SDCA, 1999). There is a defence of legal professional privilege to s. 128A but not to s. 128B.

It is advisable to retain a record of the stamp duty return (which has been approved by your client) for auditing purposes for four years from the stamping of the instrument. Unfortunately the drop boxes selected in the return are not shown in the printed version and this issue has been brought to the attention of the Revenue by the Law Society Taxation Committee.

7.2.2 EFFECT OF A DOCUMENT NOT BEING STAMPED

Section 127 of the SDCA provides that if an instrument is not duly stamped:

(a) Such instrument cannot be used as evidence in court in civil or arbitral proceedings until any duty and penalties are paid. An unstamped document can be produced in criminal proceedings;

(b) It will not be acceptable to the Land Registry when applying for registration of ownership; and

(c) A purchaser is not obliged to accept an unstamped deed. In fact, an unstamped deed is not a good link in a chain of title.

Prior to the Finance Act, 2012, instruments that had been adjudicated were considered to be duly stamped but instruments that had been 'straight stamped' were not considered to be duly stamped.

Section 127 of the SDCA has been amended by the 2012 Act so that all instruments executed on or after 7 July 2012 and stamped using the e-stamping system are considered to be duly stamped. This change is of considerable benefit to solicitors, who otherwise would have to satisfy themselves as to the sufficiency of the stamping of documents. Solicitors will have to ensure that instruments executed before 7 July 2012 (unless bearing an adjudication stamp) have been duly stamped.

7.2.3 CATEGORIES OF STAMP DUTIES

7.2.3.1 Ad valorem duty and revenue certificates in deeds

'Ad valorem' is a Latin term meaning 'by value' and is used to describe a rate of stamp duty that is proportionate to the value of the transaction involved. Schedule 1 to the SDCA, 1999 identifies the rate of duty applicable to various instruments, whether ad valorem, fixed, or exempt from duty. Prior to 7 July 2012 the amount of duty applicable to a particular instrument often depended on that instrument containing a particular certificate. The concept of certification in deeds was introduced in the Finance Act, 1910. Under this Act lower rates of stamp duty were introduced for property transactions under a certain value and, in the absence of what became commonly known as a 'Finance Act certificate', the maximum rate of duty was payable.

Certification in deeds was subsequently expanded to identify:

(a) the type of property being transferred under a deed, for example whether residential or non-residential;

(b) the nature of the transaction involved;

(c) whether an exemption from stamp duty applied; or

(d) whether a relief from stamp duty could be claimed.

The rationale behind certification in deeds was that the maximum rate of stamp duty would be chargeable unless the correct certification to support the lower rate or exemption being claimed was used. It should be noted that prior to 7 July 2012 the insertion of an incorrect certificate was an offence (SDCA, 1999, s. 17). With effect from 7 July 2012, however, there is no longer a requirement for the inclusion of such certificates in stampable instruments. Section 17 SDCA has been abolished in respect of instruments executed on or after that date.

As stamp duty certificates are no longer required in deeds, the Conveyancing Committee of the Law Society, in the December 2015 edition of the *Gazette*, recommends that solicitors obtain a written record of instructions as to stamp duty. A suggested precedent record sheet is available on the precedent page in the members' area of the Law Society website (www.lawsociety.ie/solicitors/practising/precedents). This may then be retained on file by way of a future record, in addition to the copy printout available from the Revenue e-stamping system.

7.2.4 THE CHARGE TO STAMP DUTY—TERRITORIALITY

Stamp duty is a tax/charge on certain written documents known as instruments which are listed under one of the headings as specified in Schedule 1 to the SDCA, 1999 and which are executed in the State or which relate to property situate in the State. 'Instrument' is defined in s. 1 as including every written document. The most usual types of instruments on which stamp duty arises are deeds effecting transfers of lands or dwelling-houses, by conveyance, transfer, assignment, or lease. Once a document exists, it then becomes important to determine if it is possible for an exposure to stamp duty to arise. There must be a link between the document and Ireland. Territoriality is decided by ascertaining whether the document:

(a) is executed in the State; or

(b) relates to any property situate in the State; or

(c) relates to any matter or thing 'done or to be done' in the State.

If the document is linked to Ireland in one or more of these ways, it will be exposed to Irish stamp duty. The nationality or residence of the parties to the instrument is irrelevant for stamp duty purposes. If any instrument listed in Schedule 1 of the SDCA, 1999 is executed in the State or relates to property situate in the State or relates to any matter or thing done or to be done in the State then it is chargeable to stamp duty.

A document is regarded as executed in the State if the formalities required to make it a legally effective document are completed in Ireland. For stamp duty purposes, executed means signed and/or sealed where appropriate.

7.2.5 CONVEYANCE ON SALE

Once a document exists and that document is within the Irish territorial limits indicated earlier, an exposure to stamp duty will arise if the document is one of those listed in the First Schedule to the SDCA. As previously stated, the documents listed in this schedule are referred to as 'heads of charge'.

The amount of stamp duty payable on any instrument depends on the purpose of that instrument. A document is chargeable to stamp duty if it comes within the heads of charge contained in the SDCA, 1999, as amended. The most common heads of charge, that is, the basic categories of stamp duty, together with examples of how stamp duty is calculated under the head, are set out in the following text. The two main heads of charge for conveyancers include a conveyance on sale and a lease. A mortgage is no longer a head of charge.

Some of the heads of charge are subject to ad valorem duty and some of them are exposed to fixed type duty. Whether the stamp duty is charged at the ad valorem rates or the fixed duty rates depends on how the transaction evidenced or recorded in the instrument is classified. Conveyances on sale of shares are exposed to stamp duty at the rate of 1 per cent. Conveyances of insurance policies (for more than two years and with an Irish risk) are exposed to stamp duty at the rate of 0.1 per cent.

The most important head of charge in stamp duties is the 'conveyance on sale' head which deals with the sale of real property (houses, commercial premises, factory, farms, etc.), and these are exposed to stamp duty at the ad valorem rate. Property is defined in s. 1 of the SDCA, 1999 to include:

> *every instrument, and every decree or order (including a decree or order for, or having the effect of an order for, foreclosure) of any court or of any commissioners, whereby any property, or any estate or interest in any property, on the sale or compulsory acquisition of that property or that interest is transferred to or vested in a purchaser, or any other person, or any other person on such purchaser's behalf or by such purchaser's direction.*

Thus, any document that is used to convey or transfer ownership of property to include houses, apartments or sites with agreement to build, land, and so on will attract stamp duty at the ad valorem rate. It also applies to non-residential property such as land or housing sites without residential buildings, commercial premises, and so on. For a 'Conveyance' to be a Schedule 1 SDCA instrument it must either be 'on sale' or operate as a 'voluntary disposition' under s. 30 SDCA.

To be 'on sale' there must be parties competent to contract, mutual assent, property, a vendor/donor and purchaser/donee, and a price or consideration.

Consideration for stamp duty purposes can take the form of cash, shares, satisfaction of debt, assumption of liabilities, or an exchange of property.

In addition, the following instruments are treated as a conveyance on sale:

- a declaration of trust by a vendor in favour of a purchaser;
- a release by a life tenant of his life interest to the remainderman;
- a release by the remainderman of his remainder interest to the life tenant;
- the grant of an option.

7.2.6 RATES OF STAMP DUTY

There are a number of categories of rates. The first three are as follows:

(a) Conveyance on sale of residential property. This is dealt with at **7.3.2**.

(b) A higher rate of stamp duty of 15 per cent applies where a purchaser buys 10 or more residential units (houses or duplexes) at the one time or over a twelve-month period. This measure was introduced in 20 May 2021 to discourage investment funds from buying up housing estates. The increased rate of 15 per cent (from 10% in 2021) increased since 2 October 2024, does not apply when purchasing residential units in Apartment blocks or to the purchase of/leasing to of properties by a Housing Authority, the Housing Agency or other approved Housing Bodies.

(c) Conveyance on sale of commercial and other non-residential property. The rates are set out at **7.2.7**. These rates apply to conveyances on sale not covered in (a) or (b) or in any other head of charge provided in the legislation. This head of charge applies in situations involving non-residential elements of a conveyance on sale containing mixed residential and non-residential property.

The remaining categories of rates of stamp duties relate to conveyances on sale of stocks and marketable securities, policies of insurance, and CREST transfers on sale, and are not dealt with in this text.

7.2.7 RATES OF STAMP DUTY ON CONVEYANCE ON SALE OR LEASE PREMIUMS OF COMMERCIAL AND OTHER NON-RESIDENTIAL PROPERTY FOR INSTRUMENTS EXECUTED AFTER 9 OCTOBER 2019

In the case of non-residential property, the rate of stamp duty is 7.5 per cent. This rate applies to instruments executed on or after 9 October 2019. This single rate of 7.5 per cent applies to the entire amount of the consideration attributable to non-residential property.

Section 83D of the SDCA, as introduced in the Finance Act, 2017, provides for a Residential Development stamp duty refund scheme where land that is chargeable at the 7.5 per cent commercial and other non-residential rate of stamp duty is subsequently developed for residential purposes. It operates to effectively reduce the rate of stamp duty to a minimum of 2 per cent on certain residential property transfers. The claim is submitted under the e-payment claim section of ROS. The time allowed to commence building works has been extended to 31 December 2025.

The scheme applies to both one-off houses and larger housing developments. The accountable person can lodge the claim themselves using 'My Account' or the solicitor can lodge the claim on their behalf. In the latter case, refunds are made to the solicitor's account as filer.

The system requires a declaration to be furnished. The accountable person is the appropriate person to make the declaration. A number of documents are required to make the claim, as set out in the *Revenue Stamp Duty Manual*, but solicitors should particularly note that a certified copy of the deed and the stamp certificate is required, and therefore a copy of these items should be retained on the solicitor's file.

7.2.7.1 Aggregation

As a single rate of 7.5 per cent applies to non-residential property, aggregation is no longer relevant in determining the stamp duty liability where a transaction forms part of a larger transaction or of a series of transactions involving non-residential property.

Non-residential property is any property other than residential property, stocks or marketable securities, or policies of insurance. It includes sites, offices, factories, shops, public houses, land, and goodwill attached to businesses.

7.2.8 FINANCE ACT (TRANSACTION) CERTIFICATES

This was the first form of certification introduced for stamp duty purposes and is the one that practitioners will be most familiar with. Originally this certificate dealt solely with the amount or value of the transaction but later it also identified whether the property was residential or non-residential in nature. The rationale for this certificate was to prevent the breaking up of a larger transaction into a number of smaller transactions in order to avoid a higher rate of duty. However, for instruments executed on or after 7 July 2012 these certificates are no longer required to be included, and s. 17 of the SDCA has been abolished.

As they are no longer required in deeds, the Law Society Conveyancing Committee recommended in a Practice Note in the December 2015 *Gazette* that solicitors should obtain a written record of instructions as to stamp duty. A suggested precedent record sheet is available on the precedent page in the members' area of the website (www.lawsociety.ie/Solicitors/Practising/Precedents). This may then be retained on file by way of a future record in addition to the copy printout available from the Revenue e-stamping system.

7.2.9 NEGLIGENCE PROVISIONS AND THE PROFESSIONAL ADVISER

As discussed earlier, various Finance Acts have increased the scope of offences in the context of tax evasion, in particular for the professional adviser to a transaction. Any adviser who is involved in aiding and abetting a taxpayer to evade tax will be guilty of a criminal offence.

Similarly, money laundering legislation can impose a liability upon advisers who are not connected with such transactions, and in certain circumstances even if the adviser is not involved, failure to make the appropriate reports of a transaction may render the adviser liable.

Section 8 of the SDCA, 1999 in particular is relevant. Under s. 8, there is an onus to bring to the attention of the Revenue the full facts and circumstances affecting the liability of an instrument to stamp duty. If these are not included in the instrument, then the additional information must be disclosed in an accompanying statement. If the statement is incorrect, then any person employed or concerned in or about making the statement will be responsible with the parties to the instrument for the breach of duty. Thus, s. 134A provides for a penalty of €1265 plus a tax geared further penalty where a person acts deliberately or carelessly in relation to the execution of an instrument where:

- (a) All the facts and circumstances affecting the liability of the instrument to duty are not disclosed in the instrument or in a statement to which s. 8(2) applies;
- (b) An incorrect electronic or paper return under the e-stamping system is delivered; or
- (c) There is a failure to deliver an electronic or paper return under the e-stamping system

and this gives rise to an underpayment in the amount of stamp duty due and payable. Professional advisers who are unsure as to whether certain facts are relevant may express to the Revenue their uncertainty and, provided the uncertainty expressed is genuine and not a tactic to evade or avoid stamp duty, a prosecution for negligence or fraud may be avoided.

7.2.9.1 Expression of doubt: s. 8C of the SDCA

The removal of adjudication has increased the risk and burden on solicitors to ensure that the self-assessment return is correct and that the correct amount of stamp duty is paid. There is a very limited expression of doubt facility if there is a genuine doubt on the treatment of a matter. To utilise the expression of doubt facility the expression of doubt box must be ticked on the return. Section 8C of the SDCA allows an accountable person, who is in doubt about the application of stamp duty to an instrument, to lodge a letter of expression of doubt with the Revenue. If the expression of doubt ('EOD') is accepted by the Revenue as genuine, late filing interest will not apply to any duty payable on resolution of the doubt.

A letter of EOD must be clearly identified as a letter of expression of doubt and must meet certain additional criteria to be valid and must:

(a) set out full details of the facts and circumstances affecting the stamp duty liability of the instrument;

(b) make reference to the provisions of the law giving rise to the doubt;

(c) identify the amount of stamp duty in doubt in respect of the instrument to which the expression of doubt relates;

(d) be accompanied by any relevant supporting documentation.

This letter may be lodged with the Revenue at the Stamp Duty Office, Dublin Castle.

Both the letter of EOD and the electronic or paper return relating to the instrument must be lodged before the expiration of thirty days after the first execution of the instrument.

The Revenue has enhanced the right to reject the expression of doubt under s. 8C (4) SDCA, 1999, which contains a non-exhaustive list of grounds on which the expression can be rejected. The Revenue may reject an EOD as not being genuine. Section 8C sets out situations where an expression of doubt will not be accepted by the Revenue to include:

(a) where the Revenue have issued general guidelines on the matter;

(b) where the Revenue are of the opinion that the matter is otherwise sufficiently free from doubt as not to warrant an EOD; or

(c) where the Revenue are of the opinion that the accountable person was acting with a view to the evasion or avoidance of duty.

The Revenue will notify the accountable person if an expression of doubt is not accepted as genuine. On receipt of the notification, an amended return must be filed together with payment of the additional duty and interest. A right of appeal exists against the decision to reject the expression of doubt.

7.2.10 TAILTE EIREANN (PREVIOUSLY THE PROPERTY REGISTRATION AUTHORITY) AND STAMP DUTY ON DOCUMENTS

Section 64 of the Registration of Deeds and Title Act, 2006 amends s. 104 of the Registration of Title Act, 1964. After the commencement of this section on 4 November 2006 the Registrar no longer has a 'duty' to check the stamp duty on each deed but may now proceed to register a deed unless there are 'reasonable grounds for suspecting' that stamp duty, or the correct amount of stamp duty, has not been paid.

7.3 Residential Property

Residential property is defined in s. 1 of the SDCA, 1999 as a building or part of a building that, at the date of the instrument of conveyance or lease, was used or was suitable for use as a dwelling, or was in the course of being constructed or adapted for use as a dwelling. It includes also the normal domestic outhouses, garden, and so on, up to one acre. A rate of 1 per cent applies on the conveyance on sale or lease of residential property where the consideration does not exceed €1,000,000. Any excess over €1,000,000 up to €1,500,000 is liable to stamp duty at the rate of 2 per cent and any excess over €1,500,000 is liable to the stamp duty at the rate of 6 per cent.

7.3.1 RATES OF STAMP DUTY

Prior to the Finance Act, 2011 the rate of stamp duty applying to residential property depended on whether the residential property was a new or second-hand house or apartment, and the category of person buying it, that is, whether a first time buyer or an owner occupier, or an investor. This is no longer the case. The rates have changed regularly over recent years and the rates applicable are as stated earlier.

7.3.2 RESIDENTIAL PROPERTY RATES OF STAMP DUTY

The stamp duty regime for residential property was substantially amended and simplified by the Finance Act, 2010. The amount of stamp duty, that is, the rate of stamp duty payable, depends on the price/consideration paid or the market value where the price paid is less than the market value of the property. However, there is an increased rate of 15 per cent if a purchaser buys ten or more residential houses or duplexes at the one time or cumulative in a twelve-month period. This rate applies to the bulk purchase of houses or duplexes (ten or more). The 15 per cent rate will be triggered on the purchase of the tenth property. This will apply on cumulative purchases of ten or more houses, and on ten purchases of ten separate properties over a twelve-month period. The increased rate will apply retrospectively to the other nine units on the purchase of the tenth unit. Any property acquired prior to 20 May 2021 will count towards the threshold of ten units, but the 15 per cent rate will apply only to the units acquired on or after 2 October 2024.

Aggregate consideration	**Rate of stamp duty**
Aggregate consideration not exceeding €1,000,000	1%
Excess over €1,000,000 up to €1,500,000	2%
Excess over €1,500,000	6%

7.3.2.1 Sample

Edwin purchases a house for €1,500,000.

The stamp duty payable is calculated as follows:

First €1,000,000	@ 1%	€10,000
Excess €500,000	@ 2%	€10,000
Total stamp duty		€20,000

'Residential property' is defined in s. 1 of the SDCA, 1999 as a building or part of a building which, at the date of the execution of the conveyance or lease, was used or was suitable for use as a dwelling. It also includes curtilage (that is, the normal domestic outhouses, yard, or garden) up to one acre exclusive of the site of the residential property.

7.3.2.2 15 per cent rate of stamp duty on cumulative purchase of ten or more housing units in a twelve-month period

The standard rates of stamp duty for residential property are 1 per cent on values up to €1 million, 2 per cent on values exceeding €1 million up to €1.5 million and 6% on values over €1.5 million; s. 31E of the SDCA 1999, which took effect from 20 May 2021, provides for a higher 10 per cent rate of stamp duty to be charged on the acquisition of certain residential property. This rate was subsequently increased to 15% from 2 October 2024. The 15 per cent rate of duty applies to the acquisition of individual residential units such as houses and duplexes but not to apartments, where a person acquires at least ten such units during a twelve-month period. The intention of the legislation is to dissuade bulk buying of residential property and is aimed at direct purchase plus indirect acquisition via companies, partnerships, or Irish real estate funds.

Section 31E was introduced by the Finance (Covid-19 and Miscellaneous Provisions) Act 2021 and came into effect on 20 May 2021.

A 'Residential Unit' is defined in s. 31E as a residential property situated in the State comprising an individual dwelling. As defined in s. 1 SDCA 1999 it is essentially a building, or part of a building, that was in use as, or was suitable for use as, a dwelling, or was in the course of being constructed or adapted for use as a dwelling, when it was conveyed or leased.

The 15 per cent rate can therefore apply to the acquisition of residential units that have not yet been completed. A residential unit also includes curtilage up to one acre in area.

'Apartment Block' is defined as a multi-storey residential property that comprises or will comprise not less than three apartments with grouped or common access.

The definition of relevant residential unit specifically excludes a residential unit in an apartment block.

The legislation provides that where there are a number of individual purchases either on a single unit or fewer than ten-unit basis, the 15 per cent charge applies when a tenth unit is acquired by the person, or by a person connected with them, within a twelve-month period.

Units purchased prior to 20 May 2021 will count towards triggering the threshold of ten, but the new rate of 15 per cent will only apply to units acquired on or after 20 May 2021.

The following are outside the scope of the 15 per cent rate of stamp duty:

(a) Section 31E(7) contains a specific exclusion from the 15 per cent rate for apartments, that is, for residential units in apartment blocks.

(b) Certain social housing leases: in certain circumstances the 15 per cent rate will not apply to relevant residential units that are leased to a local authority for onward leasing to a household that qualifies for social housing support. This includes the leasing of residential units to Housing Authorities, the Housing Agency, and other approved housing bodies.

An excellent article by Julia Considine in the August/September 2021 issue of the Gazette, entitled 'New Stamping Ground', provides a welcome comment on the new legislation.

In accordance with s 31E (5) of the SDCA 1999, a residential unit is a 'relevant residential unit' where:

(a) the residential unit was acquired on or after 20 May 2021, and

(b) at least ten residential units have been acquired, either on the same day, or by aggregating any units acquired during the twelve-month period immediately preceding that date.

7.3.3 AGGREGATION

Aggregation applies in determining the stamp duty liability where a transaction forms part of a larger transaction or of a series of transactions involving residential property. The stamp duty liability is calculated on the basis of the aggregate consideration. The duty is then apportioned between the separate properties that are transferred by separate instruments and the apportionment is pro rata to the consideration for each property.

Where two or more residential properties are transferred as part of one or more connected transactions and the combined consideration exceeds €1,000,000, each of the instruments is stamped on the combined consideration valuation; that is, the instruments cannot be stamped separately to avail of the lower rate.

7.3.3.1 The rent-a-room scheme

Under the rent-a-room scheme, gross annual rental income of less than €14,000 is exempt from tax where a room or rooms in a person's principal private residence is/are let as residential accommodation, subject to a number of conditions. If the rental payments received for renting the room exceed the threshold (currently €14,000) the full amount is taxable.

The Finance Act, 2018 introduced a minimum rental period of twenty-eight days to exclude short-term lettings from the relief. However, the relief will still apply to the provision of short-term accommodation for respite cases, care for incapacitated individuals, foreign students, and providing digs for at least four days a week for at least four consecutive weeks. The rules relevant to the relief are contained in s. 216A TCA 1997.

7.3.4 NEW HOUSES AND APARTMENTS

Residential property includes houses and apartments and any site that is bought with a connected agreement to build residential property on it.

The purchase of a site with (or as part of) an arrangement to build a house or apartment on it, will attract stamp duty at the residential property rate on the total of the site cost and the building cost.

However, if a site is purchased with no connected arrangement to build a house or apartment on it, then stamp duty is charged on the site cost at the non-residential rate.

The stamp duty position relating to the purchase of what is in effect a new house or apartment depends on the nature of the contracts entered into. The deed may be giving effect to a contract to purchase:

(a) a site with a connected building agreement;

(b) a partially completed house; or

(c) a completed house.

The stamp duty implications of dealing with new houses and apartments are currently exactly the same as the rates applicable to second-hand residential property.

It is important to remember that the building agreement will be inclusive of VAT and that the VAT element should be deducted from the overall cost before calculating stamp duty.

Sample stamp duty calculation:

Purchase of new house at Hammurabi Crescent, Donnybrook,
Dublin 4,

Purchase price	€500,000.00
Site fine (contract for sale)	€50,000.00
Building agreement (including VAT 13.5%)	€450,000.00
Combined contract price	€500,000.00

Deduct VAT from the combined contract price (i.e. €500,000 divided by 113.5 and multiplied by 100)

VAT-exclusive purchase price is €440,528.63.

A clear reference to the VAT element must be in the site contract to enable deduction of VAT on the site fine. Otherwise deduct VAT on the building agreement only.

7.3.4.1 Purchase of site with connected building agreement

Section 29 SDCA

Section 29 charges stamp duty when a site is being sold and, in connection with the sale, a house or an apartment has been, is being, or is to be built on that site. The stamp duty charge arises only where the sale of the site and the building of the house or apartment are part of an arrangement or are connected in some way. Stamp duty in such cases is paid on the aggregate of the consideration paid for:

(a) the site; and

(b) the construction works, that is, the consideration paid in respect of building the house/apartment on the site.

At the time the deed giving effect to the purchase of the site is made, the construction work may not have commenced, or may have been commenced and not have been completed. In any event, because the deed is giving effect to a contract to purchase a site, the deed must only recite the consideration provided for in the contract to purchase the site.

Example

X entered into a contract to buy a site from Y, a vendor/developer, for €50,000. A building agreement was also entered into with Y whereby Y undertook to build a house on the site for X for €150,000. Y would not have sold the site to X if X had not entered into the building agreement. After the construction works were completed a deed giving effect to the purchase of the site was executed. Though the deed recited a consideration of €50,000, the stampable consideration is €200,000. As the property is residential property the stamp duty applicable is €2, 000 (€200,000 @ 1%).

Section 29 applies to the acquisition of a site where there is an arrangement to build a house on the site. Section 53 of the 1999 Act deals with similar provisions where a lease is granted with a connected agreement to build residential property (usually an apartment).

7.3.4.2 Exemptions from s. 29

Section 29 does not apply to the following:

(a) The purchaser is buying the site and it can be shown that there is no connection or arrangement between the purchase of the site and the building of a house or apartment on that site, for example where a person buys a site and employs a builder unconnected with the sale of the site.

(b) Transfers or leases of sites on which the transferee will build a house by his or her own labour. However, if the Revenue Commissioners are not satisfied with the genuineness of a particular transaction it is open to them to invoke the anti-avoidance provisions contained in s. 29(3) dealt with at **7.3.4.5**.

(c) Purchase of a partially completed house (discussed in more detail later).

(d) Purchase of a completed new house (discussed in more detail later).

(e) The rules set out in s. 29 and s. 53 do not apply to non-residential property, for example stocks, marketable securities, offices, factories.

(f) Simpliciter, in the case of a new house, s. 29 and s. 53 apply if the building agreement and the Contract for Sale are connected in some way. Section 29 and s. 53 do not apply if there is no connection between the building agreement and the Contract for Sale.

Purchase of a partially completed house

Where a person enters into a contract for the purchase of a partially completed building and where it is shown to the satisfaction of the Revenue Commissioners that there is no connection between the sale of the partially completed house and the employment of the builder chosen to complete the construction work, stamp duty will be based on the amount paid for the partially completed house. The deed giving effect to this contract must recite the consideration provided for in the contract.

Example

A decides to build a house for his daughter on his own land using direct labour. After the building works had been commenced A ran out of money. All building work ceased. Sometime later A agreed to sell the partially completed house to C for €330,000. C employs his own builder to complete the house. The deed giving effect to the contract will recite a consideration of €330,000. As there is no connection between the sale of the partially completed house and the builder chosen to complete the house, this section (s. 29) does not apply. The stampable consideration is €330,000 and, as the property being transferred is residential property, the stamp duty payable is €3300 (€330,000 @ 1%).

Purchase of a completed new house

Section 29 does not apply where the contract is a contract to purchase a new house which has already been completed. In these circumstances there can be no connection or arrangement between the sale of the site and the building agreement. Where the deed is giving effect to a contract to purchase a completed new house, the deed must recite the consideration provided for in the contract.

Example

X builds a house on his land in 2022. As soon as the house is built he sells it for €295,000. The deed will recite a consideration of €295,000 and, as the property being sold is residential property, the stamp duty payable is €2950 (€295,000 @ 1 %).

7.3.4.3 Definitions: s. 29(1)

This provision is self-explanatory.

7.3.4.4 Charge to stamp duty: s. 29(2)

Stamp duty is chargeable where land is being sold and, in connection with that sale, a house or an apartment has been, is being, or is to be built on that land. The stamp duty charge arises only where the sale of the land and the building of the house or apartment or part of an arrangement are connected in some way.

The question of the existence of the arrangement, insofar as the transfer of the site and the building of the house or apartment on that land are concerned, will be determined by the facts in each case.

7.3.4.5 Anti-avoidance measure: s. 29(3)

Where the building of a house or apartment has commenced prior to the execution of the instrument affecting the sale (i.e. the deed of transfer), such house or apartment will be deemed to be within the category of houses or apartments which are built, are being built, or are to be built for the purposes of s. 29(2).

7.3.4.6 Leases: s. 53

Section 53 applies to a lease combined with building agreement for dwelling-house or apartment.

Section 53 is similar to s. 29 except that it applies where a 'lease' rather than a 'conveyance' is made of land combined with an agreement to build residential property (usually an apartment).

7.3.5 MIXED USE PROPERTY

7.3.5.1 Apportionment (s. 45 of the SDCA, 1999)

Section 45 of the SDCA sets out how the consideration for a sale is to be apportioned in certain circumstances.

If the property being purchased is partly residential and partly non-residential, that is, mixed use property, the consideration should be apportioned between the residential and the non-residential elements and the relevant rate of stamp duty applied to each portion of the consideration: ss 45(2) and 52(5) of the SDCA, 1999. The consideration must be apportioned on a just and reasonable basis between the residential and non-residential elements of the property. The vendor must provide a form headed 'Apportionment Statement' which should be retained by the purchaser's solicitor.

For such instruments, where an incorrect apportionment is included in the stamp duty return filed under the e-stamping system, penalties relating to the filing of an incorrect return will be incurred (see s. 14(a)).

In a mixed use property situation the residential property part of the transaction is not aggregated with the non-residential portion for the purposes of determining the appropriate rate of duty. The consideration should be apportioned between the residential and non-residential elements on a just and reasonable basis and each type of property is to be separately certified to the applicable threshold, and the appropriate rate of duty is chargeable in respect of each of the residential and non-residential parts of the transaction. Basically, you pay stamp duty for the residential part of the property at the stamp duty rate applicable to transfers of residential property. You pay stamp duty for the non-residential part at the stamp duty rate for non-residential property (other than policies of insurance).

7.3.5.2 Apportionment details

Apportionment details are required (a) where a mixed use property is sold for one consideration or (b) where the sale of a wholly residential property or a mixed use property forms part of a larger transaction or a series of transactions. Both sides prepare and sign a separate apportionment. A suggested format for the furnishing of apportionment details is set out below. While this will no longer be presented to the Revenue, it should be retained on file in the event of a Revenue audit. In the case of (b), the aggregate consideration (including that portion attributable to contents) should also be apportioned where necessary as between the residential element and non-residential element comprised in the larger transaction or series of transactions.

These details are delivered under s. 8(2) of the Stamp Duties Consolidation Act, 1999—as required by s. 16(2) of the Stamp Duties Consolidation Act, 1999—because the property in question consists partly of an interest in residential property.

Re: Conveyance/Lease Dated: **Parties:**

Apportionment by the Vendor(s)/Lessor(s):

In relation to the above-mentioned sale/lease:

1. I/We state that the 'aggregate consideration'* is: €____________________
2. I/We estimate the 'residential consideration'** to be: €____________________
3. The basis for the estimate at 2 above is as follows:

____

____

____

Signed: ____________________ Date: ____________________

Signed: ____________________ Date: ____________________

Apportionment by the Purchaser(s)/Lessee(s):

In relation to the above-mentioned sale/lease:

- I/We state that the 'aggregate consideration'* is: €____________________
- I/We estimate the 'residential consideration'** to be: €____________________
- The basis for the estimate at 2 above is as follows:

____

____

____

Signed: ____________________ Date: ____________________

Signed: ____________________ Date: ____________________

*As that term is defined in section 45(2)/52(5) of the Stamp Duties Consolidation Act, 1999.

**As that term is defined in section 16(1) of the Stamp Duties Consolidation Act, 1999.

Note: Any other facts or circumstances affecting the liability of the instrument to stamp duty should be disclosed, unless contained in the deed.

Where the property is mixed, that is, part residential and part non-residential, for example living quarters over a shop or a farm sold together with the farmhouse, the residential rate of stamp duty will apply only to the residential element.

The apportionment form is available on the Revenue website.

Sample calculation

Rory buys a building for €1,200,000 (net of VAT). It comprises a retail shop at ground floor level and a residential apartment overhead that he will live in. The amount of consideration attributable to the residential apartment is €300,000 and the shop is €900,000.

The stamp duty on the deed is:

Retail shop	€900,000 @ 7.5%	€67,500
Residential apartment	€300,000 @ 1%	€3000
Total stamp duty		€70,500

Total stamp duty on shop and apartment is €70,500.

The apportionment details form set out earlier would have to be completed.

7.3.5.3 Anti-avoidance—asset splitting (s. 45A SDCA, 1999) simultaneous transactions

Before the Finance Act, 2005 the stamp duty rate on a dwelling-house could be reduced by splitting the transaction. This arose where a house or an apartment is purchased by more than one purchaser and each purchaser takes a separate conveyance or transfer of the house or apartment in order to avail of the lower rate of stamp duty. Generally, where there are a number of sales between two parties at or about the same time, irrespective of whether there is a single contract or several contracts, there is a strong presumption that each individual conveyance must form part of a larger transaction or of a series of transactions. The Finance Act, 2005 introduced an anti-avoidance provision with effect from 3 February 2005. Section 45A of the SDCA, 1999 was introduced to counter attempts at avoidance where a house or an apartment is purchased by more than one purchaser and each purchaser takes a separate conveyance or transfer of an interest in the house or apartment in order to avail of lower stamp duty rates. It provides that if an existing interest in a dwelling-house is transferred by more than one instrument executed within a period of twelve months, the instruments will be deemed to form part of a larger transaction. In addition, if the 'first transfer' of an interest in a dwelling-house (occurring before or after 1 March 2005) is followed by a 'subsequent transfer' of other interests in the same dwelling-house within a twelve-month period, the transferee of the first transfer will be liable to a clawback penalty together with interest at the rate of 0.0219 per cent per day from the date of execution of the instrument to the date the clawback is paid. The purpose of the section is to state beyond any doubt that the stamp duty on such conveyances or transfers will be determined on the basis of the value of the whole house or apartment for instruments executed on or after 5 November 2007. This section also extends to gifts made in a similar manner.

7.3.6 STAMP DUTY ON CONTENTS AND FIXTURES

Generally, stamp duty is not paid on the purchase of house contents—for example, carpets, curtains, and so on—which will pass by delivery and are not included in the deed of assurance. Section 45A of the SDCA, 1999 as amended provides that the contents of residential property are not taken into account in determining the rate of stamp duty on the consideration attributable to that residential property. However, the total consideration must be apportioned on a bona fide basis between the contents and the property. The contents pass by delivery so no stamp duty is payable. In the event that the Revenue makes a finding that the property element has been undervalued, the Revenue has a right to impose penalties.

7.4 Stamp Duty Evasion

The Conveyancing Committee of the Law Society has, in various Practice Notes to the profession, pointed out the sanctions that will be incurred by solicitors who engage in stamp duty evasion on behalf of their clients. They advise that practitioners should be aware that apportionment of sale consideration in transactions relating to the sale of residential properties inclusive of contents should be made on the basis that realistic and correct values are attributed to such contents based, if necessary, on valuations from reputable auctioneers. Any apportionments made on the basis of spurious or excessive valuations of contents in such transactions clearly constitute evasion and are in breach of Revenue guidelines. Practitioners are also reminded of the powers available to the Revenue Commissioners to impose substantial financial penalties and other sanctions not only against the parties involved in such transactions but also against their solicitors and other professional advisers. The Law Society also condemns the practice on the part of purchasers' solicitors of engaging in and assisting in the practice of deliberately inflating the sale price of properties in excess of their real price to facilitate purchasers seeking and obtaining increased loans to finance purchase of property. This practice is not in accordance with good conveyancing practice and also constitutes fraudulent and unprofessional conduct, which would render practitioners assisting in such practice liable to serious sanctions by the Law Society.

7.5 Mortgage Head of Charge

Previously where property was purchased with the aid of a mortgage, stamp duty was chargeable on both the deed of assurance and on the mortgage deed.

However, there is no stamp duty payable for mortgage deeds executed on or after 7 December 2006. The mortgage head of charge in Schedule 1 to the SDCA, 1999 is abolished. Mortgage deeds covered by these provisions include primary collateral, additional, and equitable mortgages together with transfer of mortgages. This also applies to further advances made on or after 7 December 2007 in relation to existing mortgages.

7.6 Lease Head of Charge

The lease head of charge applies to the creation of leases and not to the assignment of pre-existing leasehold interests, which are stampable under the conveyance on sale head of charge. Stamp duty under the lease head of charge consists of two distinct charges:

(a) duty on any premium paid for the granting of the lease; and

(b) duty on the rent payable on the lease.

Both of these charges to stamp duty can, and frequently do, arise on the same transaction. The duty chargeable on the premium is at the rate for residential or non-residential property as appropriate. The rate of stamp duty on rent depends on the length of the term of the lease in question. A lease is chargeable to stamp duty under paragraph 3 of the 'Lease' head of charge in the SDCA, 1999.

7.6.1 RENT

The rate of stamp duty payable on rents depends on whether the lease is of residential or non-residential property. A lease for any indefinite term, or not exceeding thirty-five years, of a house or apartment is exempt from stamp duty where the annual rent does not exceed €40,000 per year. There is no requirement to file stamp duty returns when this exemption applies. In all other cases the rate of stamp duty is determined by the term or length of the lease and the rent paid.

The rate of stamp duty payable on the annual rent depends on the period of the lease and is as follows:

1. Where the lease does not exceed thirty-five years, or is indefinite (and the annual rent exceeds €40,000), stamp duty is chargeable at the rate of 1 per cent of the average annual rent.
2. Where the lease exceeds 35 years but does not exceed 100 years, stamp duty is chargeable at the rate of 6 per cent of the average annual rent.
3. Where the lease exceeds 100 years, stamp duty is chargeable at the rate of 12 per cent of the average annual rent.

In all cases duty is rounded down to the nearest euro.

If there is a rent review clause in the lease, an additional fixed duty of €12.50 is payable.

7.6.2 PREMIUM

In addition to any rent, a lease may also provide for the payment of a premium also known as a 'fine'. This is usually a one-off capital payment payable to the landlord by the tenant as part of the consideration for granting the lease. It is paid at the commencement of the lease. Where both a premium and a rent are paid stamp duty is payable on both. The rate of stamp duty applicable to the premium depends on the type of property covered by the lease and is essentially the same as the ad valorem rate applicable to conveyances on sale. The rate reliefs and exemptions have changed frequently over the years. For residential property the stamp duty rate on the lease premium is 1 per cent on the first million euro and 2 per cent on any excess over one million euro. For non-residential property the stamp duty payable by the lessee charged on the premium component of a lease is currently 7.5 per cent.

7.7 Conveyance by Way of a Sub-Sale

The provisions relating to sub-sales are contained in the SDCA, 1999, s. 46. The relief applies in the situation where the owner of property X contracts to sell property to Y, and no deed of assurance has been executed on foot of the contract, then, prior to completion of this contract, Y agrees to sell the property or part of it to a sub-purchaser Z and, therefore, another contract exists between the purchaser Y for the further sale of the same property or part of it to a sub-purchaser Z. If, by the direction of the purchaser Y the vendor X conveys the property directly to the sub-purchaser Z, stamp duty is payable on the consideration paid by the sub-purchaser Z, that is, on the conveyance to the sub-purchaser Z only on the amount of the consideration passing between the sub-purchaser Z and the purchaser Y irrespective of whether it is greater or smaller than the consideration paid to the vendor X. The legislation allows for a chain of sub-purchasers to be involved. As the conveyance is between the original vendor and the sub-purchaser, the cooperation of the vendor is required for this relief to operate.

Sample sub-sale:

Alan contracts to sell his house in Donnybrook to Bob for €500,000. Before the property is conveyed to him, Bob contracts to sell the same property to Christian for €600,000. Under Bob's direction, Alan conveys the property by a single conveyance on sale directly to Christian, with Bob joining in to transfer any beneficial interest he may have. Stamp duty is charged on the conveyance on sale to Christian only in respect of the consideration of the €600,000 paid by Christian to Bob.

The property is residential.

Stamp duty is payable as follows:

€600,000 @ 1% is €6000.

Stamp duty payable is €6000.

7.7.1 EXCHANGES OF PROPERTY

The law concerning exchanges is now contained in the SDCA, 1999, s. 37, which provides that where an exchange of immovable property (that is, land and buildings) is effected, full ad valorem stamp duty will be charged on the value of all the property being transferred. Previously, stamp duty was payable only on the inequality of value in the property which was the subject matter of the exchange. These provisions apply in cases where immovable property is exchanged for other immovable property. They also apply where some consideration was paid, for example, where the properties were of unequal value. In effect, therefore, deeds of exchange are chargeable to stamp duty based on the value of lands and buildings therein conveyed. The value of any other property or any equality money paid is ignored. Where there is more than one deed recording the exchange each deed bears stamp duty based on the value of the lands or buildings which it conveys. Where immovable property situate in the State is exchanged for foreign property, immoveable or otherwise, stamp duty is payable on the value of the Irish property only.

7.7.2 DEEDS OF FAMILY ARRANGEMENT

Deeds of family arrangement are used when the beneficiaries under a will or the persons entitled to a share on intestacy decide to rearrange the benefits by means of substitution and exchange. Such deeds are executed by the beneficiaries, and the legal personal representative then proceeds to distribute and vest the property in the beneficiaries by means of a deed of assent which was exempt from stamp duty. In the decision of Ms Justice Baker delivered on 30 July 2018 in the case of *Re Estate of Hannon* [2018] IEHC 482, she noted that the practice of executing a deed of family arrangement for the distribution of an estate other than in accordance with the wishes of a testator, or in accordance with the entitlement on intestacy, is long established. However, where any beneficial interest passes under the terms of a deed of family arrangement, then full ad valorem stamp duty is payable. This category of instrument has sometimes been overlooked in relation to stamping, as the Land Registry is precluded from seeking production of same when registering transmissions on death by virtue of s. 54(2) of the Succession Act, 1965 and s. 61(3) of the Registration of Title Act, 1964. These sections provide that 'it shall not be the duty of the Registrar, nor shall he be entitled to call for any information as to why any assent or transfer is or was made and shall be bound to assume that the personal representative is or was acting in relation to the application, assent or transfer correctly and within his powers'. This has generated a mistaken belief that deeds of family arrangement in respect of registered land for deaths occurring on or after 1 July 1966 do not attract stamp duty because they do not have to be produced in order to vest good title in a beneficiary. This is not the case. Great care should be taken to ensure that they are fully stamped in accordance with the statutory provisions previously specified. Even though the deed of family arrangement, duly stamped, may not be produced to the Land Registry, it still forms part of the title deeds to the property and must be retained. In addition these deeds should be entered into within two years of the date of death to ensure that they do not constitute a disposal for capital gains tax purposes. See also para 15.3 of the Wills, Probate & Estates OUP Manual.

7.8 Fixed Duties

The fixed duty charge of €12.50 was abolished under the Finance Act, 2007 in respect of instruments executed on or after 2 April 2007 in relation to the following heads of charge in Schedule 1 of the SDCA, 1999:

Conveyance or Transfer of any kind not already described in Schedule 1.

Exchange (other than an exchange chargeable under s. 37 of the SDCA, 1999. This section imposes a charge to ad valorem duty on exchanges involving immovable property.)

Release or Renunciation of any property, or of any right or interest in any property (other than an instrument which operates as sale or a gift).

Surrender of any property or of any right or interest in any property (other than an instrument which operates as a sale or gift).

There is no need to present such instruments to the Revenue prior to being lodged in either the Land Registry or the Registry of Deeds.

7.8.1 STAMP DUTY ON GIFTS—VOLUNTARY DISPOSITIONS INTER VIVOS: SECTION 30 OF THE SDCA

A transfer by way of a voluntary gift inter vivos is chargeable to stamp duty in the same way as a transfer on sale with the market value of the property being substituted for the consideration.

Where property is transferred as a gift, or for less than its full value, stamp duty is charged on the market value of the property transferred. This is the price that the property would attain if sold on the open market. A voluntary disposition is not a conveyance on sale as there is no sale (SDCA, 1999, s. 30). However, it is chargeable to stamp duty as if it were a conveyance on sale, and the market value of the property being conveyed or transferred determines the rate of duty payable. In the case of land and buildings, residential and non-residential, the rates of stamp duty in the case of a voluntary disposition are the same as those that apply to conveyances or transfers on sale. For instruments executed on or after 7 July 2012 where an incorrect apportionment is included in the stamp duty return filed under the e-stamping system, penalties relating to the incorrect filing of a return will be incurred (see s. 134A). Prior to 7 July 2012, s. 30(3) of the SDCA, 1999 provided that a voluntary deed must be lodged for adjudication with the Revenue Commissioners. Adjudication is now abolished in respect of all instruments executed on or after 7 July 2012. The mode of valuing property for the purposes of the SDCA, 1999, s. 30 is set out in ss 18 and 19. In the case of an instrument which operates as a voluntary disposition inter vivos, all parties are accountable for the payment of stamp duty (s. 30(1) and s. 54(1)).

Section 8(5) of the SDCA imposes an obligation on all parties to a voluntary transfer to ensure that the Revenue are aware from the stamp duty return delivered under the e-stamping system that the transfer is by way of gift, and the market value must be set out in the return. If the parties to the instrument fail to provide this information they are regarded as having acted deliberately for the purpose of s. 134 A(2)(a) until the contrary is proven.

7.8.2 INFORMATION FROM TAILTE EIREANN ('TE'), PREVIOUSLY THE PROPERTY REGISTRATION AUTHORITY ('PRA') AND TE REQUIREMENTS FOR FOLIO NUMBERS IN STAMPING CERTIFICATES

A new s. 137A of the SDCA, 1999 was introduced by the Finance Act, 2010 to allow the Revenue to obtain information from the Property Registration Authority as might be required by the Revenue for the purposes of the SDCA, 1999. In addition, the Revenue are also required to provide to the Property Registration Authority, at such intervals and as requested, such information as might be required by the PRA to consider stamp duty in relation to documents presented for registration.

Tailte Eireann was established on 1 March 2023 from a merger of the property Registration Authority, The Valuation Office and Ordinance Survey Ireland.

In the December 2018 edition of the *Gazette*, practitioners' attention was drawn to the PRA Legal Office Notice No 1 of 2018, 'Query management/review and rejection of dealings'.

Paragraph 6 of the appendix to the notice provides that an application to the PRA should be rejected if, among other things, no stamp certificate or other evidence of Revenue stamping is lodged. It also lists a number of other grounds for rejection, including that the relevant folio number is not inserted on the stamp certificate. The PRA has advised the Conveyancing Committee that it will now enforce these provisions.

The Committee has written to the PRA with a view to persuading it to change its practice and reverse its decision to enforce this requirement. The Committee is of the view that enforcing this requirement will add hugely to the administrative burden of the profession and indeed to that of the Land Registry itself. The provision of a folio number is optional in the Revenue stamping system but practitioners should be aware that the PRA have now made it a compulsory requirement.

In a subsequent update outlined in the August/Gazette under the heading 'Land Registry Matters—Update August 2019', the Land Registry acknowledge that there may be some cases where a folio number cannot be entered in the stamping system, where the vendor's title is not yet registered. However, where there is a folio number available it must be entered by the filer, or the dealing/application for registration will be rejected. The Land Registry advise that in the case of a transfer of part, the number of the parent folio should be entered.

In the case of the transfer of multiple folios, the stamping system allows for up to five folios to be entered. The Revenue suggest that where there are more than five folio numbers involved the first four should be entered and the text '& Others' should be entered in the field for the fifth folio number. The Land Registry have confirmed that they do not have any difficulty with this.

The Committee reiterates its disagreement with the Land Registry on this issue and is still of the view that if entry of a folio number is not compulsory in the stamping system, it should not be compulsory in the registration system.

7.8.3 RESTING IN CONTRACT: SECTION 31A OF THE SDCA

7.8.3.1 Licence agreements S31B and agreements for more than 35 years: s. 50A

The Finance Act, 2013 changed the previously used legitimate stamp duty avoidance scheme where, instead of taking a conveyance or transfer of land, the full purchase price was paid by or on completion and the purchaser relied on the contract, that is, the transaction 'rested on contract'. In that way no stamp duty was paid unless at some time in the future the purchaser sought a conveyance or transfer. A number of the previous tax planning opportunities have now been closed with the commencement of s. 31A of the SDCA.

Section 31A of the SDCA as inserted by the Finance Act, 2013 provides that a charge to stamp duty will arise on a contract or agreement for the sale of an estate or interest in land in the State where 25 per cent or more of the consideration for the sale has been paid to the holder of the estate or interest. The charge will arise where a stamp duty return has not been filed and stamp duty paid in respect of a conveyance or transfer of the lands concerned within thirty days after that amount of consideration has been paid. This charge under s. 31A applies to instruments executed on or after 13 February 2013. However, the charge will not apply where an instrument is executed solely in pursuance of a binding contract or agreement entered into before 13 February 2013.

A subsequent conveyance or transfer will not be chargeable to stamp duty.

The contract or agreement for sale is chargeable to stamp duty as if it were a conveyance or transfer of the estate or interest where a payment which amounts to 25 per cent or more of the consideration for the sale has been paid. The charge does not apply where, within thirty days of the date of the payment of 25 per cent or more of the consideration:

(a) an electronic stamp duty return is filed in relation to a conveyance or transfer made in conformity with the contract or agreement for sale; and

(b) the stamp duty chargeable on the conveyance or transfer has been paid to the Revenue.

The Revenue will refund any duty paid on the contract if the contract is later rescinded or annulled. While this section does not specify the time limit for submitting claims for a refund, a four-year time limit is provided by s. 159A from the date the contract is stamped in respect of a valid claim for a refund. Interest may arise on the refund (s. 159B of the SDCA).

Section 45 of the Finance Act, 2018 amends ss 31 and 31A of the SDCA 1999. As already stated, these sections impose a stamp duty charge in certain circumstances at the stage when an agreement or contract is signed and then provide a 'credit' for the stamp duty paid if there is a subsequent conveyance or transfer on sale. Instead of transferring the stamp duty paid on the contract to the later executed instrument of conveyance or transfer the Revenue will issue a stamp certificate stating that the later instrument is not chargeable with stamp duty.

Similarly, this will also apply to licences given to builders by developers to enter onto lands to develop, that is, to build houses, apartments, or other non-residential buildings, or to carry out any engineering or other operations to adapt it for materially altered use. The stamp duty is assessed on the market value of the land. This is provided for in s. 31B of the SDCA, which provides that a charge to stamp duty will arise on certain licence agreements relating to land in the State under which the licensee is allowed to carry out development on that land and 25 per cent or more of the market value of the land is paid to the licensor, other than as consideration for the sale of all or part of the land. The charge under s. 31B applies to instruments executed on or after 13 February 2013.

The charge will also apply where long leases greater than thirty-five years are created under an agreement for lease as provided for in s. 50A. For example, instead of executing a lease (by signing and/or sealing or both), the purchaser may execute an Agreement for Lease. This Agreement for Lease sets out the terms to be included in the Lease. Stamp duty is payable on the consideration set out in the Agreement if the agreement is for a period longer than thirty-five years or for an indefinite period or the Agreement is for any period over thirty-five years where 25 per cent of the consideration in the Agreement is paid.

The overall effect of these three sections is that contracts, building licences, and agreements for leases in excess of thirty-five years are to be treated as conveyances for sale/leases in certain circumstances.

7.9 Exemptions and Reliefs

Certain instruments are exempted from the charge to stamp duty, or bear a reduced amount of stamp duty, or enjoy benefit from a relief. Part 7 of the SDCA, 1999 lists both the instruments that are exempt from stamp duty and the reliefs from stamp duty available in certain situations. Prior to the termination of the adjudication process for instruments executed on or after 7 July 2012, in order to benefit from an exemption or relief, the instrument may or may not have had to be presented for adjudication to the Revenue. For instruments executed on or after 7 July 2012 a self-assessed return must be filed under the e-stamping system in order to benefit from an exemption or relief.

In most cases the exemption or relief is claimed when filing returns. Some exemptions and reliefs do not however require a return. It is important to keep records to support any claim for entitlement to an exemption. The terms of the exemption or the relief must be met on the date of execution of the instrument. However, in, say, the case of an agricultural qualification as required for young trained farmer's relief and relief for leases of farmland, for example, certain qualifying criteria must be adhered to for a number of years for certain exemptions to apply in order to avoid clawback.

If the exemption or relief is general then the instrument is not liable to stamp duty under any head of charge in Schedule 1.

The following are instruments for which a self-assessed stamp duty return must be filed under the e-stamping system in order to obtain the exemptions and reliefs available.

The main exemptions and reliefs are contained in Part 7 of the SDCA and samples of these are as follows:

1. Associated companies relief (s. 79 SDCA)
2. Young trained farmers relief (s. 81AA SDCA)
3. Transfers between spouses and civil partners (s. 96 SDCA)
4. Certain transfers by cohabitants (s. 97A SDCA)
5. Consanguinity relief for agricultural land (Sch 1 SDCA)
6. Charities (s. 82 SDCA)
7. Commercial woodlands relief (s. 95 SDCA)
8. Reconstruction and amalgamation relief (s. 80 SDCA).

7.9.1 SECTION 79 SDCA ASSOCIATED COMPANIES

Conveyances and transfers of property between certain bodies corporate and instruments dealing with the reconstruction and amalgamation of companies are exempt from stamp duties (SDCA, 1999, ss 79 and 80 respectively). Section 79 of the SDCA, 1999 grants a relief from stamp duty on certain transfers of property between These transactions usually involve the transfer of shares or an undertaking from one Company to another in return for the issue of shares. The relief does not apply to the leasing of property between such entities. The relief also applies to voluntary dispositions and dispositions between all 'bodies corporate' which include industrial and provident societies, limited and unlimited companies, and foreign companies. Section 79 of the SDCA, 1999, contains claw back provisions providing that a claw back of the exemption will now apply if any of the three tests of ownership cease to be met within two years after the date the instrument is executed. The following conditions must be satisfied before the relief will be granted. The instrument in respect of which the relief is sought must convey or transfer a beneficial interest in property from one body corporate to another:

(a) One company must own beneficially 90 per cent or more of the ordinary share capital of the other company, or a third company owns over 90 per cent of the ordinary share capital of both, directly or indirectly;

(b) The company must be entitled to 90 per cent or more of the profits available for distribution to the shareholders of the other company;

(c) The company must be entitled to 90 per cent or more of the assets available for distribution to the shareholders of the other company on its winding up.

It is further provided that stamp duty exemption will be denied between two companies in a 90 per cent relationship if the instrument or transfer is executed in pursuance of or in connection with any arrangement whereby any part of the consideration is to be provided or received by any person who or which is not a company in a 90 per cent relationship with either the transferor or the transferee though meeting all three tests.

In relation to stamp duty relief for company reconstruction and/or amalgamations set out in s. 80 of the SDCA, 1999, a self-assessed stamp duty return must be filed in relation to the instrument in respect of which the relief is claimed. Section 68 of the Finance Act, 2004 provides that in relation to the conveyance or transfer on sale head (immovable property) where this forms part of the transfer of an undertaking, the s. 80 exemption will only apply if there has been an actual conveyance to the transferor company before the reconstruction or amalgamation.

7.9.2 LAND ACQUIRED BY APPROVED SPORT BODIES

Stamp duty is not chargeable on any conveyance, transfer, or lease of land to an approved sport body approved under s. 235 of the Taxes Consolidation Act, 1997 where the land will be used for the sole purpose of promoting athletic or amateur games or sports. The relief is now contained in s. 82B of the SDCA, 1999. A self-assessed stamp duty return must be filed under the e-stamping system in relation to the instrument in respect of which the exemption is sought.

7.9.3 TRANSFER OF STOCK OR MARKETABLE SECURITIES UNDER €1000

The transfer of certain stock or marketable securities where the consideration paid is €1000 or less qualifies for an exemption from the 1 per cent rate of stamp duty payable on stock transfer forms.

7.9.4 TRANSFERS BETWEEN SPOUSES/CIVIL PARTNERS/CERTAIN QUALIFIED COHABITANTS

The Civil Partnership and Certain Rights and Obligations of Cohabitants Act, 2010 ('the 2010 Act'), which came into effect on 1 January 2011, did not include any tax provisions, and the taxation measures required were published in the Finance (No 3) Act, 2011, which applies from 1 January 2011. The Act provided that the tax treatment of registered civil partners mirrors that of married couples. Section 96 of the SDCA, 1999 (as amended) provides that a conveyance or transfer or lease of any property between spouses/civil partners is exempt from stamp duty **unless** the transfer is a transfer referred to in s. 46(1) to (4) of the SDCA (i.e. it involves a third party or a sub-sale), whether the property is transferred by a spouse/civil partner or spouses/civil partners of a marriage to either spouse/civil partner or to both spouses/civil partners of that marriage/civil partnership. If any other person is a party to the instrument the exemption does not apply. However a stamp duty return must be filed and the exemption claimed on the return when availing of the exemption from stamp duty under s. 96 SDCA.

Section 14 of the Family Home Protection Act, 1976 (as amended) exempts from stamp duty an assurance of a family/shared home into the **joint names** of both spouses/civil partners. An application form for registration both in the Land Registry and Registry of Deeds of such assurance is also exempt from stamp duty. There is no requirement to file a stamp duty return if the instrument creates a joint tenancy of a family home/shared home to claim the exemption. The one firm of solicitors may act for both parties in s. 14 transactions.

In contrast, where any property, which is **not** a family/shared home, is transferred between spouses/civil partners although the relevant deed of assurance is exempt from stamp duty, the Registry of Deeds application forms of these assurances are liable to stamp duty at the rate of €50. In addition, both parties must instruct a separate legal firm to act on their behalf. These provisions are now contained in s. 96 of the SDCA, 1999. The exemption from stamp duty will not apply if the property is transferred to any person other than a spouse/civil partner. Spouses/civil partners do not cease to be spouses/civil partners as a result of a deed of separation or a decree of judicial separation or on the dissolution of the civil partnership.

Section 97A of the SDCA exempts from stamp duty certain transfers of property between former cohabitants. All transfers of property from one cohabitant to his or her cohabitant made pursuant to an order under s. 174 of the Civil Partnership and Certain Rights and Obligations of Cohabitants Act, 2010 are exempt from stamp duty. The exemption only applies to transfers between the cohabitants. If any other person is a party to the instrument the exemption does not apply. The property must be transferred on or after 1 January 2011 pursuant to a Property Adjustment Order.

Stamp duty returns must be filed and the exemption is claimed on the return. The s. 174 Order must be kept to hand to claim the exemption.

7.9.5 CERTAIN TRANSFERS FOLLOWING THE DISSOLUTION OF MARRIAGE OR CIVIL PARTNERSHIP AND CERTAIN TRANSFERS BY QUALIFIED COHABITANTS

It is provided in s. 97 of the SDCA, 1999 that certain conveyances following the dissolution of marriage or the dissolution of a civil partnership are not chargeable to stamp duty where the conveyance is on foot of certain specified court orders. Section 97 provides that stamp duty is not chargeable on an instrument by which property is transferred pursuant to:

(1) a relief order under s. 23 of the Family Law Act, 1995 made following the dissolution of marriage; or

(2) an order under Part III of the Family Law (Divorce) Act, 1996; or

(3) where property is transferred between former spouses pursuant to a foreign court order or other determination to like effect made on or after 10 February 2000, which is similar to an order referred to at (1) or (2) above of a court under the law of another territory made or in consequence of the dissolution of a marriage, being a dissolution that is entitled to be recognised as valid in the State; or

(4) an order under Part 12 of the Civil Partnership and Certain Rights and Obligation of Cohabitants Act, 2010 which deals with property being transferred by a cohabitant to their cohabitant on or after 1 January 2011 under a Property Adjustment Order.

After divorce, spouses cease to be such, and therefore enjoy an exemption from stamp duty only if the provisions of s. 97 above apply. The exemption does not apply in relation to an instrument by which any part of or beneficial interest in the property concerned is transferred to a person other than the spouses concerned. If any other person is a party to the instrument the exemption does not apply.

Section 97A of the SDCA, 1999 provides for an exemption from stamp duty where a property is transferred pursuant to an order under s. 174 of the 2010 Act by a cohabitant to his or her cohabitant. If any other person is a party to the instrument the exemption does not apply. This section applies to transfers made on or after 1 January 2011.

7.9.6 CONVEYANCES ON SALE AND VOLUNTARY DISPOSITIONS TO YOUNG TRAINED FARMERS

Section 81AA of the SDCA provides an exemption from stamp duty where agricultural land, including such farm buildings, farmhouses, and mansion houses occupied therewith, is conveyed/transferred to young trained farmers. The relief can be claimed regardless of whether the land is acquired by gift or on a purchase. The relief provides for a full exemption from stamp duty on the acquisition or transfer of farmland and agricultural buildings to certain young trained farmers who are under the age of 35 years and who hold the relevant agricultural qualification. Essentially there are three aspects to being a qualifying trained farmer: age, agricultural qualification, and the use of the land.

The purpose of the relief is to encourage the transfer of lands into the hands of a younger, more trained generation of farmers. It constitutes EU State aid and must comply with EU State aid rules. The relevant State aid rules are contained in Commission Regulations (EU) No 702/2014—in particular Chapter 111, s. 1, Article 180 dealing with 'Start-up aid for young farmers and the development of small farms'.

The parties to the deed do not have to be related for the relief to apply. The relief applies to both conveyances on sale and voluntary dispositions executed after 2 April 2007, and has been extended by the Finance Act, 2024 to transfers executed on or before 31 December 2028 subject to the finalisation of issues relating to the Agricultural Block Exemption Regulations at EU level.

The relief, although applying to both sales and gifts, does not apply to leases or where a power of revocation exists. A power to revoke the transfer, whether it is contained in the instrument conveying or transferring the lands or otherwise, will disqualify the young trained farmer from the relief. To be a young trained farmer, an individual must show that he or she was under the age of 35 at the date of execution of the instrument and that he or she has completed one of the qualifying farming courses set out in Schedule 2B to the SDCA, 1999 and in s. 81AA of the Act and has satisfied the EU State aid conditions. In addition a transferee must intend to spend at least 50 per cent of their normal working time farming the transferred land and retain ownership for a period of at least five years from the date of execution of the deed of transfer.

In order to qualify for the relief a self-assessed return must be filed under the e-stamping system in relation to the instrument in respect of which the relief is sought.

The relief also applies where the agricultural land is conveyed or transferred to joint owners where all satisfy the conditions for granting the relief (SDCA, 1999, s. 81(4)). The only exception to this rule is where the land is being transferred into the joint ownership of a husband and wife or to a civil partner. In such cases only one of the spouses or civil partners must be a young trained farmer and meet the conditions set out earlier. The section provides a revised list of qualifications, establishments, and revision to the standards of those qualifications. The Finance Act, 2007 included changes relating to education criteria and a simplified refund procedure governing the relief for young trained farmers contained in s. 81AA of the SDCA, 1999. To qualify as a young trained farmer the minimum requirement will be a FETAC Level 6 Advanced Certificate in Agriculture, rather than a minimum number of hours of training. The qualifying agricultural qualifications are listed in Schedule 2B of Revenue eBrief No 187/18 dated 19 October 2018, which deals with the stamp duty implications of transfers of land to young trained farmers.

When the deed transferring the land is executed, the transferee must hold a relevant agricultural qualification as outlined above. However, a person who obtains a relevant agricultural qualification within the period of three years after the date on which the deed transferring the land is executed will be able to claim a refund of the stamp duty paid. The date of the award of the qualification is accepted as the date on which the person becomes the holder of the qualification.

Furthermore, if the farmer receives land, pays stamp duty, and subsequently qualifies as a young trained farmer, the farmer will be required to retain and farm the land for a period of five years from the date which the claim for a refund of duty is made to the Revenue. Also, there will be no requirement that a refund be made within a set time period.

It appears that the Minister has tightened up the minimum educational requirements for young trained farmers to ensure that only genuine farmers qualify for the relief. Only agricultural land can qualify for the relief. However, agricultural land includes such farmhouses and buildings and the land on which they are situated as are of a character appropriate to the land.

The Finance Act, 2017 introduced a condition that a young trained farmer must submit a business plan to Teagasc and must come within the EU definition of 'micro, small and medium enterprises' to claim young trained farmers relief. Section 46 of the Finance Act, 2018 provides that where a person achieves the relevant agricultural qualification to be treated as a young trained farmer after the date of execution of the instrument transferring the lands and can claim a repayment of stamp duty, such a person must submit a business plan to Teagasc and come within the EU Regulations meaning of micro or small size enterprise before a repayment of stamp duty can be claimed. The young trained farmer must also be registered for Income Tax.

A practice note in the Jan/Feb 2020 issue of the Gazette reminds practitioners that since 1 January 2019 there is a limit of €70,000 in State Aid that may be claimed by a person claiming the young trained farmer relief from stamp duty, as the relief from stamp duty is regarded as State aid. Consanguinity relief (**16.9.7**), where the rate of stamp duty is reduced to 1 per cent from 7.5 per cent, is frequently available to young trained farmers and is also deemed to be State aid. Therefore, while a deed might have a nil liability to stamp duty arising from young trained farmer relief, consanguinity relief, if available, should also be claimed in order to reduce the amount of State aid that will be counted towards the limit of €70,000.

7.9.7 CONSANGUINITY RELIEF

Special consanguinity relief is available when transferring farmland between certain family members. This has the effect of reducing stamp duty to 1 per cent on family farm transfers that qualify for the relief. Previously a stamp duty relief known as consanguinity relief was available where a relationship existed between the parties to the deed. This relief was available in the case of either a sale or a gift of property between certain related persons and the instrument was stamped at 50 per cent, the specified rate for such instrument. The relief was not available in relation to a lease or the transfer of stocks or marketable securities.

Consanguinity relief is no longer available for instruments transferring or conveying residential property executed on or after 8 December 2010 or for non-residential property **apart** from agricultural land after 31 December 2015.

When consanguinity relief applies for farm transfers the rate of stamp duty on the instrument is reduced from 7.5 per cent to 1 per cent. This relief is due to expire on 31 December 2028.

In the case of farming land, consanguinity relief continues to apply to instruments executed:

1. on or after 1 January 2016 in respect of transfers or conveyances of land by a person of any age; and
2. on or after 1 January 2016 and before 24 December 2017 where executed by a person who has not reached the age of 67 years at the date of the transfer or

conveyance. Where the transferees are co-owners of the land they must all be under the age of 67 years at the date of the transfer or conveyance.

3. On or after 25 December 2017 and up to 31 December 2028, a person of any age, subject to the conditions set out below.

The conditions for availing of the relief are as follows. The individual to whom the farmland is being transferred or conveyed must be an active farmer and must from the date of execution of the transfer or conveyance:

1. farm the land for a period of not less than six years; or
2. lease it for a period of not less than six years to an individual who will farm the land, or lease the land to a partnership or to a company whose main shareholder and working director farms the land on behalf of the company.

The person who farms the land (including the partners or working director in the case of a company), or the individual to whom the land is leased, must:

(a) be the holder of (or within a period of four years from the date of the deed of transfer/conveyance, become the holder of) a qualification set out in Schedule 2, 2A, or 2B of the SDCA, 1999; or

(b) spend not less than 50 per cent of the individual's normal working time farming land including the land being transferred. The Revenue accepts that 'normal working time' approximates to forty hours per week. This will enable farmers with off-farm employment to qualify for the relief provided they spend a minimum of twenty hours per week working on the farm.

(c) The land must be farmed on a commercial basis with a view to the realisation of profits from the land.

In order to avail of the relief, each of the persons to whom the property is transferred must be related to each of the transferors to the required degree. The degree of relationship is mainly based on direct ancestry and extends to nephews and nieces but does not include cousins or in-laws. The relief is provided for in paragraph 15 in Schedule 1 to the SDCA, 1999, and the list of related persons who may qualify for consanguinity relief includes a lineal descendant, parent, grandparent, step-parent, husband or wife, brother or sister of a parent or brother or sister, or lineal descendant of a parent, husband or wife, or brother or sister.

'Lineal descendant' is also now defined in s. 1, in relation to a conveyance or transfer (whether on sale or as a voluntary disposition inter vivos), to include a person who, as transferee, is a child of the transferor. 'Child' would be interpreted in the context of the above definition and will also include a child as defined in s. 2 of the Adoption Act, 2010. This would include as a relative for the purpose of consanguinity relief a foster brother or foster nephew, foster uncle, or similar.

7.9.8 FAMILY FARM TRANSFER RELIEF

Section 83B of the SDCA, 1999 provides for an exemption from stamp duty on certain transfers of farmland from a child to a parent in the context of certain family arrangements to which the provisions of s. 599 of the Taxes Consolidation Act, 1997, as amended, apply for capital gains tax purposes. A child includes a child of a deceased child, certain nephews, nieces, and foster children. A self-assessed stamp duty return must be filed under the e-stamping system in order to obtain the exemption.

7.9.9 FARM CONSOLIDATION RELIEF

The purpose of Farm Consolidation Relief is to encourage the consolidation of farm holdings, to reduce fragmentation, and to improve the operation and viability of farms. Teagasc is required to certify that the purchases, sales, and transfers, that is, the disposals and acquisitions of land, are being carried out for genuine consolidation purposes. A number of conditions apply; for example, they must intend to retain ownership of the land and use the land for farming for a period of at least five years from the date the relief is claimed and a Farm Restructuring Certificate (a Consolidation Certificate) must be obtained from Teagasc.

Section 81C SDCA revived the relief. The relief constitutes EU State Aid and must comply with State Aid rules. The relief is available where farm holdings are consolidated by way of linked sales and purchases of land and where land is transferred as a gift or by way of exchange. It is basically available to farmers who buy and sell agricultural land in order to consolidate their holdings. Stamp duty at a reduced rate of 1 per cent (usual rate 7.5 per cent) is applied to the excess of the value of the land acquired over the value of the land disposed of, where the acquisition and disposal take place within a 24-month period of each other. The relief has been extended to 31 December 2028 pending finalisation of issues relating to EU Agricultural Block Exemption Regulations.

7.9.10 COMMERCIAL WOODLANDS

Section 95 of the SDCA, 1999 provides partial relief from stamp duty in respect of certain instruments relating to the sale or lease of lands on which commercial woodlands/trees are growing. The relief previously only applied to a sale or lease of land and was not available in the case of a gift. In a recent appeal before the Appeal Commissioners, they determined that the relief is also applicable to a conveyance or transfer operating as a voluntary disposition. Accordingly, the relief will now apply where the conveyance or transfer is on sale or the conveyance or transfer operates as a voluntary disposition (gift).

The trees must be growing on a substantial part of the land. While 'substantial' is not defined in the legislation, the Revenue will consider each case on its merit. A substantial part is regarded as not less than 75 per cent of the land. The woodlands must be managed on a commercial basis and with a view to making a profit.

The relief applies to the portion of the consideration which represents the value of the trees growing on the lands. An apportionment of the consideration between the land and the trees growing on the lands is required.

7.9.11 CHARITIES

Section 82 of the SDCA, 1999 provides an exemption from stamp duty for conveyances, transfers, and leases of lands which will be used for charitable purposes in the State or Northern Ireland to a body of persons established solely for charitable purposes or to the trustees of a trust so established.

The appropriate charity ('CHY') number must be quoted on the instrument. If charity exemption status has not already been obtained an application form must be completed and the exemption status obtained.

On receipt of the CHY number a self-assessed stamp duty return must be filed under the e-stamping system to obtain the exemption.

7.9.12 TRANSFERS BY HOUSING AUTHORITY OR AFFORDABLE HOME PARTNERSHIP NOW STAMPABLE

Paragraph 3 of Schedule 1 to the Stamp Duty (E-stamping of Instruments) Regulations, 2009 (SI 476/2009) lists instruments that do not have to be stamped using the e-stamping system. They include instruments giving effect to the conveyance, transfer, or lease of a house, building, or land to or by a housing authority or the Affordable Homes Partnership ('AHP').

However, with effect from 1 April 2011, s. 64 of the Finance Act, 2011 (which amended s. 106B SDCA, 1999):

(a) removed the stamp duty exemption that applied on the transfer of property by a housing authority or the AHP; and

(b) limited the stamp duty payable on such transfers to a maximum of €100.

As a result of these changes, paragraph 3 of the Stamp Duty (E-stamping of Instruments) Regulations, 2009 (SI 476/2009) has been amended by the Stamp Duty (E-stamping of Instruments) (Amendment) Regulations, 2011 (SI 87/2011). These regulations now provide that only transfers to a housing authority or to the AHP do *not* have to be stamped.

Accordingly, any instrument executed on or after 1 April 2011 that gives effect to the conveyance, transfer, or lease of a house, building, or land by a housing authority or the Affordable Homes Partnership must be stamped through the e-stamping system and any stamp duty, up to a maximum of €100, must be paid.

(See the Law Society *Gazette* Practice Note of June 2011.)

7.10 Adjudication

Section 20 of the SDCA, 1999 provides for the accountable person to include an assessment of the duty in the return filed in relation to an instrument under the e-stamping system and also enables the Revenue, in certain circumstances, to assess the amount of duty chargeable on an instrument. The Finance Act, 2012 abolished the requirement for adjudication for instruments executed on or after 7 July 2012. Prior to that, in order to benefit from an exemption or relief from stamp duty, the instrument had to be presented to the Revenue for adjudication. Adjudication of an instrument for stamp duty purposes meant that the Revenue Commissioners determined the correct amount of stamp duty that owed on the instrument, if any. The adjudication stamp will appear on many deeds executed on or before that date.

Adjudication is no longer possible in respect of instruments executed on or after 7 July 2012, nor can adjudication be requested by the Revenue or the taxpayer. For instruments executed on or after that date a self-assessed stamp duty return must be filed under the e-stamping system in order to obtain the exemption or relief.

Although the Revenue no longer retain the power to adjudicate documents, they have the power to require the taxpayer to produce the instrument together with such evidence (including statutory declarations similar to those routinely required in adjudicated transactions) as they deem necessary in order to establish that the instrument has been properly stamped. In addition, the Finance Act, 2012 gave the Revenue new powers to inspect and require the production of documents held by, or on behalf of, an accountable person which are backed up with significant penalties for non-compliance. The removal of adjudication has increased the risk and burden on practitioners to ensure that the self-assessment return is correct and that the correct amount of stamp duty has been paid.

7.11 New Stamping System

7.11.1 E-STAMPING

The Revenue Commissioners commenced the operation of an e-stamping system on 30 December 2009 in accordance with SI 476/2009 entitled Stamp Duty (e-Stamping of Instruments) Regulations, 2009. Details of the system, which also provides details for paying stamp duty, can be found on the Revenue website (www.revenue.ie).

The new system, called e-stamping, applies to every document required to be stamped. Each solicitor should register with the Revenue Online System ('ROS') as, in order to use the e-stamping system, solicitors must be registered with ROS. Practitioners must also set up a Revenue debit instruction to authorise the online payment of stamp duty.

On 1 June 2011 it became mandatory to file stamp duty returns through ROS (subject to very limited exceptions) and to make payment of stamp duty through ROS.

On 1 June 2011, the e-stamping regulations were amended to remove the optional ability to file a paper form of stamp duty return as an alternative to an electronic stamp duty return. The Revenue have made regulations under s. 17A of the SDCA, 1999 on mandatory electronic stamp duty returns and payment of stamp duty (Stamp Duty (E-stamping of Instruments) (Amendment) (No. 2) Regulations, 2011 (SI 222/2011). The Revenue have made the following regulations in relation to the filing of self-assessed returns under the e-stamping system—The Stamp Duty (E-stamping of Instruments and Self-assessment) Regulations, 2012 (SI 234/2012).

The amended regulations allow the Revenue to exempt a person from having to pay and file electronically where they are satisfied that the person does not have the capacity to do so. Incapacity is limited to cases where there is insufficient access to the internet or where an individual is prevented by reason of age or physical or mental infirmity from filing and paying electronically. A person aggrieved by the failure of the Revenue to exempt them from having to pay and file electronically can bring an appeal to the Appeal Commissioners.

In order to file a stamp duty return through ROS it will be necessary to include the PPS number for individuals (or tax reference number for others) of all the parties to the document to be stamped even if the parties to the deed are non-resident. Practitioners should start collecting this information as soon as possible in all transactions involving the potential stamping of an instrument, and preferably before the instrument is executed (which should be verified where possible), to enable the instrument to be stamped. Otherwise there is a real risk that late filing and interest charges will arise. Returns with incorrect PPS or tax reference numbers will be rejected by the Revenue.

The PPS number is an individual's unique reference number for all dealings with the public services, including tax, education, and so on. However, a PPS number does not become an individual's tax reference number until such time as it has been registered with the Revenue as that individual's tax reference number. Consequently, if a PPS number is input into an e-stamping return before it is registered as a tax reference number with the Revenue, it will not be recognised by—and the return will be rejected by—the e-stamping system. In addition, the Local Property Tax ID number is required since 30 November 2013 for residential property.

As most people are already registered for tax with the Revenue, the easiest way to check a tax reference number is to obtain a copy of recent correspondence from the Revenue to the client, for example a tax credit certificate or PAYE balancing statement, or a notice of assessment in the case of an individual.

As and from 7 December 2015 a tax reference type is no longer a mandatory field when completing an e-stamping return.

The Revenue has also advised of two further changes to the e-stamping system as follows:

1. Where the effective date of execution is equal to or later than 24 November 2018, the 'size of property' field will no longer be displayed on the drop down menu.
2. For 'type of instrument' on the 'fixed duty' screen there is now only one option for instruments executed on or after 31 December 2007, which is a lease for stamped agreement. Underneath 'type of instrument' a new field will be displayed: 'Document ID of the Agreement for Lease'. The filer will have to enter this Document ID. The reason for the change is that most of the fixed duties as previously referred to in the drop down menu have not applied since 2007.

These are set out in the Law Society ezine of December 2018 (Issue 103).

The main changes introduced under the new system include:

(a) a comprehensive stamp duty return setting out all relevant particulars and information required to calculate duty and issue the stamp;

(b) a new form of stamp;

(c) a facility to stamp deeds online;

(d) the extension of tax reference number requirements to apply to all instrument types;

(e) more reliance by the Revenue on post-stamping checks and audits.

7.11.2 STAMP DUTY RETURNS

Stamp duty returns must be completed and filed electronically for every instrument executed on or after 1 June 2011, with a few exceptions. On execution of an instrument that requires stamping, the practitioner files a stamp duty return with the Revenue on behalf of the client together with any stamp duty payable. This return must be filed electronically or in paper format (the latter in limited circumstances only). The completed stamp duty return will contain all the information needed to calculate the stamp duty and to stamp the instrument. On receipt of the return and payment when validated by the Revenue, the Revenue electronically issues the practitioner with a stamp certificate which must then be printed and attached to the instrument to denote that it has been stamped. If a paper return is made the stamp certificate will issue in hard copy. The return will be used to generate the stamp.

The former foil/holograph stamp is replaced by the stamp certificate.

A stamp duty return should not be filed in the case of any of the following instruments:

1. An instrument creating a joint tenancy between spouses or civil partners to which s. 14 of the Family Home Protection Act, 1976 applies.
2. A conveyance, transfer, or lease of a house, building, or land by or to a Housing Authority or the Affordable Homes Partnership to which s. 106B (Housing Authorities and Affordable Homes Partnership) of the SDCA applies.
3. A lease for any indefinite term or any term not exceeding thirty-five years to which paragraph (1) under the heading 'lease' in Schedule 1 to the SDCA applies, or an instrument to which s. 108B (National Asset Management Agency) of the SDCA applies.

7.11.3 STAMP CERTIFICATE FORMAT

Each stamp certificate bears its own unique security number and other specific details that will associate it solely and clearly with one particular instrument only. The stamp certificate will need to be printed in paper form whether the return was submitted in electronic or paper format. Returns filed electronically, and completed correctly, will result in the immediate issue of a stamp certificate online in cases not subject to adjudication.

Returns filed in paper format will result in the issue of a stamp certificate by post some days later. A facility to amend details on a submitted return is provided for both electronic and paper returns.

An instrument is considered to be duly stamped when the stamp certificate is attached to it.

The stamp certificate contains the Revenue logo and the following elements:

(a) stamp certificate security number (stamp certificate ID). The security number will be alpha-numeric and will always have twenty digits and be in the following format: 12-0123456-A12B-DDMMYY-A;

(b) document ID number;

(c) date of instrument;

(d) parties' names;

(e) address and folio number (if registered) of the property;

(f) chargeable consideration;

(g) duty (including for leases the rental element) and all penalty amounts, whether mitigated in full or in part;

(h) reliefs applied;

(i) adjudication marker;

(j) date of issue of stamp certificate;

(k) counterpart marker.

Should a stamp certificate be lost or need to be verified, the e-stamping system will allow the Revenue to issue duplicate stamp certificates and to verify the authenticity of a stamp certificate.

Under the new system the instrument itself will not be presented to the Revenue before stamping except in certain cases, such as in refund applications, in penalty mitigations, where additional information is required, or where the case is subject to an expression of doubt or the case is selected by the Revenue for assurance check or audit.

Even in cases where the instrument is presented, the Revenue will use the return to calculate the duty payable and to generate a stamp certificate. Any instrument or documentation presented to the Revenue in support of the return will be sent back to the practitioner pending issue of the stamp certificate.

As previously mentioned at **16.8.2**, the Property Registration Authority have advised the Conveyancing Committee that one of the grounds for rejecting applications is if the relevant folio number is not inserted on the stamp certificate. In a Practice Note in the November 2018 edition of the *Gazette* practitioners were advised that they should be aware of the position and the stance of the PRA.

7.11.4 LOST DEEDS

Under the pre-ROS system a deed on which stamp duty had been paid was sometimes lost. It was then necessary to produce a substitute deed to prove the owner's title to the property. In such cases the Revenue would agree to stamp the substitute deed without the stamp duty being paid a second time, provided adequate evidence could be produced to show that the original deed was properly stamped. The claimant would usually have to produce a statutory declaration giving evidence in relation to the lost deed.

Under the e-stamping system a return is filed on ROS and a record of the return will be on record. The stamp certificate with its unique ID number and security code can be reprinted.

7.11.5 RECENT CHANGES TO E-STAMPING

In a Practice Note in the January 2016 edition of the *Gazette* the Law Society Taxation Committee outlined the changes made to e-stamping screens applicable since 7 December 2015 by the National Stamps Office, which are as follows:

1. A tax reference type for the parties to the instrument will no longer be required when completing an e-stamping return. However, in a small number of cases (less than 1 per cent) the tax reference type may be sought by the e-stamping system for verification purposes.

2. Re individuals: PPS numbers received from the Department of Social Protection and not registered for any tax will continue to require registration by the

National Stamp Duty Office ('NSDP') prior to the number being used on an e-stamping return.

3. Re foreign companies: foreign companies which are not (or were not at any time in the past) registered for tax will continue to have to apply to the NSDO for a tax reference number.
4. The 'consideration' field on the ROS dropdown window has been increased to allow input of eleven digits preceding the decimal point (e.g. the system will in future accept a consideration up to a maximum of €99, 999, 999, and 999.00).
5. The local authority 'field' in the Address Details section of the e-stamping return (for residential property) can now be amended where a change of address entry is made.
6. The only option available in the 'type of instrument' drop down menu for 'fixed duties' is 'Document ID of the Agreement for Lease'. The filer will have to enter the Document ID number. This is so because most of the fixed duties have not applied since 2007.
7. Where the effective date (i.e. later of date of execution and date of escrow) is equal to or later than 24 November 2018, the 'size of property' field will no longer be displayed.

The above information and further information on tax reference numbers and other stamp duty issues is available on the Revenue website.

7.12 Stamping Deed of Assurance of Derelict/Uninhabitable Property

A derelict uninhabitable property falls outside the charge to Local Property Tax ('LPT'), and thus in most cases will not have an LPT ID number, which is required to stamp the deed of assurance of such a property at the residential rate of stamp duty. The Revenue has outlined a new procedure for obtaining a property ID number in such cases. The procedure is reproduced below and can be found in the FAQs on Stamp Duty on the Revenue website.

The Revenue requirement for an uninhabitable property for LPT purposes is that it is not suitable for use as a dwelling—but note that the stamp duty definition is different.

A Revenue guide on the distinction entitled 'Interaction of LPT (Local Property Tax)l and stamp duty' is available in the FAQs on Interaction of Stamp Duty and LPT Sample on the Revenue website.

Sample Case Study

Query:

I am filing a return online for a derelict/uninhabitable property. What do I do if I have no LPT (Local Property Tax) ID number?

Answer:

A derelict house falls within the definition of 'residential property' for stamp duty purposes. In order to file the stamp duty return online, the following steps need to be taken:

1. As it is the responsibility of the vendor to provide the purchaser with an LPT property ID, the vendor should contact the LPT branch in the Revenue by telephoning 1890 200 255 (or 353 1 7023049 if calling from abroad) or emailing lpt@revenue, explain the situation (that is, sale of a derelict house and an LPT property ID number needed in order to file the stamp duty return online), and request them to create an LPT property ID number for the vendor. The LPT Branch

will need the vendor's tax reference number and the address of the property being sold and may request supporting documentation to confirm the status of the property.

2. Once the vendor has provided you with the LPT property ID, you should file the stamp duty return online through ROS, inserting the LPT property ID number in the appropriate screen.

The Revenue have confirmed that the above procedure should be followed in the case of houses that are not suitable for use as a dwelling ('uninhabitable houses').

7.13 Exemptions

There are many instruments exempt from Stamp Duty.

7.13.1 HOUSES ACQUIRED BY LOCAL AUTHORITIES OR FROM INDUSTRIAL AND PROVIDENT SOCIETIES

Section 93 provides an exemption for conveyances, transfers, and leases by local authorities under the provisions of the Housing Act, 1966 to 2008.

7.13.2 APPROVED HOUSING BODY

Section 93A provides an exemption for conveyances, transfers, and leases to an approved Housing Body.

7.13.3 PURCHASE OF LAND FROM LAND COMMISSION

Section 94 provides that the purchase by Qualified Persons of land from the Land Commission is exempt from Stamp Duty on that land where the instrument contains a charge on the land or on which an order is endorsed in favour of the Irish Land Commission.

7.14 'Consideration'

The 'conveyance on sale' head in Sch. 1 provides that *ad valorem* duty is to be chargeable on the 'amount or value of the consideration'.

In most cases the consideration will be the purchase price for the property being conveyed. In some circumstances (i.e. a voluntary disposition or gift) the consideration will not be on the face of the instrument. Sections 44 and 55 govern the situations where at the date of a conveyance, transfer, or lease, the appropriate consideration cannot be ascertained. This could be because part of the consideration is deferred, or the rent payable is partly conditional on the turnover in the demised premises.

Different rates apply for instruments where s 29(4)(a) or s 53(4)(a) applies.

Where the Revenue Commissioners are not able to determine the consideration, in such circumstances Revenue will use a multiple of between five and ten times the market value of the land to calculate the Stamp Duty payable. If it is subsequently proved that this amounts to an excess, a refund of any excess may be available if the application for a refund is made within the appropriate three-year time period.

7.14.1 UNASCERTAINABLE CONSIDERATION OR RENT (SECTIONS 44 AND 55)

Where the consideration in respect of a conveyance or transfer cannot be ascertained, the legislation provides that Stamp Duty will be based on the value of the consideration that could be obtained from a purchaser paying full value; that is, the **open market value of the property** is substituted for the unascertainable consideration. This will apply in the case of a voluntary disposition or any other disposition where the consideration is inadequate.

Section 44 provides for the situation where consideration cannot be ascertained with regard to a sale. Where the consideration cannot be ascertained at the date of execution of a conveyance, Stamp Duty is chargeable on the amount or value of the consideration that could be obtained from a purchaser paying full consideration for such sale. The market value of the property is imposed as consideration.

Section 55 contains the provisions that apply to leases where the consideration (either rent, premium, or both) cannot be ascertained. Market values are imposed for the unascertainable part. Section 55 provides for the substitution of a market consideration or rent in circumstances where a consideration or rent cannot be ascertained on the date of execution of a conveyance or lease.

In the case of a lease in respect of which the rent is unascertainable and no premium is payable, Stamp Duty will be payable on the full market rent that the property would currently obtain; that is, the open market rental value is used. When a lease provides for a payment of a premium and rent both of which are unascertainable, Stamp Duty will be payable on the full consideration *other than rent* that would be payable on the open market for the leasehold interest; that is, if both are unascertainable, consideration is determined by the value of a market premium on the basis that no rent is payable.

The substitution of a market consideration (s 44) or rent or premium (s 55) means that a charge to duty can be applied. In determining whether or not a consideration or rent is ascertainable for the purposes of ss 44 and 55, the contingency principle should **not** be used.

The following examples illustrate the point:

- A conveyance with a stated consideration of €200,000. The provisions of ss 44 and 55 do not apply because the consideration is ascertainable.
- A conveyance with a stated consideration of €200,000 plus a percentage of future profits. The provisions of s 44 apply because the consideration is unascertainable. The property being conveyed should be valued for the consideration that a purchaser paying full consideration would pay and duty charged accordingly.
- A conveyance with a stated consideration of €200,000 plus a percentage of future profits up to a maximum of €20,000. The provisions of s 44 apply because the consideration is unascertainable. Duty should not be charged on a contingent consideration of €220,000. Instead, the property being conveyed should be valued for the consideration that a purchaser paying full consideration would pay and duty charged accordingly.

Once a premium or rent contains a contingent element (i.e. a sum that may be paid if certain conditions are met) the provisions of s 55 apply and the market value will be imposed.

7.14.2 CONSIDERATION OTHER THAN FOR MONEY

'Marketable Security' and 'Stock' are defined in s 1 and include any shares, loan stock, and gilts (Irish and foreign). Note that government stocks and securities (Irish and foreign) and EC securities are exempt from Stamp Duty (s. 89).

Section 40(2) provides that 'where the consideration, or any part of the consideration, for a conveyance on sale of any property, consists of any security not being a marketable security, the conveyance shall be charged with ad valorem duty as a conveyance on sale of that property for a consideration equal to the value of that property on the date of execution of the conveyance'.

Example: A transfers a parcel of land to B in consideration of 20,000 ordinary shares in X Limited (value €250,000). Stamp Duty is payable on the conveyance of the land based on the value of the shares (€250,000 × 7.5% = €18,750).

7.14.3 DEBTS—CONVEYANCE IN SATISFACTION OF A DEBT

Section 41 provides that a transfer of property in satisfaction of a debt is chargeable as a conveyance on sale based upon the amount of the debt.

Example: A transfers land valued at €50,000 to B in satisfaction of a debt of €60,000 owed by A to B. Stamp Duty is payable on €60,000 @ 7.5% = €4500.

A conveyance of property by the executors of a will in discharge of a pecuniary legacy is a conveyance on sale, on the grounds that the legatee is entitled to money from the estate and the conveyance is in consideration of the money (*Dawson v IRC* [1905] 2 IR 69).

Consideration in the form of debts is to be valued based on the amount due upon the security for principal and interest on the date of the instrument (s. 41).

It is the date of the instrument which is relevant for valuation of the consideration in the above cases.

7.14.4 CONVEYANCE WHERE DEBT TAKEN OVER/ASSUMPTION OF LIABILITY

Section 41 also provides for the situation where property is transferred subject to a liability being taken over; for example, where a house is sold subject to the purchaser taking over the existing mortgage. Where this occurs, the liability taken over **is added** to the money paid to establish the chargeable consideration.

Example: Jane agrees to buy Sean's farm (value €250,000 with mortgage of €130,000) for €120,000 and also agrees to take over the mortgage liability. Stamp Duty is chargeable on the €120,000 cash plus the €130,000 liability assumed (i.e. €250,000).

Section 41(2) applies to a situation where property is conveyed subject certainly or contingently to the payment or transfer of any money or stock whether it is a charge or incumbrance or not. Where, in a situation that falls within s. 41, stock of a company is being transferred and the transferee procures either directly or indirectly the payment/discharge of any indebtedness of the company or any connected company (as defined in TCA, 1997, s. 10) and the main or one of the main purposes of the arrangement is to secure a tax advantage, then the consideration shall be treated as including the payment of any cash, the transfer of stock (if applicable), and an amount equal to the amount of the indebtedness.

7.14.5 FOREIGN CURRENCY

If consideration is expressed in a foreign currency, s. 9 provides that the duty is calculated on the value of the money in that foreign currency according to the rate of exchange at the date of the execution of the instrument.

7.14.6 PERIODICAL PAYMENTS OF CONSIDERATION

Section 42 contains provisions to apply in cases where the consideration is expressed to be payable periodically (e.g. €10,000 per annum for 20 years). These provisions specify what amount of the consideration is to be charged to Stamp Duty.

7.14.6.1 Section 42(1)

Where the consideration is payable for a definite period not exceeding twenty years and the total payable is ascertainable, duty is charged on the total payable.

In *Hotung v Stamps Revenue Collector* [1965] AC 766, the Privy Council held that the duty is to be calculated on the nominal total of the instalments payable and not by reference to their value at the date of the sale (i.e. the amount of the instalments' total is not to be discounted).

Example: €10,000 per annum for ten years. Stamp Duty is charged on €100,000 (€10,000 × 10) @ 7.5% = €7500.

7.14.6.2 Section 42(2)

Where there is a definite period exceeding twenty years, the duty is charged on the total payable during the first twenty years after the date of the instrument.

Example: If the consideration for a sale is annual payments of €10,000 each, payable for twenty-five years, the chargeable consideration will be limited to €200,000 (i.e. €10,000 × 20).

In *Western United Investment Company Limited v IRC* [1958] All ER 257, Upjohn J held that where the agreement for sale of shares provided for the £5.5 million agreed consideration to be paid over 125 years by annual instalments of £44,000, and further provided in clause 3 that, in the event of default in any payment, all the unpaid instalments should immediately become due, the Inland Revenue Commission could not apply the contingency principle to the default clause and assess the entire £5.5 million: 'there should be disregarded those terms of sale such as clause 3 which becomes effective only when the other terms of sale are broken.'

It seems that interest on the periodical payments may not be included in the amount on which duty is payable (*Hotung v Collector of Stamp Revenue* [1965] AC 775).

7.15 Value Added Tax

The chargeable consideration for Stamp Duty purposes is the VAT-exclusive amount.

7.16 Covenants to Improve

Section 43 provides that any covenant in a conveyance on sale by the purchaser to improve or add to the property conveyed, or any other covenant by him relating to the subject matter of the conveyance, **shall not be chargeable as consideration**.

This section was applied in the case of *Kimbers & Co v IRC* [1936] 1 KB 132, where the Inland Revenue Commission unsuccessfully sought to charge duty on a conveyance of a building site, which was conditional upon a building contract between the same parties, for a house on the site based on the total consideration for the site and the building work.

7.17 Mortgaged Property

In the case of a voluntary transfer of property subject to a mortgage, the Revenue Commissioners will deduct the mortgage liability in arriving at the value of the benefit passing and Stamp Duty will be charged on the **net benefit taken** (i.e. the value of the equity of redemption). The provisions of ss. 30 and 41 must be considered.

7.17.1 GIFT OF MORTGAGED PROPERTY—NO CONSIDERATION

Example: A makes a gift of property to B. The property is valued at €270,000 but is subject to a mortgage of €40,000.

Value of property:	€270,000
Mortgage:	€ 40,000
Equity of redemption:	€230,000

In this example, duty would be assessed on the value of the equity of redemption (€230,000). However, if the amount of the mortgage being assumed by the donee is greater in amount than the value of the equity of redemption, the Revenue Commissioners will assess duty on the amount of the mortgage (by treating the instrument as a 'conveyance on sale' and applying the provisions of s. 41 (assumption of liabilities)).

Example: A makes a gift of property to B. The property is valued at €270,000 and is subject to a mortgage of €240,000.

Value of property:	€270,000
Mortgage:	€240,000
Equity of redemption:	€30,000

In this case duty will be assessed on the €240,000 mortgage, treating the instrument as a 'conveyance on sale' and applying the provisions of s. 41.

7.17.2 GIFT OF MORTGAGED PROPERTY—PART PAYMENT

If, instead of gifting property to someone outright, that person partly pays for the property, the calculation of Stamp Duty is somewhat different. The provisions of s. 41 apply and any debt or liability taken over is added to the consideration payable, to determine the total consideration liable to duty.

Example: A sells a house to B for €240,000. The value of the house is €270,000 and the property is subject to a mortgage of €30,000. B will take over the mortgage.

Duty is assessed on the instrument as a 'conveyance on sale' (and not as a voluntary disposition *inter vivos*) for a consideration of:

$$€240,000\,\text{cash} + €30,000\,\text{mortgage} = €270,000\big(\text{s. }41\big).$$

The duty paid is therefore €270,000 @ 1% = €2700.

The treatment of mortgages in gift cases is anomalous when compared to the treatment of debts in a sale case.

Example: A sells property which is worth €270,000, and which is liable to a mortgage of €30,000, to B. The purchase price is to be €240,000 (which is equal to the equity of redemption).

Value of property:	€270,000
Mortgage:	€30,000
Equity of redemption:	€240,000
Consideration paid:	€240,000

In this case, being a sale (and not a gift, since full consideration is paid), the debt being assumed by the purchaser is added to the €240,000 cash consideration to determine the total chargeable consideration for Stamp Duty purposes.

The duty is therefore assessed on:

Consideration	€240,000
Mortgage assumed	€30,000
Liable to duty	€270,000

If A had made a gift of the property to B, only €240,000 (i.e. the equity of redemption) would be liable to duty.

Even in the case of gifts, there is an inequality between the treatment of part consideration in the form of a mortgage assumed and in the form of money paid.

Compare the following scenarios. No allowance is made in Stamp Duty law for partial consideration, except in the case of liabilities charged on the gifted property.

Mortgage assumed		**Part cash payment**	
Value of property	€290,000	Value of property	€290,000
Mortgage assumed	(€40,000)	Cash paid	(€40,000)
Gift of equity	€250,000	Gift of equity	€250,000
Stamp duty on €250,000		**Stamp duty on**	
		€250,000 + €40,000 = €290,000	
€250,000 @ 1% = €2500		€290,000 @ 1% = €2900	

7.18 Voluntary Leases (i.e. Gifts) (Section 54)

As in the case of conveyances of property, specific provisions are contained in the legislation to deal with leases which confer a substantial benefit to the lessee. The provisions are contained in s. 54 and are designed to permit Stamp Duty to be assessed on the capital value of any benefit passing to the lessee.

If a lease, by reason of the inadequacy of the rent reserved or the premium charged, or by reason of any other circumstances, confers a substantial benefit on the lessee, it is to be assessed as a voluntary disposition.

Section 54(2) provides that, where a lease operates as a voluntary disposition, duty is to be assessed on the lease by reference to 'the minimum amount or value that would be necessary in order that the lease, any rent thereunder remaining unchanged, would not be a lease operating as a voluntary disposition inter vivos'.

In other words, where a lease operates as a voluntary disposition (i.e. confers a substantial benefit), a capital payment, of an amount equal to the amount of the benefit passing, will be imputed to the lease and that capital payment will be subject to Stamp Duty in the same way as if it were a premium payable under the terms of the lease.

Example: A lets his grocery shop to his brother B for three years at an annual rent of €45,000. No premium is payable. If let on the open market on such terms (i.e. no premium, three-year term), a rent of €90,000 per annum would be obtainable.

The full market value, 'with the rent thereunder remaining unchanged', would result in a premium of €120,000 (€45,000 per annum rent deficit x three years, discounted) which would need to be reserved in the lease.

Duty would be charged as follows:

Rent	€45,000 × 1% (less than 35 years)	=	€450
Deemed premium:	€120,000 × 7.5%	=	€9000
Total			€9450

7.19 Partition or Division

A partition or division of property occurs where property which was owned jointly is conveyed by the joint owners in separate parcels into their separate names. As in the case of an exchange, a partition or division is not a 'sale' per se.

Schedule 1 contains the head 'partition or division' and provides that duty is only payable in the case specified in s. 38. Section 38 provides that whereupon the partition or division of any 'real or heritable property' any consideration exceeding €130 is given for equality, the principal instrument effecting the partition or division is to be charged with the same ad valorem Stamp Duty as a conveyance on sale for the consideration.

7.19.1 REAL OR HERITABLE PROPERTY

'Real or heritable property' has been held to refer only to freehold property (*IRC v Littlewoods Mail Order Stores Ltd* [1962] 2 WLR 1228).

A partition or division of leasehold property (where equality money is paid) by assignment into different parts would appear to be chargeable as a conveyance on sale of the more valuable part in consideration of the equality money paid—the same result as above. However, there is authority (*MacLeod v IRC* (1885) 12 R (Ct of Sess) 1045) that such an instrument may not be charged as a sale and is therefore exempt.

Example: A and B are co-owners of land held in fee simple. The value of the lands is €240,000. They wish to partition the lands, A taking a part worth €140,000 and B the remaining part worth €100,000. A agrees to pay €20,000 equality money to B.

Section 38 will apply to the stamping of the instrument of partition and the duty thereon will be as on a conveyance on sale for €20,000 consideration (i.e., €20,000 × 7.5% = €1500).

7.19.2 VOLUNTARY PARTITION OR DIVISION

A partition or division which, by reason of the inadequacy of the equality money, is more beneficial to one party than the other may be chargeable to Stamp Duty as a voluntary disposition under the provisions of s. 30.

Example: If in the above example A only paid €5000 equality money, the resulting split would be unequal.

A		**B**	
	140,000		€100,000
Less equality money paid	(€5000)	Plus equality money paid	€5000
	€135,000		**€105,000**

The instrument would in such case be deemed voluntary and duty would be assessed on the value of the beneficial interest passing (€140,000 less €120,000 already owned = €20,000).

7.20 Sub-Sales: Anti-Avoidance

Because s. 46(1) and (2) offer significant relief from Stamp Duty, stringent anti-avoidance measures have been introduced. These are contained in s. 46(4), (5) and (6) and have been developed through case law. These anti-avoidance measures are an attempt to prevent the manipulation of straightforward two-party sales into sub-sales by interposing an associate or relative of the purchaser.

Section 46(4) provides that the consideration moving from the sub-purchaser shall be ascertained '*without regard to the value of any covenant, power, condition or arrangement relating to the subject matter of the conveyance which was not in the contract entered into by the original seller*' and without regard to any periodical payments that would otherwise be charged under s. 42(2).

Section 46(5) provides that instruments effecting sub-sales shall not qualify for consanguinity relief.

Section 46(6) provides that any conveyance to which s. 46(4) applies is to be deemed a voluntary conveyance, and so chargeable based on the market value of the property conveyed.

Example: C wishes to buy property from A for €130,000. He requests his brother B to sign the contract with A and then C contracts to buy from B. The consideration expressed in the sub-purchase agreement between B and C is twenty annual payments of €1300 followed in the twenty-first year by a final instalment of €200,000 (total consideration €226,000, which presumably would have a current actuarial value of €130,000). Alternatively, B could have placed a restrictive covenant in his contract with C and thereby considerably reduced the sale price payable to B by C.

In the absence of the anti-avoidance provisions in s. 46(4), (5) and (6), duty might only be chargeable on the consideration moving from C to B, based on the provisions in s. 42(2)—namely, on the first twenty instalments only (i.e., €26,000).

Because the anti-avoidance provisions apply, the conveyance is deemed to be a voluntary disposition (s. 46(6)) and the instrument is charged to Stamp Duty based on the market value of the property passing.

It would seem that in the event of s. 30 applying to the instrument (either by virtue of the inadequacy of the consideration passing or because the anti-avoidance provisions apply), only one charge to Stamp Duty would arise on the instrument (as compared with two charges where the instrument fails to qualify as a sub-sale at all).

Warning: If the consideration passing between C and B could be shown to be inadequate, then even in the absence of s. 46(4) and (6), the general voluntary disposition provisions in s. 30 would apply and the conveyance would be charged to duty based on the value of the property passing and not by reference to the consideration moving from C.

The relief is stated to apply where the purchaser contracts to sell 'the same' property to the sub-purchaser. In *Fthereforell Limited v IRC* [1962] 3 All ER 685 it was held that where shares had been reduced to nominal value by the creation of new rights prior to being sub-sold, the property could not be described as the same, and therefore the provisions of s. 46(1) did not apply.

7.21 Administrative Matters

7.21.1 ESCROW

A document may, however, be executed by all the parties but be held in 'escrow', meaning that it is only to become operative on the performance of an outstanding condition. In such cases the time for stamping only arises when the condition is satisfied and the instrument is released from escrow and delivered. The Revenue Commissioners will require evidence of the existence of the escrow.

7.21.2 PENALTIES (SECTION 1078 TCA, 1997)

Section 133 provides that Section 1078 of TCA 1997 provides that a person shall be guilty of an offence if he or she knowingly and wilfully delivers incorrect information in connection with tax (including Stamp Duty) or knowingly aids, abets, assists, incites, or induces another person to do so.

A person guilty of an offence under the section is liable:

(1) on summary conviction, to a fine not exceeding €5000, or imprisonment not exceeding 12 months or both, or

(2) on indictment, to a fine not exceeding €126,970 or imprisonment not exceeding five years, or both.

Sections 987(4), 1061, 1062, 1063, 1064, 1065, 1066, and 1068 of TCA, 1997 apply to fines or penalties under the Act or otherwise related to stamp duty.

Note also that the provisions of s. 1068 of TCA, 1997 (publication of names of tax defaulters) apply to Stamp Duty.

7.21.3 ASSESSMENT BY REVENUE—RETURN NOT MADE

Section 20(2) also allows the Revenue Commissioners to make assessments of duty that to the best of their knowledge, information (which can include information from the Gardaí), and belief ought to be charged on an instrument when an accountable person fails to make an electronic or paper filing. The accountable person must pay the stamp duty specified in the assessment together with any applicable interest.

7.21.4 AMENDED RETURN

Section 20(9) provides that an amended return must contain an assessment to be substituted for the earlier assessment.

7.22 Disclosure of Relevant Facts (Section 8)

Section 8 provides that 'all the facts and circumstances affecting the liability of any instrument to duty, or the amount of the duty with which any instrument is chargeable, are to be fully and truly set forth in the instrument'.

In the case of e-stamping, information is included on the return and a statement is not required to be delivered. Instead, all of the facts and circumstances related to the instrument must be retained by the accountable person for a period of six years from the date of stamping and such information must be made available to Revenue upon request.

7.22.1 PENALTIES FOR NON-DISCLOSURE

Section 8(4A) provides that the penalty for failing to include in an instrument or in the related statement all of the facts and circumstances of which the person is aware, or failing to fully and truly set out the facts and circumstances affecting the Stamp Duty liability of the instrument, is **€3000**.

Penalties may also arise under s. 134A where an accountable person acts carelessly or deliberately in the disclosure of relevant information for stamp duty purposes.

7.22.2 INNOCENT MISREPRESENTATION

Section 8(4) provides that where an instrument or statement innocently contains a misstatement, any person who executed the instrument is deemed to have acted negligently where such fact later comes to his notice, or would have if he has acted reasonably, unless the Revenue Commissioners are informed without reasonable delay.

7.22.3 VOLUNTARY DISPOSITIONS

Section 8(5) provides that where an instrument operates as a voluntary disposition, unless such fact, including a statement of value, is brought to the attention of the Revenue Commissioners in the stamp duty return, any person who executed the instrument shall be presumed, until the contract is proved, to have acted deliberately for the purposes of s. 134A(2)(a).

7.22.4 POWERS OF INSPECTION (SECTION 128)

Section 128 provides that every person who is a party to any instrument, or who has in his or her custody or control any document which if examined might:

(a) secure any duty, or

(b) prove or lead to the discovery of any fraud, negligence or omission in relation to any duty, must, within fourteen days of receiving a written request from the Revenue Commissioners:

(c) provide such information as the Revenue Commissioners deem necessary, and

(d) permit inspection of the document and the taking of copies, and so on, if necessary.

Failure to comply results in an offence and the provisions of the TCA, 1997 will apply.

7.23 Stamp Duty Audit

Records are required to be retained for stamp duty audit purposes. The purpose of an audit is to ensure that the stamp duty return is correct and the correct Stamp Duty has been paid or that post-stamping conditions have been satisfied for relief granted. The audit is of the accountable person.

To facilitate audits, records must be retained for six years from the later of the date the return was made or the date the stamp duty was paid (s. 8(2) and s. 128A).

Under s. 128A an accountable person is obliged to retain records relating to the stamp duty and to any relief or exemption claimed for a six-year period. A penalty of €3000 will apply for failure to maintain records.

The records must enable Revenue to verify the facts and circumstances of transactions presented in the Stamp Duty return.

Revenue has the power to enter premises or a place of business for the purposes of auditing a return under s. 128B. An accountable person or his employees may be requested to produce records and other documents. Penalties apply for a failure by an accountable person to produce such records.

7.24 Appeals

7.24.1 AMOUNT OF DUTY

Section 21 allows a person to appeal the assessment of the Revenue Commissioners relating to the amount of stamp duty properly payable on an instrument. Appeals must be made in writing within thirty days after the date of the assessment of the duty. The appeal will be determined by the Appeal Commissioners.

No appeal can be made against an assessment made by an accountable person, or where an accountable person has agreed the assessment with Revenue. If an error has been made by an accountable person, then an amended return may be filed rather than an appeal being made.

The appeal is made to the Appeal Commissioners whose determination is final, unless the matter is appealed by means of a case stated to the High Court (on a point of law only).

Where no return is made, or Revenue are dissatisfied with the return made and make an assessment, then in order to appeal the assessment the accountable person must file a return (if he had failed to file one) and pay the duty (together with any surcharge and interest or other costs levied regarding the collection of the stamp duty) prior to making the appeal.

7.24.2 REFUNDS—S159A

A claim for a refund/repayment must be made within four years of the date of stamping an instrument.

Interest will only be payable on a refund under s. 159B where the repayment is not made by Revenue within ninety-three days of receiving a valid claim for a refund. Any interest would be payable from the ninety-fourth day to the date of repayment. However, interest will be payable from the date giving rise to the repayment where Revenue have made an error in operating stamp duty. The interest rate is 0.011 per cent per day or part of a day. Interest that would amount to less than €10 is not payable.

7.24.3 MAKING ENQUIRIES—TIME PERIODS—S159C

Revenue have four years from the date of stamping of an instrument to raise an assessment or make enquiries in relation to underpayment of stamp duty.

This time period does not apply where there is fraud or neglect.

CHAPTER 8

CAPITAL GAINS TAX AND CONVEYANCING—OTHER TAX CHARGES

8.1 Introduction to Chapter 8

This chapter deals with capital gains tax ('CGT'), initially as it arises in a typical conveyancing transaction, then moving on to deal with calculating the capital gain on other types of asset.

In conveyancing, where the consideration exceeds either €1,000,000 in the case of residential houses and apartments as defined or €500,000 in disposals of all other Irish land and buildings including commercial property, a clearance certificate pursuant to s. 980 of the Taxes Consolidation Act, 1997 is required by a purchaser's solicitor.

Alternatively, 15 per cent from the purchase price must be deducted and paid to the Revenue Commissioners (withholding tax) where such clearance certificate is not provided by the person disposing of the asset. An online application system for vendors to apply for a CG50A and for purchasers filing a CG50B is available since June 2020. However, for customers who are non e-enabled the Revenue continue to support paper based applications.

In addition, a new clearance procedure to operate in non-resident vendor cases was put in place by Revenue from 24 October 2022. The process for dealing with requests for clearance for CGT when there is a non-resident vendor is outlined in the Tax and Duty Manual (TDM) Part 45-01-05. An online application on ROS will result in an acknowledgement recording the start of the thirty-five-day period.

In addition to capital gains tax (and stamp duty and CAT, dealt with in previous chapters, and VAT, to be dealt with in **Chapter 9**), charges under various other taxes may arise. These include but are not limited to: charges arising under the Local Government (Charges) Act, 2009; the Local Government (Household Charges) Act, 2011; and the Finance (Local Property Tax) Act, 2012, and water charges as provided for under the Environment (Miscellaneous Provisions) Act, 2015, as amended by the Water Services Act, 2017.

In the April 2016 edition of the *Gazette* the Conveyancing Committee advised that, in cases where records required for conveyancing transactions are maintained only online, it is the online record that is conclusive and that can be accepted by a purchaser's solicitor. A purchaser's solicitor may accept a photocopy, colour copy, or printout, or review the online record—for example, the LPT online record, BER certificates or NPPR certificates of exemption, or waiver or certificates of registration of septic tanks. The emailed soft copy of both the email and the attachment is sufficient for conveyancing purposes and can be printed out and placed with the title deeds. There is no need for either a purchaser's or a vendor's solicitor to certify a copy as being a copy of the original.

8.2 Introduction to Capital Gains Tax

Capital gains tax ('CGT') was introduced in 1974. It is a tax on the gain arising on the disposal of a capital asset by a chargeable person to include land, buildings, and shares in a company on or after 6 April 1974. Because it is a tax on disposals (i.e. not just a sale), gifts come within its scope. The standard rate of tax is currently 33 per cent. Various other rates apply; for example, a rate of 40 per cent applies to certain foreign life assurance policies and units in offshore funds, while rates of 12.5 per cent and 15 per cent apply to certain venture capital fund managers. Other rates apply in exceptional cases, for example windfall tax, which is charged at the rate of 80 per cent. In addition Section 597AA inserted by the Finance Act, 2015 of the Taxes Consolidation Act, 1999 ('the TCA, 1999') introduced a revised CGT relief for entrepreneurs, 'entrepreneur relief', disposing of certain business assets. It provides that a reduced rate of 10 per cent CGT applies from 1 January 2017 in respect of a chargeable gain or gains arising on the disposal of qualifying business assets. This is reduced from the normal rate of 33 per cent. There is a lifetime chargeable gain limit of €1m, and the current standard rate of 33 per cent CGT applies to gains in excess of this amount.

Certain assets are excluded from the tax and some gains are relieved from the tax.

There is an allowance for inflation when calculating the gain for assets which were acquired and certain expenditures (enhancement expenditures) that had been incurred before 31 December 2002.

However, this relief, known as indexation relief, will apply only for the period of ownership of the asset and enhancement expenditure incurred up to 31 December 2002. Gains accruing to persons are chargeable to capital gains tax, whereas gains accruing to companies are generally chargeable to corporation tax (except in the case of development land).

The taxation of capital gains is incorporated into the Taxes Consolidation Act, 1997 ('the TCA, 1997') as amended by subsequent Finance Acts. Previously, it was governed by the Capital Gains Tax Act, 1975 and the Corporation Tax Act, 1976 as amended by the capital gains tax (Amendment) Act, 1978 and subsequent Finance Acts. The Finance Act, 2012 introduced full self-assessment for chargeable persons and obliges the disponer or their agent to self-assess when making a tax return and the legislation allows for penalties where no self-assessment is made. If registered for capital gains tax then the tax must be paid online using ROS or My Account.

Assets include all forms of property, including land, shares, and buildings (TCA 1997, s. 532).

Certain assets are not chargeable assets (e.g. euro currency or wasting assets) and some gains are not chargeable gains as an exception or relief may apply (for example, generally, no CGT applies on a principal private residence used wholly as residential premises).

8.3 Scope of Capital Gains Tax

Section 28 of the Capital Gains Tax Act, 1975 provides that tax shall be charged in respect of *chargeable gains* computed in accordance with the Act and accruing to a *person* on the *disposal* of *assets*. It is necessary for all of these four conditions to arise in order for a charge to capital gains tax to arise (subject to a limited number of exceptions). Since the introduction of the calendar tax year by s. 77 of the Finance Act, 2001, this year of assessment now runs from 1 January to the following 31 December. The date of payment of CGT is triggered by the date the contract is made (TCA 1997 s. 542). If it is a conditional contract then the relevant date is the date the condition is satisfied.

The tax year is divided into two periods for payment purposes as follows:

- in the initial period 1 January to 30 November both inclusive;
- in the later period 1 December to 31 December both inclusive.

The due date for payment of capital gains tax is now as follows:

- disposals in the initial period: tax is due by 15 December in the same tax year;
- disposals in the later period: tax is due by 31 January in the following tax year.

Capital gains that arise for persons other than companies are chargeable to CGT and capital gains that arise for companies are generally chargeable to corporation tax (with some exceptions; e.g. companies are chargeable to CGT on chargeable gains from disposals of development land).

Self-assessment rules apply to CGT for all persons—both self-employed and individuals who receive payment under the PAYE system (e.g. employees and recipients of pensions). A person is obliged to pay and file CGT without being requested to do so by the Revenue Commissioners.

Example:

A contract is signed on 1 October 2023 and the conveyance is executed on 2 December 2023. When is the CGT payable?

As the contract was signed on 1 October 2023 and does not appear to be conditional, this contract falls within the initial period and the CGT must be paid on or before 15 December 2023.

If the contract is not signed until 2 December 2023, CGT would be payable on 31 January 2024.

Payment is made to the Collector General.

CGT can be returned as part of the income tax return or, where a tax return is not otherwise required, on a CGT return (Form CG1). The return must be submitted by 31 October in the year following the tax year in which the disposal is made.

The file date is extended if ROS is used, usually to mid-November (the date is announced annually by the Revenue).

A return must be filed even if no tax is due where a person has used losses or claimed a relief.

Self-employed persons file the income tax self-assessment form (form 11), employees file a form 12, partnerships file a form 1 (firms), and companies file a form CT1 which is also used for corporation tax purposes. If a person is not required to make an income tax return (e.g. a non-resident individual selling their Irish holiday home; a person who is not obliged to submit an income tax return; a person exempt from income tax) then that person files a form CG1.

If CGT is not returned and paid when due, late payment interest at the rate of 0.0219 per cent per day/part day is payable until the tax is paid. In addition, if a CGT return is not filed when due on the 31 October, this being the file date, the following surcharges apply:

(i) If the return is filed up to two months late: 5 per cent of the tax due subject to a maximum of €12,695.

(ii) If the return is filed more than two months late: 10 per cent of the tax due subject to a maximum of €63,485.

Companies

For companies, where gains are chargeable to corporation tax, the due date for payment is determined by reference to the accounting period in which the gain accrues.

Example:

Audrey fails to file her CGT return by 31 October 2023 in relation to a €7,000 CGT liability that arose from a disposal in 2022. She realises this mistake and files the return by 30 November 2023. As this is within two months of the filing date she is subject to a 5 per cent surcharge, calculated as €7,000 * 5% = €350.

Full self-assessment applies. If the Revenue raise an assessment and a person is not happy with an assessment (the Revenue decision on the return), he/she can appeal the assessment to the Appeal Commissioners within thirty days of the notice of the assessment.

8.4 Persons Chargeable

A person's liability to capital gains tax generally depends on the following factors: domicile, residence, and ordinary residence, and the location and type of the asset disposed of. Any person who is resident or ordinarily resident and domiciled in the State for a year of assessment is liable to tax on chargeable gains accruing on all disposals of chargeable assets worldwide made during that year. The same applies to a company in respect of the chargeable gains accruing to it for a chargeable period during which it resided in the State.

In relation to a person who is resident or ordinarily resident in the State but is not domiciled in the State, gains realised on disposals of assets situated outside the State and foreign assets are liable to Irish CGT tax only to the extent that the gains are remitted to this country and such gains are not chargeable to tax until so remitted.

Everyone is liable to capital gains tax on the disposal of Irish land.

Where someone is neither resident nor ordinarily resident nor domiciled in Ireland they are chargeable on gains on specified Irish assets only, for example land and buildings in the State or minerals in the State.

8.4.1 RESIDENCE

A statutory definition of residence is set out in s. 819(1) of the TCA, 1997.

Residence status for Irish tax purposes is determined by the number of days a person is present in the State during a given tax year. Section 819(1) sets out the two basic tests of residence. A person will be tax resident in the State in a tax year if:

(a) he or she is present in the State for a period amounting to 183 days or more in that calendar tax year—the current year test; or

(b) he or she is present in the State for 280 days taking the current and preceding calendar years together—the two-year test. An individual who is present in the State for thirty days or less in a tax year will not be treated as resident for that year unless he or she elects to be resident.

Up to the end of 2009 an individual was deemed to be present in the State for a day if he or she was in the State at the end of a day, that is, midnight (a 'Cinderella' test). Effectively it was the nights spent in the State which were counted. From 2009 forward a taxpayer is 'present in the State' for a day if he or she is present at any time during that day.

Example:

If Joan, an Australian national, spends 121 days in Ireland in 2021 and 160 days in Ireland in 2022, she will be tax resident in Ireland for 2022. If she had spent just twenty days in Ireland in 2021 these days would not be counted when doing the residence test and she would not be resident in 2022.

8.4.2 ORDINARY RESIDENCE

Section 820(1) of the TCA, 1997 contains the definition of ordinary residence. This refers to an individual's pattern of residence over a number of tax years. If a person has been resident in the State for three consecutive tax years, he or she is regarded as ordinary resident for the beginning of the fourth tax year. Ordinary residence implies a greater degree of permanence than simply being resident. Once an individual becomes ordinary resident in the State he or she will remain ordinary resident until or unless he or she is non-resident for three consecutive years.

Example:

Simon arrived in Ireland from Australia in January 2020 and has remained in Ireland ever since. As he is tax resident in Ireland in 2020, 2021, and 2022 he will be ordinarily tax resident in Ireland from 2023 onwards.

8.4.3 DOMICILE

The TCA, 1997 does not contain a definition of domicile. This is because domicile is a common law legal term rather than a tax specific term. Under common law, every person must have a domicile. A person can have only one domicile at any particular time but cannot be without a domicile. There are three kinds of domicile:

1. Domicile of origin.
2. Domicile of choice.
3. Domicile of dependence.

It is broadly interpreted as meaning residence in a particular country with the intention of residing permanently in that country. A person is born with a domicile of origin but this can be changed by the actions of a person to a domicile of choice.

8.4.4 ASSETS

All forms of property wheresoever situate are assets for the purpose of capital gains tax. Assets include land; houses; other buildings; sites be they developed or green field and with or without planning permission; minerals; exploration rights; unquoted shares in any of the above; shares in a company; incorporeal property, for example, goodwill or an option; and any interest in property, including a lease. However, Irish currency is not an asset for the purpose of the tax; nor are prize bonds or lottery and gaming winnings or gains from the disposal of Irish government stocks or securities and gains from the disposal of one's principal private residence.

8.4.5 DISPOSAL AND DATE OF DISPOSAL AND ACQUISITION

The disposal of an asset includes any transfer of ownership of the asset by way of sale, exchange, gift, or settlement on trustees. A part disposal occurs where less than the whole of an asset is disposed of or an interest in an asset is transferred, for example the granting of a lease at a premium. Disposals which are not made at 'arm's length', for example gifts, are deemed to have been made at market value.

The main rules for determining the time/date of disposal and acquisition for capital gains tax purposes are as follows:

1. For a disposal under an unconditional contract the date of disposal and acquisition is the date of the contract, and not the completion date.
2. Where the contract is subject to a condition, the date of disposal and acquisition is the date the condition is satisfied, not the completion date. A contract is conditional if a condition must be satisfied before an obligation to perform the contract arises. For example, where the acquisition of land is subject to the purchaser obtaining planning permission, the time of the disposal and acquisition is the date the permission is obtained.

A disposal includes a sale, a transfer, a gift, or any other method by which a person ceases to own or have an interest in an asset. A disposal includes the granting of an option over an asset (TCA 1997, s. 534).

8.4.5.1 Death

Death is not treated as a disposal for CGT purposes (TCA 1997, s. 573). The beneficiary (the person acquiring the asset on the death) is treated as acquiring the asset at its market value at the date of death.

8.4.5.2 Gift/disposal not at 'arm's length'

When an asset is disposed of otherwise than for full consideration by way of a bargain made at arm's length, for example there is a full or partial gift of the asset, for CGT purposes the transaction is treated as a disposal of the asset for a consideration equal to the asset's market value at that time.

CGT is calculated on the market value of the asset.

The original purchase cost (or deemed cost if it was a gift) of the asset is known as the base cost. This may be adjusted for inflation if it was acquired prior to 31 December 2002.

If an asset was acquired before 6 April 1974 the market value at 6 April 1974 has to be used as the base cost when calculating CGT on a disposal of the asset and not the original price and costs of acquisition. CGT was only introduced in 1974.

8.4.6 INDEXATION RELIEF (ADJUSTMENT FOR INFLATION): SECTION 556 OF THE TCA, 1997

Each year up to 2003 the Revenue issued indexation factors which were based on the consumer price index and compensated for inflation. Indexation relief permitted the effects of inflation to be taken into account in computing chargeable gains. There is an allowance for inflation when calculating the gain for assets which were acquired and certain enhancement expenditure that had been incurred prior to 31 December 2002. This is achieved by multiplying the cost of purchasing the asset and enhancement expenditure by an indexation factor determined by the tax year in which the asset was acquired or the expenditure incurred. Indexation relief was not available for disposals made within twelve months of acquisition. If the expenditure incurred in acquiring or enhancing an asset was incurred more than twelve months before its disposal, the amount of that expenditure was adjusted to take account of inflation. The adjustment was made by multiplying the relevant item of allowable expenditure by a factor 'the multiplier' which reflects the change in the all items consumer index during the period since the asset was incurred and the year of assessment in which the disposal is made. A table of multipliers for the year ending 2002 is available in Appendix 8.1 and is available on the Revenue website. The indexation table is based on the tax year in which the asset was acquired (columns on the left side) and the tax year in which it was sold (top of the table). Indexation relief can only be claimed if the assets being disposed of were owned before 31 December 2002.

Assets owned at 6 April 1974 are deemed to have been disposed of and reacquired on that date. Thus if an asset was acquired before 6 April 1974, its market value on that date is used as the base cost. Indexation relief applies to all assets without exception but is restricted in the case of development land. However, no allowance for inflation will be allowed for future years of ownership from 31 December 2002, and indexation relief will apply only for the period of ownership of an asset up to 31 December 2002.

8.4.6.1 Example of indexation

Land is bought on 15 June 1980. This is in the tax year 1980–81. It is disposed of on 12 May 2000. This is in the tax year ending 5 April 2001. The indexation factor is 2.833. There is no indexation if you sell within twelve months of purchasing an asset.

The Finance Act, 2003 abolished inflation indexation with effect from 3 December 2002. The 2003 indexation factors are used for 2003 and later years, and have not been increased since 2003.

Indexation Relief applied to the following:

(a) The purchase price or market value of the asset at the date of acquisition.

(b) The costs incurred in acquiring the asset, such as solicitors and auctioneer's fees, and stamp duty.

(c) The cost of enhancing the value of the asset.

(d) The cost of disposing of the asset.

Indexation Relief is only available for costs paid up to 31 December 2002 and will not apply to any costs paid in 2003 and later years.

Restrictions on use of indexation:

There are restrictions on the use of indexation. Indexation cannot be used:

(a) to convert a monetary gain into a loss or a monetary loss into a gain—instead the disposal is treated as a no gain–no loss situation; or

(b) to increase a monetary loss—the actual loss is the loss that can be used.

Example:

On a disposal of an asset bought in 2001 Jonathan makes an actual gain of €2,000 but when he calculates his CGT liability using the indexation factors he calculates that he has made a loss of €5,000. Due to the restriction on the use of indexation in these circumstances Jonathan cannot claim this loss and instead for CGT purposes he is treated as if the disposal of the asset was a no gain–no loss situation.

8.4.7 ANNUAL PERSONAL EXEMPTION

There is an annual exemption of €1,270 per individual, which is not transferable between spouses/civil partners. The first €1,270 of an individual's net gain (that is, gains less loss including losses brought forward from earlier years) is not chargeable. If either individual cannot utilise the exemption it cannot be transferred to the other. The annual exemption applies to individuals only—companies, trustees, or other non-corporate bodies are not entitled to it. See also **8.7.1** for more details.

8.4.8 SAMPLE COMPUTATION OF GAIN

The three main headings for CGT deductions are:

- the cost of acquisition together with any incidental costs;
- enhancement expenditure;
- incidental costs of disposal.

The amount of chargeable gain or an allowable loss is determined by deducting any allowable expenditure from the consideration received for the disposal.

The capital gain is the difference between:

(a) the consideration for the disposal of the asset or the deemed consideration (for example market value in the case of a gift or disposal between connected persons); and

(b) the cost of acquisition of the asset or its market value if not acquired at arm's length and any expenditure incurred on its which is reflected in the state of the asset at the time of disposal: expenditure to establish, preserve, or defend legal title. This may be adjusted to take account of inflation; and also

(c) the incidental costs of making the disposal, such as legal fees and selling costs, may be deducted.

Section 542 of the TCA, 1997 provides that where the disposal occurs by contract the date of disposal is the date of the contract and is not the date of the subsequent deed of assurance.

The following is a sample layout of a capital gains tax computation in relation to an asset:

Niall Murray—Capital Gains Tax computation for 2023

8.4.8.1 Facts

Niall Murray, a developer, sold lands for €1,000,000 on 31 December 2022, paying costs of sale of €20,000. He had inherited the land in May 2006, at which time the land was valued at €400,000.

Sales			€1,000,000
Less			
Allowable costs of sale	€20,000		
Original cost/market value at date of acquisition	€400,000		
No indexation post-2003			
No enhancement expenditure			
Less			
Allowable costs of sale			
Base cost			€420,000
	Gain		€580,000
	Less annual allowance		€1,270
	Taxable Gain		€578,730

Capital Gains Tax @ 33% €190,980.9

8.4.8.2 Sample CGT layout for computation

TAX YEAR 31 December 20.

1. Date of disposal (generally the date of the Contract for Sale)	
2. Description of asset	
3. Date of acquisition	€
4. Disposal consideration Less	
5. Incidental costs of disposal (if any)	
6. Net disposal consideration (4 - 5)	
Deduct allowable costs of sale	€

continued

continued

7 & 8. Original cost of acquisition of asset market value as at date of acquisition	X Multiplier INDEXED @ (X Multiplier)
Incidental costs of acquisition/purchase	Indexed to 2003
9 & 10. Enhancement expenditure	Indexed to 2003 X Multiplier
11. Total indexed cost	
12. Capital gain/loss after indexation (6–11)	
13. Actual monetary gain (or loss)	
14 & 15. Chargeable gain	
If these are any unused losses from previous year insert the amount here	
Calculation of capital gains tax payable	
16. Total chargeable gains net of allowable losses	
17. Less annual personal exemption €1,270	
Less relief (if any)	
Net Chargeable gain	

Capital Gains Tax payable: Taxable gain @ 33%. (In 2025)

8.4.8.3 Shares

Example:

Shares were purchased by Jamie on 2 December 1980 for €4,000. Jamie sold the shares on 10 May 2023 for €15,000. The costs of sale were €2,000.

Does Jamie have any CGT liability?

Sale Price		15,000
Less:		
Costs of sale	2,000	
Base cost: €4,000		
Multiplied by indexation factor (80/81) * 3.240	12,960	
Total deductions		(14,960)
Gain		40
Less loss relief carried forward	nil	
Less annual allowance		(€1,270)
Taxable gain		nil
Tax @ 33%		nil

Example 2:

John sold shares for €10,000 on 1 October 2023. The costs of sale were €3,000. John had purchased the shares in February 2000 for €5,000 and the acquisition costs were €1,000.

Calculate any tax payable and identify the pay and file deadline.

Sale Price			10,000
less Costs of sale		3,000	
less Purchase price or market value			
(99/2000)	5,000*1.193	5,965	
& Costs of purchase			
(99/2000)	1,000*1.193	1,193	
(indexed to 2003)			
less Enhancement expenditure			
total deductions			(10,158)
equals loss or gain			(158)

Calculate actual gain/loss without indexation

Sale Price			10,000
less Costs of sale		3,000	
less Purchase price or market value			
(99/2000)		5,000	
& Costs of purchase			
(99/2000)	1,000	1,000	
(indexed to 2003)			
less Enhancement expenditure			
total deductions			(9,000)
equals loss or gain			1,000

8.4.8.4 Shares—special rules

When shares are being disposed of, shares of the same class are treated as if the shares first purchased are the shares first sold; this is known as the first in–first out basis (TCA 1997, s. 580).

Example:

John holds 20,000 shares in ABC Limited which he has bought over the past ten years, purchasing 2,000 shares at a time since 2002. He decides to sell 5000 shares. These shares being disposed of will be treated as 2000 shares bought in 2002, 2000 shares bought in 2003 and 1000 shares bought in 2004.

8.4.9 INCIDENTAL COSTS OF DISPOSAL AND ACQUISITION

Section 552 TCA 1997 provides the basic rules for determining the expenditure to be allowed in computing chargeable gains. Section 552(2) TCA 1997 contains a definition of 'incidental costs' of acquisition and disposal. The list is exhaustive, that is, no other expenditure is allowable. Incidental costs of disposal mean the expenditure wholly and exclusively incurred for the purposes of the disposal. The disposal consideration is the value of the consideration received on disposal, for example the sale price in the case of a sale at arm's length. If the disposal is not made by a bargain at arm's length then the consideration is equal to its market value at the time of disposal. It is the consideration which was given wholly and exclusively for the acquisition of the asset.

Any disposal proceeds received in foreign currency must be converted to Irish currency by reference to the rate of exchange at the time of the disposal.

The following costs are allowable deductions as outlined in s. 552(2) TCA 1997 and should be noted when doing the capital gains tax computation. The costs incurred by the person in disposing of the asset—for example legal and valuation fees. They may be deducted from the consideration received for the disposal:

(a) Fees, commission or remuneration paid for the professional services of any of surveyor, valuer, auctioneer, accountant, agent, or legal adviser so far as the expenditure is wholly and exclusively incurred for the purposes of the acquisition or disposal.

(b) The costs of transfer or conveyance (including stamp duty) and the cost of advertising to find a seller or buyer.

(c) The costs reasonably incurred in making any valuation or apportionment required for the purpose of computing the chargeable gain or allowable loss.

Allowable expenditure is divided into the following categories:

(a) Cost of acquisition, i.e. the consideration which was given wholly and exclusively for the acquisition of the asset, plus the incidental costs of acquiring the asset; or, if the disponer created the asset (e.g. copyright or the goodwill of a business), the expenditure incurred in creating it.

(b) Additional expenditure,

That is expenditure incurred for the purpose of enhancing the value of the asset that is reflected in the state or nature of the asset at the time of disposal; and expenditure to establish and maintain legal title to the assets or an interest or right over it and

If the asset was acquired by inheritance on a death, by way of gift, or on a transfer from a trust, it is the market value at the date of death, gift, or transfer that is to be used. If the asset was acquired prior to 6 April 1974 the allowable cost to be entered in the computation is the market value as at 6 April 1974. In the case of a part disposal of an asset, only part of the original cost is allowed.

Items included in (a) and (b) may be adjusted to take account of inflation.

Note: on or after 2003, the multiplier is 1.

8.4.10 ENHANCEMENT EXPENDITURE

Enhancement expenditure is the cost of additions to the asset, after the date of acquisition, which adds to the value of the asset and is reflected in the state or nature of the asset at the date of sale. Expenditure must be reflected in the State of the asset at the time of disposal. Interest paid is not an allowable deduction for capital gains tax purposes.

Where enhancement expenditure has been incurred on an asset, the cost and each subsequent item of enhancement expenditure are treated as separate assets for the purposes of indexation relief. The chargeable gain is calculated as the difference between the various items of expenditure, that is, both original cost and enhancement expenditure as adjusted for indexation and the sale proceeds.

Generally, expenditure qualifies as 'enhancement' if it includes an element of improvement: for example, building a new garage, conservatory, landscaping, or an attic conversion is 'enhancement', whereas routine maintenance such as painting or rewiring a house is not.

It also includes expenditure incurred to establish, preserve, or defend legal title. To be deducted the expenditure must not have proved futile or have wasted away before disposal.

It should be noted that deductions may only be made in respect of expenditure wholly and exclusively incurred in connection with the acquisition, enhancement, or disposal of an asset.

Expenditure that is allowable for income tax purposes cannot also be deducted for CGT purposes (TCA 1997, s. 554).

8.4.11 LOSSES

Where there is a loss on a disposal, it will generally be allowable if the gain on the same transaction would be chargeable. Special provisions apply in relation to development land.

Losses on development land can be offset against gains on all disposals. However, gains on development land can only be offset by losses on development land.

Where an asset qualified for capital allowances, a balancing charge or allowance will be calculated at the time the asset is disposed. For CGT purposes any loss on such an asset will only cover any loss not already covered by a capital allowance.

No CGT is payable on a loss. All chargeable gains in a tax year are aggregated and losses on disposals of assets in the current tax year can be set off against other gains made in the same tax year (TCA 1997, s. 546). A person pays CGT based on the net balance.

Example 1:

Amy sold in 2023 three apartments that she had purchased as investments and rented out in 2005. She made a gain of €4000 on apartment A, a gain of €7000 on apartment B and a loss of €5000 on apartment C. When calculating her chargeable gains Amy will be able to deduct the €5000 loss from the gains of €11,000 and will pay CGT based on the net gain of €6000.

If a loss cannot be used in the current year (e.g. a person has made a loss and does not dispose of any other asset in the same tax year), the loss can be carried forward and set against future chargeable gains.

Example 2:

Using the same facts as in the Amy example above, but this time there is a loss of €15,000 on apartment C:

When calculating her chargeable gains Amy will be able to deduct the €15,000 loss from the gains of €11,000 and there will be no CGT payable in 2023. Amy has unused losses of €4000 that she can carry forward and set off against future chargeable gains.

8.5 Disposals on a Death

Death does not give rise to a capital gains tax liability. Section 573 of the TCA, 1997 deals with the passing of assets on a death. The assets which a deceased person was competent to dispose of are deemed to be acquired on his or her death by the legal personal representative (LPR) or by the beneficiary at the market value at the date of death. The deemed transfer at market value at the date of death does not give rise to a chargeable disposal for capital gains tax purposes and accordingly no liability will attach to the estate of the deceased in respect of any gains realised on the asset over his or her lifetime. The converse is also true in that no allowable losses are crystallised on a death.

The base cost for the purposes of a subsequent disposal, by the LPR or by the beneficiaries, of an asset acquired on death will be the market value at the date of death, irrespective of when the death occurred, and indexation relief is applied from the date of death to this base cost. If the death occurred before 6 April 1974, then the market value at 6 April 1974 will form the base cost.

If the personal representative sells any property during the administration of the estate, there may be a liability to capital gains tax—but only to the extent that the value of the property in question has increased between the date of death and the date of sale. Any gain or loss arising on the sale by the LPR accrues to the estate of the deceased and not to any beneficiary. In such circumstances the LPR will not have the benefit of any personal allowances that might ordinarily arise to a taxpayer and cannot pass any gain or loss onto a beneficiary.

The distribution of property by the personal representative to the beneficiaries does not give rise to a capital gains tax liability.

If the LPR is disposing of property to which beneficiaries are absolutely entitled, then it is necessary for the beneficiary with the LPR to prove that the beneficiary has become beneficially entitled to the property so that the LPR is in effect acting as a bare trustee for the beneficiary. This can be shown by the LPR vesting the property in the beneficiary prior to the sale so as to enable the beneficiary sell the property in their own right or by the LPR completing a declaration of trust confirming that the LPR holds the property for the beneficiary who is beneficially entitled in possession and that it is not held by the LPR in the course of the administration. The effect of this is that for CGT calculation purposes any gain or loss accrues to the beneficiary who has the benefit of the personal allowance.

Section 104 of the Capital Acquisitions Tax Consolidation Act, 2003 provides that if CGT and CAT payable on the acquisition of a property by way of gift or inheritance arise on the same property on the same event, the person paying the CAT can credit the amount of CGT paid by the disponer (the person making the gift) against his CAT liability. The credit granted for CGT paid will cease to apply and there will be a clawback of the relief where the property the subject matter of the gift or inheritance is disposed of within two years.

8.6 Development Land

Development land means land, including a building, in the State which is disposed of for a price higher than its current use value. The higher value is known as development value. Development land is land with development potential. Special provisions apply to chargeable gains arising from disposals of development land (see ss 648–653 of the TCA, 1997). Development land is defined for capital gains tax purposes and the test relates to the value of the land rather than its use. The current use value is the market value of the land assuming it is unlawful to carry out development (other than development of a minor nature). The current use value may be defined as the amount which would be the market value of the land if its value were calculated on the basis that it was at that time, and would remain, unlawful to carry out any development in relation to the land other than development of a minor nature. The special provisions include restrictions on indexation, rollover relief, and relief for losses.

8.6.1 RESTRICTION ON RELIEF

In relation to development land, indexation relief is confined to the amount of the current use value of the land at the time of acquisition or at 6 April 1974, if acquired prior to that date. One can allow but cannot index the development value. Enhancement expenditure is allowed but cannot be indexed. Only those parts of incidental costs of purchase relating to the current use value can be indexed; the balance costs are allowed, but cannot be indexed. The rules relating to restriction of indexation and loss relief, and restriction of availability of roll over relief, which normally apply to the sale of development land, are specifically excluded from operation where the total sales consideration (not the amount of the gain) does not exceed €19,050 in any year of assessment. This special relief is restricted to an individual and is not available to a company.

Where an individual sells, for example, part of his or her garden to a builder who builds a house on it, a charge to capital gains tax arises. Normally when an individual disposes of his or her principal private residence and a garden or gardens of up to one acre (excluding the site of the house), then any gain on such a disposal is exempt from capital gains tax. However, where a dwelling-house or garden or part of a garden is sold for greater than its current use value, then this constitutes the sale of development land and the principal private residence relief will only apply to the current use value. In general terms, the difference between the consideration and the current use value is liable to capital gains tax.

8.6.2 WINDFALL GAINS TAX

Section 649B TCA 1997 provides that an 80 per cent rate applies to gains attributable to a relevant planning decision. Such a decision has two elements: a rezoning and a decision to allow a material contravention of a development plan. A rezoning means a change under the Planning and Development Act 2000 from non-development lad use to development land use. This change is one from agricultural and amenity uses to residential, commercial, or industrial uses or a mixture of such uses. This section applies to disposal made in the period beginning on 30 October 2009 and ending on 31 December 2014. The Finance Act, 2010 widened the scope of the provisions by introducing a relevant planning decision, which includes both a rezoning and a material contravention of a development plan. This change applies to decisions made on or after 4 February 2010.

A relevant planning decision will, in general terms, mean a change in the zoning of land from non-development land use to another development land use, including a mixture of such uses.

It also applies to a decision to grant permission for a development that would materially contravene a development plan. The 80 per cent rate is charged on the amount by which the land increased in value as a result of the relevant planning decision. The remainder of the gain will be taxed at the 33 per cent rate with effect from 7 December 2013.

The windfall tax will not apply in relation to gains derived from relevant planning decisions where:

(a) the disposal of land occurs as a result of a compulsory purchase order;

(b) the disposal is by a company in which NAMA owns any part of the ordinary share capital, or by a company which is an effective 75 per cent subsidiary of such company;

(c) the disposal is of a site of 0.4047 hectares or less whose market value at date of disposal does not exceed €250,000, other than where the disposal forms part of a larger transaction or of a series of transactions. This exemption applies regardless of whether planning permission has been granted for the disposal.

There are provisions included to ensure that the 80 per cent charge cannot be sidestepped by a transfer between connected persons.

The Revenue Commissioners can be contacted in order to provide full information as to the definitions above but it may be necessary to consult with the relevant local authority to establish if a relevant planning decision has been taken in any particular case.

8.7 Exemptions and Reliefs

8.7.1 SMALL GAINS EXEMPTION

There is an annual exemption of €1,270 per individual which is not transferable between spouses or civil partners. A husband and wife and two civil partners are separate persons for capital gains tax purposes and their gains and losses should be computed separately. The residence status of each spouse or civil partner must be considered individually to decide whether or not that person is chargeable to capital gains tax. It is the first €1,270 of an individual's net gain (gains less losses, including losses brought forward from earlier years) that is exempt. The chargeable gains accruing to a married woman/civil partner in any year of assessment during which she is living with her husband/civil partner will be assessed on the husband/civil partner unless an application for separate assessment for capital gains tax purposes has been made. The relief only applies to individuals; companies, trustees, or other non-corporate bodies are not entitled to it.

By virtue of the Finance (No 3) Act, 2011 the tax treatment of registered civil partners, which applies from 1 January 2011, mirrors that of married couples. Civil partners can be assessed jointly to CGT on chargeable gains accruing in a year of assessment during which they are living together, and the CGT will be assessed and charged on the civil partner who is the nominated civil partner.

8.7.2 DISPOSAL OF A SITE FROM A PARENT TO A CHILD

A capital gains tax exemption for the disposal of a site by a parent (or both parents simultaneously) to a child of the transferor or on the transfer of a site by a civil partner (or both civil partners simultaneously) to a child where the transfer is to enable the child to construct his or her principal private residence on the site is provided for in s. 603A inserted into the TCA, 1997. The area of the site must not exceed one acre (0.4047 of a hectare) and the value of the site must not exceed €500,000. Section 603A of the TCA, 1997 has been extended by including 'foster child' as defined at **8.7.6.1** in the definition of a child of a parent and this takes effect from 31 March 2006. Section 28 of the Finance Act, 2018 further amends s. 603A to allow both a child and his or her spouse or civil partner to avail of the relief. The amendment applies to disposals made on or after 1 January 2019. No capital gains tax is payable on the disposal of a site from a parent/civil partner to a child and his or her spouse or civil partner where the site is valued at €500,000 or less, and the purpose of the transfer is to enable the child to build a principal place of residence on the land which the child will occupy as his or her only or main residence. If the value of the site exceeds €500,000, there is no provision for relief up to that amount, so that capital gains tax is payable in the normal way. The word 'site' is not defined in s. 603A, except by reference to 'land'. On a subsequent sale of the site (other than a disposal to a spouse or civil partner), the child pays capital gains tax on the site transfer unless he or she can show that a dwelling-house was built on the site and he or she occupied it as his or her only or main residence for a period of at least three years. If the child disposes of the site without building the dwelling-house and occupying it for at least three years the child must at that stage pay capital gains tax on the site transfer. The area of the site must not exceed 0.4047 hectare (one acre) exclusive of the area on which the house is to be built.

8.7.3 PRINCIPAL PRIVATE RESIDENCE RELIEF

Generally, any gain arising on the disposal of the main residence of an individual is exempt from capital gains tax. Grounds up to 0.405 hectares (one acre), (exclusive of the site of the house), around the house are also exempt. This exemption is contained in the TCA, 1997, s. 604.

When the private residence comprises development land (it includes the disposal of a garden or part of a garden of a principal private residence) and the consideration exceeds €19,050, the private residence relief is restricted to the current use value of the property.

If there is more than 0.405 hectares (one acre), then the 0.405 hectares (acre) to be taken into account is that which would be most suitable for occupation and enjoyment with the residence.

The exemption is available if the dwelling-house, or part of the dwelling-house, was occupied by the individual as his or her only or main residence throughout the period of ownership, or under certain circumstances, as the sole residence of a dependent relative.

In the case of a married couple/civil partners living together, only one house can qualify as the principal private residence of both spouses/civil partners. A person with two or more residences will nominate which one will qualify for relief and will agree this with the Revenue.

There is full relief only where the owner has occupied the house throughout the period of ownership. Full relief may not be due if only part of the house has been used as the individual's residence, in which case an apportionment is made to arrive at the exempt portion of the total gain (partial relief). This may happen where the house is used partly as a home and partly for business purposes or where rooms in the house have been let.

However, availing of the rent-a-room scheme introduced by the Finance Act, 2001 will not affect an individual's full entitlement to principal private residence relief on the subsequent disposal of the property.

Restrictions apply if the person has not always lived in the property, as a person can only claim for the time lived in the property. There are special provisions in the legislation setting out certain circumstances in which the individual is deemed to have occupied the premises; for example, where the individual is required, because of work commitments, to reside outside the State or elsewhere in the State, principal private residence relief may be available, because of the 'deemed occupation' principle. However, a period of the past twelve months before a principal private residence is sold is deemed to be the period of occupancy even though the individual may not have been actually living in it during that period. Periods of foreign or local employment will only qualify as periods of occupation if the individual occupies the residence both before and after the periods as their only or main residence and has no other house eligible for exemption. The relief does not apply where the house was acquired wholly or mainly for the purposes of making a gain on disposal.

The following are examples of absences considered as living in the property.

A person will be considered to have lived in the property where:

(a) They could not live in the property because their employer required them to live elsewhere.

(b) They have a job all the duties of which were performed outside Ireland.

(c) Their PPR remained unoccupied as they were either receiving care in a hospital, nursing home, or convalescent home, or are resident in a retirement home on a fee paying basis.

8.7.4 HOUSE OCCUPIED BY DEPENDENT RELATIVE

The principal private residence relief is also available to a gain arising on the disposal of a second dwelling owned by an individual and occupied without payment by a dependent relative as his or her principal private residence. A relief from CGT is available where the disponer disposes a property that he/she provided free use of to a dependent relative. A dependent relative is a relative of the owner or his or her spouse/civil partner who is either incapacitated by old age or infirmity from maintaining himself, or the widowed father or mother of the individual or his or her spouse/civil partner whether or not he/she is incapacitated by old age or infirmity.

8.7.5 SEPARATED OR DIVORCED SPOUSES AND SPOUSES INTER VIVOS AND SEPARATED CIVIL PARTNERS

Inter vivos disposals between spouses/civil partners are dealt with in the TCA, 1997, s. 1028, which provides that no capital gains tax will arise on transfers between spouses/civil partners provided they are living together. In effect, an inter vivos transfer between spouses/civil partners is ignored for tax purposes. When, at a further date, the transferee spouse/civil partner disposes of the asset, that spouse/civil partner will be deemed to have acquired the asset at the same time and for the same cost as the transferring spouse/civil partner.

Where assets are transferred between separated or divorced spouses in certain specified circumstances by virtue of, or in consequence of, a deed of separation or an order made or following judicial separation or an order made under Part III of the Family Law (Divorce) Act, 1996, such disposal will not give rise to a capital gains tax liability (see ss 1030 and 1031 of the TCA, 1997). This relief now applies to civil partners under Part 12 of the 2010 Act, which provides that a charge to capital gains tax does not arise where a person disposing of a civil asset is a former civil partner following a court order on the dissolution of the civil partnership. Similarly, a charge to CGT does not arise where a person disposes of an asset to a former cohabitant as a consequence of a court order under Part 15 of the 2010 Act.

8.7.6 RETIREMENT RELIEF

8.7.6.1 Disposal of a business or farm within the family

Certain gains arising on the disposal of 'qualifying assets' by an individual who has attained the age of 55 years and has owned the assets for ten years or more may be exempt from capital gains tax if certain conditions are satisfied (see TCA, 1997, s. 599). This relief is commonly referred to as 'retirement relief', but there is no requirement that the individual in question should actually retire from the business or farming. The amount of relief that will be available depends upon whether the assets are disposed of to the individual's children or, alternatively, to third parties.

Up to 31 October 2013, irrespective of the amount of the consideration for the disposal, total relief from capital gains tax could be claimed by an individual aged 55 or over on the disposal to his or her child of the whole or part of his or her qualifying asset, for example farm or business assets or shares in the family company. A disposal to a niece or nephew who has worked full-time on the farm or in the business for the previous five years similarly qualified for the relief.

The Finance Act, 2011 introduced measures to promote the early transfer of family farms. From 1 January 2014 full retirement relief from capital gains tax on transfers within the family will be maintained for individuals aged between 55 and 66 years. The Act introduced an upper limit of €3,000,000 on retirement relief for business and farm assets disposed of within the family where the individual transferring ownership is over 66 years. Where the market value of the asset disposed of to the child is more than €3,000,000 relief will be given as if the consideration was €3,000,000.

Post-Budget 2024 an upper limit of €10m was introduced for transfers within a family for individuals aged between 55 and 69 years.

An upper limit of €3m on retirement relief for business and farm assets disposed of within the family will be given where the person disposing is over 70 years.

The relief is clawed back where the child disposes of the asset within six years of the date of acquisition from his or her parent.

Section 71 extends the retirement relief of s. 599 (disposals within the family of business or farm) by including, along with the favourite nephew or niece provisions, a 'foster child'—same definition as appears in the capital acquisitions tax legislation.

For this purpose, the term 'child' includes not only the favourite nephew or niece but also a foster child, who is defined as:

> (ii) *an individual (in this paragraph referred to as the 'first mentioned individual') who resided with, was under the care of and was maintained at the expense of the individual making the disposal throughout—*
>
> - *a period of five years, or*
> - *periods which together comprised at least five years*
>
> *before the first mentioned individual attained the age of eighteen years but only if such claim is not based on the uncorroborated testimony of one witness.*

Although the legislation now applies, and a 'foster child' can qualify for relief under these provisions, there must be corroborating evidence of his or her residence, and so on. For the future, we should advise clients in this situation to keep records of time, expenditure, and any other factors which might be regarded as evidence. This relief is now extended to the child of a deceased child and to a child as defined in s. 2 Adoption Act, 2010, a stepchild, or a child of a civil partner. In the case of a nephew or a niece they must have worked full-time in running or assisting in the running of the business concerned for a minimum of five years ending on the date of the disposal.

8.7.6.2 Disposal of a business or farm outside the family

The retirement relief provisions in s. 598 of the TCA, 1997 were amended by subsequent Finance Acts. This section provides that from 1 January 2014, where the sale proceeds on the 'qualifying assets' do not exceed (currently) €750,000, total relief from capital gains tax may be claimed from gains accruing to an individual aged between 55 and 65 years on the disposal of the whole or part of his or her business assets or farm or shares in his or her family company, owned for ten or more years, subject to certain conditions.

Since 1 January 2025 the age limits are 55–69 years and over 70 years. The amounts remain the same, viz €750,000 and €500,000.

The Finance Act, 2010 amended the retirement relief provisions. The amendments clarified the position that an individual can come within the scope of the retirement relief provisions on the proceeds of a disposal of shares pursuant to a qualifying redemption, repayment, or purchase by a family company of its own shares. Therefore, the payments will fall within the scope of the €750,000 threshold relevant to CGT retirement relief.

The upper limit for retirement relief for business and farming assets transferred outside the family is reduced from €750,000 to €500,000 for individuals aged over 70 years. Where the individual disposing of the asset is 70 years or over and the consideration exceeds €500,000 marginal relief applies so as to limit the amount of CGT payable to one half the amount of the consideration and €500,000. Where the individual disposing of the asset is 66 years or over and the consideration does not exceed €500,000 relief is given in respect of the full amount of the CGT chargeable. The reduction of the amount to €500,000 given to individuals aged 70 or over applies to dispositions on or after 1 January 2025. The €750,000 and €500,000 thresholds are lifetime limits.

8.7.6.3 Retirement relief and leases

The relief was extended to disposals of farmland which has been leased prior to disposal. To qualify, the land must:

- have been leased for no longer than five years prior to disposal;
- have been owned and used for farmland by the disponer for ten years prior to the initial letting; and
- be disposed of to the person leasing the land.

This charge applies only to disposals to individuals other than qualifying family members as no value cap is placed on the relief relating to qualifying disposals to a child/favourite niece/nephew/foster child as per **8.15.4.1**.

8.7.6.4 Relief for disposal of property purchased between 7 December 2011 and 31 December 2014 (acquisition relief)

The Finance Act, 2011 introduced a new relief from capital gains tax in respect of properties purchased between 7 December 2011 and 31 December 2014. Where the property was held for more than seven years no capital gains tax will arise on any gain attributable to that seven-year period. The Revenue has confirmed that this relief is not extended beyond 31 December 2014. If the property is held for less than seven years but for more than four years and was disposed of after 1 January 2018 it was exempt from CGT.

Partial relief is available if the property is owned for more than seven years. For example, if the property was bought in January 2012 and sold in January 2022, the property would have been held for ten years, and thus any gain will be reduced by 7/10th and 3/10th is taxable.

8.7.6.5 Revised entrepreneur relief (10% rate)

Section 597AA TCA, 1997 (inserted by the Finance Act 2015) introduced a new entrepreneur relief and provides for a reduced rate of CGT of 10 per cent in respect of a chargeable gain or chargeable gains arising on the disposal of certain qualifying business assets made by an individual on or after 1 January 2016 up to a lifetime cap of €1m. This is reduced from the normal CGT rate of 33 per cent. This relief replaced the entrepreneur relief that applied for the years 2014 and 2015. During this period, which is for disposals from 1 January to 31 December 2016, the rate was 20 per cent.

The chargeable business must be owned by that individual for a minimum period of three years prior to the disposal of those assets.

The relief will not apply to disposals of chargeable business assets by companies or to disposals of development lands or a business consisting of dealing in or developing land, a business consisting of the letting of land or buildings, or holding investments.

Where the business is carried on by a private company, individuals seeking to qualify for the relief must own not less than 5 per cent of the shares of the company and at least 5 per cent of the shares to a holding company which owns 100 per cent of the company. The shareholder must be a full-time working director of the company for a minimum of three years prior to the disposal of the chargeable asset.

The reduced rate of CGT of 10 per cent applies up to €1 million on gains for qualifying business assets owned for a continuous period of three years in the five years immediately prior to the disposal (TCA 1997, s. 597AA).

What is a qualifying business?

A business other than:

(a) a business holding securities or assets as investments; or

(b) a business that holds development land; or

(c) a business that develops land or is letting land.

Lifetime limit €1 million

It must be a disposal after 1 January 2017.

It must be a disposal of:

- chargeable business assets.
- in a qualifying business.
- by a relevant individual.

What is a 'relevant individual'?

A 'Relevant Individual' is an individual who has been the beneficial owner of chargeable business assets for a continuous period of at least three years in the five years immediately prior to the disposal of the assets.

Qualifying shares

Some shares qualify for the 10 per cent rate: these are ordinary shares in a company whose business is wholly or mainly a qualifying business or are shares in a holding company for a qualifying group; the individual must own at least 5 per cent of the ordinary share capital and must be a qualifying person.

Qualifying person

In this case a 'qualifying person' is an individual who is (or has been) an employee or director of a company: who spends at least 50 per cent of his working time working for the company in a managerial or technical capacity; and who has served in that capacity for a continuous period of three years in the five-year period immediately prior to the disposal of the chargeable business assets.

8.8 Certificates of Clearance

Capital gains tax (withholding tax)

Section 980 of the TCA, 1997 as amended by subsequent Finance Acts contains provisions regarding obtaining capital gains tax clearance certificates. Section 980 provides that on the disposal of land and buildings in the State (including leasehold interests), mineral assets in the State, exploration/exploitation rights on the Irish continental shelf, unquoted shares deriving their value from these assets, or goodwill of a trade carried on in the State where the consideration exceeds a certain amount (currently €1,000,000 for houses and apartments and €500,000 for all other properties), the person 'by or through whom' the payment is made (the purchaser or the purchaser's solicitor) must withhold and remit capital gains tax at 15 per cent to the Collector General, unless the vendor produces a clearance certificate issued under s. 980(8) TCA97 (Form CG50A). This certificate does not indicate that the Revenue are satisfied with the CGT position; it merely provides that the purchaser need not deduct the 15 per cent withholding tax. This 15 per cent of the gross purchase consideration must be withheld and paid directly to the Revenue Commissioners regardless of whether a gain arises on the disposal of the asset in question. However, there is no need to deduct any tax unless the sale proceeds exceed either €1,000,000 in the case of houses and apartments and €500,000 in all other cases.

Section 980 of the TCA, 1997 provides that the purchaser must deliver an account of the payment, and the amount deducted from the payment, within thirty days of the date of payment, and remit the 15 per cent to the Revenue. This also provides that if the 15 per cent has not been paid within the period of thirty days the Revenue can assess the purchaser for that amount. Where the 15 per cent is paid within the thirty days that amount will be allowed as a credit against the capital gains tax liability of the vendor.

A Form CG50 A is not required if the asset being sold is land on which a new house has been or is in the course of being built and one of the general certificates listed in s. 980(8A) TCA 97 applies.

The Revenue Commissioners under the TCA, 1997, s. 916 must issue a clearance certificate with a copy to the purchaser if they are satisfied that the vendor is resident in the State or that capital gains tax is not payable or that capital gains tax chargeable in respect of the disposal (and any previous disposals) has already been paid. In the latter two instances, the vendor's solicitor must demonstrate to the vendor's Inspector of Taxes with supporting computation, payment, and so on that the relevant condition is satisfied. For example, in the case of an application by a non-resident vendor the solicitor must show that either no capital gains tax is payable, or, if tax is payable, the solicitor must attach a computation of the tax payable and pay any such tax together with any tax chargeable on any gain accruing in any earlier year on a previous disposal of the asset. *The grounds for the application must be clearly marked on the Form CG50 and only one of the three available options should be specified.* The clearance certificate is given on a Form CG50A. Anti-avoidance provisions are in place to ensure that this requirement is not avoided by negotiating a number of contracts, each for a consideration of less than €1,000,000 or €500,000. The provisions contained in s. 980 apply to all sales, whether by an Irish resident or by a non-resident. However, the legislation is principally enacted to ensure that capital gains tax is collected on sales of Irish property by non-residents. Tax deducted is treated as payment on account of the eventual capital gains tax liability.

When the consideration is of a kind from which the 15 per cent deduction cannot be made and the vendor does not produce a clearance certificate, the person acquiring the asset must, within seven days of the time at which the acquisition is made, notify the Revenue Commissioners in writing of the acquisition and give particulars of the asset acquired, the consideration for acquiring the asset, the market value of the consideration, and the name and address of the person making the disposal. In addition the person must pay to the Revenue Commissioners an amount of capital gains tax equal to 15 per cent of the market value. In all cases the vendor's solicitor must submit a Form CG50 applying for a CG50A immediately the contracts are signed and where the consideration exceeds €1,000,000 where a dwelling-house or apartment is being sold or €500,000 when any other property is being sold.

Where the withholding tax of 15 per cent is withheld, the purchaser's solicitor should give a completed form CG50B to the vendor's solicitor, and when a receipt for the payment issues from the Revenue this should also be provided to the vendor's solicitor to facilitate the vendor in claiming the tax withheld as a credit against any capital gains tax that may be due.

Since June 2020 the Revenue have introduced a system for the online processing of the CG50A and CG50B forms. Applications for CG50A and CG50B forms can be submitted online through ROS or My Account. The Revenue will continue to accept paper applications but the turnabout time for the issuing of the CG50A will be approximately ten days from 1 June 2021.

8.8.1 PROCEDURE FOR OBTAINING CAPITAL GAINS TAX CLEARANCE CERTIFICATES (CG50A) ON OR AFTER JUNE 2020

Since June 2020 the online CG50 application system is available for:

(a) vendors applying for an eCG50A certificate, and

(b) purchasers filing an eCG50B form.

Online processing significantly improves the turnaround time for applicants seeking a CG50A certificate. Resident applicants can receive an immediate turnaround on their application, in general.

For customers who are non-e-enabled the Revenue continues to support paper based applications, but with a slower turnaround time.

Section 980 TCA 1997 outlines in detail the process of withholding tax on certain disposals. It provides that on the payment of consideration for acquiring certain assets a purchaser must withhold 15 per cent of the consideration and pay this to the Revenue unless the vendor can produce a CG50A.

Where the consideration of the disposal of certain assets exceeds €1,000,000 in the case of houses and apartments and €500,000 in all other cases, the person paying that consideration must deduct 15 per cent and remit it to the Revenue Commissioners unless the vendor produces a capital gains tax clearance certificate (Form CG50A). The assets in question are specified in s. 980(2) of the TCA, 1997 and in **8.4.4**. In practice, the Revenue Commissioners will not issue a CG50A after the consideration has been paid and under no circumstances should an undertaking be accepted from a vendor's solicitor to produce a certificate after completion.

Since June 2021 applicants applying for a Form CG50A need to be registered on ROS or My Account, unless their agent/solicitor submits the application on their behalf via ROS. All applicants must be, or have previously been, registered for CGT prior to making the application.

There are three separate bases on which the clearance may be granted:

1. The applicant is Irish resident.
2. The is no CGT due.
3. The CGT due has been paid.

If the vendor is Irish resident this should be the only basis selected for the application as the other options (no CGT or CGT paid) all have additional submission requirements.

The following details must be provided for **resident** vendors:

(a) Name and PPSN/TRN (Tax Reference Number) of all the vendors. For multiple vendors all vendors will need to be registered for CGT.

(b) Name and address of all purchasers. (PPSN/TRN of purchasers is optional).

(c) Signed copy of the Contract for Sale.

(d) Asset address or Ordnance Survey Ireland grid reference.

There may be requirement for:

1. Consideration value documents (if consideration amount is different from the value in the contract).
2. Ownership documents (if complex ownership dates exist, e.g. share purchases).
3. Closing dates elapsed documents (if the closing date on the contract has elapsed an explanation for the late application is required).
4. A letter of undertaking to furnish signed contracts (if unsigned contracts have been submitted).

The following declarations by the vendor may be needed:

1. Confirmation if the asset was obtained by gift, inheritance, or neither.
2. If the asset was obtained by gift or inheritance, a confirmation that obligations under the Capital Acquisitions Tax Consolidation Act 2003 (CATCA 2003) were met will be required.
3. Confirmation that any tax obligations owing which relate to the asset are fulfilled. Certain obligations may have a future pay and file deadline—for example, rental income—and these will need to be specified in the application if they have not yet been fulfilled. This point links to the new CGT clearance procedure for non-residents discussed at **8.8.3** although it is not specifically directed at non-residents.

The Revenue notes that the question at 3 above can be used by agents to ensure that they are not personally liable for potential taxes arising from the sale of an asset by a non-resident vendor under s. 1034 or s. 1043 TCA, 1997.

Non- resident vendors are required to provide:

1. CGT Computations.
2. CGT payment receipt (if CGT is due).
3. A letter of undertaking to pay any CGT due if they have not paid it yet.

Non-resident vendors are dealt with at **8.8.3**.

If the eCG50 form indicates that there are taxes due, the tax must be paid to get the clearance. The Tax Duty Manual (TDM 42-03-01a updated in January 2022) indicates that the Revenue will then have thirty days from the date of the application for the certificate to decide if an intervention is warranted. This timeline is shorter than the thirty-five working days envisaged in the non-resident vendor clearance process.

The ROS system allows the upload of various documents to support the application. Mandatory supporting documentation are as follows:

1. Signed Contract for Sale (or unsigned contract plus a letter of undertaking from the solicitor that signed contracts will be supplied within two weeks).

The following supporting documents are required depending on the complexity of the application:

a. Two letters of undertaking from the solicitor: one for applicants not submitting a signed contract and one for applicants whose solicitor will pay the CGT liability after the consideration has been paid.

b. CGT calculations for applicants who select 'No CGT due' or 'CGT is paid' in their declaration reasons for obtaining a CG50A.

c. Asset acquisition documentation if there is more than one date; or complex acquisition dates, for example, multiple vendors each with their own acquisition date; or various dates of share purchase.

Sometimes a vendor will refuse to furnish Form CG50A, arguing that a particular property was not liable for capital gains tax by reason of being the vendor's only or main residence. The legal position is quite clear. The question of whether a particular transaction is or is not liable to capital gains tax is not relevant. A purchaser is not required to make any enquiries about the vendor's tax liability and is not obliged to consider any information about it that may be given to him. All that is relevant is the amount of the consideration. If it exceeds a certain threshold (currently €1,000,000 for houses and apartments and €500,000 for all other property), the purchaser's solicitor must insist on getting Form CG50A or make the deduction prescribed by the Act from the amount of the purchase money paid. A solicitor should not offer or accept an undertaking to furnish CG50A.

8.8.2 NEW HOUSES AND CAPITAL GAINS TAX CLEARANCE

There is one exception to the rule that Form CG50A must be produced where all the relevant conditions apply, in order to avoid withholding tax. If the asset being sold is land on which a new house has been built or land on which a new house is in the course of construction, other certificates can be used.

As an alternative to obtaining Form CG50A where the vendor (the builder) is disposing of a newly constructed house, production of any one of the following certificates will exempt the purchaser from deducting the 15 per cent withholding tax:

(a) A copy current notification of determination issued to the vendor under the TCA, 1997, s. 531; (C2 Clearance Certificate—subcontractors) indicating a 0 per cent rate;

(b) A copy current tax clearance certificate issued to the vendor under ss 1094 and 1095 of the TCA, 1997 or for licence application; or

(c) A copy current tax clearance certificate issued to the vendor for the particular purposes of the TCA, 1997, s. 980.

If the appropriate tax clearance certificate Form CG50A or those referred to at (a), (b), and (c) above are not produced by the vendor, the person acquiring such asset is obliged on payment of the consideration to deduct 15 per cent of the consideration and remit that amount to the Revenue Commissioners.

8.8.3 NON-RESIDENT VENDOR CGT CLEARANCE POST 24 OCTOBER 2022

It is important to deal with the issue of obtaining Revenue clearance in relation to a disposal by a non-resident vendor at the early stage of a transaction and not regard same as a mere completion item, in order to prevent the withholding tax applying. An individual, who is neither resident, ordinarily resident, or domiciled in the State is chargeable to Irish capital gains tax on the disposal of certain 'specified Irish assets'. The specified assets are listed in the TCA, 1997, s. 29 and are as follows:

(a) land in Ireland which includes not just actual land but any interest in land such as buildings or leases in land.

(b) minerals in Ireland or any rights, interests, or other assets in relation to minerals or mining searching for minerals. In addition it includes exploration or exploitation rights in the Irish continental shelf which are deemed to be assets situated in the State.

(c) shares deriving their value or greater part of their value directly or indirectly from mining or from assets listed in paragraphs (a) and (b) above other than shares quoted on a stock exchange.

Therefore where a non-resident individual disposes a s. 29 specified asset they will be within the charge to Irish CGT and they will have a liability to CGT in respect of any gain arising. If the non-resident client does not pay any CGT in respect of the asset being disposed of the Revenue can collect the CGT from the Irish solicitor.

All solicitors through whom CGT/income tax payments are made on behalf of non-resident individuals assessable and chargeable to CGT/income tax should be aware of the provisions of s. 1034 and s. 1043 of the TCA, 1997, which apply equally to income tax and capital gains tax. Essentially these sections provide that a solicitor may have a secondary liability to capital gains tax and or income tax in circumstances where they act for a non-resident vendor in relation to the sale of a property in the State.

Section 1034 of the TCA, 1997 provides that, in the case of a non-resident individual assessable and chargeable to CGT and income tax, capital gains tax and income tax can be assessed:

> *in the name of any trustee, guardian or committee of such person, or of any factor, agent, receiver, branch or manager, whether such factor, agent, receiver, branch or manager has the receipt of the profits or gains or not, in like manner and to the like amount as such non-resident person would be assessed and charged if such a person were resident in the State and in the actual receipt of such profits or gains.*

The extent of any liability for the non-resident individual is the same as if he/she were actually resident in the State. The imposition of a charge on their representative (solicitor) in such cases leads to a liability for the representative where the non-resident vendor does not discharge any CGT liability arising in respect of the asset being disposed of.

The Revenue interprets s. 1034 widely as applying to any representative of any kind in Ireland. If an Irish resident solicitor acts as an agent for a non-resident vendor he or she needs to bear in mind that this may result in a tax liability under s. 1034. The term 'agent' is not defined and, in light of the fact that the 'agent' can be assessed for the non-resident's capital gains tax liability regardless of the fact that it is not in receipt of the proceeds of sale, solicitors should be particularly cautious in relation to this section.

Prior to 24 October 2022 the recommended practice for a solicitor acting for a non-resident vendor in the case of a disposal of a specified asset, and who is in receipt of the sale proceeds, was not to release the proceeds to his or her client until:

(a) the relevant capital gains tax returns have been filed with the Revenue;

(b) the outstanding capital gains tax has been paid;

(c) a nil notice of assessment has issued form the Revenue; and

(d) the Revenue have issued a 'no audit' letter following a review of the return.

Essentially, the no audit letter is a letter which states that, based on the information that is contained in the tax return for the non-resident, it is not intended to carry out an audit. It might be prudent for a solicitor to ensure that any tax is paid even though Form CG50A is not required.

REQUESTS FOR CLEARANCE TO DISTRIBUTE SALE PROCEEDS—Capital Gains Tax and non-resident vendors

Position post 24 October 2022

A new Revenue clearance procedure in non-resident cases operates from 24 October 2022. The new process is outlined in Revenue Tax Duty Manual (TDM) 45-01-05. The clearance procedure outlined deals mainly with issues arising in relation to disposals of land and building in the State. All other relevant disposals of s. 29 TCA 1997 assets will be dealt with on a case by case basis by the Revenue.

The TDM sets out how the clearance request should be submitted and the necessary documentation that must accompany a valid clearance request. A new online process to manage these application requests for clearance has been established on ROS. It is necessary for the solicitor seeking clearance to have a TAIN (a Transaction Advisory Identification Number or a Tax Agent Identification Number) and register for ROS. The solicitor must then link to each non-resident client who is the subject of the clearance request. The 'linking' will be done by the Revenue as part of the clearance process and the relevant documentation listed below should be submitted with the clearance request. The request (including the documentation/confirmations) and the necessary attachments should be submitted via My Enquiries on ROS.

It is recommended that reference is made to the requirements set out in the TDM in the irrevocable retainer and authority to be signed by the client to their solicitor at the onset of the transaction.

When the request is submitted, the applicant (solicitor) will receive an automated reply stating that if the Revenue do not respond within thirty-five working days, the solicitor can distribute the sale proceeds to the non-resident vendor.

There will be no requirement for a further letter from the Revenue to issue providing clearance to the applicant solicitor. The automated letter will be sufficient to allow the solicitor to distribute after the timeframe of thirty-five working days has elapsed and no contact has been made by the Revenue in relation to the application for clearance. Basically, if nothing is heard from the Revenue within thirty-five working days, the sale proceed can be paid out.

In making a clearance request to the Revenue the solicitor should be satisfied that a complete and accurate submission has been made which should include all the following documentation, completed in full:

1. Form CG1 for the tax year in which the disposal takes place.
2. CGT computation of tax. The computation should include a breakdown of base cost, enhancement value, details of losses carried forward, and so on.
3. Full payment of CGT liability (if any).
4. Contract for Sale as evidence of proceeds.
5. Details on how the property was used during the course of the ownership.
6. If the property was rented during the period of ownership, confirmation that all relevant income tax returns have been filed and all relevant taxes paid.

A declaration of non-residence by the non-resident must also be submitted confirming that:

(a) They will spend less than 183 days in the State and

(b) They will spend less than 280 days in the State in the year of disposal and year preceding disposal.

It is important to remember that although the clearance process outlined above applies solely to the sale of land and buildings situated in the State, a solicitor who acts in relation to the sale of a company deriving most of its value from Irish land for a non-resident vendor is however still liable for any CGT on sale. There are specific residence rules for bodies of persons such as personal representatives (they take their residence from the deceased under s. 573 TCA 1997) and trusts. The new process outlined in the TDM above operates from 24 October 2022 and will be subject to ongoing review by the Revenue. Further information is available on Revenue eBrief 192/22.

8.8.4 PURCHASE IN TRUST

Circumstances can arise where a purchaser does not want to reveal its identity to a vendor, or where this may not have been finally decided, say in the context of a group of companies. The Revenue has agreed that the inclusion of 'in trust' details for the purchaser on the application form will not prevent the issue of a clearance certificate.

The purchaser's solicitors must however furnish the name and address of the purchaser to the Revenue Office that issued the certificate immediately on the closing of the sale.

8.9 Other Property Taxes and Charges on Property

Since 2009 a number of additional property-based taxes and charges have been introduced, including:

- The Local Government (Charges) Act, 2009, which brought in the Non-principal private residence annual charge;
- The Local Government (Household Charges) Act, 2011, which brought in an annual charge for all dwellings;
- The Finance (Local Property Tax) Act, 2012, as amended by the Local Property Tax (Amendment) Act, 2021, which brought in Local Property Tax (LPT);
- The Environment (Miscellaneous Provisions) Act, 2015, which brought in water charges;
- The Urban Regeneration and Housing Act, 2015, which brought in the vacant site levy. The Finance Act 2021 replaced this tax by introducing a residential zoned land tax which will take effect in 2024;
- The Finance Bill, 2022, which brought in a new Vacant Homes Tax (VHT) to be introduced in 2023.

8.10 Local Property Tax ('LPT')

8.10.1 INTRODUCTION

This tax was brought in by the Finance (Local Property Tax) Act 2012, which was subsequently amended by the Local Property Tax (Amendment) Act 2021. The Act governs the application of Local Property Tax to residential property as defined. LPT is due and payable by the person who is liable on the liability date and the amount on which LPT is chargeable is the market value that the property could *reasonably* be expected to fetch on a sale in the open market on the valuation date. The 2021 Act introduced certain changes in relation to LPT due in 2022. These apply to property valued on 1 November 2021. The revaluation of homes has been deferred on many occasions, resulting in one valuation period from 2013 to 2021. The new valuation period applies to LPT for 2022 to 2025. Homeowners were obliged to submit a self-assessed valuation of their property and submit a LPT return by 7 November 2021. Unlike non-principal private residences (NPPR) charges, discussed at **8.2.5**, under s. 124 of the Finance (Local Property Act) Act 2012 there is no time limit on the charge.

8.10.2 APPLICATION OF LOCAL PROPERTY TAX

The Local Property Tax came into effect on 1 July 2013 (2012 Act) following the passing of the Finance (Local Property Tax) Act, 2012 as amended by the Finance (Local Property Tax) Amendment Act, 2013. As the tax did not come into effect until July 2013, for that year, 2013, the LPT was payable for the last six months of the year and not the full twelve months as is now the case. Unless it is outside of the scope of the LPT charge or is exempt from the charge, all residential property as defined in the legislation that is sold after 1 May 2013 is chargeable to LPT in respect of that liability date.

The 2012 Act was subsequently amended by the Finance (Local Property Tax) (Amendment) Act 2021 (the 2021 Act), which contains provisions for a new valuation period which commenced on 1 November 2021 and will apply for a period of four years from 1 January 2022 to 31 December 2025.

Although the LPT is a tax on residential property, unlike the NPPR (see para **8.11**), LPT is administered and collected by the Revenue Commissioners rather than the local authority.

In addition, the LPT, unlike the NPPR and household charge, is not a fixed charge and is based on a self-assessment of the value of the property. The owner of the property on the valuation date is responsible for valuing the property, filing the return, and paying the tax. The liability and valuation date for the LPT for 2013 was 1 May 2013 and for subsequent years is 1 November in the preceding year.

The current applicable valuation date is 1 November 2021. The valuation of the property as at 1 November 2021 determines the LPT charge for the years 2022 to 2025 and property owners were required to submit valuations of their property by 7 November 2021. No further valuation is required until 2025. The owner of the property on 1 November of the preceding year is liable for the year; for example, the owner on the 1 November 2022 is liable for 2023 LPT. The LPT charge will not be affected by any general increase or decrease in property prices during the new valuation period of 2022 to 2025.

In a practice note published in the Gazette of 30 June 2023 practitioners were reminded that by virtue of s127 of the Finance (Local Property Tax) Act 2012 that a sale of property includes a transfer for no consideration or consideration which is significantly less than the chargeable value of the residential property at the time of the transfer. In this situation where a liable person does not pay LPT in accordance with s126 that any unpaid LPT shall remain a charge on the relevant residential property to which it relates.

Revenue advise that the new owner of a property where the LPT charge is not satisfied before the transfer of ownership takes place will receive an encumbered asset as the charge remains on the property.

Revenue has highlighted that the pursuit of outstanding liabilities after transfer is standard practice and the LPT clearance process must be followed in all cases before the property is transferred

8.10.2.1 Penalties for non-compliance

A return must be made in respect of the LPT. Failure to file a return can result in a penalty of up to €3,000 and late payment attracts interest at a rate of 0.0219 per cent or 8 per cent per annum, in line with other taxes. In addition, a €500 fixed penalty may be imposed on a vendor who does not provide information to a purchaser about the chargeable value of the property that he or she has declared to the Revenue. A vendor could also be liable to a separate penalty of the amount of the additional LPT that is payable for making a false statement to obtain a reduction in the LPT payable.

In addition, a purchaser could be liable to a penalty for failure to submit a revised chargeable value where it appears to them that the value that was declared to the Revenue by the vendor could not reasonably have been arrived at. This penalty would be the amount of the additional tax payable as a result of the correct value being declared, subject to a maximum penalty of €3,000.

The LPT is, as stated, a self-assessed tax based on the owner's assessment of the market value of the property on the valuation date. The Revenue has introduced a revised banded system details of which can be downloaded from the Revenue website (www.revenue.ie). There are currently nineteen bands for properties valued up to €1.75 million. In addition, the Revenue provided in September 2017 a most helpful guide under the heading 'LPT Guidelines for the Sale or Transfer of ownership of a relevant residential property' effective from 1 September 2017 to 31 October 2021, which should be downloaded from the Revenue website. Following the introduction of the new LPT valuation period, which commenced on 1 November 2021 and which applies for the period of four years from 1 January 2022 to 2025, the Revenue have confirmed that they will introduce revised guidelines for the transfer of property during the new valuation period these are available on the Revenue website.

The Revenue has increased the general clearance thresholds for LPT to "€500,000 (Dublin) and €400,000 (elsewhere)" and this has the effect of reducing the number of cases requiring specific clearance for the purpose of closing property sales.

8.10.2.2 Valuation date and duration of valuation

The usual valuation rule applicable to LPT is that the chargeable value of a residential property is established on a valuation date. Thus, the chargeable value established on the first valuation date of 31 May 2013 applied in relation to the years 2013 (from 1 July 2013) to 2021. The chargeable value established on the second valuation date, 1 November 2021, applies in relation to the years 2022 to 2025. The chargeable value established in relation to a property that becomes a residential property after 1 November 2021 applies from the following 1 November liability date until 1 November 2025.

As the value declared for the preceding valuation date applies for LPT purposes until the next valuation date, a vendor is required to provide a purchaser with details of the chargeable value/valuation band he or she declared in relation to the immediately preceding valuation date. This valuation is the relevant valuation for the next liability date.

8.10.2.3 LPT interest

Section 149 of the Finance (Local Property Tax) Act 2012 provides that interest shall be payable on unpaid LPT. The rate of interest amounts to 0.0219 per cent per day or 8 per cent per annum.

Although there is an interest column in the property history screen (PHS), as interest is calculated on a daily basis, the interest (if any) due on unpaid LPT is seldom if ever shown on the PHS. Solicitors should not rely on the PHS in this regard.

Where a property is being sold and there are arrears of interest, the vendor's solicitor should make an application to the Revenue at lpt@revenue.ie to calculate the amount of interest due, which should be paid on closing. It is imperative to verify all interest is cleared as interest is a charge on the property.

If the LPT is to be paid from the proceeds of sale and an undertaking is being given in this regard, care should be taken by both the solicitor for the vendor and the purchaser to ensure that any such undertaking includes arrears of interest due and that the interest is paid.

Otherwise the PHS will show that the LPT has been paid but will then show the amount(s) outstanding and due for interest, which will remain a charge.

In all cases where the PHS shows that the LPT has been deferred, a change has been made whereby since 25 October 2021, interest on deferred liabilities will be calculated on a weekly basis, and the amount of interest due will be reflected in the liable person's online records and also on the PHS. In such cases an application should also be made to the Revenue well in advance of closing a sale to calculate the amount of interest due. The Revenue have indicated that a new format PHS has been designed that will highlight by use of a footnote that interest is accruing on outstanding liabilities.

The Revenue have provided a new PHS in their online service that provides property owners with a statement of their LPT matters that they can access on ROS. This statement does not however provide details of the valuation band declared for LPT purposes at the last valuation date or the position in relation to the household charge.

This statement is therefore not acceptable for conveyancing purposes in lieu of the printout of the vendor's property history screen from the LPT online system. Practitioners should advise their vendor clients accordingly and request that they produce a printout of the up-to-date property history screen to provide for the purchaser.

8.10.3 EFFECT ON LPT WHERE THE DATE ON THE PURCHASE DEED IS NOT THE DATE OF CLOSING

On the sale of residential property, the liable person for LPT is the owner of the property on the liability date being 1 November in each year. Accordingly, the owner of the property on 1 November 2021 is the liable person for the 2022 LPT.

Issues may arise whereby a vendor closes a sale before a liability date (1 November) but the purchaser dates the deed after the liability date. In this situation it would appear to the Revenue that the vendor is the liable person for the following year's LPT. Section 11 (1) of the Finance (Local Property Tax) Act 2012 provides that the 'relevant date' is the date on which the purchaser is entitled to take immediate possession of the such property (for a period that may equal or exceed twenty years) or is entitled to the rent (unless from a local authority or approved housing body) of such property (for a period that may equal or exceed twenty years).

It is enough that the purchaser is entitled to take possession although they may not have actually taken possession. The Revenue agree that the vendor should not be held liable for the purchaser's LPT in such cases but they cannot change the records until such time as they make enquiries of both the vendor and the purchaser as to when the purchaser was entitled to possession.

The vendor's solicitor should contact the Revenue as soon as they become aware of the issue and supply evidence to the Revenue as to when the purchaser was entitled to go into possession—this can include the date closing funds were transferred, the date of closing searches, the date of redemption of the vendor's mortgage, etc. The Revenue will then make enquiries of both parties.

8.10.4 WHO IS LIABLE FOR PAYMENT OF THE LPT?

A person's liability to LPT depends on their connection to the property, Section 11 provides that the liability to pay the LPT falls upon any person who:

Holds any estate, interest or right in a relevant residential property entitling the person to—

- *The immediate possession of such property for a period that may equal or exceed 20 years, or*
- *The receipt of rents or profits of such property for a period that may equal or exceed 20 years.*

The owner of a residential property on the liability date (which is 1 May 2013 for the tax year 2013 and 1 November thereafter) is liable to pay the LPT. There are many different categories of owners.

1. Joint owners will have a joint and several liability even if they do not live in the property. Joint owners are required to nominate one of the joint owners as the designated liable person
2. Tenants and Leaseholders/Landlords: a rent paying tenants holding under a lease of more than twenty years is liable for the LPT but in the case of properties leased for twenty years or **less**, to a rent paying tenant, the tenant does not have to pay LPT and the landlord is liable. However, if leasing from a local authority there is no exposure to LPT.
3. If the property is leased to local authorities and approved housing bodies the property owner is liable for LPT if the lease is for less than twenty years or was entered into on or after 22 July 2021.
4. A person who has a right of residence for life or for twenty or more years to live in the property to the exclusion of all others is liable to LPT.
5. If a person has no legal title to the property but has acquired (or is acquiring) title by adverse possession he or she will be liable to LPT. The Revenue have indicated that a person who has occupied a property on a rent-free basis without challenge, and has a *prima facie* right to register title under the adverse possession legislation (which normally occurs after twelve years' unchallenged occupation) will be the liable person.

While the Revenue are conscious that difficulties can arise in terms of establishing the ownership of property, the LPT deals with this by placing the onus of proof on the taxpayer. Section 11 of the Finance (Local Property Tax) Act, 2012 (FLPTA, 2012) provides that the absence of documentary evidence of title to property shall not preclude an assessment and it will be presumed that a person who is in occupation of a relevant residential property, or in receipt of the rents or profits, is a liable person.

The following is s. 11(3) reproduced in full to give an idea of the wide-reaching implications of who is liable to pay the LPT:

> *Without prejudice to subsections (1) and (2) the following persons shall for the purposes of this Act be liable persons in relation to a relevant residential property (the 'property')*
>
> - *a person having an equitable or beneficial estate, interest or right in the property that entitles the person to the possession or receipt referred to in subsection 1(a) or (b)*
> - *a trustee that holds the property by an estate, interest or right in the property that entitles the Trustee or a beneficiary to the possession or receipt referred to in subsection 1(a) or (b)*
> - *a trustee or other person having a power to appoint in the property, an estate, interest or right that entitles a person to the possession or receipt referred to in subsection 1(a) or (b)*
> - *A person having an exclusive right of residence in the property for*
>   - *His or her life or the life or lives of one or more or*
>   - *A period that may equal or exceed 20 years*
> - *The personal representative of the estate of a person who was a liable person by virtue of any of the preceding provisions of this section*
> - *a person occupying the property with the right to be registered, pursuant to the Registration of Title Act 1964, in respect of any estate, interest or right that would entitle the person to the possession or receipt referred to in subsection 1(a) or (b).*

Subsection 4 provides:

> *For the avoidance of doubt in a case where a person is a trustee as referred to in subsection (3) (b), that person shall, for the purposes of this Act, be a liable person in relation to the relevant residential property concerned notwithstanding that the one or more beneficiaries under the trust is or are, for the purposes for this Act, also a liable person or persons in relation to that property.*

What is clear from this is that there may at any time be several liable persons all of whom are responsible to discharge the LPT and all of whom may be targeted by the Revenue. It is also clear from this that the provisions of the Act have implications for those involved in the administration of trusts and estates.

8.10.5 LPT AND THE LEGAL PERSONAL REPRESENTATIVE AND TRUSTEES

There is no doubt that a legal personal representative of a person who was subject to the charge is a liable person under s. 11 of the Act.

The Act does not however specify that the liability does not arise until after a grant of representation has been extracted and so it is possible that an executor of an estate, who has power from the date of death of a deceased, may be liable for the charge from the date of death while a legal personal representative ('LPR') of an intestate deceased would not be liable from that date.

However, the Finance (Local Property Tax) Amendment Act, 2013 in s. 4 amends the primary Act in relation to who is a liable person and creates a period of grace for the estate of an intestate deceased (or an estate where the executor has predeceased the deceased) for twelve months if no grant has been extracted in that time. Once the twelve months are up, then any person in occupation or in receipt of rent from the property is liable. The same provision is not available for the executor of an estate.

A deferral of the LPT is available to the LPR of an estate in circumstances where there is no grant of representation in the first twelve months after death, where the deceased himself had deferred the LPT, or where there was an outstanding liability to the charge as at the deceased's date of death.

In any event the LPT will be due for payment when the LPR is in a position to transfer the property to a beneficiary or distribute the proceeds from the sale of the property, or, at the very latest, three years from the date of death of the deceased. In addition, a trustee is liable for the payment, as is a beneficiary entitled to possession.

The Revenue have suggested that where multiple parties are liable then they must all agree as to who should file the return and pay the tax.

8.10.6 UNPAID CRYSTALLISED LIABILITIES—LPT AND SOLICITOR'S OBLIGATION

Section 123 of the Finance (Local Property Tax) Act, 2012 provides that any unpaid LPT, and interest, or other monetary penalty amount that is due and unpaid by a liable person shall be and remain a charge on the relevant residential property to which it relates, and shall continue to apply without a time limit until such time as it is paid in full. This was confirmed in s. 126(1) of the 2012 Act as amended by s. 12(e) of the Finance (Local Property Tax) (Amendment) Act, 2013, which provided that a vendor of residential property must, before completion of the sale of the property, pay any LPT, penalties, and accrued interest due in respect of the property. These must be paid notwithstanding that a sale of the property is completed before the tax is payable. This statutory obligation on the vendor does not mean that the amount of the LPT already paid by the vendor cannot be apportioned between the vendor and purchaser on closing. The Conveyancing Committee of the Law Society in a Practice Note in the June 2013 edition of the *Gazette* confirmed that the apportionment between the vendor and purchaser of the LPT should be done except where an exemption from LPT applies. The precedent wording of the special condition dealing with the apportionment of LPT as between the vendor and the purchaser is dealt with at **6.2.9**. Therefore, before a sale of residential property is completed, a vendor is required to pay upfront any unpaid LPT due in respect of a liability date falling before the date of the sale, even if, in the ordinary course of events, such liability would not yet be payable. The liability that has crystallised at this stage comprises unpaid LPT, accrued interest, and any penalty amount that has been imposed in relation to a vendor's self-assessment or a Revenue assessment. In addition, all outstanding returns must be filed. Any outstanding crystallised liability that is not paid by the vendor before the completion of the sale is a charge on the property. In addition, where the household charge for 2012 has not been paid or has been part paid prior 1 July 2013 the arrears amount (including late payment penalties) has now been increased to €200 and is included as part of the LPT liability in respect of the property. In effect, the arrears of the household charge become an LPT charge and so become part of the outstanding crystallised liability. As from 1 July 2013 these arrears are being collected by the Revenue. Details of any arrears of the household charge will appear on the LPT Property History screen. See **8.11.2**.

The LPT is a charge on property; however, unlike most charges to include the NPPR and the household charge that have a twelve-year life span, there is no time limit for the LPT and the normal provisions of the Statute of Limitations will not apply. It is important therefore when dealing with a sale or transfer of a property to receive confirmation from the Revenue that same has been discharged. There is also a 'snitch clause' in the legislation in that a purchaser will be bound to inform the Revenue of vendors who have placed a much lower value on their property than the sale price. Offending vendors will be fined €500 if they refuse to reveal to the purchaser the band in which they valued the property for the purposes of the LPT. In turn the purchaser must file a revised chargeable value return and valuation where it appears to him or her that the valuation declared by the vendor to the Revenue was too low given the circumstances at the valuation date. This penalty will be the amount of the additional LPT payable as a result of the correct value being declared, subject to a maximum penalty of €3,000.

It is important to be mindful of these points when acting in the administration of an estate, and more particularly when acting for a vendor/purchaser in a conveyancing transaction.

8.10.7 RESIDENTIAL PROPERTY AND EXEMPT PROPERTY

It is important for a vendor's solicitor to determine if the property in sale meets the definition of residential property or relevant residential property as defined in the LPT Act. LPT is charged on the market value of such property and issues may arise as to whether a property is a residential property, how certain properties are to be valued, and the components of a property that are to be valued for LPT purposes. Section 2 of the 2012 Act as amended by ss 4(b) and 5 of the Finance (Local Property Tax) (Amendment) Act 2021 which inserted a new s. 2A in the 2012 Act and defines 'residential property' as:

1. *Any building which is in use as, or is suitable for use as, a dwelling.*
2. *A shed, outhouse, garage or other building which is appurtenant to or usually enjoyed with a residential property shall be considered, for the purposes of this Act, to form part of the residential property.*
3. *Subject to subsection (4), yards, garden and other land appurtenant to or usually enjoyed with a residential property as its garden or grounds shall be considered, for the purposes of this Act to form part of the residential property.*
4. *Where the total area of the yards, gardens and other lands, referred to in subsection (3), exceeds 0.4047 hectares, only those parts of such yards, gardens and other lands, which would be the most suitable for occupation and enjoyment with the dwelling, up to the total area (exclusive of the area at ground level, of the building referred to in subsection (1)) shall form part of the residential property.*

'Relevant residential property' is defined as a building in the State that is a residential property on a liability date.

There were eleven exemptions from LPT available for the first valuation period from 2013 to 2021. Four of these have expired and are not available for the second valuation period of 2022 to 2025. Sections 4–10 of the LPT Act set out a number of properties that will not be regarded as a relevant residential property for the purposes of the Act. An LPT exemption will be available for the following properties if they meet the qualifying conditions, some of which are limited in relation to time:

- Commercial properties that are or can be used as a dwelling and are fully subject to commercial rates. An example of this is a guesthouse. This exemption does not apply if the property is exempt from the payment of commercial rates to a local authority.
- A property vacated by their owner for at least twelve months due to their long-term physical or mental infirmity, that is certified by a medical practitioner, or alternatively, where the medical practitioner—if it is for less than twelve months—certifies that the person is unlikely to return to the property. Prior to 2021 this exemption only applied if the property was not occupied by another person. Since 2022 the exemption applies if someone lives in the property and they are not a joint owner of the property. For example, they may be a tenant, relative, or friend.
- Residential property owned by a charity or similar public body that is used solely or primarily as residential accommodation in connection with recreational activities that are an integral part of the body's charitable purpose and providing special needs accommodation.
- A residential property purchased or built or adapted for use as the main or sole residence of a permanently incapacitated individual who has received an award from the Personal Injuries Assessment Board or a court or who is a beneficiary under a trust established for that purpose.
- Mobile homes, vehicles, and vessels.
- Residential properties having a significant level of pyrite damage are exempt for a temporary period of at least six years. The Finance (Local Property Tax) (Pyrite Exemption) Regulations, 2013 (SI 147/2013) stipulated how properties are to be tested to establish whether they have been affected by a significant level of pyrite induced damage and providing for the issue of certificates by a competent person where this has been established. This exemption is being phased out and will not be available for new applicants after 22 July 2023.

Properties built using defective concrete blocks may be exempt if they are confirmed to be eligible for the Defective Concrete Blocks Grant Scheme or if the builder or an insurance company has carried out remediation work required or provided funds for it.

- Certain institutional dwellings, to include registered nursing homes, hospitals, prisons, army barracks, boarding schools, and so on.

Where an exemption from LPT applies, and the LPT will therefore not arise, evidence of entitlement to the exemption should be furnished by the relevant party, if necessary in the form of a statutory declaration. It is possible to check online what the LPT status of a property is.

To recap:

1. If the property meets the definition of relevant residential property on a liability date, currently 1 November, then the LPT is payable. Confirmation from the Revenue that the tax has been paid should be furnished by way of an up-to-date property history printout from the online Revenue system.
2. If the property did not meet the definition of relevant residential property on the liability date then the vendor should furnish a statutory declaration confirming this and giving the reason, together with a copy confirmation from the Revenue by way of a printout from ROS that there are no outstanding amounts of LPT payable (if applicable).

Previous exemptions from LPT 2013–2021

Many of the exemptions available for LPT no longer apply. These include the following:

(a) New and previously unused property purchased from a builder or developer between 1 January and before 1 November 2021.

(b) Residential properties built and owned by a builder or developer but unsold.

This LPT exemption applied to properties constructed and owned by a builder or developer and remained unsold and was contained in s. 6 of the Finance (Local Property Tax) Act 2012. It previously applied to a builders' trading stock and is no longer available beyond 2021. Section 6 of the 2012 Act was amended by s. 10 of the Finance (Local Property Tax) (Amendment) Act 2021 by the substitution of 'as a relevant residential property in relation to the liability dates in the years 2013 to 2020' for 'as relevant residential property'.

If builders or developers have houses suitable for use as a dwelling on a liability date (that is, 1 November in any year), they must now register them with the Revenue, and, as owners on the relevant liability date, must pay the LPT due in respect of those properties.

A builder or developer who owns a house suitable for use as a dwelling on a liability date is, in respect of that (finished) house, in the same position as any other owner of a residential property.

A property that becomes suitable for use as a dwelling after 1 November in any year in a valuation period will not be liable for LPT until the following 1 November. The property will be valued as of the valuation date for the valuation period, which is 1 November 2021 in the current valuation period. For example, if a new house is built and becomes suitable for use as a dwelling on 1 July 2023 the property will become liable to LPT for the first time on 1 November 2023, but the valuation date is 1 November 2021.

(c) Properties in unfinished housing estates (commonly called 'ghost estates').

(d) Properties purchased and occupied as a home in 2013 as exempt from LPT until 2021 if the owner continued to own it as their sole or main residence.

The exemption from LPT is no longer available for properties listed from a to d above.

8.10.8 CONVEYANCING COMMITTEE GUIDELINES FOR LPT

In a Practice Note in the June 2013 edition of the *Gazette* the Conveyancing Committee provided guidelines for dealing with LPT in the context of including a special condition in the Contract for Sale dealing with the apportionment of LPT and providing for the amendment of general conditions 27 and 8(c) of the general conditions (now general conditions 23 and 6(f) in the 2019 edition).

The Practice Note contained the following guidelines for practitioners.

The vendor should be advised to:

- Submit all outstanding LPT returns and print off their confirmation of payment if they are paying their LPT online.
- Pay all outstanding tax, interest, and penalties; this applies even if the tax is being paid by instalments.
- Advise those vendors who are paying LPT by deduction at source from salary that they will not be given credit for amounts paid during the year until their employers file P35s after the end of the relevant tax year. If they are selling within the tax year, they will have to pay the full amount of LPT for the year upfront before closing, and later claim a refund from the Revenue of any amount deducted at source. If they know they intend selling during the course of a particular year, they might prefer to alter their method of payment so as to avoid the inconvenience of such a double payment.
- It is recommended that a vendor would furnish a purchaser at the pre-contract stage with a note of the value band declared for a property by the vendor. Advise vendors to keep a copy of their returns for this purpose.
- Self-correct any return where there has been an under declaration of value.
- Provide the purchaser with such information about the tax arising on the previous valuation date as is relevant to the purchaser. This is usually given through a vendor's solicitor by providing the property history screen printout.
- Ascertain if the agreed sale price comes within the general clearance or whether specific clearance is required.

The purchaser should:

- Obtain any relevant information from the vendor. The Revenue suggest this includes the property ID, valuation band, basis for valuation, and details of any exemption claimed.
- Confirm that there is no outstanding tax, interest, or penalties.
- Where the property is sold within a valuation period, consider whether the valuation declared by the vendor appears to have been reasonably and honestly made. If not, the purchaser's own estimate of the property's valuation should be used at the following liability date.
- Ascertain from the vendor if the agreed sales price comes within general clearance and, if not, whether formal clearance has been obtained.

In a Practice Note in the October 2013 edition of the *Gazette* the Conveyancing Committee confirmed that it was successful in getting the Revenue to accept that purchasers must be given some assurance that the property they purchase is not subject to a charge in respect of a vendor's unpaid LPT where the value declared by the vendor on a LPT return is less than the subsequent sale price. The Revenue on 1 September 2017 issued a revised publication 'Guidelines for the sale or transfer of ownership of a relevant residential property' which should be consulted by practitioners and which is available on the Revenue website, www.revenue.ie/en/tax/lpt/sale-transfer-property.html. These are currently being updated. The Revenue will not issue a certificate of discharge for LPT and instead a system of general and specific clearance has been agreed to facilitate a purchaser to satisfy themselves that the property is not subject to a charge.

8.10.9 LPT REVENUE CLEARANCE

LPT Revenue clearance must be obtained by the vendor on the sale of residential property. It is important to note that the clearance provisions are intended to facilitate purchasers. A purchaser is given an assurance that there is no charge on the property but the Revenue reserve the right to pursue a vendor for pre-sale liabilities where clearance has been obtained on the basis of false information or inadequate disclosure.

There are two types of Revenue clearance: general clearance and specific clearance. The property does not qualify for either general or specific clearance where there are outstanding or deferred LPT liabilities, or outstanding household charge liabilities and/or outstanding LPT returns.

The assurance is provided in one of two ways:

1. **General clearance—**subject to three conditions

   This general clearance should cover the vast majority of sales. The easiest way to check that the property is fully compliant is by logging in to LPT Online to review the LPT records and LPT status of the property. The Revenue are not directly involved in this clearance process and general clearance from 13 November 2023 applies if either of the following conditions are met:

   - The sale price is "€500,000 (Dublin) and €400,000 (elsewhere)" or less; or

   Condition 2 is split into parts A and B. Where either part A or B is satisfied. general clearance applies.

2. **Condition 2(A) applies if your property was liable for LPT on 1 May 2013.**

   The Sale price does not exceed:

   - The upper limit of the valuation band by 125 per cent (or 125 per cent above the actual declared value for properties above Band 19) declared as of 1 May 2013; and
   - The upper limit of the valuation band by 25 per cent (or 25 per cent above the actual declared value for properties above Band 19) declared as of 1 November 2021.

3. **Condition 2(B) applies if your property was not liable for LPT on 1 May 2013.**

   Sale price does not exceed:

   - 25 per cent of the upper limit of the valuation band (or 25 per cent above the actual declared value for properties above Band 19) declared as of 1 November 2021.

The three conditions can be described as allowable valuation margin, expenditure enhancement to a property, and sale of a comparable property.

The Revenue has provided an update on the general clearance conditions for LPT in a note on 27 August 2024. These changes increase the number of cases where general clearance applies without having to refer the matter to the Revenue. They expanded the allowable valuation margin from 2022 in situations where the property is sold for €400,000 or less.

8.10.9.1 How to obtain general clearance

Prior to the sale, a vendor's solicitor can obtain general clearance from the LPT online system using the client's PPSN, the property ID, and the PIN. The Property Access Number (PAN) can be retrieved on the Payment History screen. If this information is not to hand an application can be made to the Revenue to reissue these details.

The Payment History screen can then be printed off to show that there is no outstanding liabilities or returns. This provides comfort to the purchaser that the vendor is fully compliant for LPT. If an exemption has been claimed this will be indicated in the printout.

8.10.9.2 Specific revenue clearance in certain circumstances

Revenue will provide specific written clearance on request from the vendor where the conditions specified in 1, 2(A), and 2(B) above do not apply but the vendor nevertheless claims that the valuation made at the valuation date was made in good faith. An application for specific clearance should be made to the Revenue by completing Form LPT5, Application for Specific Pre-Sale Clearance.

It should be noted that:

(a) This request for clearance is conducted by secure email (pre-registration with the Revenue is required) using form LPT5 (which is confusingly called 'Application for Specific Pre-Sale Clearance').

(b) Application is made following agreement of the sale price but in advance of closing.

(c) Revenue will either issue a written clearance (where satisfied that there was no under declaration of the chargeable value), which the vendor must furnish to the purchaser on or before closing, or make an assessment on the vendor (where not satisfied that the valuation band/chargeable value that was declared was reasonable), which then becomes part of the standard online clearance process and which should be paid online by the vendor in advance of closing and the usual evidence of payment produced to the purchaser on or before closing.

8.10.10 LPT CLEARANCE IN SECOND AND SUBSEQUENT SALES

In cases where specific clearance has been applied for and granted, the valuation band originally declared will be the relevant band until the next valuation date. The 'specific clearance' indicator is included in the LPT History details screen. The date the specific clearance was granted is also included.

Where there is more than one sale in a valuation period and general clearance applied on the first sale, this is sufficient to confirm the declared valuation for any and all subsequent sales within the valuation period.

If the subsequent transfer would not meet the general clearance condition and if the vendor does not have specific clearance for a previous sale an application should be made to the Revenue for specific clearance.

The Revenue will issue a confirmation that the conditions for general clearance are satisfied and that, accordingly, the Revenue band remains the valuation band originally declared. This will confirm that all LPT and household charge liabilities have been paid and returns filed and that the property valuation was reasonable. This LPT clearance should be retained with the title documents, as it should be produced on any subsequent sales within the valuation period.

In circumstances where the sale meets the general clearance criteria, the standard general clearance process should be applied.

Where general clearance conditions were not met for the first sale in the period, specific clearance should have been requested from the Revenue.

If the current vendor does not have a copy of a specific clearance approval for the first sale and the property does not now qualify for general clearance the vendor should submit an application for specific clearance.

An exemption from LPT may have been claimed in the first or subsequent sale. The vendor may not be able to provide confirmation as they did not make the claim. The vendor should request approval from the Revenue of the exemption claimed.

8.10.11 DERELICT/UNINHABITABLE PROPERTY

A derelict or uninhabitable property falls outside the chare to LPT and so, in most cases, will not have an LPT property ID number. Properties that were uninhabitable or unsuitable for use as a dwelling, as at 1 November 2021 are not liable for LPT for 2022.

A derelict or an uninhabitable house falls within the definition of 'residential property' for stamp duty purposes. In order to file the stamp duty return online, an LPT property ID number will be required. The vendor should contact the Revenue to obtain a LPT ID number to enable stamping. The Revenue may require supporting documentation to confirm the status of the property.

8.11 Non-Principal Private Residence Tax and the Household Charge

The Local Government (Charges) Act, 2009 (NPPR) And The Local Government (Household Charges) Act, 2011

8.11.1 INTRODUCTION

In essence these provided for an annual local government charge of €200 on non-principal private residences, such as investment/rental properties, vacant investment properties, and holiday homes, and an annual charge of €100 on residential property respectively. The appropriate receipts or certificates of exemption had to be produced to the purchaser on completion. While both of these charges are now abolished they still remain a charge on residential property and will remain so for twelve years. In the case of the NPPR charge the purchaser's solicitor should ensure that the relevant certificate of discharge, or a certificate of exemption, is obtained at closing from the local authority. A receipt or declaration made by the vendor is not sufficient. However, a declaration can be provided where the property does not come within the ambit of the Act.

While any unpaid NPPR is a charge on the property under the Act, the Act has however provided for the expiration of the charge after twelve years. There is now a phased expiry of the NPPR charge, late payment fees, and the charge on property. Since 1 August 2021 the amount due for same will reduce every year until the liability and charge on property expires completely on 1 April 2025. The 2009 Act is due to be repealed on the 31 March 2025. Certificates of Discharge and Certificates of Exemption are still required until 31 March 2025 for the purpose of a sale for years for which the liability and charge on property have not yet expired and for the amount remaining liable on that date. Since 1 April 2022 the new maximum amount payable is €3,330.00.

The household charge was abolished on 1 January 2013. Any outstanding household charge plus interest and penalties unpaid on 1 July 2013 were converted into LPT of €200 due and payable on that date. This is collected and pursued by the Revenue through the LPT system. Any arrears will show as outstanding on the LPT property history screen and are collected by the Revenue through the LPT system. Purchasers will insist on any arrears being discharged by a vendor prior to closing.

8.11.2 THE LOCAL GOVERNMENT (CHARGES) ACT, 2009 (NPPR) CHARGE

The NPPR charge was introduced by the Local Government (Charges) Act, 2009 ('the 2009 Act') and affects and continues to affect the sale of certain residential property as defined in the 2009 Act, being in essence NPPR, from 31 July 2009. Section 3 of the 2009 Act applied an annual charge of €200 to the owners of all Irish non-principal private residences. The charge was payable to the relevant local authority in which the NPPR was located. Liability to pay the charge was determined on the basis of ownership of the property in question on a single day each year. The date is called the 'liability date'.

For the year 2009, 31 July was the liability date. For the years 2010, 2011, 2012, and 2013, 31 March was set as the liability date. The charge must be paid within two months of the liability date. Liability falls on all co-owners of the property but payment by any one co-owner discharges the liability of all co-owners.

Residential property was defined in s. 2 of the 2009 and the main type of residential property liable for the charge was private rented property, vacant property (except new but unsold property), apartments, flats, maisonettes, bedsits, and holiday homes.

If the property met with the definition of residential property and no exemptions applied then the NPPR charge was payable.

If the vendor was claiming an exemption from payment of the charge, s. 8 of the 2009 Act provided that the owner of a residential property may apply to the relevant local authority for a certificate of exemption in relation to any liability date specifying the reason why the charge was not payable.

Exemptions from the charge included the following:

(a) An individual's sole or main residence including a house where the individual is claiming a tax relief under the 'rent-a-room' scheme;

(b) A building of particular heritage which is an 'approved building' by the Minister of the Environment, Heritage, and Local Government and the Revenue Commissioners;

(c) A building forming part of the trading stock of a business (only if it has not previously been let or used as a dwelling);

(d) A building occupied under a shared ownership lease;

(e) A building leased to a housing authority or the Health Service Executive;

(f) A mobile home, caravan, or vehicle;

(g) Properties which through judicial separation or divorce become the principal residence of the other spouse or civil partner;

(h) The owner was incapacitated by long-term mental or physical infirmity and as a result was obliged to vacate his/her sole or main residence and to reside in a property not owned by him/herself;

(i) The property was occupied rent-free by a relative of the owner as their sole or main residence and the owner resided in a different sole or main residence located within 2 kilometres;

(j) Any year where the liability date falls after the date of death of the owner, and the grant of representation had not issued before the liability date.

(k) The property was subject to an exclusive right of residence.

Further exemptions may also apply.

Any unpaid NPPR charge is a charge on property for a period of twelve years. Section 7(1) of the 2009 Act provides that any charge or late payment fee due and unpaid by an owner of residential property shall be and shall remain a charge on the property to which it relates. However, s. 7(2) provides that the property shall not, as against a bona fide purchaser for full consideration in money or money's worth or a mortgagee, remain charged with or liable to the payment of such unpaid NPPR charge or late payment fee after the expiration of twelve years from the date upon which the amount concerned fell due.

The penalties in relation to this charge were particularly high. For example, if there was a liability to the NPPR charge from 2009 to 2013 and no payment has been made, a total amount of €7320 (including late payment fees) was due on 1 September 2014 if the tax remained unpaid.

In a practice briefing in the August/September 2021 issue of the Gazette the Conveyancing Committee advise that there will be a phased expiry of NPPR charges, the late payment fees, and the charge on property. From 1 August 2021, the amount due for same will reduce every year until the liability and charge on property expires completely on 1 April 2025.

The portion of unpaid NPPR liability and charge on property in respect of the year of charge and the amount due is as follows:

1. 2009 (€2070 due) expired on 31 July 2021.
2. 2010 (€1830 due) expired on 31 March 2022.
3. 2011 (€1470 due) expires after 31 March 2023.
4. 2012 (€1110 due) expires after 31 March 2024.
5. 2013 (€750 due) expires after 31 March 2025.
6. After 1st April 2025 No NPPR due.

Since 1 April 2024 the maximum amount outstanding is €750.

The whole of the Local Government (Charges) Act will be repealed on 31 March 2025.

8.11.3 PRE 31 MARCH 2025 REQUIREMENTS FOR CONVEYANCING SOLICITORS RE NPPR AS OUTLINED IN LAW SOCIETY GUIDELINES

If the vendor can claim an exemption on a particular liability date or where the charge or tax is paid and there is statutory provision for issuing a receipt, then the vendor must furnish on closing:

> *For the period from 1 August 2021 until 31 March 2025 a certificate of exemption/waiver/discharge will be required from the local authority for the purpose of a sale for the years for which the liability and charge on property have not yet expired and for the amount remaining liable on that date. There is a statutory provision for obtaining these certificates. If they are not obtained a purchaser cannot be certain that a property is not subject to a charge for any unpaid NPPR or household charge. Essentially in the case where an exemption applies the vendor may apply to the local authority for a certificate of exemption in relation to any liability date specifying the reasons the charge was not payable. On the other hand, if the property meets the definition of residential property and an exemption does not apply then the NPPR tax is payable and the vendor must apply to the local authority for a certificate of discharge from the local authority for each liability date. The years 2009 and 2010 are no longer included in certificates of exemption or discharge.*
>
> *Local authorities have been instructed not to accept payments in respect of both the 2009 and 2010 NPPR charge, as both have expired, and have further been instructed to refund any payments made in respect of the years 2009 and 2010.*

There are situations where the property does not come within the ambit of the 2009 Act because, for example, it does not meet the definition of residential property or relevant residential property (it is uninhabitable, for example, or is part of trading stock) in which case the Act does not apply and the property is not subject to the charge. This is not an exemption situation and a certificate of exemption is not necessary and will not issue from the local authority. In these situations the vendor's solicitor must provide on closing a statutory declaration of the vendor setting out the basis and giving the reasons why the property does not come within the ambit of the 2009 Act.

In view of the uncertainty as to when a statutory declaration as opposed to a certificate of exemption/waiver/discharge was required the Law Society issued a Practice Note in the January/February 2014 edition of the Law Society *Gazette* clarifying the position, see **8.10.9**. The Conveyancing Committee in a later Practice Notes in the April 2018 Gazette and also in May 2019 outlined the requirements and documents that should be sought and obtained and this is dealt with further at **8.10.5**.

8.11.4 NPPR CHARGE AND THE POSITION OF THE LEGAL PERSONAL REPRESENTATIVE

There was considerable confusion as to the position of a personal representative in relation to the NPPR charge. In particular, concerns were raised as to how property where the owner was deceased was to be treated where the grant of representation had not yet been granted. The Conveyancing Committee of the Law Society in a Practice Note in the March 2011 issue of the Law Society *Gazette* clarified the position as follows:

> *It is only when a grant of representation issues in a deceased's estate that a personal representative becomes liable for the charge. Where there is a property whose owner is deceased there is no person meeting the definition of owner in the Local Government (Charges) Act until letters of administration or probate have been granted. Where letters of administration are required, the person who is granted administration becomes the owner for the purposes of the Act. In a probate case, the executor becomes the owner on the issuing of the grant of probate. Only at that point does liability commence and liability lies with the owner that is the personal representative.*

The Act provides that the personal representative does not have any liability to pay the NPPR charge in a relevant year if the grant of representation has not issued by the liability date (i.e. 31 March). Late payment fees which had been accruing up to the point of death ceased, provided that the personal representative of the deceased discharged the full amount of the NPPR charge and late payment fees due up to the date of death within three months of the date of the grant of representation to the estate of the deceased. In the interim the property was treated as if it had no owner.

There is no waiver in the case of an insolvent estate and the insolvency of the estate would not negate the owner's liability.

The Local Government (Charges) Act, 2009 was amended by s. 19 of the Local Government (Household Charges) Act, 2011 by inserting a new s. 8A that transposes certain similar provisions of the 2011 Act into the 2009 Act. It provides that:

- A vendor's failure to pay the NPPR charge under the 2009 Act before completion of the sale is an offence carrying a Class C fine on summary conviction.
- The definition of 'vendor' includes an agent of the owner who receives the sale proceeds or part thereof on behalf of the owner, or who provides legal advice to the owner in a voluntary or below market value transfer. This will include a solicitor or auctioneer receiving a deposit or booking deposit on behalf of a vendor in the sale of a non-principal private residence. They will become liable to conviction of an offence and payment of a Class C fine if the sale is closed without the amount of any outstanding charge and arrears and late payment fees having been paid to the local authority.
- Section 8A (4) of the 2009 Act (as inserted by the 2011 Act) provides that on or before the completion of a sale of residential property the vendor of that residential property shall, in respect of that residential property, give to the purchaser a certificate of exemption or a certificate of discharge as may be appropriate in respect of each year in which a liability date fell since the date of the last sale of the property. A sale includes a voluntary transfer. Prior to this, during the years 2009–2011 if there was no liability to the NPPR charge, a statutory declaration confirming that the property was a principal private residence was (in accordance with recommended practice) provided by the vendor. However, as a result of s. 8A (4) the vendor is required to provide either a certificate of exemption or a certificate of discharge on the sale of a property to which the legislation applied for each year in which a liability date fell since the date of the last sale of the property.

8.11.5 ABOLITION OF NPPR HOUSEHOLD CHARGES/ REQUIREMENTS ON CLOSING

Both the NPPR and the household charge dealt with at **8.11.6** were abolished with effect from 1 January 2014 and 1 January 2013 respectively. Nevertheless, any unpaid NPPR or household charge remains a charge on property for a period of twelve years from the due date for payment of the charge after which a bona fide purchaser takes free of the charge. If a residential property is sold, the vendor is liable to pay all outstanding charges, late payment fees, and interest due before completion of the sale. 'Vendor' is defined to include a solicitor as agent of the owner who receives the proceeds of sale or provides legal advice to the owner. A sale includes a CPO or gift.

Therefore, despite the current abolition of both the household and the NPPR charges, vendors and their solicitors will still have to deal with both of these charges for a period of twelve years from the last due date.

Under the legislation, a vendor is obliged to give to the purchaser either a certificate of discharge, a certificate of exemption, or a certificate of waiver in respect of the NPPR charge. An up-to-date receipt or a declaration made by the vendor is not sufficient (except where the property does not come within the ambit of the 2009 Act). Applications for certificates in relation to the NPPR charge should be made to the NPPR section of the relevant local authority. The Law Society *Gazette* of 5 April 2012 sets out the procedures for applying for the relevant certificate regarding the household charge. The January 2014 edition of the *Gazette* sets out the requirements for certificates of waiver/exemption/discharge or declaration that legislation does not apply in respect of NPPR, household charge, and LPT.

The April 2018 edition of the *Gazette* contains revised recommendations regarding the NPPR charges. The 2009 Act did not provide that a form of certification was required in the event that the property was exempt from the charge—that is to say, if the property was the principal private residence of an owner on a liability date. The 2011 Act however amended s. 8 of the 2009 Act by the insertion of s. 8A(4) with effect from 1 January 2012, to provide that on or before the completion date of the sale of a residential property, the vendor of that residential property shall, in respect of that residential property, give to the purchaser (a) a certificate of discharge or (b) a certificate of exemption, as may be appropriate, in respect of each year in which a liability date fell since the date of the last sale of the property.

Problems have arisen in connection with properties that were purchased in the years 2009, 2010, and 2011 before the coming into force of the 2011 Act and that are now being sold. This is because prior to 1 January 2012 it was not possible to obtain a certificate of exemption from the local authority in respect of the property concerned for any liability date as indeed the requirement to furnish a certificate of exemption/discharge was only introduced in the 2011 Act. The Law Society had advised that a purchaser of a residential property (prior to the coming into force of the 2011 Act) should seek a statutory declaration from the vendor confirming that the provisions of the 2009 Act did not apply, if such was the case, because the property was the sole or principal residence of the vendor.

The committee have reviewed the NPPR legislation and have confirmed in the said Practice Note of April 2018 that a certificate of exemption need only be provided in respect of each year in which a liability fell since the date of the last sale of the property.

In the event of a sale in the years 2009 to 2011, it was the recommended practice to obtain a statutory declaration from the vendor confirming that the property was occupied by that individual as their sole or main residence and was accordingly exempt from the charge. Therefore, in the absence of any reason to question the validity of the statutory declaration, a purchaser should be entitled to rely on this statutory declaration and to seek a certificate of exemption only in respect of the liability dates since the date of the last sale of the property. This is particularly true in the case of a bona fide purchaser for value.

The Local Government (Charges) Act will be repealed on 31 March 2025 as aforesaid. In a Practice Note in the July 2021 *Gazette* the Conveyancing Committee advise that it is of the opinion that it is reasonable for a solicitor to advise a purchaser acquiring property for full consideration in money or money's worth to proceed with a purchase without raising any requisition or objection in relation to any NPPR charge outstanding following the expiry of twelve years from its liability date.

8.11.6 THE LOCAL GOVERNMENT (HOUSEHOLD CHARGE) ACT, 2011

The Local Government (household charge) Act, 2011 (enacted 19 December 2011) introduced a new household charge set at €100 for 2012 as a temporary measure pending the introduction of the Local Property Tax. It was a €100 flat tax chargeable on 1 January

2012 and to be paid by 31 March 2012. Section 3 of the Act provided that in 2012 and in each subsequent year the owner as defined of a residential property shall pay an annual household charge to the relevant local authority. Section 4 set out a list of exemptions and waivers and s. 9 dealt with applications for certificates of exemption or certificates of waiver. The provisions of s. 9 mean, in effect, that certificates of waiver and certificates of discharge will be required in connection with sales of residential property.

Section 8 provided that any unpaid charge, late payment fee, or late payment interest due shall be a charge on the property to which it relates. This is important for conveyancing purposes as it will fall within the remit of general condition 6(f) of the General Conditions of Sale 2019 edition. As against a bona fide purchaser for value or a mortgagee, the property shall not remain charged after the expiration of twelve years from the date upon which the amount owing fell due. Essentially the property is liable to the household charge if on the liability date (1 January 2012) the property met the definition of residential property and the vendor cannot claim an exemption or waiver.

The Conveyancing Committee in a Practice Note in the Law Society *Gazettes* of January/February 2012, April 2012, and November 2018 issued guidelines to practitioners in relation to these new charges. Because the Act provided that the household charge is a charge on the property to which it relates, solicitors should, on or before closing a transaction, seek confirmation of whether the property in sale is liable to the charge and, if so, obtain a certificate of discharge of the statutory charge on the property to place with the title deeds. If it is claimed by a vendor that the property is not liable to the local authority household charge, the purchaser's solicitor should seek confirmation of this by way of either a certificate of exemption or a certificate of waiver, as appropriate. If the property does not meet the definition of residential property then the vendor must furnish a statutory declaration confirming this and giving the reason.

The household charge however ceased to apply from 1 January 2013. Where the household charge for 2012 has not been paid prior to 7 July 2013, the arrears amount (including late payment penalties) has now increased to €200 and is included as part of the Local Property Tax liability in respect of the property. In effect the arrears of the household charge were converted to a Local Property Tax charge of €200 and so become part of the outstanding 'crystallised' liability. In addition, since 7 July 2013 these arrears are being collected by the Revenue rather than by the local authority. The statutory requirement to provide a certificate of discharge, exemption, or waiver from the household charge was repealed by s. 73 (3) (a) of the Local Government Reform Act, 2014 with effect from 27 January 2014. It is still possible to obtain a certificate of discharge or waiver or exemption from the household charge support unit by email: support@householdcharge.ie, or by phone: (1890) 357357.

Property owners can pay the €200 arrears by accessing the Revenue's online system using their PPSN/Tax registration number, LPT property ID number, and pin. Alternatively, they can pay by cheque or postal order, which should be sent to The Revenue Commissioners, LPT Branch, PO Box 1, Limerick. They should confirm that the payment is for household charge arrears. If the charge was paid after 1 July 2013, then it is a Local Property Tax and not a household charge and the evidence of payment is the usual LPT printout.

Household charge arrears now appear on the Revenue's online LPT History Screen and any arrears (for the year 2012) are collected by the Revenue through the LPT system and will be shown as outstanding on the LPT Property History screen. Purchasers will insist on any arrears being discharged by a vendor prior to closing.

The Conveyancing Committee in practice notes of October 2018 and July 2021 outlines the problem that arise in situations where owners (including previous owners on title) had not declared a relevant property for the purposes of the household charge. In these cases, the Revenue amends the Property History screen to reflect unpaid arrears. Where it is the current owner of the property who did not declare it, the matter is dealt with in the usual way by discharging the arrears due prior to any sale of the property.

However, a difficulty arises where the person who owned the property as of 1 January 2012 (the liability date for the 2012 charge) did not declare the property for household charge purposes and the Revenue did not discover the failure to declare until after that previous owner had sold it.

The current owner of the property may have been unaware of the outstanding charge and is now placed in the position of being unable to close a sale of the property to a current purchaser without addressing the question of the outstanding arrears that are properly the liability of another person (i.e. the owner as of 1 January 2012). This is a matter of title on which the current vendor must satisfy a purchaser before closing because any unpaid arrears are a charge on property for a period of twelve years after they fell due.

The Committee asked the Revenue to review that problem that arises in particular where there was on the face of the LPT property history screen no household charge due at the time a purchaser closed the sale of a property, but Revenue later find out that a previous owner had mis-declared or not declared for household charge and the arrears due by the previous owner are then placed on the property history screen as arrears. This prevents the current owner from selling the property without addressing the previous owner's liability, as unpaid household charge is a charge on the property.

The Law Society's view is that:

1. A current owner in the case outlined above should not be required to discharge another taxpayer's liability where the LPT Property History screen showed no outstanding arrears of household charge at the time they purchased the property;
2. It is the responsibility of the Revenue to pursue the owner as of 1 January 2012 for any outstanding household charge and for any failure to declare the property for household charge at that time;

The Revenue has acknowledged to the Conveyancing Committee that where the household charge liability comes to light after the date of sale, and the sum due was the liability of a previous owner, the Revenue would not expect the current owner to be liable for same.

They suggested that, in cases where sums due were the liability of a previous owner but have been put on the property history screen as arrears following a Revenue audit, Revenue can put an indicator on the property history screen saying that this sum is not a charge on the property.

The Committee agrees that, as a matter of practice, this would be sufficient evidence for title purposes that there is no claim by the Revenue against the property and that Revenue will pursue the matter with the previous owner as a debt due.

The Revenue are to put a process in place to reflect that there is no charge on the property even though the property history screen says there are arrears due, and an IT development is needed for this. Until the process and IT has been put in place, the Revenue have confirmed that solicitors for vendors in this situation should contact them as early as possible in a transaction at lpt@revenue.ie to have the matter resolved by provision of a letter confirming that Revenue has no charge on the property.

8.12 Vacant Homes Tax (VHT)

Section 84 of the Finance Act 2022 introduced a new Part 22B into the TCA a new VHT and effective from 1 November 2022. It applies to buildings which are residential properties for the purposes of LPT. This means that it does not apply to derelict properties or properties unsuitable for use as a dwelling and consequentially not liable for LPT. The tax is on a self-assessment basis and is administered by the Revenue.

VHT applies to a residential property for a chargeable period in which the residential property is in use as a dwelling or occupied for less than thirty days in a chargeable period i.e. a twelve-month period. A chargeable period is a 12 month period beginning on 1 November and ending on 31 October each year. The tax applies to residential properties which are vacant for twelve months or more. The legislation includes a number of exemptions to ensure that owners are not unfairly charged if the property is vacant for a genuine reason. These will include the following:

(a) properties currently listed for sale or recently sold during the chargeable period;

(b) properties vacant due to the occupier ceasing to occupy the property due to a physical or mental infirmity requiring long-term care and who had occupied the property as their sole or main residence prior to the cessation of occupation;

(c) properties vacant as a result of structural works, substantial repairs, or significant refurbishment work for a period of not less than six months in the chargeable period and subject to certain other conditions;

(d) a property that was the subject of a relevant tenancy for a period of not less than thirty days during the chargeable period;

(e) a property in respect of which no Local Property Tax was payable;

(f) a property where the death occurs of the person who was, immediately prior to their death, the chargeable person in relation to the property, that person having occupied the property as their sole or main residence.

Records should be maintained if intending to rely on an exemption from VHT. These may include books, accounts, documents, and any other data relating to the use of a residential property during a chargeable period.

The current rate of VHT is charged at a rate equal to seven times (previously five and three times) the property's existing basic Local Property Tax rate, excluding LPT local adjustment factors.. The legislation provides that the amount of VHT to be charged in respect of a residential property for a chargeable period shall be the amount represented by 'A' in the formula **A=B x 3** where B is the amount of LPT payable in respect of the residential property in relation to the liability date falling in the year in which the chargeable period commences, before any local authority adjustment.

The tax is due and payable on or before 1 January in the year immediately following the end of the chargeable period. The first chargeable period for the VHT commenced on 1 November 2022 and ended on 31 October 2023. For that chargeable period, a VHT return was be due by 7 November 2023 and the tax was payable by 1 January 2024.

8.13 Residential Zoned Land Tax (Previously Vacant Site Levy)

A vacant site levy was introduced in the Urban Regeneration and Housing Act 2015. The purpose of the introduction of the levy was to stimulate the development of housing and to eliminate the hoarding of land. It provided for a levy to be charged on each vacant site which has been entered on the vacant site register for which a market value is determined. It applies to residential land (more than 0.4047 hectares) where there is a need for housing in the area, or the site is suitable for housing and the majority of the site has not been in use for an extended period of time. It also applies to regeneration land (other than residential land), where the majority of the site has not been in use for an extended period of time or the site is having a negative impact on existing amenities or on the character of the area.

Once a vacant site has been identified, it must be vacant for a period of twelve months prior to being placed on the register.

The amount of the vacant site levy in 2018 was initially 3 per cent of the market value of the site as determined. The levy was increased to 7 per cent in 2019.

The residential zoned land tax will apply to land which has not been developed for housing but is serviced and zoned for residential development. The tax will be 3 per cent of the market value of the land and it will be collected by the Revenue. In the meantime the vacant site levy continues to apply.

A residential zoned land tax (RZLT) was introduced in the Finance Act 2021 with the purpose of activating vacant lands for residential purposes and will replace the vacant site levy in 2024. The process to identify lands to which the tax applies is now under way and the tax will be payable from 1 February 2025.

The objective of the tax is to activate land that is serviced and zoned for residential use or mixed use, including residential use, in order to increase housing supply and to ensure regeneration of vacant and idle lands in urban locations.

The RZLT process has two parts:

(i) identification and mapping of the land in scope for the tax. This is undertaken by local authorities through the publication of draft and supplemental maps; and

(ii) administration of the tax, which is to be undertaken by the Revenue Commissioners from 2024.

The tax will be 3 per cent of the market value of the land and will apply from 1 February 2025.

A vacant site is either:

(a) Residential land (more than 0.4047 hectares), where there is a need for housing in the area, the site is suitable for housing, and the majority of the site has not been in use for an extended period of time.

(b) Regeneration land (other than residential land), where the majority of the site has not been in use for an extended period of time, or the site is having a negative impact on existing amenities or on the character of the area.

The RZLT replaces the vacant site levy (VSL), which was introduced in the Urban Regeneration and Housing Act 2015 with the purpose of stimulating the development of housing and to eliminate the hoarding of land. The Act provides for the establishment and maintenance of a register of vacant sites by each individual planning authority and for the charging of an annual levy on such properties.

The amount of the VSL in 2018 was 3 per cent of the market value of the site as determined. This was increased to 7 per cent in 2019. The VSL continues to apply until the RZLT commences on 1 February 2025. The standard Requisitions on Title have been amended in April 2025 to deal with this tax.

8.14 Water Charges

Water charges were provided for under s. 48 of the Environment (Miscellaneous Provisions) Act, 2015, which commenced on 1 January 2016. The Law Society has issued a number of Practice Notes on the topic in the December 2015, March 2016, and February 2017 editions of the *Gazette* respectively. Section 48 inserted s. 3A into the Water Services Act, 2014, under which an obligation was placed on the vendor's solicitors to discharge any unpaid water charges from the proceeds of sale.

Section 5(1) (b) (ii) of the Water Services Act, 2017 has now repealed s. 3A of the Water Services Act, 2014. There is no longer an obligation on the vendor's solicitors to make enquiries of Irish Water about amounts due and/or to discharge arrears from sale proceeds. The 2019 edition of the Requisitions on Title at requisition 2 outlines the current requirements in relation to water services/local authority services.

A Practice Note in the December 2018 edition of the *Gazette* provides an Irish Water update. This Practice Note confirms that while Irish Water assumed responsibility for water and waste infrastructure which was previously vested in local authorities, Irish Water is not responsible for surface water pipes or water attenuating systems, responsibility for which remains with the local authority.

Irish Water has confirmed to the Conveyancing Committee that solicitors acting for purchasers of second-hand dwellings may continue to rely on a letter previously issued by a local authority confirming that roads and services are in charge as evidence that the applicable water infrastructure is now vested in Irish Water.

In addition Irish Water has confirmed that, where a local authority issues a letter confirming that the roads immediately abutting the property are in charge, Irish Water accepts responsibility for the water infrastructure servicing the property, even where the letter states that the local authority is no longer responsible for the water infrastructure. This issue, to include obtaining certificates of registration of septic tanks from Protect Our Waters, is dealt with in more detail in **Chapter 7**.

Water charges are currently not applicable but it is intended to introduce a charge for excessive water use from October 2023.

8.15 Conveyancing Fees

The following is a list of conveyancing fees payable to the Property Registration Authority for both registered and unregistered transactions.

8.15.1 LAND REGISTRY FEES

Land Registration (Fees) Order, 2012. These fees are effective from 1 January 2012.

1. **Fee scale for transfers on sale**

Value		**Fee**
€1	€50,000	€400
€50,001	€200,000	€600
€200,001	€400,000	€700
In excess of €400,000	€50,000	€800

2. **Other registrations affecting registered land**

a.	Voluntary transfers	€130
b.	Opening a new folio or subdivision of parent folio	€75
c.	Charge	€175
d.	Transfer order	€130
e.	Transmissions on death	€130
f.	Section 49 application	€130
g.	First registration in Form 3	€130
h.	First registration other than application in Form 3	€500
i.	Caution/Inhibition	€40
j.	Priority entry	€40
k.	Release of burden/charge	€40
l.	Any other registration not specified above	€40

3. **Other services**

1.	Special registration map	€40
2.	Copy folio with file/title plan (sealed and certified)	€40

3.	Copy instrument, affidavit, order, or ruling	€40
4.	Names index search	€5
5.	Approval of scheme map (where lodged in electronic form)	€130
6.	Approval of scheme map lodged for the first time	€300
7.	Approval of revision of scheme map	€50

4. **Miscellaneous**

(a)	Administration fee on refused, abandoned, or withdrawn dealings	€50

8.15.2 REGISTRY OF DEEDS FEES

On 1 May 2008, the Registry of Deeds (Fees) Order, 2008 came into operation. The most commonly used applications are as follows:

1.	Registration of a deed/application form	€50
2.	Registration of a vacated mortgage	€20
3.	Resubmission of a deed and application	€20
4.	Certified copy memorial or application form	€20

The fees order can be viewed on the Authority's website at www.prai.ie.

All Registry of Deeds fees must be paid directly to the Registry of Deeds at Henrietta Street, Dublin 7.

Appendix 8.1 Multiplier Table for Capital Gains Tax

Capital Gains Tax	Multipliers									
Year Expenditure Incurred	Capital Gains Tax Multiplier for Disposals Years ended 5 April 1993 to 31 December 2002									
	Y/e 5 April 1996	Y/e 5 April 1997	Y/e 5 April 1998	Y/e 5 April 1999	Y/e 5 April 2000	Y/e 5 April 2001	Short Y/e 31 Dec 2001	Y/e 31 Dec 2002	Y/e 31 Dec 2003	Y/e 31 Dec 2004 et seq/
1974/75	5.899	6.017	6.112	6.215	6.313	6.582	6.930	7.180	7.528	7.528
1975/76	4.764	4.860	4.936	5.020	5.099	5.316	5.597	5.799	6.080	6.080
1976/77	4.104	4.187	4.253	4.325	4.393	4.580	4.822	4.996	5.238	5.238
1977/78	3.518	3.589	3.646	3.707	3.766	3.926	4.133	4.283	4.490	4.490
1978/79	3.250	3.316	3.368	3.425	3.479	3.627	3.819	3.956	4.148	4.148
1979/80	2.933	2.992	3.039	3.090	3.139	3.272	3.445	3.570	3.742	3.742
1980/81	2.539	2.590	2.631	2.675	2.718	2.833	2.983	3.091	3.240	3.240
1981/82	2.099	2.141	2.174	2.211	2.246	2.342	2.465	2.554	2.678	2.678
1982/83	1.765	1.801	1.829	1.860	1.890	1.970	2.074	2.149	2.253	2.253
1983/84	1.570	1.601	1.627	1.654	1.680	1.752	1.844	1.911	2.003	2.003
1984/85	1.425	1.454	1.477	1.502	1.525	1.590	1.674	1.735	1.819	1.819
1985/86	1.342	1.369	1.390	1.414	1.436	1.497	1.577	1.633	1.713	1.713
1986/87	1.283	1.309	1.330	1.352	1.373	1.432	1.507	1.562	1.637	1.637
1987/88	1.241	1.266	1.285	1.307	1.328	1.384	1.457	1.510	1.583	1.583
1988/89	1.217	1.242	1.261	1.282	1.303	1.358	1.430	1.481	1.553	1.553
1989/90	1.178	1.202	1.221	1.241	1.261	1.314	1.384	1.434	1.503	1.503
1990/91	1.130	1.153	1.171	1.191	1.210	1.261	1.328	1.376	1.442	1.442
1991/92	1.102	1.124	1.142	1.161	1.179	1.229	1.294	1.341	1.406	1.406
1992/93	1.063	1.084	1.101	1.120	1.138	1.186	1.249	1.294	1.356	1.356
1993/94	1.043	1.064	1.081	1.099	1.117	1.164	1.226	1.270	1.331	1.331
1994/95	1.026	1.046	1.063	1.081	1.098	1.144	1.205	1.248	1.309	1.309
1995/96	—	1.021	1.037	1.054	1.071	1.116	1.175	1.218	1.277	1.277
1996/97	—	—	1.016	1.033	1.050	1.094	1.152	1.194	1.251	1.251
1997/98	—	—	—	1.017	1.033	1.077	1.134	1.175	1.232	1.232
1998/99	—	—	—	—	1.016	1.059	1.115	1.156	1.212	1.212
1999/00	—	—	—	—	—	1.043	1.098	1.138	1.193	1.193
2000/01	—	—	—	—	—	—	1.053	1.091	1.144	1.144
2001	—	—	—	—	—	—	—	1.037	1.087	1.087
2002	—	—	—	—	—	—	—	—	1.049	1.049
2003 et seq										1.000

Note: in the 'Year Expenditure Incurred' column, for all years to 2000/2001 inclusive, a year means a 12-month period commencing on 6 April and ending on the following 5 April. The 'Short year' 2001 covers the period 6 April 2001 to 31 December 2001. With effect from 1 January 2002 the income tax year is the calendar year, i.e. 2002 refers to the year ended 31 December 2002.

Indexation is not available on expenditure incurred within 12 months prior to the date of disposal. Indexation relief will *only* apply for the period of ownership of the asset up to 31 December 2002 for any disposals made on or after 1 January 2003.

Appendix 8.2 CERTIFICATES OF WAIVER/EXEMPTION/ DISCHARGE OR DECLARATION THAT LEGISLATION DOES NOT APPLY: NPPR, HOUSEHOLD CHARGE, LPT

CONVEYANCING COMMITTEE

Certificates of waiver/exemption/discharge or declaration that legislation does not apply: NPPR, household charge, LPT

It appears to the committee that there is significant confusion among practitioners about the circumstances in which certificates of waiver/exemption/discharge from the NPPR charge or the household charge must be obtained, and when it is appropriate to obtain a declaration from a vendor (or a purchaser in some cases) as to the non-applicability of the relevant piece of legislation. It appears to the committee that exemptions (from a charge or tax that would otherwise be due) are being confused with situations where the relevant act does not apply at all.

It is necessary to distinguish between:

1) Situations where the relevant legislation makes statutory provision for a specific exemption or waiver and provides for the issue of a certificate in relation to same or where it provides for issue of a certificate of discharge following payment of the relevant charge or tax, and
2) Situations where a property does not come within the ambit of the relevant legislation because, for example, it does not meet the definition of 'residential property' or 'relevant residential property' as set out in the different pieces of legislation (either because it is uninhabitable, is part of trading stock, and so on), in which case the relevant act does not apply and the property is not subject to the charge. This second situation is not an exemption situation and a certificate of exemption is not necessary and will not be issued.

The committee wishes to clarify that its practice note published in the June 2013 issue of the *Gazette* (p50) relates to cases that come within the ambit of the relevant legislation and where the legislation provides for a waiver or exemption in certain circumstances or where the charge or tax is paid and there is statutory provision for issuing a receipt, that is, cases described in paragraph 1 above. The committee confirms that certificates of waiver/exemption/discharge should be obtained in those cases, as there is specific statutory provision for them and, if they are not obtained, a purchaser cannot be certain that a property is not subject to a charge for any unpaid NPPR or household charge. A declaration from a vendor as to entitlement to a waiver or exemption is not sufficient, and a receipt for payment by itself is not sufficient in these cases.

To deal with the situations described in paragraph 2 above, the committee's first practice note on NPPR published in the September 2009 *Gazette* (p44) recommended that a statutory declaration should be obtained if it is claimed that the charge does not apply. Although not repeated in subsequent practice notes, the committee understands that this has also become common practice in relation to cases where it is claimed that the household charge and the local property tax do not apply, and the committee recommends this extension of this practice.

The committee has set out in a table the circumstances in which the various certificates or declarations are appropriate. This can be accessed in the members' area of the Society's website by clicking on 'Committees', 'Conveyancing Committee', 'Resources' (in the box titled 'Additional information') and scrolling down the Resources page to click on 'Conveyancing guidelines'.

Source: <https://www.lawsociety.ie/Documents/committees/conveyancing/CertificatesOfWaiver-etc-notApply-JanFeb2014.pdf.>

To view the Practice Note please visit: <https://www.lawsociety.ie/Solicitors/Practising/Practice-Notes/Certificates-of-waiverexemptiondischarge-or-declaration-that-legislation-does-not-apply-NPPR-household-charge-LPT/#.U6lWy5RdXTo>.

CHAPTER 9

VALUE ADDED TAX

9.1 General Introduction to VAT

9.1.1 BACKGROUND

Value Added Tax ('VAT') was introduced into Ireland on 1 November 1972 as one of the conditions of Ireland's accession to the European Economic Community. Irish VAT legislation is embodied primarily in the Value Added Tax Consolidation Act 2010 ('VCA') and various European Community Directives and Regulations and Irish Regulations. (References to sections of the Act refer to the VCA.)

An EU Member State's own national VAT legislation may only vary from obligations set out in EU VAT legislation where derogation is permitted and has been granted. In the absence of a derogation a person may seek to rely on EU legislation where he or she feels national legislation has not properly reflected the EU provision.

9.1.2 HOW VAT OPERATES

VAT is a transaction-based tax. Fundamentally, VAT is paid on the *value added* at each stage of the chain from production to consumption. The VAT that is levied at each stage in the chain is reported to the Revenue Commissioners (referred to as 'Output' VAT) on a periodic basis.

In order to tax the 'value added' by a supplier, the supplier can deduct from his or her Output VAT the VAT that they incur on resale purchases and most other business expenses (referred to as 'Input' VAT).

Each supplier must file regular VAT returns on which the supplier's Output VAT and Input VAT are declared. If Output VAT exceeds Input VAT, payment of the difference must be made to the Revenue Commissioners. If Input VAT exceeds Output VAT, the difference will be repaid by the Revenue Commissioners.

When considering any supply from a VAT perspective it is essential to establish the following:

What? What is being supplied?	Different rules and rates apply to goods and services as well as situations where several items are being supplied together.
Where? Where is the transaction taxable?	The Place of Supply is determined under a series of rules (there are separate rules for goods and for services). The Place of Supply dictates the VAT regime (if any) that will apply to the transaction.

How? How much is taxable, i.e. what is the taxable amount and what is the rate applicable?	The taxable amount @ the applicable VAT rate gives the amount of VAT due.
When? When is the transaction regarded as taking place?	This dictates when the tax is due and when it must be paid and the rate to be applied.

9.1.3 WHAT IS THE SCOPE OF VAT AND HOW IS IT APPLIED?

9.1.3.1 General scope of VAT

Irish VAT arises on the supply of goods or services:

(a) made within the State;

(b) by a taxable person acting as such;

(c) in the course or furtherance of business;

(d) for consideration.

Where any of these elements is missing, the transaction is not subject to Irish VAT.

Example

Gerry decides to sell his car, which he uses every day to travel to work. Gerry has spent a lot of time upgrading the car and it is highly customised for performance. Is the sale subject to VAT?

Answer: No. The sale by a person of his car or his principal private residence would not be subject to VAT as this is not being done in the course or furtherance of business.

Example

Patricia decides to sell her family home. The house is her principal private residence. Is the sale subject to VAT?

Answer: No. The sale is not being made in the course of a business so does not fall within the scope of VAT.

In contrast, if Patricia were to build a new house on part of her garden with the intention of selling it, then the sale of that new house would fall within the scope of VAT.

Irish VAT also arises on:

- the arrival of goods into Ireland from jurisdictions outside the EU—referred to as VAT on imports;
- the acquisition of goods into Ireland from other EU Member States; and
- services received in Ireland from both other EU Member States and non-EU territories (in relation to the second and third bullet points the trader must self-account for that VAT, referred to commonly as 'reverse charge' VAT).

Supplies of goods and/or services in the course of business are, as we have seen, subject to VAT, as are importations and intra-EU acquisitions. However, the VCA provides that certain supplies shall nevertheless be exempt from VAT.

9.1.3.2 Exemptions

The exemptions are listed in Schedule 1 to the VCA and include:

(a) medical care services;

(b) public transport services;

(c) social welfare services;

(d) education;

(e) activities of public radio and television bodies (excluding advertising);

(f) live theatrical and musical performances;

(g) fund-raising activities of certain non-profit making organisations;

(h) insurance and banking services together with related agency services;

(i) supply of stocks and shares and related agency activities.

9.1.3.3 Supplies of goods subject to VAT

In general, a supply of goods takes place where there has been a transfer of ownership of goods by agreement. Goods are defined (s 2) as all movable and immovable objects, but this does not include things in action, or money. References to goods include references to both new and used goods. The legislation also contains specific provisions which hold that certain transactions are regarded as being a supply of goods, such as electricity, gas, heat, refrigeration, and ventilation.

A self-supply of goods takes place when a person either appropriates goods from his or her business for a non-business use (e.g. takes goods from his or her shop for his or her own use) or, in the case of movable goods, applies the goods from a taxable to an exempt activity. A self-supply is also liable to VAT and the trader must charge himself or herself VAT based on the tax exclusive cost of acquiring or manufacturing the goods that have been self-supplied.

Certain transactions are not regarded as constituting a supply of goods. These include the transfer of ownership of goods as security for a loan (particularly relevant when mortgaging a property) and the transfer of ownership of goods in connection with the transfer of a business or part of a business.

9.1.3.4 Supplies of services subject to VAT

A supply in relation to a service means:

> *the performance or omission of any act or the toleration of any situation other than (a) the supply of goods and (b) other than a transaction specified in Section 20 or 22(c).*

This definition is sufficiently wide so as to encompass all VATable transactions which are not treated as a supply of goods for VAT purposes.

9.1.4 WHERE IS THE TRANSACTION TAXABLE?

Only supplies of goods and services effected within the State can be subject to Irish VAT. It is essential, therefore, to determine the place where the supply of goods or the supply of services has taken place (the Place of Supply), and the legislation provides a series of rules to determine this. In the context of immovable goods these rules include the following:

- Immovable goods—taxed where the goods are located.
- Services connected to supplies of immovable goods—taxed where the goods are located.

9.1.5 HOW MUCH?

The taxable amount is set out in Part 5 VCA. Fundamentally, the taxable amount is the total consideration which the person supplying the goods or services is entitled to receive, including all taxes, commissions, costs, and charges whatsoever (excluding the VAT itself, of course).

Where the consideration is not entirely in money then the taxable amount is the amount of money that might reasonably be expected to be charged at the open market price.

Example

Motors Ltd has sold a new car to Helen for €30,000 and agreed to take Helen's existing car in part exchange. Helen will pay €20,000 in cash and her trade in has been valued at €10,000.

Even though Motors Ltd will only receive €20,000 it will be subject to VAT on €30,000 (the market value of the new car).

There are specific rules that address situations where goods or services are given away free of charge, and which also confer on the Revenue the power to impose a market value in certain situations relating to transactions between connected parties.

Once the taxable amount is established then the appropriate VAT rate is applied to it to compute the VAT due.

Currently (2023) the rates applicable are:

(a) Zero (the Zero Rate)—mostly food and drink, children's clothing and footwear, medicine (VCA s. 46(1)(b) and Schedule 2);

(b) 4.8 per cent—supply of livestock (s 46(1)(d));

(c) 13.5 per cent (the Reduced Rate)—sale, maintenance, and repair of property; tour guide services; short-term hire of cars, boats, and caravans; general repair and maintenance services; certain personal services and certain flour-based bakery products (s 46(1)(c) and Schedule 3);

(d) 23 per cent (the Standard Rate)—all goods and services not listed in the Schedules 1–3 inclusive: VCA s. 46(1)(a). Property rents when taxable are subject to this rate of VAT.

(e) 9 per cent (the Second Reduced Rate)—newspapers and periodicals; certain eBooks, eNewspapers, and ePeriodicals (certain publications are excluded); and the provision, by a person other than a non-profit making organisation, of facilities for taking part in sport.

For the period from 1 November 2020 to 28 February 2023, the following items are subject to the second reduced rate of VAT: catering and restaurant supplies (excluding alcohol, soft drinks, and bottled water); hot takeaway food and hot tea and coffee; hotel lettings, for example, guesthouses, caravan parks, or camping sites; admissions to cinemas, theatres, certain musical performances, museums, art galleries, or exhibitions; amusement services of the kind normally supplied in fairgrounds or amusement parks; admission to an open farm; hairdressing services; and certain printed matter such as brochures, leaflets, catalogues, or printed music (excluding books).

For the period from 1 May 2022 to 28 February 2023, the following items were subject to the second reduced rate: the supply of electricity and the supply of gas used for domestic or industrial heating or lighting, whether in gaseous or liquid form (with certain exclusions).

9.1.6 WHEN? ACCOUNTING FOR VAT

9.1.6.1 Basis of accounting for output VAT

When a trader is completing his periodic VAT return, he must calculate the amount of Output Tax arising in the period. There are two bases under which output VAT may be calculated: the Invoice Basis and the Monies Received Basis (or Cash Receipts Basis).

Invoice basis

Under the Invoice Basis, a trader must pay output VAT to the Revenue based on the sales invoices issued (or which should have issued) in the VAT period, irrespective of whether the invoice has been paid or not. For supplies which do not require an invoice to be issued, VAT is due at the time the goods or services are supplied.

Monies received basis

Under the cash receipts basis, VAT is only payable to Revenue when the cash is received by the trader.

The cash basis is only available to traders whose turnover from the supply of goods or services to customers not registered for VAT exceeds 90 per cent of total turnover, or to traders whose annual turnover does not exceed €2,000,000.

The main advantage of the cash receipts basis over the invoice basis is that the trader only accounts for the output VAT when they themselves have been paid, whereas a trader on the invoice basis must pay over VAT at the due date whether or not they have been paid.

9.1.6.2 Issuing VAT invoices

When a taxable person supplies taxable goods or services to a person who is in business (or to the State or a Local Authority or a body established by statute) a VAT invoice must be issued by the 15th of the month following the month in which the goods or services are supplied. The invoice must contain certain specified details, including:

(a) the name, address, and VAT registration number of the supplier;

(b) the name and address of the person to whom the supply is made;

(c) the date of issue of the invoice;

(d) a sequential number;

(e) the date on which the goods or services were supplied;

(f) a description of the goods or services supplied;

(g) the quantity or volume of goods supplied;

(h) the consideration exclusive of VAT for the supply; and

(i) the rate of VAT applicable to the supply.

Other details are required in relation to specific transactions; for example, when supplying most legal services to businesses based within the EU but outside Ireland, the customer's non-Irish VAT number must be included on the fee note, as well as an indication that the recipient must account for the VAT arising on the supply. There is no requirement to issue an invoice for supplies to a private individual (i.e. a person not acting in a business capacity), but the supplier may issue an invoice if they so wish.

As mentioned, the requirement to issue an invoice is normally triggered by the completion of the supply of the goods or services in question. It should be noted, however, that the receipt of a payment (for example a deposit, pre-payment, or retainer) in advance of completion of the supply is deemed to be a supply in that amount and therefore triggers an obligation to issue an invoice and account for VAT in relation to the amount received.

Example

ABC Limited agrees to sell the freehold to a new store to Retail Ltd for €1.5m. Under the sale agreement a deposit of €150,000 is payable in March 2020 (deposit paid to ABC Ltd, i.e. not held in escrow) and the sale will close in May 2020.

The deposit is deemed to create a supply and so the invoice relating to the payment must be raised by 15 April 2020 at the latest.

The invoice in respect of the balance is triggered when the sale closes in May 2020 and so must be issued by 15 June 2020 at the latest.

9.1.6.3 VAT returns

The majority of traders are required to file VAT returns for each two-month taxable period, those periods being based on a calendar year (i.e. January–February, March–April, May–June, July–August, September–October, and November–December).

Certain traders may be granted permission by the Collector General to file an annual return, a biannual return, a quarterly return, or a thrice annual return depending on the size of their annual VAT liability.

Returns must be completed and returned to the Revenue Commissioners by the nineteenth day of the month following the end of the filing period in question so (extended to the twenty-third when filing electronically); for example, the September/October return must be filed via ROS (Revenue Online Service) on or before 23 November.

The VAT charged by a person on the supply of goods or services (together with any VAT he is deemed to have charged) is known as 'Output' tax. The VAT payable by a person on goods and services supplied to him is known as 'Input' tax. When filing a VAT return, a person may claim credit for 'Input tax' against 'Output tax' arising, paying the excess only to the Revenue. If allowable 'input tax' in any accounting period exceeds the 'output tax', the person is entitled to a refund of the difference from the Revenue Commissioners.

Example

A solicitor bills fees of €25,000 (excl VAT @ 23 per cent) in the period March/April 2020. During that period, he purchased a laptop costing €2000 (excl VAT @ 23 per cent). The VAT return will show the following:

		Price (€)	**VAT (€)**
Output VAT (Box T1)	Supplies—fees	25,000	5750
Less: Input VAT (Box T2	Purchases—laptop	(2000)	(460)
Net VAT payable (Box T3)	Tax payable for the period		5290

9.1.7 INPUT CREDIT—VCA PART 8 CHAPTER 1

A taxable person can generally obtain an input credit for any VAT borne on purchases of goods for resale and most business expenses when they relate to VATable supplies. However, an input credit is not allowed for the following:

(a) The provision of food, drink, accommodation, or other personal services supplied to the taxable person or his or her agent or employee; for example, VAT on hotel bills incurred while a solicitor is on circuit is not recoverable.

(b) Entertainment expenses.

(c) The purchase, lease, or hire of cars and petrol otherwise than as stock in trade (except car hire firms and driving schools). (A proportion of the VAT incurred on new cars purchased subsequent to 1 January 2009 with a CO_2 emission of less than 156g/km may also be reclaimed.)

Generally, a trader is prohibited from claiming input tax on costs associated with exempt sales. A trader who makes an exempt sale of property or an exempt letting will therefore be prohibited from taking a deduction for VAT incurred on costs such as estate agents' fees, legal fees, and any costs incurred in preparing the property for sale.

9.1.8 RECORDS

A taxable person must keep records in such form and containing such information as is necessary so that his liability to VAT (output VAT) and the credits (input VAT) to which he is entitled for taxable purchases can be checked. Records must be maintained for six years from the date of the transaction to which they relate.

Records relating to property transactions must be retained by a taxable person for the entire period that they hold an interest plus six years thereafter.

Revenue officials have powers enabling them to:

(a) enter premises;

(b) seek production of the relevant business records and inspect them;

(c) make extracts or remove them for a reasonable period; and

(d) seek assistance from any person on the premises.

Generally, notice of any intention to inspect records is given.

9.2 VAT and Property Transactions

9.2.1 INTRODUCTION

In this text the term 'property' has been used for convenience. VAT law refers to 'Immovable Goods', which is given the same meaning as 'Immovable Property' as defined under EU VAT Regulations. Immovable Property is defined in s. 2 VCA and Article 13b VAT Directive 2006/112/EC as:

(a) any specific part of the earth, on or below its surface, over which title and possession can be created;

(b) any building or construction fixed to or in the ground above or below sea level which cannot be easily dismantled or removes;

(c) any item that has been installed and makes up an integral part of a building or construction without which the building or construction is incomplete, such as doors, windows, roofs, staircases and lifts;

(d) any item, equipment or machine permanently installed in a building or construction which cannot be moved without destroying or altering the building or construction.

From the introduction of VAT w.e.f. 1 November 1972 to 30 June 2008 a framework of rules (now commonly referred to as the 'Old Rule') applied to property related transactions. Following a long consultation process a new framework for VAT on property was introduced coming into effect on 1 July 2008 (and now commonly referred to as the 'New Rules').

It was also necessary to bridge the gap between the old and new frameworks and therefore a number of Transitional Rules also came into effect w.e.f. 1 July 2008.

9.2.2 THE 'OLD RULES'

The framework of VAT on property rules applicable from the introduction of VAT in Ireland on 1 Nov 1972 up to 30 June 2008 (commonly referred to as the 'Old Rules') can be summarised as follows:

- Sales of an interest in property were subject to VAT only where a number of conditions were met. These conditions were as follows: (i) the property had to be developed or redeveloped on or after 1 November 1972; (ii) the sale had to be in the course of a business; (iii) the vendor had to be entitled to recover input VAT incurred on the acquisition or development of the property; (iv) the vendor had to hold an interest in the property; and (v) the vendor had to dispose of an interest in the property.

  An 'interest' was defined as any interest that was for a period of ten years or more. Where the conditions were not met the sale was exempt and there was no provision to opt to tax it.

- Lettings of ten years or more were treated as if they were a sale and were subject to VAT where the conditions set out above were met; otherwise they were exempt. Where a letting of ten years or more was subject to VAT a capital value was placed on the lease and VAT was charged upfront on the commencement of the lease based on that capital value. The rents themselves then passed without further charge to VAT. There were a number of methods available to compute this capital value.

Having to pay VAT upfront on a lease could place significant cash-flow pressure on a tenant having to fund the payment of VAT to the landlord and then wait for a refund from Revenue (if entitled to it). Consequently, a facility known as the 4A facility was introduced. In advance, of the transaction the landlord and the tenant could apply to Revenue for authorisation to apply the facility to a letting. If granted, the tenant did not have to pay the VAT to the landlord and instead self-accounted for the VAT on their VAT return (a form of reverse charge).

Specific rules applied to the surrender or assignment of lettings of ten years or more but broadly they were treated in a similar manner to the creation of a letting of ten years or more. Specific rules also applied to any premium or reverse-premium applicable.

One further feature of the treatment of lettings of ten years or more was the treatment of the reversionary interest created when the letting was granted. Essentially, the landlord was regarded as taking a self-supply of the reversionary interest. If the letting was for twenty years or more the self-supply was deemed to be nil, and no VAT arose. However, for lettings of between ten and twenty years the landlord was liable to VAT on the value of the reversionary interest, which was essentially the market value of the property less the capital value placed on the letting.

Example

In 2005 Patrick purchases a newly built warehouse valued at €2m plus VAT. He has found a tenant willing to rent the unit for fifteen years. Patrick's adviser has informed him that the capital value of the lease is €1.5m. If Patrick proceeds with the letting, he will be regarded as taking a self-supply of the reversionary interest valued at €2m – €1.5m = €500,000, resulting in a VAT liability @ 13.5 per cent of €67,500. This is Patrick's liability.

- Lettings of less than ten years were exempt from VAT (with certain exceptions, for example holiday homes, hotel rooms, car parks). There was a facility for a landlord to 'waive' this exemption and if doing so the landlord would then charge VAT at the standard rate on the rents as they fell due.

Where a landlord waived their exemption, the waiver applied to all their lettings for periods of less than ten years, so whether to waive or not had to be carefully considered. As always with VAT there were certain exceptions where a waiver could be applied to a specific letting only.

A landlord was entitled to cancel their waiver. On cancellation, however, a 'waiver cancellation adjustment' arose. Essentially, the landlord had to compare the amount of VAT he had deducted as Input VAT because they had waived (for example VAT reclaimed on acquisition, development, redevelopment, maintenance, etc. of the property) and the VAT paid as Output VAT on the rents arising from the waiver during the life of the waiver. Where Input VAT exceeded Output VAT the difference had to be repaid to Revenue.

9.2.3 THE 'NEW RULES'

Following a long consultation process, a new framework was introduced w.e.f. 1 July 2008. This new framework takes a very different approach, which can be summarised as follows:

- First supply of properties within five years of their completion are subject to VAT. Second or subsequent sales within this five-year window may or may not be subject to VAT depending on various circumstances. This category includes freehold interests but also 'freehold equivalent' interests, freehold equivalent interests being essentially a very long leasehold interest.

- Where a supply is not subject to VAT the vendor and purchaser may however jointly 'opt to tax' a specific transaction, but there are specific circumstances where a joint option to tax is not permitted.
- All lettings (other than freehold equivalent lettings and specific lettings such as holiday homes, hotel rooms, car parks, and toll roads, for example) are exempt from VAT. A landlord may however 'opt to tax' a specific letting. Unlike the old waiver, opting to tax can be done on a letting-by-letting basis. Unlike the joint option for sales, the option for a letting is the landlord's prerogative. There are specific circumstances where an opt to tax is however prohibited.
- The New Rules also introduced a Capital Goods Scheme for VAT on property transactions. Prior to the CGS a deduction on property transactions depended solely on the person's entitlement to deduct at the time the VAT relating to the property was incurred. Unless a person changed the use of the property to a fully exempt or non-business use there was no further adjustment throughout the person's period of ownership of that property. The Capital Goods Scheme fundamentally changed this position, requiring an annual check to be performed in terms of the person's right to deduct and adjusting the amount the person has recovered in relation to the property (be it positively or negatively) arising from any change in that entitlement.
- The New Rules also include specific measures to address transactions (on or after 1 July 2008) in properties which existed before 1 July 2008. The most significant of these relate to the treatment of what are commonly referred to as 'legacy leases'. These are leases of ten years or more which were granted before 1 July 2008 and therefore taxed upfront based on a capital value. There are also specific rules relating to transactions in certain reversionary interests and in properties which were the subject of a waiver.

9.2.4 ESTABLISHING A PROPERTY'S VAT HISTORY

Before you can determine what VAT, if any, is applicable to a contemplated property transaction, it is essential to establish the VAT history of the property. This VAT history will inform:

- whether a sale is taxable (or not) and, if not, whether a joint option to tax should be sought or not;
- whether a letting should be exempt or whether the landlord should opt to tax;
- whether there is a positive or negative Capital Goods Scheme impact;
- whether or not the specific transitional rules apply.

Given the complexity of the VAT on property system it is imperative that both the solicitors acting for the vendor and for the purchaser are apprised of the VAT position at a pre-contract stage. To assist practitioners in this regard, the Conveyancing and Taxation Committees of the Law Society jointly issued VAT pre-contract enquiries which were first posted on the Law Society website in May 2009 and may be accessed by logging onto the member's area of that website. As these enquiries are updated on a regular basis, practitioners should ensure that the most up-to-date version available on the website is used in each individual transaction. Although the enquiries are to be raised by the purchaser's solicitor, in a joint Practice Note issued in the May 2009 *Gazette*, the Conveyancing and Taxation Committees stated that it was their view that the enquiries would prove a useful tool for the vendor's solicitor in establishing the VAT position in each individual transaction, thereby assisting the vendor's solicitor in correctly drafting the Contract for Sale. It is, therefore, advisable that, on receiving instructions regarding the sale of the property, the vendor's solicitor would liaise with the vendor and, if necessary, the vendor's taxation adviser, in order to complete the questionnaire.

The purchaser's solicitor should carefully consider the responses to the enquiries received from the vendor and ensure that the purchaser is fully aware of the VAT implications of the transaction. On completion, the purchaser's solicitor ought to seek confirmation from the vendor's solicitor that the replies to the enquiries are still accurate and correct.

As the enquiries are composed of a series of very detailed questions regarding the VAT history of the property, it is strongly advised that, unless the solicitor in question is an expert in VAT or the transaction is a straightforward one, the vendor should be advised to engage the services of a VAT specialist or a tax adviser. Equally, the purchaser's solicitor, if he or she does not feel competent to analyse the information furnished by the vendor and advise on the consequences of the same for the VAT treatment of the transaction, ought to advise the purchaser to seek specialist assistance.

9.3 Property Transactions on or after 1 July 2008

9.3.1 INTRODUCTION

The current framework of rules relating to the application of VAT to property transactions came into effect on 1 July 2008 and applies to all transactions on or after that date.

There are however a number of specific rules which are required to address transactions that involve certain interests in property that were in existence on 1 July 2008 (commonly referred to as Transitional Rules). The transactions covered by these specific rules include:

- the surrender and assignment of legacy leases (i.e. leases of ten years or more created pre-1 July 2008);
- lettings involving a property that subject to a waiver of exemption that was in place on 1 July 2008;
- a sale of a reversionary interest created when a legacy lease was created;
- a sale of a property that was subject to a waiver of exemption in place on 1 July 2008.

These categories of transactions are examined later. In this section we shall examine the standard rules that apply to property transactions.

9.3.2 LETTINGS

9.3.2.1 What is a letting?

The VCA uses the term 'letting'. That term is not specifically defined, though its meaning has been considered by various courts. A common thread running through the various judgments is that the characteristics of a letting are as follows:

1. There is a defined area of the property.
2. The owner of that property assigns the right to occupy that space to the tenant or licensee.
3. There is an agreement for a fixed term.
4. There is a payment by the tenant or licensee in return for the rights of occupation.
5. The agreement is for the passive provision of space.
6. The owner of the property assigns to the tenant/licensee the right to exclude other persons from that part of the property.

From a VAT perspective it is the characteristics of the agreement that are important rather than whether it is referred to as a lease or a licence or indeed whether it is a written or verbal agreement.

A transaction that does not amount to a letting is simply regarded as a standard service from a VAT perspective, and outside the specific VAT on property rules. They are subject to VAT at the standard rate, currently 23 per cent.

Example

Gumdrop operates a mobile sweet cart. Treepark Shopping Centre grants Gumdrop a licence to operate its sweet cart at its shopping centre at a daily rate of €200. Gumdrop can locate the cart at any of the four entrances to the centre or the central concourse but there are conditions as to how far from the entrance it can be located, times of operation, and so on. Treepark also has the right to request Gumdrop to move the cart to a different location in the centre. Is this a letting?

Answer: No. The agreement is missing a number of the key hallmarks of a letting; in particular, there is no defined specific area and no exclusive use. The daily fee would be subject to VAT @ the standard rate (presently 23%).

Certain transactions are excluded from the specific VAT provisions relating to lettings. These include hotel and holiday accommodation (subject to VAT at the second reduced rate, currently 9 per cent), operator-run car parks, and road/bridge toll charges (subject to VAT at the standard rate, currently 23 per cent).

Lettings which amount to a Freehold Equivalent are treated as a sale rather than a letting and therefore the rules applicable to sales rather than lettings apply to this type of letting.

9.3.2.2 Freehold equivalent lettings

VCA Part 3 Chapter 1 specifies that a supply in relation to immovable goods shall be regarded as including

> *the transfer in substance of (a) the right to dispose of immovable goods as owner or (b) the right to dispose of immovable goods.*

Consequently, a letting which amounts to a freehold equivalent is regarded as a sale and is subject to the VAT provisions relating to property sales (see paragraph xxx below).

A 'freehold equivalent' is defined as:

> *An interest in immovable goods other than a freehold interest the transfer of which constitutes a supply of immovable goods in accordance with VCA Part 3 Chapter 1.*

Example

On 1 July 2022 BarCo grants a 500-year lease to CoffCo. This will be regarded as a sale rather than a letting.

9.3.2.3 VAT and lettings

From 1 July 2008 all lettings created (other than those to which specific transitional rules apply and other than freehold equivalent interests) are exempt from VAT (paragraph 11 Schedule 1).

A landlord may however opt to tax the letting, in which case VAT @ the standard rate (presently 23%) is applied to the rents as they fall due.

9.3.2.4 The landlord's option to tax a letting

The detailed provisions relating to the Option to Tax are contained in s. 97 VCA. In summary:

- The option is exercised on a letting-by-letting basis (the decision to opt to tax or not must therefore be made each time there is a letting and only applies to that specific letting).
- An option can be exercised or cancelled at any time during the letting.
- The option can be exercised by either including an appropriate provision in writing within the letting agreement or issuing a document to the tenant notifying him that VAT is chargeable on the rents.

- There is no requirement to notify the Revenue of the option.
- An option cannot be exercised in respect of a letting of residential accommodation.
- An option cannot be exercised where the tenant is connected to the landlord **unless** the tenant is entitled to claim an input VAT credit for at least 90 per cent of the VAT that would arise on the rents.
- An option to tax is terminated by a written agreement between landlord and tenant that the option is terminated or by the delivery by the landlord of a document notifying the tenant that the option is terminated.
- An option is automatically terminated when the landlord and the tenant become connected, unless the tenant is entitled to claim an input VAT credit for at least 90 per cent of the VAT that would arise on the rents.
- An option is automatically terminated where the landlord or a person connected with the landlord occupies the property, unless the person connected is entitled to claim an input VAT credit for at least 90 per cent of the VAT that would arise on the rents.
- A trader in the process of developing a property with a view to letting is deemed to option upon claiming an input deduction for VAT incurred on the development. Should the trader (landlord) subsequently make a letting and not actually opt to tax, the deemed option is terminated.

When a landlord opts to tax and the tenant is a VAT registered person, Department of State or Local Authority body established by statute, or a person engaged in VAT exempt activities, he is required to issue a VAT invoice in respect of the rents. Alternatively, he can issue a one-off statement stating the dates the rent falls due and the VAT thereon.

Why would a landlord opt to tax?

This is an obvious question: why would someone choose to tax a transaction when it could be regarded as exempt? The answer is that the decision to opt to tax or not will dictate the landlord's input VAT deduction entitlement.

A person is prohibited from recovering VAT incurred on costs that relate directly to an exempt transaction. Where a landlord grants a VAT exempt letting (i.e. where he does not opt to tax) the landlord cannot recover any of the VAT incurred on the costs associated thereto, such as legal fees, tax advice, and estate agent's fees.

More importantly, however, he or she also loses the right to a deduction entitlement in relation to the cost of acquiring and/or developing the property (or if already deducted on the basis of 'intention' they would be obliged to repay such VAT). The amount of this deduction entitlement loss is dictated by the Capital Goods Scheme (examined below).

9.3.2.5 Tenant's VAT status

While it is the landlord's prerogative to Opt to Tax or not, obviously the ability of the tenant to recover VAT arising on the rents has an impact on the decision.

Commercially, it may make sense for the tenant to agree to pay a premium to the landlord to cover any CGS (and other tax) adjustment the landlord will incur should he not opt to tax rather than incurring VAT at the standard rate on all the rents payable under the lease for the duration of the lease.

9.3.2.6 Premium

Where the tenant pays a lump sum to the landlord at the commencement of one of these lettings the treatment of that payment is dictated by the treatment of the rents, that is, where the landlord has opted to tax, then the payment is subject to VAT; where the landlord has not opted to tax the payment is exempt.

Where the landlord makes a payment to the tenant the matter is more complex. Revenue accepts that where the tenant does not make any supply in relation to obtaining the payment (i.e. does not give any rights or undertakings) then the payment is not subject to VAT. Where a supply is made then VAT will arise. The nature of the agreement relating to the payment will determine the VAT treatment in each individual instance.

A bona fide rent-free period does not give rise to a VAT event; however, the landlord should ensure the opt to tax is in place and not terminated during that period, otherwise a CGS adjustment may arise.

9.3.2.7 Subsequent surrender and assignments

The surrender or assignment of these leases (i.e. created since 1 July 2008) does not trigger a VAT event in relation to the letting itself (note this is very different to the treatment of a surrender or assignment of a legacy lease which is examined later). However, see **9.3.4.6** below regarding any tenant works.

Where the tenant pays a lump sum to the landlord to take the surrender, the treatment of that payment will follow that of the rents; that is, where the landlord has opted to tax then the payment is subject to VAT, and where the landlord has not opted the payment is exempt.

Where the lease is surrendered, however, the landlord will need to consider any CGS impact in relation to any subsequent use of the property, including any re-lettings.

Where the lease is assigned, the landlord needs to consider whether or not he and the new tenant are 'connected'; if so, will this cause the termination of any option to tax he has in place.

9.3.2.8 Lettings—summary VAT considerations

Option to Tax	Letting is exempt unless the landlord opts to tax. If the landlord is opting to tax, he/she is required to notify the tenant in writing.
Who accounts?	Landlord will levy VAT on the rents (standard rate presently 23%). Lease should provide that the VAT will be paid (generally on presentation of a VAT invoice). Lease needs to be clear as to whether the agreed rent is inclusive or exclusive of VAT.
Other issues	Landlord may wish to restrict the tenant from assigning the lease to a person connected with the landlord. Landlord may wish to restrict the right of the tenant to undertake works. Tenant may wish to have an obligation included that the landlord will take on a CGS relating to tenant works.
Premium	Tenant pays landlord—treatment follows that of the rents. Landlord pays tenant—not subject to VAT unless tenant regarded as providing some form of service for that payment.

9.3.3 SALES

9.3.3.1 Sales—general provisions

Sales of new properties (including properties which have been sufficiently redeveloped so as to render them new) which are completed on or after 1 July 2008 are subject to the New Rules.

Since 1 July 2008, s. 94 deals with sales of property. You may recall that from a VAT perspective all sales of goods for consideration by a taxable person acting in that capacity are subject to VAT (s 3). However, s. 94(2) operates by stipulating that the following sales of immovable goods are *not* subject to VAT:

- where the property has not been developed within a twenty-year period prior to the sale;
- where the sale of completed immovable goods takes place more than five years from the date of the most recent completion;
- where it is a second or subsequent sale of completed immovable goods within five years of completion, the property has been occupied for at least twenty-four months post completion, and there has been no development since completion, or if there was development that development was minor;
- where in the case of a building the building was completed more than five years prior to the sale and there has been development of the property within five years prior to the sale but that development was only minor.

In principle, therefore, sales not falling within these categories *are* subject to VAT at the reduced rate, currently 13.5 per cent.

There are a number of terms used earlier which are specifically defined.

Development

'Development' in relation to any land is defined in s. 2 as meaning

> *the construction, demolition, extension, alteration or reconstruction of any building on the land, or (b) the carrying out of any engineering or other operation in, on, over or under the land to adapt it for materially altered use.*

Minor development

Minor development is development where

> *such development did not and was not intended to adapt the building for a materially altered use,* and *(ii) the cost of such development did not exceed 25% of the consideration for that supply.*

Refurbishment

Refurbishment is defined as 'development on a previously completed building, structure or engineering work'.

Completed

'Completed' is defined in s. 94(1) as meaning that

> *the development of those goods has reached the state, apart from only such finishing or fitting work that would normally be carried out by or on behalf of the person who will use them, where the goods can effectively be used for the purposes for which the goods were designed, and the utility services required for those purposes are connected to the goods.*

Occupied

'Occupied' is also defined by s. 94(1) and means

> *occupied and fully in use following completion, where that use is one for which planning permission for the development of those goods was granted, and (b) where those goods are let, occupied and fully in such use by the tenant.*

9.3.3.2 Joint option to tax

Each of the categories noted earlier is not, as stated, subject to VAT. Section 94(5) however provides that where both the supplier and the purchaser are taxable persons within the State, they can jointly opt to tax the transaction. *Note:* the provision refers only to purchasers who are 'taxable persons', which is essentially persons who are in business; the ability to opt is therefore not enjoyed where a buyer is not in business.

In relation to a joint opt to tax:

- The agreement must be in writing.
- It must be entered into no later than the fifteenth day of the month following the month in which the supply occurs.
- The purchaser becomes the accountable person, that is, the supplier does not charge the VAT; rather the purchaser self-accounts (i.e. charges the VAT to themselves) under a reverse charge.

Why would the parties choose to tax a transaction that would otherwise be exempt from VAT?

Generally, input VAT is not deductible in connection with an exempt supply. Therefore, where a sale of immovable goods is exempt from VAT, the vendor cannot recover VAT incurred on estate agency fees, legal fees, tax advice, and so on in connection with that sale.

Similarly, where the sale is exempt there is a loss of input credit in respect of any VAT incurred by the vendor on the acquisition and/or development of the property. This loss of deduction entitlement is addressed under the Capital Goods Scheme regime, which was also introduced on 1 July 2008. In making an exempt supply the supplier may be required to make a Capital Goods Scheme clawback payment or may miss out on a Capital Goods Scheme repayment. The Capital Goods Scheme is examined later.

9.3.3.3 Sales subject to VAT

Having considered the categories of supplies of property that are not subject to VAT, the following are the key supplies of property that *are* subject to VAT. These are subject to VAT at the reduced rate, currently 13.5 per cent.

- The first sale of a new or transformed building within the first five years from completion will be subject to VAT. A transformed building is one which has been rendered 'new' through development.
- The second or subsequent sale of a new or transformed building within the first five years following completion will also be subject to VAT unless the property has been occupied for a period of twenty-four months in that period.
- A supply of an incomplete property is subject to VAT (the five-year rule only applies to completed buildings).
- A supply of property which would be exempt from VAT but where both parties have exercised the joint option for taxation (see earlier).
- The sale of undeveloped property is generally not subject to VAT. However, s. 94(3) provides that where a person supplies property to a person and in connection with that supply enters into an agreement with that person or somebody connected with that person to carry out a development of that property then the sale is subject to VAT.

Example

Sahel Ltd constructs two new retail units, the construction of which is completed on 1 July 2019. Sahel Ltd concludes the sale of the freehold of Unit 1 to Gobi Ltd on 1 August 2019. Is this sale subject to VAT?

Answer: Yes. This is the first sale of a newly constructed building occurring within five years of completion, so it is subject to VAT.

In 2022 Gobi Ltd agrees to sell the unit. Is this sale subject to VAT?

Answer: No. This is a second sale within five years of completion but as it has been occupied for more than two years it is exempt. Gobi and the purchaser may jointly opt to tax the sale.

Example

Sahel Ltd occupies Unit 2 itself from September 2019, using it as a depot for its distribution business. In October 2021 it finally secures a purchaser. Will the sale be taxable?

Answer: Yes. This is the first sale of the unit, so the 'occupancy' test does not apply. As the first sale is taking place within five years of completion it is subject to VAT.

Note: a property is commonly referred to as 'new' within that first five-year window from its completion.

Example

Clawail Ltd owns a site. It sought and obtained planning permission to build a number of retail units on the site. The company however no longer wishes to proceed with the development itself. No works of any kind have taken place on the site. Newbuild Ltd enters an agreement with Clawail Ltd under which it will develop and put the retail units on the market. The prospective purchaser will be required to (i) purchase the site from Clawail Ltd; and (ii) enter into a building agreement with Newbuild Ltd. When Clawail Ltd sells the sites to the buyers will those sales be subject to VAT?

Answer: Yes. While the sale by Clawail Ltd would be of an undeveloped site (note: planning permission of itself does not constitute development), s. 94(3) will apply as the sale is connected with an agreement to subsequently develop the site.

Important note: The extent of any works on a property is therefore crucial from several perspectives. Where the works are simply repairs and maintenance then they do not need to be considered further. Works that constitute development may render a property 'new' and therefore start a five-year window from completion (with the consequence that a sale within that window is likely to be subject to VAT). However, where the works are development but are only minor development then they are not regarded as commencing a five-year window.

Time of supply

The time of supply is obviously an important date, as it is the status of the property on that date that will determine its liability to VAT or not etc. It also dictates when any related invoice must be issued and when any VAT arising will be accounted for.

Under VAT rules a supply of goods takes place where there is a transfer by agreement of ownership of the goods. Typically, in relation to property, this will occur when the Contract for Sale is completed.

It is important to note that it is not necessary that legal title be transferred; it is sufficient that the purchaser acquires the right to dispose of the property as owner to trigger a supply for VAT purposes.

A sale will typically involve the payment of a deposit and the balance then being payable on closing. As we have seen, the time of supply for VAT purposes will be on closing. However, specific VAT rules deem the deposit to be a supply in itself, and therefore VAT will arise on the deposit at the time it is paid. VAT on the balance then falls due at closing. This rule applies where a pre-payment/deposit is made available to the vendor.

You will note the definition of supply includes a 'by agreement' requirement. As a consequence, there are specific rules to capture transactions under a compulsory purchase or as settlement of a debt so that they are specifically subject to VAT.

9.3.3.4 Sale of residential property

The general rules outlined earlier are varied when the property in question is a residential property.

VCA s. 94(8) specifically sets aside the provisions in subsection (2), that is, the five- and two-year rules, and provides that the first supply of 'a dwelling' by the developer ('the person who developed the immovable goods in the course of a business of developing immovable goods') or a person connected with the developer is subject to VAT providing that person was entitled to a deduction on the acquisition and/or development of the property.

Example

Cathbest Limited buys a site in 2015, obtains planning permission for three townhouses, and completes the construction of the houses on 30 September 2006. The market still being slow, it rents out the houses and finally, in October 2022, puts them on the market. They all sell by 31 December 2022. Are these sales subject to VAT?

Answer: Yes. Under the general rules, as this is a first sale and it is taking place more than five years from completion, the sale would be exempt. However, s. 94(8) kicks in and the sale is specifically subject to VAT.

9.3.3.5 Sales—summary VAT considerations

Works?	What works have been undertaken? • When were those works undertaken? • What were those works? • Do those works constitute development and, if so, when were they complete and would they be regarded as minor?
Taxable or not?	• First sale within five years of completion. • Second or subsequent sale within five years of completion—was it occupied; if so for how long? • Is the vendor operating a waiver (see later)—if so, should the waiver be cancelled prior to sale?
Jointly opt or not?	• Is the purchaser in a position to opt? • What are the CGS consequences for the vendor? • If advising the purchaser, establish benefit to purchaser for agreeing.
Who accounts?	• Sale of new building, taxable sale of partially developed lands, sales deemed to be subject to VAT—vendor must charge the VAT and report it to Revenue. • Sale that has been jointly opted to tax—purchaser must self-account on a reverse charge basis.

Warning: Do not issue a VAT invoice earlier than is necessary, otherwise you may needlessly accelerate the time VAT becomes due.

9.3.4 THE CAPITAL GOODS SCHEME ('CGS')

9.3.4.1 Introduction

VCA s. 2 defines a 'capital good' as 'developed immovable goods' and includes refurbishment within the meaning of section 63(1), and a reference to a capital good includes a reference to any part thereof. 'Refurbishment' is defined as 'development on a previously completed building, structure or engineering work'.

The CGS works, in general, on the basis that the appropriate amount of deductible VAT is reclaimed upfront and an annual adjustment is made at the end of each succeeding interval to the extent that the usage of the property varies from the usage in the initial interval when the input VAT was deducted. Generally speaking, where the annual taxable usage in an interval is less than the taxable usage in the initial interval then an amount of VAT is payable, which is, in effect, a clawback of a proportion of the VAT deducted in the initial interval. Where the taxable usage in an interval is greater than the taxable usage in the initial interval then an additional amount of VAT is deductible.

A critical point to note is that it is only the cost of developing *immovable* goods that is included in a CGS. While this does include professional fees (architects, estate agents, legal fees, and so on), it does not include the cost of movable goods such as furniture, carpets, and so on incurred as part of the development/redevelopment.

A property which is also a capital good has a 'VAT life', this being the adjustment period during which the owner of the property is required to continuously review their deduction entitlement which was exercised on the acquisition or development of that property. More importantly, a sale of such a property within this adjustment period may trigger a clawback or additional deduction depending on the particular circumstances and so the decision to jointly opt to tax a sale or to opt to tax a letting is very much linked to the Capital Goods Scheme (CGS) status of that property.

The adjustment periods are as follows:

- the general adjustment period—twenty intervals;
- refurbishment—ten intervals;
- Legacy leases—various (depends on the original length of the lease, subject to a maximum of twenty intervals and, in the case of a surrender or assignments, the remaining intervals at that time).

9.3.4.2 What are the CGS intervals?

An interval is a fixed period of time in respect of which the CGS owner must review their deduction entitlement. The VCA defines the following intervals:

Initial interval	The 12 months immediately following the completion or purchase of the property is known as the 'initial interval'.
Second interval	The period from the end of the initial interval to the trader's financial year-end.
Third and subsequent intervals	Each successive period to the trader's next accounting year-end following the second or subsequent interval.

In the initial interval the use of the property is examined. If it is for a fully taxable use, then all VAT is recoverable; if it is for fully exempt use, no VAT is recoverable; and if it has a 'mixed use' (i.e. both a taxable and exempt use), then an element of the VAT incurred is deductible.

At the end of the initial interval an adjustment is performed to take account of any change in deductibility which occurred within twelve months of the acquisition of the property. This is fundamental to the intent of the CGS, which is to try and link the amount of VAT deducted to the use of property over the VAT life of the property.

In each of the following intervals an adjustment is made *if* the taxable use of the property varies from the use in the initial interval (as adjusted).

Example

In June 2019 Trated Ltd purchases the freehold in a new building for €10m plus €1.35m VAT. This VAT is recoverable in full in 2019 if the building is used wholly for taxable purposes in that initial interval. For the remaining VAT life of the property, the VAT deduction entitlement of Trated Ltd must be reviewed under the CGS.

The VAT life of a freehold interest is deemed to be twenty intervals; therefore, for every interval, Trated Ltd will review its recovery entitlement of one-twentieth of the VAT initially recovered, i.e. €1.35m ÷ 20 (€67,500).

In 2020 if Trated Ltd continues to use the property fully for taxable purposes no adjustment needs to be made in these years.

However, let us assume that in 2022 Trated Ltd creates a VAT exempt letting of 30 per cent of the property for a five-year period. That part of the property has therefore been moved to an exempt use and an adjustment will arise. Trated Ltd will therefore have to pay an amount under the CGS of €20,250 to Revenue ((€1.35m ÷ 20) × 30 per cent) for the tax year 2022. For each subsequent interval that the exempt letting continues, Trated Ltd will have to pay an amount of €20,250.

Example

The following comprehensive example is taken from Revenue's Tax and Duty Manual VAT—Capital Goods Scheme (Example 6 therein), which illustrates a number of the key features of the Capital Goods Scheme and how variations in the trader's deductibility entitlement are handled by the CGS.

ABC Ltd acquired a property on 13 September 2014. Its accounting year ends 31 December. ABC Ltd claimed in full the VAT it incurred on the acquisition:

Total tax incurred = €1,350,000

Base tax amount = €67,500 (€1,350,000/20). This is the total tax incurred divided by the number of intervals in the adjustment period.

However, when ABC Ltd reviewed its actual deductible entitlement for its initial interval it noted it was 80 per cent. It therefore had to review its deduction taken as follows:

Total reviewed deductible amount = €1,080,000.

Reference deduction amount = €54,000 (€1,080,000/20). This is calculated by dividing the total reviewed deductible amount by the number of intervals in the adjustment period and is used for any calculations required at the end of the second or subsequent intervals. The reference deduction amount is the same for the second and each subsequent interval.

Where the deductible amount for the second or any subsequent interval (known as the 'interval deductible amount') differs from this amount, an adjustment will be required.

Second interval—no adjustment

For the second interval (which ends on 31 December 2015) ABC's taxable use was 80 per cent. (This is known as the 'proportion of deductible use' for the interval.) As this is the same as the use for the initial interval, no adjustment is required.

Third, fourth, and fifth interval—no adjustment

For the third (ending 31 December 2016), fourth (ending 31 December 2017), and fifth (ending 31 December 2018) intervals, the 'proportion of deductible' use was still 80 per cent, so adjustments are not required for those intervals.

Sixth and seventh interval—change in taxable use—VAT payable on adjustment

For the sixth interval (ending 31 December 2019) the 'proportion of deductible use' due to a change in ABC's business mix is reduced to 70 per cent. As this differs from 80 per cent (use during initial interval) an adjustment is required. In order to carry out the calculation, ABC is obliged to calculate the 'interval deductible amount', which is the 'proportion of deductible use' for that interval multiplied by the 'base tax amount' c 67,500 × 70 per cent = c €47,250.

The adjustment is the difference between the 'reference deduction amount' and the 'interval deductible amount':

C – D

(C – reference deduction amount; D = interval deductible amount)

€54,000 – €47,250 = €6750.

As C is greater than D, €6750 is payable to the Revenue as tax due for the taxable period following the end of the interval, which is January/February 2016.

For the seventh interval (ending 31 December 2020) the proportion of deductible use was 70 per cent. Again, an adjustment is required:

$$C - D$$

$$€54{,}000 - €47{,}250 = €6750$$

As C is greater than D, €6750 is payable as tax due for the taxable period following the end of the interval, which is January/February 2021.

Eighth and nine intervals—no adjustment required

Trading mix changes again so that ABC's entitlement returns to 80 per cent. For the eighth (ending 31 December 2021) and ninth intervals (ending 31 December 2022) the 'proportion of deductible use' for the interval was 80 per cent, so no adjustment required.

Tenth interval—change in taxable use—VAT deductible on adjustment

For the tenth interval (ending 31 December 2023) the 'proportion of deductible use' changes again due to a further change in the business mix and ABC is now entitled to 95 per cent. As this differs from 80 per cent (use during the initial interval) an adjustment is required. Similar to the above, the 'interval deductible amount' is €67,500 × 95 per cent = €64,125.

Adjustment for the interval—

$$C - D$$

$$€54{,}000 - €64{,}125 = €10{,}125$$

As D is greater than C, €10,125 is given as a VAT credit to ABC by the Revenue for the taxable period following the end of the interval, which is January/February 2024.

For the remainder of the intervals the 'proportion of deductible use' is 80 per cent, which means there are no adjustments made at the end of all the intervals. The twentieth interval ends on 31 December 2029. After this date there are no further obligations under the scheme.

Interval	*Amt Deducted*	*Total Rev Deduction Amt*	*Adjustment*	*VAT*
1	€1,350,000	€1,080,000	€270,000	Payable
	€67,500 €54,000	= base tax amount = reference deductible amount		
Interval	*Ref Deduction*	*Interval Deduction*	*Adjustment*	*VAT*
2	€54,000	€54,000		
3	€54,000	€54,000		
4	€54,000	€54,000		
5	€54,000	€54,000		
6	€54,000	€47,250	€6750	Payable
7	€54,000	€47,250	€6750	Payable
8	€54,000	€54,000		
9	€54,000	€54,000		
10	€54,000	€64,125	–€10,125	Repayable
11	€54,000	€54,000		

Interval	*Ref Deduction*	*Interval Deduction*	*Adjustment*	*VAT*
12	€54,000	€54,000		
13	€54,000	€54,000		
14	€54,000	€54,000		
15	€54,000	€54,000		
16	€54,000	€54,000		
17	€54,000	€54,000		
18	€54,000	€54,000		
19	€54,000	€54,000		
20	€54,000	€54,000		

9.3.4.3 'Big swing'

Normally an adjustment (i.e. a payment or repayment of an amount of VAT depending on variation in usage) is made on an annual basis. An exception arises however where in any interval other than the initial interval the proportion of tax deductible differs by more than 50 per cent from the initial interval proportion of tax deductible: then the owner of the property must perform an adjustment covering all of the remaining intervals, not just the current one.

Example

Trixy Limited incurs VAT of €400,000 when it acquires a property. As Trixy was engaged in fully VATable activities it recovered this VAT in full. The base tax amount is therefore €20,000—(€400,000/20), one-twentieth of the amount initially recovered.

If in year 10 the property is used for only 40 per cent taxable purposes (i.e. 60 per cent exempt purposes) then the adjustment which is made is not just for year 10 but is in respect of the entire remainder of the VAT life of the property.

The adjustment of €132,000 which must be paid to the Revenue is calculated as €20,000 × 60 per cent × 11 = €132,000. (Note: if Trixy's deduction moves from 40 per cent in the future, then any adjustment is referenced to a base amount of €8,000 (€20,000 × 40 per cent) per interval thereafter.)

9.3.4.4 Refurbishment/development

The development/refurbishment of an existing property creates its own Capital Good and so there can be two or more Capital Goods relating to the same building: the acquisition/development of the building, and the monies spent on refurbishing the building. 'Refurbishment' is defined as 'development on a previously completed building, structure or engineering work'.

The CGS adjustment period for refurbishment is just ten years.

9.3.4.5 Keeping CGS records

Section 64(12) of the VCA requires Capital Goods owners to create and maintain a record in respect of each Capital Good and s. 85(1) provides an obligation to retain these records together with the taxpayer's existing records. This document is referred to in the legislation as a 'Capital Good record' and is a form of 'VAT passport'.

This VAT passport is essential in order to allow traders to calculate the amount of any annual adjustment and, as we will see later, compute the amount on which VAT is chargeable on certain assignments or surrenders.

9.3.4.6 Tenant works

There will be instances where a tenant undertakes works on a property and where those works will constitute refurbishment.

From the tenant's perspective they will have created a Capital Good with a ten-interval VAT life. The same general rules as outlined earlier will similarly apply to the tenant's capital good.

An issue will arise for the tenant where they surrender or assign a lease in respect of which the VAT life on tenant works has not expired at the time of surrender/assignment. Unless the tenant can get the agreement of the landlord (in the case of a surrender) or the new tenant (in the case of an assignment) to 'step into his shoes' and take on the tenant's CGS obligations in relation to the refurbishment for the remainder of the VAT life then at the time of surrender/assignment, the tenant will incur a VAT liability in accordance with the formula:

$$\frac{B \times N}{T}$$

Where B = the total reviewed deductible amount in relation to the capital good (the refurbishment).

N = the number of full intervals remaining in the VAT life of the Capital Good plus one.

T = the total number of intervals (i.e. ten).

The only other option available to the tenant to avoid a clawback is to destroy the works that were undertaken, in which case no clawback arises.

9.3.4.7 Multiple CGS on the same property

A property can have a number of Capital Goods Schemes open simultaneously.

Example

BatCo constructs new offices in 2014. An extension is added in 2016 and then a mezzanine floor is added in 2022.

There will therefore be three different CGSs open: (1) a twenty-year adjustment period commencing in 2014 for the construction; (2) a ten-year adjustment period commencing in 2016 for refurbishment for the extension; and (3) a ten-year adjustment period commencing in 2022 for the mezzanine.

It is also possible for a landlord to own a Capital Good (the building itself) and the tenant to own a Capital Good (the refurbishment if carried out by the tenant), both relating to the same property.

9.3.4.8 Capital Goods Scheme—residential property

You recall that where a person applies a property (capital good) to a VAT exempt use it will trigger an adjustment under the CGS and where the variation in the person's deduction entitlement swings by more than 50 per cent a full adjustment (rather than an interval-by-interval adjustment) is triggered. You might also recall that since 1 July 2008 lettings are exempt from VAT and that while the landlord generally has a right to opt to tax, an opt to tax is prohibited when it is residential accommodation.

VCA s. 94(8)(c) varies the general rules above in the case of a developer and residential property with the effect that a developer who lets a residential property:

- will not incur a 'big swing' adjustment;
- will incur an adjustment payment on an interval-by-interval basis; and
- will always have to charge VAT on the sale (by him or a person connected to him) of the property.

9.3.4.9 Capital Goods Scheme—interaction with sales and lettings

Sales

At the time of sale, the first issue to be addressed from a VAT perspective is whether or not the sale is taxable. If the sale is taxable (see earlier) then the vendor should review his CGS position for that property as he may be entitled to an additional deduction.

Example

Minx Limited incurs €400,000 VAT on the construction of a new building in 2019 but it cannot recover any of the VAT because it is engaged in a wholly exempt business. It continues to use the building for exempt purposes until it sells the building in 2022. This is the first sale following completion and is within five years of that completion, so it is subject to VAT.

At the time of sale, say there are sixteen full intervals left. As the sale is VATable Minx Limited will be obliged to levy VAT at 13.5 per cent on the consideration. However, Minx Limited will also be entitled to a deduction of 17*/20ths of the input VAT (€300,000) under the CGS. It will claim this input VAT at the time of sale of the property.

**16 plus 1 as per the relevant formula in the legislation.*

Where the sale of the property is exempt it is necessary to determine whether or not it is worthwhile for both parties to exercise a joint option for taxation in relation to the sale. Essentially, this will depend on the CGS position of the property together with commercial considerations. VAT incurred on the costs of sale of a taxable sale or an opted sale is recoverable, whereas VAT on the costs of sale is not recoverable when that sale is exempt.

Example

Brush Ltd purchased a building in 2010 and the VAT incurred of €400,000 was recovered in full. Having used the building for taxable purposes since acquiring it, the company sells the building in 2021 for €5m.

The sale is exempt from VAT (more than five years from completion). Brush Ltd and the purchaser now face a choice.

If both parties do not jointly exercise an option for taxation, Brush will incur a VAT cost under the CGS. The VAT cost for Brush is €200,000 (400,000/20 × 10*).

(**The number of years remaining in the VAT life of the property is nine plus one as per the formula stated in legislation.*)

But what of the purchaser? If the purchaser agrees to jointly exercise an option to tax, they will incur VAT of €675,000 (€5m × 13.5 per cent), which may or may not be recoverable by them. If they do not agree, then they do not incur this VAT. The commercial dynamic then becomes clear. Obviously, it should not be assumed that a purchaser will agree to a joint option for taxation even where he has a full deduction entitlement.

Where the purchaser does not have VAT recovery (or restricted recovery) it may be worth agreeing to uplift the price to cover the CGS adjustment cost the vendor will have to pay if the sale is not opted. From the tenant's perspective this could still be a lower cost than incurring VAT on the rents over the lifetime of the letting.

Lettings

The position is similar for landlords when contemplating a letting. Where a letting is exempt from VAT, which is the standard position since 1 July 2008, the landlord will not be entitled to recover VAT incurred on the acquisition, development, and management of the property in question. A landlord must therefore carefully consider the impact of an exempt letting in terms of any CGS adjustment that would arise.

Where a property has not been developed within the previous twenty years its adjustment period has expired and therefore there can be no clawback under the CGS if an exempt letting is granted. Similarly, if a landlord did not incur any VAT on the acquisition of a property, then there would be no CGS adjustment arising should he make an exempt letting (as no VAT has been recovered).

While the decision to opt to tax is the landlord's alone, a landlord must be aware of the impact of opting to tax on his/her tenant. Where a landlord opts to tax then VAT will arise at the standard rate (presently 23%) on the rents. Should a tenant not be in a position to recover all that VAT then this would represent a very significant cost to the tenant and will impact on their willingness to enter a commercial arrangement with the landlord.

9.4 Property held on 1 July 2008—Transitional Rules

9.4.1 INTRODUCTION

As a general principle, any letting or any sale on or after 1 July 2008 will follow the new framework which we examined earlier. There are however a number of exceptions to which specific rules apply (commonly referred to as Transitional Rules). The transactions covered by these specific rules include:

- Lettings involving a property that was subject to a waiver of exemption in place on 1 July 2008.
- A sale of a property that was subject to a waiver of exemption in place on 1 July 2008.
- The surrender and assignment of legacy leases (I.e. leases of ten years or more created pre 1 July 2008).
- A sale of a reversionary interest created when a legacy lease was created.
- The sale of interests in properties acquired pre 1 July 2008 and held on 1 July 2008.

9.4.2 WAIVERS—LETTINGS AND SALES OF PROPERTIES THAT ARE SUBJECT TO A WAIVER OF EXEMPTION IN PLACE ON 1 JULY 2008

9.4.2.1 Introduction

Prior to 1 July 2008 lettings which were for periods of less than ten years were exempt from VAT. A landlord could however waive that exemption. Unlike the present opt to tax system, a person who waived exemption did so with respect to all such lettings and it was therefore a significant decision. While no new waivers are permitted after 1 July 2008, a trader with a waiver in place prior to 1 July 2008 is, subject to the rules in relation to connected persons, permitted to keep that waiver in place.

Where a landlord has a waiver in place it cannot extend to any letting of a property acquired or developed on or after 1 July 2008 (though a waiver can cover a property where the waiver was in place on 18 February 2008 and the property was undergoing development on that date even if completion did not take place until after 1 July 2008).

9.4.2.2 Lettings of 'waived' properties

All new lettings of properties falling within the waiver will be treated under the waiver rules, irrespective of their duration (i.e. the old ten-year rule does not apply, but of course excluding freehold equivalents).

Where a letting is subject to a Waiver of Exemption the opt to tax regime does not apply to that letting; nor is an annual CGS review required.

A landlord may have a portfolio of properties which includes properties held on 1 July 2008 and to which the waiver applies and properties to which the waiver does not apply (which could include for example properties acquired after 1 July 2008 and properties held prior to 1 July 2008 that were subject to legacy leases). It is important to note that the rules applicable to waived properties only apply to the properties held on 1 July 2008 which were the subject of the waiver: any new letting of other properties in the portfolio are subject to the 'normal' rules (i.e. the letting will be exempt and the landlord may opt to tax the letting).

Example

Mike purchased a retail property 'A' in 2006 and has rented it out. Mike waived his exemption and has been charging VAT on the rents. In January 2022 Mike purchased a second retail unit, Unit 'B'. This is an old unit, and he did not incur VAT. In February 2022 Mike finds a new tenant who agrees to rent both unit A (€2,000 per month) and unit B (€1,250 per month). Will Mike have to charge VAT?

Answer: It is necessary to consider each unit separately as each is a separate letting. With respect to Unit A, this property was owned by Mike on 1 July 2008 and was subject to a waiver at that time. Any new letting, including the letting in 2022, is covered by that waiver and therefore VAT at the standard rate applies to this rent. As we will see, Mike could cancel this waiver, in which case the new letting would not be subject to VAT. However, there are consequences to cancelling a waiver, as we shall see.

Unit B was acquired by Mike after 1 July 2008 and so is not covered by the waiver. This letting is exempt from VAT. Mike may opt to tax this letting if he wishes.

Where a waiver is in place, VAT at the standard rate (currently 23%) is applied to the rents as they fall due.

As a general rule, a waiver cannot be extended to a residential letting (the exception being situations where the landlord had a waiver in place as at 2 February 2007 and the property has not been developed since that date).

9.4.2.3 Cancellation of a waiver

A landlord can cancel their waiver should they wish. On cancellation a look-back takes place. Under the look-back any excess must be repaid to the Revenue. This arises if the VAT recovered by the landlord on the acquisition/development relating to properties to which the waiver relates exceeds the VAT paid to the Revenue on the letting.

Important note: The waiver regime is a very different regime to the CGS. The waiver regime considers VAT reclaimed and VAT paid. When the VAT paid equals the amount of VAT reclaimed the waiver can be cancelled without any further cost. The CGS focuses only on the VAT deducted, adjusting the amount recovered up or down in line with the use of the property, interval by interval; there is no credit for VAT charged on the rents.

Specific measures ensure that the CGS does not also apply where this waiver cancellation look-back applies.

In certain instances, a waiver will be cancelled automatically. Section 96(8) of the VCA provides that where a person has a letting in respect of which a waiver is in place, that waiver will be cancelled with immediate effect if the parties are/become connected and the tenant does not have over 90 per cent VAT recovery. However, by way of exception, if the parties can establish that, on the basis of the VAT already charged to the tenant and the VAT to be charged in the future, an amount equivalent to the VAT recovered by the landlord would be charged to the tenant within the first twelve years of the letting, then the waiver can remain in place. To benefit from this exception, the waiver must have been in place prior to 18 February 2008, or the property was owned by the landlord on 18 February 2008 and was 'in the course of development' on that day, or the landlord himself held a long lease (i.e. a lease of ten years or more) granted to him between 18 February 2008 and 30 June 2008 by an unrelated person.

Example

Alba Ltd acquires a building and incurs VAT of €1 million. In January 2004 Alba Ltd puts a six-year short-term letting in place with Bineva Ltd (a related company with only 35 per cent VAT recovery). Between January 2004 and June 2008 Alba Ltd has charged VAT of €300,000 to the tenant.

In July 2008 this waiver of exemption terminates unless the annual VAT charged by Alba Ltd to Bineva Ltd exceeds €77,778:

$$\frac{€1,000,000 - €300,000}{12 - 3}$$

If the annual VAT charged exceeds €77,778 then the waiver may stay in place but if not, it will terminate, triggering an immediate repayment of the difference between the VAT recovered and VAT paid (here €700,000) to Revenue.

Where a particular letting no longer qualifies for the waiver (e.g. it no longer meets the twelve-year test) then there is a deemed cancellation of the waiver in relation to that property and a look-back specific to that particular property takes place. Where the VAT reclaimed exceeds the VAT paid on that property then a payment of the difference must be made to Revenue.

Specific measures were introduced by the Finance Act (No 2), 2008 to address situations where a landlord with a waiver in place and a tenant become members of a VAT group. Essentially a waiver cancellation clawback is triggered when they become members of a VAT group unless the group enjoys at least 90 per cent VAT input deduction entitlement.

9.4.2.4 Sales of waived properties

Great care is needed regarding the sale of a property that is the subject of a waiver of exemption. The starting point is that the standard rules apply to the sale (i.e. sale outside the first five years post completion is not subject to VAT and so on).

The vendor however must make a critical choice. They can first cancel their waiver and then proceed with the sale, or they can sell the property, which is then followed by a cancellation of the waiver.

Critical to this decision is the 'waiver cancellation adjustment'. On cancellation of a waiver the landlord must compare all the input VAT deducted/reclaimed over the lifetime of the waiver with the VAT paid on the rents as a consequence of having the waiver in place. Where the input VAT deducted exceeds the VAT paid on the rents then the deficit must be refunded to the Revenue upon the cancellation of the waiver.

Important note: When a general waiver cancellation adjustment is made, any subsequent sale of that property is not subject to VAT (provided of course it has not been redeveloped in the interim and become subject to the exercise of a joint option for taxation).

Where the sale takes place before the waiver is cancelled and the sale is subject to VAT then the VAT on the sale can be added to the VAT paid on the rents when computing the waiver cancellation adjustment. This may of course eliminate or at least significantly reduce the waiver cancellation adjustment.

When a landlord sells a property that has been the subject of a waiver before they cancel their waiver there is a deemed cancellation of their waiver in relation to the specific property. If the landlord has no remaining properties that have been subject to a waiver, then they are deemed to have fully cancelled their waiver.

Example

TomCo purchased a building in 2006 and incurred VAT of €1m.

TomCo granted a nine-year lease to Tenant A of the entire property and waived exemption. In 2015 TomCo granted a new seven-year lease of the entire building to Tenant B and continued the waiver. The total VAT paid on the rents from both Tenant A and Tenant B is €750,000. The property is presently vacant and TomCo decides to sell the property and has received an offer of €8m.

If TomCo proceeds to sell the building without exercising the joint option to tax, then the sale is exempt from VAT. However, there is an automatic cancellation of its waiver, and a waiver cancellation adjustment arises. TomCo must therefore pay €250,000 (being VAT claimed as a consequence of the waiver €1m - VAT paid on the rents as a consequence of the waiver €750,000).

If TomCo cancels its waiver before the sale, then a similar waiver cancellation adjustment will arise, and the sale is specifically outside the scope of VAT.

If, however, TomCo does not waive exemption prior to the sale and jointly opts to tax the sale then a waiver cancellation payment is avoided. While the sale will trigger a cancellation of the waiver the VAT claimed, that is, €1m, is exceeded by the VAT paid of €1.758m (being €50,000 on rents + €1.08m VAT on the sale), so no clawback arises.

It is also important to note that the waiver cancellation is a completely separate exercise to any adjustment required under the Capital Goods Scheme. Where a sale is exempt and not opted then any consequential CGS adjustment must also be paid. The VAT claimed on those works must be included as input VAT reclaimed in the waiver cancellation adjustment. However, any CGS adjustment that does arise can then be included (as VAT paid) in the waiver cancellation adjustment.

9.4.3 LEGACY LEASES—SURRENDERS AND ASSIGNMENTS OF +10-YEAR LEASES GRANTED PRE-1 JULY 2008

9.4.3.1 Introduction

Section 95 of the VCA contains transitional measures relating to a post-1 July 2008 surrender or assignment of ten years + leases granted pre 1 July 2008. Essentially, specific CGS rules apply to legacy leases. Section 95 provides that these leases are to be regarded as Capital Goods; however, the landlord is relieved from conducting the annual look-back and adjustment generally required under the CGS.

Should the landlord (or tenant) undertake any refurbishment works on the property then those works are subject to all the normal CGS rules.

The CGS adjustment period (i.e. standard number of intervals) for a legacy lease is twenty years or the number of full years remaining in that interest from the date when it was created or last assigned pre 1 July 2008, whichever is the shorter. However, if the property has been developed (which according to the Revenue is to be regarded as meaning developed to completion, that is, it does not apply to development that is refurbishment) since it was acquired then the twenty-year life runs from the date of the most recent development.

In the case of the first assignment or surrender of a legacy lease after 1 July 2008 then the CGS adjustment period is *the number of full years remaining in the adjustment period* ***plus one***:

- The adjustment period where the lease was not previously surrendered or assigned is 20 years from its creation or the number of full years if the lease is for a period of less than 20 years.
- The adjustment period where the lease had been assigned prior to 1 July 2008 is 20 years from that date of assignment or the period remaining in the lease when the assigned occurred if shorter.

In the case of the second or subsequent assignment of a legacy lease after 1 July 2008 the adjustment period is *the number of full years remaining in the adjustment period* ***plus one*** as obtained under the rule in the previous paragraph.

9.4.3.2 VAT treatment—surrenders and assignments of legacy leases

Where the person surrendering or assigning a legacy lease was entitled to deduct input VAT on the acquisition of their interest or development of that property then the assignment or surrender will be subject to VAT.

Where the person surrendering or assigning a legacy lease was not entitled to deduct input VAT on the acquisition of their interest or development of that property then the assignment or surrender is not subject to VAT. In these instances, however, both the vendor and the purchaser can jointly exercise an option for taxation in relation to the surrender or assignment. NOTE: this differs from a landlord's option to tax a letting in that *both* the existing tenant and the landlord/new tenant as the case may be must jointly agree to exercise the option for taxation. Also, the landlord's option to tax relates to a supply of a service whereas the joint option for taxation relates to a supply of goods.

Section 95(8)(a) of the VCA dictates the amount on which VAT must be levied in relation to surrenders or assignments of legacy leases that are subject to VAT including those where a joint option for taxation has been exercised. The taxable amount is based on a formula as follows:

$$\frac{T \times N}{Y}$$

Where T = the total tax incurred on his acquisition of the lease by the existing tenant making the surrender/assignment

N = the number of full intervals plus one remaining in the adjustment period (see comments above)

Y = the total number of intervals in the adjustment period.

Example

Berga Limited took a twenty-five-year lease in a warehouse unit on 1 July 2003 and VAT of €450,000 was incurred on the lease. On 1 October 2009 Berga Limited agreed to assign the lease to Bria Limited.

T = €450,000

N = Number of full intervals plus *one* = 13 + 1 = 14 (the adjustment period is 20 years, there are 6 years and 3 months expired leaving 13 years and 9 months in the adjustment period).

Y = 20 (note while the lease is a 25-year lease the adjustment period is capped at 20 years).

VAT arising on the assignment = 450,000 × 14/20 = €315,000.

9.4.3.3 Accounting for VAT on the surrender/assignment of legacy leases

The provisions of VCA s. 95(8) apply to these surrenders and assignments. As a consequence, where the recipient (landlord or new tenant as the case may be) is an accountable person, a Department of State, or a Local Authority, or a person engaged in exempt lettings, then a reverse charge applies in relation to the VAT arising on the supply. This means the existing tenant does not levy the VAT; instead the recipient is obliged to self-account for the VAT. If the recipient is not already registered for VAT, he would be obliged to register for VAT and report the reverse charge. In terms of potential VAT clauses this is an important point as it is essential to be aware of who has the responsibility to report the VAT and to provide accordingly.

Where VCA s. 95(8) applies there is also a requirement to hand over a document (this is not a VAT invoice). The document must stipulate the VAT value of the interest being surrendered or assigned, the amount of VAT arising, and the number of intervals remaining in the adjustment period (VAT life).

Taking the example above and assuming a VAT rate of 13.5 per cent, this would be:

Value = €2,333,334 and

VAT = €315,000 and

Adjustment Period = 14

Note: The landlord or new tenant, as the case may be, is regarded as taking on a Capital Good. Their initial interval will be a twelve-month period commencing on the date of the surrender or assignment.

9.4.3.4 Tenant works

A tenant holding a legacy lease may have undertaken works on the property which constitute refurbishment. As a consequence, the tenant will have created a Capital Good with a ten-interval VAT life. The same general rules as outlined earlier will similarly apply to the tenant's Capital Good.

Where the tenant surrenders or assigns a lease in respect of which he holds an unexpired Tenant Works Capital Good, unless the tenant can get the agreement of the landlord (in the case of a surrender) or the new tenant (in the case of an assignment) to step into his shoes and take on the remainder of the Capital Good, then at the time of surrender/assignment an additional VAT liability of the remaining CGS value is triggered. This liability cannot be passed on by the tenant to the landlord or new tenant.

Where the Tenant Works are destroyed then no clawback arises.

Note: The assignment/surrender of the lease and the taking on of a CGS relating to Tenant Works are two separate matters and should be addressed separately.

9.4.3.5 Premium

Where the existing tenant pays a premium to the landlord (in the case of a surrender) or new tenant (in the case of an assignment) it is outside the scope of VAT; any VAT arising is based on the CGS-based formula outlined earlier.

Where the landlord (in the case of a surrender) or the new tenant (in the case of an assignment) pays a premium to the existing tenant it is subject to VAT at the standard rate, currently 23 per cent (as it is regarded as a payment in respect of the tenant giving up his entitlement to the lease).

9.4.4 REVERSIONARY INTERESTS

9.4.4.1 Introduction

We saw earlier that under the Old Rules, when a person created a letting which was for a period of ten years or more (i.e. legacy leases), they were regarded as simultaneously taking a self-supply of the reversionary interest in the property. Here the reversionary interest was essentially the total interest held by the landlord in the property less the letting interest just granted.

From a VAT perspective the reversionary interest was regarded as having passed outside the scope of VAT and therefore any subsequent disposal of that reversionary interest (or part thereof) was not subject to VAT.

9.4.4.2 Sale of a reversionary interest

The New Rules preserve this historic treatment providing the property has not been developed or redeveloped by or on behalf of the landlord. In summary:

- Where the property has not been so developed then the sale of the reversionary interest on or after 1 July 2008 is not subject to VAT.
- Where it has been developed or redeveloped by or on behalf of the landlord then the normal rules apply.

Important Note

This rule only applies to reversionary interests created on the granting of a legacy lease pre 1 July 2008. It does apply for example apply to the sale of a reversion interest created when a twenty-year lease was granted in, say, 2015.

9.4.5 SALES OF INTERESTS HELD ON 1 JULY 2008

VCA s. 95 deals with the transitional measures which have been introduced to deal with interests in properties acquired pre 1 July 2008 and held on 1 July 2008 ('Interests' include freehold interests and what were commonly referred to as legacy leases, which we examined earlier).

Where a property was incomplete on 1 July 2008 then the new rules apply when that property is sold post 1 July 2008.

Important note: s 95 contains specific provisions and therefore where a particular transaction does not fall within its remit the general rules as detailed in s. 94 then apply.

VCA s. 95(3) provides that in relation to freehold and freehold equivalent interests the following applies:

- Where the vendor was not entitled to deduct any VAT on the acquisition and/or development of the property prior to 1 July 2008 and there has been no development of that property on or after 1 July 2008, the sale is *not* subject to VAT.
- Where the vendor was not entitled to deduct any VAT on the acquisition and/or development of the property prior to 1 July 2008 and there has been development of that property on or after 1 July 2008 but that development is minor, the sale is *not* subject to VAT.
- Where the transaction is not subject to VAT a joint option for taxation can be exercised. In relation to a joint option for taxation:
  - the agreement must be in writing;
  - it must be entered into no later than the fifteenth day of the month following the month in which the supply occurs;
  - the purchaser becomes the accountable person, that is, the supplier does not charge the VAT; rather, the purchaser self-accounts (i.e. charges the VAT to itself) under a reverse charge.

From the above, where the vendor was entitled to an input deduction, the specific measures of s. 95 do not apply and so the new general rules detailed in s. 94 do, meaning the first sale of a new or transformed (i.e. development works that have rendered it new) building within the first five years from completion will be subject to VAT. VAT at the reduced rate applies, currently 13.5 per cent, while the second or subsequent sale of a new or transformed building within the first five years following completion will also be subject to VAT unless the property has been occupied for a period of twenty-four months in that period.

Example

Colco Ltd built a new retail unit in 2007 at a cost of €1m plus VAT. The work was complete in June 2007 and Colco Ltd opened for business on 1 July 2007. In December 2011 the company is being wound up and it agrees to sell the unit for €750k plus VAT. Is the sale subject to VAT?

The property was held on 1 July 2008 and is therefore a transitional property. As Colco Ltd would have been entitled to recover VAT on the build cost, the new rules apply. Given that this is the first sale since completion and is within five years thereof, the sale is subject to VAT.

If the sale was delayed to 30 July 2012, then it would be outside the five-year window and would be exempt. Vendor and purchaser may, however, jointly exercise an option for taxation in relation to the sale.

The special provisions of s. 94(3) apply to transitional properties also, so where a person supplies a transitional property to a person and in connection with that supply enters into an agreement with that person or somebody connected with that person to carry out a development of those goods then the sale is subject to VAT.

9.4.6 CAPITAL GOODS SCHEME—TRANSITIONAL PROPERTIES

Transitional properties (their development and subsequent work thereon) are capital goods for the purposes of the CGS, that is, they have a VAT life; however, certain of the obligations under the CGS are set aside and certain specific measures are applied. These variations to the general rules can be summarised as follows:

- The adjustment period for freehold and freehold equivalent interests held on 1 July 2008 is a period of twenty years from the acquisition of that interest. Where the property has been developed post acquisition but prior to 1 July 2008 then the adjustment period is twenty years from the most recent development.
- There is no requirement to conduct the annual review normally required (but any development/refurbishment post 1 July 2008 would be subject to the normal CGS rules).
- If on or after 23 February 2010 a transitional property is used for the first time or there is a change of use in the property of more than 50 percentage points, the 'big swing' adjustment will apply.
- Where the person makes an exempt letting of a transitional property, they are required to make a deductibility adjustment (s 95(4)(a) refers): see **16.19.4.9** regarding deductibility adjustments.
- There is no requirement to make a CGS adjustment (a deductibility adjustment arises instead) where the person exercises an option to tax or terminates an option to tax in respect of a letting of that property (but see **16.19.4.9**).
- Where a transitional property is sold within its adjustment period the CGS *must* be considered. Where the sale is within the adjustment period applicable to the property then:
  - where a sale is exempt from VAT the vendor may incur a VAT payment adjustment under the CGS;
  - where a sale is taxable the vendor will preserve his deduction entitlement, and where he was entitled to recover less than 100 per cent, he would be entitled to an additional deduction under the CGS.

9.5 Specific Transactions

9.5.1 LETTINGS AND SALES BY MORTGAGEE IN POSSESSION, LIQUIDATOR, OR RECEIVER

When a MIP, liquidator, or receiver is appointed, the defaulter must furnish the MIP, liquidator, or receiver with the Capital Goods Record for the property. The MIP, liquidator, or receiver is treated as the Capital Goods Owner and is responsible for all obligations of the defaulter under the CGS. Therefore, if the property is sold by the MIP, liquidator, or receiver then:

- If the property is 'new' and therefore subject to VAT, the MIP, liquidator, or receiver must levy the VAT and report that VAT to the Revenue.
- If the property is 'old' and the sale is exempt and the exempt sale gives rise to a clawback of VAT under the CGS, the MIP, liquidator, or receiver must pay the amount due to the Revenue.
- If the property is old, the MIP, liquidator, or receiver may enter a joint option to tax.

Where an MIP, liquidator, or receiver lets a property they can exercise the landlord's option to tax in respect of the letting. Where an MIP, liquidator, or receiver takes possession of a property which is subject to lettings, the MIP, liquidator, or receiver is entitled to the rents and is obliged to account for VAT on the rents if the letting is taxable.

9.5.2 RENT TO BUY

These are schemes whereby potential purchasers are attracted by initial periods of renting. It should be noted that as the conditions of these schemes can vary significantly, each should be examined on their own merits. Commonly, however, they feature:

- An upfront payment.
- The prospective purchaser renting the property for a defined period of time.
- At the end of the rental period, they can exercise an option to purchase the property at an agreed price or walk away.
- The final price paid will generally be net of the upfront payment and some or all of the rental payments.

Revenue's Tax and Duty VAT Manual—VAT Immovable Goods Rent to Buy sets out the Revenue's general position regarding Rent to Buy schemes. Essentially, Revenue views these agreements as being a multiple supply, that is, two supplies, being (1) the granting of an option to purchase the property at an agreed price and (2) the granting of a lease (of course, if the occupier decides to exercise the option there will also be a sale). The consideration for these supplies must therefore be apportioned between these two supplies and is taxed accordingly.

With regard to the option to purchase, the VAT treatment will follow that of the underlying supply (i.e. if the option is granted on undeveloped land, it is exempt from VAT/if the sale of the property would be subject to VAT, then the option is also taxable).

With regard to the letting of the property, the letting of property is exempt from VAT in accordance with paragraph II Schedule 1 to the VAT Act, 1972 (as amended) (now paragraph 11 Schedule 1 VCA). The landlord's option to tax cannot apply to the letting of residential property as per s. 7A(4) VAT Act (now s. 97(4) VCA).

The Revenue regards any upfront payment as a payment in respect of the granting of an option to purchase the property, unless refunded at the end of the scheme. The monthly payments made are regarded as consideration for the letting of the property but where the amount paid exceeds the market rent then any excess is regarded as being in respect of the option. In such cases it is then necessary to split the payment between the rent element (exempt) and the option element (taxable or exempt, as mentioned above).

If the purchaser does not exercise the option to buy there are no further VAT implications in relation to the transaction. If the option to purchase is exercised then generally, as the vendor is the person who developed the property, the sale will be subject to VAT.

9.5.3 PROPERTY DEVELOPERS RENTING OUT RESIDENTIAL PROPERTIES

Where on or after 1 July 2008 a landlord develops residential properties with the intention to sell (i.e. intending to make a taxable supply), the developer is entitled to recover in full the VAT incurred on the development costs as it is incurred. Where, for whatever reason, subsequent to completion of the development the developer decides to let the properties (which will of course be an exempt letting), then the developer must make a CGS adjustment on a yearly basis from the second interval and for each subsequent interval during which the property is let by way of repaying one-twentieth of the input VAT recovered in each of the years in which an adjustment is required. The eventual sale of the property will always be subject to VAT and no CGS adjustment will be made upon sale. This is of cash-flow benefit to the developer.

Where residential properties, built with the intention of sale, were completed prior to 1 July 2008 but were instead let prior to 1 July 2008, then a deductibility adjustment (equal to a full clawback of input VAT) arises upon first letting. The subsequent sale would be liable to VAT and an adjustment made whereby a proportion of the input VAT previously clawed back would become available to the vendor.

In their Tax and Duty VAT Manual—Immovable Goods Property Developers Letting Out Residential Accommodation, the Revenue have indicated that they are prepared to accept in the circumstances set out in their guidance that a property may be regarded as not having been completed until it has been rented. Therefore, where properties have been developed for sale and were completed prior to 1 July 2008 but were first let subsequent to 1 July 2008 Revenue are prepared to accept that completion occurred after 1 July 2008. In such cases the benefit of the annual CGS adjustment becomes available to the developer as opposed to a full deductibility adjustment arising upon first letting.

9.5.4 TRANSFER OF BUSINESS

9.5.4.1 Introduction

VCA contains special measures regarding the Transfer of a Business or part of a business. Essentially, the transfer of goods, intangibles and goodwill as part of a transfer of a business is regarded as outside the scope of VAT. The assets being transferred can include a freehold interest or a leasehold interest in a property. The transfer of a property portfolio may constitute a transfer of a business or part thereof. Similarly, the sale of, say, a freehold interest in a property that is subject to a letting(s) may also constitute a transfer of a business.

9.5.4.2 Sales as part of a transfer of a business

Where ownership of a property transfers as part of a transfer of business the supply is regarded as outside the scope of VAT (s 20(2)(c) applies).

While the sale itself may not be subject to VAT there may be obligations under the CGS to be addressed.

The issue of deductibility of VAT incurred on the costs of the disposal can be complex and care is needed; an entitlement to deduction should not be presumed.

CGS adjustments—transfer in the period the property is regarded as 'new'

Where the property is new (i.e. is being sold within five years of its most recent completion) and where the transferor was entitled to a full deduction, then he has no CGS adjustment to contend with. If, however, he had a prior restricted deduction entitlement he will be entitled to a further deduction under the CGS, as he is regarded as making a taxable sale.

The transferee is regarded as supplying the property to themselves and they must therefore charge themselves VAT, this being the amount of VAT that would have been charged to them if VAT had been charged by the transferor. If their deduction entitlement is less than 100 per cent they must pay over the difference to the Revenue. Clearly, in these situations, the value of the property must be distinguished within the overall consideration being paid for the business.

Example

A Ltd agrees to sell its business (including its business premises) to B Ltd. Assume VAT of €400,000 would have been charged to B Ltd on the supply of the premises but for transfer of business relief.

B Ltd has 50 per cent recovery. B Ltd will be required to pay €200,000 to Revenue (400k @ 50%) at the time of the transfer.

The transferee starts a new twenty-interval CGS (VAT life) from the date of acquisition.

CGS adjustments—transfer in the period the property is not regarded as 'new'

Unlike the previous scenario where the property is outside its 'new' period the transferee is regarded as stepping into the shoes of the transferor. They therefore take on the existing CGS (VAT life) of the property (i.e. if there were, say, eight intervals left when sold, the transferee will take on those remaining eight intervals).

Note: care is always required to establish whether a transaction qualifies for transfer of business or not. Where it does not then the vendor needs to establish whether or not they should charge VAT and if it is an exempt sale the parties need to agree on whether they will jointly opt to tax or not.

9.5.4.3 Transfer of a legacy lease as part of a transfer of business

Where a legacy lease transfers in connection with a transfer of a business and the transferor had an entitlement to deduct VAT incurred on the acquisition or that lease and that transfer, or assignment, would otherwise be taxable in the absence of transfer of business then the transferee steps into the shoes of the transferor. There is no new twenty-year life, and the transferee is liable for CGS obligations for the remainder of the VAT life of the legacy lease CGS.

9.5.4.4 Property transferring under transfer of business and impact on waiver cancellation

A cancellation of an existing waiver may be triggered by the sale of a property that is subject to transfer of business rules (s 96(12)). We saw earlier that the cancellation of a waiver triggers a look-back that may result in a cancellation adjustment having to be paid to Revenue. Where this occurs Revenue will give credit in calculating the cancellation sum as follows:

- Where the sale would have been taxable but for TOB, a credit is given for VAT at reduced rate: currently 13.5 per cent of the sales consideration.
- Where the sale would have been exempt but for TOB, a credit is given for the VAT taken on by the purchaser under the CGS, that is, the liability that would arise for the transferee if the transferee immediately diverted the property to an exempt use.

9.5.4.5 Transfers of let properties and transfer of business rules

The transfer of a let property may be regarded as being a transfer of a business or part thereof. Vacant units may qualify where it was let or partially let on a continuing basis, but the Revenue will not accept that the transfer of a vacant unit that has never been let qualifies. The following is an excerpt from the Revenue's Tax and Duty VAT Manual—Transfer of Business containing a number of very useful examples.

Specific rules applying to transfers of property—Examples

1. *A transfer of an immovable good which is subject to: a. an existing letting agreement b. an agreement to lease, or c. a licence to occupy, comes within TOB provisions, as together those assets are capable of constituting an independent business or undertaking.*
2. *A transfer of an immovable good, of itself, without any additional assets (such as a letting agreement), which together with the immovable good, would constitute an independent undertaking cannot come within TOB, regardless of how the immovable good had been used prior to its transfer.*
3. *The transfer of a let property to the tenant will not be regarded as coming within TOB provisions as the only asset being transferred in those circumstances is the property itself and the transfer of a property without any additional assets, which together with the property would constitute an independent undertaking, cannot come within TOB, regardless of how the property had been used prior to its transfer.*
4. *The transfer of a retail premises together with the stock and fittings used in that retail business falls within the provisions of TOB.*
5. *The transfer of the assets of a letting business which includes property which is part let, part vacant and part undeveloped, by a single vendor in one transaction to a single purchaser, falls within the TOB provisions. The assets in question must however be shown to be assets of the letting business rather than assets of a separate business such as a development business.*

For the purposes of determining if a property is an asset of the letting business it will be necessary to show that the property was to be developed with the intention of being used for the purposes of that letting business. The appropriate CGS treatment should be applied to each property transferred.

6. *Where a number of persons co-own a property which is let, the transfer by one of the co-owners of an interest in the property, whether to another co-owner or to a third party, is treated as falling within the scope of TOB.*
7. *Where an option to acquire an immovable good is purchased the VAT treatment of that option will follow the treatment of the transfer of the immovable good to which the option applies so that, if the transfer of the immovable good falls within the TOB provisions so too will the sale of the option to acquire those immovable goods.*

To note: In the case of a transfer of property consisting of multiple units, the appropriate CGS treatment should be applied to each unit on an individual basis.

9.6 Suggested General Approach to Dealing with VAT and Property Transactions

9.6.1 INTRODUCTION

The rules relating to VAT and property transactions are extensive and complex, containing many standard rules, many exceptions to those standard rules, and indeed exceptions to exceptions. In tackling any VAT on property question we recommend taking the following approach:

1. Establish if the transaction is happening in the course or furtherance of a business. If not, then it is not subject to VAT.

Example

Tom decides to sell his principal private residence. He purchased the house in June 2021 for Euro 450,000 and the sale closes on 1 Dec 2022 for Euro 600,000. Is the sale subject to VAT?

No. Tom is selling his own private residence and is not doing so in the course of a business. The sale is therefore not subject to VAT.

2. Establish if the transaction constitutes a transfer of business or as part of a transfer of business—if it does it will not be subject to VAT, but specific rules and requirements for vendor and purchaser apply.
3. Where the transaction is within the scope of VAT:
    - Identify the type of transaction it is from a VAT perspective—is it a letting or it a sale?
    - Establish the VAT history of the property—the information required will depend on the type of transaction. The responses to the Pre-Contract VAT Enquiries are key.
    - Classify the transaction—use the categories set out in the tables below. Classification will determine whether or not the transaction is taxable and, if it is taxable, who must levy and account for the VAT (as well as the taxable amount and VAT rate).
    - Be aware that specific rules apply where the transaction is:
        - The sale of a reversion interest created when a Legacy Lease was created.
        - The surrender or assignment of a Legacy Lease.
        - The letting of a property that is still subject to a waiver of exemption.
        - The sale of a property that is the subject of a waiver.

- If the transaction is not subject to VAT, then consider:
  - If an opt to tax is possible and, if so, if it should it be exercised (largely this will depend on the CGS consequences where the transaction is exempt or where an opt to tax is exercised).
- Keep in mind there are a number of anti-avoidance measures (including):
  - Special rules where the transactions are between connected persons.
  - A sale that would otherwise not be subject to VAT is deemed taxable when there is an agreement with the purchaser, or someone connected with the purchaser to subsequently develop the property.
  - Where a landlord and a tenant or sub-tenant are/become connected.

9.6.2 TABLE 1—LETTINGS

Standard Rules		
	Description	Treatment
Category 1	Does not amount to a 'letting' from a VAT perspective.	Not subject to the VAT on property rules. Fees charged are taxable at the standard rate (presently 23%).
Category 2	Letting—Freehold equivalent interest (Example: a 99-year lease)	Treated as a sale—see rules applicable to sales.
Category 3	Letting (Other than freehold equivalent or categories 4–7 below)	Exempt—landlord has an option to tax
Rules Applicable to Specific Transactions		
Category 4	Surrender or assignment of a lease created on or after 1 July 2008	Not a VATable event in itself. Care required if a premium, reverse premium, or other payment being made. Specific rules regarding tenant works. Impact on landlord's CGS must be assessed.
Category 5	Surrender or assignment of a legacy lease (lease of ten years or more created prior to 1 July 2008)	Detailed specific rules apply—9.4.3 above.
Category 6	Surrender or assignment of a lease of <10 years created before 1 July 2008	Not a VAT event in itself—care required if a premium, reverse premium, or other payment is being made. Note—the specific rules applicable to legacy leases do not apply to this category.
Category 7	New letting of a 'waived property'	Detailed specific rules apply. Rents on the new letting are subject to VAT at the standard rate. Landlord can cancel their waiver in which case rents are exempt from VAT, but a waiver cancellation payment may arise.

9.6.3 TABLE 2—SALES

Standard Rules		
	Description	Treatment
Category 1A	First sale of a new non-residential property	Sale within five years of completion—Subject to VAT at the reduced rate (presently 13.5%). Sale outside this five-year window—Exempt (joint option to tax may be possible).
Category 1B	First sale of residential property post completion	First sale within five years of completion—subject to VAT at the reduced rate (presently 13.5%). First sale (at any time) by a developer (or person connected to the developer) who was entitled to input VAT deduction on that development—subject to VAT at the reduced rate (presently 13.5%). First sale outside five-year window and not falling within the above rule—Exempt (joint option to tax may be possible).
Category 2A	Second or subsequent sale or non-residential property within five years of completion	Subject to VAT (unless it meets the occupancy test in which case it is exempt from VAT).
Category 2B	Second or subsequent sale or residential property	Sale within five years of completion—Subject to VAT (unless it meets the occupancy test in which case it is exempt from VAT). However, a second/third sale at any time by a person connected with the developer who was entitled to input VAT deduction on that development—Subject to VAT at the reduced rate (presently 13.5%).
Category 3	Sale of undeveloped property or property last developed over twenty years ago (see also Category 5)	Not subject to VAT. Possibility of joint option to tax.
Rules Applicable in Specific Circumstances		
Category 4	Sale of reversionary interest created when a legacy lease was created pre-1 July 2008	Not subject to VAT. If however the property has been developed or redeveloped by or on behalf of the landlord then standard rules apply. Other types of reversionary interest are subject to the standard rules.
Category 5	Sale of undeveloped/ otherwise not taxable property where in connection with the sale there is an agreement with the purchaser, or someone connected to the purchaser to subsequently develop the property	Sale deemed to be subject to VAT.

CHAPTER 10

INCOME TAX

10.1 Business Taxation

The following chapters on taxation will give an overview of the principles and concepts that apply to income tax for individuals and partners in a partnership, and to corporation tax and chargeable gains for companies.

Tax is a method of collection of money from persons and corporate entities to pay for services provided by the State. Different rules apply to different types of taxes.

The primary sources of legislation for income tax and corporation tax are the Taxes Consolidation Act 1997 as amended ('TCA 1997'), the Finance Acts, and various statutory instruments. These chapters have been prepared using the Finance Act 2024 and the taxes may have been amended since this date, so the current legislation should always be ascertained and reviewed when addressing and advising on taxation matters.

The government agency responsible for the collection of tax is the Revenue Commissioners. The administration and collection of taxation has been gradually moving online using the Revenue Online Service (ROS) and PAYE Anytime facilities of the Revenue Commissioners. The Revenue Commissioners issue a number of guidance notes and briefings on their interpretation of taxation. Much of this information can be obtained on their website (<www.revenue.ie>).

10.2 An Introduction to Income Tax

Income tax is payable by individuals on annual income (profits and gains of a business and any other sources of income) earned in a tax year.

A tax year runs from 1 January to 31 December.

For an employee, income tax is deducted from salary through the PAYE (Pay as You Earn) system.

Self-employed persons pay their own tax directly to the Revenue Commissioners using the self-assessment system and by filing a Form 11 with the Revenue Commissioners. The self-assessment system applies to self-employed persons and to other persons who receive income from sources where all of the tax cannot be collected under the PAYE system.

Example:

John's main source of income is his job as a mechanic in a local garage but he also has rental income of €15,000 each year from three apartments he bought in 2020.

His Schedule E source income (income from his employment) is subject to PAYE and his employer deducts income tax, the universal social charge, and pay related social insurance (PRSI) at source directly from John's salary.

John must separately declare the Schedule D Case V income (rental income) to Revenue and Revenue will determine whether it will deduct this additional tax from him using the PAYE system by making an adjustment to his tax credits and tax bands. If the rental income is not deducted using the PAYE system John will have to file a tax return and pay the tax directly to Revenue using the self-assessment system and completing a Form 12 (if specifically requested by Revenue) or Form 11 annual tax return. A Form 11 will be required if the net assessable non-PAYE income is in excess of €5000 or the person has total gross income from non-PAYE sources of €30,000 or more.

10.3 Who Must Pay Irish Income Tax?

This depends on whether an individual is resident, ordinarily resident, or domiciled in Ireland. An individual who is resident, ordinarily resident, or domiciled in the State is liable to income tax in respect of his/her total worldwide income.

10.3.1 RESIDENCE

A person is resident for Irish tax purposes if they spend:

(a) 183 days in Ireland in a tax year; or

(b) 280 days over two years (when you count the number of days spent in Ireland in the current and the preceding tax year, if it is 280 or more the person will be resident for the current year—if a person spends less than thirty days in Ireland in a tax year then these days are ignored).

A day, for the residence test, is a day in which the person is in Ireland at any time in a day.

Example:

Anne came to Ireland on 15 December 2023 and left in March 2024. She was not treated as tax resident in Ireland as she had not been present for 183 days in Ireland in either 2023 or 2024. Her time in Ireland in 2023 is ignored as it was for less than thirty days.

If Anne had stayed until 20 March 2025 she would have been tax resident in Ireland in the tax year 2024, as she spent more than 183 days in Ireland in 2024 (365 days). She would also have been tax resident for 2025, as she spent more than 280 days over two years: 365 days in 2024 and 79 days in 2025.

10.3.2 ORDINARILY RESIDENT

An individual who has been resident in Ireland for three consecutive tax years becomes ordinarily resident in Ireland from the beginning of the fourth tax year.

Example:

Mark moved to Ireland in February 2021 and remained here until December 2024. He was tax resident for 2021, 2022, and 2023 and he became ordinarily resident in Ireland in 2024.

An individual who has been ordinarily resident in Ireland ceases to be so at the end of the third consecutive tax year in which he/she is not resident in Ireland.

Example:

Mark left Ireland on 30 December 2024 and returned to New Zealand. He will not cease to be ordinarily resident in Ireland until the tax year 2028 (as he ceases to be tax resident in 2024).

10.3.3 DOMICILE

Domicile is a legal concept. It is generally interpreted as meaning living in a particular country with the intention of residing permanently in that country.

10.3.4 DOUBLE TAXATION

Generally under a tax treaty, where income is taxable in two different states, either an exemption for tax is provided in one State or alternatively the tax paid in one of the states is permitted as a tax credit against tax in the other State.

For the purposes of this chapter it is assumed that the individuals are resident, ordinarily resident, and domiciled in Ireland.

10.4 Tax Rates

Each year in the budget the government announce the tax rates for the next tax year. Currently a tax year runs from 1 January to 31 December. The tax rates for the tax year 1 January to 31 December 2025 are as follows (TCA 1997, s. 15):

(a) For single, widowed, or a surviving civil partner, the first €44,000 of income is taxed at 20 per cent and the balance of income is taxed at 40 per cent.

(b) For single, widowed, or a surviving civil partner qualifying for the single person child carer tax credit, the first €48,000 of income is taxed at 20 per cent and the balance of income is taxed at 40 per cent.

(c) For married or civil partners where one spouse/civil partner only has income, the first €53,000 of income is taxed at 20 per cent and the balance of income is taxed at 40 per cent.

(d) For married or civil partners where both spouses/civil partners have income, the first €53,000 (plus an additional €35,000 maximum or the amount of the second income if less) (i.e. up to €88,000 of income) is taxed at 20 per cent and the balance of income is taxed at 40 per cent.

Examples:

Single—2025

Mary is single and has employment income of €50,000 payable under the PAYE system. Her income tax is as follows (ignoring all tax credits, allowances, and reliefs):

€44,000 * 20% = 8800

€6,000 * 40% = 2400

€50,000 results in €11,200 income tax.

Single and qualify for single person child carer credit in 2025

If Mary had a daughter and qualified for the single person child carer tax credit her income tax is as follows (ignoring all tax credits, allowances, and reliefs):

€48,000 * 20% = 9600

€2,000 * 40% = 800

€50,000 results in €10,400 income tax.

Married one spouse with income in 2025

If Mary was married and she was the only spouse working her income tax is as follows (ignoring all tax credits, allowances, and reliefs):

€50,000 * 20% = 10000

€50,000 results in €10,000 income tax.

Married two spouses with income in 2025

If Mary was married and her spouse Ron also earned €50,000 as a self-employed butcher, their combined income tax is as follows (ignoring all tax credits, allowances, and reliefs), assuming that Ron is assessed for both their incomes:

€88,000 * 20% = 17,600

€12,000 * 40% = 4,800

€100,000 results in €22,400 income tax

10.4.1 EXEMPTIONS FROM INCOME TAX

An exemption from having to pay income tax applies to persons over sixty-five years of age that have total income of less than €18,000 if single or widowed or €36,000 if married/civil partners in 2025. These limits are increased for dependent children.

10.5 Tax Credits

Tax credits are available under tax legislation and can be used to reduce the tax payable by an individual. There are numerous credits dependent on certain circumstances and conditions. Some of these credits are detailed below.

10.5.1 PERSONAL TAX CREDITS FOR 2025

This is a tax credit available to every individual tax resident in Ireland and the level of the credit is based on the civil status of the person—whether the individual is single, widowed, married, or a civil partner.

A single person is entitled to a tax credit of €2000.

Married persons or civil partners who are jointly assessed to tax are entitled to a tax credit of €4000.

A widowed person or surviving civil partner is entitled to a tax credit as follows:

(a) in the year of death of the spouse/civil partner the tax credit is €4000; and

(b) thereafter if no qualifying children the tax credit is €2540.

Various rates apply to a widowed person or surviving civil partner with a qualifying child, with the rates dependent on the year the person was bereaved.

Examples:

Mary is single and is entitled to a tax credit of €2000 as a deduction against her income tax liability.

Mary and Ron are married and jointly assessed to tax and are entitled to a tax credit of €4000 as a deduction against their income tax liability.

Jennifer who lost her husband Michael in June 2025 is entitled to a tax credit of €4000 in 2025 and as she has no children, she will be entitled to a tax credit of €2540 in 2025 and thereafter (subject to .any changes in tax rules or rates).

10.5.2 SINGLE PERSON CHILD CARER TAX CREDIT

An individual is entitled to a single person child carer tax credit of €1900 if the individual is single; a widow or widower; a surviving civil partner; a divorced, separated, or deserted parent, or in a dissolved civil partnership; and the individual is the primary carer and has the custody of a child (which includes a stepchild or an adopted child) and the child resides with the individual for the greater part of a year and the individual maintains the child at his or her own expense.

The child must reside with the claimant for the whole or greater part (more than six months) of the year of assessment. If the child was born in the year of assessment, he or she must reside with the claimant for the greater part of the period from when he or she was born. A child can only be the subject of one claim, and a claimant can only make a claim for one child for a year of assessment irrespective of the number of children that reside with them.

Example:

Mary is single and has a daughter and qualifies for the single person child carer tax credit. Her income for the year is €50,000 and her income tax is as follows (ignoring allowances and reliefs):

€48,000 * 20% = 9600

€2,000 * 40% = 800

€50,000 results in €10,400 income tax.

Less:

Tax credits:

Single:	(2000)
Single person carer credit	(1900)
Net tax	6500

10.5.3 PAYE TAX CREDIT

A PAYE tax credit of €2000 is available for deduction against income that is subject to the PAYE system. If a person has PAYE income of less than €10000 only an amount equivalent to 20 per cent of the actual PAYE income can be deducted as a tax credit.

Example:

Maeve gets a part-time job over the Christmas of 2025 and receives €800 in payment under the PAYE system. The maximum PAYE tax credit that Maeve can claim is €800 * 20% = 160.

If Maeve had employment income of €5000 paid under the PAYE system she will be entitled to a PAYE credit of 1000 (5000 * 20% = 1000).

If Maeve had employment income of €15,000 paid under the PAYE system she will be entitled to a PAYE credit of 2000 (maximum).

Example:

Mary is single, earns €50,000 (subject to PAYE) in 2025, and has a daughter and qualifies for the single person child carer tax credit. Her income tax is as follows:

€48,000 * 20% = 9600

€2000 * 40% = 800

€50,000 results in €10,400 income tax.

Less:

Tax credits:

Single:	(2000)
PAYE	(2000)
Single person carer credit	(1900)
Net tax	4500

There are restrictions and conditions on a spouse, civil partner, or child obtaining the PAYE credit when the income is paid by the spouse, civil partner, or parent, or a partnership of the spouse or parent.

10.5.4 EARNED INCOME TAX CREDIT

An earned income tax credit of €2000 is available for deduction against trade income under Schedule D Case I or II. To claim the full tax credit trade income must be €10000. For income below that level the earned income tax credit is 20 per cent of the earned income.

The maximum tax credit between the PAYE tax credit and the earned income tax credit is €2000 if a person also has income subject to PAYE.

10.5.5 PENSION CONTRIBUTIONS

Tax relief is available, currently against the highest rate of tax payable by a person, for payments into a pension. The relief is based on the age of the taxpayer and is capped at a percentage of a person's net relevant earnings (employment income or self-employed earnings after deduction of losses and capital allowances). There is an overall limit/cap on net relevant earnings of €115,000 that can be used when calculating the tax relief.

Age	% of Net Relevant Earnings
Up to 30	15%
30 up to 40	20%
40 up to 50	25%
50 up to 55	30%
55 up to 60	35%
60 and upwards	40%

Example:

John is a forty-five-year old self-employed dentist who has earnings of €225,000 and has paid €60,000 into his pension fund in 2025. He can claim tax relief on 25 per cent of €115,000 = €28,750. He will get tax relief of €11,500 on the pension payment (€28,750 * 40%) in 2025.

10.5.6 PROFESSIONAL SERVICES

Income tax at the standard rate (currently 20%) is deducted from payments made for professional, services by government departments, State bodies, local authorities, and other specified bodies (TCA 1997, sections 520–529). Legal services provided by solicitors are professional services and tax is deducted, known as professional services withholding tax (PSWT), when an invoice is being paid. A credit for the tax deducted is given against the income tax liability of the year in which PSWT is deducted. In certain hardship circumstances a refund of the PSWT may apply.

10.5.7 OTHER TAX RELIEFS

Other tax reliefs include:

(a) Medical insurance premiums

(b) Tax relief on films

(c) Tax relief for loan interest

(d) Medical expenses.

10.6 Types of Income

Different tax rules apply depending on the type of income and how the income is earned. Different types of income are divided into different schedules, and within Schedule D into different classes. This chapter will primarily focus on Schedule D and Schedule E income when discussing income tax.

10.6.1 SCHEDULE D

Schedule D covers income tax and sources of income are divided into a number of classes:

(a) Case I—trade income;

(b) Case II—income from a profession;

(c) Case III—discounts, interest, annual payments (excluding deposit interest received under a deduction of tax (which is taxed under Case IV)), dividends on credit union regular share accounts (special share accounts are taxed under Case IV), and income from foreign securities and possessions that do not suffer Irish tax at source, for example foreign rental income dividends and interest, foreign employment;

(d) Case IV—annual profits or gains not falling into another category as well as shares issued instead of dividends and interest subject to deposit interest retention tax (DIRT) from financial institutions; and

(e) Case V—rental income within the State.

For the purposes of this chapter Schedule D Cases I and II will be dealt with together and will be called income from a business.

10.6.2 SCHEDULE E

Schedule E covers income received from employment and most people will be familiar with this tax if they have ever been an employee. It covers payments received from the employer—for example salary, cash bonus—and benefits in kind, for example payment of health insurance for the employee and occupational pensions. The employer deducts income tax, PRSI, and the Universal Social Charge from the salary payment and pays it directly to the Revenue Commissioners, and the balance remaining is paid to the employee. Details of the deductions are set out in the payslip. Each year the Revenue issues a statement of tax credits for each individual and employers are informed of the tax bands and tax credits applicable to employees to facilitate the deduction of the correct tax. Most employees pay tax by deduction under the PAYE scheme, where the tax is deducted by the employer from the salary payable to the employee.

10.6.3 SCHEDULE F

Schedule F covers Irish dividend income from an Irish company received by an Irish individual or partnership. See Corporation Tax chapter elsewhere in this book.

10.7 Deposit Interest & Deposit Interest Retention Tax (DIRT) (Scheduled D Case IV)

For the tax year 2025 the rate of DIRT was 33 per cent.

Generally, a financial institution is obliged to deduct DIRT from any interest paid on a deposit account and the saver receives the net interest amount. For taxation purposes the person is taxed on the gross income and can claim a credit for the DIRT deducted against the income tax on the deposit interest.

The deduction of DIRT satisfies the income tax liability of an individual for the income tax payable on the interest received.

Deposit interest that is subject to DIRT is exempt from the Universal Social Charge (USC) and it is therefore necessary to exclude deposit interest subject to DIRT when calculating the USC charge. However, gross interest must be included when calculating a person's reckonable income that is used to calculate the amount of PRSI that an individual must pay.

Example:

Emer has been saving to purchase her own home and has a deposit account with a bank in Ireland in 2025 on which she has received net interest of €8000 as the bank has deducted DIRT of 33 per cent on her gross interest.

For income tax purposes Emer will pay tax on the gross interest received under Schedule D Case IV. The DIRT must be added back to the net interest to calculate the tax payable and Emer will receive a credit for the DIRT amount.

€8000 = 67% so €11,940.30 is the gross amount. DIRT is €3940.30.

Companies can open a deposit account and receive interest payments without deduction of DIRT.

An exemption from DIRT applies to (i) an individual (or his spouse or civil partner) aged sixty-five or over where their total income does not exceed the income tax exemption limit (total income of less than €18,000 if single or widowed or €36,000 if married/civil partners plus an additional amount for dependent children) or (ii) if permanently incapacitated due to a physical or mental disability, (iii) payment under the Mother and Baby Institutions Payment Scheme. A declaration to confirm eligibility for the exemption must be made to the financial institution.

Example:

Income Tax for Married Couples—PAYE Income and Deposit Interest in 2025.

In addition to the net deposit interest of €8000, Emer has PAYE income of €50,000. She is married and her spouse also works and has PAYE income of €60,000. Emer is jointly assessed for income tax purposes. Assume €22,000 tax has been deducted under PAYE. For the tax year 2025, what is their income tax liability?

Steps:

1. Identify the different sources of income.
2. Identify the relevant tax bands and rates of tax.
3. Ascertain if any tax credits are available.
4. Ascertain if any losses are available.
5. Ascertain if any reliefs or allowances are available.

Sources of income 2025:

Schedule D Case IV—deposit interest

€8,000 = 67% so €11,940.30 is the gross amount. DIRT is €3940.30 (33%).

Schedule E – employment income

PAYE income €50,000 – self

PAYE income €60,000 – spouse

Total €110,000.

Total income:

€11,940.30	Schedule D Case IV	pay tax on gross income
€110,000	Schedule E	
€121,940.30	Total income	

Relevant Tax Band:

Married – 2 incomes – tax year 2025.

For married or civil partners where both spouses/civil partners have income, the first €53,000 (plus an additional €35,000 maximum or the amount of the second income if less) (i.e. up to €88,000 of income) is taxed at 20 per cent and the balance of income is taxed at 40 per cent.

€88,000 * 20%, balance at 40%, Deposit Interest at 33%.

Tax credits available

Married couple	€4000
PAYE self	€2000
PAYE spouse	€2000

Losses – no information

Reliefs/allowances – no information

Tax calculation

Total income:	€121,940.30
Taxed as follows:	
€88,000 * 20%	17,600
€11,940.30* 33%	3940.30
22,000 * 40%	8,800
Total:	€30,340.30

Less Tax credits:	
Personal credit	€4000
PAYE self	€2000
PAYE spouse	€2000
	€8000
	€22,340.30
Less DIRT paid	(€3940.30)
Less PAYE paid	(€22,000.00)
Net income tax payable/refund	(€3600)

10.8 Rental Income—Schedule D Case V

In calculating the amount of rental income liable to income tax, certain deductions and expenses are permitted to be deducted from the rental income. Deductions can include any rent paid on the property (the property could be sub-let); any rates payable, goods and services provided to the tenant, maintenance costs, repairs, insurance, capital allowances on fixtures and fittings (at a rate of 12.5 per cent) and interest on money borrowed to purchase, improve, or replace property if the property has been registered with the Residential Tenancies Board.

Example:

James has invested in two houses and he rents them out to professionals each year. He took out mortgages to pay for the houses and he pays mortgage repayments totalling €30,000 each year, of which €10,000 relates to interest on the mortgages. He received rental income of €15,000 in 2025. He spent €3000 maintaining the houses.

He will be able to claim a deduction of €3000 in expenses and €10,000 for the interest payment from the income of €15,000, leaving him with a net rental income of €2000 liable to income tax.

10.9 Income from a Business—Schedule D Cases I and II

Schedule D Case I and II relate to the rules on the taxation of the income that arises on a trade/profession (a business).

A person is taxed based on the annual accounts of the business. The annual accounts in the tax year are used and the date of the annual accounts does not matter for an ongoing business: tax is paid on accounts of twelve months ending in a tax year—for example a year ended 31 March, 30 June, 30 September, 31 December or any other date can be used. Special rules apply on the commencement and cessation of a business (see below).

Tax on other income is based on the income earned in a tax year (1 January to 31 December).

Taxable profits are the business turnover (gross income/sales excluding VAT if VAT registered) less deductible allowable business expenses that are used wholly and exclusively for the business.

10.9.1 PERMITTED DEDUCTIONS AND ADD BACKS

Day to day running costs and expenditure and business expenses incurred in making a profit are deductible subject to certain rules. Examples of deductible expenses include light and heat, telephone, broadband, mobile charges, rent, and accountancy fees.

Pre-trading expenses incurred in the three-year period prior to commencing business are deductible when calculating the business income. They are treated as having been incurred when the business commences.

A claim cannot be made for private expenses—these are expenses not used wholly and exclusively for the business, any personal expenses, and business entertainment expenses. Only certain food and subsistence expenses are allowable. Where expenses relate to both business and private use the amount must be apportioned to exclude the private use.

Capital expenditure is not deductible but instead a capital allowance may be available (see **10.9.4.2**).

Claims can only be made for expenses actually incurred and for which receipts have been retained.

Example:

Aidan is a self-employed software designer. He operates out of an office in his home. He cannot claim a deduction for all of his heating and electricity bills. He will need to apportion the bills between private (home) usage and his office (business) usage.

He cannot seek a deduction for his daily lunch when he is working out of his home office. He may be able to seek a deduction for his food expenses if he is away from the office working on site for a client.

10.9.2 DRAWINGS—HOW CAN A SELF-EMPLOYED PERSON GET MONEY OUT OF THE BUSINESS

An individual pays tax on the net profits of the business without taking account of any drawings removed by the owner from the business.

Drawings cover all payments and items taken by the owner from the business—this would include any salary, bonus, cash, or stock withdrawals.

Drawings are not valid deductions from the income of the business for taxation purposes and must be added back to the profits to calculate the taxable profits of the business.

Drawings are treated as a withdrawal of capital from the business and the drawings will be recorded in the balance sheet of the business.

10.9.3 CALCULATING TAX ON SCHEDULE D CASE I AND II INCOME

It is necessary to start with the net profit figure in the financial accounts of the business—the profit and loss account for a twelve-month period ending in the tax year (see **10.10.1** and **10.10.2** for special rules on commencement or cessation of a business).

The business expenses should be reviewed to ascertain if all of them are deductible for tax purposes.

If the accounts have made a deduction for depreciation then this deduction will not be allowed for tax purposes and this expense will need to be added back to ascertain the taxable profits. A person may be able to make a claim for capital allowances instead (see **10.9.4.2**).

If the accounts have made a deduction for drawings then this deduction will not be allowed for tax purposes and the drawings will need to be added back to ascertain the taxable profits.

10.9.3.1 Steps

1. Identify the different sources of income.
2. Adjust income for tax purposes if necessary.
   - (a) Are all expenses deductible?
   - (b) Check for depreciation
   - (c) Check for drawings

3. Identify the relevant tax bands and rates of tax.
4. Ascertain if any tax credits are available.
5. Ascertain if any losses are available.
6. Ascertain if any reliefs or allowances are available.

Example:

Aidan has made a net profit for the year ended 30 September 2025 of €25,000, having taken a salary of €2000 each month from his software business. Calculate his income tax liability on the basis that he has no other source of income and he is single, aged twenty-five.

Steps:

1. Identify the different sources of income—Schedule D Case I only.
2. Adjust income for tax purposes—€24,000 taken by way of drawings.
3. Identify the relevant tax bands and rates of tax—single: €44,000 * 20 per cent, balance at 40 per cent.
4. Ascertain if any tax credits are available—single €2000 and earned income credit.
5. Ascertain if any losses are available—none.
6. Ascertain if any reliefs or allowances are available—no information.

Schedule D Case I

Net profit:

25,000

24,000 add back drawings (2,000 * 12)

49,000 adjusted profits for tax purposes

Taxed as follows:

44,000 * 20%	8800
5,000 * 40%	2000
49,000	10,800

Less Tax credit

Personal	2000
Earned Income	2000
Net tax payable	€6800

10.9.4 DEPRECIATION VERSUS CAPITAL ALLOWANCES

10.9.4.1 Depreciation

Depreciation is a wear and tear allowance calculated using accounting rules to determine the rate at which an asset should be written down in value over the life of an asset. Different rates of depreciation will apply to different assets, for example a building, a motor vehicle, and computer software: a building will last many years while a motor vehicle or a laptop or software may only have a short life.

Deprecation is not a valid deduction for taxation purposes and any deduction for depreciation must be added back to the net profits of the business to calculate the adjusted profits for taxation purposes.

A capital allowance may instead be claimed against the taxable income if certain conditions are satisfied.

10.9.4.2 Capital allowances

Capital expenditure is expenditure on assets that have a lasting use, for example a photocopier or a new office building.

The full capital expenditure cannot be deducted from the trading profits of the business in the year in which it is acquired. Instead an allowance, called a capital allowance, is deductible.

Capital allowances are calculated on different categories of assets at different rates: for example, at 12.5 per cent each year on the cost of plant and machinery.

There is a maximum cap on the net cost of a motor vehicle for capital allowances purposes. The current cap is €24,000 and whether an allowance is available and the amount of capital allowance is linked to the carbon emission level of the vehicle. There are enhanced allowances for electric vehicles.

When an asset is disposed of a check is done to ascertain if a further allowance is required (a balancing allowance) or whether the taxpayer needs to pay back any capital allowances to the Revenue (a balancing charge).

Example:

Máiread runs a retail shop. In January 2025 she purchased machinery for use in the shop at a cost of €12,000.

Capital allowance is calculated on a straight line basis on plant and machinery at a rate of 12.5 per cent of the net cost of the asset if the asset is used in the business.

Máiread will be able to seek a deduction for capital allowance on the machinery of €12,000 * 12.5% = €1500 in 2025. She will not be entitled to deduct the full €12,000 in 2025.

An accelerated capital allowance, at 100 per cent, can be claimed on certain items.

10.10 Special Rules

10.10.1 COMMENCEMENT OF A BUSINESS

There are special start-up rules for new businesses that must be followed for the first three years in business.

In the first year of business income tax is payable on the profits from the date of commencement of the business until 31 December in that year (s. 66 of the TCA 1997).

In the second year in business the profits to be assessed are those in a set of accounts made up in that tax year for a twelve-month period, for example accounts made up to 31 March, 30 June, 30 September in that tax year, or if there are more than one set of accounts those made up to the latest date, or if no accounts the actual profits from 1 January to 31 December in that tax year.

In the third year and onwards in business the profits liable to income tax are those profits assessed on a set of accounts of twelve months ending in a tax year.

A special relief applies in the third year which allows a person to make a claim to have the third-year profits reduced by any excess profits in year two (the excess profits are calculated as being profits assessed in year two which exceeded the actual profits in year two if calculated on an actual basis from 1 January to 31 December in year two). A claim for the relief must be made in writing by 31 October following the third year of business, that is, on the same date as a paper tax return must be filed.

If the excess profits in year two are greater than the taxable profits in year three any remaining year two excess can be carried forward and used against future profits.

10.10.2 CEASING IN BUSINESS

In the final year, tax is payable on profits from 1 January to the cessation date.

In the previous year, the profit situation is reassessed, and if the actual profits for the year from 1 January to 31 December exceed the profits in the financial year accounts then the actual profits figure must be used to calculate the income tax payable. The onus is on the taxpayer to do this calculation and pay over the revised tax liability.

10.10.3 SHORT-LIVED BUSINESSES

Where a business only lasts three years (i.e. starts and ceases within three tax years) a special provision is available that allows a taxable person to elect that the taxable profits for the three years cannot exceed the actual profits earned in the three years.

10.10.4 CHANGE OF ACCOUNTING YEAR END

If a person changes the accounting year end date this must be notified to the Revenue. A taxpayer is obliged to review the preceding year under s. 65 of the TCA 1997 to ascertain what the profits would have been had the new accounting year end date been used. If the profits using the new date exceed the original profits additional tax must be paid.

10.11 Losses

10.11.1 INCOME FROM A BUSINESS—SCHEDULE D CASE I AND II

A loss incurred in a trade or profession in a current tax year can be used as follows in accordance with sections 381 to 390 of the TCA 1997:

(a) Against **any other income** chargeable to tax in the same year; and

(b) Any remaining unutilised loss can be carried forward and set off against future profits of the **same trade or profession** in the future.

Restrictions on the use of losses to a maximum of €31,750 (or the actual loss if lower) in a year have been introduced since Finance Act 2015 when an individual carries on a trade or profession in a non-active capacity (TCA 1997, sections 381B and 381C).

Examples:

Prior Year Losses

Mark has been in business for many years. He owns two shoe shops but the businesses have been suffering in recent years. He made a loss of €3000 in 2023 and €4000 in 2024 and for 2025 he has made a small profit of €10,000.

Mark can utilise the losses that he made in the business in 2023 and 2024 to reduce his taxable income in 2025, leaving him €3000 liable to income tax (€10,000 - €7000).

Same Year Losses

Ruth runs a craft shop and she is struggling. Luckily she made some property investments in 2016 and she is generating some rental income of €20,000 in 2025 that she is surviving on as her craft shop has made a loss of €5000 in the financial year ending 31 October 2025.

Ruth can utilise the loss from her business against the rental income so that only €15,000 of the rental income is liable to income tax.

10.11.2 TERMINAL LOSS RELIEF

In the case of a business that is being shut down and discontinued, special loss rules apply, which are called terminal loss relief rules (TCA 1997, s. 385).

Terminal loss relief can be claimed for losses made in the last twelve-month period of the trade or profession. How the relief works is that there is a look back at the profits made in the business and the losses can be carried back and set against profits made in the business for the three years of assessment prior to the tax year in which the discontinuance occurs.

Example:

Ryan's business has reduced considerably in 2025 as many other stores closed in the shopping centre and he has very few customers. Ryan decides to shut down his business. He has losses of €20,000 for 2025.

He had made small profits in recent years: €4000 in 2024, €6000 in 2023, and €6000 in 2022.

He can claim terminal loss relief and utilise the €20,000 losses against his profits for 2024, 2023, and 2022. He can utilise €16,000 of these losses to eliminate the profits in these years.

10.11.3 LOSSES AND CAPITAL ALLOWANCES—CONNECTION

Capital allowances can be used to create or to increase a loss in a business if there are any capital allowances remaining after they have been set off against any balancing charges in the same tax year.

10.11.4 SCHEDULE D CASE IV

These losses can only be set against other Schedule D Case IV income or carried forward and can only be offset against future Schedule D Case IV income.

10.11.5 SCHEDULE D CASE V

Rental losses on property in the State are carried forward and can be offset only against rental income from property in the State.

10.12 Tax Incentives for Investors

There are a number of tax incentives in place to encourage investment in business and to encourage the formation of business operating through companies. These include:

10.12.1 EMPLOYMENT AND INVESTMENT INCENTIVE (EII)—INCOME TAX RELIEF

A tax relief applies for making investments in certain qualifying companies. A person can get income tax relief for making an investment in certain corporate trades. Relief is available for each individual of up to €500,000 per annum (minimum four-year holding period) if certain conditions are met. Revenue guidance should always be reviewed as this relief is subject to changes.

10.12.2 START-UP CAPITAL INCENTIVE (SCI)

A €500,000 lifetime limit is available for a qualifying company (a micro enterprise) to raise funds from family members and the family members to obtain tax relief on the investment. The shares must be issued within seven years of commencement.

10.12.3 START-UP RELIEF FOR ENTREPRENEURS (SURE)

A special tax relief is available to individuals who start up and work full time in their own company that engages in a qualifying business. The relief applies by enabling the individual to claim back the income tax paid in the previous six years to invest equity by subscribing for shares in the new company. Up to €100,000 can be recovered in the current year and each of the previous six years.

10.12.4 OTHER RELIEFS

Other reliefs include tax relief on investments in films and relief for investment in renewable energy generation.

10.12.5 HIGH INCOME EARNER RESTRICTIONS

Where an individual is held to be a 'high income individual' restrictions are imposed on certain reliefs that the individual can claim.

The purpose of the legislation is to ensure that high income individuals do not use specified reliefs to reduce significantly the amount of tax that they pay and to ensure that tax at an effective rate of 30 per cent is paid in a tax year.

The restrictions apply to a person who has income of €125,000 and receives specified reliefs totalling €80,000. The specified reliefs are set out in legislation.

10.13 Universal Social Charge (USC)

This is a charge payable on gross income (after a deduction for certain capital allowances and losses) before pension contributions.

An exemption from the USC applies in 2025 where an individual's total income for the year does not exceed €13,000. Once this income threshold is reached all of the income is liable to the USC.

Income that is subject to DIRT is not liable to the USC.

Certain Department of Social Protection payments and similar payments paid by other government departments are also exempt from the USC.

The 2025 USC rates are detailed below.

10.13.1 STANDARD RATE

(a) Income up to €12,012	0.5%
(b) Income from €12,012.01 to €27,382 (€15,370)	2%
(c) Income from €27,382.01 to €70,044 (€42,662)	3%
(d) Income above €70,044	8%

10.13.2 SPECIAL REDUCED RATE

A special reduced rate applies for individuals aged seventy years or more and for individuals who hold a full medical card (in each case if their aggregate income for the year is €60,000 or less).

(a) Income up to €12,012	0.5%; and
(b) Income above €12,012	2%.

Regardless of age, persons with non-PAYE income above €100,000 pay an extra 3 per cent surcharge on this income (excluding income subject to PAYE) that exceeds €100,000 in a year. This means that a rate of 11 per cent applies to such income in 2025.

Examples:

Catherine, aged thirty-two, earns €60,000 PAYE income and €2000 gross deposit interest that is subject to DIRT. She does not hold a medical card.

She will have to pay USC on €60,000 calculated as follows:

€12,012 * 0.5% =	60.06
€15,370 * 2% =	307.40
€32,618 * 3% =	978.54
€60,000	€1346

Joan is aged seventy-two and has a pension of €58,000.

She will have to pay USC on €58,000 calculated as follows:

€12,012 * 0.5% =	60.06
€45,988 * 2% =	919.76
€58,000	€979.82

Ciaran is aged fifty-two, earns €160,000 in his own business and has €2000 gross deposit interest that is subject to DIRT.

He will have to pay USC on €160,000 calculated as follows:

€12,012 * 0.5% =	60.06
€15,370 * 2% =	307.40
€42,662* 3% =	1279.86
€29,956* 8% =	2396.48
€60,000 *11% =	6600.00
€160,000	€10,643.80

10.14 Pay Related Social Insurance (PRSI)

PRSI is calculated on an employee's reckonable pay. Reckonable pay is the gross money pay plus notional pay (benefit in kind) if applicable. PRSI applies to all income of a person subject to the exclusions outlined below.

The PRSI contributions for a self-employed person are paid on the person's gross income less capital allowances and allowable pension deductions. Self-employed persons pay PRSI on all sources of income. Trade losses carried forward cannot be deducted against gross income when determining the PRSI payable.

While PRSI is collected by the Revenue, it is administered by the Department of Social Protection.

10.14.1 RATES OF PRSI

The 2025 rates are as follows:

(a) For employees—under Category A1 the current rate is 4.1 per cent increasing to 4.2 per cent on 1 October 2025.

(b) An employee is exempt from PRSI if his income is below €352 per week. If the income is above €352 per week, it is all subject to PRSI. Special rules apply between €352 and €424 per week.

(c) An employer must also make a PRSI payment for his employees: an employer pays at the rate of 8.9 per cent (9 per cent on 1 October 2025) on income up to €527 and 11.15 per cent (11.25 per cent on 1 October 2025) on income above this level.

(d) For self-employed persons the rate is 4.1 per cent for the year 2025 (4.2 per cent on 1 October 2025) with a minimum amount of €650 payable. An exemption applies if total income is less than €5,000.

Example:

Aine is a self-employed hat designer and runs a retail shop selling her hats. She has the following income in 2025:

Income from a retail shop of €40,000

Deposit interest €10,000

Rental income €20,000

Her PRSI liability for 2025 will be €40,000 + €10,000 + €20,000 = €70,000 * 4.1% * 9/12 = €2152.50 plus €70,000 * 4.2% * 3/12 = 735 totalling €2,887.50

10.15 Administration and Payment of Income Tax

10.15.1 TAX REGISTRATION—REGISTERING FOR TAX

A person (including a company) must notify the Revenue Commissioners when he/it has started in business. Registration can be managed through Revenue' eRegistration service using myAccount or ROS.

The form TR1 is the registration form that applies to individuals, partnerships, trusts, or unincorporated bodies to register for income tax, employer's PAYE/PRSI, VAT, and Relevant Contracts Tax.

Information that must be filed in the Form TR1 includes the following:

(a) General details about the individual: name, address, PPS number, gender, nationality, date of birth, contact details.

(b) Business details: business address, business details, legal form, commencement date, accounts details, rental details of premises, and adviser details.

(c) Confirmation of registration for income tax purposes.

(d) Details for registration of Value Added Tax (VAT).

(e) Details for registration as an employer for PAYE/PRSI purposes.

(f) Details for registration for Relevant Contracts Tax (RCT) purposes.

The form TR2 is the registration form that applies to companies to register for corporation tax, employer's PAYE/PRSI, VAT, and RCT.

Income tax is the tax payable on the profits of the business.

If a person is to be engaged as an employee of a business, the business must register as an employer, register to operate the PAYE system, and register for PRSI.

A business must also register for VAT if it is a taxable person and in 2025 the annual turnover exceeds €85,000 in relation to the supply of goods or €42,500 in relation to the supply of services. Other rates apply for intra community distance sales and making acquisitions from other EU Member States.

The tax reference for an individual will be the PPS number—Personal Public Service number.

10.15.2 PRELIMINARY TAX

Employees have income tax, PRSI, and USC deducted directly from their salary by their employer. A similar system does not apply for self-employed persons so a different system is used.

Preliminary tax is an estimate of the tax due for the full tax year and must be paid by 31 October (early November, for example 12, 13, or 14 November, if using ROS to pay and file online) in the tax year. Revenue announce the ROS extension deadline each year.

The payment of preliminary tax must include a payment for PRSI and USC.

To avoid paying interest a certain minimum payment must be made:

(a) 90 per cent of the current year final tax liability (e.g. 90% of 2025 tax liability for the tax year 2025); or

(b) 100 per cent of the preceding year's final tax liability (e.g. 100% of 2024 liability); or

(c) 105 per cent of the year predating the preceding year's final tax liability (e.g. 105% of 2023 liability) if you pay by direct debit and the 105 per cent tax liability was not nil.

Example:

How much preliminary tax does Jane have to pay if she estimates that her tax liability for 2025 is €24,000? Her tax liability for 2024 was €30,000 and for 2023 it was €20,000.

Choices:

2025: 24,000 * 90% =	21,600;
2024 30,000 * 100% =	30,000 or
2023 20,000 * 105% =	21,000 and pay by direct debit.

If the 90 per cent formula is used and this estimate becomes incorrect when the final tax is calculated and 90 per cent of the final tax liability is greater than the payment made, the taxpayer will then be ***liable to interest*** (0.0219 per cent per day or part of a day) on the difference between the payment made and the actual final tax liability. The full tax liability also becomes immediately due and payable from the 31 October preliminary tax date.

Example:

Gerry pays €45,000 in preliminary tax for his 2025 income tax liability. This was calculated based on 90 per cent of his 2025 tax liability, which he estimated to be €50,000 (€50,000 * 90% = €45,000). The actual 2025 liability turns out to be €65,000 (90% = €58,500).

This means that he has underpaid the preliminary tax by €13,500.

Interest is due on the underpayment of €13,500 * 0.0219% * number of days from 31 October 2025 until the date the €13,500 plus interest is paid.

The underpayment also triggers the payment of his full 2025 liability as it becomes due and payable from 31 October 2025 and interest will run on the full amount until it is paid.

Some relief is available where the amount is underpaid by less than 5 per cent (or €3175 maximum) and it is paid by 31 December. Also, if the amount underpaid is not more than €635 then interest is not payable as €635 is the permitted margin of error.

It is the taxpayer's responsibility to make the necessary payments and filings under the self-assessment system. The tax payment should be made to the Collector General.

10.15.3 PAY AND FILE SYSTEM—PAYMENT OF TAX AND MAKING A TAX RETURN

A person who has a business and also has PAYE employment income only needs to file one income tax return that covers all sources of income. Proprietary directors and other persons notified by the Revenue are also obliged to file a tax return.

Tax law provides for both civil penalties and criminal sanctions for the failure to make a return or making a false return or claiming allowances and relief to which a person is not entitled. See below.

There is a set date for the payment of income tax and the filing of income tax returns. The 'pay and file' date is 31 October in each tax year.

On 31 October a person liable to the self-assessment system must:

(a) pay preliminary income tax, USC, and PRSI for the current tax year;

(b) file an income tax and CGT tax return (Form 11) for the previous tax year;

(c) pay any balance of income tax, USC, and PRSI from the previous tax year; and

(d) pay in full any CAT on benefits received with a valuation date of before 31 August.

By paying and filing on ROS the date is extended to early November (the date is announced annually by the Revenue).

In the tax year 2025 for an ongoing business:

(a) preliminary tax for the tax year 2025 has to be paid by 31 October 2025;

(b) the tax return for tax year 2024 must be filed by 31 October 2025; and

(c) the balance of the tax due for the tax year 2024 must be paid by 31 October 2025.

By paying and filing on ROS the date is generally extended to early November 2025 (date to be announced).

10.15.4 METHODS OF FILING A TAX RETURN

Taxpayers can file their returns in a paper or electronic format.

10.15.4.1 Revenue Online Service (ROS)

Tax filing can be done electronically, and payment can be made electronically using the Revenue Online Service (ROS) accessible on www.revenue.ie. Certain taxpayers are obliged to make payments to the Revenue and file their tax returns online using the ROS system. The pay and file date is extended as an incentive to those who pay and file using ROS.

10.15.4.2 New business

For a new business extended time is granted for the filing of the first tax return. The tax return for the first year and second year of business can be filed at the same time if the person or his spouse was not carrying on another business in the tax year in which the new business was set up.

10.15.5 LATE FILING OF RETURN—CONSEQUENCES—SURCHARGE

If a person fails to file the tax return by the pay and file date then a surcharge is imposed on the person. The amount of the surcharge depends on the lateness of the return filing date.

If the return is filed within two months of the return filing date (i.e. by 31 December) a surcharge of 5 per cent of the tax up to a maximum of €12,695 is payable in addition to the tax liability for the tax year. If the return is filed more than two months of the return filing date (i.e. after 31 December in the tax year) a surcharge of 10 per cent of the tax up to a maximum of €63,485 is payable in addition to the tax liability for the tax year.

10.15.6 LATE PAYMENT OF TAX—CONSEQUENCES—INTEREST

Interest at a rate of 0.0219 per cent per day or part of a day is imposed if tax is not paid on time and continues to accrue until the tax is paid. Civil and criminal penalties can also arise in the case of a late filing of a return or a failure to file a return.

Example:

Joe, a sole trader, fails to file and pay his income tax liability for the tax year 2024 by the ROS deadline in November 2025. He has trading income of €60,000; he is single, aged thirty two, and has no other source of income. Assume that his total income tax, USC, and PRSI liability is €25,000.

What are the consequences:

a. if he pays by 30 November 2025?
b. if he pays by 13 January 2026?

Surcharge

a. if he pays by 30 November 2025?

   A surcharge of 5 per cent of the tax up to a maximum of €12,695.

   €25,000 * 5% = €1250

b. if he pays by 13 January 2026?

   A surcharge of 10 per cent of the tax up to a maximum of €63,485.

   €25,000 * 10% = €2500

Interest

Interest at a rate of 0.0219% per day or part of a day is payable until the tax is paid.

a. if he pays by 30 November 2025?

   Due 31 October 2025 – paid 30 November 2025

   30 days * 0.0219% * amount not paid

b. if he pays by 13 January 2026?

   Due 31 October 2025 – paid 13 January 2026

   30 + 31 + 13 = 74 days * 0.0219% * amount not paid.

10.15.7 ASSESSMENT

Full self-assessment is required by tax payers when making the tax return filing. A tax payer must include a self-assessment of the tax payable for the tax year in the tax return.

An individual has an option to file a tax return by 31 August in advance of the pay and file date to enable the Revenue to do the self-assessment for the tax payer.

If a taxpayer files electronically using ROS and uses the calculation of liability provided by ROS in the self-assessment, interest or penalties will not apply if the assessment is incorrect due to any error or mistake that might arise from using the ROS calculated assessment figures.

If a person fails to include a tax self-assessment a fixed penalty of €250 will be imposed, and a fixed penalty of €100 will be imposed if a person does not amend a self-assessment when this is necessary.

An assessment will issue from the Revenue after the return has been submitted. If a person is not happy with an assessment (the Revenue decision on the return) he/she can appeal the assessment to the Appeal Commissioners within thirty days of the notice of the assessment.

10.16 Obligations to Keep Records

Every person must keep full and accurate records for tax purposes; this includes records of all businesses from their commencement. The records must be sufficient to enable the taxpayer to make a proper return of income for tax purposes.

The records must include books of accounts that record all purchases and sales of goods and services and all amounts received and all amounts paid out. They should show cash introduced to the business (capital), details of debtors and creditors, and all items of expenditure and drawings from the business.

Supporting records, for example invoices, bank statements, cheque stubs, and receipts, must be retained, as well as records of all drawings—all amounts of cash withdrawn from the business or cheques drawn on the business bank account for personal use.

The business prepares its financial statements based on its profit and loss account and balance sheet.

Records must be retained for at least six years.

Failure to keep proper records is an offence with a risk of a fine or imprisonment.

10.17 Expression of Doubt

If a person is unsure about a tax matter when filing a tax return a person may express doubt provided that the return is submitted on time (i.e. by the return filing date for the tax year or if a company for the accounting period involved). The doubt over the tax treatment of the income must be genuine, having checked the tax legislation and guidance notes issued by Revenue. If Revenue rejects an expression of doubt a person can appeal that decision.

If the doubt is genuine and Revenue decides to treat the income in a different manner to the manner in which the taxpayer treated the matter, a person will not be penalised, as he has pointed out the doubt to Revenue.

10.18 Anti-Avoidance

There are extensive anti-avoidance rules provided for in legislation in Ireland to prevent persons taking certain steps or participating in certain transactions to minimise or avoid paying tax.

10.19 Revenue Powers

Revenue has extensive powers to enforce tax legislation, including:

(a) to carry out inspections;

(b) to request information from taxpayers and from third parties;

(c) to enter premises;

(d) to make enquiries and ask questions;

(e) to carry out investigations; and

(f) to carry out audits—to verify returns, income, and entitlement to tax credits, reliefs, and allowances.

10.20 Penalties

Both civil penalties and criminal sanctions can be imposed for:

(a) the failure to make a return;

(b) the making of a false return;

(c) facilitating the making of a false return; or

(d) claiming tax credits, allowances, or reliefs which are not due.

In addition, various penalties are imposed by the Revenue based on when the failure or incorrect return is notified to the Revenue, and whether it is a voluntary disclosure, an unprompted, or a prompted qualifying disclosure (where the disclosure is made after Revenue notify a taxpayer that an audit is to be carried out). Mitigation of penalties may apply where a taxpayer co-operates with Revenue and also are based on what caused an incorrect return to be filed—was it deliberate behaviour or was it carelessness? The penalties also are determined by the number of notifications a taxpayer has had to make to the Revenue—it is a one-off or has the taxpayer a history of having to make disclosures?

10.21 Taxation of a Partnership

For taxation purposes a partnership is not treated as a separate person that must pay tax. The partnership is not a separate legal entity.

The rules governing the taxation of partnerships are set out in the Taxes Consolidation Act 1997 (TCA 1997) as amended and the various Finance Acts. References in this chapter to legislation are to the TCA 1997 unless otherwise indicated.

10.21.1 INCOME TAX

For taxation purposes the partnership prepares its own business accounts—a profit and loss account and a balance sheet for the business of the partnership using the income tax rules as they apply to individuals.

Partnership income is calculated as if the partnership is a separate business.

Expenses incurred wholly and exclusively in operating the partnership trade are deductible business expenses.

The net profit of the partnership is calculated and is then divided between the partners in accordance with whatever profit-sharing agreement the partners have made.

Each partner's tax liability will be calculated using the income tax rules outlined in the income tax chapter with the share of the profit of the partnership treated as a separate (several) trade of the individual and this separate trade will be included in the self-assessment return (Form 11) of each partner as Schedule D Case I or II income.

The assets of the partnership are treated as the assets of the individual partners apportioned in the same manner as the profit share of the partnership.

10.21.2 CAPITAL ALLOWANCES

A partner is entitled to his/her share of the capital allowances attributable to the partnership trade and is liable to tax on his/her share of the partnership's balancing charges (if any) for each year of assessment in which he/she is a partner.

Capital allowances are calculated for the partnership and then allocated to each partner. The appropriate share of the allowances is the amount computed in accordance with the profit-sharing ratio included in the partnership agreement for the tax year.

The separate trade for a partner commences when the partnership commences to trade (or the partner joins an existing partnership) and ceases when a person ceases to be a partner in the partnership or the partnership ceases to carry on a trade. The commencement and cessation rules outlined in the income tax chapter will apply to this several trade.

10.21.3 LOSSES

Losses are allocated to the partners in accordance with the agreed profit/loss share arrangement in the partnership agreement. Each partner is responsible for claiming the loss relief appropriate to his own personal circumstances and may make his/her own decision as to the form of the loss relief claim of his/her several trade. Terminal loss relief may be available on cessation of the partnership as a severable trade.

10.21.4 DRAWINGS

Any drawings or salary of a partner deducted by the partnership in calculating its net profit must be added back as the partners will be taxed on the net profit of the partnership without a deduction for drawings (which would include partnership salaries).

A partner is taxed on his/her share of the net profit of the partnership and not on any drawings taken from the partnership or on a partner's salary.

Any drawings or salary taken from the partnership is treated as a removal of capital from the partnership and is not an income deduction but a capital deduction that should be reflected in the balance sheet of the partnership and the capital accounts of the partnership.

Example:

Adam, Barry, and Caroline are partners in ABC partnership and each took drawings from the partnership of €10,000 in 2025. The net profit of the partnership after deducting the drawings was €60,000.

Calculate Caroline's share of the partnership profits. Under the partnership agreement Caroline is entitled to 30 per cent of the partnership profits.

Partnership profits	60,000
Add back drawings	30,000
Adjusted profits	90,000

Caroline's share of partnership profits is €90,000 * 30% = €27,000.

10.21.5 RETURN

The partnership must file a partnership tax return—a Form 1 (firms) providing details of the accounts of the partnership. The individual partners do not then need to file extracts from the same accounts in the Form 11 that each partner must file.

The precedent partner is required to make the partnership's return of income before the relevant income tax pay and file deadline for that year (31 October). This is a return of information as no income tax is payable by the partnership.

10.21.6 EXAMPLES

Example 1:

John is a partner with Marie and Amy and together they operate a dental practice as a partnership. The partnership agreement provides that the income of the partnership is to be allocated as follows: Marie (40%), Amy (30%), John (30%). The net profits of the partnership for 2025 are €90,000.

John also has rental income of €8000 from which he had to pay €3000 in maintaining the property.

John is single and has no PAYE income.

Calculate John's tax liability.

Schedule D Case I

Share of the partnership income is treated as a several trade and John is taxed on such income under Schedule D Case I—as a separate business:

€90,000 adjusted net profits of the partnership.

John's share under partnership agreement = 30 per cent so his income is €27,000.

Several trade €27,000.

Schedule D Case V—rental interest

8000	income
(3000)	expenses
5000	net income

Total Income:

27,000

5000

32,000

Income Tax:

32,000 @ 20% = 6400

Less Tax Credits

Personal	2000
Earned Income	2000
Net	2400

PRSI

32,000 * 4.1% * 9/12	984.00
32,000 * 4.2% * 3/12	336.00
	1320

USC

First 12,012 * 0.5% = 60.06

Next 15,370 * 2% = 307.40

Balance 4618 * 3% = 138.54

USC total	506
Total payable	€4226

Example 2:

Profit and Loss account of ARC Partnership as at 31/8/2025

Sales	800,000
Cost of Sales	(450,000)
Gross Profit	350,000
Expenses	(200,000)
Profit before tax	150,000

The expenses include depreciation of €50,000 on plant and machinery that was calculated at 20 per cent of the initial cost of €250,000.

Aidan Rooney is a partner in ARC Partnership and he is entitled to 35 per cent of the partnership profits.

Aidan also has rental income of €90,000 from which he had to pay €15,000 in maintaining the property in 2025. Aidan is single, aged fifty-two, and has no PAYE income.

Calculate Aidan's tax liability for 2025.

Partnership profits

Profits before tax as per P & L account	150,000
Add back depreciation	50,000
Adjusted profits for tax purposes	200,000
Available deduction	
Less Capital Allowance	(31,250*)
Taxable amount	168,750

*Capital allowance is calculated at €250,000 * 12.5% = €31,250 on the plant and machinery—it is calculated at 12.5% on a straight line basis.

Schedule D Case I

Share of the partnership income is treated as a several trade and Aidan is taxed on such income under Schedule D Case I as a separate business:

€200,000 adjusted net profits of the partnership.

Aidan's share under partnership agreement = 35% so his income is €70,000.

Aidan's share of capital allowances = 35% so he can claim €31,250 * 35% = €10,937.50 rounded to €10,938.

Several trade	€70,000
Capital Allowance	€10,938

Schedule D Case V –rental interest

90,000	gross income
(15,000)	expenses
75,000	net income

Total Income:

70,000	several trade
(10,938)	capital allowance
59,062	net taxable
75,000	rental income
134,062	Net income

Income Tax: 2025

Initial 44,000 @ 20% = 8,800

Balance 90,062 @ 40% = 36,024.80

Total	44,824.80
Less Tax Credits	
Personal	(2000)
Earned Income	(2000)
Net	€40,824.80

PRSI

134, 062 (total income less capital allowance) * 4.1% * 9/12 =	€4122.41
134, 062 (total income less capital allowance) * 4.2% * 3/12 =	€1407.65
	€5530.06

USC

134,062 (total income less capital allowance)

First 12,012 * 0.5% =	60.06
Next 15,370 * 2% =	307.40
Next 42,662 * 3% =	1279.86
Next 29,956*8% =	2396.48
Last 34,062 *11% =	3746.82

Total USC	€7790.62
Total	€54,145.48

10.21.7 CHARGEABLE GAINS—PARTNERSHIP ASSETS

Partners are assessed and charged separately on gains accruing from the disposal of partnership assets. The assets of the partnership are treated as the assets of the partners and disposals by the partnership are treated as disposals by the partners.

Gains that accrue on a disposal of partnership assets are apportioned between the partners and assessed and charged on the partners.

A partnership is required to include in the partnership return (Form 1 (firms)) details of its chargeable gains and chargeable assets acquired.

When a partner disposes of his interest in a partnership this is treated as a disposal of a chargeable asset of the partnership and Capital Gains Tax ('CGT') may be payable by the disposing partner. Goodwill is a chargeable asset and any gain accruing to a disposing partner on the disposal of his interest in the partnership that is attributable to goodwill will be chargeable to CGT. Stock in trade and work in progress consideration will not be liable to CGT. CGT is covered in more detail elsewhere in this book.

CHAPTER 11

CORPORATION TAX

11.1 Introduction

This chapter will look at the rules that relate to the taxation of an Irish business that operates through a company. Rather than pay income tax and capital gains tax, certain trading income and chargeable gains of a company are liable to corporation tax. The primary sources of legislation for corporation tax are the Taxes Consolidation Act 1997 as amended ('TCA 1997'), the Finance Acts, and various statutory instruments.

The starting point for calculating the profits of a company for taxation purposes is the financial statements (profit and loss account and balance sheet) of the company. Certain adjustments are made to the profit and loss account—adding back of non-qualifying deductions and making certain permitted deductions for taxation purposes. Corporation tax is calculated on the adjusted profit figures.

The self-assessment system applies to companies, which means that a company must file a tax return and pay the corporation tax without being requested to do so by Revenue.

Corporation tax covers both income profits and most chargeable gains, so the capital gains of a company are calculated in accordance with the capital gains tax rules but are chargeable to corporation tax and are generally not chargeable to capital gains tax.

Disposals of development land are chargeable to capital gains tax.

11.2 Liability to Irish Corporation Tax

If a company is resident in Ireland it is liable to corporation tax. For a non-Irish-resident company, under s. 25 of the TCA 1997 the income and chargeable gains attributable to a branch or agency in the Republic of Ireland are chargeable to Irish corporation tax. Since 1 January 2015 all companies incorporated in Ireland are Irish tax resident except if not so regarded under a tax treaty.

An Irish-incorporated company will be liable to Irish tax if it is not regarded as tax resident in a tax treaty jurisdiction because it is not incorporated there.

A new s. 23A of the TCA 1997 came into effect on 1 January 2015 and provides that all newly incorporated companies will be Irish tax resident if incorporated in Ireland except if not so regarded under a tax treaty. Companies not incorporated in Ireland but with central management and control of the company in Ireland will also continue to be Irish tax resident.

11.3 How to Register for Corporation Tax

Companies must take steps to register for tax.

11.3.1 TAX REGISTRATION—FORM TR2

The form TR2 is the registration form that applies to companies to register for corporation tax, employer's PAYE/PRSI, VAT, and Relevant Contracts Tax. It must be completed by a company (and other entities) and filed with Revenue.

It must include the following details:

(a) company name and business name;

(b) registered address;

(c) business address;

(d) contact details;

(e) legal format of the entity;

(f) registration date;

(g) Companies Registration Office number;

(h) commencement date;

(i) accounts date;

(j) type of business;

(k) intention to have online sales;

(l) usage of plastic bags;

(m) director details;

(n) company secretary details;

(o) shareholder details (15 per cent or more beneficial interest);

(p) adviser details;

(q) property rental details;

(r) previous owner details (if applicable) and

(s) tick boxes to register for corporation tax, VAT (with detailed questions to be answered), PAYE/PRSI, RCT, CGT, and related information.

A company will be given a taxation reference number by the Revenue Commissioners.

A company must register directors and employees for PAYE purposes and deduct PAYE, USC, and PRSI on employee and certain director salary payments.

11.3.2 ADDITIONAL COMPANY FILING ON FORMATION—STATEMENT OF PARTICULARS

A statement of particulars has to be furnished to Revenue under s. 882 TCA 1997 (Form 11F CRO) within thirty days of commencing to carry on a business. It must contain the following information:

(a) company name;

(b) address—registered and business addresses;

(c) secretary details;

(d) commencement date;

(e) company accounting date;

(f) nature of the business;

(g) whether an incorporated company is claiming to be not tax resident; and

(h) whether it has any related company.

Any material changes must be notified to Revenue within thirty days of the change. A failure to file the statement can result in a notification from the Revenue Commissioners to the Companies Registration Office which can result in the company being struck off for failing to comply with this filing obligation.

11.4 Tax Rates

Income tax is not chargeable on the income of a company; instead a company pays corporation tax on its profits, which includes both income and chargeable gains.

The standard corporation tax rate for trading companies is **12.5 per cent** (TCA 1997, s. 21). The 12.5 per cent rate applies to the trading income of a company. A minimum effective rate of 15 per cent applies from 31 December 2024 for companies with a turnover of more than €750 million per year under the EU Minimum Tax Directive (implemented in Ireland in Finance Act 2024) which brings into effect OECD Two Pillar agreement rules. Ireland has chosen to apply the Qualified Domestic Top-up Tax.

The corporation tax rate for certain designated activities (excepted trades), for example working minerals, petroleum activities, and dealing in or developing lands, is 25 per cent (TCA 1997, s. 21A).

The corporation tax rate is also 25 per cent for the following non-trading income:

(a) Schedule D Case III income—interest not taxed at source, foreign income;

(b) Schedule D Case IV—royalties and other sources of income; and

(c) Schedule D Case V income—rental income from land and buildings.

Example:

The profits of Bright Sparks Limited relating to its retail shop will be liable to corporation tax at 12.5 per cent.

If Bright Sparks Limited purchased an office and rented this out to another person, this income would not relate to its trading business and would be taxed as rental income at a rate of 25 per cent.

11.5 Calculation of Corporation Tax

Corporation tax is payable on the taxable profits of a company for an accounting period.

11.5.1 WHAT IS AN ACCOUNTING PERIOD?

An accounting period is determined by tax rules and generally is of twelve months' duration chosen by the company.

An accounting period starts when a company:

(a) commences to carry on a trade;

(b) becomes resident in Ireland;

(c) acquires its first source of income; or

(d) commences to be wound up.

An accounting period is deemed to end:

(a) twelve months after the period commences;

(b) on a company's specified accounting date;

(c) on a company ceasing to trade; or

(d) on a company being wound up.

Example:

ABC Limited commences to trade on 1 April 2025. This starts an accounting period. If the company wishes to make up its accounts to 31 December 2025, the accounting period ends on that date; otherwise the accounting period will end twelve months from the start of the accounting period, 31 March 2026.

11.5.2 COMPANY PROFITS

The starting point to calculating a company's corporation tax is to review the profits of a company for an accounting period and to review the income and expenses to ascertain if all are applicable for corporation tax purposes.

11.5.3 DEDUCTIONS

Expenses wholly and exclusively used for the business of the company and expenses incurred for the purposes of the business are deductible. Personal deductions and other specified deductions are not permitted—for example, business entertainment expenses are not deductible. Pre-trading expenses incurred within three years of commencement can be deducted if they were incurred for the purposes of the business. Depreciation is not a qualifying deduction.

11.5.4 DEPRECIATION AND CAPITAL ALLOWANCES

Depreciation does not qualify as a deduction from income for taxation purposes and so the depreciation figure deducted as an expense in the profit and loss account must be added back to the profit figure to determine the profit figure for taxation purposes.

Instead, a deduction is available for capital allowances on capital assets. A tax calculation must be done on the capital assets of the company to ascertain if any of them can avail of capital allowances.

The rates for deductions for capital allowances are set out in tax legislation and are divided into different categories, including plant and machinery, industrial building, and motor vehicles.

Example:

- A furnace costs €10 million and will last five years. At that time assume the cost of demolition is the same as the value of the material that is left.
- If preparing a five-year set of accounts, the cost of the furnace would be €10 million.
- The use of the furnace is over the five years for €10 million, so €2 million per year would be deductible in the accounts.
- The depreciated value of the furnace after one year shown in the balance sheet is €8 million, after two years is €6 million, and so on.

The €2 million depreciation figure in the profit and loss account must be added back.

The furnace would constitute plant and machinery for capital allowances, so the applicable rate is 12.5 per cent for capital allowances.

The capital allowance deductible for taxable purposes for year one will therefore be €10 million * 12.5%= €1,250,000 and it is this figure that is deductible from the adjusted profits for taxation purposes, not the €2 million in the accounts.

11.5.5 CHARGES ON INCOME

Certain interest payments, royalty payments, and other annual payments are treated as charges on income. They are not deductible as expenses of the company when calculating company profits but are separately deductible as charges from the corporation tax profits.

In certain circumstances the company may have to deduct income tax from the payments and pay it over to Revenue.

11.5.6 REVIEW OF FINANCIAL STATEMENTS: PROFIT & LOSS A/C TO 31/1/2025

Sales	663,000
Cost of Sales	(523,000)
Gross Profit	140,000
Expenses	(95,000)
Profit before tax	45,000
Tax on profits	(8,000)
Profit after tax	37,000
Dividends	(10,000)
Retained Profits	27,000

If the figures in the profit and loss account are used, the corporation tax on €45,000 * 12.5 per cent would have been €5625.

This therefore indicates that certain expenses of the company have been added back for taxation purposes (€19,000) as the taxation is €64,000 * 12.5 per cent = €8000.

11.6 Start-Up Exemption

Relief is available for the first five years of trading for trading income and certain gains on new qualifying start-up companies that are commenced up to the end of 2026. The effect of the relief is that a qualifying start-up company can earn €480,000 tax free per year for the first five years if it has paid (or is deemed to have been paid) sufficient employer's PRSI.

Relief from corporation tax and chargeable gains may be available where the total corporation tax liability in any of the first five accounting periods does not exceed €60,000.

The value of the relief is based on the amount of employer's PRSI paid (or deemed paid) by the company in the accounting period. It is based on a maximum of €5000 PRSI per employee.

If the paid employer's PRSI is less than the corporation tax liability the relief is restricted to match the employer's PRSI paid.

Example:

ZZZ Limited was set up by Aidan in November 2025 as a new business that qualifies for the start-up exemption. It has a corporation tax liability for the accounting period ended 31 October 2026 of €20,000.

ZZZ Limited has paid or been deemed to pay €8000 in employer's PRSI in the same period.

ZZZ Limited can get an exemption from corporation tax for the PRSI paid and it only has to pay corporation tax on the balance (€20,000 – €8000) = €12,000.

If ZZZ Limited had paid €20,000 or more in employer's PRSI no corporation tax would have been payable.

There are certain conditions that must be complied with for the relief to apply. It will not apply to an existing trade taken over by a new company, it does not apply to service companies, and it does not apply to companies that must pay corporation tax at 25 per cent on trading income.

11.7 Preliminary Tax

Preliminary tax for an accounting period is due on the twenty-first day of the month preceding when the accounting period ends (except for large companies, as outlined below). Generally, this is the twenty-first day of the eleventh month of the accounting period.

To avoid an interest charge the preliminary tax must be 90 per cent of the final tax liability. There is a facility to top up the preliminary tax if there is a disposal of an asset and a chargeable gain arises after the preliminary tax is paid. If payments are made via ROS the payment date is extended by two days to the twenty-third of the month.

The balance of the tax is due by the twenty-first day of the ninth month after the accounting period ends. If a company is late paying or pays less than the appropriate preliminary tax amount, the total tax is deemed due from the preliminary tax date.

Example:
Bright Sparks Limited accounts are made up to 30 September; this means that the preliminary tax must be paid by 21 August (as it is a small company) and the balance of the tax must be paid and the tax return filed by 21 June after the end of the accounting period.

11.7.1 LARGE COMPANY—SPLIT PAYMENT OF PRELIMINARY TAX

A large company is a company which has had a corporation tax liability of more than €200,000 in the previous accounting period.

Preliminary tax is paid in two instalments by a large company. The first payment is due on the twenty-first day of the sixth month of the accounting period. The payment must be 50 per cent of the corporation tax of the previous accounting period or 45 per cent of the current period's corporation tax liability. The second payment is due on the twenty-first day of the eleventh month of the accounting period and it must be of such amount that will bring the total payment to 90 per cent of the corporation tax liability of the current period. For an accounting period of less than seven months the large company must pay all of the preliminary tax in one payment.

Example:
IOU Limited is very successful and has had a corporation tax liability of more than €350,000 in its accounting period ended 31 August 2024, so for the accounting period ended 31 August 2025 it will need to pay the following preliminary tax payments:

21 February 2025 – 45 per cent of current accounting period's liability (or 50 per cent of prior year corporation tax liability); and

21 July 2025 – so much as will bring the total preliminary tax payment to 90 per cent of current accounting period's corporation tax liability.

11.7.2 SMALL COMPANY

A small company is a company which had a corporation tax liability of less than €200,000 in the previous accounting period. Such a company can calculate its preliminary tax based on 100 per cent of the prior period's corporation tax liability or to 90 per cent of the corporation tax liability of the current period. The preliminary tax is payable by the twenty-first day of the eleventh month of the accounting period (or the twenty-first day of the month before the end of the accounting period if the accounting period is less than twelve months).

11.7.3 START-UP COMPANIES

New or start-up companies with a corporation tax liability of €200,000 or less are not required to pay preliminary tax for the first accounting period and can pay the tax at the same time as filing the tax return, which is by the twenty-first day of the ninth month after the accounting period ends.

Example:

Bright Sparks Limited has a corporation tax liability of €8000 for its first accounting period and is not required to pay preliminary tax for its first accounting period that ends on 30 September 2024, and it can pay the €8000 corporation tax when it files the corporation tax return (form CT1) by 21 June 2025.

11.8 Tax Return and Payment of Balance of Corporation Tax

A company must file a tax return, a form CT1, by the twenty-first day of the ninth month after the accounting period ends. The balance of the tax liability must be paid by this date also. If the return is filed and the tax paid using ROS the deadline is extended to the twenty-third day of the ninth month. Generally, all companies are obliged to file and pay using ROS.

Example:

ZZZ Limited accounts are made up to 31 October; this means that the preliminary tax must be paid by 21 September (as it is a small company) and the balance of the tax must be paid and the tax return filed by 21 July after the end of the accounting period.

11.8.1 SURCHARGE

If a company fails to file the form CT1 tax return by the due date a surcharge is imposed, which is determined by how late the company is in filing the return.

The surcharge is calculated in the same way as it is for income tax:

(a) if the return is filed within two months of the return filing date, a surcharge of 5 per cent of the tax up to a maximum of €12,695 is payable in addition to the tax liability for the tax year; and

(b) if the return is filed more than two months after the return filing date, a surcharge of 10 per cent of the tax up to a maximum of €63,485 is payable in addition to the tax liability for the tax year.

11.8.2 INTEREST

Interest will be payable on any late payment at the rate of 0.0291 per cent per day or part of a day.

11.8.3 FAILURE TO INCLUDE INFORMATION

A surcharge may also be payable if a company fails to include certain information in its return in relation to reliefs that it is claiming and the company becomes aware that it has failed to include the information and fails to provide it to Revenue. The surcharge is calculated at 5 per cent of the tax up to a maximum of €12,695 and is payable in addition to the tax liability for the tax year.

11.8.4 RESTRICTIONS ON RELIEFS AND ALLOWANCES FOR LATE FILING

If a return is filed late this has consequences on the reliefs and allowances that a company can claim. The reliefs and allowances that are impacted include group relief, trading losses, and certain capital losses.

If the return is filed within two months of the return filing date reliefs and allowances are **restricted by 25 per cent** subject to a maximum of €31,740 for each relief and allowance. If the return is filed more than two months after the return, filing date reliefs and allowances are **restricted by 50 per cent** subject to a maximum of €158,715 for each.

Example:

XYZ Limited has trading losses of €10,000 and it has other income of €40,000 taxable at 12.5 per cent. It delays in filing its tax return, form CT1, and it files one month later than it should.

The consequences of this will mean that the trading losses will be restricted to €7500.

In addition, XYZ Limited will have to pay a surcharge of 5 per cent of the tax up to a maximum of €12,695 as well as the tax liability for the tax year.

Interest per day or part of a day at 0.0219 per cent on the unpaid tax is also due.

11.9 Trading Losses—Schedule D Case I or II

Losses cannot be set off against other personal income of the shareholders.

For companies with income taxed at 25 per cent, losses may be offset against the company's other profits before charges in the same accounting period and against the company's profits for the *immediately preceding* accounting period of the same length on a euro-for-euro basis (TCA 1997, s. 396). Any unused trade loss can be carried forward and can be set against future trading profit of the same trade.

For companies with income taxed at 12.5 per cent, losses from income liable to tax at 12.5 per cent may be offset against the company's other trading profits taxable at 12.5 per cent before charges in the same accounting period and against the company's trading profits taxable at 12.5 per cent for the immediately preceding accounting period of the same length on a euro-for-euro basis (TCA 1997, s. 396 A). Any unused trade loss can be used against income not taxable at 12.5 per cent on a value basis for the same accounting period and immediately preceding accounting period, and any remaining can be carried forward and can be set against future trading profit of the same trade.

If the company is a member of a group of companies, the losses can be surrendered to other members of the group.

Example:

Bright Sparks Limited made a loss of €50,000 for 31 December 2025. The loss can be set off against other trading income taxable at 12.5 per cent for the twelve months ending 31 December 2025 and the trading income taxable at 12.5 per cent for the twelve months ending 31 December 2024.

Any unused trading loss may be set off against the company's non-trading income, but only on a value basis, and if any losses remain they can be carried forward against future trade profits.

Example:

Bright Sparks Limited has unused trading losses of €25,000 (this trade is taxable at 12.5 per cent) and it has investment income of €40,000 (taxable at 25 per cent) in 2025. It can get relief for the loss at a rate of 12.5 per cent (€25,000 *12.5 per cent = €3125) and deduct this from the investment income tax of €40,000 * 25 per cent = €10,000, leaving €6875 tax payable. This means that €12,500 of the trading losses can be offset against the €40,000 investment income, leaving €27,500 taxable at 25 per cent = €6875 corporation tax payable.

11.9.1 ORDER FOR USE OF LOSSES

Generally, under the legislation, losses must be used in a specific order.

For a trading loss on a trade taxable at 12.5 per cent, the following order would be used:

(a) use losses carried forward from a previous accounting period for the same trade against the profits of the trade;

(b) then use current period losses for offset against current period trading income taxed at 12.5 per cent;

(c) if any losses remaining carry back against income (in a preceding accounting period of equal length) taxed at 12.5 per cent;

(d) then use current period losses for offset against current period trading income and gains not taxed at 12.5 per cent on a value basis;

(e) if any losses remain carry back against income and gains (in a preceding accounting period of equal length) not taxed at 12.5 per cent on a value basis; and

(f) any remaining losses are available to be carried forward against future profits from the same trade.

11.9.2 TERMINAL LOSS RELIEF

If a company ceased to trade and made a loss in its last accounting period, it can seek to carry this loss back against income from the same trade in the preceding three years.

11.9.3 SCHEDULE D CASE IV

A loss made on Schedule D Case IV income can be set against other Case IV income in the same accounting period and any unused loss can be carried forward against future Case IV income.

11.9.4 SCHEDULE D CASE V

A Schedule D Case V loss can be carried back against Case V income in a preceding accounting period of equal length and any unused loss can be carried forward against future Case V income.

11.10 Group Relief

Group relief may be claimed where companies are members of the same group.

Members of a group may surrender current year trading losses, excess charges on income, excess management expenses (in the case of investment companies), and excess capital allowances in rental property.

A group for group loss relief applies if one company is a 75 per cent subsidiary of the other (i.e. one company owns 75 per cent of the shares in the other company) or two or more companies are 75 per cent subsidiaries of another company. The parent company must be beneficially entitled to not less than 75 per cent of the profits available for distribution and 75 per cent of the assets available for distribution on a winding up.

All the companies must be resident in the Republic of Ireland or in the European Economic Area and be in a country with which Ireland has a tax treaty. Group relief is also available to members of a consortium if the loss-making company is owned by the consortium. A company is able to hand over (surrender) its trading loss to another member of the group.

Example:

DE Limited and FG Limited are 100 per cent subsidiaries of ABC Limited.

DE Limited has a loss of €20,000, FG Limited has a loss of €5,000, and ABC Limited has a profit of €150,000. Each of the companies make their accounts up to 31 December each year, each of the companies are Irish-incorporated, and all of the companies qualify as trading companies that pay tax on their trading income as 12.5 per cent.

DE Limited can surrender the losses of €20,000 to ABC Limited to reduce its profits to €130,000.

FG Limited can also surrender its losses of €5000 to ABC Limited to further reduce its profits to €125,000.

11.11 Inter-Group Payments

A group for inter-group payments is a 51 per cent group; that is, if one company is a 51 per cent subsidiary of the other (i.e. one company owns 51 per cent of the shares in the other company) or two or more companies are 51 per cent subsidiaries of another company. A member of a group is permitted to make certain payments to another member of a group without deducting tax in certain circumstances. For example; interest payments and royalties may be paid gross, that is, without deduction of tax, if a group relationship exists.

11.12 Taxation of Dividends

11.12.1 IF AN IRISH COMPANY RECEIVES DIVIDENDS

No tax is payable on dividends received from other Irish resident companies.

Dividends received from a foreign company that is tax resident within the EU or in a country with which Ireland has a tax treaty which are paid out of trading profits are liable to corporation tax at 12.5 per cent.

Otherwise, foreign dividends are generally liable to corporation tax at 25 per cent.

11.12.2 IF A COMPANY PAYS A DIVIDEND

If a company declares and pays a dividend, the recipients will be liable to income tax on the dividend received.

The company that declares and pays the dividend may have to deduct dividend withholding tax on the dividend (currently at a rate of 25 per cent) and pay this directly to Revenue (before the fourteenth day after the month of the payment of the dividend). A voucher detailing the dividend withholding tax must be provided to the shareholders.

The company cannot seek a deduction from corporation tax for the dividend paid and the payment must be made out of after tax profits (profits available for distribution) that are subject to company law rules.

Example:

G2G Ltd: Profit & Loss A/c to 31/3/2025

Sales	663,000
Cost of sales	(523,000)
Gross profit	140,000
Expenses	(95,000)
Profit before tax	45,000
Tax on profits	(8000)
Profit after tax	37,000
Dividends	(10,000)
Retained profits	27,000

What are the taxation implications of the payment of the €10,000 in dividends?

G2G Limited does not get any deduction from its profits to pay the dividends.

The company must withhold dividend withholding tax at a rate of 25 per cent when paying the dividends to its shareholders (subject to certain exceptions).

The gross dividend is €10,000; 25 per cent will be withheld as dividend withholding tax (€2500) and paid over to the Revenue Commissioners before the fourteenth day after the month in which the dividend was made with the balance of €7500 paid out to the shareholders with a voucher showing the dividend withholding tax deducted that the shareholder can use as evidence of their entitlement to a credit for the dividend tax deducted.

The shareholders in receipt of the dividends are taxed under the income tax rules on the gross dividend paid and they will get a credit for any dividend withholding tax.

11.12.3 PAYMENT OF A SALARY/BONUS VERSUS PAYMENT OF A DIVIDEND

Should a shareholder be paid a dividend or a salary/bonus payment? Is there any difference for the company or for the individual?

A tax deduction may be available for the company for the payment of a salary or bonus to an employee or director of the company. However, employer's PRSI may also be payable on the salary or bonus except where a payment is made to a proprietary director (a director who controls 15 per cent or more of the shares in the company and who must pay the PRSI him/herself as a self-employed person).

Example:

A company makes a payment of a bonus to Celia, an employee, of €8000 on 31 January 2025; this payment may be subject to an employer's PRSI payment (PRSI 11.15 per cent * €8000 = €892).

If Celia was a proprietary director (she is a director and she can control more than 15 per cent of the shares), Celia will pay the PRSI and not the company.

Example:

HHH Limited has pre-tax profits of €10,000 and wishes to make a payment of €2000 to Alison an employee for all of her hard work in setting up the company and assisting in launching the first product. Alison holds 25 per cent shares in the company and is a director.

Should HHH Limited pay a bonus to Alison or should it declare a dividend?

There is a corporation tax saving of €250 for the company by paying a bonus rather than a dividend as it can take a deduction for the bonus from its trading income, which reduces its trading income for corporation tax purposes.

HHH Limited must withhold dividend withholding tax at the standard rate (25 per cent) from the dividend if it decides to pay a dividend—€2000 * 25 per cent = €500—and pay this over to Revenue.

In this example Alison pays the same tax irrespective of whether she receives a bonus or dividend, but the company makes a corporation tax saving by paying a deductible bonus rather than paying a dividend.

There is a corporation tax saving of €250 for the company by paying a bonus rather than a dividend as it can take a deduction for the bonus from its trading income, which reduces its trading income for corporation tax purposes.

HHH Limited must withhold dividend withholding tax at the standard rate (25 per cent) from the dividend if it decides to pay a dividend—€2000 * 25 per cent = €500—and pay this over to Revenue.

In this example Alison pays the same tax irrespective of whether she receives a bonus or dividend, but the company makes a corporation tax saving by paying a deductible bonus rather than paying a dividend.

Is there any other reason why a company may pay a dividend?

Reasons include providing a return for its shareholders or to avoid a close company surcharge.

11.13 Close Company

11.13.1 WHAT IS A CLOSE COMPANY?

A close company is an Irish resident company under the control of its directors who are participators or under the control of five or fewer participators.

A **participator** is someone who has an interest in the income or capital of a company. A participator is deemed to own the shares and interest of his/her associates when determining interests in the company.

An **associate** includes the spouse/civil partner, direct relatives and partners, and trustees of a participator.

11.13.2 RESTRICTIONS ON A CLOSE COMPANY

Corporation Tax rules impose a number of restrictions on close companies.

11.13.2.1 Expenses for free benefits

If a company incurs an expense in providing any benefit to a participator, the amount of the expense will not be deductible for corporation tax purposes and instead the benefit will be treated as a distribution by the company to the participator and the participator will have to pay tax on the distribution.

11.13.2.2 Interest payments

Interest paid to directors or their associates above a specified rate may be treated as a distribution.

11.13.2.3 Loans to participators

There are certain rules and negative consequences on loans provided by a company to participators or their associates. Tax must be deducted on loans provided to participators or their associates and if a loan is forgiven, the grossed-up amount is treated as income of the participator or his associate.

11.13.2.4 Close company surcharge

Surcharges are imposed on a close company that does not make distributions to its shareholders.

If a company has after tax investment income or rental income (passive income) available for distribution to its shareholders and it does not distribute the income within eighteen months of the end of the accounting year then a surcharge is imposed on the company if the amount of the undistributed passive income is more than €2000 and the company is not precluded by law from distributing the income.

The surcharge is 20 per cent of the undistributed investment and rental income. For trading companies the undistributed income can be reduced by 7.5 per cent before the surcharge is calculated.

Example:

ABC Limited is a close company and it has, after paying tax, rental income of €20,000 and deposit interest of €10,000 unrelated to the trading income for the year ended 31 July 2025.

As ABC Limited is a trading company the income can be reduced by 7.5 per cent before the surcharge is calculated.

If ABC Limited does not distribute this income by 31 January 2027 it will be subject to a surcharge of €30,000 – 2250 (30,000 * 7.5 per cent) = €27,750 * 20 per cent = €5550.

A close company that is a service company (professional company) is also liable to a surcharge that is calculated differently.

The surcharge is 20 per cent of the rental income and investment income (passive income) available for distribution and an additional 15 per cent of half the distributable trading income.

For trading companies the undistributed income can be reduced by 7.5 per cent before the surcharge is calculated.

Example:

ZZZ Limited is an architectural practice operating as a company owned by two brothers and it has €40,000 in after tax rental and investment income and €55,000 trading income for the year ended 30 September 2025. If it does not distribute this income by 31 March 2027 it will be subject to a surcharge:

$$40{,}000 - 3{,}000\left(40{,}000 * 7.5\,\text{per cent}\right) = 37{,}000 = \text{passive income}$$

$$55{,}000/2 = €27{,}500 = \text{half trading income}$$

$$20\,\text{per cent} * €37{,}000 = €7400;\text{and}$$

$$15\,\text{per cent} * €27{,}500 = €4125.$$

Total surcharge €11,525.

To avoid the surcharge a company must make a distribution within 18 months of the end of the accounting date if it has profits available for distribution that it can legally distribute.

11.14 Reliefs

There are a number of incentives and reliefs available to encourage and attract businesses to be set up as companies, and some reliefs are only available to companies.

For example, a 30 per cent tax credit is available for qualifying research and development expenditure for companies engaged in in-house qualifying research and development undertaken within the European Economic Area. The credit may be set against the company's corporation tax liability and is available on a group basis in the case of a group of companies.

11.15 Companies Chargeable Gains

11.15.1 CHARGEABLE GAINS LIABLE TO CAPITAL GAINS TAX

Gains of an Irish resident company that arise on the disposal of development land are charged to capital gains tax (CGT).

Gains that arise for a non-resident company on the disposal of certain non-trading assets situated in the State (Republic of Ireland) are liable to CGT.

11.15.2 CHARGEABLE TO CORPORATION TAX

All other gains (i.e. non-development land gains) of an Irish resident company are charged to corporation tax.

Gains accruing to a non-resident company on the disposal of assets situated in Ireland and used for the purpose of a trade carried on by it in the State through a branch or agency are liable to corporation tax.

11.15.3 AMOUNT ON WHICH TAX IS PAID

The amount of the chargeable gain liability is calculated using CGT rules.

As the rate of corporation tax and the rate of CGT are different, a notional amount of gain is calculated so that when this notional gain is charged at the rate of corporation tax applicable to the company, the correct amount of chargeable gain liability is assessed.

Example:

XYZ Limited calculates that it has a capital gain in 2025 of €20,000 * 33 per cent = €6600. The rate of corporation tax for XYZ Limited is 12.5 per cent as it is a trading company.

The amount of the gain to be considered for the corporation tax assessment is an amount that when taxed at 12.5 per cent will equal €6600.

The notional amount will have to be €52,800 as 12.5 per cent of €52,800 equals €6600.

11.15.4 PAYMENT OF TAX ON CHARGEABLE GAIN

The liability for a company's chargeable gains is assessed for the accounting period in which the gain accrued and is included in the Form C1 as part of the corporation tax return for the accounting period.

11.15.5 LOSSES

11.15.5.1 Trading losses

Trading losses may only be offset against trading income for the same and immediately preceding accounting period of the same length on a euro-for-euro basis. See above under corporation tax losses.

Any unused trading loss may be offset against non-trading income, including chargeable gains, but only on a value basis as different tax rates apply to trading income and chargeable gains.

Example:

ABC Limited has an unused trading loss in 2025 of €200,000 and a chargeable gain of €200,000. ABC Limited can get relief for the loss at the rate of 12.5 per cent against the liability on the chargeable gain.

Tax due on the chargeable gain is €200,000 * 33 per cent = €66,000 and ABC Limited can claim loss relief of €25,000 (€200,000 trading loss * 12.5 per cent) as a deduction against the €66,000 chargeable gain, leaving it with a net liability of €41,000 to be paid.

11.15.5.2 Losses on the disposal of assets

Losses of a company on non-development land assets may be offset against chargeable gains (but not development land gains) of the company in the current accounting period. Any unused balance can be carried forward for use against any future chargeable gains.

Losses on the disposal of development land can be offset against gains arising on other assets. Any unused balance can be carried forward for use against any future chargeable gains.

11.15.5.3 Groups

A group for CGT purposes applies if one company is a 75 per cent subsidiary of the other (i.e. one company owns 75 per cent of the shares in the other company) or two or more companies are 75 per cent subsidiaries of another company.

Sales of assets between companies within a group are treated as resulting in a no loss/no gain situation. Instead, a company on leaving a group pays the tax on the chargeable gain.

CHAPTER 12

TAXATION AND THE CONVEYANCERS' RESPONSIBILITIES

12.1 Introduction

This chapter deals with the various taxation issues that may arise in a typical conveyancing transaction. Any or indeed all of the following taxes may have to be considered by both the vendor's and the purchaser's solicitors when consulted to sell or buy a property on behalf of a client:

- stamp duty;
- capital gains tax;
- capital acquisitions tax;
- property charges arising under the Local Government (Charges) Act, 2009, the Local Government (Household Charges) Act, 2011, the Finance (Local Property Tax) Act, 2012;
- water charges as provided for under the Environment (Miscellaneous Provisions) Act, 2015, as amended by the Water Services Act, 2017;
- value added tax (VAT).

In the April 2016 edition of the *Gazette* the Conveyancing Committee advised, in cases where records required for conveyancing transactions are maintained only online, it is the online record that is conclusive and can be accepted by a purchaser's solicitor. A purchaser's solicitor may accept a photocopy, coloured copy, or printout, or review the online record, for example local property tax (LPT) online record, BER certificates or non-principal private residence (NPPR) certificates of exemption, or waiver or certificates of registration of septic tanks. The emailed soft copy of both the email and the attachment is sufficient for conveyancing purposes and can be printed out and placed with the title deeds. There is no need for either a purchaser's or a vendor's solicitor to certify a copy as being a copy of the original.

12.2 Conveyancing Taxation Checklist

12.2.1 STAMP DUTIES

Stamp Duty is a duty charged on certain written documents known as 'instruments' listed in Schedule 1 of the SDCA 1999. With the exception of the CREST share transfer system, where no document exists, the general rule is that there is no exposure to stamp duty. If assets can be transferred without the use of a document, stamp duty can be avoided on the transaction.

12.2.2 CAPITAL GAINS TAX

Does the consideration exceed €1,000,000 in the case of residential houses and apartments as defined or €500,000 in disposals of all other Irish land and buildings including commercial property? If it does, a clearance certificate pursuant to s. 980 of the Taxes Consolidation Act, 1997 is required by a purchaser's solicitor. Alternatively, 15 per cent from the purchase price must be deducted and paid to the Revenue Commissioners (withholding tax) where such clearance certificate is not provided by the person disposing of the asset. An online application system for vendors to apply for a CG50A and for purchasers filing a CG50B is available since June 2020. However, for customers who are non e-enabled the Revenue continue to support paper based applications.

In addition, a new clearance procedure to operate in non-resident vendor cases has been put in place by the Revenue and applies from 24 October 2022. The process for dealing with requests for clearance for capital gains tax (CGT) when there is a non-resident vendor is outlined in the Tax and Duty Manual (TDM) Part 45-01-05. An online application on the Revenue Online System (ROS) will result in acknowledgement recording the start of the thirty-five-day period.

12.2.3 CAPITAL ACQUISITIONS TAX ('CAT')

Prior to 3 April 2010, s. 60 and s. 61 of the Capital Acquisitions Tax Consolidation Act, 2003 provided that CAT was a charge on property for twelve years. However, since 3 April 2010, it is no longer a charge on property.

However, an exception was made for applications made to Tailte Eireann (previously the Property Registration Authority) Land Registry section, to register property held by way of adverse possession; this is the only remaining instance where a certificate of discharge from CAT is required. Under s. 62(2) of the Capital Acquisitions Tax Consolidation Act, 2003, a clearance certificate of discharge from CAT (Form CA12) should be obtained for such applications before a title based on adverse possession will be registered. A self-certification option is available for small properties which come within prescribed limits of value and are not part of a larger property.

12.2.4 THE FINANCE (LOCAL PROPERTY TAX) ACT 2012 AS AMENDED BY THE LOCAL PROPERTY TAX (AMENDMENT) ACT 2021

This Act governs the application of LPT to residential property as defined. LPT is due and payable by the person who is liable on the liability date and the amount on which LPT is chargeable is the market value that the property could *reasonably* be expected to fetch on a sale in the open market on the valuation date. The 2021 Act introduced certain changes in relation to LPT that is due in 2022. These apply to property valued on 1 November 2021. The revaluation of homes has been deferred on many occasions resulting in one valuation period from 2013 to 2021. The new valuation period will apply to LPT for 2022 to 2025. Homeowners were obliged to submit a self-assessed valuation of their property and submit a LPT return by 7 November 2021. Unlike NPPR charges (see **12.2.5**), under s. 124 of the Finance (Local Property Act) Act 2012, there is no time limit on the charge. There were eleven exemptions from LPT available for the valuation period from 2013 to 2021. Four of these exemptions have expired and are not available for the new valuation period 2022–2025. These include new or unused property purchased from a builder or developer, builders or developers with properties built but unused, properties in unfinished housing estates (ghost estates), and property purchased as a home in 2013. Seven LPT exemptions however are available in both valuation periods.

12.2.5 THE LOCAL GOVERNMENT (CHARGES) ACT, 2009 (NPPR) AND THE LOCAL GOVERNMENT (HOUSEHOLD CHARGES) ACT, 2011

In essence these provided for an annual local government charge of €200 on non-principal private residences, such as investment/rental properties, vacant investment properties, and holiday homes, and an annual charge of €100 on residential property, respectively. The appropriate receipts or certificates of exemption had to be produced to the purchaser on completion. While both of these charges are now abolished they did remain a charge on residential property and did expire after twelve years. In the case of the NPPR charge the purchaser's solicitor should no longer ensure that the relevant certificate of discharge, or a certificate of exemption, is obtained at closing from the local authority. A receipt or declaration made by the vendor is not sufficient. However, a declaration can be provided where the property does not come within the ambit of the Act.

The household charge was abolished on 1 January 2013. Any outstanding household charge plus interest and penalties unpaid on 1 July 2013 were converted into LPT of €200 due and payable on that date. This is collected and pursued by the Revenue through the LPT system. Any arrears will show as outstanding on the LPT property history screen and are collected by the Revenue through the LPT system. Purchasers will insist on any arrears being discharged by a vendor prior to closing.

12.2.6 VACANT HOMES TAX

A new vacant homes tax (VHT) applies from 2023. Section 84 of the Finance Act 2022 introduced a new Part 22B into the Taxes Consolidation Act (TCA) which provides that a VHT is to apply in respect of a residential property for a chargeable period in which the residential property is in use as a dwelling for less than thirty days in a twelve-month period. The tax is calculated at a rate equal to seven times, previously five and three times, the standard LPT liability applicable to the property. A number of exemptions apply to properties which are unoccupied for genuine reasons, for example, a sale during the chargeable period, illness, long term or significant refurbishment. The tax is self-assessed and administered by the Revenue Commissioners. The first chargeable period for the VHT commenced on 1 November 2022 and ended on 31 October 2023. For that chargeable period a VHT return was due by 7 November 2023 and the tax was payable by 1 January 2024.

12.2.7 RESIDENTIAL ZONED LAND TAX (PREVIOUSLY VACANT SITE LEVY)

A vacant site levy was introduced in the Urban Regeneration and Housing Act 2015. The purpose of the introduction of the levy was to stimulate the development of housing and to eliminate the hoarding of land. It provided for a levy to be charged on each vacant site which has been entered on the vacant site register for which a market value is determined. It applies to residential land (more than 0.4047 hectares) where there is a need for housing in the area, or where the site is suitable for housing and the majority of the site has not been in use for an extended period of time. It also applies to regeneration land (other than residential land) where the majority of the site has not been in use for an extended period of time or the site is having a negative impact on existing amenities or on the character of the area.

Once a vacant site has been identified, it must be vacant for a period of twelve months prior to being placed on the register.

The amount of the vacant site levy in 2018 was initially 3 per cent of the market value of the site as determined. The levy was increased to 7 per cent in 2019.

The Residential Zoned Land Tax as introduced by the Finance Act 2021 will replace the vacant site levy on 1 February 2025. The process to identify land to which the tax applies is now under way and the tax is payable from 1 February 2025. The Residential Zoned Land Tax will apply to land which has not been developed for housing but is serviced and zoned for residential development. The tax is 3 per cent of the market value of the land and it will be collected by the Revenue.

12.2.8 WATER CHARGES

Water charges were provided for under s. 48 of the Environment (Miscellaneous Provisions) Act, 2015, which commenced on 1 January 2012. The Law Society has issued a number of Practice Notes on the topic in the December 2015, March 2016, and February 2017 editions of the *Gazette*, respectively. Section 48 inserted s. 3A into the Water Services Act, 2014, under which an obligation was placed on the vendor's solicitors to discharge any unpaid water charges from the proceeds of sale.

Section 5(1) (b) (ii) of the Water Services Act, 2017 has now repealed s. 3A of the Water Services Act, 2014. There is no longer an obligation on the vendor's solicitors to make enquiries of Irish Water about amounts due and/or to discharge arrears from sale proceeds. The 2019 edition of the Requisitions on Title at requisition 2 outlines the current requirements in relation to water services/local authority services.

A Practice Note in the December 2018 edition of the *Gazette* provides an Irish Water update. This Practice Note confirms that while Irish Water assumed responsibility for water and waste infrastructure which was previously vested in local authorities, Irish Water is not responsible for surface water pipes or water attenuating systems, the responsibility for which remains with the local authority.

Irish Water has confirmed to the Conveyancing Committee that solicitors acting for purchasers of second-hand dwellings may continue to rely on a letter previously issued by a local authority confirming that roads and services are in charge as evidence that the applicable water infrastructure is now vested in Irish Water.

In addition, Irish Water has confirmed that, where a local authority issues a letter confirming that the roads immediately abutting the property are in charge, Irish Water accepts responsibility for the water infrastructure servicing the property, even where the letter states that the local authority is no longer responsible for the water infrastructure. This issue, to include obtaining certificates of registration of septic tanks from Protect Our Waters, is dealt with in more detail in **Chapter 7**.

Water charges are currently not applicable but it is intended to introduce a charge for excessive water use from October 2025.

12.2.9 VAT

The manner in which VAT is levied upon property transactions was dramatically altered with the introduction on 1 July 2008 of a new VAT on property system. The manner in which the new rules apply to the sale of freehold and 'freehold equivalent interests' is examined in detail later in this chapter. Given the complexity of this new VAT on property system and its potential fundamentally to affect the financial position of the vendor and the purchaser, it is imperative that both the solicitors acting for the vendor and the purchaser are apprised of the VAT position at a pre-contract stage. In order to assist practitioners in this regard, the Conveyancing and the Taxation Committees of the Law Society jointly issued VAT pre-contract enquiries, which were first posted on the Law Society website in May 2009 and may be accessed by logging onto the members' area of that website. As these enquiries are updated on a regular basis, practitioners should ensure that the most up-to-date version available on the website is used in each individual transaction.

Although the enquiries are to be raised by the purchaser's solicitor, in a joint Practice Note issued in the May 2009 *Gazette*, the Conveyancing and Taxation Committees stated that it was their view that the enquiries would prove a useful tool for the vendor's solicitor in establishing the VAT position in each individual transaction, thereby assisting the vendor's solicitor in correctly drafting the contract for sale. It is, therefore, advisable that, on receiving instructions regarding the sale of the property, the vendor's solicitor would liaise with the vendor and, if necessary, the vendor's taxation adviser, in order to complete the questionnaire. The purchaser's solicitor should carefully consider the responses to the enquiries received from the vendor and ensure that the purchaser is fully aware of the VAT implications of the transaction. On completion, the purchaser's solicitor ought to seek confirmation from the vendor's solicitor that the replies to the enquiries are still accurate and correct. As the enquiries comprise a series of very detailed questions regarding the VAT history of the property, it is strongly advised that, unless the solicitor in question is an expert in VAT or the transaction is a straightforward one, the vendor should be advised to engage the services of a VAT specialist or a tax adviser. Equally, the purchaser's solicitor, if he or she does not feel competent to analyse the information furnished by the vendor and advise on the consequences of the same for the VAT treatment of the transaction, ought to advise the purchaser to seek specialist assistance. VAT is not dealt with further in this book.

12.2.10 PROBATE TAX

Was there a death on title between 18 June 1993 and 6 December 2000 where the surviving spouse inherited a life interest that will now cease or has ceased within the past twelve years? If there was, a clearance certificate of discharge from probate tax (PT2) must be obtained from the vendor. Probate tax was abolished with effect from 6 December 2000. However, if a spouse received a limited (life) interest in property with the remainder to a third party after the death of the spouse, the probate tax was deferred or postponed until after the death of the surviving spouse. It was deferred until the remainder interest crystallised, that is, on the death of the surviving spouse, and becomes a charge on the property for a period of twelve years once it has crystallised on the life tenant's death.

12.3 Stamp Duties

12.3.1 INTRODUCTION

The current law relating to stamp duty is principally contained in the Stamp Duties Consolidation Act, 1999 ('the SDCA 1999'), which became law on 15 December 1999, and subsequent amending Finance Acts. Prior to this the law of stamp duty was found *inter alia* in the Stamp Act, 1891 and substantive amendments were made in subsequent Finance Acts.

Stamp duty is a tax on 'instruments'; that is to say, on various types of written documents, and not on transactions. If there is no instrument or document to stamp then no stamp duty can arise unless the legislation provides otherwise. When dealing with the question of whether a stamp duty exposure arises, the first question that needs to be asked is: 'is there a document?' These documents are referred to as 'instruments' in the stamp duty code. Not every instrument is liable to stamp duty. To be liable an instrument must be listed under one of the headings in Schedule 1 to the SDCA, 1999, which contains a list of those instruments liable to stamp duty. The documents listed in this Schedule are usually referred to as 'heads of charge'. The three main heads of charge are *conveyance on sale, lease, and mortgage*. Schedule 1 also specifies the appropriate rates of duty, which may be ad valorem or fixed, applicable to each instrument. The rates of stamp duty outlined at **12.4.2** in respect of residential property apply to instruments (written documents) executed (signed, sealed, and delivered) on or after 8 December 2010.

12.3.1.1 Ad valorem

When a document is charged to stamp duty at the ad valorem rate, the value of the property is subject to stamp duty based on the appropriate table of rates and will depend on the type of the property, whether residential or non-residential. Currently the rate of stamp duty applicable to residential property is 1 per cent where the consideration does not exceed €1,000,000, 2 per cent on any excess over €1,000,000 up to €1,500,000 and 6% on any excess value over €1,500,000.

Stamp Duty at the rate of 15 per cent is payable on the cumulative purchase of ten or more residential houses in a twelve-month period. This rate applies since 2 October 2024.

A flat rate of 7.5 per cent applies to instruments executed on or after 9 October 2019 in relation to all non-residential/commercial/agricultural property (other than policies of insurance). There is a refund scheme available to reduce the 7.5 per cent rate of stamp duty to 2 per cent on certain residential development property transfers. This scheme has been extended to 31 December 2025.

There is no stamp duty payable on contents as these pass by delivery.

12.3.1.2 Fixed

When a document is charged to stamp duty at the fixed rate, stamp duty of €12.50 is payable. An example would be a duplicate or counterpart lease.

12.3.2 THE MANDATORY NATURE OF STAMP DUTY; THE FINANCE ACTS, 1991 AND 2012; AND PENALTIES

With effect from 1 November 1991 the payment of stamp duty became mandatory. Prior to this date the payment of both ad valorem and fixed duties was voluntary. This was so because although a liability arose to stamp instruments, the Revenue did not have any method of enforcing the payment of duty. Section 2(3) of the SDCA, 1999 provides that an instrument which is subject to stamp duty must be stamped within thirty days after it is first executed. The Finance Act, 1991 is of importance to solicitors because it created a number of obligations and imposed a duty of disclosure on professional advisers and their clients in relation to the payment of stamp duty. Penalties were imposed for late stamping of instruments chargeable to duty, and surcharges were imposed where property had been undervalued in returns to the Revenue Commissioners. The Finance Act, 2012 ('the 2012 Act') introduced a range of changes in the administration of stamp duty that came into effect on 7 July 2012 in respect of instruments executed on or after that date. The provisions of the 2012 Act are now contained in ss 8, 14, 16, and 127 to 134A of the SDCA, 1999. In addition to the fact that the payment of stamp duty is compulsory s. 2) and that late payment of stamp duty will give rise to interest s. 14), ss 127 to 134A of the SDCA contain a number of provisions/penalties to help to ensure that returns are filed on time through the ROS for instruments which are chargeable to stamp duty. Late filing surcharges were introduced. Section 8 of the SDCA, 1999 provides for a penalty of €3000 for failing to file a return, setting out all of the relevant information. Section 8A of the SDCA, 1999 provides that all facts and circumstances affecting the liability to stamp duty or affecting the amount of duty are to be fully disclosed to the Revenue Commissioners in the returns. This section puts the onus on a person to bring to the attention of the Revenue Commissioners all the facts and circumstances affecting the liability of an instrument to stamp duty and these must be stated in the instrument itself. In some cases it will not be practicable for the instrument to contain all relevant facts and circumstances. In such cases it is permissible to set out any facts or circumstances not set out in the instrument in an accompanying statement. This statement is not required to be delivered to the Revenue where the instrument is stamped under the e-stamping system.

Evidence in relation to the chargeability of an instrument to duty must be retained by an accountable person for audit purposes for six years from the date of stamping of the instrument under the e-stamping system should the Revenue wish to examine it.

In addition, s. 128A provides that an accountable person is obliged to retain records relating to a stamp duty liability or to a relief or exemption claimed for a period of six years from the date a stamp duty return is filed or the date the duty is paid, whichever date is the later. The 2012 Act introduced new fixed penalties on each accountable person for failure to file a stamp duty return. The obligation would appear to apply to solicitors involved in the preparation and filing of stamp duty returns on behalf of clients.

These penalties apply to instruments executed on or after 7 July 2012. Section 8A provides for a penalty of €3000 where an incorrect electronic or paper return relating to an instrument is filed with the Revenue in circumstances where the person is aware that the facts filed are incorrect.

Section 8B provides for a penalty of €3000 where an accountable person fails to cause an electronic or paper return relating to an instrument to be filed before the time specified in s. 2(3) of the SDCA, that is, before the expiration of thirty days after the first execution of the instrument.

Section 8(3) provides that in the case of fraudulent or negligent execution of an instrument where facts affecting liability are not fully set forth in the instrument, a penalty of €1265 applies, together with the amount of difference of duty. This penalty applies to a person 'employed or concerned in or about preparation of the instrument'. This applies to solicitors and any other professional adviser to any parties executing instruments that may be liable to stamp duty.

The penalties outlined in ss 8 and 134A SDCA must be considered carefully by all practitioners. There is no de minimis threshold on the application of these penalties which could theoretically apply even where there is no stamp duty payable on the unfiled return.

Section 15 of the SDCA, 1999 reiterated the provisions of the Finance Act, 1991 in relation to surcharges imposed where the value of the property is understated to the Revenue Commissioners. This section has however been abolished in respect of instruments executed on or after 7 July 2012. For such instruments where an undervaluation of property is included in the stamp duty return filed under the e-stamping system, penalties relating to the filing of an incorrect return will be incurred s. 134A).

12.3.2.1 Penalties for late filing of returns: the Finance Act, 2012

Section 14 of the SDCA, 1999

An instrument that is chargeable to stamp duty must be duly stamped within thirty days after its first execution, otherwise penalties for late filing will be imposed s. 2 and s. 14 of the SDCA, 1999 refer). Where the correct amount of stamp duty is not paid within the time limit set down in s. 2 of the SDCA, that is, if the deed is stamped after thirty days from the date of first execution of the instrument under s. 14 SDCA, 1999 interest is payable at the rate of 0.0219 per cent per day or part of a day. The 2012 Act did not change the specified return date for the filing of stamp duty returns, which is thirty days after first execution; nor was the rate of late filing interest (0.0219 per cent) changed. The Revenue has confirmed that they will continue to accept returns filed up to forty-four days after first execution, in line with previous practice.

Section 14A of the SDCA, 1999: late filing of returns

The penalty regime for stamp duty has undergone a very substantial change since the Finance Act, 2012 became law on 7 July 2012. A self-assessment regime was introduced and, for instruments executed on or after that date, a new late filing surcharge was introduced. Solicitors must continue to file e-stamping returns as previously. The e-stamping system will ensure that returns for instruments executed on or after 7 July 2012 will be treated automatically on a self-assessed basis. Adjudication was abolished and the Revenue will no longer examine instruments prior to stamping and the stamp certificate will issue immediately after the return is lodged, provided all charges are paid. The new system of penalties include tax geared surcharges for late filing of returns, tax geared penalties for failing to file a return, and a number of other penalties that will not be dealt with in this text.

The new surcharge is based on a percentage increase of the stamp duty payable and is subject to a grading of the surcharge by reference to the length of the delay in filing the stamp duty return as well as being subject to an overall cap on the level of the surcharge.

The surcharge

For instruments executed on or after 7 July 2012 a new late filing surcharge applies equal to 5 per cent of the unpaid duty where the stamp duty return is filed after the specified return date (44 days) subject to a maximum of €12,695. Where the stamp duty return is filed later than ninety-two days of the date of execution of the instrument a late filing surcharge of 10 per cent of the unpaid duty applies subject to a maximum of €63,485. The surcharge is not a penalty and therefore forms part of a stamp duty charge. Late filing interest is charged on the amount of the original stamp duty liability plus the surcharge amount.

On 1 June 2011 it became mandatory to file stamp duty returns online using the ROS subject to very limited exceptions. Payment of stamp duty must also be made online from that date by ROS or in limited cases payment can be made by electronic fund transfer ('EFT').

Section 134A SDCA, 1999 penalties: solicitors' liability and obligations

In cases of fraud or negligence penalties will also apply. A voluntary conveyance must be brought to the attention of the Revenue by ticking the relevant box in the return. Failure to do so will result in a presumption of negligence or of acting deliberately under s. 134A SDCA, 1999. Tax geared penalties apply in addition to a fixed penalty of €1265 in instances of fraud and negligence. The penalty is determined by the number of defaults by the person, whether the category of default is deliberate or careless (failure to take reasonable care) but not deliberate, the level of cooperation, and whether a prompted or unprompted qualifying disclosure is made. The penalty can be 100 per cent of the underpayment.

If an error is neither deliberate nor careless, action must be taken without undue delay on spotting the error to rectify same to prevent it being treated as a deliberate action.

Other obligations to be aware of include s. 129 SDCA, 1999, which provides that any person who enrols, enters, or registers an instrument that is not properly stamped will incur a penalty of €630.

Mitigation of penalties under s. 1065 of the TCA, 1997 applies to stamp duty penalties.

Pursuant to s. 128 SDCA, 1999 there is an obligation to produce documents, provide information, and permit access to Revenue officials. Failure to comply is an offence under s. 1078 TCA. Section 129A SDCA, 1999 provides an obligation to retain records of a true return for six years from the date the tax was paid or return made. This is subject to a penalty of €3000 for failure to comply. Failure to produce records where a relevant person (including a solicitor) is retaining records on an accountable person's behalf can lead to a penalty of €19,045 plus €2535 per day until compliance. Employees of a relevant person can also be held liable s. 128B SDCA, 1999). There is a defence of legal professional privilege to s. 128A but not to s. 128B.

It is advisable to retain a record of the stamp duty return (which has been approved by your client) for auditing purposes for four years from the stamping of the instrument. Unfortunately the drop boxes selected in the return are not shown in the printed version and this issue has been brought to the attention of the Revenue by the Law Society Taxation Committee.

12.3.2.2 Effect of a document not being stamped

Section 127 of the SDCA provides that if an instrument is not duly stamped:

(a) Such instrument cannot be used as evidence in court in civil or arbitral proceedings until any duty and penalties are paid. An unstamped document can be produced in criminal proceedings;

(b) It will not be acceptable to the Land Registry when applying for registration of ownership; and

(c) A purchaser is not obliged to accept an unstamped deed. In fact an unstamped deed is not a good link in a chain of title.

Prior to the Finance Act, 2012 instruments that had been adjudicated were considered to be duly stamped but instruments that had been 'straight stamped' were not considered to be duly stamped.

Section 127 of the SDCA has been amended by the 2012 Act so that all instruments executed on or after 7 July 2012 and stamped using the e-stamping system are considered to be duly stamped. This change is of considerable benefit to solicitors, who otherwise would have to satisfy themselves as to the sufficiency of the stamping of documents. Solicitors will have to ensure that instruments executed before 7 July 2012 (unless bearing an adjudication stamp) have been duly stamped.

12.3.2.3 Categories of stamp duties

Ad valorem duty and Revenue certificates in deeds

'Ad valorem' is a Latin term meaning 'by value' and is used to describe a rate of stamp duty that is proportionate to the value of the transaction involved. Schedule 1 to the SDCA, 1999 identifies the rate of duty applicable to various instruments, whether ad valorem, fixed, or exempt from duty. Prior to 7 July 2012 the amount of duty applicable to a particular instrument often depended on that instrument containing a particular certificate. The concept of certification in deeds was introduced in the Finance Act, 1910. Under this Act lower rates of stamp duty were introduced for property transactions under a certain value and, in the absence of what became commonly known as a 'Finance Act certificate', the maximum rate of duty was payable.

Certification in deeds was subsequently expanded to identify:

(a) the type of property being transferred under a deed, for example whether residential or non-residential;

(b) the nature of the transaction involved;

(c) whether an exemption from stamp duty applied; or

(d) whether a relief from stamp duty could be claimed.

The rationale behind certification in deeds was that the maximum rate of stamp duty would be chargeable unless the correct certification to support the lower rate or exemption being claimed was used. It should be noted that prior to 7 July 2012 the insertion of an incorrect certificate was an offence (SDCA, 1999, s. 17). With effect from 7 July 2012 however there is no longer a requirement for the inclusion of such certificates in stampable instruments. Section 17 SDCA has been abolished in respect of instruments executed on or after that date.

As stamp duty certificates are no longer required in deeds, the Conveyancing Committee of the Law Society in the December 2015 edition of the *Gazette* recommends that solicitors obtain a written record of instructions as to stamp duty. A suggested precedent record sheet is available on the precedent page in the members' area of the Law Society website (www.lawsociety.ie/solicitors/practising/precedents).This may then be retained on file by way of a future record, in addition to the copy printout available from the Revenue e-stamping system.

12.3.2.4 The charge to stamp duty—territoriality

Stamp duty is a tax/charge on certain written documents known as instruments which are listed under one of the headings as specified in Schedule 1 to the SDCA, 1999 and which is executed in the State or which relates to property situate in the State. 'Instrument' is defined in s. 1 as including every written document. The most usual types of instruments on which stamp duty arises are deeds effecting transfers of lands or dwelling-houses, by conveyance, transfer, assignment, or lease. Once a document exists, it then becomes important to determine if it is possible for an exposure to stamp duty to arise. There must be a link between the document and Ireland. Territoriality is decided by ascertaining whether the document:

(a) is executed in the State; or

(b) relates to any property situate in the State; or

(c) relates to any matter or thing 'done or to be done' in the State.

If the document is linked to Ireland in one or more of these ways, it will be exposed to Irish stamp duty. The nationality or residence of the parties to the instrument is irrelevant for stamp duty purposes. If any instrument listed in Schedule 1 of the SDCA, 1999 is executed in the State or relates to property situate in the State or relates to any matter or thing done or to be done in the State then it is chargeable to stamp duty.

A document is regarded as executed in the State if the formalities required to make it a legally effective document are completed in Ireland. For stamp duty purposes executed means signed and/or sealed where appropriate.

12.3.2.5 Conveyance on sale

Once a document exists and that document is within the Irish territorial limits indicated earlier, an exposure to stamp duty will arise if the document is one of those listed in the First Schedule to the SDCA. As previously stated, the documents listed in this schedule are referred to as 'heads of charge'.

The amount of stamp duty payable on any instrument depends on the purpose of that instrument. A document is chargeable to stamp duty if it comes within the heads of charge contained in the SDCA, 1999, as amended. The most common heads of charge, that is the basic categories of stamp duty, together with examples of how stamp duty is calculated under the head, are set out in the following text. The two main heads of charge for conveyancers include a conveyance on sale and a lease. A mortgage is no longer a head of charge.

Some of the heads of charge are subject to ad valorem duty and some of them are exposed to fixed type duty. Whether the stamp duty is charged at the ad valorem rates or the fixed duty rates depends on how the transaction evidenced or recorded in the instrument is classified. Conveyances on sale of shares are exposed to stamp duty at the rate of 1 per cent. Conveyances of insurance policies (for more than two years and with an Irish risk) are exposed to stamp duty at the rate of 0.1 per cent.

The most important head of charge in stamp duties is the 'conveyance on sale' head which deals with the sale of real property (houses, commercial premises, factory, farms, etc.), and these are exposed to stamp duty at the ad valorem rate. Property is defined in s. 1 of the SDCA, 1999 to include:

> *every instrument, and every decree or order (including a decree or order for, or having the effect of an order for, foreclosure) of any court or of any commissioners, whereby any property, or any estate or interest in any property, on the sale or compulsory acquisition of that property or that interest is transferred to or vested in a purchaser, or any other person, or any other person on such purchaser's behalf or by such purchaser's direction.*

Thus, any document that is used to convey or transfer ownership of property to include houses, apartments or sites with agreement to build, land, and so on will attract stamp duty at the ad valorem rate. It also applies to non-residential property such as land or housing sites without residential buildings, commercial premises, and so on. For a 'Conveyance' to be a Schedule 1 SDCA instrument it must be either 'on sale' or operate as a 'voluntary disposition' under s. 30 SDCA.

To be 'on sale' there must be parties competent to contract, mutual assent, property, a vendor/donor and purchaser/donee, and a price or consideration.

Consideration for stamp duty purposes can take the form of cash, shares, satisfaction of debt, assumption of liabilities, or an exchange of property.

In addition the following instruments are treated as a conveyance on sale:

- a declaration of trust by a vendor in favour of a purchaser;
- a release by a life tenant of his life interest to the remainderman;
- a release by the remainderman of his remainder interest to the life tenant;
- the grant of an option.

12.3.2.6 Rates of stamp duty

There are a number of categories of rates. The first three are as follows:

(a) Conveyance on sale of residential property. This is dealt with at **12.4.2**.

(b) A higher rate of stamp duty of 15 per cent applies where a purchaser buys ten or more residential units (houses or duplexes) at the one time or over a twelve-month period. This rate increased to 15 per cent from 10 per cent since 2 October 2024. This measure was introduced in 20 May 2021 to discourage investment funds from buying up housing estates. The increased rate of 15 per cent does not apply when purchasing residential units in apartment blocks or to the purchase of/leasing to of properties by a housing authority, the Housing Agency, or other approved housing bodies.

(c) Conveyance on sale of commercial and other non-residential property. The rates are set out at **12.3.2.7**. These rates apply to conveyances on sale not covered in (a) or (b) or in any other head of charge provided in the legislation. This head of charge applies in situations involving non-residential elements of a conveyance on sale containing mixed residential and non-residential property.

The remaining categories of rates of stamp duties relate to conveyances on sale of stocks and marketable securities, policies of insurance, and CREST transfers on sale, and are not dealt with in this text.

12.3.2.7 Rates of stamp duty on conveyance on sale or lease premiums of commercial and other non-residential property for instruments executed after 9 October 2019

In the case of non-residential property, the rate of stamp duty is 7.5 per cent. This rate applies to instruments executed on or after 9 October 2019. This single rate of 7.5 per cent applies to the entire amount of the consideration attributable to non-residential property.

Section 83D of the SDCA, as introduced in the Finance Act, 2017, provides for a residential development stamp duty refund scheme where land that is chargeable at the 7.5 per cent commercial and other non-residential rate of stamp duty is subsequently developed for residential purposes. It operates to effectively reduce the rate of stamp duty to a minimum of 2 per cent on certain residential property transfers. The claim is submitted under the e-payment claim section of ROS. The time allowed to commence building works has been extended to 31 December 2025.

The scheme applies to both one-off houses and larger housing developments. The accountable person can lodge the claim themselves using 'My Account' or the solicitor can lodge the claim on their behalf. In the latter case, refunds are made to the solicitor's account as filer.

The system requires a declaration to be furnished. The accountable person is the appropriate person to make the declaration. A number of documents are required to make the claim as set out in the *Revenue Stamp Duty Manual*, but solicitors should particularly note that a certified copy of the deed and the stamp certificate is required, and therefore a copy of these items should be retained on the solicitor's file.

Aggregation

As a single rate of 7.5 per cent applies to non-residential property, aggregation is no longer relevant in determining the stamp duty liability where a transaction forms part of a larger transaction or of a series of transactions involving non-residential property.

Non-residential property is any property other than residential property, stocks or marketable securities, or policies of insurance. It includes sites, offices, factories, shops, public houses, land, and goodwill attached to businesses.

12.3.2.8 Finance Act (transaction) certificates

This was the first form of certification introduced for stamp duty purposes and one that practitioners will be most familiar with. Originally this certificate dealt solely with the amount or value of the transaction but later it also identified whether the property was residential or non-residential in nature. The rationale for this certificate was to prevent the breaking up of a larger transaction into a number of smaller transactions in order to avoid a higher rate of duty. However, for instruments executed on or after 7 July 2012 these certificates are no longer required to be included and s. 17 of the SDCA has been abolished.

As they are no longer required in deeds, the Law Society Conveyancing Committee recommended in a Practice Note in the December 2015 *Gazette* that solicitors should obtain a written record of instructions as to stamp duty. A suggested precedent record sheet is available on the precedent page in the members' area of the website (www.lawsociety.ie/Solicitors/Practising/Precedents). This may then be retained on file by way of a future record in addition to the copy printout available from the Revenue e-stamping system.

12.3.2.9 Negligence provisions and the professional adviser

As discussed earlier, various Finance Acts have increased the scope of offences in the context of tax evasion, in particular for the professional adviser to a transaction. Any adviser who is involved in aiding and abetting a taxpayer to evade tax will be guilty of a criminal offence.

Similarly, money laundering legislation can impose a liability upon advisers who are not connected with such transactions, and in certain circumstances even if the adviser is not involved, failure to make the appropriate reports of a transaction may render the adviser liable.

Section 8 of the SDCA, 1999 in particular is relevant. Under s. 8, there is an onus to bring to the attention of the Revenue the full facts and circumstances affecting the liability of an instrument to stamp duty. If these are not included in the instrument then the additional information must be disclosed in an accompanying statement. If the statement is incorrect, then any person employed or concerned in or about making the statement will be responsible with the parties to the instrument for the breach of duty. Thus, s. 134A provides for a penalty of €1265 plus a tax geared further penalty where a person acts deliberately or carelessly in relation to the execution of an instrument where:

(a) all the facts and circumstances affecting the liability of the instrument to duty are not disclosed in the instrument or in a statement to which s. 8(2) applies;

(b) an incorrect electronic or paper return under the e-stamping system is delivered, or

(c) there is a failure to deliver an electronic or paper return under the e-stamping system which gives rise to an underpayment in the amount of stamp duty due and payable. Professional advisers who are unsure as to whether certain facts are relevant may express to the Revenue their uncertainty and, provided the uncertainty expressed is genuine and not a tactic to evade or avoid stamp duty, a prosecution for negligence or fraud may be avoided.

Expression of doubt: s. 8C of the SDCA

The removal of adjudication has increased the risk and burden on solicitors to ensure that the self-assessment return is correct and that the correct amount of stamp duty is paid. There is a very limited expression of doubt facility if there is a genuine doubt on the treatment of a matter. To utilise the expression of doubt facility the expression of doubt box must be ticked on the return. Section 8C of the SDCA allows an accountable person, who is in doubt about the application of stamp duty to an instrument, to lodge a letter of expression of doubt with the Revenue. If the expression of doubt ('EOD') is accepted by the Revenue as genuine, late filing interest will not apply to any duty payable on resolution of the doubt.

A letter of EOD must be clearly identified as a letter of expression of doubt, must meet certain additional criteria to be valid, and must:

(a) set out full details of the facts and circumstances affecting the stamp duty liability of the instrument;

(b) make reference to the provisions of the law giving rise to the doubt;

(c) identify the amount of stamp duty in doubt in respect of the instrument to which the expression of doubt relates;

(d) be accompanied by any relevant supporting documentation.

This letter may be lodged with the Revenue at the Stamp Duty Office, Dublin Castle.

Both the letter of EOD and the electronic or paper return relating to the instrument must be lodged before the expiration of thirty days after the first execution of the instrument.

The Revenue has enhanced the right to reject the expression of doubt under s. 8C (4) SDCA, 1999, which contains a non-exhaustive list of grounds on which the expression can be rejected. The Revenue may reject an EOD as not being genuine. Section 8C sets out situations where an expression of doubt will not be accepted by the Revenue to include:

(a) where the Revenue have issued general guidelines on the matter;

(b) where the Revenue are of the opinion that the matter is otherwise sufficiently free from doubt as not to warrant an EOD; or

(c) where the Revenue are of the opinion that the accountable person was acting with a view to the evasion or avoidance of duty.

The Revenue will notify the accountable person if an expression of doubt is not accepted as genuine. On receipt of the notification, an amended return must be filed together with payment of the additional duty and interest. A right of appeal exists against the decision to reject the expression of doubt.

12.3.2.10 Tailte Eireann (TE), previously the Property Registration Authority and stamp duty on documents

Section 64 of the Registration of Deeds and Title Act, 2006 amends s. 104 of the Registration of Title Act, 1964. After the commencement of this section on 4 November 2006 the Registrar no longer has a 'duty' to check the stamp duty on each deed but may now proceed to register a deed unless there are 'reasonable grounds for suspecting' that stamp duty, or the correct amount of stamp duty, has not been paid.

12.4 Residential Property

Residential property is defined in s. 1 of the SDCA, 1999 as a building or part of a building that, at the date of the instrument of conveyance, was used or was suitable for use as a dwelling, or was in the course of being constructed or adapted for use as a dwelling. It includes also the normal domestic outhouses, garden, and so on up to one acre. A rate of 1 per cent applies on the conveyance on sale of residential property where the consideration does not exceed €1,000,000. Any excess up to €1,500,000 is liable to stamp duty at the rate of 2 per cent and any excess over €1,500,000 is liable to stamp duty at the rate of 6 per cent.

12.4.1 RATES OF STAMP DUTY

Prior to the Finance Act, 2011 the rate of stamp duty applying to residential property depended on whether the residential property was a new or second-hand house or apartment, and the category of person buying it, that is, whether a first time buyer or an owner occupier or an investor. This is no longer the case. The rates have changed regularly over recent years and the rates applicable are as stated earlier.

12.4.2 RESIDENTIAL PROPERTY RATES OF STAMP DUTY

The stamp duty regime for residential property was substantially amended and simplified by the Finance Act, 2010. The amount of stamp duty, that is, the rate of stamp duty payable, depends on the price/consideration paid or the market value where the price paid is less than the market value of the property. However, there is an increased rate of 15 per cent if a purchaser buys ten or more residential houses or duplexes at the one time or cumulative in a twelve-month period. This rate applies to the bulk purchase of houses or duplexes (ten or more). The 15 per cent rate will be triggered on the purchase of the tenth property. This will apply on cumulative purchases of ten or more houses, and on ten purchases of ten separate properties over a twelve-month period. The increased rate will apply retrospectively to the other nine units on the purchase of the tenth unit. Any property acquired prior to 20 May 2021 will count towards the threshold of ten units, but the 15 per cent rate will apply only to the units acquired on or after 2 October 2024.

Aggregate Consideration	Rate of Stamp Duty
Aggregate Consideration not exceeding €1,000,000	1%
Excess over €1,000,000 up to €1,500,000	2%
Excess over €1,500,000	6%

Sample

Edwin purchases a house for €1,500,000.

The stamp duty payable is calculated as follows:

First €1,000,000	@ 1%	€10,000
Excess €500,000	@ 2%	€10,000
Total stamp duty		€20,000

'Residential property' is defined in s. 1 of the SDCA, 1999 as a building or part of a building which, at the date of the execution of the conveyance or lease, was used or was suitable for use as a dwelling. It also includes curtilage (i.e. the normal domestic outhouses, yard, or garden) up to one acre exclusive of the site of the residential property.

12.4.2.1 15 per cent rate of stamp duty on cumulative purchase of ten or more housing units in a twelve-month period

The standard rates of stamp duty for residential property are 1 per cent on values up to €1m, 2 per cent on values up to €1.5m and 6% on values exceeding €1.5m. Section 31E of the SDCA 1999, which took effect from 2 October 2024, provides for a higher 15 per cent rate of stamp duty to be charged on the acquisition of certain residential property. The 15 per cent rate of duty applies to the acquisition of individual residential units such as houses and duplexes but not to apartments, where a person acquires at least ten such units during a twelve-month period. The intention of the legislation is to dissuade bulk buying of residential property and is aimed at direct purchase plus indirect acquisition via companies, partnerships, or Irish real estate funds.

Section 31E was introduced by the Finance (Covid-19 and Miscellaneous Provisions) Act 2021 and came into effect on 20 May 2021.

A 'Residential Unit' is defined in s. 31E as a residential property situated in the State comprising an individual dwelling. As defined in s. 1 SDCA 1999 it is essentially a building, or part of a building that was in use as, or was suitable for use as a dwelling, or was in the course of being constructed or adapted for use as a dwelling, when it was conveyed or leased.

The 15 per cent rate can therefore apply to the acquisition of residential units that have not yet been completed. A residential unit also includes curtilage up to one acre in area.

It also defines an 'apartment block' as a multi storey residential property that comprises or will comprise not less than three apartments with grouped or common access.

The definition of relevant residential unit specifically excludes a residential unit in an apartment block.

The legislation provides that where a number of individual purchases either on a single unit or less than ten-unit basis, the 15 per cent charge applies when a tenth unit is acquired by the person, or by a person connected with them, within a twelve-month period.

Units purchased prior to 20 May 2021 will count towards triggering the threshold of ten, but the new rate of 15 per cent will only apply to units acquired on or after 2 October 2024.

The following are outside the scope of the 15 per cent rate of stamp duty:

(a) Section 31E(7) contains a specific exclusion from the 15 per cent rate for apartments, that is, for residential units in apartment blocks.

(b) Certain social housing leases. In certain circumstances the 15 per cent rate will not apply to relevant residential units that are leased to a local authority for onward leasing to a household that qualifies for social housing support. This includes the leasing of residential units to Housing Authorities, the Housing Agency, and other approved housing bodies.

An excellent article by Julia Considine in the August/September 2021 issue of the Gazette provides a welcome comment on the new legislation, entitled 'New Stamping Ground'.

In accordance with s 31E(5) of the SDCA 1999, a residential unit is a 'relevant residential unit' where:

(a) the residential unit was acquired on or after 20 May 2021, and

(b) at least ten residential units have been acquired, either on the same day or by aggregating any units acquired during the twelve-month period immediately preceding that date.

12.4.2.2 Aggregation

Aggregation applies in determining the stamp duty liability where a transaction forms part of a larger transaction or of a series of transactions involving residential property. The stamp duty liability is calculated on the basis of the aggregate consideration.

The duty is then apportioned between the separate properties that are transferred by separate instruments and the apportionment is pro rata to the consideration for each property.

Where two or more residential properties are transferred as part of one or more connected transactions and the combined consideration exceeds €1,000,000, each of the instruments is stamped on the combined consideration valuation; that is, the instruments cannot be stamped separately to avail of the lower rate.

12.4.2.3 The rent-a-room scheme

Under the rent-a-room scheme, gross annual rental income of less than €14,000 is exempt from tax where a room or rooms in a person's principal private residence is/are let as residential accommodation, subject to a number of conditions. If the rental payments received for renting the room exceed the threshold (currently €14,000), the full amount is taxable.

The Finance Act, 2018 introduced a minimum rental period of twenty-eight days to exclude short-term lettings from the relief. However, the relief will still apply to the provision of short-term accommodation for respite cases, care for incapacitated individuals, foreign students, and providing digs for at least four days a week for at least four consecutive weeks. The rules relevant to the relief are contained in s. 216A TCA 1997. This is dealt with in greater detail at **12.5.3.2**.

12.4.3 NEW HOUSES AND APARTMENTS

The stamp duty implications of dealing with new houses and apartments are currently exactly the same as the rates applicable to second-hand residential property. Residential property includes houses and apartments and any site that is bought with a connected agreement to build residential property on it.

The purchase of a site with (or as part of) an arrangement to build a house or apartment on it will attract stamp duty at the residential property rate on the total of the site cost and the building cost.

However, if a site is purchased with no connected arrangement to build a house or apartment on it, then stamp duty is charged on the site cost at the non-residential rate.

12.4.4 MIXED USE PROPERTY

12.4.4.1 Apportionment (s. 45 of the SDCA, 1999)

Section 45 of the SDCA sets out how the consideration for a sale is to be apportioned in certain circumstances.

If the property being purchased is partly residential and partly non-residential, that is, mixed use property, the consideration should be apportioned between the residential and the non-residential elements and the relevant rate of stamp duty applied to each portion of the consideration: ss 45(2) and 52(5) of the SDCA, 1999. The consideration must be apportioned on a just and reasonable basis between the residential and non-residential elements of the property. The vendor must provide a form headed 'Apportionment Statement' which should be retained by the purchaser's solicitor.

For such instruments, where an incorrect apportionment is included in the stamp duty return filed under the e-stamping system, penalties relating to the filing of an incorrect return will be incurred (see s. 14(a)).

In a mixed use property situation the residential property part of the transaction is not aggregated with the non-residential portion for the purposes of determining the appropriate rate of duty. The consideration should be apportioned between the residential and non-residential elements on a just and reasonable basis and each type of property is to be separately certified to the applicable threshold and the appropriate rate of duty is chargeable in respect of each of the residential and non-residential parts of the transaction. Basically you pay stamp duty for the residential part of the property at the stamp duty rate applicable to transfers of residential property. You pay stamp duty for the non-residential part at the stamp duty rate for non-residential property (other than policies of insurance).

12.4.4.2 Apportionment details

Apportionment details are required (a) where a mixed use property is sold for one consideration or (b) where the sale of a wholly residential property or a mixed use property forms part of a larger transaction or a series of transactions. Both sides prepare and sign a separate apportionment. A suggested format for the furnishing of apportionment details is set out below. While this will no longer be presented to the Revenue it should be retained on file in the event of a Revenue audit. In the case of (b), the aggregate consideration (including that portion attributable to contents) should also be apportioned where necessary as between the residential element and non-residential element comprised in the larger transaction or series of transactions.

These details are delivered under s. 8(2) of the Stamp Duties Consolidation Act, 1999—as required by s. 16(2) of the Stamp Duties Consolidation Act, 1999—because the property in question consists partly of an interest in residential property.

Re: Conveyance/Lease Dated: Parties:

Apportionment by the Vendor(s)/Lessor(s):

In relation to the above-mentioned sale/lease:

1. I/We state that the 'aggregate consideration'* is: €____________________
2. I/We estimate the 'residential consideration'** to be: €____________________
3. The basis for the estimate at 2 above is as follows:

____

____

____

Signed: ____________________ Date: ____________________

Signed: ____________________ Date: ____________________

Apportionment by the Purchaser(s)/Lessee(s):

In relation to the above-mentioned sale/lease:

- I/We state that the 'aggregate consideration'* is: €____________________
- I/We estimate the 'residential consideration'** to be: €____________________
- The basis for the estimate at 2 above is as follows:

____

____

____

Signed: ____________________ Date: ____________________

Signed: ____________________ Date: ____________________

Note: Any other facts or circumstances affecting the liability of the instrument to stamp duty should be disclosed, unless contained in the deed.

*As that term is defined in s. 45(2)/52(5) of the Stamp Duties Consolidation Act, 1999.

**As that term is defined in s. 16(1) of the Stamp Duties Consolidation Act, 1999.

Where the property is mixed, that is, part residential and part non-residential—for example, living quarters over a shop or a farm sold together with the farmhouse—the residential rate of stamp duty will apply only to the residential element.

The apportionment form is available on the Revenue website.

Sample calculation

Rory buys a building for €1,200,000 (net of VAT). It comprises a retail shop at ground floor level and a residential apartment overhead that he will live in. The amount of consideration attributable to the residential apartment is €300,000 and that attributable to the shop is €900,000.

The stamp duty on the deed is:

Retail shop	€900,000 @ 7.5%	€67,500
Residential apartment	€300,000 @ 1%	€3000
Total stamp duty		€70,500

Total stamp duty on shop and apartment is €70,500.

The apportionment details form set out earlier would have to be completed.

12.4.4.3 Anti-avoidance—asset splitting (s. 45A SDCA, 1999) simultaneous transactions

Before the Finance Act, 2005, the stamp duty rate on a dwelling-house could be reduced by splitting the transaction. This arose where a house or an apartment is purchased by more than one purchaser and each purchaser takes a separate conveyance or transfer of the house or apartment in order to avail of the lower rate of stamp duty. Generally, where there are a number of sales between two parties at or about the same time, irrespective of whether there is a single contract or several contracts, there is a strong presumption that each individual conveyance must form part of a larger transaction or of a series of transactions. The Finance Act, 2005 introduced an anti-avoidance provision with effect from 3 February 2005. Section 45A of the SDCA, 1999 was introduced to counter attempts at avoidance where a house or an apartment is purchased by more than one purchaser and each purchaser takes a separate conveyance or transfer of an interest in the house or apartment in order to avail of lower stamp duty rates. It provides that if an existing interest in a dwelling-house is transferred by more than one instrument executed within a period of twelve months, the instruments will be deemed to form part of a larger transaction. In addition, if the 'first transfer' of an interest in a dwelling-house (occurring before or after 1 March 2005) is followed by a 'subsequent transfer' of other interests in the same dwelling-house within a twelve-month period, the transferee of the first transfer will be liable to a clawback penalty together with interest at the rate of 0.0219 per cent per day from the date of execution of the instrument to the date the clawback is paid. The purpose of the section is to state beyond any doubt that the stamp duty on such conveyances or transfers will be determined on the basis of the value of the whole house or apartment for instruments executed on or after 5 November 2007. This section also extends to gifts made in a similar manner.

12.4.5 STAMP DUTY ON CONTENTS AND FIXTURES

Generally, stamp duty is not paid on the purchase of house contents, for example, carpets, curtains, and so on, which will pass by delivery and are not included in the deed of assurance. Section 45A of the SDCA, 1999 as amended provides that the contents of residential property are not taken into account in determining the rate of stamp duty on the consideration attributable to that residential property. However, the total consideration must be apportioned on a bona fide basis between the contents and the property. The contents pass by delivery so no stamp duty is payable. In the event that the Revenue makes a finding that the property element has been undervalued, the Revenue has a right to impose penalties.

12.4.5.1 Vacant homes tax

Section 84 of the Finance Act 2022 introduced into the TCA a new vacant homes tax (VHT) effective since 1 November 2022. It applies to buildings which are residential properties for the purposes of local property tax (LPT). This means that it will not apply to derelict properties or properties unsuitable for use as a dwelling and consequentially not liable for LPT. The tax is self-assessment and administered by the Revenue.

VHT applies to a residential property for a chargeable period in which the residential property is in use as a dwelling or occupied for less than thirty days in a twelve-month period. The tax applies to residential properties which are vacant for twelve months or more. The legislation includes a number of exemptions to ensure that owners are not unfairly charged if the property is vacant for a genuine reason. These include the following:

(a) properties currently listed for sale or recently sold during the chargeable period;

(b) properties vacant due to the occupier ceasing to occupy the property due to a physical or mental infirmity requiring long-term care and who had occupied the property as their sole or main residence prior to the cessation of occupation;

(c) properties vacant as a result of structural works, substantial repairs or significant refurbishment work for a period of not less than six months in the chargeable period and subject to certain other conditions;

(d) a property that was the subject of a relevant tenancy for a period of not less than thirty days during the chargeable period;

(e) a property in respect of which no local property tax (LPT) was payable;

(f) a property where the death occurs of the person who was, immediately prior to their death, the chargeable person in relation to the property, that person having occupied the property as their sole or main residence.

Records should be maintained if intending to rely on an exemption from VHT. These may include books, accounts, documents, and any other data relating to the use of a residential property during a chargeable period.

The rate of VHT is charged at a rate equal to seven times the property's existing basic local property tax rate, excluding LPT local adjustment factors. The legislation provides that the amount of VHT to be charged in respect of a residential property for a chargeable period shall be the amount represented by 'A' in the formula **A=B x 3** where B is the amount of LPT payable in respect of the residential property in relation to the liability date falling in the year in which the chargeable period commences, before any local authority adjustment.

A chargeable period is a 12 month period beginning on 1 November and ending on 31 October each year.

The tax is due and payable on or before 1 January in the year immediately following the end of the chargeable period. The first chargeable period for the VHT commenced on 1 November 2022 and ended on 31 October 2023. For that chargeable period, a VHT return was due by 7 November 2023 and the tax was payable by 1 January 2024.

12.4.5.2 Residential Zoned Land Tax

A Residential Zoned Land Tax (RZLT) was introduced in the Finance Act 2021 with the purpose of activating vacant lands for residential purposes. The process to identify lands to which the tax applies is under way at the time of writing and the tax is payable from 1 February 2025.

The objective of the tax is to activate land that is serviced and zoned for residential use or mixed use, including residential use, in order to increase housing supply and to ensure regeneration of vacant and idle lands in urban locations.

The RZLT process has two parts:

(i) Identification and mapping of the land in scope for the tax. This is undertaken by Local Authorities through the publication of draft and supplemental maps;

(ii) administration of the tax, to be undertaken by the Revenue Commissioners from 2024.

The tax will be 3 per cent of the market value of the land.

A vacant site is either:

(a) Residential land (more than 0.4047 hectares) where there is a need for housing in the area. The site is suitable for housing and the majority of the site has not been in use for an extended period of time.

(b) Regeneration land (other than residential land) where the majority of the site has not been in use for an extended period of time, or the site is having a negative impact on existing amenities or on the character of the area.

The RZLT replaces the vacant site levy (VSL), which was introduced in the Urban Regeneration and Housing Act 2015 with the purpose of stimulating the development of housing and to eliminate the hoarding of land. The Act provides for the establishment and maintenance of a register of vacant sites by each individual planning authority and for the charging of an annual levy on such properties.

The amount of the VSL in 2018 was 3 per cent of the market value of the site as determined. This was increased to 7 per cent in 2019. The VSL applies until the RZLT commenced on 1 February 2025. The standard Requisitions on Title will be amended in due course to deal with this tax.

12.4.6 STAMP DUTY EVASION

The Conveyancing Committee of the Law Society has, in various Practice Notes to the profession, pointed out the sanctions that will be incurred by solicitors who engage in stamp duty evasion on behalf of their clients. They advise that practitioners should be aware that apportionment of sale consideration in transactions relating to the sale of residential properties inclusive of contents should be made on the basis that realistic and correct values are attributed to such contents based, if necessary, on valuations from reputable auctioneers. Any apportionments made on the basis of spurious or excessive valuations of contents in such transactions clearly constitute evasion and are in breach of Revenue guidelines. Practitioners are also reminded of the powers available to the Revenue Commissioners to impose substantial financial penalties and other sanctions not only against the parties involved in such transactions but also against their solicitors and other professional advisers. The Law Society also condemns the practice on the part of purchasers' solicitors of engaging in and assisting in the practice of deliberately inflating the sale price of properties in excess of their real price to facilitate purchasers seeking and obtaining increased loans to finance purchase of property. This practice is not in accordance with good conveyancing practice and also constitutes fraudulent and unprofessional conduct, which would render practitioners assisting in such practice liable to serious sanctions by the Law Society.

12.5 Mortgage Head of Charge

Previously where property was purchased with the aid of a mortgage, stamp duty was chargeable on both the deed of assurance and on the mortgage deed.

However, there is no stamp duty payable for mortgage deeds executed on or after 7 December 2006. The mortgage head of charge in Schedule 1 to the SDCA, 1999 is abolished. Mortgage deeds covered by these provisions include primary collateral, additional, and equitable mortgages together with transfer of mortgages. This also applies to further advances made on or after 7 December 2007 in relation to existing mortgages.

12.6 Lease Head of Charge

The lease head of charge applies to the creation of leases and not to the assignment of pre-existing leasehold interests, which are stampable under the conveyance on sale head of charge. Stamp duty under the lease head of charge consists of two distinct charges:

(a) duty on any premium paid for the granting of the lease; and

(b) duty on the rent payable on the lease.

Both of these charges to stamp duty can, and frequently do, arise on the same transaction. The duty chargeable on the premium is at the rate for residential or non-residential property as appropriate. The rate of stamp duty on rent depends on the length of the term of the lease in question. A lease is chargeable to stamp duty under paragraph 3 of the 'Lease' head of charge in the SDCA, 1999.

12.6.1 RENT

The rate of stamp duty payable on rents depends on whether the lease is of residential or non-residential property. A lease for any indefinite term, or not exceeding thirty-five years, of a house or apartment is exempt from stamp duty where the annual rent does not exceed €40,000 per year. There is no requirement to file stamp duty returns when this exemption applies. In all other cases the rate of stamp duty is determined by the term or length of the lease and the rent paid.

The rate of stamp duty payable on the annual rent depends on the period of the lease and is as follows:

1. Where the lease does not exceed 35 years, or is indefinite (and the annual rent exceeds €40,000) stamp duty is chargeable at the rate of 1 per cent of the average annual rent.
2. Where the lease exceeds 35 years but does not exceed 100 years, stamp duty is chargeable at the rate of 6 per cent of the average annual rent.
3. Where the lease exceeds 100 years, stamp duty is chargeable at the rate of 12 per cent of the average annual rent.

In all cases duty is rounded down to the nearest euro.

If there is a rent review clause in the lease, an additional fixed duty of €12.50 is payable.

12.6.2 PREMIUM

In addition to any rent, a lease may also provide for the payment of a premium also known as a 'fine'. This is usually a one-off capital payment payable to the landlord by the tenant as part of the consideration for granting the lease. It is paid at the commencement of the lease. Where both a premium and a rent are paid stamp duty is payable on both. The rate of stamp duty applicable to the premium depends on the type of property covered by the lease and is essentially the same as the ad valorem rate applicable to conveyances on sale. The rate reliefs and exemptions have changed frequently over the years. For residential property the stamp duty rate on the lease premium is 1 per cent on the first million euro and 2 per cent up to €1.5 million and 6% on the excess. For non-residential property the stamp duty payable by the Lessee charged on the premium component of a lease is currently 7.5 per cent.

12.7 Conveyance by Way of a Sub-Sale

The provisions relating to sub-sales are contained in the SDCA, 1999, s. 46. The relief applies in the situation where the owner of property X contracts to sell property to Y, and no deed of assurance has been executed on foot of the contract: then, prior to completion of this contract Y agrees to sell the property or part of it, to a sub-purchaser Z and, therefore, another contract exists between the purchaser Y for the further sale of the same property or part of it to a sub-purchaser Z. If, by the direction of the purchaser Y the vendor X conveys the property directly to the sub-purchaser Z, stamp duty is payable on the consideration paid by the sub-purchaser Z, that is, on the conveyance to the sub-purchaser Z only on the amount of the consideration passing between the sub-purchaser Z and the purchaser Y irrespective of whether it is greater or smaller than the consideration paid to the vendor X. The legislation allows for a chain of sub-purchasers to be involved. As the conveyance is between the original vendor and the sub-purchaser, the cooperation of the vendor is required for this relief to operate.

Sample sub-sale

Alan contracts to sell his house in Donnybrook to Bob for €500,000. Before the property is conveyed to him Bob contracts to sell the same property to Christian for €600,000. Under Bob's direction, Alan conveys the property by a single conveyance on sale directly to Christian, with Bob joining in to transfer any beneficial interest he may have. Stamp duty is charged on the conveyance on sale to Christian only in respect of the consideration of the €600,000 paid by Christian to Bob.

The property is residential.

Stamp duty is payable as follows:

€600,000 @ 1 per cent is €6000.

Stamp duty payable is €6000.

12.7.1 EXCHANGES OF PROPERTY

The law concerning exchanges is now contained in the SDCA, 1999, s. 37, which provides that where an exchange of immovable property (that is land and buildings) is effected, full ad valorem stamp duty will be charged on the value of all the property being transferred. Previously, stamp duty was payable only on the inequality of value in the property which was the subject matter of the exchange. These provisions apply in cases where immovable property is exchanged for other immovable property. They also apply where some consideration was paid, for example where the properties were of unequal value. In effect, therefore, deeds of exchange are chargeable to stamp duty based on the value of lands and buildings therein conveyed. The value of any other property or any equality money paid is ignored. Where there is more than one deed recording the exchange each deed bears stamp duty based on the value of the lands or buildings which it conveys. Where immovable property situate in the State is exchanged for foreign property immoveable or otherwise, stamp duty is payable on the value of the Irish property only.

12.7.2 DEEDS OF FAMILY ARRANGEMENT

Deeds of family arrangement are used when the beneficiaries under a will or the persons entitled to a share on intestacy decide to rearrange the benefits by means of substitution and exchange. Such deeds are executed by the beneficiaries, and the legal personal representative then proceeds to distribute and vest the property in the beneficiaries by means of a deed of assent which was exempt from stamp duty. In the decision of Ms Justice Baker delivered on 30 July 2018 in the case of *Re Estate of Hannon* [2018] IEHC 482, she noted that the practice of executing a deed of family arrangement for the distribution of an estate other than in accordance with the wishes of a testator, or in accordance with the entitlement on intestacy, is long established. However, where any beneficial interest passes under the terms of a deed of family arrangement, full ad valorem stamp duty is payable. This category of instrument has sometimes been overlooked in relation to stamping, as the Land Registry is precluded from seeking production of same when registering transmissions on death by virtue of s. 54(2) of the Succession Act, 1965 and s. 61(3) of the Registration of Title Act, 1964. These sections provide that 'it shall not be the duty of the Registrar, nor shall he be entitled to call for any information as to why any assent or transfer is or was made and shall be bound to assume that the personal representative is or was acting in relation to the application, assent or transfer correctly and within his powers'. This has generated a mistaken belief that deeds of family arrangement in respect of registered land for deaths occurring on or after 1 July 1966 do not attract stamp duty because they do not have to be produced in order to vest good title in a beneficiary. This is not the case. Great care should be taken to ensure that they are fully stamped in accordance with the statutory provisions previously specified. Even though the deed of family arrangement, duly stamped, may not be produced to the Land Registry, it still forms part of the title deeds to the property and must be retained. In addition, these deeds should be entered into within two years of the date of death to ensure that they do not constitute a disposal for capital gains tax purposes.

12.8 Fixed Duties

The fixed duty charge of €12.50 was abolished under the Finance Act, 2007 in respect of instruments executed on or after 2 April 2007 in relation to the following heads of charge in Schedule 1 of the SDCA, 1999:

Conveyance or Transfer of any kind not already described in Schedule 1.

Exchange (other than an exchange chargeable under s. 37 of the SDCA, 1999. This section imposes a charge to ad valorem duty on exchanges involving immovable property.)

Release or Renunciation of any property, or of any right or interest in any property (other than an instrument which operates as sale or a gift).

Surrender of any property or of any right or interest in any property (other than an instrument which operates as a sale or gift).

There is no need to present such instruments to the Revenue prior to being lodged in either the Land Registry or the Registry of Deeds.

12.8.1 STAMP DUTY ON GIFTS—VOLUNTARY DISPOSITIONS INTER VIVOS: S 30 OF THE SDCA

A transfer by way of a voluntary gift inter vivos is chargeable to stamp duty in the same way as a transfer on sale with the market value of the property being substituted for the consideration.

Where property is transferred as a gift, or for less than its full value, stamp duty is charged on the market value of the property transferred. This is the price that the property would attain if sold on the open market. A voluntary disposition is not a conveyance on sale as there is no sale (SDCA, 1999, s. 30). However, it is chargeable to stamp duty as if it were a conveyance on sale and the market value of the property being conveyed or transferred determines the rate of duty payable. In the case of land and buildings, residential and non-residential, the rates of stamp duty in the case of a voluntary disposition are the same as those that apply to conveyances or transfers on sale. For instruments executed on or after 7 July 2012 where an incorrect apportionment is included in the stamp duty return filed under the e-stamping system penalties relating to the incorrect filing of a return will be incurred (see s. 134A). Prior to 7 July 2012 s. 30(3) of the SDCA, 1999 provided that a voluntary deed must be lodged for adjudication with the Revenue Commissioners. Adjudication is now abolished in respect of all instruments executed on or after 7 July 2012. The mode of valuing property for the purposes of the SDCA, 1999, s. 30 is set out in ss 18 and 19. In the case of an instrument which operates as a voluntary disposition inter vivos, all parties are accountable for the payment of stamp duty s. 30(1) and s. 54(1)).

Section 8(5) of the SDCA imposes an obligation on all parties to a voluntary transfer to ensure that the Revenue are aware from the stamp duty return delivered under the e-stamping system that the transfer is by way of gift and the market value must be set out in the return. If the parties to the instrument fail to provide this information they are regarded as having acted deliberately for the purpose of s. 134 A(2)(a) until the contrary is proven.

12.8.2 INFORMATION FROM TAILTE EIREANN (TE) AND TE REQUIREMENTS FOR FOLIO NUMBERS IN STAMPING CERTIFICATES

A new s.137A of the SDCA, 1999 was introduced by the Finance Act, 2010 to allow the Revenue to obtain information from the Property Registration Authority as might be required by the Revenue for the purposes of the SDCA, 1999. In addition, the Revenue are also required to furnish details to the Property Registration Authority, at such intervals and as requested, such information as might be required by the PRA to consider stamp duty in relation to documents presented for registration.

Tailte Eireann was established on 1 March 2022 from a merger of the Property Registration Authority, The Valuation Office and Ordinance Survey Ireland.

In the December 2018 edition of the *Gazette* practitioners' attention was drawn to the PRA Legal Office Notice No. 1 of 2018 'Query management/review and rejection of dealings'.

Paragraph 6 of the appendix to the notice provides that an application to the PRA should be rejected if, among other things, no stamp certificate or other evidence of Revenue stamping is lodged. It also lists a number of other grounds for rejection, including that the relevant folio number is not inserted on the stamp certificate. The PRA has advised the Conveyancing Committee that it will now enforce these provisions.

The Committee has written to the PRA with a view to persuading it to change its practice and reverse its decision to enforce this requirement. The Committee is of the view that enforcing this requirement will add hugely to the administrative burden of the profession and indeed to that of the Land Registry itself. The provision of a folio number is optional in the Revenue stamping system but practitioners should be aware that the PRA have now made it a compulsory requirement.

In a subsequent update outlined in the August/Gazette under the heading 'Land Registry Matters—Update August 2019' the Land Registry acknowledge that there may be some cases where a folio number cannot be entered in the stamping system, where the vendor's title is not yet registered. However, where there is a folio number available, it must be entered by the filer, or the dealing/application for registration will be rejected. The Land Registry advise that in the case of a transfer of part, the number of the parent folio should be entered.

In the case of the transfer of multiple folios, the stamping system allows for up to five folios to be entered. The Revenue suggest that where there are more than five folio numbers involved the first four should be entered and the text '& Others' should be entered in the field for the fifth folio number. The Land Registry have confirmed that they do not have any difficulty with this.

The Committee reiterates its disagreement with the Land Registry on this issue and is still of the view that if entry of a folio number is not compulsory to the stamping system, it should not be compulsory in the registration system.

12.8.3 RESTING IN CONTRACT: S 31A OF THE SDCA

12.8.3.1 Licence agreements S31B and agreements for more than 35 years: s. 50A

The Finance Act, 2013 changed the previously used legitimate stamp duty avoidance scheme whereby instead of taking a conveyance or transfer of land, the full purchase price was paid by or on completion and the purchaser relied on the contract, that is, the transaction 'rested on contract'. In that way no stamp duty was paid unless at some time in the future the purchaser sought a conveyance or transfer. A number of the previous tax planning opportunities have now been closed with the commencement of s. 31A of the SDCA.

Section 31A of the SDCA as inserted by the Finance Act, 2013 provides that a charge to stamp duty will arise on a contract or agreement for the sale of an estate or interest in land in the State where 25 per cent or more of the consideration for the sale has been paid to the holder of the estate or interest. The charge will arise where a stamp duty return has not been filed and stamp duty paid in respect of a conveyance or transfer of the lands concerned within 30 days after that amount of consideration has been paid. This charge under s. 31A applies to instruments executed on or after 13 February 2013. However, the charge will not apply where an instrument is executed solely in pursuance of a binding contract or agreement entered into before 13 February 2013.

A subsequent conveyance or transfer will not be chargeable to stamp duty.

The contract or agreement for sale is chargeable to stamp duty as if it were a conveyance or transfer of the estate or interest where a payment which amounts to 25 per cent or more of the consideration for the sale has been paid. The charge does not apply where, within thirty days of the date of the payment of 25 per cent or more of the consideration:

(a) an electronic stamp duty return is filed in relation to a conveyance or transfer made in conformity with the contract or agreement for sale; and

(b) the stamp duty chargeable on the conveyance or transfer has been paid to the Revenue.

The Revenue will refund any duty paid on the contract if the contract is later rescinded or annulled. While this section does not specify the time limit for submitting claims for a refund, a four-year time limit is provided by s. 159A from the date the contract is stamped in respect of a valid claim for a refund. Interest may arise on the refund s. 159B of the SDCA).

Section 45 of the Finance Act, 2018 amends ss 31 and 31A of the SDCA 1999. As already stated, these sections impose a stamp duty charge in certain circumstances at the stage when an agreement or contract is signed and then provide a 'credit' for the stamp duty paid if there is a subsequent conveyance or transfer on sale. Instead of transferring the stamp duty paid on the contract to the later executed instrument of conveyance or transfer the Revenue will issue a stamp certificate stating that the later instrument is not chargeable with stamp duty.

Similarly, this will apply to licences given to builders by developers to enter onto lands to develop, that is, to build houses, apartments, or other non-residential buildings, or carrying out any engineering or other operations to adapt it for materially altered use. The stamp duty is assessed on the market value of the land. This is provided for in s. 31B of the SDCA, which provides that a charge to stamp duty will arise on certain licence agreements relating to land in the State under which the licensee is allowed to carry out development on that land and 25 per cent or more of the market value of the land is paid to the licensor, other than as consideration for the sale of all or part of the land. The charge under s. 31B applies to instruments executed on or after 13 February 2013.

The charge will also apply where long leases greater than thirty-five years are created under an agreement for lease as provided for in s. 50A. For example, instead of executing a lease (by signing and/or sealing or both), the purchaser may execute an agreement for lease. This sets out the terms to be included in the lease. Stamp duty is payable on the consideration set out in the agreement if the agreement is for a period longer than thirty-five years or for an indefinite period or if the agreement is for any period over thirty-five years where 25 per cent of the consideration in the agreement is paid.

The overall effect of these three sections is that contracts, building licences, and Agreements for Leases in excess of thirty-five years are to be treated as conveyances for sale/leases in certain circumstances.

12.9 Exemptions and Reliefs

Certain instruments are exempted from the charge to stamp duty, or bear a reduced amount of stamp duty, or enjoy benefit from a relief. Part 7 of the SDCA, 1999 lists both the instruments that are exempt from stamp duty and the reliefs from stamp duty available in certain situations. Prior to the termination of the adjudication process for instruments executed on or after 7 July 2012, in order to benefit from an exemption or relief, the instrument may or may not have had to be presented for adjudication to the Revenue. For instruments executed on or after 7 July 2012 a self-assessed return must be filed under the e-stamping system in order to benefit from an exemption or relief.

In most cases the exemption or relief is claimed when filing returns. Some exemptions and reliefs do not however require a return. It is important to keep records to support any claim for entitlement to an exemption. The terms of the exemption or the relief must be met on the date of execution of the instrument. However, in, for example, the case of an agricultural qualification as required for young trained farmer's relief and relief for leases of farmland, certain qualifying criteria must be adhered to for a number of years for certain exemptions to apply in order to avoid clawback.

If the exemption or relief is general then the instrument is not liable to stamp duty under any head of charge in Schedule 1.

The following are instruments of which a self-assessed stamp duty return must be filed under the e-stamping system in order to obtain the exemptions and reliefs available.

The main exemptions and reliefs are contained in Part 7 of the SDCA, and samples of these are as follows:

1. Associated companies relief s. 79 SDCA)
2. Young trained farmers relief s. 81AA SDCA)
3. Transfers between spouses and civil partners s. 96 SDCA)
4. Certain transfers by cohabitants s. 97A SDCA)
5. Consanguinity relief for agricultural land (Sch 1 SDCA)
6. Charities s. 82 SDCA)
7. Commercial woodlands relief s. 95 SDCA)
8. Reconstruction and amalgamation relief s. 80 SDCA).

12.9.1 SECTION 79 SDCA ASSOCIATED COMPANIES

Conveyances and transfers of property between certain bodies corporate and instruments dealing with the reconstruction and amalgamation of companies are exempt from stamp duties (SDCA, 1999, ss 79 and 80 respectively). Section 79 of the SDCA, 1999 grants a relief from stamp duty on certain transfers of property between These transactions usually involve the transfer of shares or an undertaking from one company to another in return for the issue of shares. The relief does not apply to the leasing of property between such entities. The relief also applies to voluntary dispositions and dispositions between all 'bodies corporate', which include industrial and provident societies, limited and unlimited companies, and foreign companies. Section 79 of the SDCA, 1999 contains clawback provisions providing that a clawback of the exemption will now apply if any of the three tests of ownership cease to be met within two years after the date the instrument is executed. The following conditions must be satisfied before the relief will be granted. The instrument in respect of which the relief is sought must convey or transfer a beneficial interest in property from one body corporate to another:

(a) One company must own beneficially 90 per cent or more of the ordinary share capital of the other company, or a third company owns over 90 per cent of the ordinary share capital of both, directly or indirectly;

(b) The company must be entitled to 90 per cent or more of the profits available for distribution to the shareholders of the other company;

(c) The company must be entitled to 90 per cent or more of the assets available for distribution to the shareholders of the other company on its winding up.

It is further provided that stamp duty exemption will be denied between two companies in a 90 per cent relationship if the instrument or transfer is executed in pursuance of or in connection with any arrangement whereby any part of the consideration is to be provided or received by any person who or which is not a company in a 90 per cent relationship with either the transferor or the transferee though meeting all three tests.

In relation to stamp duty relief for company reconstruction and or amalgamations set out in s. 80 of the SDCA, 1999, a self-assessed stamp duty return must be filed in relation to the instrument in respect of which the relief is claimed. Section 68 of the Finance Act, 2004 provides that in relation to the conveyance or transfer on sale head (immovable property) where this forms part of the transfer of an undertaking, the s. 80 exemption will only apply if there has been an actual conveyance to the transferor company before the reconstruction or amalgamation.

12.9.2 LAND ACQUIRED BY APPROVED SPORT BODIES

Stamp duty is not chargeable on any conveyance, transfer, or lease of land to an approved sport body approved under s. 235 of the Taxes Consolidation Act, 1997 where the land will be used for the sole purpose of promoting athletic or amateur games or sports. The relief is now contained in s. 82B of the SDCA, 1999. A self-assessed stamp duty return must be filed under the e-stamping system in relation to the instrument in respect of which the exemption is sought.

12.9.3 TRANSFER OF STOCK OR MARKETABLE SECURITIES UNDER €1000

The transfer of certain stock or marketable securities where the consideration paid is €1000 or less qualifies for an exemption from the 1 per cent rate of stamp duty payable on stock transfer forms.

12.9.4 TRANSFERS BETWEEN SPOUSES/CIVIL PARTNERS/CERTAIN QUALIFIED COHABITANTS

The Civil Partnership and Certain Rights and Obligations of Cohabitants Act, 2010 ('the 2010 Act'), which came into effect on 1 January 2011, did not include any tax provisions, and the taxation measures required were published in the Finance (No 3) Act, 2011, which applies from 1 January 2011. The Act provided that the tax treatment of registered civil partners mirrors that of married couples. Section 96 of the SDCA, 1999 (as amended) provides that a conveyance or transfer or lease of any property between spouses/civil partners is exempt from stamp duty **unless** the transfer is a transfer referred to in s. 46(1) to (4) of the SDCA (i.e. it involves a third party or a sub-sale), whether the property is transferred by a spouse/civil partner or spouses/civil partners of a marriage to either spouse/civil partner or to both spouses/civil partners of that marriage/civil partnership. If any other person is a party to the instrument the exemption does not apply. However, a stamp duty return must be filed and the exemption claimed on the return when availing of the exemption from stamp duty under s. 96 SDCA.

Section 14 of the Family Home Protection Act, 1976 (as amended) exempts from stamp duty an assurance of a family/shared home into the **joint names** of both spouses/civil partners. An application form for registration both in the Land Registry and the Registry of Deeds of such assurance is also exempt from stamp duty. There is no requirement to file a stamp duty return if the instrument creates a joint tenancy of a family home/shared home to claim the exemption. The one firm of solicitors may act for both parties in s. 14 transactions.

In contrast, where any property which is **not** a family/shared home is transferred between spouses/civil partners although the relevant deed of assurance is exempt from stamp duty, the Registry of Deeds application forms of these assurances are liable to stamp duty at the rate of €50. In addition both parties must instruct a separate legal firm to act on their behalf. These provisions are now contained in s. 96 of the SDCA, 1999. The exemption from stamp duty will not apply if the property is transferred to any person other than a spouse/civil partner. Spouses/civil partners do not cease to be spouses/civil partners as a result of a deed of separation or a decree of judicial separation or on the dissolution of the civil partnership.

Section 97A of the SDCA exempts from stamp duty certain transfers of property between former cohabitants. All transfers of property from one cohabitant to his or her cohabitant made pursuant to an order under s. 174 of the Civil Partnership and Certain Rights and Obligations of Cohabitants Act, 2010 are exempt from stamp duty. The exemption only applies to transfers between the cohabitants. If any other person is a party to the instrument the exemption does not apply. The property must be transferred on or after 1 January 2011 pursuant to a Property Adjustment Order.

Stamp duty returns must be filed and the exemption is claimed on the return. The s. 174 Order must be kept to hand to claim the exemption.

12.9.5 CERTAIN TRANSFERS FOLLOWING THE DISSOLUTION OF MARRIAGE OR CIVIL PARTNERSHIP AND CERTAIN TRANSFERS BY QUALIFIED COHABITANTS

It is provided in s. 97 of the SDCA, 1999 that certain conveyances following the dissolution of marriage or the dissolution of a civil partnership are not chargeable to stamp duty where the conveyance is on foot of certain specified court orders. Section 97 provides that stamp duty is not chargeable on an instrument by which property is transferred pursuant to:

(1) a relief order under s. 23 of the Family Law Act, 1995 made following the dissolution of marriage; or

(2) an order under Part III of the Family Law (Divorce) Act, 1996; or

(3) where property is transferred between former spouses pursuant to a foreign court order or other determination to like effect made on or after 10 February 2000, which is similar to an order referred to at (1) or (2) above of a court under the law of another territory made or in consequence of the dissolution of a marriage, being a dissolution that is entitled to be recognised as valid in the State; or

(4) an order under Part 12 of the Civil Partnership and Certain Rights and Obligation of Cohabitants Act, 2010 which deals with property being transferred by a cohabitant to their cohabitant on or after 1 January 2011 under a Property Adjustment Order.

After divorce, spouses cease to be such, and therefore enjoy an exemption from stamp duty only if the provisions of s. 97 above apply. The exemption does not apply in relation to an instrument by which any part of or beneficial interest in the property concerned is transferred to a person other than the spouses concerned. If any other person is a party to the instrument the exemption does not apply.

Section 97A of the SDCA, 1999 provides for an exemption from stamp duty where a property is transferred pursuant to an order under s. 174 of the 2010 Act by a cohabitant to his or her cohabitant. If any other person is a party to the instrument the exemption does not apply. This section applies to transfers made on or after 1 January 2011.

12.9.6 CONVEYANCES ON SALE AND VOLUNTARY DISPOSITIONS TO YOUNG TRAINED FARMERS

Section 81AA of the SDCA provides an exemption from stamp duty where agricultural land, including such farm buildings, farmhouses, and mansion houses occupied therewith, is conveyed/transferred to young trained farmers. The relief can be claimed regardless of whether the land is acquired by gift or on a purchase. The relief provides for a full exemption from stamp duty on the acquisition or transfers of farmland and agricultural buildings to certain young trained farmers who are under the age of thirty-five years and who hold the relevant agricultural qualification. Essentially there are three aspects to being a qualifying trained farmer: age, agricultural qualification, and the use of the land.

The purpose of the relief is to encourage the transfer of lands into the hands of a younger, more trained generation of farmers. It constitutes EU State aid and must comply with EU State aid rules. The relevant State aid rules are contained in Commission Regulations (EU) No. 702/2014—in particular, Chapter 111, s. 1, Article 180 dealing with 'Start-up aid for young farmers and the development of small farms'.

The parties to the deed do not have to be related for the relief to apply. The relief applies to both conveyances on sale and voluntary dispositions executed after 2 April 2007, and has been extended by the Finance Act, 2024 to transfers executed on or before 31 December 2028 subject to the finalisation of issues relating to the Agricultural Block Exemption Regulations at EU level.

The relief, although applying to both sales and gifts, does not apply to leases or where a power of revocation exists. A power to revoke the transfer, whether it is contained in the instrument conveying or transferring the lands or otherwise, will disqualify the young trained farmer from the relief. To be a young trained farmer, an individual must show that he or she was under the age of thirty-five at the date of execution of the instrument and that he or she has completed one of the qualifying farming courses set out in Schedule 2B to the SDCA, 1999 and in s. 81AA of the Act and has satisfied the EU State aid conditions. In addition a transferee must intend to spend at least 50 per cent of their normal working time farming the transferred land and retain ownership for a period of at least five years from the date of execution of the deed of transfer.

In order to qualify for the relief a self-assessed return must be filed under the e-stamping system in relation to the instrument in respect of which the relief is sought.

The relief also applies where the agricultural land is conveyed or transferred to joint owners where all satisfy the conditions for granting the relief (SDCA, 1999, s. 81(4)). The only exception to this rule is where the land is being transferred into the joint ownership of a husband and wife or to a civil partner. In such cases only one of the spouses or civil partners must be a young trained farmer and meet the conditions set out earlier. The section provides a revised list of qualifications, establishments, and revision to the standards of those qualifications. The Finance Act, 2007 included changes relating to education criteria and a simplified refund procedure governing the relief for young trained farmers contained in s. 81AA of the SDCA, 1999. To qualify as a young trained farmer the minimum requirement will be a FETAC Level 6 Advanced Certificate in Agriculture, rather than a minimum number of hours of training. The qualifying agricultural qualifications are listed in Schedule 2B of Revenue eBrief No. 187/18 dated 19 October 2018, which deals with the stamp duty implications of transfers of land to young trained farmers.

When the deed transferring the land is executed, the transferee must hold a relevant agricultural qualification, as outlined above. However, a person who obtains a relevant agricultural qualification within the period of three years after the date on which the deed transferring the land is executed will be able to claim a refund of the stamp duty paid. The date of the award of the qualification is accepted as the date the person becomes the holder of the qualification.

Furthermore, if the farmer receives land, pays stamp duty, and subsequently qualifies as a young trained farmer, the farmer will be required to retain and farm the land for a period of five years from the date which the claim for a refund of duty is made to the Revenue. Also, there will be no requirement that a refund be made within a set time period.

It appears that the Minister has tightened up the minimum educational requirements for young trained farmers to ensure that only genuine farmers qualify for the relief. Only agricultural land can qualify for the relief. However, agricultural land includes such farmhouses and buildings and the land on which they are situated as are of a character appropriate to the land.

The Finance Act, 2017 introduced a condition that a young trained farmer must submit a business plan to Teagasc and must come within the EU definition of 'micro, small and medium enterprises' to claim young trained farmers relief. Section 46 of the Finance Act, 2018 provides that where a person achieves the relevant agricultural qualification to be treated as a young trained farmer after the date of execution of the instrument transferring the lands and who can claim a repayment of stamp duty, such a person must submit a business plan to Teagasc and come within the EU Regulations' meaning of micro or small size enterprise before a repayment of stamp duty can be claimed. The young trained farmer must also be registered for income tax.

A Practice Note in the Jan/Feb 2020 issue of the *Gazette* reminds practitioners that since 1 January 2019 there is a limit of €70,000 in State aid that may be claimed by a person claiming the young trained farmer relief from stamp duty as the relief from stamp duty is regarded as State aid. Consanguinity relief (**12.9.7**), where the rate of stamp duty is reduced to 1 per cent from 7.5 per cent, is frequently available to young trained farmers and is also deemed to be State aid. Therefore, while a deed might have a nil liability to stamp duty arising from young trained farmer relief, consanguinity relief, if available, should also be claimed in order to reduce the amount of State aid that will be counted towards the limit of €70,000.

12.9.7 CONSANGUINITY RELIEF

Special consanguinity relief is available when transferring farmland between certain family members. This has the effect of reducing stamp duty to 1 per cent on family farm transfers that qualify for the relief. Previously a stamp duty relief known as consanguinity relief was available where a relationship existed between the parties to the deed, and this is known as consanguinity relief. This relief was available in the case of either a sale or a gift of property between certain related persons and where the instrument was stamped at 50 per cent, the specified rate for such instrument. The relief was not available in relation to a lease or the transfer of stocks or marketable securities.

Consanguinity relief is no longer available for instruments transferring or conveying residential property executed on or after 8 December 2010 or for non-residential property **apart** from agricultural land after 31 December 2015.

When consanguinity relief applies for farm transfers the rate of stamp duty on the instrument is reduced from 7.5 per cent to 1 per cent. This relief is due to expire on 31 December 2028.

In the case of farming land consanguinity relief continues to apply to instruments executed:

1. on or after 1 January 2016 in respect of transfers or conveyances of land by a person of any age; and
2. on or after 1 January 2016 and before 24 December 2017 executed by a person who has not reached the age of 67 years at the date of the transfer or conveyance.

Where the transferees are co-owners of the land they must all be under the age of 67 years at the date of the transfer or conveyance;

3. on or after 25 December 2017 and up to 31 December 2028 by a person of any age subject to the conditions set out below.

The conditions for availing of the relief are as follows: the individual to whom the farmland is being transferred or conveyed must be an active farmer and must from the date of execution of the transfer or conveyance:

1. farm the land for a period of not less than six years; or
2. lease it for a period of not less than six years to an individual who will farm the land, or lease the land to a partnership or to a company whose main shareholder and working director farms the land on behalf of the company.

The person who farms the land (including the partners or working director in the case of a company), or the individual, to whom the land is leased, must:

(a) be the holder of (or within a period of four years from the date of the deed of transfer/conveyance, become the holder of) a qualification set out in Schedule 2, 2A, or 2B of the SDCA, 1999; or

(b) spend not less than 50 per cent of the individual's normal working time farming land including the land being transferred. The Revenue accepts that 'normal working time' approximates to forty hours per week. This will enable farmers with off-farm employment to qualify for the relief provided they spend a minimum of twenty hours per week working on the farm;

(c) The land must be farmed on a commercial basis with a view to the realisation of profits from the land.

In order to avail of the relief, each of the persons to whom the property is transferred must be related to each of the transferors to the required degree. The degree of relationship is mainly based on direct ancestry and extends to nephews and nieces but does not include cousins or in-laws. The relief is provided for in paragraph 15 in Schedule 1 to the SDCA, 1999, and the list of related persons who may qualify for consanguinity relief includes a lineal descendant, parent, grandparent, step-parent, husband or wife, brother or sister of a parent or brother or sister, or lineal descendant of a parent, husband or wife, or brother or sister.

'Lineal descendant' is also now defined in s. 1, in relation to a conveyance or transfer (whether on sale or as a voluntary disposition inter vivos), to include a person who, as transferee, is a child of the transferor. The 'child' would be interpreted in the context of the above definition and will also include a child as defined in s. 2 of the Adoption Act, 2010. This would include as a relative, for the purpose of consanguinity relief, a foster brother or foster nephew, foster uncle, and so on.

12.9.8 FAMILY FARM TRANSFER RELIEF

Section 83B of the SDCA, 1999 provides for an exemption from stamp duty on certain transfers of farmland from a child to a parent in the context of certain family arrangements to which the provisions of s. 599 of the Taxes Consolidation Act, 1997, as amended, apply for capital gains tax purposes. A child includes a child of a deceased child, and certain nephews, nieces, and foster children. A self-assessed stamp duty return must be filed under the e-stamping system in order to obtain the exemption.

12.9.9 FARM CONSOLIDATION RELIEF

The purpose of Farm Consolidation Relief is to encourage the consolidation of farm holdings, to reduce fragmentation, and to improve the operation and viability of farms. Teagasc is required to certify that the purchase, sales and transfers, that is, the disposals and acquisitions of land, are being carried out for genuine consolidation purposes. A number of conditions apply; for example, they must intend to retain ownership of the land and use the land for farming for a period of at least five years from the date the relief is claimed and a Farm Restructuring Certificate (a Consolidation Certificate) must be obtained from Teagasc.

Section 81C SDCA revived the relief. The relief constitutes an EU State aid and must comply with State aid rules. The relief is available where farm holdings are consolidated by way of linked sales and purchases of land and where land is transferred as a gift or by way of exchange. It is basically available to farmers who buy and sell agricultural land in order to consolidate their holdings. Stamp duty at a reduced rate of 1 per cent (usual rate 7.5 per cent) is applied to the excess of the value of the land acquired over the value of the land disposed of, where the acquisition and disposal take place within a twenty-four-month period of each other. The relief has been extended to 31 December 2028 pending finalisation of issues relating to EU Agricultural Block Exemption Regulations.

12.9.10 COMMERCIAL WOODLANDS

Section 95 of the SDCA, 1999 provides partial relief from stamp duty in respect of certain instruments relating to the sale or lease of lands on which commercial woodlands/trees are growing. The relief previously only applied to a sale or lease of land and was not available in the case of a gift. In a recent appeal before the Appeal Commissioners, they determined that the relief is also applicable to a conveyance or transfer operating as a voluntary disposition. Accordingly, the relief will now apply where the conveyance or transfer is on sale or the conveyance or transfer operates as a voluntary disposition (gift).

The trees must be growing on a substantial part of the land. While 'substantial' is not defined in the legislation, the Revenue will consider each case on its merit. A substantial part is regarded as not less than 75 per cent of the land. The woodlands must be managed on a commercial basis and with a view to making a profit.

The relief applies to the portion of the consideration which represents the value of the trees growing on the lands. An apportionment of the consideration between the land and the trees growing on the lands is required.

12.9.11 CHARITIES

Section 82 of the SDCA, 1999 provides an exemption from stamp duty for conveyances, transfers, and leases of lands which will be used for charitable purposes in the State or Northern Ireland to a body of persons established solely for charitable purposes or to the trustees of a trust so established.

The appropriate charity ('CHY') number must be quoted on the instrument. If charity exemption status has not already been obtained an application form must be completed and the exemption status obtained.

On receipt of the CHY number a self-assessed stamp duty return must be filed under the e-stamping system to obtain the exemption.

12.9.12 TRANSFERS BY HOUSING AUTHORITY OR AFFORDABLE HOME PARTNERSHIP NOW STAMPABLE

Paragraph 3 of Schedule 1 to the Stamp Duty (E-stamping of Instruments) Regulations, 2009 (SI 476/2009) lists instruments that do not have to be stamped using the e-stamping system. They include instruments giving effect to the conveyance, transfer, or lease of a house, building, or land to or by a housing authority or the Affordable Homes Partnership ('AHP').

However, with effect from 1 April 2011, s. 64 of the Finance Act, 2011 (which amended s. 106B SDCA, 1999):

(a) removed the stamp duty exemption that applied on the transfer of property by a housing authority or the AHP; and

(b) limited the stamp duty payable on such transfers to a maximum of €100.

As a result of these changes, paragraph 3 of the Stamp Duty (E-stamping of Instruments) Regulations, 2009 (SI 476/2009) has been amended by the Stamp Duty (E-stamping of Instruments) (Amendment) Regulations, 2011 (SI 87/2011). These regulations now provide that only transfers to a housing authority or to the AHP do *not* have to be stamped.

Accordingly, any instrument executed on or after 1 April 2011 that gives effect to the conveyance, transfer, or lease of a house, building, or land by a housing authority or the Affordable Homes Partnership must be stamped through the e-stamping system and any stamp duty, up to a maximum of €100, must be paid. (See the Law Society *Gazette* Practice Note of June 2011.)

12.10 Adjudication

Section 20 of the SDCA, 1999 provides for the accountable person to include an assessment of the duty in the return filed in relation to an instrument under the e-stamping system and also enables the Revenue, in certain circumstances, to assess the amount of duty chargeable on an instrument. The Finance Act, 2012 abolished the requirement for adjudication for instruments executed on or after 7 July 2012. Prior to that, in order to benefit from an exemption or relief from stamp duty the instrument had to be presented to the Revenue for adjudication. Adjudication of an instrument for stamp duty purposes meant that the Revenue Commissioners determined the correct amount of stamp duty that owed on the instrument, if any. The adjudication stamp will appear on many deeds executed on or before that date.

Adjudication is no longer possible in respect of instruments executed on or after 7 July 2012; nor can adjudication be requested by the Revenue or the taxpayer. For instruments executed on or after that date a self-assessed stamp duty return must be filed under the e-stamping system in order to obtain the exemption or relief.

Although the Revenue no longer retain the power to adjudicate documents, they have the power to require the taxpayer to produce the instrument together with such evidence (including statutory declarations similar to those routinely required in adjudicated transactions) as they deem necessary in order to establish that the instrument has been properly stamped. In addition the Finance Act, 2012 gave the Revenue new powers to inspect and require the production of documents held by, or on behalf of, an accountable person, which are backed up with significant penalties for non-compliance. The removal of adjudication has increased the risk and burden on practitioners to ensure that the self-assessment return is correct and that the correct amount of stamp duty has been paid.

12.11 New Stamping System

12.11.1 E-STAMPING

The Revenue Commissioners commenced the operation of an e-stamping system on 30 December 2009 in accordance with SI 476/2009 entitled Stamp Duty (e-Stamping of Instruments) Regulations, 2009. Details of the system, which also provides details for paying stamp duty, can be found on the Revenue website (www.revenue.ie).

The new system, called e-stamping, applies to every document that requires to be stamped. Each solicitor should register with the Revenue Online System ('ROS') as, in order to use the e-stamping system, solicitors must be registered with ROS. Practitioners must also set up a Revenue debit instruction to authorise the online payment of stamp duty.

On 1 June 2011 it became mandatory to file stamp duty returns through ROS (subject to very limited exceptions) and to make payment of stamp duty through ROS.

On 1 June 2011, the e-stamping regulations were amended to remove the optional ability to file a paper form of stamp duty return as an alternative to an electronic stamp duty return. The Revenue have made regulations under s. 17A of the SDCA, 1999 on mandatory electronic stamp duty returns and payment of stamp duty (Stamp Duty (E-stamping of Instruments) (Amendment) (No 2) Regulations, 2011 (SI 222/2011)). The Revenue have made the following regulations in relation to the filing of self-assessed returns under the e-stamping system—The Stamp Duty (E-stamping of Instruments and Self-assessment) Regulations, 2012 (SI 234/2012).

The amended regulations allow the Revenue to exempt a person from having to pay and file electronically where they are satisfied that the person does not have the capacity to do so. Incapacity is limited to cases where there is insufficient access to the internet or where an individual is prevented by reason of age or physical or mental infirmity from filing and paying electronically. A person aggrieved by the failure of the Revenue to exempt them from having to pay and file electronically can bring an appeal to the Appeal Commissioners.

In order to file a stamp duty return through ROS it will be necessary to include the PPS number for individuals (or tax reference number for others) of all the parties to the document to be stamped even if the parties to the deed are non-resident. Practitioners should start collecting this information as soon as possible in all transactions involving the potential stamping of an instrument, and preferably before the instrument is executed (which should be verified where possible) to enable the instrument be stamped. Otherwise there is a real risk that late filing and interest charges will arise. Returns with incorrect PPS or tax reference numbers will be rejected by the Revenue.

The PPS number is an individual's unique reference number for all dealings with the public services, including tax, education, and so on. However, a PPS number does not become an individual's tax reference number until such time as it has been registered with the Revenue as that individual's tax reference number. Consequently, if a PPS number is input into an e-stamping return before it is registered as a tax reference number with the Revenue, it will not be recognised by, and the return will be rejected by, the e-stamping system. In addition, the local property tax ID number is required since 30 November 2013 for residential property.

As most people are already registered for tax with the Revenue, the easiest way to check a tax reference number is to obtain a copy of recent correspondence from the Revenue to the client, for example a tax credit certificate or PAYE balancing statement, or a notice of assessment in the case of an individual.

As and from 7 December 2015 a tax reference type is no longer a mandatory field when completing an e-stamping return.

The Revenue has also advised of two further changes to the e-stamping system as follows:

1. Where the effective date of execution is equal to or later than 24 November 2018 the 'size of property' field will no longer be displayed on the drop down menu.
2. For 'type of instrument' on the 'fixed duty' screen there is now only one option for instruments executed on or after 31 December 2007, which is a lease for stamped agreement. Underneath 'type of instrument' a new field will be displayed: 'Document ID of the Agreement for Lease'. The filer will have to enter this Document ID. The reason for the change is that most of the fixed duties as previously referred to in the drop down menu have not applied since 2007.

These are set out in the Law Society ezine of December 2018 (Issue 103).

The main changes introduced under the new system include:

(a) a comprehensive stamp duty return setting out all relevant particulars and information required to calculate duty and issue the stamp;

(b) a new form of stamp;

(c) a facility to stamp deeds online;

(d) the extension of tax reference number requirements to apply to all instrument types;

(e) more reliance by the Revenue on post-stamping checks and audits.

12.11.2 STAMP DUTY RETURNS

Stamp duty returns must be completed and filed electronically for every instrument executed on or after 1 June 2011, with a few exceptions. On execution of an instrument that requires stamping, the practitioner files a stamp duty return with the Revenue on behalf of the client together with any stamp duty payable. This return must be filed electronically or in paper format (the latter in limited circumstances only). The completed stamp duty return will contain all the information needed to calculate the stamp duty and to stamp the instrument. On receipt of the return and payment when validated by the Revenue, the Revenue electronically issues the practitioner with a stamp certificate, which must then be printed and attached to the instrument to denote that it has been stamped. If a paper return is made the stamp certificate will issue in hard copy. The return will be used to generate the stamp.

The former foil/holograph stamp is replaced by the stamp certificate.

A stamp duty return should not be filed in the case of any of the following instruments:

1. An instrument creating a joint tenancy between spouses or civil partners to which s. 14 of the Family Home Protection Act, 1976 applies.
2. A conveyance, transfer, or lease of a house, building, or land by or to a Housing Authority or the Affordable Homes Partnership to which s. 106B (Housing Authorities and Affordable Homes Partnership) of the SDCA applies.
3. A lease for any indefinite term or any term not exceeding thirty-five years to which paragraph (1) under the heading 'lease' in Schedule 1 to the SDCA applies, or an instrument to which s. 108B (National Asset Management Agency) of the SDCA applies.

12.11.3 STAMP CERTIFICATE FORMAT

Each stamp certificate bears its own unique security number and other specific details that will associate it solely and clearly with one particular instrument only. The stamp certificate will need to be printed in paper form whether the return was submitted in electronic or in paper format. Returns filed electronically, and completed correctly, will result in the immediate issue of a stamp certificate online in cases not subject to adjudication.

Returns filed in paper format will result in the issue of a stamp certificate by post some days later. A facility to amend details on a submitted return is provided for both electronic and paper returns.

An instrument is considered to be duly stamped when the stamp certificate is attached to it.

The stamp certificate contains the Revenue logo and the following elements:

(a) stamp certificate security number (stamp certificate ID). The security number will be alpha numeric and will always have twenty digits and be in the following format: 12-0123456-A12B-DDMMYY-A;

(b) document ID number;

(c) date of instrument;

(d) parties' names;

(e) address and folio number (if registered) of the property;

(f) chargeable consideration;

(g) duty (including for leases the rental element) and all penalty amounts, whether mitigated in full or in part;

(h) reliefs applied;

(i) adjudication marker;

(j) date of issue of stamp certificate;

(k) counterpart marker.

Should a stamp certificate be lost or need to be verified, the e-stamping system will allow the Revenue to issue duplicate stamp certificates and to verify the authenticity of a stamp certificate.

Under the new system the instrument itself will not be presented to the Revenue before stamping except in certain cases, such as in refund applications, penalty mitigations, where additional information is required, or where the case is subject to an expression of doubt or the case is selected by the Revenue for assurance check or audit.

Even in cases where the instrument is presented, the Revenue will use the return to calculate the duty payable and to generate a stamp certificate. Any instrument or documentation presented to the Revenue in support of the return will be sent back to the practitioner pending issue of the stamp certificate.

As previously mentioned at **12.8.2**, the Property Registration Authority have advised the Conveyancing Committee that one of the grounds for rejecting applications is if the relevant folio number is not inserted on the stamp certificate. In a Practice Note in the November 2018 edition of the *Gazette* practitioners were advised that they should be aware of the position and the stance of the PRA.

12.11.4 LOST DEEDS

Under the pre-ROS system a deed on which stamp duty had been paid was sometimes lost. It was then necessary to produce a substitute deed to prove the owner's title to the property. In such cases the Revenue would agree to stamp the substitute deed without the stamp duty being paid a second time, provided adequate evidence could be produced to show that the original deed was properly stamped. The claimant would usually have to produce a statutory declaration giving evidence in relation to the lost deed.

Under the e-stamping system a return is filed on ROS and a record of the return will be on record. The stamp certificate, with its unique ID number and security code, can be reprinted.

12.11.5 RECENT CHANGES TO E-STAMPING

In a Practice Note in the January 2016 edition of the *Gazette* the Law Society Taxation Committee outlined the changes made to e-stamping screens applicable since 7 December 2015 by the National Stamps Office, which are as follows:

1. A tax reference type for the parties to the instrument will no longer be required when completing an e-stamping return. However, in a small number of cases (less than 1 per cent) the tax reference type may be sought by the e-stamping system for verification purposes.
2. Re individuals: PPS Numbers received from the Department of Social Protection and not registered for any tax will continue to require registration by the National Stamp Duty Office ('NSDP') prior to the number being used on an e-stamping return.
3. Re foreign companies: foreign companies which are not (or were not at any time in the past) registered for tax will continue to have to apply to the NSDO for a tax reference number.
4. The 'consideration' field on the ROS dropdown window has been increased to allow input of eleven digits preceding the decimal point (e.g. the system will in future accept a consideration up to a maximum of €99,999,999,999.00).
5. The 'local authority' field in the 'address details' section of the e-stamping return (for residential property) can now be amended where a change of address entry is made.
6. The only option available in the 'type of instrument' drop down menu for 'fixed duties' is 'Document ID of the Agreement for Lease'. The filer will have to enter the Document ID number. This is so because most of the fixed duties have not applied since 2007.
7. Where the effective date (i.e. later of date of execution and date of escrow) is equal to or later than 24 November 2018 the 'size of property' field will no longer be displayed.

The above information and further information on tax reference numbers and other stamp duty issues is available on the Revenue website.

12.12 Stamping Deed of Assurance of Derelict/Uninhabitable Property

A derelict uninhabitable property falls outside the charge to LPT, and thus, in most cases, will not have an LPT ID number, which is required to stamp the deed of assurance of such a property at the residential rate of stamp duty. The Revenue has outlined a new procedure for obtaining a property ID number in such cases. The procedure is reproduced below and can be found in the FAQs on stamp duty on the Revenue website.

The Revenue requirements for an uninhabitable property for LPT purposes are that it is not suitable for use as a dwelling, but note that the stamp duty definition is different.

A Revenue guide on the distinction entitled 'Interaction of LPTl and stamp duty' is available in the FAQs on Interaction of Stamp Duty and LPT Sample on the Revenue website.

Sample Case Study

Query:

I am filing a return online for a derelict/uninhabitable property. What do I do if I have no LPT ID number?

Answer:

A derelict house falls within the definition of 'residential property' for stamp duty purposes. In order to file the stamp duty return online, the following steps need to be taken:

1. As it is the responsibility of the vendor to provide the purchaser with an LPT property ID, the vendor should contact the LPT branch of the Revenue by telephoning 1890 200 255 (or 353 1 7023049 if calling from abroad) or emailing

lpt@revenue. Explain the situation (that is, sale of a derelict house and an LPT property ID number is needed in order to file the stamp duty return online) and request them to create an LPT property ID number for the vendor. The LPT Branch will need the vendor's tax reference number and the address of the property being sold and may request supporting documentation to confirm the status of the property.

2. Once the vendor has provided you with the LPT property ID, you should file the stamp duty return online through ROS, inserting the LPT property ID number in the appropriate screen.

The Revenue have confirmed that the above procedure should be followed in the case of houses that are not suitable for use as a dwelling ('uninhabitable houses').

12.13 Capital Gains Tax

Capital gains tax ('CGT') was introduced in 1974. It is a tax on the gain arising on the disposal of a capital asset by a chargeable person, to include land, buildings, and shares in a company, on or after 6 April 1974. Because it is a tax on disposals (i.e. not just a sale), gifts come within its scope. The standard rate of tax is currently 33 per cent. Various other rates apply; for example, a rate of 40 per cent applies to certain foreign life assurance policies and units in offshore funds, while rates of 12.5 per cent and 15 per cent apply to certain venture capital fund managers. Other rates apply in exceptional cases, for example windfall tax, which is charged at the rate of 80 per cent. In addition, s 597AA inserted by the Finance Act, 2015 of the Taxes Consolidation Act, 1999 ('the TCA, 1999') introduced a revised CGT relief for entrepreneurs, 'entrepreneur relief', disposing of certain business assets. It provides that a reduced rate of 10 per cent CGT applies from 1 January 2017 in respect of a chargeable gain or gains arising on the disposal of qualifying business assets. This is reduced from the normal rate of 33 per cent. There is a lifetime chargeable gain limit of €1m, and the current standard rate of 33 per cent CGT applies to gains in excess of this amount.

Certain assets are excluded from the tax and some gains are relieved from the tax. There is an allowance for inflation when calculating the gain for assets which were acquired and certain expenditures (enhancement expenditures) that had been incurred before 31 December 2002.

However, this relief known as indexation relief will apply only for the period of ownership of the asset and enhancement expenditure incurred up to 31 December 2002. Gains accruing to persons are chargeable to CGT, whereas gains accruing to companies are generally chargeable to corporation tax (except in the case of development land).

The taxation of capital gains is incorporated into the Taxes Consolidation Act, 1997 ('the TCA, 1997') as amended by subsequent Finance Acts. Previously, it was governed by the Capital Gains Tax Act, 1975 and the Corporation Tax Act, 1976 as amended by the Capital Gains Tax (Amendment) Act, 1978 and subsequent Finance Acts. The Finance Act, 2012 introduced full self-assessment for chargeable persons and obliges the disponer or their agent to self-assess when making a tax return and the legislation allows for penalties where no self-assessment is made. If registered for CGT then the tax must be paid online using ROS or My Account.

12.13.1 SCOPE OF CAPITAL GAINS TAX

Section 28 of the Capital Gains Tax Act, 1975 provides that tax shall be charged in respect of *chargeable gains* computed in accordance with the Act and accruing to a *person* on the *disposal* of *assets*. It is necessary for all of these four conditions to arise in order for a charge to CGT to arise (subject to a limited number of exceptions). Since the introduction of the calendar tax year by s. 77 of the Finance Act, 2001, this year of assessment now runs from

1 January to the following 31 December. The date of payment of CGT is triggered by the date the contract is made (TCA 1997 s. 542). If it is a conditional contract then the relevant date is the date the condition is satisfied.

The tax year is divided into two periods for payment purposes as follows:

- in the initial period, 1 January to 30 November both inclusive;
- in the later period, 1 December to 31 December both inclusive.

The due date for payment of CGT is now as follows:

- disposals in the initial period: tax is due by 15 December in the same tax year;
- disposals in the later period: tax is due by 31 January in the following tax year.

CGT can be returned as part of the income tax return or, where a tax return is not otherwise required, on a CGT return (Form CG1). The return must be submitted by 31 October in the year following the tax year in which the disposal is made. The file date is extended if ROS is used usually to mid- November (the date is announced annually by the Revenue).

If CGT is not returned and paid when due, late payment interest at the rate of 0.0219 per cent per day/part day is payable until the tax is paid. In addition, if a CGT return is not filed when due on the 31 October, this being the file date, the following surcharges apply:

(i) If the return is filed up to two months late: 5 per cent of the tax due subject to a maximum of €12,695.

(ii) If the return is filed more than two months late: 10 per cent of the tax due subject to a maximum of €63,485.

12.13.2 PERSONS CHARGEABLE

A person's liability to CGT generally depends on the following factors, namely domicile, residence, and ordinary residence, and the location and type of the asset disposed of. Any person who is resident or ordinarily resident and domiciled in the State for a year of assessment is liable to tax on chargeable gains accruing on all disposals of chargeable assets worldwide made during that year. The same applies to a company in respect of the chargeable gains accruing to it for a chargeable period during which it resided in the State.

In relation to a person who is resident or ordinarily resident in the State but is not domiciled in the State, gains realised on disposals of assets situated outside the State and foreign assets are liable to Irish CGT tax only to the extent that the gains are remitted to this country and such gains are not chargeable to tax until so remitted. Everyone is liable to CGT on the disposal of Irish land. Where someone is neither resident nor ordinarily resident nor domiciled in Ireland they are chargeable on gains on specified Irish assets only, for example land and buildings in the State, minerals in the State.

12.13.2.1 Residence

A statutory definition of residence is set out in s. 819(1) of the TCA, 1997.

Residence status for Irish tax purposes is determined by the number of days a person is present in the State during a given tax year. Section 819(1) sets out the two basic tests of residence. A person will be tax resident in the State in a tax year if:

(a) he or she is present in the State for a period amounting to 183 days or more in that calendar tax year—the current year test; or

(b) he or she is present in the State for 280 days taking the current and preceding calendar years together—the two-year test. An individual who is present in the State for 30 days or less in a tax year will not be treated as resident for that year unless he or she elects to be resident.

Up to the end of 2009 an individual was deemed to be present in the State for a day if he or she was in the State at the end of a day—midnight (a 'Cinderella' test). Effectively it was the nights spent in the State which were counted. From 2009 forward a taxpayer is 'present in the State' for a day if he or she is present at any time during that day.

12.13.2.2 Ordinary residence

Section 820(1) of the TCA, 1997 contains the definition of ordinary residence. This refers to an individual's pattern of residence over a number of tax years. If a person has been resident in the State for three consecutive tax years, he or she is regarded as ordinarily resident for the beginning of the fourth tax year. Ordinary residence implies a greater degree of permanence than simply being resident. Once an individual becomes ordinarily resident in the State he or she will remain ordinarily resident until or unless he or she is non-resident for three consecutive years.

12.13.2.3 Domicile

The TCA, 1997 does not contain a definition of domicile. This is because domicile is a common law legal term rather than a tax specific term. Under common law, every person must have a domicile. A person can have only one domicile at any particular time but cannot be without a domicile. There are three kinds of domicile:

1. Domicile of origin.
2. Domicile of choice.
3. Domicile of dependence.

It is broadly interpreted as meaning residence in a particular country with the intention of residing permanently in that country.

12.13.2.4 Assets

All forms of property wheresoever situate are assets for the purpose of CGT. Assets include land, houses, other buildings, sites be they developed or green field and with or without planning permission, minerals, exploration rights, unquoted shares in any of the above, shares in a company, incorporeal property, for example goodwill or an option, and any interest in property, including a lease. However, Irish currency is not an asset for the purpose of the tax; nor are prize bonds or lottery and gaming winnings or gains from the disposal of Irish government stocks or securities and gains from the disposal of one's principal private residence.

12.13.2.5 Disposals and date of disposal and acquisition

The disposal of an asset includes any transfer of ownership of the asset by way of sale, exchange, gift, or settlement on trustees. A part disposal occurs where less than the whole of an asset is disposed of or an interest in an asset is transferred; for example, the granting of a lease at a premium. Disposals which are not made at 'arm's length', for example gifts, are deemed to have been made at market value.

The main rules for determining the time/date of disposal and acquisition for CGT purposes are as follows:

1. For a disposal under an unconditional contract the date of disposal and acquisition is the date of the contract, and not the completion date.
2. Where the contract is subject to a condition, the date of disposal and acquisition is the date the condition is satisfied, not the completion date. A contract is conditional if a condition must be satisfied before an obligation to perform the contract arises. For example, where the acquisition of land is subject to the purchaser obtaining planning permission, the time of the disposal and acquisition is the date the permission is obtained.

12.13.2.6 Indexation relief (adjustment for inflation): s. 556 of the TCA, 1997

Each year up to 2003 the Revenue issued indexation factors which were based on the consumer price index and compensated for inflation. Indexation relief permitted the effects of inflation to be taken into account in computing chargeable gains. There is an allowance for inflation when calculating the gain for assets which were acquired and certain enhancement expenditure that had been incurred prior to 31 December 2002. This is achieved by multiplying the cost of purchasing the asset and enhancement expenditure by an indexation factor determined by the tax year in which the asset was acquired or the expenditure incurred. Indexation relief was not available for disposals made within twelve months of acquisition. If the expenditure incurred in acquiring or enhancing an asset was incurred more than twelve months before its disposal, the amount of that expenditure was adjusted to take account of inflation. The adjustment was made by multiplying the relevant item of allowable expenditure by a factor, 'the multiplier', which reflects the change in the all items consumer index during the period since the asset was incurred and the year of assessment in which the disposal is made. A table of multipliers for the year ending 2002 is available in Appendix 12.1 and is available on the Revenue website. The indexation table is based on the tax year in which the asset was acquired (columns on the left side) and the tax year in which it was sold (top of the table). Indexation relief can only be claimed if the assets being disposed of were owned before 31 December 2002.

Assets owned at 6 April 1974 are deemed to have been disposed of and reacquired on that date. Thus if an asset was acquired before 6 April 1974, its market value on that date is used as the base cost. Indexation relief applies to all assets without exception but is restricted in the case of development land. However, no allowance for inflation will be allowed for future years of ownership from 31 December 2002, and indexation relief will apply only for the period of ownership of an asset up to 31 December 2002.

Example of indexation

Land is bought on 15 June 1980. This is in the tax year 1980–1981. It is disposed of on 12 May 2000. This is in the tax year ending 5 April 2001. The indexation factor is 2.833. There is no indexation if you sell within twelve months of purchasing an asset.

The Finance Act, 2003 abolished inflation indexation with effect from 3 December 2002. The 2003 indexation factors are used for 2003 and later years, and have not been increased since 2003.

Indexation relief applied to the following:

(a) The purchase price or market value of the asset at the date of acquisition.

(b) The costs incurred in acquiring the asset, such as solicitors and auctioneer's fees, and stamp duty.

(c) The cost of enhancing the value of the asset.

(d) The cost of disposing of the asset.

Indexation Relief is only available for costs paid up to 31 December 2002 and will not apply to any costs paid in 2003 and later years.

12.13.2.7 Annual personal exemption

There is an annual exemption of €1270 per individual which is not transferable between spouses/civil partners. The first €1270 of an individual's net gain (that is, gains less loss including losses brought forward from earlier years) is not chargeable. If either individual cannot utilise the exemption it cannot be transferred to the other. The annual exemption applies to individuals only—companies, trustees, or other non-corporate bodies are not entitled to it.

12.13.2.8 Sample computation of gain

The three main headings for CGT deductions are:

- the cost of acquisition together with any incidental costs;
- enhancement expenditure;
- incidental costs of disposal.

The amount of chargeable gain or an allowable loss is determined by deducting any allowable expenditure from the consideration received for the disposal.

The capital gain is the difference between:

(a) the consideration for the disposal of the asset or the deemed consideration (for example market value in the case of a gift or disposal between connected persons); and

(b) the cost of acquisition of the asset or its market value if not acquired at arm's length and any expenditure incurred on it which is reflected in the state of the asset at the time of disposal: expenditure to establish, preserve, or defend legal title. This may be adjusted to take account of inflation; and

(c) the incidental costs of making the disposal, such as legal fees and selling costs may also be deducted.

Section 542 of the TCA, 1997 provides that where the disposal occurs by contract the date of disposal is the date of the contract and not the date of the subsequent deed of assurance.

The following is a sample layout of a CGT computation in relation to an asset.

Niall Murray—Capital Gains Tax computation for 2023

Facts

Niall Murray, a developer, sold lands for €1,000,000 on 31 December 2022, paying costs of sale of €20,000. He had inherited the land in May 2006, at which time the land was valued at €400,000.

Sale proceeds			€1,000,000
Less			
Allowable costs of sale	€20,000		
Original cost/market value at date of acquisition	€400,000		
No indexation post-2003			
No enhancement expenditure			
Base cost			€420,000
		Gain	€580,000
		Less annual allowance	€1270
		Taxable Gain	€578,730

Capital Gains Tax @ 33% €190,980.9

Sample CGT layout for computation

TAX YEAR 31 December 20.

1. Date of Disposal (generally the date of the Contract for Sale)
2. Description of Asset
3. Date of Acquisition

Computation. €

4. Disposal consideration

Less

5. Incidental costs of Disposal (if any)

6. Net Disposal consideration (4–5)

Deduct allowable costs of sale	€
7 & 8. Original cost of acquisition of asset market value as at date of acquisition	X Multiplier INDEXED @ (X Multiplier)
Incidental costs of acquisition/purchase	Indexed to 2003
9 & 10. Enhancement expenditure	Indexed to 2003
	X Multiplier

11. Total indexed cost

12. Capital Gain/Loss after indexation (6–11)

13. Actual monetary gain (or loss)

14 & 15. Chargeable gain

14 & 15. Allowable loss

If these are any unused losses from previous year insert the amount here

Calculation of Capital Gains Tax payable

16. Total chargeable gains net of allowable losses

17. Less annual personal exemption €1270

Less relief (if any)

Net Chargeable gain

Capital Gains Tax payable: Taxable gain @ 33%. (In 2025)

12.13.2.9 Incidental costs of disposal and acquisition

Section 552 TCA 1997 provides the basic rules for determining the expenditure to be allowed in computing chargeable gains. Section 552(2) TCA 1997 contains a definition of 'Incidental costs' of acquisition and disposal. The list is exhaustive; that is to say, no other expenditure is allowable. Incidental costs of disposal mean the expenditure wholly and exclusively incurred for the purposes of the disposal. The disposal consideration is the value of the consideration received on disposal, for example the sale price in the case of a sale at arm's length. If the disposal is not made by a bargain at arm's length then the consideration is equal to its market value at the time of disposal. It is the consideration which was given wholly and exclusively for the acquisition of the asset. Any disposal proceeds received in foreign currency must be converted to Irish currency by reference to the rate of exchange at the time of the disposal. The following costs are allowable deductions as outlined in s. 552(2) TCA 1997 and should be noted when doing the CGT computation. They may be deducted from the consideration received for the disposal:

(a) Fees, commission or remuneration paid for the professional services of any of surveyor, valuer, auctioneer, accountant, agent, or legal adviser so far as the expenditure is wholly and exclusively incurred for the purposes of the acquisition or disposal.

(b) The costs of transfer or conveyance (including stamp duty) and the cost of advertising to find a seller or buyer.

(c) The costs reasonably incurred in making any valuation or apportionment required for the purpose of computing the chargeable gain or allowable loss.

Allowable expenditure is divided into the following categories:

(a) Cost of acquisition, that is, the consideration which was given wholly and exclusively for the acquisition of the asset, plus the incidental costs of acquiring the asset; or, if the disponer created the asset (e.g. copyright or the goodwill of a business), the expenditure incurred in creating it.

(b) Additional expenditure, that is, expenditure incurred for the purpose of enhancing the value of the asset that is reflected in the state or nature of the asset at the time of disposal, and expenditure to establish and maintain legal title to the assets or an interest or right over it.

If the asset was acquired by inheritance on a death, by way of gift. or on a transfer from a trust, it is the market value at the date of death, gift, or transfer that is to be used. If the asset was acquired prior to 6 April 1974 the allowable cost to be entered in the computation is the market value as at 6 April 1974. In the case of a part disposal of an asset, only part of the original cost is allowed.

Items included in (a) and (b) may be adjusted to take account of inflation.

Note: On or after 2003, the multiplier is 1.

12.14 Enhancement Expenditure

Enhancement expenditure is the cost of additions to the asset, after the date of acquisition, which adds to the value of the asset and is reflected in the state or nature of the asset at the date of sale. Expenditure must be reflected in the state of the asset at the time of disposal. Interest paid is not an allowable deduction for CGT purposes. Where enhancement expenditure has been incurred on an asset, the cost and each subsequent item of enhancement expenditure is treated as separate assets for the purposes of indexation relief. The chargeable gain is calculated as the difference between the various items of expenditure that is both original cost and enhancement expenditure as adjusted for indexation and the sale proceeds. Generally, expenditure qualifies as 'enhancement' if it includes an element of improvement; for example, building a new garage or conservatory, landscaping, or an attic conversion is 'enhancement', whereas routine maintenance such as painting or rewiring a house is not. It also includes expenditure incurred to establish, preserve, or defend legal title. To be deducted, the expenditure must not have proved futile or have wasted away before disposal.

It should be noted that deductions may only be made in respect of expenditure wholly and exclusively incurred in connection with the acquisition, enhancement, or disposal of an asset.

12.15 Losses

Where there is a loss on a disposal, it will generally be allowable if the gain on the same transaction would be chargeable. Special provisions apply in relation to development land.

12.15.1 DISPOSALS ON A DEATH

Death does not give rise to a CGT liability. Section 573 of the TCA, 1997 deals with the passing of assets on a death. The assets which a deceased person was competent to dispose of are deemed to be acquired on his or her death by the legal personal representative (LPR) or by the beneficiary at the market value at the date of death. The deemed transfer at market value at the date of death does not give rise to a chargeable disposal for CGT purposes and accordingly, no liability will attach to the estate of the deceased in respect of any gains realised on the asset over his or her lifetime. The converse is also true in that no allowable losses are crystallised on a death.

The base cost for the purposes of a subsequent disposal, by the LPR or by the beneficiaries, of an asset acquired on death will be the market value at the date of death, irrespective of when the death occurred, and indexation relief is applied from the date of death to this base cost. If the death occurred before 6 April 1974, then the market value at 6 April 1974 will form the base cost. If the personal representative sells any property during the administration of the estate, there may be a liability to capital gains tax—but only to the extent that the value of the property in question has increased between the date of death and the date of sale. Any gain or loss arising on the sale by the LPR accrues to the estate of the deceased and not to any beneficiary. In such circumstances the LPR will not have the benefit of any personal allowances that might ordinarily arise to a taxpayer and cannot pass any gain or loss onto a beneficiary. The distribution of property by the personal representative to the beneficiaries does not give rise to a CGT liability.

If the LPR is disposing of property to which beneficiaries are absolutely entitled, then it is necessary for the beneficiary with the LPR to prove that the beneficiary has become beneficially entitled to the property so that the LPR is in effect acting as a bare trustee for the beneficiary. This can be shown by the LPR vesting the property in the beneficiary prior to the sale so as to enable the beneficiary sell the property in their own right or by the LPR completing a declaration of trust confirming that the LPR holds the property for the beneficiary who is beneficially entitled in possession and that it is not held by the LPR in the course of the administration. The effect of this is that for CGT calculation purposes any gain or loss accrues to the beneficiary who has the benefit of the personal allowance.

Section 104 of the Capital Acquisitions Tax Consolidation Act, 2003 provides that if CGT and CAT payable on the acquisition of a property by way of gift or inheritance arise on the same property on the same event the person paying the CAT can credit the amount of CGT paid by the disponer (the person making the gift) against his CAT liability. The credit granted for CGT paid will cease to apply and there will be a clawback of the relief where the property the subject matter of the gift or inheritance is disposed of within two years.

12.15.2 DEVELOPMENT LAND

Development land means land, including a building, in the State which is disposed of for a price higher than its current use value. The higher value is known as development value. Development land is land with development potential. Special provisions apply to chargeable gains arising from disposals of development land (see ss 648–653 of the TCA, 1997). Development land is defined for CGT purposes and the test relates to the value of the land rather than its use. The current use value is the market value of the land assuming it is unlawful to carry out development (other than development of a minor nature). The current use value may be defined as the amount which would be the market value of the land if its value were calculated on the basis that it was at that time, and would remain, unlawful to carry out any development in relation to the land other than development of a minor nature. The special provisions include restrictions on indexation, rollover relief, and relief for losses.

12.15.2.1 Restriction on relief

In relation to development land, indexation relief is confined to the amount of the current use value of the land at the time of acquisition or at 6 April 1974, if acquired prior to that date. One can allow but cannot index the development value. Enhancement expenditure is allowed but cannot be indexed. Only those parts of incidental costs of purchase relating to the current use value can be indexed; the balance costs are allowed, but cannot be indexed. The rules relating to restriction of indexation and loss relief, and restriction of availability of rollover relief, which normally apply to the sale of development land, are specifically excluded from operation where the total sales consideration (not the amount of the gain) does not exceed €19,050 in any year of assessment. This special relief is restricted to an individual and is not available to a company.

Where an individual sells, for example, part of his or her garden to a builder who builds a house on it, a charge to CGT arises. Normally when an individual disposes of his or her principal private residence and a garden or gardens of up to one acre (excluding the site of the house), then any gain on such a disposal is exempt from CGT. However, where a dwelling-house or garden or part of a garden is sold for greater than its current use value, then this constitutes the sale of development land and the principal private residence relief will only apply to the current use value. In general terms the difference between the consideration and the current use value is liable to CGT.

12.15.2.2 Windfall gains tax

Section 649B TCA 1997 provides that an 80 per cent rate applies to gains attributable to a relevant planning decision. Such a decision has two elements: a rezoning and a decision to allow a material contravention of a development plan. A rezoning means a change under the Planning and Development Act 2000 from non-development lad use to development land use. This change is one from agricultural and amenity uses to residential, commercial, or industrial uses or a mixture of such uses. This section applies to disposal made in the period beginning on 30 October 2009 and ending on 31 December 2014. The Finance Act, 2010 widened the scope of the provisions by introducing a relevant planning decision which includes both a rezoning and a material contravention of a development plan. This change applies to decisions made on or after 4 February 2010.

A relevant planning decision will, in general terms, mean a change in the zoning of land from non-development land use to another development land use, including a mixture of such uses.

It also applies to a decision to grant permission for a development that would materially contravene a development plan. The 80 per cent rate is charged on the amount by which the land increased in value as a result of the relevant planning decision. The remainder of the gain will be taxed at the 33 per cent rate with effect from 7 December 2013.

The windfall tax will not apply in relation to gains derived from relevant planning decisions where:

(a) the disposal of land occurs as a result of a compulsory purchase order;

(b) the disposal is by a company in which NAMA owns any part of the ordinary share capital, or by a company which is an effective 75 per cent subsidiary of such company;

(c) the disposal is of a site of 0.4047 hectares or less whose market value at date of disposal does not exceed €250,000, other than where the disposal forms part of a larger transaction or of a series of transactions. This exemption applies regardless of whether planning permission has been granted for the disposal.

There are provisions included to ensure that the 80 per cent charge cannot be sidestepped by a transfer between connected persons.

The Revenue Commissioners can be contacted in order to provide full information as to the definitions above but it may be necessary to consult with the relevant local authority to establish if a relevant planning decision has been taken in any particular case.

12.15.3 EXEMPTIONS AND RELIEFS

12.15.3.1 Personal exemption

There is an annual exemption of €1270 per individual which is not transferable between spouses or civil partners. A husband and wife and two civil partners are separate persons for CGT purposes and their gains and losses should be computed separately. The residence status of each spouse or civil partner must be considered individually to decide whether or not that person is chargeable to CGT. It is the first €1270 of an individual's net gain (gains less losses, including losses brought forward from earlier years) that is exempt. The chargeable gains accruing to a married woman/civil partner in any year of assessment during which she is living with her husband/civil partner will be assessed on the husband/civil partner unless an application for separate assessment for CGT purposes has been made. The relief only applies to individuals; companies, trustees, or other non-corporate bodies are not entitled to it.

By virtue of the Finance (No 3) Act, 2011 the tax treatment of registered civil partners, which applies from 1 January 2011, mirrors that of married couples. Civil partners can be assessed jointly to CGT on chargeable gains accruing in a year of assessment during which they are living together, and the CGT will be assessed and charged on the civil partner who is the nominated civil partner.

12.15.3.2 Disposals of a site from a parent to a child

A CGT exemption for the disposal of a site by a parent (or both parents simultaneously) to a child of the transferor or on the transfer of a site by a civil partner (or both civil partners simultaneously) to a child where the transfer is to enable the child to construct his or her principal private residence on the site is provided for in s. 603A inserted into the TCA, 1997. The area of the site must not exceed 1 acre (0.4047 of a hectare) and the value of the site must not exceed €500,000. Section 603A of the TCA, 1997 has been extended by including 'foster child' as defined at **12.15.4.1** in the definition of a child of a parent and this takes effect from 31 March 2006. Section 28 of the Finance Act, 2018 further amends s. 603A to allow both a child and his or her spouse or civil partner to avail of the relief. The amendment applies to disposals made on or after 1 January 2019. No CGT is payable on the disposal of a site from a parent/civil partner to a child and his or her spouse or civil partner where the site is valued at €500,000 or less, and the purpose of the transfer is to enable the child to build a principal place of residence on the land which the child will occupy as his or her only or main residence. If the value of the site exceeds €500,000, there is no provision for relief up to that amount, so that CGT is payable in the normal way. The word 'site' is not defined in s. 603A, except by reference to 'land'. On a subsequent sale of the site (other than a disposal to a spouse or civil partner), the child pays CGT on the site transfer unless he or she can show that a dwelling-house was built on the site and he or she occupied it as his or her only or main residence for a period of at least three years. If the child disposes of the site without building the dwelling-house and occupying it for at least three years the child must at that stage pay capital gains tax on the site transfer. The area of the site must not exceed 0.4047 hectare (one acre) exclusive of the area on which the house is to be built.

12.15.3.3 Principal Private Residence (PPR) relief

Generally any gain arising on the disposal of the main residence of an individual is exempt from CGT. Grounds up to 0.405 hectares (one acre), (exclusive of the site of the house), around the house are also exempt. This exemption is contained in the TCA, 1997, s. 604.

If there is more than 0.405 hectares (one acre), then the 0.405 hectares (acre) to be taken into account is that which would be most suitable for occupation and enjoyment with the residence. The exemption is available if the dwelling-house, or part of the dwelling-house, was occupied by the individual as his or her only or main residence throughout the period of ownership, or under certain circumstances, as the sole residence of a dependent relative. In the case of a married couple/civil partners living together, only one house can qualify as the principal private residence of both spouses/civil partners. A person with two or more residences will nominate which one will qualify for relief and will agree this with the Revenue. There is full relief only where the owner has occupied the house throughout the period of ownership. Full relief may not be due if only part of the house has been used as the individual's residence, in which case an apportionment is made to arrive at the exempt portion of the total gain (partial relief). This may happen where the house is used partly as a home and partly for business purposes or where rooms in the house have been let.

However, availing of the rent-a-room scheme introduced by the Finance Act, 2001 will not affect an individual's full entitlement to principal private residence relief on the subsequent disposal of the property.

Restrictions apply if the person has not always lived in the property and can only claim for the time lived in the property. There are special provisions in the legislation setting out certain circumstances in which the individual is deemed to have occupied the premises; for example, where the individual is required, because of work commitments, to reside outside the State or elsewhere in the State, principal private residence relief may be available, because of the 'deemed occupation' principle. However a period of the past twelve months before a principal private residence is sold is deemed to be the period of occupancy even though the individual may not have been actually living in it during that period. Periods of foreign or local employment will only qualify as periods of occupation if the individual occupies the residence both before and after the periods as their only or main residence and has no other house eligible for exemption. The relief does not apply where the house was acquired wholly or mainly for the purposes of making a gain on disposal.

The following are examples of absences considered as living in the property.

A person will be considered to have lived in the property where:

(a) They could not live in the property because their employer required them to live elsewhere.

(b) They have a job all the duties of which were performed outside Ireland.

(c) Their PPR remained unoccupied as they were either receiving care in a hospital, nursing home, or convalescent home, or are resident in a retirement home on a fee paying basis.

12.15.3.4 House occupied by dependent relative

The principal private residence relief is also available to a gain arising on the disposal of a second dwelling owned by an individual and occupied without payment by a dependent relative as his or her principal private residence. A relief from CGT is available where the disponer disposes a property that he/she provided free use of to a dependent relative. A dependent relative is a relative of the owner or his or her spouse/civil partner who is either incapacitated by old age or infirmity from maintaining himself, or the widowed father or mother of the individual or his or her spouse/civil partner whether or not he/she is incapacitated by old age or infirmity.

12.15.3.5 Separated or divorced spouses and spouses inter vivos, and separated civil partners

Inter vivos disposals between spouses/civil partners are dealt with in the TCA, 1997, s. 1028, which provides that no CGT will arise on transfers between spouses/civil partners provided they are living together. In effect, an inter vivos transfer between spouses/civil partners is ignored for tax purposes. When, at a further date, the transferee spouse/civil partner disposes of the asset, that spouse/civil partner will be deemed to have acquired the asset at the same time and for the same cost as the transferring spouse/civil partner.

Where assets are transferred between separated or divorced spouses in certain specified circumstances by virtue of, or in consequence of, a deed of separation or an order made or following judicial separation or an order made under Part III of the Family Law (Divorce) Act, 1996, such disposal will not give rise to a CGT liability (see ss 1030 and 1031 of the TCA, 1997). This relief now applies to civil partners under Part 12 of the 2010 Act which provides that a charge to CGT does not arise where a person disposing of a civil asset is a former civil partner following a court order on the dissolution of the civil partnership. Similarly, a charge to CGT does not arise where a person disposes of an asset to a former cohabitant as a consequence of a court order under Part 15 of the 2010 Act.

12.15.4 RETIREMENT RELIEF

12.15.4.1 Disposal of a business or farm within the family

Certain gains arising on the disposal of 'qualifying assets' by an individual who has attained the age of 55 years and has owned the assets for ten years or more may be exempt from capital gains tax if certain conditions are satisfied (see TCA, 1997, s. 599). This relief is commonly referred to as 'retirement relief', but there is no requirement that the individual in question should actually retire from the business or farming. The amount of relief that will be available depends upon whether the assets are disposed of to the individual's children or, alternatively, to third parties.

Up to 31 October 2013, irrespective of the amount of the consideration for the disposal, total relief from capital gains tax could be claimed by an individual aged 55 or over on the disposal to his or her child of the whole or part of his or her qualifying asset, for example farm or business assets or shares in the family company. A disposal to a niece or nephew who has worked full time on the farm or in the business for the previous five years similarly qualified for the relief.

The Finance Act, 2011 introduced measures to promote the early transfer of family farms. From 1 January 2014 full retirement relief from capital gains tax on transfers within the family will be maintained for individuals aged between 55 and 66 years. The Act introduced an upper limit of €3,000,000 on retirement relief for business and farm assets disposed of within the family where the individual transferring ownership is over 66 years old. Where the market value of the asset disposed of to the child is more than €3,000,000 relief will be given as if the consideration was €3,000,000.

The Finance Act 2024 introduced an upper limit of €10,000,000 for transfers within a family of qualifying assets, for individuals aged between 55 and 69 years. An upper limit of €3,000,000 on Retirement Relief for business and farm assets disposed of within a family will be given where the person disposing is over 70 years. These changes came into effect from 1 January 2025.

The relief is clawed back where the child disposes of the asset within six years of the date of acquisition from his or her parent.

Section 71 extends the retirement relief of s. 599 (disposals within the family of business or farm) by including along with the favourite nephew or niece provisions a 'foster child'—same definition as appears in the capital acquisitions tax (CAT) legislation.

For this purpose, the term 'child' includes not only the favourite nephew or niece but also includes a foster child, who is defined as:

> *(ii) an individual (in this paragraph referred to as the 'first mentioned individual') who resided with, was under the care of and was maintained at the expense of the individual making the disposal throughout—*
>
> - *a period of five years, or*
> - *periods which together comprised at least five years*
>
> *before the first mentioned individual attained the age of eighteen years but only if such claim is not based on the uncorroborated testimony of one witness.*

Although the legislation now applies, and a 'foster child' can qualify for relief under these provisions, there must be corroborating evidence of his or her residence, and so on. For the future, we should advise clients in this situation to keep records of time, expenditure, and any other factors which might be regarded as evidence. This relief is now extended to the child of a deceased child and to a child as defined in s. 2 Adoption Act, 2010, a stepchild, or a child of a civil partner. In the case of a nephew or a niece they must have worked full time in running or assisting in the running of the business concerned for a minimum of five years ending on the date of the disposal.

To recap, From 1 January 2025, the new rules in respect of a disposal to a child are as follows:

1. Age 55 to 69 years- relief restricted to €10m. Full CGT relief up to €10m value, excess chargeable to CGT.
2. Age 70 years plus upwards- Full relief up €3m value, excess chargeable to CGT.

12.15.4.2 Disposal of a business or farm outside the family

The retirement relief provisions in s. 598 of the TCA, 1997 were amended by subsequent Finance Acts. The Finance Act 2024 provides that from 1 January 2025 where the sale proceeds on the 'qualifying assets' do not exceed (currently) €750,000 total relief from CGT may be claimed from gains accruing to an individual aged between 55 and 69 years on the disposal of the whole or part of his or her business assets or farm or shares in his or her family company, owned for ten or more years, subject to certain conditions.

The Finance Act, 2010 amended the retirement relief provisions. The amendments clarified the position that an individual can come within the scope of the retirement relief provisions on the proceeds of a disposal of shares pursuant to a qualifying redemption, repayment, or purchase by a family company of its own shares. Therefore the payments will fall within the scope of the €750,000 threshold relevant to CGT retirement relief.

The upper limit for retirement relief for business and farming assets transferred outside the family is reduced from €750,000 to €500,000 for individuals aged over 70 years. The reduction of the amount to €500,000 given to individuals aged 70 or over applies to dispositions on or after 1 January 2025. The €750,000 and €500,000 thresholds are lifetime limits.

12.15.4.3 Retirement relief

The relief was extended to disposals of farmland which has been leased prior to disposal. To qualify, the land must:

- have been leased for no longer than five years prior to disposal;
- have been owned and used for farmland by the disponer for ten years prior to the initial letting; and
- be disposed of to the person leasing the land.

This charge applies only to disposals to individuals other than qualifying family members as no value cap is placed on the relief relating to qualifying disposals to a child/favourite niece/nephew/foster child as per **12.15.4.1**.

12.15.4.4 Relief for disposal of property purchased between 7 December 2011 and 31 December 2014

The Finance Act, 2011 introduced a new relief from CGT in respect of properties purchased between 7 December 2011 and 31 December 2014. Where the property was held for more than seven years no capital gains tax will arise on any gain attributable to that seven-year period. The Revenue has confirmed that this relief is not extended beyond 31 December 2014. If the property is held for less than 7 years but for more than 4 years and was disposed of after 1 January 2018 it was exempt from CGT.

Partial relief is available if the property is owned for more than seven years. For example if the property was bought in January 2012 and sold in January 2022, the property would have been held for 10 years, and thus any gain will be reduced by 7/10th and 3/10th is taxable.

12.15.4.5 Revised entrepreneur relief

Section 597AA TCA, 1997 (inserted by the Finance Act 2015) introduced a new entrepreneur relief and provides for a reduced rate of CGT of 10 per cent in respect of a chargeable gain or chargeable gains arising on the disposal of certain qualifying business assets made by an individual on or after 1 January 2016 up to a lifetime cap of €1m. This is reduced from the normal CGT rate of 33 per cent. This relief replaced the Entrepreneur Relief that applied for the years 2014 and 2015. During this period, which is for disposals from 1 January to 31 December 2016, the rate is 20 per cent.

The chargeable business must be owned by that individual for a minimum period of three years prior to the disposal of those assets.

The relief will not apply to disposals of chargeable business assets by companies or to disposals of development lands or a business consisting of dealing in or developing land, a business consisting of the letting of land or buildings, or holding investments.

Where the business is carried on by a private company, individuals seeking to qualify for the relief must own not less than 5 per cent of the shares of the company and at least 5 per cent of the shares to a holding company which owns 100 per cent of the company. The shareholder must be a full-time working director of the company for a minimum of three years prior to the disposal of the chargeable asset.

12.15.4.6 Certificates of clearance

Capital Gains Tax (withholding tax)

Section 980 of the TCA, 1997 as amended by subsequent Finance Acts contains provisions regarding obtaining capital gains tax clearance certificates. Section 980 provides that on the disposal of land and buildings in the State (including leasehold interests), mineral assets in the State, exploration/exploitation rights on the Irish Continental Shelf, unquoted shares deriving their value from these assets, goodwill of a trade carried on in the State where the consideration exceeds a certain amount (currently €1,000,000 for houses and apartments and €500,000 for all other properties), the person 'by or through whom' the payment is made (the purchaser or the purchaser's solicitor), must withhold and remit capital gains tax at 15 per cent to the Collector General, unless the vendor produces a clearance certificate issued under s. 980(8) TCA97 (Form CG50A). This certificate does not indicate that the Revenue are satisfied with the CGT position; it merely provides that the purchaser need not deduct the 15 per cent withholding tax. This 15 per cent of the gross purchase consideration must be withheld and paid directly to the Revenue Commissioners regardless of whether a gain arises on the disposal of the asset in question. However, there is no need to deduct any tax unless the sale proceeds exceed either €1,000,000 in the case of houses and apartments and €500,000 in all other cases.

Section 980 of the TCA, 1997 provides that the purchaser must deliver an account of the payment, and the amount deducted from the payment, within thirty days of the date of payment, and remit the 15 per cent to the Revenue. This also provides that if the 15 per cent has not been paid within the period of thirty days the Revenue can assess the purchaser for that amount. Where the 15 per cent is paid within the thirty days that amount will be allowed as a credit against the capital gains tax liability of the vendor.

A Form CG50 A is not required if the asset being sold is land on which a new house has been or is in the course of being built and one of the general certificates listed in s. 980(8A) TCA 97 applies.

The Revenue Commissioners under the TCA, 1997, s. 916 must issue a clearance certificate with a copy to the purchaser if they are satisfied that the vendor is resident in the State or that capital gains tax is not payable or that capital gains tax chargeable in respect of the disposal (and any previous disposals) has already been paid. In the latter two instances, the vendor's solicitor must demonstrate to the vendor's Inspector of Taxes with supporting computation, payment, and so on that the relevant condition is satisfied. For example, in the case of an application by a non-resident vendor the solicitor must show that either no capital gains tax is payable or, if tax is payable, must attach a computation of the tax payable and pay any such tax together with any tax chargeable on any gain accruing in any earlier year on a previous disposal of the asset. *The grounds for the application must be clearly marked on the Form CG50 and only one of the three available options should be specified.* The clearance certificate is given on a Form CG50A. Anti-avoidance provisions are in place to ensure that this requirement is not avoided by negotiating a number of contracts, each for a consideration of less than €1,000,000 or €500,000. The provisions contained in s. 980 apply to all sales whether by an Irish resident or by a non-resident. However, the legislation is principally enacted to ensure that capital gains tax is collected on sales of Irish property by non-residents. Tax deducted is treated as payment on account of the eventual capital gains tax liability.

When the consideration is of a kind from which the 15 per cent deduction cannot be made and the vendor does not produce a clearance certificate, the person acquiring the asset must, within seven days of the time at which the acquisition is made, notify the Revenue Commissioners in writing of the acquisition and give particulars of the asset acquired, the consideration for acquiring the asset, the market value of the consideration, and the name and address of the person making the disposal. In addition the person must pay to the Revenue Commissioners an amount of capital gains tax equal to 15 per cent of the market value. In all cases the vendor's solicitor must submit a Form CG50 applying for a CG50A immediately the contracts are signed and where the consideration exceeds €1,000,000 where a dwelling-house or apartment is being sold or €500,000 when any other property is being sold.

Where the withholding tax of 15 per cent is withheld, the purchaser's solicitor should give a completed form CG50B to the vendor's solicitor, and when a receipt for the payment issues from the Revenue this should also be provided to the vendor's solicitor to facilitate the vendor in claiming the tax withheld as a credit against any capital gains tax that may be due.

Since June 2020 the Revenue have introduced a system for the online processing of the CG50A and CG50B forms. Applications for CG50A and CG50B forms can be submitted online through ROS or My Account. The Revenue will continue to accept paper applications but the turnaround time for the issuing of the CG50A is approximately ten days from 1 June 2021.

12.15.4.7 Procedure for obtaining capital gains tax clearance certificates (CG50A) on or after June 2020

Since June 2020 the online CG50 application system is available for:

(a) Vendors applying for an eCG50A certificate, and

(b) Purchasers filing an eCG50B form.

Online processing significantly improves the turnaround time for applicants seeking a CG50A certificate. Resident applicants can receive an immediate turnaround on their application, in general.

For customers who are non-e-enabled the Revenue continues to support paper based applications, but with a slower turnaround time.

Section 980 TCA 1997 outlines in detail the process of withholding tax on certain disposals. It provides that on the payment of consideration for acquiring certain assets a purchaser must withhold 15 per cent of the consideration and pay this to the Revenue unless the vendor can produce a CG50A.

Where the consideration of the disposal of certain assets exceeds €1,000,000 in the case of houses and apartments and €500,000 in all other cases, the person paying that consideration must deduct 15 per cent and remit it to the Revenue Commissioners unless the vendor produces a capital gains tax clearance certificate (Form CG50A). The assets in question are specified in s. 980(2) of the TCA, 1997 and in **12.13.2.4**. In practice, the Revenue Commissioners will not issue a CG50A after the consideration has been paid and under no circumstances should an undertaking be accepted from a vendor's solicitor to produce a certificate after completion.

Since June 2021 applicants applying for a Form CG50A need to be registered on ROS or My Account, unless their agent/solicitor submits the application on their behalf via ROS. All applicants must be, or have previously been, registered for CGT prior to making the application.

There are 3 separate bases on which the clearance may be granted:

1. The applicant is Irish resident.
2. The is no CGT due, or
3. The CGT due has been paid.

If the vendor is Irish resident this should be the only basis selected for the application as the other options (no CGT or CGT paid) all have additional submission requirements.

The following details must be provided for **resident** vendors:

(a) Name and PPSN/TRN (Tax Reference Number) of all the vendors. For multiple vendors all vendors will need to be registered for CGT.

(b) Name and address of all purchasers. (PPSN/TRN of purchasers is optional).

(c) Signed copy of the contract for sale.

(d) Asset address or Ordinance Survey Ireland grid reference.

There may be requirement for:

1. Consideration value documents (if consideration amount is different from the value in the contract).
2. Ownership documents (if complex ownership dates exist, for example share purchases).
3. Closing dates elapsed documents (if the closing date on the contract has elapsed an explanation for the late application is required).
4. A letter of undertaking to furnish signed contracts (if unsigned contracts have been submitted).

The following declarations by the vendor may be needed:

1. Confirmation if the asset was obtained by gift, inheritance, or neither.
2. If the asset was obtained by gift or inheritance, a confirmation that obligations under the Capital Acquisitions Tax Consolidation Act 2003 (CATCA 2003) were met will be required.
3. Confirmation that any tax obligations owing which relate to the asset are fulfilled. Certain obligations may have a future pay and file deadline—for example, rental income—and these will need to be specified in the application if they have not yet been fulfilled. This point links to the new CGT clearance procedure for non-residents discussed at **12.15.4.9**, although it is not specifically directed at non-residents.

Revenue note that the question at 3 above can be used by agents to ensure that they are not personally liable for potential taxes arising from the sale of an asset by a non-resident vendor under s. 1034 or s. 1043 TCA 1997.

Non- resident vendors are required to provide:

1. CGT computations.
2. CGT payment receipt (if CGT is due).
3. A letter of undertaking to pay any CGT due if they have not paid it yet.

Non-resident vendors are dealt with at **12.15.4.9**.

If the eCG50 form indicates that there are taxes due, the tax must be paid to get the clearance. The Tax Duty Manual (TDM 42-03-01a, updated in January 2022) indicates that Revenue will then have thirty days from the date of the application for the certificate to decide if an intervention is warranted. This timeline is shorter than the thirty-five working days envisaged in the non-resident vendor clearance process.

The ROS system allows the upload of various documents to support the application. Mandatory supporting documentation are as follows:

1. Signed contract for sale (or unsigned contract plus a letter of undertaking from the solicitor hat signed contracts will be supplied within two weeks).

The following supporting documents are required depending on the complexity of the application:

a. Two letters of undertaking from the solicitor: one for applicants not submitting a signed contract and one for applicants whose solicitor will pay the CGT liability after the consideration has been paid.

b. CGT calculations for applicants who select 'no CGT due' or 'CGT is paid' in their declaration reasons for obtaining a CG50A.

c. Asset acquisition documentation if there is more than one date or complex acquisition dates, such as multiple vendors each with their own acquisition date, or various dates of share purchase.

Sometimes a vendor will refuse to furnish Form CG50A, arguing that a particular property was not liable for capital gains tax by reason of being the vendor's only or main residence. The legal position is quite clear. The question of whether a particular transaction is or is not liable to capital gains tax is not relevant. A purchaser is not required to make any enquiries about the vendor's tax liability and is not obliged to consider any information about it that may be given to him. All that is relevant is the amount of the consideration. If it exceeds a certain threshold (currently €1,000,000 for houses and apartments and €500,000 for all other property), the purchaser's solicitor must insist on getting Form CG50A or make the deduction prescribed by the Act from the amount of the purchase money paid. A solicitor should not offer or accept an undertaking to furnish CG50A.

12.15.4.8 New houses and capital gains tax

There is one exception to the rule that Form CG50A must be produced where all the relevant conditions apply, in order to avoid withholding tax. If the asset being sold is land on which a new house has been built or land on which a new house is in the course of construction, other certificates can be used.

As an alternative to obtaining Form CG50A where the vendor (the builder) is disposing of a newly constructed house, production of any one of the following certificates will exempt the purchaser from deducting the 15 per cent withholding tax:

(a) A copy current notification of determination issued to the vendor under the TCA, 1997, s. 531I; (C2 Clearance Certificate—subcontractors) indicating a 0 per cent rate.

(b) A copy current tax clearance certificate issued to the vendor under ss 1094 and 1095 of the TCA, 1997; or for licence application.

(c) A copy current tax clearance certificate issued to the vendor for the particular purposes of the TCA, 1997, s. 980.

If the appropriate tax clearance certificate Form CG50A or those referred to at (a), (b), and (c) above are not produced by the vendor, the person acquiring such asset is obliged on payment of the consideration to deduct 15 per cent of the consideration and remit that amount to the Revenue Commissioners.

12.15.4.9 Non-resident vendor (CGT clearance post 24 October 2022)

It is important to deal with the issue of obtaining Revenue clearance in relation to a disposal by a non-resident vendor at the early stage of a transaction and not regard same as a mere completion item, in order to prevent the withholding tax applying. An individual who is neither resident, ordinarily resident, or domiciled in the State is chargeable to Irish capital gains tax on the disposal of certain 'specified Irish assets'. The specified assets are listed in the TCA, 1997, s. 29 and are as follows:

(a) Land in Ireland, which includes not just actual land but any interest in land such as buildings or leases in land.

(b) Minerals in Ireland, or any rights, interests, or other assets in relation to minerals or mining searching for minerals. In addition it includes exploration or exploitation rights in the Irish Continental Shelf, which are deemed to be assets situated in the State.

(c) Shares deriving their value or greater part of their value directly or indirectly from mining or from assets listed in paragraphs (a) and (b) above other than shares quoted on a stock exchange.

Therefore where a non-resident individual disposes a s. 29 specified asset they will be within the charge to Irish CGT and they will have a liability to CGT in respect of any gain arising. If the non-resident client does not pay any CGT in respect of the asset being disposed of the Revenue can collect the CGT from the Irish Solicitor.

All solicitors through whom CGT/income tax payments are made on behalf of non-resident individuals assessable and chargeable to CGT/income tax should be aware of the provisions of s. 1034 and s. 1043 of the TCA, 1997, which apply equally to income tax and capital gains tax. Essentially these sections provide that a solicitor may have a secondary liability to capital gains tax and or income tax in circumstances where they act for a non-resident vendor in relation to the sale of a property in the State.

Section 1034 of the TCA, 1997 provides that, in the case of a non-resident, individual assessable and chargeable to CGT and income tax, capital gains tax and income tax can be assessed:

> *in the name of any trustee, guardian or committee of such person, or of any factor, agent, receiver, branch or manager, whether such factor, agent, receiver, branch or manager has the receipt of the profits or gains or not, in like manner and to the like amount as such non-resident person would be assessed and charged if such a person were resident in the State and in the actual receipt of such profits or gains.*

The extent of any liability for the non-resident individual is the same as if he/she were actually resident in the State. The imposition of a charge on their representative (solicitor) in such cases leads to a liability for the representative where the non-resident vendor does not discharge any CGT liability arising in respect of the asset being disposed of.

The Revenue interprets s. 1034 widely as applying to any representative of any kind in Ireland. If an Irish resident solicitor acts as an agent for a non-resident vendor he or she needs to bear in mind that this may result in a tax liability under s. 1034. The term 'agent' is not defined and, in light of the fact that the 'agent' can be assessed for the non-resident's capital gains tax liability, regardless of the fact that it is not in receipt of the proceeds of sale, solicitors should be particularly cautious in relation to this section.

Prior to 24 October 2022 the recommended practice for a solicitor acting for a non-resident vendor in the case of a disposal of a specified asset, and who is in receipt of the sale proceeds, was not to release the proceeds to his or her client until:

(a) the relevant capital gains tax returns have been filed with the Revenue;

(b) the outstanding capital gains tax has been paid;

(c) a nil notice of assessment has issued form the Revenue; and

(d) the Revenue have issued a 'no audit' letter following a review of the return.

Essentially, the no audit letter is a letter which states that, based on the information that is contained in the tax return for the non-resident, it is not intended to carry out an audit. It might be prudent for a solicitor to ensure that any tax is paid even though Form CG50A is not required.

REQUESTS FOR CLEARANCE TO DISTRIBUTE SALE PROCEEDS: Capital Gains Tax and non -resident vendors

Position post 24 October 2022

A new Revenue clearance procedure in non- resident cases operate from 24 October 2022. The new process is outlined in Revenue Tax Duty Manual (TDM) 45-01-05. The clearance procedure outlined deals mainly with issues arising in relation to disposals of land and building in the State. All other relevant disposals of s. 29 TCA 1997 assets will be dealt with on a case by case basis by the Revenue.

The TDM sets out how the clearance request should be submitted and the necessary documentation that must accompany a valid clearance request. A new online process to manage these application requests for clearance has been established on ROS. It is necessary for the solicitor seeking clearance to have a TAIN (a Transaction Advisory Identification Number or a Tax Agent Identification Number) and register for ROS. The solicitor must then link to each non-resident client who is the subject of the clearance request. The 'linking' will be done by the Revenue as part of the clearance process and the relevant documentation listed below should be submitted with the clearance request. The request (including the documentation/confirmations) and the necessary attachments should be submitted via My Enquiries on ROS.

It is recommended that reference is made to the requirements set out in the TDM in the irrevocable retainer and authority to be signed by the client to their solicitor at the onset of the transaction.

When the request is submitted, the applicant (solicitor) will receive an automated reply stating that if Revenue do not respond within thirty-five working days, the solicitor can distribute the sale proceeds to the non-resident vendor.

There will be no requirement for a further letter from the Revenue to issue providing clearance to the applicant solicitor. The automated letter will be sufficient to allow the solicitor to distribute after the timeframe of thirty-five working days has elapsed and no contact has been made by the Revenue in relation to the application for clearance. Basically, if nothing is heard from the Revenue within thirty-five working days, the sale proceed can be paid out.

In making a clearance request to the Revenue the solicitor should be satisfied that a complete and accurate submission has been made, which should include all the following documentation completed in full:

1. Form CG1 for the tax year in which the disposal takes place.
2. CGT computation of tax. The computation should include a breakdown of base cost, enhancement value, details of losses carried forward, and so on.
3. Full payment of CGT liability (if any).
4. Contract for Sale as evidence of proceeds.
5. Details on how the property was used during the course of the ownership.
6. If the property was rented during the period of ownership, confirmation that all relevant income tax returns have been filed and all relevant taxes paid.

A declaration of non-residence by the non-resident must also be submitted confirming that:

(a) they will spend less than 183 days in the State and

(b) they will spend less than 280 days in the State in the year of disposal and year preceding disposal.

It is important to remember that although the clearance process outlined above applies solely to the sale of land and buildings situated in the State, a solicitor who acts in relation to the sale of a company deriving most of its value from Irish land for a non-resident vendor is still liable for any CGT on sale. There are specific residence rules for bodies of persons such as personal representatives (they take their residence from the deceased under s. 573 TCA 1997) and trusts. The new process outlined in the TDM above operates from 24 October 2022 and will be subject to ongoing review by the Revenue. Further information is available on Revenue eBrief 192/22.

12.15.4.10 Purchase in trust

Circumstances can arise where a purchaser does not want to reveal its identity to a vendor or where this may not have been finally decided; say, in the context of a group of companies. The Revenue has agreed that the inclusion of 'in trust' details for the purchaser on the application form will not prevent the issue of a clearance certificate.

The purchaser's solicitors must however furnish the name and address of the purchaser to the Revenue Office that issued the certificate immediately on the closing of the sale.

12.16 Capital Acquisitions Tax

Since 28 February 1974, gift tax is payable on certain gifts made during the lifetime of the donor. A gift is taken when a donee becomes beneficially entitled in possession to some property and does not give any or gives less than the full consideration for it.

Inheritance tax is charged on the taxable value of a taxable inheritance taken by a successor where the date of the inheritance is on or after 1 April 1975.

For the purpose of gift tax and inheritance tax, the relationship between the person who provided the gift or inheritance (the disponer) and the person who receives the gift or inheritance (the donee/beneficiary/successor) determines the maximum tax-free threshold, known as the 'group threshold'. Three group thresholds were introduced on 1 December 1999 in respect of gifts and inheritances. These thresholds are indexed by reference to the consumer price index.

The indexed group thresholds for the year 2025 are set out in the following table:

Group	Relationship to disponer	Amount
A	Child, stepchild, foster child, a natural adopted child, and a child adopted under the Adoption Acts, 1952 to 1991 or under a foreign adoption a grandchild, the minor child of a deceased child.	€400,000
B	Lineal ancestors and lineal descendants, brothers and sisters, and the child of a brother or sister.	€40,000
C	Any donee or beneficiary who does not come under group A or group B.	€20,000

12.16.1 THE CALCULATION OF GIFT TAX AND INHERITANCE TAX

All gifts and inheritances taken by a donee or beneficiary on or after 5 December 1991 which come within the same group threshold are aggregated to determine the amount of tax payable on the current gift or inheritance. This means that if an individual receives a gift or an inheritance on or after 5 December 2001, any prior gifts or inheritances received by that individual before 5 December 1991 will be completely ignored in calculating the tax. This change applies to gifts and inheritances taken on or after 5 December 2001. The rate of tax is 33 per cent (at the time of writing in 2025) and applies to both gift tax and inheritance tax for gifts or inheritances received on or after 2 October 2024.

12.16.2 CAPITAL ACQUISITIONS TAX CLEARANCE CERTIFICATES

Prior to 3 April 2010 CAT was a charge on the property comprised in the taxable gift or inheritance for a period of twelve years. The charge had priority over all other charges and interests created by the donee/successor.

Section 60 of the Capital Acquisitions Tax Consolidation Act, 2003 ('the CAT Act') gave the Revenue not only the right to follow the person accountable for tax but also a right against the property of which the benefit consists at the valuation date. This section also provided that tax due and payable in respect of a taxable gift or taxable inheritance was and remained a charge on the property of which the taxable benefit consists at the valuation date.

Because of this charge for tax on the property comprised in the benefit it was imperative for a solicitor acting for a purchaser to obtain from the vendor's solicitor a clearance certificate of discharge from CAT, particularly where the title showed a death within the past twelve years s. 61 of the CAT Act).

Section 147(1) (r) of the Finance Act, 2010 deleted ss 60 and 61 of the CAT Act with effect from 3 April 2010 being the date of the passing of the Finance Act, 2010. Certificates of clearance were obtained from the Revenue under the provisions of s. 61 of the CAT Act as appropriate. Since 3 April 2010 CAT is no longer a charge on property in respect of which gift or inheritance tax is due to be paid and clearance certificates will no longer issue from the Revenue. This change to the legislation is retrospective in its application from 3 April 2010.

The Finance Act also abolished the concept of secondary liability for the tax due, except in the case of non-resident beneficiaries.

12.17 Certificates Relating to Registration of Title Based on Possession. Section 62(2) Capital Acquisitions Tax Consolidation Act, 2003 (Form CA12)

Despite the abolition of CAT being a charge on property, an exception was made for an application to Tailte Eireann (previously the Property Registration Authority ('the PRA')) to register property held by way of adverse possession.

Section 146 of the Finance Act, 1994 as amended by s. 62(2) of the Capital Acquisitions Tax Consolidation Act, 2003 is of importance to practitioners and its provisions should be noted. This section provides that the Registrar of Titles in the Land Registry requires a clearance certificate of discharge from CAT (Form CA12) before applications for first registration and/or applications pursuant to s. 49 of the Registration of Title Act, 1964 based on adverse possession can be considered and registered. The requirement also relates to applications based on solicitor's certificate in Form 3. This is the only remaining instance in which a certificate of discharge from CAT is required.

Section 146 of the Finance Act, 1994 applies to all applications for registration made on or after 11 April 1994. Section 146 provides that:

1. *After the passing of this Act a person shall not be registered as owner of property in a register of ownership maintained under the Act of 1964 on foot of an application made to the Registrar on or after the 11th day of April 1994 which is:*

   (A) *Based on possession and*

   (B) *Made under the Rules of 1972, or any other rule made for carrying into effect the objects of the Act of 1964, unless the applicant produces to the Registrar a certificate issued by the Commissioners to the effect that the Commissioners are satisfied:*

      (1) *That the property did not become charged with gift tax or inheritance tax during the relevant period (defined as a period commencing on the 28 February 1974 and ending on the date registration was made).*

      (2) *That any charge for Gift Tax or Inheritance Tax to which the property became subject during that period has been discharged, or will (to the extent that it has not been discharged) be discharged within a time considered by the Commissioners to be reasonable.*

      (3) *In the case of an application for registration in relation to which a solicitor's certificate is produced for the purpose of Rule 19(3), 19(4) or Rule 35 of the Rules of 1972, the Registrar may accept that the application is not based on possession if the solicitor makes to the Registrar a declaration in writing to that effect.*

The procedure required the applicant or his/her agent to make a declaration in Revenue Form CA 12 that no charge to CAT arose in the period from the date of registration of the registered owner or 28 February 1974 (whichever is later) to the date of registration of the applicant.

The application of the section to minor boundary amendments, certain low value transactions, and statutory authorities was ameliorated by s. 128 of the Finance Act, 1996. There is now provision in s. 62 of the Capital Acquisitions Act, 2003 at subsections (7) and (8) for certification *by the solicitor* in Revenue Form IT 76.

The certificate is lodged directly in the Land Registry.

The self-certification option is available for small properties which come within prescribed limits of value and size and are not part of a larger property. The prescribed limits are:

1. €19,050 in a case where the area occupied by the property does not exceed five hectares.
2. €127,000 in a case where the applicant is a statutory authority.

There is an exception to the rule that the small property being registered should not be part of a larger property which exceeds the limits above and it applies if the sole purpose of the application for registration is the rectification of the register to take account of small mapping errors not exceeding 500 square metres in area or €2540 in value, and the application is not part of a series of related applications relating to a larger holding of property exceeding either of these limits.

All other cases continue to require a certificate in Form CA 12 and the considerations in Richard Grogan's article continue to apply.

Many tax problems can arise on even the most routine possessory title application to the Land Registry. When taking instructions in relation to such applications or when considering whether to extract representation on the death of a person on title, the tax implications should be considered and the client should be duly advised.

To reiterate, the requirement to furnish a CAT clearance certificate to Tailte Eireann for the registration of title based on adverse possession to certify that the property did not become charged to CAT during the relevant period or that any tax arising will be paid still remains despite the abolition of the requirement to obtain CAT clearance certificates.

12.18 The Local Government (Charges) Act, 2009 (NPPR Charge)

The NPPR charge was introduced by the Local Government (Charges) Act, 2009 ('the 2009 Act') and affects and continues to affect the sale of certain residential property as defined in the 2009 Act, being in essence non-principal private residences (NPPR), from 31 July 2009. Section 3 of the 2009 Act applied an annual charge of €200 to the owners of all Irish non-principal private residences. The charge was payable to the relevant local authority in which the NPPR was locate. Liability to pay the charge was determined on the basis of ownership of the property in question on a single day each year. The date is called the 'liability date'.

For the year 2009, 31 July was the liability date. For the years 2010, 2011, 2012, and 2013, 31 March was set as the liability date. The charge must be paid within two months of the liability date. Liability falls on all co-owners of the property but payment by any one co-owner discharges the liability of all co-owners.

Residential property was defined in s. 2 of the 2009 and the main types of residential property liable for the charge were private rented property, vacant property (except new but unsold property), apartments, flats, maisonettes, bedsits, and holiday homes.

If the property met the definition of residential property and no exemptions applied then the NPPR charge was payable.

If the vendor was claiming an exemption from payment of the charge, s. 8 of the 2009 Act provided that the owner of a residential property may apply to the relevant local authority for a certificate of exemption in relation to any liability date specifying the reason why the charge was not payable.

Exemptions from the charge included the following:

(a) An individual's sole or main residence including a house where the individual is claiming a tax relief under the 'rent-a-room' scheme.

(b) A building of particular heritage which is an 'approved building' by the Minister of the Environment, Heritage, and Local Government and the Revenue Commissioners.

(c) A building forming part of the trading stock of a business (only if it has not previously been let or used as a dwelling).

(d) A building occupied under a shared ownership lease.

(e) A building leased to a housing authority or the Health Service Executive.

(f) A mobile home, caravan, or vehicle.

(g) Properties which through judicial separation or divorce become the principal residence of the other spouse or civil partner.

(h) The owner was incapacitated by long-term mental or physical infirmity and as a result was obliged to vacate his/her sole or main residence and to reside in a property not owned by him/herself.

(i) The property was occupied rent free by a relative of the owner as their sole or main residence and the owner resided in a different sole or main residence located within 2 kilometres.

(j) Any year where the liability date falls after the date of death of the owner, and the grant of representation had not issued before the liability date.

(k) The property was subject to an exclusive right of residence.

Further exemptions may also apply.

Any unpaid NPPR charge is a charge on property for a period of twelve years. Section 7(1) of the 2009 Act provides that any charge or late payment fee due and unpaid by an owner of residential property shall be and shall remain a charge on the property to which it relates. However, s. 7(2) provides that the property shall not, as against a bona fide purchaser for full consideration in money or money's worth or a mortgagee, remain charged with or liable to the payment of such unpaid NPPR charge or late payment fee after the expiration of 12 years from the date upon which the amount concerned fell due.

The penalties in relation to this charge were particularly high. For example, if there was a liability to the NPPR charge from 2009 to 2013 and no payment has been made, a total amount of €7320 (including late payment fees) was due on 1 September 2014 if the tax remained unpaid.

In a practice briefing in the August/September 2021 issue of the *Gazette* the Conveyancing Committee advise that there will be a phased expiry of NPPR charges, the late payment fees, and the charge on property. From 1 August 2021, the amount due for same will reduce every year until the liability and charge on property expires completely on 1 April 2025.

The portion of unpaid NPPR liability and charge on property in respect of the year of charge and the amount due is as follows:

1. 2009 (€2070 due) expired on 31 July 2021.
2. 2010 (€1830 due) expired on 31 March 2022.
3. 2011 (€1470 due) expired after 31 March 2023.

4. 2012 (€1110 due) expired after 31 March 2024.
5. 2013 (€750 due) expires after 31 March 2025.
6. After 1 April 2025 no NPPR is due.

Since 1 April 2024 the maximum amount outstanding is €750.

The whole of the Local Government (Charges) Act will be repealed on 31 March 2025.

12.18.1 PRE 31 MARCH 2025 REQUIREMENTS FOR CONVEYANCING SOLICITORS RE NPPR AS OUTLINED IN LAW SOCIETY GUIDELINES

If the vendor can claim an exemption on a particular liability date or where the charge or tax is paid and there is statutory provision for issuing a receipt, then the vendor must furnish on closing:

For the period from 1 August 2021 until 31 March 2025 a certificate of exemption/waiver/discharge will be required from the local authority for the purpose of a sale for the years for which the liability and charge on property have not yet expired and for the amount remaining liable on that date. There is a statutory provision for obtaining these certificates. If they are not obtained a purchaser cannot be certain that a property is not subject to a charge for any unpaid NPPR or household charge. Essentially, in the case where an exemption applies, the vendor may apply to the local authority for a certificate of exemption in relation to any liability date specifying the reasons the charge was not payable. On the other hand, if the property meets the definition of residential property and an exemption does not apply then the NPPR tax is payable and the vendor must apply to the local authority for a certificate of discharge from the local authority for each liability date. The years 2009 and 2010 are no longer included in certificates of exemption or discharge.

Local authorities have been instructed not to accept payments in respect of both the 2009 and 2010 NPPR charge as both have expired, and have further been instructed to refund any payments made in respect of the years 2009 and 2010.

There are situations where the property does not come within the ambit of the 2009 Act because, for example, it does not meet the definition of residential property or relevant residential property (it is uninhabitable, for example, or is part of trading stock), in which case the Act does not apply and the property is not subject to the charge. This is not an exemption situation and a certificate of exemption is not necessary and will not issue from the local authority. In these situations the vendor's solicitor must provide on closing a statutory declaration of the vendor setting out the basis and giving the reasons why the property does not come within the ambit of the 2009 Act.

In view of the uncertainty as to when a statutory declaration as opposed to a certificate of exemption/waiver/discharge was required, the Law Society issued a Practice Note in the January/February 2014 edition of the Law Society *Gazette* clarifying the position: see **12.18.5.7**. The Conveyancing Committee in a later Practice Note in the April 2018 *Gazette*, and also in May 2019, outlined the requirements and documents that should be sought and obtained, and this is dealt with further at **12.18.3**.

12.18.2 NPPR CHARGE AND THE POSITION OF THE LEGAL PERSONAL REPRESENTATIVE

There was considerable confusion as to the position of a personal representative in relation to the NPPR charge. In particular, concerns were raised as to how property where the owner was deceased was to be treated where the grant of representation had not yet been granted. The Conveyancing Committee of the Law Society in a Practice Note in the March 2011 issue of the Law Society *Gazette* clarified the position as follows:

It is only when a grant of representation issues in a deceased's estate that a personal representative becomes liable for the charge. Where there is a property whose owner is deceased there is no person meeting the definition of owner in the Local Government (Charges) Act until letters of administration or probate have been granted. Where letters of administration are required, the person who is granted administration becomes the owner for the purposes of the Act. In a probate case, the executor becomes the owner on the issuing of the grant of probate. Only at that point does liability commence and liability lies with the owner that is the personal representative.

The Act provides that the personal representative does not have any liability to pay the NPPR charge in a relevant year if the grant of representation has not issued by the liability date (i.e. 31 March). Late payment fees which had been accruing up to the point of death ceased, provided that the personal representative of the deceased discharged the full amount of the NPPR charge and late payment fees due up to the date of death within three months of the date of the grant of representation to the estate of the deceased. In the interim the property was treated as if it had no owner.

There is no waiver in the case of an insolvent estate and the insolvency of the estate would not negate the owner's liability.

The Local Government (Charges) Act, 2009 was amended by s. 19 of the Local Government (Household Charges) Act, 2011 by inserting a new s. 8A that transposes certain similar provisions of the 2011 Act into the 2009 Act. It provides that:

- A vendor's failure to pay the NPPR charge under the 2009 Act before completion of the sale is an offence carrying a Class C fine on summary conviction.
- The definition of 'vendor' includes an agent of the owner who receives the sale proceeds or part thereof on behalf of the owner, or who provides legal advice to the owner in a voluntary or below market value transfer. This will include a solicitor or auctioneer receiving a deposit or booking deposit on behalf of a vendor in the sale of a non-principal private residence. They will become liable to conviction of an offence and payment of a Class C fine if the sale is closed without the amount of any outstanding charge and arrears and late payment fees having been paid to the local authority.
- Section 8A (4) of the 2009 Act (as inserted by the 2011 Act) provides that on or before the completion of a sale of residential property, the vendor of that residential property shall, in respect of that residential property, give to the purchaser a certificate of exemption or a certificate of discharge as may be appropriate in respect of each year in which a liability date fell since the date of the last sale of the property. A sale includes a voluntary transfer. Prior to this, during the years 2009–2011 if there was no liability to the NPPR charge, a statutory declaration confirming that the property was a principal private residence was (in accordance with recommended practice) provided by the vendor. However, as a result of s. 8A(4) the vendor is required to provide either a certificate of exemption or a certificate of discharge on the sale of a property to which the legislation applied for each year in which a liability date fell since the date of the last sale of the property.

12.18.3 ABOLITION OF NPPR HOUSEHOLD CHARGES/REQUIREMENTS ON CLOSING

Both the NPPR and the household charge dealt with at **12.18.4** were abolished with effect from 1 January 2014 and 1 January 2013 respectively. Nevertheless, any unpaid NPPR or household charge remain a charge on property for a period of twelve years from the due date for payment of the charge, after which a bona fide purchaser takes free of the charge. If a residential property is sold, the vendor is liable to pay all outstanding charges, late payment fees, and interest due before completion of the sale. 'Vendor' is defined to include a solicitor as agent of the owner who receives the proceeds of sale or provides legal advice to the owner. A sale includes a CPO or gift.

Therefore, despite the current abolition of both the household and the NPPR charges, vendors and their solicitors will still have to deal with both of these charges for a period of twelve years from the last due date.

Under the legislation, a vendor is obliged to give to the purchaser either a certificate of discharge, a certificate of exemption, or a certificate of waiver in respect of the NPPR charge. An up-to-date receipt or a declaration made by the vendor is not sufficient (except where the property does not come within the ambit of the 2009 Act). Applications for certificates in relation to the NPPR charge should be made to the NPPR section of the relevant local authority. The Law Society *Gazette* of 5 April 2012 sets out the procedures for applying for the relevant certificate regarding the household charge. The January 2014 edition of the *Gazette* sets out the requirements for certificates of waiver/exemption/discharge or declaration that legislation does not apply in respect of NPPR, household charge, and LPT.

The April 2018 edition of the *Gazette* contains revised recommendations regarding the NPPR charges. The 2009 Act did not provide that a form of certification was required in the event that the property was exempt from the charge—that is to say, if the property was the principal private residence of an owner on a liability date. The 2011 Act however amended s. 8 of the 2009 Act by the insertion of s. 8A(4) with effect from 1 January 2012, to provide that on or before the completion date of the sale of a residential property, the vendor of that residential property shall, in respect of that residential property, give to the purchaser (a) a certificate of discharge or (b) a certificate of exemption, as may be appropriate, in respect of each year in which a liability date fell since the date of the last sale of the property.

Problems have arisen in connection with properties that were purchased in the years 2009, 2010, and 2011 before the coming into force of the 2011 Act and that are now being sold. This is because prior to 1 January 2012 it was not possible to obtain a certificate of exemption from the local authority in respect of the property concerned for any liability date, as indeed the requirement to furnish a certificate of exemption/discharge was only introduced in the 2011 Act. The Law Society had advised that a purchaser of a residential property (prior to the coming into force of the 2011 Act) should seek a statutory declaration from the vendor confirming that the provisions of the 2009 Act did not apply, if such was the case, because the property was the sole or principal residence of the vendor.

The Committee have reviewed the NPPR legislation and have confirmed in the said Practice Note of April 2018 that a certificate of exemption need only be provided in respect of each year in which a liability fell since the date of the last sale of the property.

In the event of a sale in the years 2009 to 2011, it was the recommended practice to obtain a statutory declaration from the vendor confirming that the property was occupied by that individual as their sole or main residence and was accordingly exempt from the charge. Therefore, in the absence of any reason to question the validity of the statutory declaration, a purchaser should be entitled to rely on this statutory declaration and to seek a certificate of exemption only in respect of the liability dates since the date of the last sale of the property. This is particularly true in the case of a bona fide purchaser for value.

The Local Government (Charges) Act has been repealed on 31 March 2025 as aforesaid. In a Practice Note in the July 2021 *Gazette* the Conveyancing Committee advise that it is of the opinion that it is reasonable for a solicitor to advise a purchaser acquiring property for full consideration in money or money's worth to proceed with a purchase without raising any requisition or objection in relation to any NPPR charge outstanding following the expiry of twelve years from its liability date.

12.18.4 THE LOCAL GOVERNMENT (HOUSEHOLD CHARGE) ACT, 2011

The Local Government (Household Charge) Act, 2011 (enacted 19 December 2011) introduced a new household charge set at €100 for 2012 as a temporary measure pending the introduction of the local property tax. It was a €100 flat tax chargeable on 1 January 2012 and to be paid by 31 March 2012. Section 3 of the Act provided that in 2012 and in each subsequent year the owner as defined of a residential property shall pay an annual household charge to the relevant local authority. Section 4 set out a list of exemptions and waivers and s. 9 dealt with applications for certificates of exemption or certificates of waiver. The provisions of s. 9 mean, in effect, that certificates of waiver and certificates of discharge will be required in connection with sales of residential property.

Section 8 provided that any unpaid charge, late payment fee, or late payment interest due shall be a charge on the property to which it relates. This is important for conveyancing purposes as it will fall within the remit of general condition 6(f) of the General Conditions of Sale 2019 edition. As against a bona fide purchaser for value or a mortgagee, the property shall not remain charged after the expiration of twelve years from the date upon which the amount owing fell due. Essentially the property is liable to the household charge if on the liability date (1 January 2012) the property met the definition of residential property and the vendor cannot claim an exemption or waiver.

The Conveyancing Committee in a Practice Note in the Law Society *Gazettes* of January/ February 2012, April 2012, and November 2018 issued guidelines to practitioners in relation to these new charges. Because the Act provided that the household charge is a charge on the property to which it relates, solicitors should, on or before closing a transaction, seek confirmation of whether the property in sale is liable to the charge and, if so, obtain a certificate of discharge of the statutory charge on the property to place with the title deeds. If it is claimed by a vendor that the property is not liable to the local authority household charge, the purchaser's solicitor should seek confirmation of this by way of either a certificate of exemption or a certificate of waiver, as appropriate. If the property does not meet the definition of residential property then the vendor must furnish a statutory declaration confirming this and giving the reason.

The household charge however ceased to apply from 1 January 2013. Where the household charge for 2012 has not been paid prior to 7 July 2013 the arrears amount (including late payment penalties) has now increased to €200 and is included as part of the local property tax liability in respect of the property. In effect the arrears of the household charge was converted to a local property tax charge of €200 and so becomes part of the outstanding 'crystallised' liability. In addition, since 7 July 2013 these arrears are being collected by the Revenue rather than by the local authority. The statutory requirement to provide a certificate of discharge, exemption, or waiver from the household charge was repealed by s. 73(3)(a) of the Local Government Reform Act, 2014 with effect from 27 January 2014. It is still possible to obtain a certificate of discharge or waiver or exemption from the household charge support unit by email: support@householdcharge.ie, or by phone: (1890) 357357.

Property owners can pay the €200 arrears by accessing the Revenue's online system using their PPSN/Tax registration number, LPT property ID number, and pin. Alternatively they can pay by cheque or postal order, which should be sent to The Revenue Commissioners, LPT Branch, PO Box 1, Limerick. They should confirm that the payment is for household charge arrears. If the charge was paid after 1 July 2013 then it is a local property tax and not a household charge and the evidence of payment is the usual LPT printout.

Household charge arrears now appear on the Revenue's online LPT History Screen and any arrears (for the year 2012) are collected by the Revenue through the LPT system and will be shown as outstanding on the LPT Property History screen. Purchasers will insist on any arrears being discharged by a vendor prior to closing.

The Conveyancing Committee in practice notes of October 2018 and July 2021 outlines the problem that arises in situations where owners (including previous owners on title) had not declared a relevant property for the purposes of the household charge. In these cases the Revenue amends the Property History screen to reflect unpaid arrears. Where it is the current owner of the property who did not declare it, the matter is dealt with in the usual way by discharging the arrears due prior to any sale of the property.

However, a difficulty arises where the person who owned the property as of 1 January 2012 (the liability date for the 2012 charge) did not declare the property for household charge purposes and the Revenue did not discover the failure to declare until after that previous owner had sold it.

The current owner of the property may have been unaware of the outstanding charge and is now placed in the position of being unable to close a sale of the property to a current purchaser without addressing the question of the outstanding arrears that are properly the liability of another person (i.e. the owner as of 1 January 2012). This is a matter of title on which the current vendor must satisfy a purchaser before closing, because any unpaid arrears are a charge on property for a period of twelve years after they fell due.

The Committee asked the Revenue to review the problem that arises in particular where there was on the face of the LPT property history screen no household charge due at the time a purchaser closed the sale of a property, but Revenue later finds out that a previous owner had misdeclared or not declared for household charge and the arrears due by the previous owner are then placed on the property history screen as arrears. This prevents the current owner from selling the property without addressing the previous owner's liability, as unpaid household charge is a charge on the property.

The Law Society's view is that:

1. A current owner in the case outlined above should not be required to discharge another taxpayer's liability where the LPT Property History screen showed no outstanding arrears of household charge at the time they purchased the property.
2. It is the responsibility of the Revenue to pursue the owner as of 1 January 2012 for any outstanding household charge and for any failure to declare the property for household charge at that time.

The Revenue has acknowledged to the Conveyancing Committee that where the household charge liability comes to light after the date of sale, and the sum due was the liability of a previous owner, the Revenue would not expect the current owner to be liable for same. They suggested that, in cases where sums due were the liability of a previous owner but have been put on the property history screen as arrears following a Revenue audit, Revenue can put an indicator on the property history screen saying that this sum is not a charge on the property.

The Committee agrees that, as a matter of practice, this would be sufficient evidence for title purposes that there is no claim by the Revenue against the property and that Revenue will pursue the matter with the previous owner as a debt due.

The Revenue is to put a process in place to reflect that there is no charge on the property even though the property history screen says there are arrears due, and an IT development is needed for this. Until the process and IT has been put in place, Revenue has confirmed that solicitors for vendors in this situation should contact them as early as possible in a transaction at lpt@revenue.ie to have the matter resolved by provision of a letter confirming that Revenue has no charge on the property (Practice Note, July 2021 *Gazette*).

12.18.5 LOCAL PROPERTY TAX ('LPT')

The LPT came into effect on 1 July 2013 (2012 Act) following the passing of the Finance (Local Property Tax) Act, 2012 as amended by the Finance (Local Property Tax) Amendment Act, 2013. As the tax did not come into effect until July 2013, for that year, 2013, the LPT was payable for the last six months of the year and not the full twelve months as is now the case. Unless it is outside of the scope of the LPT charge or is exempt from the charge, all residential property as defined in the legislation that is sold after 1 May 2013 is chargeable to LPT in respect of that liability date.

The 2012 Act was subsequently amended by the Finance (Local Property Tax) (Amendment) Act 2021 (the 2021 Act) which contains provisions for a new valuation period which commenced on 1 November 2021 and will apply for a period of four years from 1 January 2022 to 31 December 2025.

Although the LPT is a tax on residential property, unlike the NPPR, LPT is administered and collected by the Revenue Commissioners rather than the local authority. In addition, the LPT, unlike the NPPR and household charge, is not a fixed charge and is based on a self-assessment of the value of the property. The owner of the property on the valuation date is responsible for valuing the property, filing the return, and paying the tax. The liability and valuation date for the LPT for 2013 was 1 May 2013 and for subsequent years is 1 November in the preceding year.

The current applicable valuation date is 1 November 2021. The valuation of the property as at 1 November 2021 determines the LPT charge for the years 2022 to 2025 and property owners were required to submit valuations of their property by 7 November 2021. No further valuation is required until 2025. The owner of the property on 1 November of the preceding year is liable for the year, for example the owner on the 1 November 2022 is liable for 2023 LPT. The LPT charge will not be affected by any general increase or decrease in property prices during the new valuation period of 2022 to 2025.

12.18.5.1 Penalties for non-compliance

A return must be made in respect of the LPT. Failure to file a return can result in a penalty of up to €3000 and late payment attracts interest at a rate of 0.0219 per cent or 8 per cent per annum, in line with other taxes. In addition, a €500 fixed penalty may be imposed on a vendor who does not provide information to a purchaser about the chargeable value of the property that he or she has declared to the Revenue. A vendor could also be liable to a separate penalty of the amount of the additional LPT that is payable for making a false statement to obtain a reduction in the LPT payable.

In addition, a purchaser could be liable to a penalty for failure to submit a revised chargeable value where it appears to them that the value that was declared to the Revenue by the vendor could nor reasonably have been arrived at. This penalty would be the amount of the additional tax payable as a result of the correct value being declared, subject to a maximum penalty of €3000.

The LPT is, as stated, a self-assessed tax based on the owner's assessment of the market value of the property on the valuation date. The Revenue has introduced a revised banded system, details of which can be downloaded from the Revenue website (www.revenue.ie). There are currently 19 bands for properties valued up to €1.75 million. In addition the Revenue provided in September 2017 a most helpful guide under the heading 'LPT Guidelines for the Sale or Transfer of ownership of a relevant residential property' effective from 1 September 2017 to 31 October 2021, which should be downloaded from the Revenue website Following the introduction of the new LPT valuation period which commenced on 1 November 2021 and which applies for the period of four years from 1 January 2022 to 2025, the Revenue have confirmed that they will introduce revised guidelines for the transfer of property during the new valuation period, see Revenue website.

The Revenue has increased the general clearance thresholds for LPT to "€500,000 (Dublin) and €400,000 (elsewhere)" and it has had the effect of reducing the number of cases requiring specific clearance for the purpose of closing property sales.

12.18.5.2 Valuation date and duration of valuation

The usual valuation rule applicable to LPT is that the chargeable value of a residential property is established on a valuation date. Thus, the chargeable value established on the first valuation date of 31 May 2013 applied in relation to the years 2013 (from 1 July 2013) to 2021. 12. The chargeable value established on the second valuation date 1 November 2021 applies in relation to the years 2022 to 2025. The chargeable value established in relation to a property that becomes a residential property after 1 November 2021 applies from the following 1 November liability date until 1 November 2025.

As the value declared for the preceding valuation date applies for LPT purposes until the next valuation date, a vendor is required to provide a purchaser with details of the chargeable value/valuation band he or she declared in relation to the immediately preceding valuation date. This valuation is the relevant valuation for the next liability date.

12.18.5.3 LPT interest

Section 149 of the Finance Local Property Tax Act 2012 provides that interest shall be payable on unpaid LPT. The rate of interest amounts to 0.0219 per cent per day or 8 per cent per annum.

Although there is an interest column in the property history screen (PHS), as interest is calculated on a daily basis, the interest (if any) due on unpaid LPT is seldom if ever shown on the PHS. Solicitors should not rely on the PHS in this regard.

Where a property is being sold and there are arrears of interest, the vendor's solicitor should make an application to the Revenue at <lpt@revenue.ie> to calculate the amount of interest due, which should be paid on closing. It is imperative to verify all interest is cleared as interest is a charge on the property.

If the LPT is to be paid from the proceeds of sale and an undertaking is being given in this regard, care should be taken by both the solicitor for the vendor and the purchaser to ensure that any such undertaking includes arrears of interest due and that the interest is paid.

Otherwise the PHS will show that the LPT has been paid but will then show the amount(s) outstanding and due for interest, which will remain a charge.

In all cases where the PHS shows that the LPT has been deferred, a change has been made whereby since 25 October 2021, interest on deferred liabilities will be calculated on a weekly basis, and the amount of interest due will be reflected in the liable person's online records and also on the PHS. In such cases an application should also be made to the Revenue well in advance of closing a sale to calculate the amount of interest due. Revenue has indicated that a new format PHS has been designed that will highlight by use of a footnote that interest is accruing on outstanding liabilities.

The Revenue have provided a new PHS in their online service that provides property owners with a statement of their LPT matters that they can access on ROS. This statement does not however provide details of the valuation band declared for LPT purposes at the last valuation date or the position in relation to the household charge.

This statement is therefore not acceptable for conveyancing purposes in lieu of the printout of the vendor's property history screen from the LPT online system. Practitioners should advise their vendor clients accordingly and request that they produce a printout of the up-to-date property history screen to provide the purchaser.

12.18.5.4 Effect on LPT where the date on the purchase deed is not the date of closing

On the sale of residential property, the liable person for LPT is the owner of the property on the liability date being 1 November in each year. Accordingly, the owner of the property on 1 November 2021 is the liable person for the 2022 LPT.

Issues may arise whereby a vendor closes a sale before a liability date (1 November) but the purchaser dates the deed after the liability date. In this situation it would appear to the Revenue that the vendor is the liable person for the following year's LPT. Section 11(1) of the Finance (Local Property Tax) Act 2012 provides that the 'relevant date' is the date on which the purchaser is entitled to take immediate possession of the such property (for a period that may equal or exceed twenty years) or is entitled to the rent (unless from a local authority or approved housing body) of such property (for a period that may equal or exceed twenty years).

It is enough that the purchaser is entitled to take possession although they may not have actually taken possession. The Revenue agree that the vendor should not be held liable for the purchaser's LPT in such cases but the Revenue cannot change the records until such time as they make enquiries of both the vendor and the purchaser as to when the purchaser was entitled to possession.

The vendor's solicitor should contact the Revenue as soon as they become aware of the issue and supply evidence to the Revenue as to when the purchaser was entitled to go into possession—this can include the date closing funds were transferred, the date of closing searches, the date of redemption of the vendor's mortgage, and so on. Revenue will then make enquiries of both parties.

12.18.5.5 Who is liable for payment of the LPT?

A person's liability to LPT depends on their connection to the property. Section 11 provides that the liability to pay the LPT falls upon any person who:

Holds any estate, interest or right in a relevant residential property entitling the person to—

- *The immediate possession of such property for a period that may equal or exceed 20 years, or*
- *The receipt of rents or profits of such property for a period that may equal or exceed 20 years.*

The owner of a residential property on the liability date (which is 1 May 2013 for the tax year 2013 and 1 November thereafter) is liable to pay the LPT. There are many different categories of owner:

1. Joint owners will have a joint and several liability even if they do not live in the property. Joint owners are required to nominate one of the joint owners as the designated liable person.
2. Tenants and Leaseholders/Landlords. A rent paying tenant holding under a lease of **more** than twenty years is liable for the LPT but in the case of properties leased for twenty years or **less** to a rent paying tenant the tenant does not have to pay LPT and the landlord is liable. However, if leasing from a local authority, there is no exposure to LPT.
3. If the property is leased to local authorities and approved housing bodies the property owner is liable for LPT if the lease is for less than twenty years or was entered into on or after 22 July 2021.
4. A person who has a right of residence for life or for twenty years or more to live in the property to the exclusion of all others is liable to LPT.
5. If a person has no legal title to the property but has acquired (or is acquiring) title by adverse possession he or she will be liable to LPT. Revenue have indicated that a person who has occupied a property on a rent free basis without challenge, and has a *prima facie* right to register title under the adverse possession legislation (which normally occurs after twelve years' unchallenged occupation), will be the liable person.

While the Revenue are conscious that difficulties can arise in terms of establishing the ownership of property, the LPT deals with this by placing the onus of proof on the taxpayer. Section 11 of the Finance (Local Property Tax) Act, 2012 (FLPTA, 2012) provides that the absence of documentary evidence of title to property shall not preclude an assessment and it will be presumed that a person who is in occupation of a relevant residential property, or in receipt of the rents or profits, is a liable person.

The following is s. 11(3) reproduced in full to give an idea of the wide-reaching implications of who is liable to pay the LPT:

Without prejudice to subsections (1) and (2) the following persons shall for the purposes of this Act be liable persons in relation to a relevant residential property (the 'property')

- *a person having an equitable or beneficial estate, interest or right in the property that entitles the person to the possession or receipt referred to in subsection 1(a) or (b)*
- *a trustee that holds the property by an estate, interest or right in the property that entitles the Trustee or a beneficiary to the possession or receipt referred to in subsection 1(a) or (b)*
- *a trustee or other person having a power to appoint in the property, an estate, interest or right that entitles a person to the possession or receipt referred to in subsection 1(a) or (b)*
- *A person having an exclusive right of residence in the property for*
  - *His or her life or the life or lives of one or more or*
  - *A period that may equal or exceed 20 years*

- *The personal representative of the estate of a person who was a liable person by virtue of any of the preceding provisions of this section*
- *a person occupying the property with the right to be registered, pursuant to the Registration of Title Act 1964, in respect of any estate, interest or right that would entitle the person to the possession or receipt referred to in subsection 1(a) or (b).*

Subsection 4 provides:

> *For the avoidance of doubt in a case where a person is a trustee as referred to in subsection (3) (b), that person shall, for the purposes of this Act, be a liable person in relation to the relevant residential property concerned notwithstanding that the one or more beneficiaries under the trust is or are, for the purposes for this Act, also a liable person or persons in relation to that property.*

What is clear from this is that there may at any time be several liable persons, all of whom are responsible to discharge the LPT and all of whom may be targeted by the Revenue. It is also clear from this that the provisions of the Act have implications for those involved in the administration of trusts and estates.

12.18.5.6 LPT and the legal personal representative and trustees

There is no doubt that a legal personal representative of a person who was subject to the charge is a liable person under s. 11 of the Act.

The Act does not however specify that the liability does not arise until after a grant of representation has been extracted and so it is possible that an executor of an estate, who has power from the date of death of a deceased, may be liable for the charge from the date of death while a legal personal representative ('LPR') of an intestate deceased would not be liable from that date.

However, the Finance (Local Property Tax) Amendment Act, 2013 in s. 4 amends the primary Act in relation to who is a liable person and creates a period of grace for the estate of an intestate deceased (or an estate where the executor has predeceased the deceased) for twelve months if no grant has been extracted in that time. Once the twelve months are up, any person in occupation or in receipt of rent from the property is liable. The same provision is not available for the executor of an estate.

A deferral of the LPT is available to the LPR of an estate in circumstances where there is no grant of representation in the first twelve months after death, where the deceased himself had deferred the LPT, or where there was an outstanding liability to the charge as at the deceased's date of death.

In any event, the LPT will be due for payment when the LPR is in a position to transfer the property to a beneficiary or distribute the proceeds from the sale of the property, or, at the very latest, three years from the date of death of the deceased. In addition, a trustee is liable for the payment, as is a beneficiary entitled to possession.

The Revenue have suggested that where multiple parties are liable, they must all agree as to who should file the return and pay the tax.

12.18.5.7 Unpaid crystallised liabilities—LPT and solicitor's obligation

Section 123 of the Finance (Local Property Tax) Act, 2012 provides that any unpaid LPT and interest or other monetary penalty amount that is due and unpaid by a liable person shall be and remain a charge on the relevant residential property to which it relates, and shall continue to apply without a time limit until such time as it is paid in full. This was confirmed in s. 126(1) of the 2012 Act as amended by s. 12(e) of the Finance (Local Property Tax) (Amendment) Act, 2013, which provided that a vendor of residential property must, before completion of the sale of the property, pay any LPT, penalties, and accrued interest due in respect of the property. These must be paid notwithstanding that a sale of the property is completed before the tax is payable. This statutory obligation on the vendor does not mean that the amount of the LPT already paid by the vendor cannot be apportioned between the vendor and purchaser on closing. The Conveyancing Committee of the Law Society in a Practice Note in the June 2013 edition of the *Gazette* confirmed that the apportionment between the vendor and purchaser of the LPT should be done except where an exemption from LPT applies. The precedent wording of the special condition dealing with the apportionment of LPT as between the vendor and the purchaser is dealt with at **6.2.9**. Therefore before a sale of residential property is completed, a vendor is required to pay upfront any unpaid LPT due in respect of a liability date falling before the date of the sale, even if, in the ordinary course of events, such liability would not yet be payable. The liability that has crystallised at this stage comprises unpaid LPT, accrued interest, and any penalty amount that has been imposed in relation to a vendor's self-assessment or a Revenue assessment. In addition, all outstanding returns must be filed. Any outstanding crystallised liability that is not paid by the vendor before the completion of the sale is a charge on the property. In addition, where the household charge for 2012 has not been paid or has been part paid prior 1 July 2013, the arrears amount (including late payment penalties) has now been increased to €200 and is included as part of the LPT liability in respect of the property. In effect, the arrears of the household charge become an LPT charge and so become part of the outstanding crystallised liability. As from 1 July 2013 these arrears are being collected by the Revenue. Details of any arrears of the household charge will appear on the LPT Property History screen. See **12.18.4**.

The LPT is a charge on property; however, unlike most charges, to include the NPPR and the household charge, that have a twelve-year life span, there is no time limit for the LPT and the normal provisions of the Statute of Limitations will not apply. It is important therefore when dealing with a sale or transfer of a property to receive confirmation from the Revenue that same has been discharged. There is also a 'snitch clause' in the legislation in that a purchaser will be bound to inform the Revenue of vendors who have placed a much lower value on their property than the sale price. Offending vendors will be fined €500 if they refuse to reveal to the purchaser the band in which they valued the property for the purposes of the LPT. In turn the purchaser must file a revised chargeable value return and valuation where it appears to him or her that the valuation declared by the vendor to the Revenue was too low given the circumstances at the valuation date. This penalty will be the amount of the additional LPT payable as a result of the correct value being declared, subject to a maximum penalty of €3000.

It is important to be mindful of these points when acting in the administration of an estate, and more particularly when acting for a vendor/purchaser in a conveyancing transaction.

12.18.5.8 Residential property and exempt property

It is important for a vendor's solicitor to determine if the property in sale meets the definition of residential property or relevant residential property as defined in the LPT Act. LPT is charged on the market value of such property and issues may arise as to whether a property is a residential property, how certain properties are to be valued, and the components of a property that are to be valued for LPT purposes. Section 2 of the 2012 Act as amended by ss 4(b) and 5 of the Finance (Local Property Tax) (Amendment) Act 2021 inserted a new s. 2A in the 2012 Act and defines 'residential property' as:

1. *Any building which is in use as, or is suitable for use as, a dwelling.*
2. *A shed, outhouse, garage or other building which is appurtenant to or usually enjoyed with a residential property shall be considered, or the purposes of this Act, to form part of the residential property.*
3. *Subject to subsection (4), yards, garden and other land appurtenant to or usually enjoyed with a residential property as its garden or grounds shall be considered, for the purposes of this Act to form part of the residential property.*
4. *Where the total area of the yards, gardens and other lands, referred to in subsection (3), exceeds 0.4047 hectares, only those parts of such yards, gardens and other lands, which*

> *would be the most suitable for occupation and enjoyment with the dwelling, up to the total area (exclusive of the area at ground level, of the building referred to in subsection (1)) shall form part of the residential property.*

'Relevant residential property' is defined as a building in the State that is a residential property on a liability date.

There were eleven exemptions from LPT available for the first valuation period from 2013 to 2021. Four of these have expired and are not available for the second valuation period of 2022 to 2025. Sections 4–10 of the LPT Act set out a number of properties that will not be regarded as a relevant residential property for the purposes of the Act. An LPT exemption will be available for the following properties, if they meet the qualifying conditions, some of which are limited in relation to time:

- Commercial properties that are or can be used as a dwelling and are fully subject to commercial rates. An example of this is a guesthouse. This exemption does not apply if the property is exempt from the payment of commercial rates to a local authority.
- A property vacated by their owner for at least twelve months due to their long-term physical or mental infirmity, that is certified by a medical practitioner, or alternatively, where the medical practitioner—if it is for less than twelve months—certifies that the person is unlikely to return to the property. Prior to 2021 this exemption only applied if the property was not occupied by another person. Since 2022 the exemption applies if someone lives in the property and they are not a joint owner of the property. For example they may be a tenant, relative, or friend.
- Residential property owned by a charity or similar public body that is used solely or primarily as residential accommodation in connection with recreational activities that are an integral part of the body's charitable purpose and providing special needs accommodation.
- A residential property purchased or built or adapted for use as the main or sole residence of a permanently incapacitated individual who has received an award from the Personal Injuries Assessment Board or a court or who is a beneficiary under a trust established for that purpose.
- Mobile homes, vehicles, and vessels.
- Residential properties having a significant level of pyrite damage are exempt for a temporary period of at least six years. The Finance (Local Property Tax) (Pyrite Exemption) Regulations, 2013 (SI 147/2013) stipulated how properties are to be tested to establish whether they have been affected by a significant level of pyrite induced damage and providing for the issue of certificates by a competent person where this has been established. This exemption has been phased out and was not available for new applicants after 22 July 2023.

  Properties built using defective concrete blocks may be exempt if they are confirmed to be eligible for the Defective Concrete Blocks Grant Scheme or if the builder or an insurance company has carried out remediation work required or provided funds for it.
- Certain institutional dwellings, to include registered nursing homes, hospitals, prisons, army barracks, boarding schools, etc.

Where an exemption from LPT applies, and the LPT will therefore not arise, evidence of entitlement to the exemption should be furnished by the relevant party, if necessary in the form of a statutory declaration. It is possible to check online what the LPT status of a property is.

To recap:

1. If the property meets the definition of relevant residential property on a liability date, currently 1 November, then the LPT is payable. Confirmation from the Revenue that the tax has been paid should be furnished by way of an up-to-date property history printout from the online Revenue system.

2. If the property did not meet the definition of relevant residential property on the liability date then the vendor should furnish a statutory declaration confirming this and giving the reason, together with a copy confirmation from the Revenue by way of a printout from ROS that there are no outstanding amounts of LPT payable (if applicable).

Previous exemptions from LPT 2013–2021

Many of the exemptions available for LPT no longer apply. These include the following:

(a) New and previously unused property purchased from a builder or developer between 1 January and before 1 November 2021.

(b) Residential properties built and owned by a builder or developer but unsold.

This LPT exemption applied to properties constructed and owned by a builder or developer and remained unsold and was contained in s. 6 of the Finance (Local Property Tax) Act 2012. It previously applied to a builder's trading stock and is no longer available beyond 2021. Section 6 of the 2012 Act was amended by s. 10 of the Finance (Local Property Tax) (Amendment) Act 2021 by the substitution of 'as a relevant residential property in relation to the liability dates in the years 2013 to 2020' for 'as relevant residential property'.

If builders or developers have houses suitable for use as a dwelling on a liability date (that is 1 November in any year), they must now register them with Revenue, and, as owners on the relevant liability date, must pay the LPT due in respect of those properties.

A builder or developer who owns a house suitable for use as a dwelling on a liability date is, in respect of that (finished) house, in the same position as any other owner of a residential property.

A property that becomes suitable for use as a dwelling after 1 November in any year in a valuation period will not be liable for LPT until the following 1 November. The property will be valued as of the valuation date for the valuation period, which is 1 November 2021 in the current valuation period. For example, if a new house is built and becomes suitable for use as a dwelling on 1 July 2023 the property will become liable to LPT for the first time on 1 November 2023, but the valuation date is 1 November 2021.

(c) Properties in unfinished housing estates, commonly called 'ghost estates'.

(d) Properties purchased and occupied as a home in 2013 as exempt from LPT until 2021 if the owner continued to own it as their sole or main residence.

The exemption from LPT is no longer available for properties listed from a to d above.

12.18.5.9 Conveyancing committee guidelines for LPT

In a Practice Note in the June 2013 edition of the *Gazette* the Conveyancing Committee provided guidelines for dealing with LPT in the context of including a special condition in the contract for sale dealing with the apportionment of LPT and providing for the amendment of general conditions 27 and 8(c) of the general conditions (now general conditions 23 and 6(f) in the 2019 edition).

The Practice Note contained the following guidelines for practitioners:

The vendor should be advised to:

- *Submit all outstanding LPT returns and print off their confirmation of payment if they are paying their LPT online.*
- *Pay all outstanding tax, interest, and penalties; this applies even if the tax is being paid by instalments.*
- *Advise those vendors who are paying LPT by deduction at source from salary that they will not be given credit for amounts paid during the year until their employers file P35s after the end of*

the relevant tax year. If they are selling within the tax year, they will have to pay the full amount of LPT for the year upfront before closing, and later claim a refund from the Revenue of any amount deducted at source. If they know they intend selling during the course of a particular year, they might prefer to alter their method of payment so as to avoid the inconvenience of such a double payment.

- *It is recommended that a vendor would furnish a purchaser at the pre-contract stage with a note of the value band declared for a property by the vendor. Advise vendors to keep a copy of their returns for this purpose.*
- *Self-correct any return where there has been an under declaration of value.*
- *Provide the purchaser with such information about the tax arising on the previous valuation date as is relevant to the purchaser. This is usually given through a vendor's solicitor by providing the property history screen printout.*
- *Ascertain if the agreed sale price comes within the general clearance or whether specific clearance is required.*

The purchaser should:

- *Obtain any relevant information from the vendor. The Revenue suggest this includes the property ID, valuation band, basis for valuation, and details of any exemption claimed.*
- *Confirm that there is no outstanding tax, interest, or penalties.*
- *Where the property is sold within a valuation period consider whether the valuation declared by the vendor appears to have been reasonably and honestly made. If not, the purchaser's own estimate of the property's valuation should be used at the following liability date.*
- *Ascertain from the vendor if the agreed sales price comes within general clearance and if not, whether formal clearance has been obtained.*

In a Practice Note in the October 2013 edition of the *Gazette* the Conveyancing Committee confirmed that it was successful in getting the Revenue to accept that purchasers must be given some assurance that the property they purchase is not subject to a charge in respect of a vendor's unpaid LPT where the value declared by the vendor on a LPT return is less than the subsequent sale price. The Revenue on 1 September 2017 issued a revised publication 'Guidelines for the sale or transfer of ownership of a relevant residential property' which should be consulted by practitioners and is available on the Revenue website, www.revenue.ie/en/tax/lpt/sale-transfer-property.html. These are currently being updated. The Revenue will not issue a certificate of discharge for LPT and instead a system of general and specific clearance has been agreed to facilitate a purchaser to satisfy themselves that the property is not subject to a charge.

12.18.5.10 LPT revenue clearance

LPT Revenue clearance must be obtained by the vendor on the sale of residential property. It is important to note that the clearance provisions are intended to facilitate purchasers. A purchaser is given an assurance that there is no charge on the property but the Revenue reserve the right to pursue a vendor for pre-sale liabilities where clearance has been obtained on the basis of false information or inadequate disclosure.

There are two types of Revenue clearance: general clearance and specific clearance. The property does not qualify for either general or specific clearance where there are outstanding or deferred LPT liabilities, or outstanding household charge liabilities and/or outstanding LPT returns.

The assurance is provided in one of two ways:

1. **General clearance**—subject to three conditions

This general clearance should cover the vast majority of sales. The easiest way to check that the property is fully compliant is by logging in to LPT online to review the LPT records and LPT status of the property. The Revenue are not directly involved in this clearance process and general clearance from 1 January 2022 applies if either of the following conditions are met:

1. The sale price is "500,000 (Dublin) and €400,000 (elsewhere)" or less or
2. **Condition 2(A) applies if your property was liable for LPT on 1 May 2013.**

   Sale price does not exceed:

   - The upper limit of the valuation band by 125 per cent (or 125 per cent above the actual declared value for properties above Band 19) declared as of 1 May 2013 and
   - The upper limit of the valuation band by 25 per cent (or 25 per cent above the actual declared value for properties above Band 19) declared as of 1 November 2021.
3. **Condition 2(B) applies if your property was not liable for LPT on 1 May 2013.**

   Sale price does not exceed:

   - 25 per cent of the upper limit of the valuation band (or 25 per cent above the actual declared value for properties above Band 19) declared as of 1 November 2021.

The three conditions can be described as allowable valuation margin, expenditure enhancement to a property, and sale of a comparable property.

The Revenue has provided an update on the general clearance conditions for LPT in a note on 27 August2024. These changes increase the number of cases where general clearance applies without having to refer the matter to the Revenue. They expanded the allowable valuation margin from 2022 in situations where the property is sold for "500,000 (Dublin) and €400,000 (elsewhere)" or less.

How to obtain general clearance

Prior to the sale a vendor's solicitor can obtain general clearance from the LPT online system using the client's PPSN, the property ID, and the PIN. The Property Access Number (PAN) can be retrieved on the Payment History Screen. If this information is not to hand an application can be made to the Revenue to reissue these details.

The Payment History Screen can then be printed off to show that there are no outstanding liabilities or returns. This provides comfort to the purchaser that the vendor is fully compliant for LPT. If an exemption has been claimed this will be indicated in the printout.

Specific revenue clearance in certain circumstances

Revenue will provide specific written clearance on request from the vendor where the conditions specified in 1, 2(A), and 2(B) above do not apply but the vendor nevertheless claims that the valuation made at the valuation date was made in good faith. An application for specific clearance should be made to the Revenue by completing Form LPT5 Application for Specific Pre-Sale Clearance.

It should be noted that:

(a) This request for clearance is conducted by secure email (pre-registration with the Revenue is required) using Form LPT5 (which is confusingly called 'Application for Specific Pre-Sale Clearance').

(b) Application is made following agreement of the sale price but in advance of closing.

(c) Revenue will either issue a written clearance (where satisfied that there was no under declaration of the chargeable value), which the vendor must furnish to the purchaser on or before closing, or make an assessment on the vendor (where not satisfied that the valuation band/chargeable value that was declared was reasonable), which then becomes part of the standard online clearance process and which should be paid online by the vendor in advance of closing and the usual evidence of payment produced to the purchaser on or before closing.

12.18.5.11 LPT clearance in second and subsequent sales

In cases where specific clearance has been applied for and granted, the valuation band originally declared will be the relevant band until the next valuation date. The 'specific clearance' indicator is included in the LPT History details screen. The date the specific clearance that was granted is also included.

Where there is more than one sale in a valuation period and general clearance applied on the first sale, this is sufficient to confirm the declared valuation for any and all subsequent sales within the valuation period.

If the subsequent transfer would not meet the general clearance condition and if the vendor does not have specific clearance for a previous sale an application should be made to the Revenue for specific clearance.

Revenue will issue a confirmation that the conditions for general clearance are satisfied and that, accordingly, the Revenue band remains the valuation band originally declared. This will confirm that all LPT and household charge liabilities have been paid and returns filed and that the property valuation was reasonable. This LPT clearance should be retained with the title documents, as it should be produced on any subsequent sales within the valuation period.

In circumstances where the sale meets the general clearance criteria, the standard general clearance process should be applied.

Where general clearance conditions were not met for the first sale in the period, specific clearance should have been requested from the Revenue.

If the current vendor does not have a copy of a specific clearance approval for the first sale and the property does not now qualify for general clearance, the vendor should submit an application for specific clearance.

An exemption from LPT may have been claimed in the first or subsequent sale. The vendor may not be able to provide confirmation as they did not make the claim. The vendor should request approval from the Revenue of the exemption claimed.

12.18.5.12 Derelict/Uninhabitable property

A derelict or uninhabitable property falls outside the chare to LPT and so, in most cases, will not have an LPT property ID number. Properties that were uninhabitable or unsuitable for use as a dwelling, as at 1 November 2021, were not liable for LPT for 2022.

A derelict or an uninhabitable house falls within the definition of 'residential property' for stamp duty purposes. In order to file the stamp duty return online, an LPT property ID number will be required. The vendor should contact the Revenue to obtain a LPT ID number to enable stamping. The Revenue may require supporting documentation to confirm the status of the property.

Appendix 12.1 Multiplier Table for Capital Gains Tax

Capital Gains Tax	Multipliers									
Year Expenditure Incurred	Capital Gains Tax Multiplier for Disposals Years ended 5 April 1993 to 31 December 2002									
	Y/e 5 April 1996	**Y/e 5 April 1997**	**Y/e 5 April 1998**	**Y/e 5 April 1999**	**Y/e 5 April 2000**	**Y/e 5 April 2001**	**Short Y/e 31 Dec 2001**	**Y/e 31 Dec 2002**	**Y/e 31 Dec 2003**	**Y/e 31 Dec 2004 et seq/**
1974/75	5.899	6.017	6.112	6.215	6.313	6.582	6.930	7.180	7.528	7.528
1975/76	4.764	4.860	4.936	5.020	5.099	5.316	5.597	5.799	6.080	6.080
1976/77	4.104	4.187	4.253	4.325	4.393	4.580	4.822	4.996	5.238	5.238
1977/78	3.518	3.589	3.646	3.707	3.766	3.926	4.133	4.283	4.490	4.490
1978/79	3.250	3.316	3.368	3.425	3.479	3.627	3.819	3.956	4.148	4.148
1979/80	2.933	2.992	3.039	3.090	3.139	3.272	3.445	3.570	3.742	3.742
1980/81	2.539	2.590	2.631	2.675	2.718	2.833	2.983	3.091	3.240	3.240
1981/82	2.099	2.141	2.174	2.211	2.246	2.342	2.465	2.554	2.678	2.678
1982/83	1.765	1.801	1.829	1.860	1.890	1.970	2.074	2.149	2.253	2.253
1983/84	1.570	1.601	1.627	1.654	1.680	1.752	1.844	1.911	2.003	2.003
1984/85	1.425	1.454	1.477	1.502	1.525	1.590	1.674	1.735	1.819	1.819
1985/86	1.342	1.369	1.390	1.414	1.436	1.497	1.577	1.633	1.713	1.713
1986/87	1.283	1.309	1.330	1.352	1.373	1.432	1.507	1.562	1.637	1.637
1987/88	1.241	1.266	1.285	1.307	1.328	1.384	1.457	1.510	1.583	1.583
1988/89	1.217	1.242	1.261	1.282	1.303	1.358	1.430	1.481	1.553	1.553
1989/90	1.178	1.202	1.221	1.241	1.261	1.314	1.384	1.434	1.503	1.503
1990/91	1.130	1.153	1.171	1.191	1.210	1.261	1.328	1.376	1.442	1.442
1991/92	1.102	1.124	1.142	1.161	1.179	1.229	1.294	1.341	1.406	1.406
1992/93	1.063	1.084	1.101	1.120	1.138	1.186	1.249	1.294	1.356	1.356
1993/94	1.043	1.064	1.081	1.099	1.117	1.164	1.226	1.270	1.331	1.331
1994/95	1.026	1.046	1.063	1.081	1.098	1.144	1.205	1.248	1.309	1.309
1995/96	—	1.021	1.037	1.054	1.071	1.116	1.175	1.218	1.277	1.277
1996/97	—	—	1.016	1.033	1.050	1.094	1.152	1.194	1.251	1.251
1997/98	—	—	—	1.017	1.033	1.077	1.134	1.175	1.232	1.232
1998/99	—	—	—	—	1.016	1.059	1.115	1.156	1.212	1.212
1999/00	—	—	—	—	—	1.043	1.098	1.138	1.193	1.193
2000/01	—	—	—	—	—	—	1.053	1.091	1.144	1.144
2001	—	—	—	—	—	—	—	1.037	1.087	1.087
2002	—	—	—	—	—	—	—	—	1.049	1.049
2003 et seq										1.000

Note: in the 'Year Expenditure Incurred' column, for all years to 2000/2001 inclusive, a year means a 12-month period commencing on 6 April and ending on the following 5 April. The 'Short year' 2001 covers the period 6 April 2001 to 31 December 2001. With effect from 1 January 2002 the income tax year is the calendar year, i.e. 2002 refers to the year ended 31 December 2002.

Indexation is not available on expenditure incurred within 12 months prior to the date of disposal. Indexation relief will *only* apply for the period of ownership of the asset up to 31 December 2002 for any disposals made on or after 1 January 2003.

Appendix 12.2 Certificates of Waiver/Exemption/Discharge or Declaration that Legislation Does Not Apply: Nppr, Household Charge, Lpt

CONVEYANCING COMMITTEE

Certificates of waiver/exemption/discharge or declaration that legislation does not apply: NPPR, household charge, LPT

It appears to the committee that there is significant confusion among practitioners about the circumstances in which certificates of waiver/exemption/discharge from the NPPR charge or the household charge must be obtained, and when it is appropriate to obtain a declaration from a vendor (or a purchaser in some cases) as to the non-applicability of the relevant piece of legislation. It appears to the committee that exemptions (from a charge or tax that would otherwise be due) are being confused with situations where the relevant act does not apply at all.

It is necessary to distinguish between:

1) Situations where the relevant legislation makes statutory provision for a specific exemption or waiver and provides for the issue of a certificate in relation to same or where it provides for issue of a certificate of discharge following payment of the relevant charge or tax, and
2) Situations where a property does not come within the ambit of the relevant legislation because, for example, it does not meet the definition of 'residential property' or 'relevant residential property' as set out in the different pieces of legislation (either because it is uninhabitable, is part of trading stock, and so on), in which case the relevant act does not apply and the property is not subject to the charge. This second situation is not an exemption situation and a certificate of exemption is not necessary and will not be issued.

The committee wishes to clarify that its practice note published in the June 2013 issue of the *Gazette* (p50) relates to cases that come within the ambit of the relevant legislation and where the legislation provides for a waiver or exemption in certain circumstances or where the charge or tax is paid and there is statutory provision for issuing a receipt, that is, cases described in paragraph 1 above. The committee confirms that certificates of waiver/exemption/discharge should be obtained in those cases, as there is specific statutory provision for them and, if they are not obtained, a purchaser cannot be certain that a property is not subject to a charge for any unpaid NPPR or household charge. A declaration from a vendor as to entitlement to a waiver or exemption is not sufficient, and a receipt for payment by itself is not sufficient in these cases.

To deal with the situations described in paragraph 2 above, the committee's first practice note on NPPR published in the September 2009 *Gazette* (p44) recommended that a statutory declaration should be obtained if it is claimed that the charge does not apply. Although not repeated in subsequent practice notes, the committee understands that this has also become common practice in relation to cases where it is claimed that the household charge and the local property tax do not apply, and the committee recommends this extension of this practice.

The committee has set out in a table the circumstances in which the various certificates or declarations are appropriate. This can be accessed in the members' area of the Society's website by clicking on 'Committees', 'Conveyancing Committee', 'Resources' (in the box titled 'Additional information') and scrolling down the Resources page to click on 'Conveyancing guidelines'.

Source: <https://www.lawsociety.ie/Documents/committees/conveyancing/CertificatesOfWaiver-etc-notApply-JanFeb2014.pdf>.

To view the Practice Note please visit: <https://www.lawsociety.ie/Solicitors/Practising/Practice-Notes/Certificates-of-waiverexemptiondischarge-or-declaration-that-legislation-does-not-apply-NPPR-household-charge-LPT/#.U6lWy5RdXTo>.

CHAPTER 13

WILLS, ESTATE PLANNING, AND TAXATION

13.1 What Is Estate Planning?

Estate planning, as its name suggests, deals with calculating and planning for the future tax liability of potential beneficiaries based on the present taxation regime, that is, planning for the transfer of assets (usually) to the next generation on death or otherwise. For the purposes of this chapter, it is assumed that the tax regime applicable is the current taxation regime and when advising clients, this should be pointed out in writing.

One of the main taxes, arising on a death, is CAT, so anyone engaging in tax planning must fully understand how CAT is currently charged, based on the relationship between disponer and beneficiary, and must know the aggregation effect of previous gifts and/or inheritances received by that beneficiary from a disponer in the same tax group, since 5 December 1991 as outlined in para 3.4. In addition, a full knowledge of all the possible exemptions and reliefs (not the same thing) that may apply in relation to certain assets and certain beneficiaries is required, including any clawback provisions that relate to same. Finally, it is imperative that a practitioner can actually calculate the estimated tax due.

In the course of the Law Society of Ireland's PPC I Probate and Taxation Module and by reference to the Law Society OUP "Wills, Probate and Estates" Manual, Chapters 1 to 5, students have learnt how to draft wills and will trusts in accordance with the client's informed instructions. In estate planning, in particular, thosee instructions should always be used with caution, and certainly they are of no specific assistance in estate planning and taxation. Thus, in this context, it is the tax effect of the legal effect of the client's wishes that need to be outlined to the client.

Estate planning requires more than merely drafting a will, even if same is done in absolute accordance with the testator's instructions. As Barron J. in Doran v Delaney [1998] 2 ILRM 1 put it so elegantly,

> *the solicitor is not a conduit pipe . . .he warrants . . . he has taken care and applied the skill and knowledge of a member of his profession . . . It is not enough that the solicitor was acting bona fides.*

Each will is a totally individual document that needs to be tailored to the client's current and reasonably foreseeable individual circumstances and requirements while minimising the tax payable on the death of that client.

When drafting a will for a client, the solicitor must first and foremost draft a will that will dispose of all of the client's property in exact accordance with his or her **informed** instructions. This includes following all of the legal requirements for the signing and witnessing of the will (as discussed in *Wills, Probate and Estates*, Chapter 2) and advising on and taking into account, for example, the possibility of lapse and dealing with s. 98, the rights of spouses and civil partners and possible applications for redress by cohabitants and children.

It is no longer sufficient, if indeed it ever was, to simply provide the client with a will in a format which will be acceptable to the Probate Office while leaving the estate or potential beneficiaries open to a very large tax bill.

Practitioners must apply their knowledge of capital taxes as outlined in the preceding chapters and elsewhere to the client's situation and be in a position to advise the client accordingly. In other words, practitioners must be able to consider the tax implications of their clients proposals and advise them, where possible, on a means of achieving these goals while minimising and/or avoiding tax liabilities.

When the client comes into the office to make a will, a marvellous opportunity for tax planning arises. The aim is to ensure that the potential tax liability of the proposed beneficiaries is reduced as far as is possible and as far as is compatible with the testator's wishes.

The important point to keep in the forefront of one's mind at this stage is that, with very few limited exceptions, the will cannot be varied later for CAT or any other tax purposes on the death of the testator.

This is the only opportunity, with the exception of disclaimers, deeds of family arrangement or agricultural relief, to reduce or avoid a tax liability. While there is limited provision to apply to court to alter or vary a trust under ss 23 and 24 of the Land and Conveyancing Law Reform Act, 2009, this is specifically not to be used with the intention of avoiding or reducing the incidence of tax.

13.1.1 POWER OF APPROPRIATION: SECTION 55 OF THE SUCCESSION ACT, 1965

Before going on to review the taxation elements, there is a general will-drafting point regarding all CAT (and indeed CGT) reliefs that needs to be considered, that is, inserting a s. 55, Succession Act, 1965 power of appropriation clause in the will.

While this is not a CAT relief per se, it is mentioned here as it is useful to have the same in a will to enable the legal personal representative to 'guide' the assets to the beneficiary/beneficiaries most likely to be able to access the relief post death. It is also very useful where appropriation could mean that Stamp Duty can be avoided.

Consider the inclusion of an express power of appropriation in a will so that assets can be directed to secure tax relief, if the opportunity arises. Under s. 55 of the Succession Act, an executor has a statutory power to appropriate any part of the estate of a deceased person in its condition in or towards satisfaction of a beneficiary's share in the estate. The statutory power requires the executors to serve notices and secure consents from the beneficiaries so it can be cumbersome to use in practice. A will can provide an express power of appropriation that does not require the notices and consents contained in the statutory power.

If an express power is included in the will, executors can direct benefits towards beneficiaries who can claim reliefs, reducing the tax on the estate; and, as noted above, an appropriation under the will is not liable to Stamp Duty.

13.1.1.1 Precedent power of appropriation

I direct that my executors shall be entitled to exercise the power of appropriation contained in Section 55 of the Succession Act, 1965 without serving any notices or securing any consents.

13.1.2 WILL TRUSTS

The solicitor must put the testator in a position where the testator is aware of all the various taxes, reliefs and exemptions and be fully au fait with the advisability or inadvisability of placing assets in trust. The question of the creation of a will trust is dealt with separately in the trusts lectures and the Will Trusts Book provided to students. It is sufficient at this stage to say that where a discretionary trust is created, the solicitor should remind the client of the taxes potentially levied on same. Taxation of Trusts and Discretionary Trust Tax ('DTT') and CGT and CAT implications on the breakup of trusts are taught as part of the Law Society Advanced Probate & Tax Advanced Elective. (is that what its called now Padraic?)

13.1.3 TAX HISTORY OF BENEFICIARIES

While a testator will of course be aware of any gifts made by him to beneficiaries, as at the date of giving instructions to a solicitor, he may not be aware of previous gifts or inheritances to beneficiaries or those which may occur at a future date from another source, and which could potentially cause a tax liability on the testator's death.

Where a testator is a parent, this information should be to hand; in most other cases, however, it will not. It is also not possible to predict future benefits from other sources. Obviously such information, as far as can be practically obtained, should be sought by the solicitor so that as complete a picture as possible of the tax consequences for beneficiaries of any will drafted can be calculated.

13.1.4 CAT INFORMED WILL DRAFTING

A thorough knowledge of CAT is essential in order to advise any testator in relation to a will, and a full discussion can be found in the preceding chapters. CAT in general will not be discussed in this chapter, but rather CAT from a will-drafting perspective and, in that regard, more from considering 'an approach' a solicitor could take when advising a client and drafting a will based on the client's informed instructions, rather than discussing substantive tax law.

13.1.4.1 Thresholds

Thresholds were discussed in para 2.5 and the current (from 2 October 2024) rates are: Group A €400,000,; Group B €40,000; Group C €20,000.

It is essential to have a thorough knowledge of the thresholds and their interrelationship with reliefs and exemptions, such as surviving spouse, favourite nephew/niece, and minor child of a deceased child.

Where appropriate, the solicitor will also take into account Finance (No. 3) Act, 2011 which put tax provisions into place following the introduction of the Civil Partnerships and Certain Rights and Obligations of Cohabitants Act, 2010.

13.2 Domicile/Residence/Ordinary Residence

In the majority of cases that solicitors deal with the client will be domiciled and resident/ ordinarily resident in Ireland, as will all the beneficiaries. However, in an increasing number of cases this will not be so. For example, the client could have retired to an apartment in Spain, while still spending a substantial amount of time each year in Ireland; or a client could be working abroad for a number of years, while holidaying either in Ireland or abroad. This chapter does not deal with international law, but in this regard, when dealing with such a client, the EU Regulation on Succession Law (no 650/2012), also known as 'Brussels IV', may be relevant.

Practitioners are referred to the article 'Succession Slalom' by Aileen Keogan in the December 2013 *Law Society Gazette* <https://www.lawsociety.ie/globalassets/documents/gazette/gazette-pdfs/gazette-2013/gaz-december.pdf> in this regard.

The Hague Convention on the International Protection of Adults, 2000, which came into force on 1 January 2009 (which Ireland ratified on 31 May 2024, and which entered into force in the State from 1 September 2024), should also be considered.

The Finance Act, 2000 replaced domicile as the intrinsic arbiter of liability to CAT with the concept of residence and ordinary residence. Domicile is still relevant as the new rules only fully came into force for non-domiciled persons on 1 December 2004. Under the current regime (CAT Consolidation Act, 2003, Sections 6 and 11) CAT is imposed on:

1. gifts or inheritances of Irish situated assets (real and personal);
2. gifts or inheritances of worldwide assets made by Irish resident or ordinarily resident donors;
3. gifts or inheritances of worldwide assets received by Irish resident or ordinarily resident beneficiaries or donees.

For a fuller explanation of the consequences of the changes brought about by the replacement of domicile with residence/ordinary residence on the charge to CAT, see 'Scope of the Capital Acquisitions Tax', Irish Tax Review (May 2001).

13.2.1 'RESIDENCE' AND 'ORDINARY RESIDENCE'

These concepts have been considered in para 1.2, but to recap: s. 2(6)(a) and (b) define 'residence' and 'ordinary residence' respectively by reference to Part 34 of the TCA, 1997 as amended.

Since the introduction of the calendar tax year by s. 77 of the Finance Act, 2001, the tax year now runs from 1 January to the following 31 December. This took effect from 1 January 2002, and was preceded by a short transitional tax 'year' for the period from 6 April to 31 December 2001.

An individual is regarded as tax resident in Ireland if in a tax year he or she is present in the State:

1. for a period or periods of 183 days or more in that tax year; or
2. for a period or periods over that tax year and the preceding tax year and amounting to 280 days or more.

If the person does not stay in the State for more than thirty days at a time that stay is not taken into account in calculating the 280 days.

An individual can also elect to be resident if he or she does not satisfy either of the two tests, provided that the individual spends more than thirty days in the State in the tax year in question and can satisfy the local inspector of taxes that he or she will be resident for the following tax year.

Before the Finance (No. 2) Act, 2008, a person was deemed to be present in Ireland if he or she was in the country at midnight (the so-called Cinderella rule), so effectively it was nights that were spent in Ireland that counted. The 2008 Act provides that for the tax year 2009 and subsequent tax years an individual shall be deemed to be present in the State for a day if he or she is in the State at any time during that day, with limited exceptions for individuals in transit or forced to be present due to force majeure circumstances outside their control.

Note: it is important to note that from 6 April 1994, having a place of abode available for use in Ireland does not make a person tax resident.

The term 'ordinary residence' is used in relation to a person's normal place of residence. Since 1994 a person will not be regarded as being ordinarily resident in Ireland until he or she has been in residence for the preceding three years.

Where an individual is not domiciled in the State, ss. 6(4) (gifts) and 11(4) (inheritances) of the CAT Consolidation Act, 2003 provide that they are not considered to be resident or ordinarily resident for CAT unless they have been resident in the State for the five tax years immediately preceding the year that the taxable event occurs and are resident or ordinarily resident in the State that year.

For example, if a non-domiciled person moved to Ireland in 2010, that person can gift non-Irish property to persons not resident or ordinarily resident in Ireland during the period 2010 to 2014 without their incurring a CAT liability.

As noted, a person is regarded as ordinarily resident in Ireland if he or she has been living in the State for the preceding three years. The individual does not cease to be ordinarily resident in Ireland until he or she has been living outside the State for the preceding three years.

Conversely, a person having acquired ordinary residence status will continue to be regarded as ordinarily resident in Ireland until that person has been non-resident for three continuous tax years.

If the non-domiciled person were to leave Ireland in 2021, he or she would be ordinarily resident until 2024 and any gift or bequest during the period 2018 to 2024 would be subject to CAT.

13.2.2 DOMICILE

Domicile is basically residence plus intention to live in a State. Thus it is a much wider concept than mere residence. Everyone has a domicile of origin/birth. The individual retains this domicile of origin unless he or she changes it, to acquire a domicile of choice or dependency.

See *T v T* [1983] IR 29 where Henchy J says that there is a rebuttable presumption that an individual always retains his or her domicile of origin. Thus, there is a very strong burden on the person who seeks to argue that a domicile of choice has been acquired. The burden, in this case, was described as resembling more a criminal standard of proof than a civil standard.

While clearly this is a very difficult burden to discharge, a person can subsequently acquire a domicile of choice. This requires an intention of permanent or indefinite residence in that place. Unfortunately, the length of time spent in the State for the purposes of residence is not decisive. See *Revenue Commissioners v Z* [1977] No 111 ITC, where an individual who had remained in Ireland for a continuous period of fourteen years was held not yet to be domiciled there.

However, if an intention of indefinite residence in the State can be demonstrated then it may be found that an individual has acquired a domicile there: see *In Re Sillar* [1956] IR 344. In this case the court had to decide whether the will of an English national who had resided in Ireland for more than forty years was to be construed in accordance with English or Irish law. Despite the fact that the testator described himself in his will as a British subject domiciled in Britain resident in Ireland, Budd J held that the testator was domiciled in Ireland, saying, *'he cannot alter the fact that he has acquired a domicile of choice by stating something to contrary'*. He went on to say:

> *from a consideration of the case law it is clear that it is a question of fact from all known circumstances whether an individual is shown by his conduct that he has formed the settled purpose of residing permanently in the domicile of choice.*

Thus, because, it has already been established that it is a question of fact and not one of law, practitioners must establish every known fact and circumstance about the client, if it appears from a cursory view of the facts, that domicile may be an issue. Practitioners may find themselves in a position of (subsequent to the client's death) giving evidence in an attempt to establish domicile. Therefore it is evident that caution must be exercised when taking instructions for a will from a client who is domiciled outside Ireland in order to be in a position to advise the client what assets will be assessable for CAT purposes.

Practitioners are referred to the case of *Claire Proes v Revenue Commissioners* V ITR 481 (High Court decision of Costello J., 5 June 1997). In this case a taxpayer had an Irish domicile of origin. She had left Ireland many years ago as a very young woman and had lived in the UK and married an English man in the UK. She had lived in various countries throughout her life, but all of them outside Ireland. She and her husband had taken up residence in the UK where they lived at the time of his death in 1982. She was obliged to leave their apartment, which had been provided for by his employer. She took up residence in a Cork holiday home which she and her husband had bought in 1970. She continued to spend a great deal of time in London with her daughters and her evidence was that she intended to move to London to live near them. She bought a property in London in 1992.

The High Court found on the above facts that the taxpayer had never intended to leave the UK permanently. Her intention to return to London was not so vague as to lead to the conclusion that she had abandoned her domicile of choice and revived her Irish domicile of origin, therefore the taxpayer was UK domiciled.

13.2.2.1 Minors

An additional point about domicile is that, minors normally assume the domicile of the father, except non-marital children, who assume the domicile of the mother. As with all beneficiaries, ensure that for the children their CAT status and in this case their domicile are all properly identified.

13.2.2.2 Relevance of domicile

Domicile remains important in the following circumstances:

1. to obtain an exemption from tax on government securities, the donee or successor must not be domiciled, resident, or ordinarily resident in the State;
2. in respect of settlements executed prior to 1 December 2000 it is the domicile not the residence of the disponer that gives rise to the charge.

13.2.2.3 Practice notes relating to domicile

Solicitors should ask the client where he or she says they are domiciled, but should be wary of inserting declarations of domicile in a will. A declaration of domicile by a testator does not carry much weight or stand up to the scrutiny of the courts if it is apparent that the declared domicile was not in fact the domicile of the deceased as of the date of death. See *In Re BL Rowan (Deceased), Rowan v Rowan & Others* III ITR 172 and *The Law & Taxation of Trusts* (Keogan, Mee & Wylie, Tottel, 2007), Chapter 23.

Solicitors should be particularly careful if they are drafting a will for a 'green card' holder living in the US. Those who hold a green card in the US, when returning on holiday, or for some other purpose, are required to sign a form that they are leaving the US for a temporary visit abroad with the intention of returning to the US. The US Federal Courts in 1999 held that this means that the individual has acquired US domicile. The US authorities subsequently utilise this signed agreement to insist that domicile has been established in the particular State. Most holders sign the form because they fear losing the green card and do not think or do not know of the consequences for them as testators.

As a consequence, the holder is both domiciled and resident in a State in the US and is taxed on global income. Further, being domiciled in the US, he or she is subject to both federal estate and gift taxes and the local State taxes. Although the federal estate tax has a generous threshold for US citizens, it does not contain many of the exemptions and reliefs that the CAT tax code contains and the rates under the unified credit system can exceed the Irish rate.

In addition, many difficulties under the double taxation agreement are determined by the country of domicile; for example, bank accounts are deemed to be locally situate in the country of domicile, and the succession rights on intestacy are different. It is understood that the US parties are enforcing this, which, in fact, is contrary to the intentions of domiciliary green card holders.

Ireland is increasingly becoming a multinational society. It is highly likely that people will die resident but not domiciled here. In making wills for such clients, it is necessary to obtain detailed advice (tax and law) from the country of domicile in relation to foreign property and the treatment there of property situate in Ireland. Advice must also be given to clients to seek legal and tax advice in their country of domicile. If clients do not wish to do this, solicitors should consider refusing to draft an Irish will unless the testator executes a disclaimer, releasing the solicitor from any liability in those circumstances.

13.2.2.4 Domicile and trusts

Since s. 138 of the Finance Act, 2000 came into force on 1 December 1999 (now incorporated in CAT Consolidation Act, 2003, s. 6 (taxable gift) and s. 11 (taxable inheritance)), there are in effect two regimes now operating with respect to trusts:

1. benefits taken under trusts established *prior to* 1 December 1999, which are subject to the old domicile rules;
2. trusts established *on or after* 1 December 1999, which are subject to the new residence-based rules.

Discretionary trusts established before 1 December 1999 are within the charge to CAT on foreign assets, if the settlor was domiciled in Ireland when the trust was created, or when appointments are made from the trust, or when the settlor dies, assuming the appointments are made after his death.

In the case of a trust established on or after 1 December 1999, if the disponer was resident or ordinarily resident on any one of these critical dates, the trust will be within the charge to CAT on foreign assets. Irish-located assets will, of course, be within the charge to tax in any event.

Tax advisers may therefore wish to consider fully dismantling foreign-domiciled settlor trusts established prior to December 1999 where the beneficiaries are resident or ordinarily resident in Ireland before there is any further change in the CAT rules.

Frequently such trusts are non-resident for Income Tax/CAT purposes, of course, and great care must be taken in relation to these trusts in the context of the recent Finance Act changes, which may have very significant implications for Income Tax and CAT. However, while it may be beneficial from the CAT point of view, the possible impact of dismantling such trusts should be considered of course under all taxation heads. (Padraic – are you happy that Practice notes relating to Domicile and US have been removed?)

13.3 Initial Fact-Gathering for CAT

Having established the residence/ordinary residence/domicile of the testator/beneficiaries the solicitor should then make a list of the client's entire assets and intended beneficiaries, noting any relevant tax points in relation to both the assets and beneficiaries.

The solicitor should list the assets and note if any reliefs may/could be made to apply to same due to the nature of the asset itself. For example:

- Is the testator bequeathing **farmland** and/or other agricultural assets?
- Is the testator bequeathing a **business** or an interest in a business?
- Is the testator bequeathing a **dwelling**?

List the beneficiaries and their blood relationship to the testator and note any possible reliefs/exemptions that may apply due to the 'type' of beneficiaries themselves. For example: favourite nephew/niece; surviving spouse; minor child of a deceased child; parent inheriting absolutely; parent inheriting within five years of a gift to a child.

List CAT groups for the various beneficiaries.

- List any prior or likely future benefits to any beneficiaries as can be practically obtained, so that as complete a picture as possible of the tax consequences for beneficiaries of any will drafted can be calculated.
- Are there any predeceased and/or non-marital/step children or child/children of a civil partner? See Finance (No. 3) Act, 2011.
- Do any of the beneficiaries fall into any special categories? For example, is there a possible favourite nephew, or surviving spouse of a predeceased spouse?
- Are there minor children or minor children of a predeceased child or minor children of a civil partner or minor children of a deceased child of a civil partner?

Once this has been done, the solicitor is then in a position to advise the client on the various possible reliefs and exemptions under the tax legislation that may or may not apply, or may be made to apply, in the particular circumstances.

Having considered the assets and beneficiaries in general regarding CAT and decided what might apply, the solicitor then needs to look in particular at any such reliefs/exemptions. While the main CAT reliefs/exemptions have been outlined in **Chapters 3–6** we will now reconsider the following main CAT reliefs and exemptions in particular, and consider how to draft a will to maximise the use of same:

1. agricultural relief;
2. business relief;
3. favourite nephew relief;
4. dwelling-house exemption;
5. insurance policies (Sections 72/73 or otherwise);
6. spouse/civil partner exemption (s. 70 CAT Consolidation Act, 2003 as amended by Schedule 3 to the Finance (No.3) Act, 2011);
7. surviving spouse/civil partner relief (see para. 6 of the Second Schedule to CAT Consolidation Act, 2003 as amended by Schedule 3 to the Finance (No.3) Act, 2011);
8. minor child of a deceased child or minor child of the deceased child of a civil partner (see para. 1 of the First Part of the Second Schedule to CAT Consolidation Act, 2003 as amended by Schedule 3 to the Finance (No.3) Act, 2011);
9. parent inheriting from a child.

13.3.1 AGRICULTURAL RELIEF

Agricultural relief has been dealt with in detail in **Chapter 4** and will not be reviewed in detail here.

However, as it is important not to forget the basics of agricultural relief when advising a testator on same in relation to a will, a brief recap on some key elements is appropriate.

Remember, to investigate whether the intended beneficiary will be able to avail of agricultural relief and be able to pass both asset (financial) and activity elements of the farmer test.

The farmer test must therefore be explained to the testator with all of its nuances; for example, for 'off-farm principle residences', bear in mind that only the equitable interest in the off-farm residence is taken into account for the farmer test. You should also remind your client that placing property in a discretionary trust or giving an interest in expectancy to a beneficiary who may otherwise obtain agricultural relief, will be included in any farmer test. It would be prudent to advise the testator to in turn advise the potential beneficiary to keep his or her non-agricultural assets to a minimum. Bear in mind, however, if the testator 'changes his mind' any such conversation with the beneficiary may be used by the beneficiary to support a s. 117 claim or a claim for proprietary estoppel.

No discussion with a testator regarding agricultural relief would be complete without explaining clawback provisions in full, and in particular the clawback relating to the 'active farmer'.

From a will-drafting/estate-planning perspective, the following should also be considered:

Check that assets that will be included in the calculation for agricultural relief fit into the definition of agricultural relief.

Any crops, trees, and underwood must be growing on the land to qualify as agricultural property. Once a crop or tree is cut it ceases to be agricultural property for the purposes of the relief.

Farm machinery, livestock, and bloodstock must be 'thereon', that is, on agricultural property. A bequest of a valuable brood animal will not qualify for relief unless the beneficiary also gets land.

Farm buildings, farmhouses, and mansion houses must be of a character appropriate to the property. They do not have to be on the property, or in the same folio, but there is an Appeal Commissioners case that indicates that they must be linked to the property in some way.

Check the area of agricultural land passing, and circumstances of the donee.

The Revenue operates an informal *de minimis* rule, and will not generally give agricultural relief on land of 2.5 acres (1 hectare approx.) or less. This seems to refer to the UK case of *Starke (executors of Brown deceased) v IRC* [1996] 1 All ER 622. In a recent case, Revenue refused the relief on a plot of 0.14 acres.

If two assets are likely to be passing via two different routes (e.g. survivorship and will) so there are two valuation dates and two farmer test computations bear in mind that all of the property coming from the estate counts towards both farmer tests.

Assets forming the part of the residue of an estate should be included in the farmer test where a beneficiary takes an inheritance of agricultural property on the date of death.

Where a beneficiary takes agricultural property by survivorship and a share in the residue, the residue (and any other benefit taken from the estate) must be included when doing the farmer test for the assets taken by survivorship.

The last Finance Act 2024 did not restate section 89 (3) and thus, it can only be presumed that this relief no longer applies. The same Act proposed a change to the activity test, which would require the disponer to have owned the property for six years and to have been an active or trained famer throughout this period. There were such strong objections from the IFA that same is being reconsidered and at the time of writing has not been resolved.

13.3.2 BUSINESS RELIEF

Business relief has been dealt with in detail in **Chapter 5** and will not be reviewed here in detail.

Where the testator indicates that there is a substantial business that he wishes to leave to any particular beneficiary it is essential that the solicitor explains the rules regarding business relief, as provided for in Chapter II of CAT Consolidation Act, 2003. Where appropriate the amendments provided for in by the Finance (No. 3) Act, 2011 (i.e. civil partners and children of civil partners have been included in the group of relatives and other persons whose shares will be counted together when valuing private company shares under s. 27 CAT Consolidation Act, 2003) should be taken into account.

The tax applies to mainstream CAT only and not to Discretionary Trust Tax (it would apply, however, to payment out of a discretionary trust), and provides for a 90 per cent relief. This is a huge relief and therefore if there is a possibility that the testator wishes to dispose of such an asset it is vital that the solicitor advising, ensures as far as possible that both the testator, the beneficiary, and of course the asset complies with all conditions. In particular, clawback should be explained in writing in detail, as it is most likely to arise in an uncertain economic market.

Points to be considered prior to finalising a will would include:

1. Make sure that sufficient qualifying business assets are passed across to each beneficiary to constitute a business or an interest in a business.
2. The relief is available for a business or interest in a business so a single asset on its own will not qualify unless it passes with a business or sufficient interest in a limited company/partnership carrying on a business.
3. If land or other asset is personally owned but used in a business not fully owned by the donor (an incorporated business or partnership), consider if relief can be secured by passing the asset with the shares or partnership interest.
4. Check for excluded assets or value if the testator is relying on business relief being available to the beneficiaries of the will.
5. Certain businesses are excluded from the relief, including a business of investing in currencies, securities, stocks or shares, land or buildings, or making or holding investments. A construction company that has lands held long term as a 'land bank' will not generally be treated as an investment where a history of building on such land banks owned by the company can be displayed.

In the CAT Business Relief Manual <https://www.revenue.ie/en/tax-professionals/tdm/capital-acquisitions-tax/cat-part12.pdf> on page 14 under 'Meaning of "Dealing"', the Revenue indicate that care should however be taken to identify a building or development company which retains and lets its completed property, as this may, over time, convert the business into one of mainly investment holding.

An asset that has not been used wholly or mainly for the purposes of the business throughout the two years to the date of the gift or inheritance (or for the entire period of ownership if it has been owned for less than two years) is an excepted asset and the value of the asset will not qualify for relief.

This provision excludes the value of dwellings from the relief (e.g. an apartment that is part of a pub or restaurant premises). The Revenue indicate that a practical approach will be taken and, for example, a car owned by a company and used by a director will not normally be excluded based on miles travelled on company business.

Note however, that the relief is not available re a new business, if it does not replace an old one.

When drafting a will to pass on a business or asset that qualifies for business relief, warn the testator, that the beneficiary needs to make sure that the business remains running, at a level that will keep it within the definition of relevant business property, for the six-year clawback period.

The relief will be withdrawn not only if the asset is sold, but also if it ceases to qualify as relevant business property during the six years after the date of gift/inheritance and does not come back into the category of relevant business property within a year.

This could occur if the trade in a company is scaled down and a trading property is rented so that it falls into the category of investments and as a result the investments held make up more than 50 per cent of the value of the company.

When estate planning for a client who has a group of companies, bear in mind that if the holding company gifts shares in a subsidiary the relief is technically not available.

To meet the ownership condition (two or five years) the gift must come from the owner.

There are a number of examples for each of these points in the Revenue CAT Manual, at Part 12, which should be reviewed prior to giving any advice.

13.3.3 FAVOURITE NEPHEW/NIECE RELIEF

This is discussed in **Chapter 6**. The Second Schedule of CAT Consolidation Act, 2003 deems the donee or successor to be a child of the disponer where certain conditions are met. In other words, once the conditions are met the group threshold of a nephew or niece moves from a Group B to a Group A threshold in relation to the qualifying assets.

This of course would give a substantially increased threshold to any proposed nephew/niece who was to be a beneficiary. Since the Finance (No. 3) Act, 2011 this relief has been extended so that it is available to the child of a civil partner of a brother or sister.

When the testator is making a will, such a nephew/niece may not immediately qualify (i.e. fulfil the conditions) but if these conditions are adequately explained to the testator, by the time of death the nephew/niece may well be able to avail of the said relief.

The conditions are that the donee is:

1. a child of a brother or sister (or a child of the civil partner of the brother or sister),
2. who has worked substantially on a full-time basis for five years ending on the date of the inheritance while carrying on or assisting in the trade, business, or profession of the donor and assisting on the property used in connection with the business.

The meaning of substantially or on a full-time basis is defined in the Second Schedule to CAT Consolidation Act, 2003, para. 7(3) as:

1. more than 24 hours a week for the disponer at the place where the business was carried on;

   or

2. more than 15 hours a week for the disponer at a place where the business, etc. was carried on and such business, etc. was carried on exclusively by the disponer, any spouse of the disponer, and the nephew/niece.

Points to consider when reviewing favourite nephew relief include:

1. *Establishing that the niece/nephew has worked on the farm/in the business substantially on a full-time basis.*

   It can be difficult to evidence that the niece or nephew has been working in the business on a full-time basis. It tends to be easier to establish the facts where a formal employer–employee relationship exists. However, often these relationships can be less formal and the niece or nephew may not be formally employed. It would be advisable for clients to have a formal employee–employer relationship in place if they wish to claim favourite nephew relief in the future.

   A very important point is that if the testator intends leaving a life interest in the property to (e.g.) a spouse and the remainder interest to the favourite nephew, then the relief may not apply In all such circumstances, the qualifying criteria must be met prior to the transfer of the life interest.

2. *Appointments out of discretionary trusts.*

   It should be noted that this relief does not apply to appointments out of discretionary trusts.

3. *Who is a niece or nephew?*

   Remember to inform the client, that the relief is limited to children of siblings of the testator and the child of a civil partner of a brother or sister. The nephew of his/her spouse is not his/her 'nephew' and is, in fact, a stranger in blood. Also remember to inform the client that under the Status of Children Act, 1987 a non-marital child of his/her sibling is a nephew/niece.

Although the relief is available for adopted nieces and nephews, *it is not available in respect of a foster child of a sibling.*

The relief can be made available, by agreement with the Revenue, in the case of the spouse/civil partner of a deceased niece or nephew provided all other conditions are met.

Non-business assets:

Where the Group A threshold has been absorbed by the business assets, it is advantageous for some assets being gifted or inherited to be classified as non-business assets as they would then be taxed as Group B benefits. The donee or successor would be able to avail to two tax-free thresholds (i.e. Group A and Group B), resulting in a total tax-free amount of up to €440,000 (€400,000together with €40,000since 2 October2024.

13.3.4 DWELLING-HOUSE EXEMPTION

This relief is to be found in s. 86 of CAT Consolidation Act, 2003 as repealed and replaced by s. 52 of the Finance Act, 2017 and further amended in subsequent Finance Acts. Dwelling-House exemption is discussed in detail at **3.13.3** and practitioners are also referred to the Revenue Tax and Duty Manual CAT Part 24 Dwelling-House Exemption <https://www.revenue.ie/en/tax-professionals/tdm/capital-acquisitions-tax/cat-part24.pdf> last updated March 2023. Since 25 December 2016 the section provides that save in very limited circumstances, the relief is now only available on inheritances. Dependent relatives are referred to in **7.5.3** and this section will focus on inheritances. In essence, where the deceased:

- lived in a dwelling referred to in the legislation as the 'relevant dwelling-house' (as defined in s. 86) as his or her main residence; and
- a beneficiary has been living in the dwelling-house with the donor for a period of at least three years prior to the death of the donor; and
- the beneficiary does not have any interest in any other dwelling, here or abroad.

then the beneficiary can inherit the dwelling free from CAT, and in addition the inheritance is not taken into account for future aggregation purposes.

Certain conditions apply, however:

1. The beneficiary cannot have a beneficial interest in any other dwelling at the date of the inheritance and must not inherit any other dwelling or any other interest in a dwelling from the deceased prior to the valuation date.
2. The beneficiary must have lived in the dwelling for the three years immediately preceding the inheritance.
3. The deceased must have been living in the dwelling at the date of death as his only or main residence. There is provision for 'deemed occupation' where the deceased or beneficiary ceases to occupy that dwelling-house for a period due to his or her mental or physical infirmity.
4. The beneficiary must reside in the dwelling as his or her only or main residence for the next six years. Some exceptions apply to the residence requirements for residents and may be applicable where the donee is over 65, dies, goes to work abroad or elsewhere in Ireland as a condition of employment, or enters a nursing home or convalescent home.

Clawback is dealt with at **3.13.7**.

When drafting a will for a testator who is leaving a dwelling-house to a beneficiary who lives in it, check if the beneficiary, has another dwelling, oris likely to obtain another dwelling before the proposed benefit is inherited, or takes a share in another dwelling under the will. For example, is there a holiday home, rental investment, or derelict property in the residue?

Dwelling-house exemption may not be available where a beneficiary inherits two properties together unless appropriate action is taken prior to the valuation date. If a beneficiary takes a principal dwelling ('relevant dwelling-house') and an interest in another dwelling, relief may not be granted, no matter how small the interest or the value of the property; thus, when drafting, watch this issue!

For example, if a child is being left the house they reside in with the parent along with a share of the residue of the estate which includes a holiday home, it may be better to give a specific bequest of the holiday home jointly to the other residuary beneficiaries.

Note also, that ownership of a rental dwelling (Irish or foreign) by a beneficiary will preclude relief.

The inheritance of a site with a derelict house may prevent a claim for CAT dwelling-house exemption. The definition of dwelling-house is similar to the definition of residential property for Stamp Duty purposes.

The following extract from Revenue Stamp Duty Work Manual <https://www.revenue.ie/en/tax-professionals/tdm/stamp-duty/stamp-duty-manual/part-01.pdf> indicates that a derelict house would be residential property:

> **What is residential property?**
>
> Residential property is defined as a building or part of a building which, at the date the conveyance or lease is executed, was used or was suitable for use as a dwelling. It includes:
>
> partially constructed/adapted dwellings, and dwellings which have not been adapted for non-residential use since construction. This would include, for example, a derelict house.

However, as this is a different Act and different tax head the Stamp Duty interpretation may not be conclusive.

Check for a future interest in another dwelling—does the beneficiary have a remainder interest in a residential property? Dwelling-house exemption is not available where a beneficiary has a beneficial interest in another dwelling. The legislation does not specify that the beneficial interest has to be vested in possession.

It is interesting to note that, contrary to the 2004 Law Reform Commission Consultation Paper on the Rights and Duties of Co-Habitees <http://www.lawreform.ie/_fileupload/consultation papers/cp32.htm> at paras 8.27 to 8.38, the Finance (No. 3) Act, 2011 does not give a CAT exemption for cohabitants in relation to the 'family home'. This could create considerable financial problems where one co-habitant dies and leaves the property to the surviving co-habitant if dwelling-house exemption does not apply. As noted at **7.5.1** the relief would not apply on a gift such as a voluntary transfer into joint names where the beneficiary is not a 'dependent relative'.

It is also eminently possible that the surviving co-habitant might not be able to avail of dwelling-house exemption. This could arise if the surviving co-habitant has a beneficial interest in another dwelling irrespective of how minor an interest or the value of the same then the relief will not apply. If advising in such a situation para. 19.9 of the Revenue CAT Manual may assist, although that refers to 'common law spouses'.

13.3.5 INSURANCE POLICIES

Insurance policies for this purpose fall into two separate categories:

1. certain 'IFSC' (Irish Financial Services Sector) insurance policies where both the disponer (testator) and beneficiary are non-ordinarily resident and domiciled; and
2. insurance policies under ss. 72 and 73 of CAT Consolidation Act, 2003 (so-called s. 60 policies).

Section 74 of CAT Consolidation Act, 2003 exempts from Inheritance and Gift Tax certain policies of life assurance issued after 1 December 1992 and comprised in the benefit at the date of the benefit where both the disponer and beneficiary are non-ordinarily resident and domiciled. Effectively, this originally enabled financial institutions operating in the IFSC to sell insurance products to clients outside the jurisdiction.

Prior to 1 January 2001, the proper law of the disposition could not be the law of the State and the assurance company had to operate within the area of the IFSC. This is no longer the case; however, both disponer and beneficiary have to be non-ordinarily resident and domiciled. Thus if clients fall into this category it might be worth their while to take out such a life insurance policy.

Insurance policies under ss. 72 and 73 of CAT Consolidation Act, 2003 (formerly called 's. 60' policies) have been discussed in para 3.7.

Briefly, they allow the disponer to take out certain insurance policies, the proceeds of which can be utilised to discharge a liability to pay Inheritance Tax (s. 72) or Gift Tax (s. 73) without tax necessarily being charged on the proceeds of the policy. These also include a policy taken out by two spouses the proceeds of which are payable on the death of the survivor of those spouses or on the simultaneous death of both.

These policies can potentially be of great benefit; however, they are not a general panacea and should not be suggested to every client '*willy nilly*', and the following points should be considered:

1. The older the disponer, the more expensive the policy. It would be particularly important, where the client is elderly, to point out to him or her that the premiums on such policies do not qualify for Income Tax relief. In short, the ideal candidates for such policies are middle-aged, wealthy testators who wish to reduce their beneficiaries' tax bill.
2. The principal benefit of the policy is that the proceeds of the policy to the extent that they are used to discharge a liability to Inheritance Tax are not aggregated to the property forming the subject-matter of the inheritance and they can potentially be of great benefit. The corollary of this of course is that any portion of the proceeds of the policy not required to discharge the inheritance forms an inheritance taken by the beneficiary and is liable for tax. Thus, the 'figures' need to be run to ensure this does not happen if at all possible.
3. For a policy to be effective for tax purposes there are certain qualifying provisions, which must be explained to the client. For example, the inheritance must be taken on or after the date of death of the insured and not later than one year after the date of death of the insured. This restriction would be an extremely important consideration to be borne in mind in the context of drafting a will leaving property upon trust with minor beneficiaries who may not become beneficially entitled in possession to the property comprised in the trust until many years after the death of the insured. So here the policies would not be of use.
4. It is of equal importance that the will contains instructions to the executors/trustees as to how the proceeds of the policy are to be applied. In particular, the will should instruct the executors to utilise the proceeds of the policy and discharge any Inheritance Tax liability arising under the terms of the will and they must be given the power to do so, that is, to appropriate the proceeds of the policy when necessary to discharge the tax liabilities of various beneficiaries.
5. In the event that the Inheritance Tax liability arises from a benefit passing outside the will, for example joint property passing by survivorship or the termination of a life interest, it is important that the trustee/executor be given power to utilise the proceeds of the policy that in all probability will form part of the estate of the deceased to discharge the liability to tax.

13.3.6 SPOUSES/CIVIL PARTNERS/QUALIFIED COHABITANTS

A major relief, which is applicable in most cases, is that, all inheritances and gifts between spouses and civil partners are exempt from CAT, as discussed at **3.11**. As noted earlier, this relief does not apply, however, to qualified cohabitants.

Qualified cohabitants have a limited relief only in relation to any property transferred under a court order under the redress scheme provided for by s. 194 of the Civil Partnership and Certain Rights Of Cohabitants Act, 2010 <http://www.irishstatutebook.ie/eli/2010/act/24/section/194/enacted/en/html#sec194> as set out in Chapter 4, para 4.7 of the OUP *Wills, Probate & Estates Manual.*

13.3.6.1 Surviving spouse/Civil partner relief

This has been discussed at **3.13**. In short, where one spouse/civil partner has died and the surviving spouse/civil partner, takes an inheritance from a relative of the deceased spouse/civil partner, the surviving spouse's/civil partner's group threshold is calculated as if the surviving spouse/civil partner had the same relationship to the disponer as the deceased spouse/civil partner.

The effect of this is that they are deemed to acquire the tax threshold of the deceased spouse/civil partner in relation to the disponer. They do not, however, acquire the deceased spouse's/civil partner's tax history. For example, my daughter-in-law, the widow of my late son, would acquire a Group A threshold instead of the Group C she would normally have but any prior benefits received by my late son would not be taken into account.

Points to consider include:

1. As noted above, this should also apply to other reliefs, such as favourite nephew relief.
2. Quite often a 'gift over' clause in a will would ensure that a surviving spouse does not benefit in an unplanned fashion should a child predecease.

However, if a testator intends making provision for a surviving spouse/civil partner of a relative it is important that they realise that their group threshold may have changed and plan accordingly. If they have moved from Group C to Group A (as in the example above) this may be of little use to them if their Group A threshold has already been exceeded.

In that case, it may be more tax efficient to provide for the children directly.

13.3.7 MINOR CHILD OF A DECEASED CHILD

It is important in light of the Finance (No. 3) Act, 2011 when considering this relief, that it now applies to the **minor** child of a deceased child of a civil partner and to the minor child of a civil partner of a deceased child (the equivalent of a step-grandchild for spouses) and the minor child of a civil partner of a deceased child of the disponer's civil partner (the equivalent of the stepchild of a deceased stepchild for spouses).

There are a number of exemptions that relate to children specifically. Points to consider include:

1. As noted, children of a civil partner have a Group A threshold. As such children are now defined as children in s. 2(1) of the Act; the child of a sibling's civil partner would be a 'nephew/niece' and thus Group B and possibly a 'favourite nephew/niece' even though there is no blood relationship at all.
2. Practitioners are aware that the Group A threshold will apply to the *minor* child of a deceased child of a disponer. This would also now apply to the minor child of a deceased child of a civil partner of a disponer. It is important to remember that this must be a child of the disponer/civil partner who is deceased. For example, if a child predeceases leaving minor children, any bequest from the parents of that child, to those minor children is Group A. Any bequest from the parents of the surviving parent of those children is not: it is still Group B. Thus, the children of a predeceased child may have different tax-free thresholds where one or more are minors and one or more are not.

3. It is important to explain to the testator that such a child must take the bequest prior to reaching the age of eighteen, if they are to avail of the relief. Any inter vivos gifts of a capital nature to a minor child must be on a 'bare' trust if they are to vest before the child turns eighteen.
4. As discussed at **3.14.10.2**, where the testator is the parent of the deceased parent of and is acting *in loco parentis* in relation to a minor child, certain payments in relation to support and maintenance are free from tax.

13.3.8 INHERITANCES TAKEN BY PARENTS ON THE DEATH OF A CHILD

There are two similar but totally separate issues arising here that should not be confused.

1. Any absolute inheritance (i.e. not a limited interest) by a parent on the death of a child/child of a civil partner is a Group A benefit.
2. This relief is extended to an absolute exemption where either or both parents made a taxable disposition to that child or where a child inherits from a parent within five years of that child subsequently dying.

Points to consider include:

1. A non-exempt gift is one exceeding €3000 that is not exempt for any other reason, for example Dwelling-House exemption. Such an inheritance is exempt from tax and is not taken into account in calculating CAT on later gifts and inheritances from any other source.
2. A situation where this may arise in practice, is where a child has been born suffering from catastrophic disabilities arising from (say) medical negligence or suffers catastrophic injuries early in life in an accident. In those situations the parents will often sue on the child's behalf and win damages including special damages. These damages are usually lodged in a trust fund for the benefit of the child, managed by the parents of that child.

   Quite often all the expenses and outlay incurred by the parents for the benefit of the child is paid back as part of the special damages and all future expenses and outlay is paid out of the trust fund. In those circumstances, should the child die leaving a large sum outstanding in the trust fund, the parents will be the people entitled, usually on intestacy, to the funds. However, they may not be able to claim the relief, unless they can show that a non-exempt gift was provided in the five years prior to the death of the child.
3. The exemption will not apply in the following circumstances:
   (a) an inheritance that has become such by reason of the disponer dying within two years from the date of a gift to his/her parent; or
   (b) an inheritance received by parents by way of, for example, an appointment from a discretionary will trust created by their child.

13.3.9 EXEMPTION RELATING TO QUALIFYING EXPENSES OF INCAPACITATED PERSONS

This was also discussed in **3.14.13**. Section 84 of the CAT Consolidation Act, 2003 exempts benefits **taken** exclusively for the purposes of discharging qualifying expenses of certain individuals. In the past, once it could be verified that benefits are being applied for such purposes, the benefits were then treated as exempt.

However, as noted in that paragraph, since 2011, the Revenue Commissioners have interpreted the phrase *'taken exclusively for the purpose of discharging qualifying expenses'* as a technical phrase referring to the intention in the mind of the disponer. An Appeal

Commissioner made a determination on 18 June 2019 (32TACD2019, <http://www.taxappeals.ie/_fileupload/Determinations/2019/32TACD2019(1).pdf>) in which he took a completely different view than Revenue. The Revenue did not appeal this determination to the High Court, but notwithstanding the view set out in the determination is not accepted by Revenue. It's position is set out in Part 22 of the Revenue CAT Manual <https://www.revenue.ie/en/tax-professionals/tdm/capital-acquisitions-tax/cat-part22.pdf>

Bearing all of this in mind, it is best practice when drafting a will on behalf of a client, to enquire as a matter of course whether any intended beneficiaries are 'permanently incapacitated by reason of physical or mental infirmity' and if so, to draft any bequest to such beneficiary identifying the bequest as being that of 'qualifying expenses' of an 'incapacitated beneficiary':

> *I give and bequeath the sum of €X (X euro) to AB and I declare that such sum should be used exclusively for the purpose of discharging qualifying expenses of AB arising from [insert name of illness/condition/incapacity].*

While, arguably, in light of the determination referred to above, this is no longer necessary, it is more straightforward to have the instruction by the testator to use the bequest in this fashion in place. This allows the solicitor to confirm both to Revenue and the beneficiary or the trustees of the beneficiary that this is the sole purpose for which the funds can be utilised.

This highlights, again, the importance of taking detailed instructions and keeping a detailed attendance.

13.3.10 GOVERNMENT SECURITIES

These are discussed at **3.14.7** and are relevant in two ways. Firstly, under s. 56 of CAT Consolidation Act, 2003, certain government stock held by the disponer can be used to pay the tax at par. The advantage of payment at par is that the current market value of the stock may be less than the par value. While this is not currently the case in 2020, it should be checked as a possibility prior to selling government stock.

Also, under s. 81 of CAT Consolidation Act, 2003, certain government securities (which would be exempt from taxation if held by a person neither domiciled nor ordinarily resident in the State) are exempt from CAT when bequeathed or given to a person neither resident nor ordinarily resident in the State. For gifts or inheritances on or after 24 February 2003, the disponer must have held the security for fifteen years.

Note that a personal representative or trustee where there is a foreign beneficiary could exercise his or her power of appropriation under s. 55 of the Succession Act to appropriate any government stock in favour of the foreign beneficiary in order to fully avail of the relief.

13.3.11 PAYMENTS FOR SUPPORT AND EDUCATION

There has been a significant 'clawing back' of the exemption provided for the support, maintenance or education of a child or child of a civil partner or other person in relation to whom they are in loco parentis ('child, etc.'). It is now limited to a child etc. under the age of 18 or, if over 18, under the age of 25 and in full-time education. If a child, etc. is living with a disability to the extent that he or she is unable to care for him or herself, there is no age limitation.

Since the passing of the Finance (No. 3) Bill, 2011 civil partners and children of civil partners are included in this relief.

These payments (as restricted) are exempt from tax where they are part of the normal expenditure of a person in the circumstances of the disponer, and if the provision is reasonable having regard to the financial circumstance of the disponer.

The relief as outlined above also applies to the receipt by a child of the disponer of money for a similar purpose when both the disponer and the other parent of that child are dead. Prior to the Finance Act, 2014 this relief was confined to orphans who were minors.

Full details of the Finance Act 2014 amendments in relation to this relief can be found on the Revenue Guide <http://www.revenue.ie/en/gains-gifts-and-inheritance/documents/cat-treatment-receipts-by-children.pdf>.

Where a trust is set up during the client's lifetime or by will it is useful to provide that the trust should allow for monies being expanded for the support, maintenance, or education of the child. See Wills Trust chapters. If both parents are dead, then such expenditure will not be deemed a gift or inheritance where the provision is such as would be part of the normal expenditure of a person in the circumstances of the disponer prior to his death, and is reasonable having regard to the financial circumstances.

13.3.12 ADDITIONAL RELIEFS AND RELATED ISSUES

These are some of the major exemptions and reliefs available in relation to CAT reviewed from a will-drafting/estate-planning perspective. However, there are some additional exemptions/reliefs and a practitioner should be in a position to advise on all such exemptions/reliefs. These would include:

1. charities (s. 76);
2. superannuation and employment benefits payable to employees (s. 80);
3. objects of national scientific, historic, or artistic interest (s. 77). (Note however the clawback and viewing provisions.)

13.4 Other Methods to Reduce CAT Liability

There are other methods of reducing a CAT liability, which one ought to advise the testator to consider, for example:

1. *Splitting the estate*. Where a testator owns a relatively large estate he may achieve a significant tax planning by splitting the estate among his children and/or grandchildren, that is, by splitting the inheritance among a larger number of children, a tax-saving opportunity arises as each can take advantage of their own thresholds.
2. *Limited estates*. While these can cause a lot of CAT problems they can be quite useful in relation to wasting assets, such as a race horse.
3. *Inter vivos gifts*. It might suit the client to dispose of a portion of his property immediately, in the knowledge that any subsequent growth in value will accrue to the donee rather than the disponer. The donee would avail of the small gift exemption but may be liable to Stamp Duty and the disponer may incur a charge to CGT (which can be set off against the donee's CAT liability).

It is crucial, however, always to act in the best interests of the client. Saving tax for a beneficiary is not the main concern—protecting the client's interests is. For example, it is not in clients' best interests to divest themselves of all or some assets during their lifetime, leaving them at the mercy of a donee's gratitude, no matter how tax efficient the transfer appeared at the time!

While it is vital to be aware of all the possible reliefs and exemptions to ascertain if any relief applies to the testator's circumstances, it is advisable not to get involved in a complicated tax- planning exercise by will unless and until the solicitor is absolutely certain that he or she is aware of the implications and consequences of what is being advised upon and until, where necessary, the solicitor has sought all necessary advice.

13.5 General Summary of Estate Planning and Taxation

To sum up for tax planning purposes, the solicitor must be in a position to advise a testator in four particular areas.

13.5.1 AVOID TAX

In other words, the solicitor should be able to advise the client on how to arrange his affairs so that his exposure to taxation is avoided; for example, if the client x owns a dwelling, to allow the intended beneficiary of the dwelling to live in the house in the hope that the beneficiary will be able to avail of dwelling-house exemption, or, in the alternative, having left a property as a specific bequest to a beneficiary and ensuring that dwelling-house exemption applies and then in the residue leaving an interest in a holiday home to all beneficiaries, thereby obviating the Dwelling-House exemption for the beneficiary of the specific bequest of a property.

This would also involve advising the client to advise the proposed beneficiary of the beneficiary's role in ensuring that he or she can avail of the relief; that is to say, by not acquiring an interest in any other property. It is completely legitimate to arrange affairs to avoid tax or so as to limit tax. This is not tax avoidance which would fall foul of anti-avoidance legislation. However, note that evasion of tax means non-disclosure and is illegal.

13.5.2 REDUCE TAX

If it is not possible for the client to completely avoid tax, the solicitor should be in a position to advise clients on how to arrange their affairs so that the tax liability is kept as low as possible. For example, if the property which is going to be liable to CAT can qualify for business relief, to ensure that both the client and the beneficiary ensure that the beneficiary will qualify for business relief. A crucial point, mentioned above but worth repeating here, is that such an arrangement may not suit the client's wider interests.

For example, if the client owns a business premises in his sole name and operates a business from the premises as a limited liability company, it may not be in the client's interest to transfer the premises to the limited liability company. In that case, if it is the client's intention that the beneficiary should inherit the premises, ensure that it can pass with the business and avail of the relief.

13.5.3 PLAN FOR TAX

Where it is not possible to either avoid or reduce the tax or where the tax has been avoided and reduced as much as possible, the solicitor should ensure that the client has enough information in order to make plans that will provide for the payment of tax.

For example, the client may wish to take out a s. 72 policy which would provide money for the payment of CAT and indeed any tax arising on death. Again, depending on the age and income of the client, it may well not be in the client's best interests to take out an expensive s. 72 policy, on which no Income Tax relief is available, merely to ensure the beneficiary's tax liability is reduced.

13.3.4 CALCULATE POTENTIAL LIABILITY

The solicitor must be in a position to advise clients very simply about likely exposure to tax and to calculate what that liability will be. It should of course be made clear to the client that the liabilities have been calculated on the basis of current legislation and estimated values. It is not generally possible to predict what will happen in the future, and changes in legislation could well introduce dramatic changes in the calculation of tax.

Therefore, it is a wise idea to put the onus on the client, should legislation change or should his own circumstances change, to come back to the solicitor. At that time the client and solicitor can discuss such changes in order to enable the solicitor to provide fresh advice taking into account any change in legislation and or any change in circumstances. If necessary or advisable the solicitor can draft a new will for execution by the client to maximise the benefit to him of such legislation or to take such change in circumstances arising into account.

It is best to so advise clients in writing by letter after execution of the will. At the very least, clients should be advised to review their wills every three years where no major legislative or life changes have occurred.

As every practitioner approaches tax planning and will drafting differently, the advice outlined above is to be taken into consideration when drafting a will and is clearly not comprehensive.

CHAPTER 14

TAXATION ISSUES IN THE ADMINISTRATION OF ESTATES

14.1 Introduction

Whenever a solicitor opens an administration file, he or she is also commencing a tax file. Benjamin Franklin once said: *'In this world nothing can be said to be certain, except Death and Taxes.'* When opening an administration file, these two certainties, are inextricably linked.

The implication of all taxes should be apparent to a practitioner in dealing with the assets in the estate. The following are some guidelines on the various taxes which will be encountered in any administration.

The taxes dealt with here are:

- capital acquisitions tax (CAT);
- income tax;
- capital gains tax (CGT); and
- stamp duty.

This chapter deals with these taxes, in the context of the responsibilities of the personal representative in the course of administering an estate, but does not attempt to provide a comprehensive explanation of the individual taxes. See the relevant chapters of this book for a more thorough explanation of CGT and stamp duty.

For income tax and CGT, the new Revenue procedure dealing with clearance in death cases will apply, and details of same can be found in Revenue Income Tax, CGT and Corporation Tax (CT) Tax and Duty Manual Part 46–01–02 Requests for Clearance in Death Cases.

The personal representative or their professional advisor makes an online clearance request to Revenue via the *MyEnquiries* portal outlining pre and post-death tax liability, confirming that all returns have been filed and taxes paid. If Revenue do not respond within thirty-five working days, the personal representative is free to distribute the estate.

14.2 Capital Acquisitions Tax

CAT has been dealt with in detail elsewhere in this book. In this chapter, the responsibilities of the personal representative will be highlighted.

14.2.1 TAXABLE INHERITANCE

As discussed in **Chapter 1**, the CAT Consolidation Act, 2003, s. 11 directs that an inheritance is deemed to be taken where:

- under or in consequence of any disposition (such as a trust)
- a person (i.e., an individual or a legal person) becomes beneficially entitled in possession on a death to any benefit otherwise, than for full consideration in money or monies worth.

In contrast to Estate Duty, which it replaced, CAT is a tax on gifts or inheritances, which is paid by the recipient of the gift/inheritance and not by the disponer's estate.

14.2.2 DATE OF DEATH AND VALUATION DATE

As practitioners are aware from **Chapter 1**, there is a distinction between the inheritance date (the date of death) and the valuation date. The CAT regime covering the administration is fixed at the inheritance date. Therefore, it is imperative to check the date of death under which the benefit was received in assessing the CAT payable.

In some circumstances, there may be discretion in regard to choosing the valuation date. Great care should be taken by solicitors in advising personal representatives in this regard. For example, a person who is not a farmer at the date of death and who is to inherit farmland/livestock, farm machinery, and so on may be able to take steps to ensure that he or she does fall within the definition of a farmer on the valuation date, which will allow him or her to take advantage of agricultural relief, as outlined in **Chapter 4**.

The closer the valuation date is to 31 August the shorter the time period the beneficiary will have in which to file a return and pay any tax due. See below at **14.2.4**.

14.2.3 ACCOUNTABILITY AND NON-RESIDENT BENEFICIARIES/ LEGAL PERSONAL REPRESENTATIVES

Prior to 14 June 2010, there was a secondary accountability whereby a disponer/personal representative could have become liable to tax, if this tax was not paid by the beneficiary of the gift/inheritance. For Irish resident beneficiaries, this secondary liability was abolished as part of a series of reforms of the administration of CAT in June 2010. The potential secondary liability to tax still arises, however, where the beneficiary resides outside the jurisdiction.

As a tax liability cannot currently be enforced outside the jurisdiction, when the Revenue Commissioners removed secondary liability in all other cases, it has been retained, in a slightly different form, where the beneficiary is non-resident. Where the personal representative resides outside the jurisdiction, the legislation provides that a solicitor practising in the State must be retained to act as 'agent' in the administration of the estate and is personally liable for the payment of the tax.

Accountability, in general, is discussed at **2.9.6**. Section 45 of CATCA, 2003 as substituted in its entirety by s. 147(1)(b) of the Finance Act, 2010 deals with accountability and provides that the person accountable is the donee or successor.

The entirely new s. 45AA as inserted by 147 (1) (d) of the Finance Act, 2010 provides for the liability of the personal representative where there are non-resident beneficiaries. It provides that where the non-resident beneficiary does not file and pay, then the personal representative in the jurisdiction (or the solicitor 'agent' appointed under s. 48(10) of the Act as inserted by 147(1)(l) of the Finance Act, 2010 where there is no personal representative resident) shall be assessable and chargeable for the tax in the same way as the beneficiary would be.

Section 45AA goes on to provide certain limitations to this and certain powers to the personal representative or solicitor to retain, sell, or mortgage the property in order to raise the tax. The limitations include protection for the personal representative where the beneficiary does not fully disclose prior benefits on enquiry from the personal representative. Also, the charge to tax only applies to property within the 'control' of the personal representative/solicitor.

It should be noted however that 'control' includes property which the personal representative/solicitor would have, but for their own neglect or default retained control over. It is unclear at present what will be considered 'neglect or default' in these circumstances.

Further limitations on liability, were provided in the Revenue CAT Tax and Duty Manual Part 02 para 2.4, which clarify that where a beneficiary fails to disclose assets outside the State that would affect their liability to CAT (for example, not disclosing non-agricultural assets in order to claim agricultural relief) then the personal representative/solicitor who has made reasonable enquiries is not liable for the extra CAT incurred. See para **14.2.3.1** below and the initial letter sent to a beneficiary in Chapter 6, para 6.8.4.2 of *Wills, Probate and Estates* (Courtney: OUP, 2022).

Finally, as outlined in **2.9.6.1**, where a personal representative/solicitor writes to the Revenue Commissioners outlining an intent to distribute and does not receive a response within a month they can distribute, having satisfied their obligations. This is assuming that they acted honestly and in good faith and did not deliberately fail to comply with their obligations.

As provided for in the Revenue TDM dealing with the Statement of Affairs (Probate) Form SA.2 (CAT Manual Part 2) a new online process, to manage these applications for clearance has been established.

Details can be found on page 7 of the Manual and a step by step guide provided in Appendix 1 of same.

A solicitor or resident personal representative can now submit their intention to distribute to non-resident beneficiaries via *MyEnquiries* on ROS. When the request is submitted the applicant will receive an automated reply stating that if Revenue do not respond within thirty days, they can distribute the benefit to the non-resident beneficiaries. This is similar to the tax clearance process mentioned in para 14.1 for CGT and income tax.

The Probate, Administration & Trusts Committee issued a Practice Note in this regard in December 2018 and same is reproduced here:

> ***Undertakings, non-resident personal representative and probate practice***
>
> *Practitioners are reminded that as soon as a Grant of Representation issues, the personal representative is absolutely entitled to receive the proceeds of any funds in any bank or other financial institution.*
>
> *A solicitor acting for such personal representative(s) should therefore, be extremely cautious in giving any undertaking concerning such funds and should avoid doing so wherever possible.*
>
> *Prior to giving any such undertaking the solicitor should obtain from each of the personal representatives the usual irrevocable authority to act and an irrevocable instruction to the financial institution concerned that the funds can only be paid through the solicitor's office.*
>
> *This instruction should be then forwarded to the financial institution concerned and confirmation should be obtained from them that they will only release the proceeds through the solicitor's office.*
>
> *This should also be done where the solicitor is acting as agent for a non-resident personal representative. In such cases under s. 48(10) of the CAT Consolidation Act, 2003 (as inserted by section 147(1) (l) of the Finance Act, 2010 and further clarified by Section 115 of the Finance Act, 2012) the solicitor shall be assessable and chargeable for the tax to the same extent as the beneficiary.*
>
> *In all such cases, this should be done as soon as early as possible after the issue arises.*
>
> ***Padraic Courtney***
>
> ***Probate Administration & Trusts Committee Secretary***

14.2.3.1 'Reasonable enquiries' to be made

The Revenue Commissioners have indicated that, in general, where a solicitor has made *reasonable enquiries,* he will only be secondarily liable, to the extent that he has control of the assets.

The Revenue view is that, if many of the beneficiaries are non-resident, the likelihood is that in the majority of cases, any property in Ireland will be sold, so the personal representative or the solicitor/agent will be holding proceeds to deal with CAT; but that is not always the case, and this was pointed out to them. For example, the family of a deceased owner of a holiday home in Ireland may wish to retain the holiday home.

The result was that they have indicated informally that where property passing to a non-resident is outside the control of the solicitor or personal representative and the solicitor/personal representative makes a reasonable effort to ascertain the extent of the property passing then the Revenue will not seek to enforce secondary liability, except to the extent of any property remaining under the solicitor's or personal representative's control.

The question then arises: What are 'reasonable enquiries' or what is 'makes a reasonable effort'?

In view of the increased responsibility attaching to acting for an estate with non-resident beneficiaries and/or personal representatives, it is important to be sure on who is non-resident.

Many clients will assume that they are resident where they (and/or their families) are currently based and will be unaware of the statutory rules. It is so easy for us as advisers to make the same error and, for example, to assume that a client who gives an Irish address is tax resident in Ireland.

Because the CAT legislation now distinguishes non-resident cases and applies a special regime, solicitors need to:

- take formal instructions on the residence position, and
- include residence declarations as part of the probate instruction paperwork.

The test for whether a person is resident or not on a particular date, for example a date of death, should be carried out for the tax year in which the date falls.

It is important that the solicitor obtain a declaration of residence and this can be included by adding the following to the standard letter sent to a beneficiary in relation to prior benefits. The declaration can be adapted to be sent to a personal representative if they are resident outside the jurisdiction:

Declaration of Residence

I, of

being a beneficiary in the Estate of deceased (herein after called 'the deceased') who died on the hereby confirm that :

I am resident (as per the definitions below) in: .... (Country)

NB: Please note that under Irish tax legislation an individual is resident in Ireland for a tax year if he is present in Ireland for 183 days or more in that tax year, or for 280 days or more across two tax years. A person will not be resident in Ireland in any tax year in which he spends 30 days or less in Ireland, and no account shall be taken of the 30 days or less for the purpose of the 280-day test.

Up to the Finance (No. 2) Act, 2008 a person was deemed to be present in Ireland if he was in the country at midnight (the 'Cinderella test') so effectively it was nights spent in Ireland that counted. The Finance (No. 2) Act, 2008 provides that, for the tax year 2009 and subsequent tax years, an individual shall be deemed to be present in the State for a day if the individual is present in the State at any time during that day, with limited exceptions for individuals in transit or forced to be present due to force majeure circumstances outside their control.

Ordinary Residence

An individual becomes ordinarily resident once he has been resident for three consecutive tax years and remains ordinarily resident in Ireland until he has been non-resident in Ireland for three consecutive tax years. However, for CAT purposes a person domiciled outside Ireland only becomes resident after five consecutive years in the country.

My permanent domicile (Country) if different from your residence:

Please read this declaration very carefully before executing it and if you are unsure on any matter please revert to us as [insert name of] Solicitors will be relying on the accuracy of your answers to same in all dealings with the Revenue

Signed: ____________________

Address: ____________________

Dated this day of 20

Witness's Signature: ____________________

Name of Witness: ____________________

Address of Witness: ____________________

Occupation of Witness: ____________________

14.2.4 FILE AND PAY DEADLINE

As noted above, self-assessment is in effect for payment of CAT. Section 46 of CATCA, 2003 provides that a person who is primarily accountable for CAT is obliged to deliver a return on 31 October of the tax year where the valuation date arises prior to 31 August in that year and on 31 October the following year where the valuation date arises after 31 August in that year.

Each year, the Revenue Commissioners have provided for an extension of this deadline where the taxpayer pays and files (note: the taxpayer must both file a return and pay the tax due) using the Revenue Online System. Practitioners should check the Revenue Website to ensure whether this discretionary extension has been granted and the date of the deadline each year. In 2024 the extension deadline was 14 November 2024. At the time of writing no extension for 2025 has yet been granted, but it is becoming the practice for it to be so granted. Therefore, come October 2025, the position should be checked.

Where any relief or exemption is claimed (other than the Small Gift Exemption, which will not apply on a death) the return must be filed online using the Revenue Online System (ROS).

14.2.4.1 Instalments

Provision is made for the payment of CAT by instalments (see **2.9.8**) and by transfer of certain government securities as discussed in **3.14.7**. The beneficiary must make a return, where the aggregation of the taxable values of all taxable benefits taken by the beneficiary (which have the same Group threshold) exceeds 80 per cent of the threshold amount that applies in the computation of tax on that aggregate. No return is required where 80 per cent of the threshold amount has not been exceeded, unless a relief is claimed. In particular, where Business Relief or agricultural relief is claimed, the taxpayer or their adviser must file an online return regardless of the taxable value of the benefit. See s. 46 (4) of the CAT Consolidation Act, 2003 as amended by s. 55 of the Finance Act, 2020.

Section 46(12) of CATCA, 2003 imposes an obligation on a person to deliver a CAT return if requested to do so by the Revenue Commissioners even if no benefit has been received. Legislation provides for a €3,000 penalty for non-production.

Normally, this is entirely the responsibility of the beneficiary but where the beneficiary is resident outside the jurisdiction the personal representative (s. 45AA), or where the personal representative is resident outside the jurisdiction the solicitor appointed (s. 48(10)), will also be obliged, if required in writing by the Revenue Commissioners, to comply with the self-assessment procedures.

14.2.5 DUTIES OF ACCOUNTABLE PERSONS

As noted above, an accountable person must, if required in writing by the Revenue Commissioners, deliver a statement stating such particulars relating to the property and such evidence as they require as may be relevant to the assessment of tax. The Revenue Commissioners may authorise a person to inspect any property comprised in a gift/ inheritance or any books, accounts, and so on relating to any property as may be relevant to the assessment of tax. Any person having the custody or possession of property, books, records, and so on must permit the authorised person to make the inspection at all reasonable times. The Revenue Commissioners have power to require additional returns from the accountable person if the return made was materially defective and to make any consequent additional assessments. Notwithstanding the introduction of the self-assessment system, the Revenue Commissioners retain the right to raise assessments and additional assessments and to correct assessments.

If an accountable person, who has made a return or additional return, becomes aware that the return was defective in a material respect, he must, within four months of becoming aware of the defect in the original return, make a new return, amend the assessment, and pay the outstanding tax. The outstanding tax due must accompany the new return. If an accountable person pays the self-assessed tax within four months of the valuation date no interest will be charged. If an accountable person makes a conditional or an incorrect tax payment, such payment will be treated as a payment on account.

14.2.6 INTEREST AND SURCHARGES FOR LATE PAYMENT

Interest on CAT has been covered in **2.9.7** and practitioners will be aware that interest is chargeable at a daily rate of 0.0219 per cent per day or part of a day (or 0.0164 per cent per day or a part of a day where the benefit consists of agricultural property or relevant business property). In addition, a surcharge for late filing of return was introduced on 14 June 2010, as outlined at **2.9.7.1**.

Interest runs from the file and pay deadline to the date of payment. The file and pay deadline would be included as a date but the date of payment would not. For example, a valuation date arising in May 2023 would trigger a pay and file deadline on 31 October 2023. If the beneficiary did not pay the CAT due (for example €10,000) and file a return until 20 December 2023 the following interest and surcharge would apply:

Surcharge for filing within two months of 5 per cent of €10,000 equals €500.

Interest on €10,000 at 0.0219 per cent per day equals €2.19 per day for 50 days (one day in October, 30 days in November and 19 days in December; the date of payment is not included) is €109.50 giving total interest and surcharges of €609.50.

While this is essentially a matter for the beneficiary, it is best practice for the personal representative and thus the solicitor advising the personal representative, on the 'triggering of the valuation date', to inform the beneficiary of their potential liability to pay and file by the due date when the valuation date arises and to ensure that the asset has passed to the beneficiary as soon as possible after the valuation date arises.

14.2.7 OTHER APPLICABLE PENALTIES

Penalties are payable for:

(1) self-assessment: failure to make returns;

(2) obstruction of person inspecting property;

(3) fraudulent or negligent returns or valuation statements;

(4) assisting or inducing incorrect returns.

If a court judgment is obtained for failure to make returns there is a further penalty for each day the failure continues.

Section 1078 of TCA, 1997 (as amended) sets out what constitutes a Revenue offence and the sanctions that can be imposed by a court on a person found guilty of such an offence. Section 142 of the Finance Act, 2005 inserted a new subsection into s. 1078 to create new offences of being knowingly concerned in the fraudulent evasion of tax or being knowingly concerned in, or being reckless as to whether or not one is concerned in, facilitating the fraudulent evasion of tax (or other Revenue offences under s. 1078). Section 1078(2), which sets out a number of specific actions or failures that constitute an offence, is also amended. Officers of a company can be charged with such offences.

Such Revenue offences carry serious penalties, being punishable on conviction on indictment by a fine of up to €126,970 or imprisonment for up to five years, or both. The section is widely drafted covering not just the evasion and attempted evasion of tax, but also 'reckless' involvement in the fraudulent evasion of tax, which involves disregarding a substantial risk such that the person is 'culpable to a high degree'. This is of particular significance to solicitors as tax advisers as the burden of proof for 'reckless' involvement is far lower than that of culpability in fraudulent behaviour.

14.2.8 SURCHARGE FOR UNDERVALUATION

Section 53 of CATCA, 2003 provides that where an accountable person delivers a return that contains an estimate of the market value of the gift/inheritance that, when expressed as a percentage of the agreed value of that asset is within any of the percentages set out below, a surcharge will be applied as follows.

Value of Asset in Return as a Percentage of 'Ascertained Value' or Actual Market Value	Surcharge
67–100%	Nil
50–66%	10%
40–49%	20%
0–39%	30%

Example: A beneficiary estimated the value of an inheritance to be €450,000 and on review by the Revenue Commissioners the 'ascertained' or actual market value was €1,000,000 and the actual tax owed was €250,000. The surcharge would be calculated as follows:

- €450,000 as a percentage of €1,000,000 is 45 per cent;
- the surcharge applying between 40 per cent and 50 per cent is 20 per cent;
- a surcharge of 20 per cent on the actual tax owed of €250,000 is €50,000, which is payable along with the actual tax owed, giving a total tax charge including surcharge of €300,000.

Interest is payable on the surcharge in the same way that it is payable on the tax due and any payment on account is taken off the interest first and not the capital sum owed.

14.2.9 APPEALS

An accountable person aggrieved by the imposition on him of a surcharge, can appeal the imposition of the surcharge within thirty days of notification to him. He can appeal on the grounds that, having regard to all the circumstances, there were sufficient grounds on which he might reasonably have based his estimate of the market value of the asset. This is the only ground for an appeal. The usual rights for the re-hearing of the appeal by the Circuit Court and on a point of law by the High Court apply.

Appeals against an assessment to CAT may arise under two headings dealt with under ss. 66 and 67 respectively of CATCA, 2003.

14.2.9.1 Market value of property (section 66 appeal)

Section 66 provides for an appeal against the Revenue Commissioners' decision on the market value of any property. This appeal will be in accordance with the procedure laid down by s. 33 of the Finance (1909–10) Act, 1910, which allows for an appeal first of all to an arbitrator appointed by the Valuation Office, and thereafter to the Circuit Court and High Court. The particulars of any stamped transfer or lease will, in any appeal under this section, be received as *prima facie* evidence of all matters and things stated in such particulars.

Appeals, in relation to the market value of any real or leasehold property, are heard by a property arbitrator appointed by the Land Values Reference Committee [such Committee is appointed under the Property Values (Arbitration and Appeals) Act 1960].

While s 66 CATCA 2003 does not mention a time limit, the time limit for an appeal under s 66 is thirty days. This thirty-day time limit is found, via s 33 Finance (1909–10) Act 1910, in Rule 5 of the Land Values (Referees) (Ireland) Rules 1911. However, Rule 6 of those Rules allows the Reference Committee absolute discretion to extend the thirty-day time limit.

Rule 9, of the Land Values (Referees) (Ireland) Rules, 1911 states that the appellant cannot rely on any grounds not set out in the notice of appeal. However, the Rule also allows the referee (arbitrator) discretion, if he/she thinks it just in the circumstances, to allow the notice of appeal to be amended.

Section 33(4) Finance (1909–10) Act 1910 states that any person aggrieved by a decision of a referee (arbitrator) may appeal such decision to the High Court within the time and manner directed by the Rules of Court.

There is no right of appeal to the Tax Appeals Commission for real property valuation disputes.

14.2.9.2 Appeals on any other ground (section 67)

Section 67 deals with an appeal for an assessment to tax on any ground other than the market value of the property. The law in relation to appeals on any other ground is now contained in the Finance (Tax Appeals) Act, 2015, which came into operation on 21 March 2016. This Act establishes the Taxation Appeals Commission (www.taxappeals.ie) and provides for a significant number of amendments to the various tax and duty Acts to standardise the appeal provisions across the various Acts and to correct any anomalies that were identified.

A taxpayer who wishes to make an appeal against a decision or assessment made by the Revenue Commissioners ('Revenue'), must submit a written notice of appeal to the Tax Appeals Commission ('the Commission') either using email or post within thirty days of the date of the assessment. A form for the purpose of making an appeal is available on, and may be downloaded from, the Commission's website. The appeal can be posted or emailed (but not both) to the Commissioners.

The decision of the Commission shall be final and conclusive unless a case is required to be stated to the High Court on a point of law. To improve the transparency of the appeals process, the Commission is required to publish anonymised versions of all of their determinations. These can be found on the TAC website: <http://taxappeals.ie/determinations/>.

Notice in writing (section 67(8))

Section 67(8) provides a procedure for the Revenue to serve notice in writing on any person whom they have reason to believe to be accountable for the payment of tax of any decision they have made in relation to the tax (for example notice to a trustee that a discretionary trust has become a chargeable discretionary trust). The person served with the notice has the right of appeal under s. 67 against such a decision of the Revenue Commissioners.

When can the taxpayer appeal? (section 68)

Section 68 sets out additional requirements in relation to gifts or inheritances taken on or after 12 February 1998. Before an appeal can be made under either s. 66 or s. 67 CATCA, the appellant must first file a return and pay the tax (and interest if any) due in respect of the benefit in the opinion of the Commissioners. Until then, no appeal can be made.

14.2.10 TAX CONSEQUENCES OF DISCLAIMERS

Disclaimers on intestacy are dealt with in para 9.10 of *Wills, Probate and Estates* (Courtney: OUP, 2022) and disclaimers in general are covered in para 16.4 of that book, while the tax consequences of disclaimers are dealt with in **3.6** of this book.

Both the legal and the tax consequences of disclaimers must be very carefully explained to a client and every effort must be made to ensure that a client fully understand the consequences of any disclaimer they may execute both in succession and taxation terms.

A donee/beneficiary is entitled to disclaim his or her right to an inheritance, or his or her legal rights under Part IX of the Succession Act. Such disclaimer is not a disposition for the purpose of CATCA, 2003. This means that it does not give rise to a claim for **inheritance** tax on the original inheritance against the person disclaiming, nor to a claim for **gift** tax on the benefit conferred by the disclaimer on the ultimate beneficiary. The ultimate beneficiary, however, takes a taxable inheritance from the deceased.

No double charge to CAT will arise if a donee or successor disclaims his title to a benefit so that it is taken by the person next entitled. However, a double charge to CAT will arise if the donee or successor, does not merely disclaim his title to a benefit, but instead, transfers the benefit to the third party or disclaims in favour of a third party.

In that case, there is a charge to CAT on the benefit taken by the first donee and a second charge to CAT on the benefit, which is passed on to the third party. If a beneficiary disclaims for a consideration, this consideration is deemed to be inherited from the deceased.

It is crucial that the solicitor fully understands the legal effect of the disclaimer drafted by him or her, particularly if the disclaimer is a disclaimer on intestacy, and the provisions of s. 72A of the Succession Act should be reviewed prior to execution of any disclaimer on intestacy. It should be noted that the solicitor should not advise the person executing the disclaimer and the person benefiting from the disclaimer.

See also the Practice Note, Gazette (August/September 1997), p. 33 on disclaimers on intestacy and the series of articles in the October/November and December 2003 Gazettes on Disclaimers and Deeds of Family Arrangement.

14.2.11 AGRICULTURAL RELIEF

As discussed in **Chapter 4** and mentioned earlier in this chapter, there is an important tax planning possibility here after death, available to a beneficiary. A beneficiary may not be a farmer at the date of death, but he could become one by the valuation date. The opposite is also possible. Therefore, extreme care must be taken that a successor/beneficiary who does qualify as 'a farmer' at the date of death continues to qualify by the valuation date. Bear in mind however that placing property into a discretionary trust or settling property to create an interest in expectation will not suffice.

Two points worth noting in relation to agricultural relief are:

(1) Any livestock, bloodstock, and farm machinery must be on agricultural land both at the date of the gift/inheritance and at the valuation date, to obtain the relief.

(2) The definition of 'agricultural property' does not include cash items, that is, proceeds of the sale of farm animals or the sale of crops grown on the land.

14.2.12 JOINT TENANTS

Section 13 of CATCA, 2003 provides that the liability to inheritance tax in respect of an inheritance taken by persons as joint tenants is the same in all respects as if they took the inheritance as tenants in common in equal shares. Joint property is covered in **Chapter 2** and *Wills, Probate and Estates*, Chapter 14.

Strictly speaking, joint property—where the asset is truly joint property—falls outside the estate and as such is not the responsibility of the personal representative, but in dealing with and acting for surviving joint tenants, the following points should be borne in mind.

- The solicitor should check the reasons for the property being placed in joint names, how the money was provided, and by whom the income was enjoyed. If necessary, the solicitor should obtain advice as to whether the property in fact passes by survivorship, or should be claimed by the personal representative as forming part of the deceased's free estate. See the Law Society Practice Note on Joint Bank Accounts (December 2008).
- In addition to inheritance tax being payable on the death of a deceased joint holder, there may also be gift tax which was due back at the date on which the property was put into joint names. This underlines the need to obtain full details to ascertain the extent of the tax liability. Even if the deceased joint holder enjoyed the income solely, it is possible that the surviving beneficiary will take an inheritance of the entire property.
- In the case of personalty, the situation can be difficult to decipher without full enquiries being made. Note the questions in the SA.2 in relation to joint property.
- Section 109 of CATCA, 2003 provides that joint accounts holding up to €50,000 (formerly €31,750) can be released to the surviving joint account holder on production of a letter of clearance (Form IT 8) unless the surviving joint account holder is the surviving spouse/civil partner. No clearance is required for a surviving spouse/civil partner. From 14 September 2020, requests for an IT8 Letter of Clearance can be made by applicants through the online Form SA.2. Where a joint holder of an account wishes to personally request IT8 Clearance, separate to the application for a grant of representation, they may do so by submitting a paper CA4 Form (Revenue Clearance application form) to the National Capital Acquisitions Tax Unit. The Form CA4 is a two-page form which does not have to be sworn. Further information on requesting IT8 Clearance is available at Guide to Completing a Statement of Affairs (Probate) Form SA.2.
- As far as a joint tenancy is concerned for tax purposes, it can be argued that a beneficiary takes a moiety (half) by survivorship. There is a possible claim for gift tax in relation to the original creation of the joint tenancy. If however the property was put into joint names prior to 5 December 1991 there will be no aggregation between the previous gift and subsequent inheritance. If a gift however is argued, evidence will be required by the Revenue Commissioners.

  At the outset of any administration the solicitor should obtain all the information as set out above and be fully satisfied as to the status of ownership.
- Where assets are greater than €50,000, the bank/financial institution will require a Death Certificate and evidence of CAT clearance. As far as the paying bank is required they will pay out to the surviving joint account holder(s), as this is usually clear from documentation setting up the joint account.

Regard must also be had to the inheritance tax implications of creating a joint tenancy. The essential questions raised by the Revenue Commissioners are:

- Who provided the joint property?
- Who gets the entire on the death of the deceased joint tenant?

To answer these questions the following points must be clarified:

(1) The source of the joint property.

(2) The relationship of the parties.

(3) Evidence to rebut or support advancement or resulting trust.

(4) In relation to personalty, how the income was dealt with.

14.2.13 CERTIFICATES OF DISCHARGE AND CLEARANCE CERTIFICATES

Certificates of Discharge from CAT were abolished on 3 April 2010 and are no longer required. The only CAT clearance certificates now issued are the form CA.12 in respect of an application on a IT8 and/or for registration of title to land, which are based on possession under s. 62 of the CATCA, 2003. Such applications will not be dealt with by the Property Registration Authority unless the Revenue Commissioners have issued a certificate to the effect that they are satisfied that any liability to inheritance tax/gift tax and probate tax charged on the land, has been paid, or will be paid within a reasonable time.

14.2.14 CAT/INHERITANCE TAX DOUBLE TAX AGREEMENT WITH THE UNITED KINGDOM

The Ireland–United Kingdom double taxation agreement (SI 279/1978) provides relief from double taxation in respect of taxes on estates of deceased persons and inheritances and on gifts. It came into force on 2 October 1978. It is not proposed to go into the details of this treaty but practitioners should be aware of when the provisions of the treaty are applicable.

14.3 Income Tax

14.3.1 INTRODUCTION

Income tax is an area that requires close attention as soon as possible after the date of death. It is an additional service that can be provided by a solicitor to a personal representative, but in most cases, an accountant should be engaged. If attended to early on in the administration, it can be dealt with as part of the general administration and winding up, but if left until the last minute it usually prolongs the finalisation of the estate and may cause serious delay in completing the administration, and may result in interest and penalties being applied.

It is important to distinguish between a PAYE taxpayer and a taxpayer who is subject to self-assessment and is a 'chargeable person'.

Where the deceased was a PAYE taxpayer without any other source of income and/or whose non-PAYE income is taxed through the PAYE system and where the sole beneficiary is the surviving spouse or civil partner, this can be relatively straightforward.

Where the deceased was a chargeable person, the liability for income tax is primarily that of the chargeable person and the personal representative has a duty to ensure both that any pre-death income tax is paid and any income tax arising during the administration is paid.

The payment of income tax is divided into preliminary tax (paid in the tax year) and a final top-up figure paid the following year. Preliminary tax is due on 31 October in the year of assessment and in order to avoid interest charges arising the preliminary tax payment must generally amount to 90 per cent of the income tax payable for that tax year, or 100 per cent of the income tax payable for the previous tax year. If the preliminary tax paid in a tax year is less than 100 per cent of the income tax due the balance of tax is generally due on or before 31 October in the year following the relevant tax year.

Section 951 TCA 1997 provides that all chargeable persons must submit an income tax return not later than 31 October following the year of assessment. Each year, 31 October is the due date for:

- The payment of preliminary tax for the current tax year.
- Filing tax returns for the previous year.
- The payment of the balance of income tax for the previous tax year.

If the deceased dies, before the specified date for making a return in any year, a return must be lodged within one year after death to avoid a surcharge for late filing.

It may be that the deceased's tax affairs were handled by an accountant or tax adviser. It is advisable to obtain the personal representatives' consent to the retention of such adviser, who will no doubt charge professional fees in finalising matters. Once the position as of the date of death is clarified, any income tax liability will be included as a debt of the estate and any certified refund will be included as an asset. The personal representative's main objective is to obtain tax clearance prior to distribution.

The main advantage to the solicitor in dealing with the issue of income tax is the retention of control over this area of the administration. It is entirely up to the solicitor acting as to how quickly matters can be resolved with the Inspector of Taxes.

The self-assessment regime has now made matters more 'user friendly'. Solicitors should not, without adequate consideration, become involved in a long and protracted income tax problem that could, with assistance, be sorted out relatively quickly.

If tax is immediately payable on death, the solicitor, in consultation with the personal representative should consider, from what source funds might same be discharged in order to avoid interest and penalties.

As noted earlier, the Revenue TDM 46–01–02 outlines the new procedure when applying for clearance in death cases and should be read carefully before proceeding.

In dealing with income tax, it is important to distinguish between pre-death liability and post-death liability.

14.3.2 PRE-DEATH LIABILITY

A personal representative must ascertain the deceased's liability to date of death and discharge all liabilities including interest to date of death. This involves not only the preparation and submission of a return from 1 January to date of death but also the submission of returns for previous years (if necessary). Where the deceased was a PAYE-only taxpayer the Revenue Form 12 can be completed by the surviving spouse or civil partner where they are the assessable spouse or civil partner.

Details of the necessary due diligence can be found in Appendix 1 of the Revenue TDM.

Revenue will have the information supplied in the Form SA.2 together with any supporting documentation uploaded with same.

Other matters that should be investigated by the personal representative are:

(1) any available reliefs (e.g. medical expenses/age allowance);

(2) refund of any overpayment of tax;

(3) any available losses that should have been claimed in the final years before death;

(4) any claims for medical expenses.

In an ideal world, the only period that would require finalisation would be the period from 1 January last to the date of death. In many instances, however, the deceased may not have been making a return (or a full return) of all assets for a number of years prior to death. Notwithstanding that, a considerable amount of work may be involved in collecting the necessary information to complete the return. In all instances:

(1) ascertain details of the deceased's Inspector of Taxes (details of the PPS number should be to hand);

(2) ascertain to what date Income Tax affairs have been settled;

(3) obtain a copy of the last return submitted by the deceased to the Inspector of Taxes.

Once the foregoing has been clarified and the Inspector's outstanding requirements have been ascertained, the solicitor (or the person dealing with income tax) will then be in a position to commence making the necessary returns. For each outstanding income tax year, consider the following.

(1) Ascertain details of all deposit interest. This may be discovered by writing to the various financial institutions (banks, building societies, etc.) seeking a Certificate of Interest and DIRT deducted.

(2) Ascertain details of any dividend income. (Note that original counterfoils will be required and if necessary duplicate counterfoils should be obtained from the various Registrars of Companies.)

(3) Ascertain details of all other income, such as rental income.

(4) Consider the various cessation rules and schedules of income.

(5) If the deceased was involved in a business, accounts will be required as of the date of death for Schedule D Case 1 or Case 2 income. Note that death causes a cessation for trade purposes, with the exception of where a widow survives to her husband's trade.

(6) If the deceased was a trader, consider any capital losses and any balancing charges which may arise as a result of cessation.

(7) Where the deceased was a trader or professional, the Inspector will look at the past two years' accounts prior to death on an actual basis.

14.3.2.1 Pre-death time periods

In relation to tax relating to periods before death, be aware of the time periods applicable. Revenue must make an assessment within three years after the end of the year of assessment in which the death occurred. However, if the grant does not issue in the same tax year as the date of death, the assessment must be made no later than two years after the end of the tax year in which the grant issues.

14.3.2.2 Surcharge

A personal representative should be aware of the possibility of the imposition of a surcharge on the liability of the deceased.

If the deceased dies before the specified date for making a return in any year, a return must be lodged within one year after death to avoid a surcharge for late filing.

The surcharge is tax based and will be equal to 5 per cent of the tax if the return is up to two months late and 10 per cent if the return is filed later than two months.

Lodgement of an appeal notice (if necessary) should be made within thirty days of the assessment to tax and the normal rules of appeal apply to a personal representative. If an assessment is made prior to death and the deceased dies within thirty days, the personal representative should consider the necessity for lodgement of an appeal.

This highlights the necessity to deal with income tax affairs of the deceased as quickly as possible in order to avoid surcharges, or the possibility of failing to lodge a notice of appeal within the time allocated.

14.3.3 POST-DEATH ADMINISTRATION PERIOD

It should be noted that personal allowances or other reliefs which are available to an individual do not apply to a personal representative. Any income arising after death is regarded as income of the personal representative (although it is not aggregated with the personal representative's personal income). If a personal representative is resident in Ireland, the worldwide income of the deceased's estate is liable to income tax in Ireland.

The administration period is in effect, the period between the date of death and the date on which the residue is ascertained. It may consist of a number of years or part only of such years, depending on the length of time taken to wind up the estate. The date of ascertainment is usually the date on which the liabilities, costs, and expenses have been paid and legacies and taxes discharged.

If all the residuary beneficiaries/persons entitled on intestacy are resident within the jurisdiction, the Inspector of Taxes will normally agree to treat these people as succeeding to the income from date of death. The income is not therefore assessed in the hands of the personal representative. If the Inspector of Taxes treats the beneficiaries as so succeeding, the income need not be included in an assessment for inheritance tax where the valuation date is later than the date of death. A letter from the Inspector of Taxes confirming that he will treat the income as income of the beneficiaries must be obtained.

If there is an income-producing asset in the hands of the personal representatives and it would be more beneficial for such to be taxed in the hands of the beneficiary, the personal representative should consider vesting such property in the beneficiary, *provided always* that there are sufficient assets to meet all liabilities. Where a residuary beneficiary is residing outside the jurisdiction, the Inspector will normally require returns for the administration period.

The distribution date will usually be the date upon which *all* the assets are available for distribution and not just the bulk of the assets. The Inspector of Taxes will not regard the estate as finalised until all the executor's/administrator's accounts have been closed off and securities transferred.

Under s. 1047 of TCA, 1997 a personal representative is liable for any pre-death income tax. Note that this is a personal liability, and the Revenue Commissioners can proceed against a personal representative. Therefore, clearances are a priority. However the tax, interest, and any penalty is payable out of the assets of the estate. The personal representative is not liable for sums owed in excess of the value of the assets.

The Inspector of Taxes has liberty to go back for any period up to ten years in investigating matters. However, if there is fraud or neglect involved there is no time limit. Such an investigation could be sparked off by the disclosure to the Revenue in the Form SA.2 of an asset previously undisclosed by the deceased.

14.4 Discretionary Trust Tax

Discretionary trust tax is dealt with on the Advanced Probate & Tax Advanced Elective. Suffice it to say now that special tax rules apply to discretionary trusts as defined in s. 2(1) of CATCA, 2003. The most common example is where a fund is held by trustees upon trust for appointment or distribution among a defined class of beneficiaries (or 'objects' of the trust), none of whom is absolutely entitled to a share in the trust funds. It should be noted that the definition of discretionary trust in CATCA, 2003 goes beyond this normal legal definition of such a trust and includes 'accumulation trusts' which are trusts where the trustees have a power to accumulate the income and are not given a discretion to pay out the income to the potential beneficiaries. This goes beyond the normal legal definition of a discretionary trust.

In such a situation one should have special regard to the following matters.

14.4.1 DATE DISCRETIONARY TRUST COMMENCES

Under s. 111 Finance Act 2012, which took effect in relation to deaths arising on or after 8 February 2012, where a discretionary trust is created under a will (or codicil) of a deceased person, the property is deemed to become subject to the trust at the date of death of the deceased.

This change to legislation followed the High Court determination in *Revenue Commissioners v Executors and Trustees of Jeannie Hammett Irvine, Christie & Others* [2005] No. 172R High Court Laffoy J. In that case, the Court determined that Discretionary Trust Tax only arose when the Trust was ascertained, usually at the end of the administration of an estate. The legislation reversed this decision and deemed the discretionary trust to commence on the death of the testator.

In this way, the charge arises at the date of death of the deceased, albeit that, the valuation date for the payment of the tax remains the same (in the case of trusts of the residue that is usually the date of ascertainment of the residue).

Therefore, if it takes a number of years to administer an estate, levies can accumulate during those years. The valuation date is the relevant date for the purposes of calculating the levy. The values at the date of death or each 31 December in the course of the administration are not relevant at that point. The date of death is merely a trigger for the tax while the valuation date is the date used for deciding what is to be taxed and the timing of the payment of the tax. Revenue have updated their internal guidelines on the effect of s. 111 Finance Act 2012 by way of Part 05 of the Revenue CAT Tax and Duty Manual <https://www.revenue.ie/en/tax-professionals/tdm/capital-acquisitions-tax/cat-part05.pdf>.

14.4.2 EXEMPTIONS

Exceptions are made where there are 'principal objects' (i.e. beneficiaries who are the spouse/civil partner, children of deceased or children of civil partner of deceased, or children of a predeceased child/child of civil partner of the deceased) under the age of twenty-one years or where one of the beneficiaries is suffering from a disability.

The beneficiary must be suffering from a severe disability and the trust must be specifically for that person. If requested, the Revenue Commissioners will issue a letter confirming that the disability is such as to exclude the trust from DTT.

Other exemptions include charitable trusts, superannuation or unit trusts, or trusts providing for the upkeep of a heritage house or garden, which are not dealt with on this course.

14.4.2.1 Improvident beneficiaries of a discretionary trust

Following representations by the Law Society, the position surrounding trusts for individuals who are because of improvidence, incapable of managing their affairs has been clarified.

This is separate from beneficiaries who because of age or incapacity are incapable of managing their affairs and covers gambling or substance addiction, vulnerable adults, and 'spendthrift' adults.

Part 05 of the Revenue CAT Tax and Duty Manual para 5.4.1 deals with the circumstances that may arise, and the proofs required by Revenue in these cases.

14.4.3 INITIAL 6 PER CENT AND ANNUAL 1 PER CENT LEVY

Chapter 2 of CAT Consolidation Act, 2003 provides for an initial levy for DTT at 6 per cent of the value of the fund comprised in the discretionary trust. This initial 6 per cent is due within four months of the valuation date, it is not subject to the usual fixed CAT file and pay deadline. This is a discretion allowed by the Revenue Commissioners and does not have a statutory basis.

If the entire trust is paid out within five years, half this initial levy (3 per cent) is refunded.

In addition, Chapter 3 of CATCA, 2003 provides for a 1 per cent annual levy on such trusts. This 1 per cent is charged on the net value of the trust fund as at 31 December each year with an exception for the first payment due within twelve months of the payment date of the initial 6 per cent.

14.4.4 PAYMENTS AND TRANSFERS OUT OF THE DISCRETIONARY TRUST

Where payments are made out of the Discretionary Trust Fund to beneficiaries, this constitutes an inheritance from the testator, for which CAT returns should be made at the appropriate time. If the payment to the beneficiary results in a liability, the return should be made and the tax paid on the appropriate date. Obviously, where there is an element of choice, the trustees of the fund can pay out at a time (for example, 1 September) that allows the greatest amount of time between date of payment and file and pay deadline.

If farmland is being appointed out of a discretionary trust fund to a beneficiary, care should be taken to ensure (if it is possible to do so) that the beneficiary is, at the date of appointment for distribution, a 'farmer' as defined in s. 89 of CATCA, 2003 so that the beneficiary will get the benefit of agricultural relief for the purpose of the inheritance. It should be noted that agricultural relief and/or Business Relief do not apply to DTT but may apply when a relevant asset is being appointed out of the trust.

14.4.5 DISCRETIONARY WILL TRUSTS AND INCOME TAX

The personal representatives or trustees of a will should consider the effect of income tax on the trust funds. The normal position is that trustees are liable for tax at the standard rate of 20 per cent on any trust income and should deduct this before paying the balance to a beneficiary. In certain cases, it may be possible, by arrangement with the relevant Inspector of Taxes, to pay the income growth to a beneficiary. Undistributed income (e.g. accumulated income in relation to a minor's share) may attract an additional tax liability of 20 per cent. While beneficiaries are responsible for their own tax liabilities, it is important to note that the beneficiary also pays income tax on any income received from the trust.

14.5 Stamp Duty

14.5.1 INTRODUCTION AND LEGISLATION

Stamp Duty in relation to assets passing on death has been dealt with in para 7.7.2 and in para 15.3 of *Wills, Probate and Estates* (Courtney: OUP, 2022). Normally stamp duty does not arise in relation to assets passing on death, but may arise where transactions take place outside the terms of the will or intestacy. As practitioners are aware, the law relating to stamp duty is principally contained in the Stamp Duties Consolidation Act, 1999 ('SDCA, 1999') as amended.

14.5.2 PENALTIES AND DUTY OF DISCLOSURE

Practitioners should be aware of the mandatory nature of stamp duty, the penalties applicable for late payment and undervaluation, and the penalties imposed on professional advisers (including solicitors) for preparing untruthful instruments.

In a nutshell, this duty of disclosure means that if a solicitor is aware that a client is in any way fraudulent or negligent (for example, receiving payments made 'under the counter'), the solicitor has a duty to disclose the relevant facts to the Revenue Commissioners. Likewise, if a solicitor has a strong suspicion that there is something about the transaction which is not correct, the solicitor appears to have a duty also to enquire further and ultimately inform the Revenue, if necessary. Breach of either of these two provisions would make the solicitor personally liable to the penalties.

14.5.3 STAMP DUTY ON ASSENTS

Under the SDCA, 1999 no stamp duty is payable on any deed of assent where property is vested in the persons entitled under the deceased's will or on intestacy. However, where the beneficiary 'pays' for the property, or the part of it, then the asset becomes a conveyance on sale and stamp duty applies.

Example: Rachel has inherited a house under Barry's will. Unfortunately, because of the debts due by Barry's estate, there are insufficient funds to meet all the liabilities as well as the bequest to Rachel. Under normal circumstances the house would be sold and the proceeds of sale after payment of outstanding debts would go to Rachel. If Rachel pays sufficient money to the personal representative(s) to discharge the debts in order to release the house, the assent vesting the house in her will be a conveyance on sale and will attract stamp duty in respect of the amount paid by Rachel.

Solicitors should ensure that such stamp duty is paid and that there is no collusion with the beneficiary for the non-payment of stamp duty.

This does not apply when a house is inherited subject to a charge under s. 47 of the Succession Act, 1965. In that case, Rachel would inherit a house subject to a mortgage and would be inheriting the deceased person's interest in the property.

14.5.4 STAMP DUTY ON DEEDS OF FAMILY ARRANGEMENT

Under a deed of family arrangement or a variation of the terms of the will (this is not an available option in Ireland save and except in very limited circumstances under the Land and Conveyancing Law Reform Act 2009) or shares on intestacy, a stamp duty liability can arise on any document completed for the purpose of passing any interest in land.

Where there is a deed of family arrangement (dealt with in Chapter 15 of *Wills, Probate and Estates*) this must be lodged with the Revenue Commissioners to enable them to adjudicate on the stamp duty payable. The Revenue Commissioners will seek a valuation of the property and based on this valuation the document will be stamped.

The question of value often causes great difficulty. If the Revenue Commissioners do not accept the valuation, which should be carried out by an appropriate person, they may refer the matter to the Valuation Office. In practice the Valuation Office's value will be accepted unless there is no urgency to register the deed.

The Valuation Office will take some time to carry out its own valuation and if this valuation is not acceptable by the parties to the deed they may appeal. However, all this takes a considerable length of time and if the difference between the lodging party's valuation and that of the Valuation Office is not significant, it may be more practical to proceed with the value as assessed by the Revenue Commissioners.

The other tax consequences of deeds of family arrangement will be dealt with below in **14.6**.

14.5.5 STAMP DUTY AND APPROPRIATION UNDER SECTION 55

In relation to stamp duty, note the provisions of s. 55(17) of the Succession Act, 1965, which states:

> *Where any property is appropriated under the provisions of this section, a conveyance thereof by the personal representatives to the person to whom it is appropriated shall not, by reason only*

that the property so conveyed is accepted by the person to whom it is conveyed in or towards the satisfaction of a legacy or a share in residuary estate, be liable to any higher Stamp Duty than that payable on a transfer of personal property for the like purpose.

Where a surviving spouse/civil partner in whose favour an appropriation has been made has made a payment into the estate to cover the excess in value of the property appropriated over his or her share in the estate (s. 56(9)), the protection of s. 55(17) against payment of stamp duty may not extend, to at least, the equality money paid, since the conveyance would then be in part, a sale.

However, as this may be classed as a transaction between spouses/civil partners and as such may be exempt from stamp duty (SDCA, 1999, s. 96), such a payment may not arise. Qualified co- habitants are not exempt from stamp duty per se, but may be exempt, if the transaction takes place arising from a court order under the Civil Partnership and Certain Rights and Obligations of Cohabitants Act, 2010.

14.6 Capital Gains Tax

14.6.1 INTRODUCTION

In a similar manner to income tax, it is important to distinguish between pre-death liability and post-death liability.

As also noted earlier, the Revenue TDM 46–01–02 outlines the new procedure when applying for clearance in death cases and should be read carefully before proceeding.

14.6.2 PRE-DEATH CAPITAL GAINS TAX ('CGT')

CGT is payable by reference to the 'time of disposal' which is dealt with in s. 542 TCA 1997. In most cases, the time of disposal is clear, and s. 542 does not have a single general rule. Instead, it provides specific rules for certain specific cases, the most important of which is the case of a disposal by contract. If an asset is disposed of under a contract, the time of disposal, is the time the contract is made and not the date on which the property is actually conveyed. If the contract is conditional, the disposal is made when the condition is satisfied.

There are 2 CGT payment dates for individuals. For the 'initial period' running from 1 January to 30 November each year CGT must be paid on or before 15 December in that year, and if the disposal occurs in the later period (in December) the CGT is due for payment by the following 31 January.

The CGT return is not due for filing until 31 October following the year of assessment. A person who files an income tax return will include the disposal in that return. A person who is not obliged to file an income tax return files a CGT return in respect of chargeable gains.

The person making the disposal is primarily liable for CGT. If a disposal is made by a personal representative of an estate, he will have a primary liability for any disposals made in the course of the administration of estate. Similarly, the trustees of a trust who make a disposal will be liable to CGT if any disposal is made by them in their capacity as trustees.

14.6.2.1 Residency and CGT

The Irish agent of a non-resident vendor will also have a secondary liability for the payment of any CGT or income tax arising in relation to a non-resident person. The liability arises regardless of *'whether such . . . agent . . . has . . . receipt of the profits or gains or not'*. Solicitors acting on behalf of non-resident personal representatives should bear this section in mind when dealing with the estate, and in particular if selling the assets from the estate or receiving the estate funds through the office client account should obtain confirmation that taxes due have been paid prior to releasing funds.

The recent Revenue Tax and Duty Manual Part 45-01-05 dealing with Requests for Clearance—Capital Gains Tax and Non-Resident Vendors should be reviewed in that case, as should the Law Society Taxation Committee's Practice Note of 25 October 2022.

A person's liability to Irish CGT generally depends on domicile, residence, and ordinary residence, and the location and type of the asset.

- An Irish domiciled and resident or ordinarily resident person is liable on all gains worldwide.
- A person who is not Irish domiciled but either resident or ordinarily resident is normally liable to Irish CGT on Irish and remitted gains, but s. 568(2) provides that personal representatives cannot claim the remittance basis on non-Irish assets.
- A person who is neither resident nor ordinarily resident is only liable to Irish CGT where gains are made on specified Irish assets, for example land in Ireland.

It should be noted that under s. 573 Taxes Consolidation Act 1997 (TCA 97) the personal representatives of a deceased person are treated for CGT purposes as if they were a single and continuing body of persons having the same residence, ordinary residence, and domicile as the deceased had at his death.

Terminal loss relief is available to the personal representatives of a deceased person if allowable capital losses arise to the deceased in the year of death. Capital losses can normally only be set against capital gains in the same year, and if there are excess losses against capital gains in future years. However, excess year of death losses may be set back against the chargeable gains for the three previous tax years, going against gains of later years first, in priority to earlier years. Any refunds generated by the loss claim will be an asset of the estate.

Disposals by the personal representatives do not result in a loss which qualifies for terminal loss relief, as such a loss is not a loss of the deceased person.

14.6.3 POST-DEATH CAPITAL GAINS TAX

When assets pass on a death they are not deemed to have been disposed of by the deceased, so the death is not an occasion of charge for CGT purposes. The assets of which the deceased person was 'competent to dispose' are deemed to be acquired by the personal representatives or other person on whom they devolve for a consideration equal to their value at the date of death.

When in the course of administration, the personal representatives dispose of assets of the estate (other than by transfer to legatees), they are liable on any gains in the normal way, that is, as a 'body of persons'.

The personal representatives are treated as a single and continuing body of persons and are deemed to have the deceased's residence, ordinary residence, and domicile at the date of death. Therefore, the personal representatives will have the same territorial exposure to CGT as the deceased.

The assets comprising the estate should be reviewed as soon as possible and a note made of the disposals that will occur for CGT purposes. Gains will generally arise on the disposal of assets by the personal representatives, the conversion of foreign currency, and occasionally on the transfer of assets to beneficiaries when the estate is being wound up.

Section 568 provides that CGT on gains accruing to personal representatives may be assessed and charged on any one or more of the personal representatives.

In the computation of gains, accruing to personal representatives on the disposal of assets, the allowable expenditure includes the expenses or a due proportion of the expenses, incurred in obtaining a grant of probate or letters of administration.

Any losses made by the personal representatives can be claimed against gains made by the personal representatives, made in the same year, or carried forward against future years. They cannot be set back or transferred to the beneficiaries.

14.6.3.1 Post-death gains checklist

1. Identify gains arising in the course of administration.
2. Check return filing dates and CGT payment dates for estate gains.
3. Calculate any CGT due and submit returns.
4. If losses arise in the estate check if they can be used in the event they arise or should be carried forward against future estate gains.
5. Transferring estate assets to beneficiaries.

14.6.3.2 Transferring estate assets to beneficiaries

No chargeable gain is deemed to accrue to the personal representatives on the transfer to a beneficiary of an asset from the estate of the deceased. Any gain which the legatee may make on a later disposal of the asset should be calculated as if the legatee acquired the asset at the date of death at its value on that date.

If, under the terms of a will, the personal representatives have power to satisfy a pecuniary legacy by the appropriation of assets to the value of that legacy, the beneficiary who takes such an asset should be dealt with in the same way as the personal representatives; that is, he should be deemed to have acquired the asset on the date of death at its value on that date.

If, on the other hand, there is no such power of appropriation, a person who is offered by the personal representatives (and accepts) an asset in satisfaction of a legacy is not regarded as acquiring the asset as legatee unless both he and the personal representatives agree that he should be deemed to have acquired it as the personal representatives acquired it; that is, he should be deemed to have acquired the asset on the date of death at its value on that date. It would follow that any future chargeable gain or allowable loss would be deemed to accrue to the beneficiary. In the absence of this agreement, the personal representatives may be regarded by the Revenue as having disposed of the asset at market value in the course of administration of the estate with a chargeable gain or allowable loss.

Section 5(1) defines 'legatee' widely, including any person taking property under a will or intestacy or partial intestacy, or by virtue of the Succession Act, 1965, whether he takes it beneficially or as trustee, and provides that a donatio mortis causa should be treated as a legacy, and not as a gift. The definition also includes cases where assets are appropriated in satisfaction of a pecuniary legacy or where a residuary legatee, instead of taking his share in cash, takes assets.

14.6.3.3 Disposal by personal representatives as bare trustees for beneficiaries

Paragraph 9.11 of the Revenue CGT Manual indicates that the residuary beneficiary or beneficiaries should be regarded as becoming absolutely entitled to property as against the personal representatives when the net residue has been ascertained.

If property is disposed of by personal representatives (other than on transfer to legatees or after appropriation to legatees) during the period of administration, any gain or loss which may arise accrues to the personal representatives.

If a particular property is appropriated during the course of the administration by the personal representatives assenting to particular assets being vested in a residuary legatee or residuary legatees jointly, and the personal representatives then dispose of those assets (say a legatee prefers to receive cash rather than an asset), they will be disposing as 'bare trustees' and not as personal representatives.

14.6.4 DOUBLE CHARGE TO CAT AND CGT

CGT is charged on any rise in value post-death. CAT is charged on the value on the valuation date. It follows that where a capital asset rises in value before the valuation date, and is sold in the course of administration, then that rise in value will be taxed twice, as both CAT and CGT arise. No set off is available under s. 104 CATCA 03 as the two taxes arise on separate events. This could mean the beneficiary being subject to up to 66 per cent tax on the value of the rise in the value of the asset.

This is, only an issue in a rising market, as it is the rise in value post-death that results in CGT due. In the past few years property prices in some areas, in particular certain areas of Dublin, have seen a significant rise in value. If the personal representatives sell property in an area in which property prices have increased, a CGT liability will arise on the sale.

The key issue affecting the level of CGT payable by the estate is the date of death value selected for the property, as it is this value that will set the base cost for CGT purposes on a subsequent sale.

When completing the Statement of Affairs (Probate) Form SA.2 practitioners should be aware of the potential for a CGT liability arising if they include a low valuation for the property in the Form SA.2 and there is a sale in the course of administration.

Example:

Joe died on 17 November 2023 and the valuer indicates that his principal private residence is valued at €500,000 to €530,000 and the asset is included in the SA.2 at a value of €500,000 (the low end of the valuer's range). A grant of probate issued on 15 February 2024 and on that date the property was valued at €550,000. On 28 February 2024, a Contract for Sale was signed selling the property for €560,000.

The valuation date for CAT purposes is the date of grant of probate. CAT is paid based on the valuation of €550,000. This is the only benefit taken by the beneficiary and the beneficiary has no available threshold, therefore, CAT of €181,500 is paid (€550,000*33%). CGT is paid on the rise in value between the date of death and the date of sale (€60,000). CGT of €19,800 is payable (€60,000*33%).

The rate of tax which has been paid on the rise in value (€50,000) between the date of death and the date of grant of probate is 66 per cent. The beneficiary has paid total tax of €201,300 on receipt of cash of €560,000.

It may be clear if there is a fast sale that the formal valuation used for the SA.2 date of death value was an underestimate (given the price paid shortly afterwards by a willing purchaser). This will result in CGT arising on a gain that is not a real commercial gain (a 'virtual' gain). In such cases the personal representatives may wish to correct the value submitted to Revenue to line up with the market value established on the sale.

If a personal representative sells a property at a price that shows a rise in value over the date of date valuation used that is substantially greater than the average increase in property prices recorded in property registers, consideration should be given to the question of whether the value used in the SA.2 was on the low side, and if so whether it can be corrected.

If a valuer provides a valuation range (e.g. €450,000 to €500,000) the personal representative's instinct may be to use the lower valuation. The adviser should check if a sale is likely and if so what price the personal representative hopes to achieve so that advice can be given on whether the use of the lower end of the valuation range will give rise to double tax.

A correction to the SA.2 information involves amending the SA.2, which can be done online.

It should be noted however that the SA.2 should only be amended in case of 'material error or omission' and that Revenue specifically state that 'fluctuations in property values after the date of death are not considered material errors'. Acceptance of an amended

Form SA.2 and generation of an amended Notice of Acknowledgment Probate does not necessarily that Revenue will accept that the corrected date of death value shown in that amended Notice of Acknowledgment Probate is the base cost for CGT purposes.

14.7 Tax Implications of Deeds of Family Arrangements

14.7.1 INTRODUCTION AND EXAMPLE

Deeds of family arrangement are quite complex and are dealt with in detail in para. 15.3 of the OUP Manual "*Wills, Probate and Estates*". While the stamp duty implications have been referred to at **14.5.4**, it is opportune to look at all the tax implications of such a deed of family arrangement, which goes outside the terms of the will/intestacy/partial intestacy.

Example: Property has been devised to three sisters as tenants in common in equal shares. One devisee voluntarily releases her share and another devisee sells her share to the third devisee, the personal representative joining in to assign the legal estate to the third devisee.

Such an arrangement between these three sisters who inherit the property equally will necessitate a deed of family arrangement involving a sale by one beneficiary of her share, and a voluntary disposition by another beneficiary of her share to the third beneficiary. Under s. 10 of the Succession Act, 1965 the personal representative will join in to assign the legal estate vested in him or her to the third beneficiary.

14.7.2 TAXATION IMPLICATIONS

14.7.2.1 Stamp duty

The deed will attract stamp duty on the following elements:

(1) on the value of one undivided third share voluntarily conveyed; and

(2) assuming that the consideration for one undivided third share conveyed by the second beneficiary represents the full value of that share, on that consideration or, alternatively, on the value of the share.

Consanguinity relief will not apply unless the property consists of farmland.

Section 8 imposes the duty to set out all the facts and circumstances affecting the liability of any instrument to duty in the instrument or in a statement attached to the instrument. There are penalties incurred by anybody who fraudulently or negligently executes any instruments not containing all the facts and circumstances. See **14.5.2**. Anybody employed or concerned in the preparation of any such instrument who fraudulently or negligently prepares it will also incur the same penalties. Thus, a practitioner will be deemed to be negligent if he or she fails to take reasonable care and has a duty of disclosure if aware that the client is in any way fraudulent or negligent.

14.7.3 CAT IMPLICATIONS

The CAT implications should also be considered. In the example above, the sister receiving the voluntary conveyance of one undivided third share of the value of the property may have to file a return, if the value of the one undivided third share (along with any aggregable prior benefits from any other Group B disponer) is in excess of the Group B threshold (currently €40,000). This is assuming that the entirety of the market value, was paid to the sister conveying her the one third undivided share of the property.

Assuming all concerned are resident in the jurisdiction, the issue of secondary liability should not arise.

14.7.4 CGT IMPLICATIONS

A further tax which ought to be considered where there is a deed of family arrangement is CGT. The question is whether the disposition by the various parties gives rise to a CGT liability. Section 573(6) of TCA, 1997 states that there is a CGT liability where a deed of family arrangement is made within two years of the date of death. There is a concession in such cases so that the disposition by the parties to the deed is deemed to be a disposition by the deceased.

In the current property market, it is possible that property prices could increase by a large amount in a two-year period and this would need to be considered in some estates.

As with all voluntary transactions, solicitors should consider the question of fraud, duress, and undue influence. Therefore, it is advisable that each party is independently advised, particularly as to the taxation consequences.

14.8 Valuation Dates

In the area of administration a number of different valuation dates may be relevant. Property may have different values for different purposes; for example, there may be special rules for establishing the value, depending on the nature of the property or the particular tax head under which it is charged. Thus the 'market value' for one tax might be different from the market value estimated by the same valuers for another tax.

14.8.1 CAT VALUATION DATES

Valuation dates for CAT have been dealt with in **Chapter 1** and practitioners will be aware that various properties may have different valuation dates in the course of an administration. The importance of the valuation date has already been dealt with earlier in this chapter at **14.2.2**. For example, for CGT, the date of death is the valuation date, while for CAT it is usually (but not always, and not for all assets) the date of the grant of representation.

The amount of CAT payable depends on the market value as at the date of the gift or on the valuation date for inheritances.

The valuation of the residuary estate, provided the estate is solvent, and following the end of the executor's year, is the date on which the residue is ascertained for the benefit of the residuary beneficiaries or next of kin. This is the date on which all the liabilities, costs, and expenses have been paid and the assets in residue have been ascertained, subject possibly to payment of final taxation and the balance of the costs of administration.

Note that this is the date when the personal representative physically 'retains' the benefit for the successor without actually delivering, paying, satisfying, or discharging the benefit. Accordingly, any delivery, payment, satisfaction, or discharge prior to the date of the entitlement to retain or the date of retention, will determine an independent earlier valuation date in respect of any property so delivered, paid, satisfied, or discharged.

Where a beneficiary receives a benefit by way of part payment, advancement, payment on account, or in any manner whatsoever before the total of such inheritance, the appropriate valuation date of each part so paid or advanced will be ascertained in accordance with the rules set out in s. 30(5) of the CAT Consolidation Act, 2003. Where tax is payable, the tax is payable on the proportion attributable to the payment or advancement.

Example of Partial Distribution/Payment on Account

Anne Burke left the residue of her estate to Ciara Dwyer, who had not received any previous gifts or inheritances and is a stranger in blood.

Ciara Dwyer places the executrix of Anne's estate, Emma Farrel, under huge pressure to advance part of the residue to her.

Emma Farrel, the executrix, 'caves in' and pays Ciara Dwyer the sum of €100,000 on account.

The total residue will be in the region of €300,000.

The tax is calculated as follows:

Payment on account	€100,000
The remainder of the residue (estimated)	€200,000
Total	€300,000
Calculation of tax	
Threshold amount (2024)	€20,000
Taxable balance	€280,000
Tax at 33%	€92,400
Portion attributable to advance €100,000/€300,000 (in this case 1/3) × €92,400	€30,800

Advance payments cannot be used to enable a beneficiary to avail of agricultural relief.

Where property is held in joint names, which pass by survivorship on the death of one joint holder, the date of death is the date of inheritance, and is usually also the valuation date.

Where property is settled and ceases to be settled on the death of the life tenant, then the date of death of the life tenant when the property vests absolutely in possession in the remainderman will be the date of the inheritance and also the valuation date.

Where the deceased was a life tenant of any property, take particular note of any liability to CAT that may arise on the death of the life tenant and note the requirement to lodge returns and pay appropriate tax within four months of the date of that death which is also the valuation date.

Note however, that the disponer is the original settlor, not the life tenant.

In selecting valuation dates for CAT purposes, it is important to have regard to any potential CGT liability that may arise on the disposal of assets in the course of the administration. In all instances practitioners should refer back to the relevant legislation and ensure that they are aware of when valuation dates arise and inform the beneficiary of the same.

14.8.1.1 Appropriation under section 55 and the valuation date

When it is decided to appropriate property in satisfaction of a legacy or of shares in the residue, the valuation date is the date of the appropriation. The rules of appropriation in s. 55 of the Succession Act, 1965, must be observed where no power to appropriate is provided for by the will. Where appropriation is not pursuant to a broader power provided for by the will, stamp duty is payable on the appropriation. Therefore the trustees or personal representatives are usually given the power in the will to appropriate property without the consent of any person.

As stated, under s. 55, even where broader powers are given in the will, the valuation date is the date of appropriation.

14.8.1.2 Appropriation determinable by revenue commissioners and the valuation date

The Revenue Commissioners can determine a valuation date and must give notice of the determination to the accountable person, for example, the donee's successor or personal representative. Notice must be in writing and can refer to the whole or any part of the inheritance.

They cannot determine a valuation date before the grant of probate has issued unless the personal representative allows a beneficiary to take beneficial possession of a specific legacy which is capable of being physically enjoyed before the grant of probate has issued. Nor can the Revenue Commissioners determine a valuation date within twelve months of the death of the deceased in view of 'the executor's year'. There is a right of appeal against a determination of a valuation date as if it were an assessment to tax.

In case of doubt, the Revenue Commissioners can determine a valuation date with the agreement in writing of the accountable person or his or her agent. That agreed valuation date will be substituted for any other valuation date.

14.8.2 CGT VALUATION DATE

The valuation date is the date of the disposal giving rise to the liability.

14.8.3 INCOME TAX

The valuation date is the date of assessment in the current year.

14.8.4 STAMP DUTY

The valuation date is the date of execution of the deed.

14.9 Revenue Clearance

A solicitor, acting for a personal representative in the administration of an estate, has a duty to that personal representative to obtain all necessary evidence that the various taxes and obligations have been discharged.

During the course of an administration, a personal representative has, in many, cases a primary responsibility for the tax which arises, and in other cases will be secondarily liable for taxes which arise during the course of administration. Accordingly, the solicitor acting should ensure that all necessary evidence is obtained that the said taxes have been discharged.

As noted earlier, unless a beneficiary resides outside the jurisdiction, CAT is a self-assessment tax and not a concern of the Legal Personal Representative.

In relation to income tax and CGT, as also noted earlier, the Revenue have introduced a new online clearance procedure when all taxes have been paid which gives the Legal Personal Representative the ability to make a submission for clearance to distribute the estate without further liability.

This is set out in detail in Revenue TDM Part 46-01-02 Requests for Clearance in Death Cases. Interestingly, it is not mandatory to apply for Estate Clearance, but a prudent solicitor/LPR would do so. However, having said that, where the LPR is quite certain that there is no outstanding income tax or CGT due, especially in a very simple Estate, is under no obligation to apply for the Estate Clearance.

Any such request for clearance, is of course only possible, where all appropriate income tax and CGT returns for both the pre-death and post-death periods have been submitted and payment of all outstanding income tax and CGT has been made.

The 'Due Diligence Questionnaire' set out in Appendix 1 of the manual sets out the detail required in each case.

Where clearance is required, but no grant of representation is needed, all property is in joint names, insurance policies are nominated, and so on, a schedule of assets would have to be provided.

INDEX

F

G

H

I

S

The manufacturer's authorised representative in the EU for product safety is Oxford University Press España S.A. of El Parque Empresarial San Fernando de Henares, Avenida de Castilla, 2 - 28830 Madrid (www.oup.es/en or product.safety@oup.com). OUP España S.A. also acts as importer into Spain of products made by the manufacturer.
Printed and bound by CPI Group (UK) Ltd, Croydon, CR0 4YY
01/09/2026
02207116-0001